The Influence of Sea Power upon History

1660-1783

Books by Alfred Thayer Mahan

The Influence of Sea Power upon
  the French Revolution and Empire, 1793-1812
Admiral Farragut
The Life of Nelson
From Sail to Stream

The Influence of Sea Power

upon History 1660-1783

BY CAPTAIN ALFRED THAYER MAHAN, D.C.L., LL.D.
UNITED STATES NAVY

INTRODUCTION BY LOUIS M. HACKER

AMERICAN CENTURY SERIES

 HILL AND WANG · NEW YORK
A division of Farrar, Straus and Giroux

Introduction

Sometimes a man meets his destiny when he is very young, as Napoleon did in Italy; sometimes it happens when he is already in middle life. The latter occurred to Albert Thayer Mahan when he was 46 years old, and only ten years short of retirement from the humdrum posts he had been holding as a captain in the virtually non-existent American Navy. For in 1886 he was called to lecture on naval history and tactics before a handful of officers at the newly-created Naval War College at Newport, Rhode Island; and out of this academic exercise was to emerge a book, four years later, that, in its way and its place, was to have as profound an effect on the world as had Darwin's *Origin of Species*.

Mahan's *The Influence of Sea Power upon History, 1660-1783* at once circled the globe, for it was translated into all the important modern languages; it was read eagerly and studied closely by every great chancellory and admiralty; it shaped the imperial policies of Germany and Japan; it supported the position of Britain that its greatness lay in its far-flung empire; and it once more turned America toward those seas where it had been a power up to 1860 but which it had abandoned to seek its destiny in the conquest of its own continent.

If the young Kaiser Wilhelm II "devoured," as he himself said,

Mahan's book, so did the young Theodore Roosevelt, and, in a later time, so did another Roosevelt; and the building and maintenance of the American Navy, in the first two decades of the twentieth century, and also in the 1930s, made possible the saving of the Atlantic community twice when threatened by the great land power of Germany. The lessons Mahan preached—although warfare today is much more complex and the control over the seas includes the air above them and the regions beneath them—are still relevant; for the politics and strategy of sea power are the keys to our safety today as they were those Britain understood and employed in the 17th and 18th centuries and, later, in the first decade of the 20th century, when she was the world's leading power and the guarantor of its peace.

The Influence of Sea Power, therefore, is a work in international politics and a treatise on the strategy of war. And if some of the immediate conditions out of which Mahan wrote have changed—we no longer seek our own security in dependent colonies but in friends and allies; we no longer can look wholly to battleships to keep the sea lanes open—his argument still remains a sound one and his book is as much a tract for the times now as it was almost seventy years ago. Certainly, it deserves reading both for the profound effects it has had upon America and for the counsels it affords. Written by a man of war, it is a guide for the maintenance of peace; for it teaches how a great country, ever alert to the protection of its safety, can keep an unstable world in balance.

Alfred Thayer Mahan, the son of an instructor of military and civil engineering at West Point, where he was born in 1840, elected to follow the sea as a career, entered Annapolis, and was graduated from it in 1859. He was in the South Atlantic and Gulf blockading squadrons during the Civil War but saw no combat; the next quarter-century he spent afloat and ashore in a service that seems to have abandoned the tradition of the sea. The old American Navy (it was not modernized until the 1880s) was a curious collection of full-rigged frigates that carried their guns in broadside as they had in Drake's day, little steam corvettes with full complements of sail, iron double-ender paddle steamers, steam sloops with iron-plated sides, and river gunboats. These ships crossed the seas to take their stations in distant waters where, presumably, they protected American commerce; for America's naval defense, up to the late 1890s, was linked not to its ships but to its shore batteries.

So, as second in command, Mahan literally sailed the *Iroquois*— a steamer rigged as a sloop—across the Atlantic, around the Horn, and across the Indian Ocean to the China Sea (the journey took nine months), to move idly from port to port, as the days and nights and years slipped drowsily by. He had his own ship but it was sold under him and he proceeded home overland by way of India, Suez, and England: it was his first encounter with the British Empire— its colonies, bases, great merchant marine, and patrolling fleets— and upon these experiences and the reflections growing out of them he was to draw so heavily when he came to write his book.

How England achieved sea power, by the use of sound strategic ideas in war, was really his theme; and how it maintained this sea power for its own security and as a force for peace was the lesson he sought to convey.

Mahan visited England again in 1894; he came this time on a modern man-of-war and as a great personage. In 1883 the first four ships of the new American Navy had been authorized; it was in command of one of them, the *Chicago*, an unarmored cruiser of 4,500 tons, but with modern armament set in turrets, that he steamed into English waters. The *Chicago* was the flagship of the "White Fleet," brave, glistening warships with their high brown superstructures and shiny white hulls, that marked the end of America's isolation from the sea. They and the armored cruisers soon to be built demonstrated the soundness of Mahan's preachments in the War against Spain four years later.

The Influence of Sea Power upon History is, in consequence, a number of things. It is a brilliant exposition of those forces and factors—geographical, physical, economic, political (in this last connection, he worried about democracies, saying, "Popular governments are not generally favorable to military expenditure, however necessary. . . .")—that govern the creation and maintenance of sea power. It is a naval history of England's rise during those early years when it met and overcame the challenges of Holland, France, and Spain by the correct use of the immutable principles of naval strategy. It seeks to demonstrate that the rise and fall of sea power, and therefore of nations, has been always linked with the commercial and military command of the sea. It states clearly and emphatically that naval power is a complex of merchant marine, overseas colonies for trading purposes and to maintain military bases, and the upkeep of a fleet ever ready to move out, in offensive combat and with overbearing power, against those nations prepared to disturb the peace. Sea power means dominance by fleets of battleships possessing striking force; and for this reason Mahan wrote slightingly of commerce-destroying warfare as an effective military tactic. Mahan underestimated the potentialities of the submarine and, fortunately for England in World War I, Germany too followed his lead, for had she had a larger undersea fleet England might have been brought low almost at once. Mahan died on December 1, 1914, at the age of 74, when the future of England was still in doubt.

All these ideas Mahan stated in an article in the English *National Review* in 1902, when he said: "It seems demonstrable, therefore, that as commerce is the engrossing and predominant interest of the world today, so, in consequence of its acquired expansion, oversea commerce, oversea political acquisition, and maritime commercial routes are now the primary objects of external policy among nations. The instrument for the maintenance of policy directed upon these objects is the navy of the several states. . . ."

At the heart of this conception is an important strategic principle; Mahan formulates it precisely almost on the last page of his book, although it is the pervasive theme that runs throughout the whole work, and it is this: "Commerce-destroying by independent cruisers depends upon wide dissemination of force. Commerce-destroying through control of a strategic centre by a great fleet depends upon concentration of force. Regarded as a primary, not as a secondary operation, the former is condemned, the latter justified, by the experience of centuries."

Today, of course, sea power is conjoined with air power and the greater mobility of land warfare has made land bases more vulnerable (witness the case of Singapore in World War II). Nevertheless, the heart of the doctrine is still sound and great striking power, in concentrated force, when directed from the sea, is properly a fundamental tenet of American policy—as it was England's in earlier centuries—and a true foundation of international peace.

LOUIS M. HACKER

Columbia University

Contents

Plans of Naval Battles

In these plans, when the capital letters A, B, C, and D are used, all positions marked by the same capital are simultaneous.

Preface

The definite object proposed in this work is an examination of the general history of Europe and America with particular reference to the effect of sea power upon the course of that history. Historians generally have been unfamiliar with the conditions of the sea, having as to it neither special interest nor special knowledge; and the profound determining influence of maritime strength upon great issues has consequently been overlooked. This is even more true of particular occasions than of the general tendency of sea power. It is easy to say in a general way, that the use and control of the sea is and has been a great factor in the history of the world; it is more troublesome to seek out and show its exact bearing at a particular juncture. Yet, unless this be done, the acknowledgment of general importance remains vague and unsubstantial; not resting, as it should, upon a collection of special instances in which the precise effect has been made clear, by an analysis of the conditions at the given moments.

A curious exemplification of this tendency to slight the bearing of maritime power upon events may be drawn from two writers of that English nation which more than any other has owed its greatness to the sea. "Twice," says Arnold in his History of Rome, "has there been witnessed the struggle of the highest individual genius against the resources and institutions of a great nation, and in both cases the nation was victorious. For seventeen years Hannibal strove against Rome, for sixteen years Napoleon strove against England; the efforts of the first ended in Zama, those of the second in Waterloo." Sir Edward Creasy, quoting this, adds: "One point, however, of the similitude between the two wars has scarcely been adequately dwelt on; that is, the remarkable parallel between the Roman general who finally defeated the great Carthaginian, and the English general who gave the last deadly overthrow to the French emperor. Scipio and Wellington both held for many years commands of high importance, but distant from the main theatres of warfare. The same country was the scene of the principal military career of each. It was in Spain that Scipio, like Wellington, successively encountered and overthrew nearly all the subordinate generals of the enemy before being opposed to the chief champion and conqueror himself. Both Scipio and Wellington restored their countrymen's confidence in arms when shaken by a series of reverses, and each of them closed a long and perilous war by a complete and overwhelming defeat of the chosen leader and the chosen veterans of the foe."

Neither of these Englishmen mentions the yet more striking coincidence, that in both cases the mastery of the sea rested with the victor. The Roman control of the water forced Hannibal to that long, perilous march through Gaul in which more than half his veteran troops wasted away; it enabled the elder Scipio, while sending his army from the Rhone on to Spain, to intercept Hannibal's communications, to return in person and face the invader at the Trebia. Throughout the war the legions passed by water, unmolested and unwearied, between Spain, which was Hannibal's base, and Italy; while the issue of the decisive battle of the Metaurus, hinging as it did upon the interior position of the Roman armies with reference to the forces of Hasdrubal and Hannibal, was ultimately due to the fact that the younger brother could not bring his succoring reinforcements by sea, but only by the land route through Gaul. Hence at the critical moment the two Carthaginian armies were separated by the length of Italy, and one was destroyed by the combined action of the Roman generals.

On the other hand, naval historians have troubled themselves little about the connection between general history and their own particular topic, limiting themselves generally to the duty of simple chroniclers of naval occurrences. This is less true of the French than of the English; the genius and training of the former people leading them to more careful inquiry into the causes of particular results and the mutual relation of events.

There is not, however, within the knowledge of the author any work that professes the particular object here sought; namely, an estimate of the effect of sea power upon the course of history and the prosperity of nations. As other histories deal with the wars, politics, social and economical conditions of countries, touching upon maritime matters only incidentally and generally unsympathetically, so the present work aims at putting maritime interests in the foreground, without divorcing them, however, from their surroundings of cause and effect in general history, but seeking to show how they modified the latter, and were modified by them.

The period embraced is from 1660, when the sailingship era, with its distinctive features, had fairly begun, to 1783, the end of the American Revolution. While the thread of general history upon which the successive maritime events is strung is intentionally slight, the effort has been to present a clear as well as accurate outline. Writing as a naval officer in full sympathy with his profession, the author has not hesitated to digress freely on questions of naval policy, strategy, and tactics; but as technical language has been avoided, it is hoped that these matters, simply presented, will be found of interest to the unprofessional reader.

A. T. MAHAN

December, 1889

Introductory

The history of Sea Power is largely, though by no means solely, a narrative of contests between nations, of mutual rivalries, of violence frequently culminating in war. The profound influence of sea commerce upon the wealth and strength of countries was clearly seen long before the true principles which governed its growth and prosperity were detected. To secure to one's own people a disproportionate share of such benefits, every effort was made to exclude others, either by the peaceful legislative methods of monopoly or prohibitory regulations, or, when these failed, by direct violence. The clash of interests, the angry feelings roused by conflicting attempts thus to appropriate the larger share, if not the whole, of the advantages of commerce, and of distant unsettled commercial regions, led to wars. On the other hand, wars arising from other causes have been greatly modified in their conduct and issue by the control of the sea. Therefore the history of sea power, while embracing in its broad sweep all that tends to make a people great upon the sea or by the sea, is largely a military history; and it is in this aspect that it will be mainly, though not exclusively, regarded in the following pages.

A study of the military history of the past, such as this, is enjoined by great military leaders as essential to correct ideas and to the skilful conduct of war in the future. Napoleon names among the campaigns to be studied by the aspiring soldier, those of Alexander, Hannibal, and Cæsar, to whom gunpowder was unknown; and there is a substantial agreement among professional writers that, while many of the conditions of war vary from age to age with the progress of weapons, there are certain teachings in the school of history which remain constant, and being, therefore, of universal application, can be elevated to the rank of general principles. For the same reason the study of the sea history of the past will be found instructive, by its illustration of the general principles of maritime war, notwithstanding the great changes that have been brought about in naval weapons by the scientific advances of the past half century, and by the introduction of steam as the motive power.

It is doubly necessary thus to study critically the history and experience of naval warfare in the days of sailing-ships, because while these will be found to afford lessons of present application and value, steam navies have as yet made no history which can be quoted as decisive in its teaching. Of the one we have much experimental knowledge; of the other, practically none. Hence theories about the naval warfare of the future are almost wholly presumptive; and although the attempt has been made to give them a more solid basis by dwelling upon the resemblance between fleets of steamships and fleets of galleys moved by oars, which have a long and well-known history, it will be well not to be carried away by this analogy until it has been thoroughly tested. The resemblance is indeed far from superficial. The feature which the steamer and the galley have in common is the ability to move in any direction independent of the wind. Such a power makes a radical distinction between those classes of vessels and the sailing-ship; for the latter can follow only a limited number of courses when the wind blows, and must remain motionless when it fails. But while it is wise to observe things that are alike, it is also wise to look for things that differ; for when the imagination is carried away by the detection of points of resemblance,—one of the most pleasing of mental persuits,—it is apt to be impatient of any divergence in its new-found parallels, and so may overlook or refuse to recognize such. Thus the galley and the steamship have in common, though unequally developed, the important characteristic mentioned, but in at least two points they differ; and in an appeal to the history of the galley for lessons as to fighting steamships, the differences as well as the likeness must be kept steadily in view, or false deductions may be made. The motive power of the galley when in use necessarily and rapidly declined, because human strength could not long maintain such exhausting efforts, and consequently tactical movements could continue but for a limited time;[1] and again, during the galley period offensive weapons were not only of short range, but were almost wholly confined to hand-to-hand encounter. These two conditions led almost necessarily to a rush upon each other, not, however, without some dexterous attempts to turn or double on the enemy, followed by a hand-to-hand *mêlée*. In such a rush and such a *mêlée* a great consensus of respectable, even eminent, naval opinion of the present day finds the necessary outcome of modern naval weapons,—a kind of Donnybrook Fair, in which, as the history of *mêlées* shows, it will be hard to know friend from foe. Whatever may prove to be the worth of this opinion, it cannot claim an historical basis in the sole fact that galley and steamship can move at any moment directly upon the enemy, and carry a beak upon their prow, regardless of the points in which galley and steamship differ. As yet this opinion is only a presumption, upon which final judgment may well be deferred until the trial of battle has given further light. Until that time there is room for the opposite view,—that a *mêlée* between numerically equal fleets, in which skill is reduced to a minimum, is not the best that can be done with the elaborate and mighty weapons of this age. The surer of himself an admiral is, the finer the tactical development of his fleet, the better his captains, the more reluctant must he necessarily be to enter into a *mêlée* with equal forces, in which all these advantages will be thrown away, chance reign supreme, and his fleet be placed on terms of equality with an assemblage of ships which have never before acted together.[2] History has lessons as to when *mêlées* are, or are not, in order.

---

[1] Thus Hermocrates of Syracuse, advocating the policy of thwarting the Athenian expedition against his city (B.C. 413) by going boldly to meet it, and keeping on the flank of its line of advance, said: "As their advance must be slow, we shall have a thousand opportunities to attack them; but if they clear their ships for action and in a body bear down expeditiously upon us, they must ply hard at their oars, and *when spent with toil* we can fall upon them."

[2] The writer must guard himself from appearing to advocate elaborate tactical movements issuing in barren demonstrations. He believes that a fleet seeking a decisive result must close with its enemy, but not until some advantage has been obtained for the collision, which will usually be gained by manœuvring, and will fall to the best drilled and managed fleet. In truth, barren results have as often followed upon headlong, close encounters as upon the most timid tactical trifling.

The galley, then, has one striking resemblance to the steamer, but differs in other important features which are not so immediately apparent and are therefore less accounted of. In the sailing-ship, on the contrary, the striking feature is the difference between it and the more modern vessel; the points of resemblance, though existing and easy to find, are not so obvious, and therefore are less heeded. This impression is enhanced by the sense of utter weakness in the sailing-ship as compared with the steamer, owing to its dependence upon the wind; forgetting that, as the former fought with its equals, the tactical lessons are valid. The galley was never reduced to impotence by a calm, and hence receives more respect in our day than the sailing-ship; yet the latter displaced it and remained supreme until the utilization of steam. The powers to injure an enemy from a great distance, to manœuvre for an unlimited length of time without wearing out the men, to devote the greater part of the crew to the offensive weapons instead of to the oar, are common to the sailing vessel and the steamer, and are at least as important, tactically considered, as the power of the galley to move in a calm or against the wind.

In tracing resemblances there is a tendency not only to overlook points of difference, but to exaggerate points of likeness,—to be fanciful. It may be so considered to point out that as the sailing-ship had guns of long range, with comparatively great penetrative power, and carronades, which were of shorter range but great smashing effect, so the modern steamer has its batteries of long-range guns and of torpedoes, the latter being effective only within a limited distance and then injuring by smashing, while the gun, as of old, aims at penetration. Yet these are distinctly tactical considerations, which must affect the plans of admirals and captains; and the analogy is real, not forced. So also both the sailing-ship and the steamer contemplate direct contact with an enemy's vessel,—the former to carry her by boarding, the latter to sink her by ramming; and to both this is the most difficult of their tasks, for to effect it the ship must be carried to a single point of the field of action, whereas projectile weapons may be used from many points of a wide area.

The relative positions of two sailing-ships, or fleets, with reference to the direction of the wind involved most important tactical questions, and were perhaps the chief care of the seamen of that age. To a superficial glance it may appear that since this has become a matter of such indifference to the steamer, no analogies to it are to be found in present conditions, and the lessons of history in this respect are valueless. A more careful consideration of the distinguishing characteristics of the lee and the weather "gage," [3] directed to their essential features and disregarding secondary details, will show that this is a mistake. The distinguishing feature of the weather-gage was that it conferred the power of giving or refusing battle at will, which in turn carries the usual advantage of an offensive attitude in the choice of the method of attack. This advantage was accompanied by certain drawbacks, such as irregularity introduced into the order, exposure to raking or enfilading cannonade, and the sacrifice of part or all of the artillery-fire of the assailant,—all which were incurred in approaching the enemy. The ship, or fleet, with the lee-gage could not attack; if it did not wish to retreat, its action was confined to the defensive, and to receiving battle on the enemy's terms. This disadvantage was compensated by the comparative ease of maintaining the order of battle undisturbed, and by a sustained artillery-fire to which the enemy for a time was unable to reply. Historically, these favorable and unfavorable characteristics have their counterpart and analogy in the offensive and defensive operations of all ages. The offence undertakes certain risks and disadvantages in order to reach and destroy the enemy; the defence, so long as it remains such, refuses the risks of advance, holds on to a careful, well-ordered position, and avails itself of the exposure to which the assailant submits himself. These radical differences between the weather and the lee gage were so clearly recognized, through the cloud of lesser details accompanying them, that the former was ordinarily chosen by the English, because their steady policy was to assail and destroy their enemy; whereas the French sought the lee-gage, because by so doing they were usually able to cripple the enemy as he approached, and thus evade decisive encounters and preserve their ships. The French, with rare exceptions, subordinated the action of the navy to other military considerations, grudged the money spent upon it, and therefore sought to economize their fleet by assuming a defensive position and limiting its efforts to the repelling of assaults. For this course the lee-gage, skilfully used, was admirably adapted so long

[3] A ship was said to have the weather-gage, or "the advantage of the wind," or "to be to windward," when the wind allowed her to steer for her opponent, and did not let the latter head straight for her. The extreme case was when the wind blew direct from one to the other; but there was a large space on either side of this line to which the term "weather-gage" applied. If the lee ship be taken as the centre of a circle, there were nearly three eighths of its area in which the other might be and still keep the advantage of the wind to a greater or less degree. Lee is the opposite of weather.

as an enemy displayed more courage than conduct; but when Rodney showed an intention to use the advantage of the wind, not merely to attack, but to make a formidable concentration on a part of the enemy's line, his wary opponent, De Guichen, changed his tactics. In the first of their three actions the Frenchman took the lee-gage; but after recognizing Rodney's purpose he manœuvred for the advantage of the wind, not to attack, but to refuse action except on his own terms. The power to assume the offensive, or to refuse battle, rests no longer with the wind, but with the party which has the greater speed; which in a fleet will depend not only upon the speed of the individual ships, but also upon their tactical uniformity of action. Henceforth the ships which have the greatest speed will have the weather-gage.

It is not therefore a vain expectation, as many think, to look for useful lessons in the history of sailing-ships as well as in that of galleys. Both have their points of resemblance to the modern ship; both have also points of essential difference, which make it impossible to cite their experiences or modes of action as tactical *precedents* to be followed. But a precedent is different from and less valuable than a principle. The former may be originally faulty, or may cease to apply through change of circumstances; the latter has its root in the essential nature of things, and, however various its application as conditions change, remains a standard to which action must conform to attain success. War has such principles; their existence is detected by the study of the past, which reveals them in successes and in failures, the same from age to age. Conditions and weapons change; but to cope with the one or successfully wield the others, respect must be had to these constant teachings of history in the tactics of the battlefield, or in those wider operations of war which are comprised under the name of strategy.

It is however in these wider operations, which embrace a whole theatre of war, and in a maritime contest may cover a large portion of the globe, that the teachings of history have a more evident and permanent value, because the conditions remain more permanent. The theatre of war may be larger or smaller, its difficulties more or less pronounced, the contending armies more or less great, the necessary movements more or less easy, but these are simply differences of scale, of degree, not of kind. As a wilderness gives place to civilization, as means of communication multiply, as roads are opened, rivers bridged, food-resources increased, the operations of war become easier, more rapid, more extensive; but the principles to which they must be conformed remain the same. When the march on foot was replaced by carrying troops in coaches, when the latter in turn gave place to railroads, the scale of distances was increased, or, if you will, the scale of time diminished; but the principles which dictated the point at which the army should be concentrated, the direction in which it should move, the part of the enemy's position which it should assail, the protection of communications, were not altered. So, on the sea, the advance from the galley timidly creeping from port to port to the sailing-ship launching out boldly to the ends of the earth, and from the latter to the steamship of our own time, has increased the scope and the rapidity of naval operations without necessarily changing the principles which should direct them; and the speech of Hermocrates twenty-three hundred years ago, before quoted, contained a correct strategic plan, which is as applicable in its principles now as it was then. Before hostile armies or fleets are brought into con*tact* (a word which perhaps better than any other indicates the dividing line between tactics and strategy), there are a number of questions to be decided, covering the whole plan of operations throughout the theatre of war. Among these are the proper function of the navy in the war; its true objective; the point or points upon which it should be concentrated; the establishment of depots of coal and supplies; the maintenance of communications between these depots and the home base; the military value of commerce-destroying as a decisive or a secondary operation of war; the system upon which commerce-destroying can be most efficiently conducted, whether by scattered cruisers or by holding in force some vital centre through which commercial shipping must pass. All these are strategic questions, and upon all these history has a great deal to say. There has been of late a valuable discussion in English naval circles as to the comparative merits of the policies of two great English admirals, Lord Howe and Lord St. Vincent, in the disposition of the English navy when at war with France. The question is purely strategic, and is not of mere historical interest; it is of vital importance now, and the principles upon which its decision rests are the same now as then. St. Vincent's policy saved England from invasion, and in the hands of Nelson and his brother admirals led straight up to Trafalgar.

It is then particularly in the field of naval strategy that the teachings of the past have a value which is in no degree lessened. They are there useful not only as illustrative of principles, but also as precedents, owing to the comparative permanence of the conditions. This is less obviously true as to tactics, when the fleets come into collision at the point to which strategic considerations have brought them. The unresting progress of mankind causes continual change in the weapons; and with that must come a continual change in the manner of fighting,—in the handling and disposition of troops or ships on the battlefield. Hence arises a tendency on the part of many connected with maritime matters to think that no advantage is to be gained from the study of former experiences; that time so used is wasted. This view, though natural, not only leaves wholly out of sight those broad strategic considerations which lead nations to put fleets afloat, which direct the sphere of their action, and so have modified and will continue to modify the history of the world, but is one-sided and narrow even as to tactics. The battles of the past succeeded or failed according as they were fought in conformity with the principles of war; and the seaman who carefully studies the causes of success or failure will not only detect and gradually assimilate these principles, but will also acquire increased aptitude in applying them to the tactical use of the ships and weapons of his own day. He will observe also that changes of tactics have not only taken place *after* changes in weapons, which necessarily is the case, but that the interval between such changes has been unduly long. This doubtless arises from the fact that an improvement of weapons is due to the energy of one or two men, while changes in tactics have to overcome the inertia of a conservative class; but it is a great evil. It can be remedied only by a candid recognition of each change, by careful study of the powers and limitations of the new ship or weapon, and by a consequent adaptation of the method of using it to the qualities it possesses, which will constitute its tactics. History shows that it is vain to hope that military men generally will be at the pains to do this, but that the one who does will go into battle with a great advantage,—a lesson in itself of no mean value.

We may therefore accept now the words of a French tactician, Morogues, who wrote a century and a quarter ago: "Naval tactics are based upon conditions the chief causes of which, namely the arms, may change; which in turn causes necessarily a change in the construction of ships, in the manner of handling them, and so finally

8

in the disposition and handling of fleets." His further statement, that "it is not a science founded upon principles absolutely invariable," is more open to criticism. It would be more correct to say that the application of its principles varies as the weapons change. The application of the principles doubtless varies also in strategy from time to time, but the variation is far less; and hence the recognition of the underlying principle is easier. This statement is of sufficient importance to our subject to receive some illustrations from historical events.

The battle of the Nile, in 1798, was not only an overwhelming victory for the English over the French fleet, but had also the decisive effect of destroying the communications between France and Napoleon's army in Egypt. In the battle itself the English admiral, Nelson, gave a most brilliant example of grand tactics, if that be, as has been defined, "the art of making good combinations preliminary to battles as well as during their progress." The particular tactical combination depended upon a condition now passed away, which was the inability of the lee ships of a fleet at anchor to come to the help of the weather ones before the latter were destroyed; but the principles which underlay the combination, namely, to choose that part of the enemy's order which can least easily be helped, and to attack it with superior forces, has not passed away. The action of Admiral Jervis at Cape St. Vincent, when with fifteen ships he won a victory over twenty-seven, was dictated by the same principle, though in this case the enemy was not at anchor, but under way. Yet men's minds are so constituted that they seem more impressed by the transiency of the conditions than by the undying principle which coped with them. In the strategic effect of Nelson's victory upon the course of the war, on the contrary, the principle involved is not only more easily recognized, but it is at once seen to be applicable to our own day. The issue of the enterprise in Egypt depended upon keeping open the communications with France. The victory of the Nile destroyed the naval force, by which alone the communications could be assured, and determined the final failure; and it is at once seen, not only that the blow was struck in accordance with the principle of striking at the enemy's line of communication, but also that the same principle is valid now, and would be equally so in the days of the galley as of the sailing-ship or steamer.

Nevertheless, a vague feeling of contempt for the past, supposed to be obsolete, combines with natural indolence to blind men even to those permanent strategic lessons which lie close to the surface of naval history. For instance, how many look upon the battle of Trafalgar, the crown of Nelson's glory and the seal of his genius, as other than an isolated event of exceptional grandeur? How many ask themselves the strategic question, "How did the ships come to be just there?" How many realize it to be the final act in a great strategic drama, extending over a year or more, in which two of the greatest leaders that ever lived, Napoleon and Nelson, were pitted against each other? At Trafalgar it was not Villeneuve that failed, but Napoleon that was vanquished; not Nelson that won, but England that was saved; and why? Because Napoleon's combinations failed, and Nelson's intuitions and activity kept the English fleet ever on the track of the enemy, and brought it up in time at the decisive moment.[4] The tactics at Trafalgar, while open to criticism in detail, were in their main features conformable to the principles of war, and their audacity was justified as well by the urgency of the case as by the results; but the great lessons of efficiency in preparation, of activity and energy in execution, and of thought and insight on the part of the English leader during the previous months, are strategic lessons, and as such they still remain good.

In these two cases events were worked out to their natural and decisive end. A third may be cited, in which, as no such definite end was reached, an opinion as to what should have been done may be open to dispute. In the war of the American Revolution, France and Spain became allies against England in 1779. The united fleets thrice appeared in the English Channel, once to the number of sixty-six sail of the line, driving the English fleet to seek refuge in its ports because far inferior in numbers. Now, the great aim of Spain was to recover Gibraltar and Jamaica; and to the former end immense efforts both by land and sea were put forth by the allies against that nearly impregnable fortress. They were fruitless. The question suggested—and it is purely one of naval strategy—is this: Would not Gibraltar have been more surely recovered by controlling the English Channel, attacking the British fleet even in its harbors, and threatening England with annihilation of commerce and invasion at home, than by far greater efforts directed against a distant and very strong outpost of her empire? The English people, from long

4 See note at end of Introductory Chapter, page 20.

immunity, were particularly sensitive to fears of invasion, and their great confidence in their fleets, if rudely shaken, would have left them proportionately disheartened. However decided, the question as a point of strategy is fair; and it is proposed in another form by a French officer of the period, who favored directing the great effort on a West India island which might be exchanged against Gibraltar. It is not, however, likely that England would have given up the key of the Mediterranean for any other foreign possession, though she might have yielded it to save her firesides and her capital. Napoleon once said that he would reconquer Pondicherry on the banks of the Vistula. Could he have controlled the English Channel, as the allied fleet did for a moment in 1779, can it be doubted that he would have conquered Gibraltar on the shores of England?

To impress more strongly the truth that history both suggests strategic study and illustrates the principles of war by the facts which it transmits, two more instances will be taken, which are more remote in time than the period specially considered in this work. How did it happen that, in two great contests between the powers of the East and of the West in the Mediterranean, in one of which the empire of the known world was at stake, the opposing fleets met on spots so near each other as Actium and Lepanto? Was this a mere coincidence, or was it due to conditions that recurred, and may recur again? [5] If the latter, it is worth while to study out the reason; for if there should again arise a great eastern power of the sea like that of Antony or of Turkey, the strategic questions would be similar. At present, indeed, it seems that the centre of sea power, resting mainly with England and France, is overwhelmingly in the West; but should any chance add to the control of the Black Sea basin, which Russia now has, the possession of the entrance to the Mediterranean, the existing strategic conditions affecting sea power would all be modified. Now, were the West arrayed against the East, England and France would go at once unopposed to the Levant, as they did in 1854, and as England alone went in 1878; in case of the change suggested, the East, as twice before, would meet the West halfway.

At a very conspicuous and momentous period of the world's history, Sea Power had a strategic bearing and weight which has

---

[5] The battle of Navarino (1827) between Turkey and the Western Powers was fought in this neighborhood.

received scant recognition. There cannot now be had the full knowledge necessary for tracing in detail its influence upon the issue of the second Punic War; but the indications which remain are sufficient to warrant the assertion that it was a determining factor. An accurate judgment upon this point cannot be formed by mastering only such facts of the particular contest as have been clearly transmitted, for as usual the naval transactions have been slightingly passed over; there is needed also familiarity with the details of general naval history in order to draw, from slight indications, correct inferences based upon a knowledge of what has been possible at periods whose history is well known. The control of the sea, however real, does not imply that an enemy's single ships or small squadrons cannot steal out of port, cannot cross more or less frequented tracts of ocean, make harassing descents upon unprotected points of a long coastline, enter blockaded harbors. On the contrary, history has shown that such evasions are always possible, to some extent, to the weaker party, however great the inequality of naval strength. It is not therefore inconsistent with the general control of the sea, or of a decisive part of it, by the Roman fleets, that the Carthaginian admiral Bomilcar in the fourth year of the war, after the stunning defeat of Cannæ, landed four thousand men and a body of elephants in south Italy; nor that in the seventh year, flying from the Roman fleet off Syracuse, he again appeared at Tarentum, then in Hannibal's hands; nor that Hannibal sent despatch vessels to Carthage; nor even that, at last, he withdrew in safety to Africa with his wasted army. None of these things prove that the government in Carthage could, if it wished, have sent Hannibal the constant support which, as a matter of fact, he did not receive; but they do tend to create a natural impression that such help could have been given. Therefore the statement, that the Roman preponderance at sea had a decisive effect upon the course of the war, needs to be made good by an examination of ascertained facts. Thus the kind and degree of its influence may be fairly estimated.

At the beginning of the war, Mommsen says, Rome controlled the seas. To whatever cause, or combination of causes, it be attributed, this essentially non-maritime state had in the first Punic War established over its sea-faring rival a naval supremacy, which still lasted. In the second war there was no naval battle of importance,—a circumstance which in itself, and still more in connection with other well-ascertained facts, indicates a superiority analogous to that which at other epochs has been marked by the same feature.

As Hannibal left no memoirs, the motives are unknown which determined him to the perilous and almost ruinous march through Gaul and across the Alps. It is certain, however, that his fleet on the coast of Spain was not strong enough to contend with that of Rome. Had it been, he might still have followed the road he actually did, for reasons that weighed with him; but had he gone by the sea, he would not have lost thirty-three thousand out of the sixty thousand veteran soldiers with whom he started.

While Hannibal was making this dangerous march, the Romans were sending to Spain, under the two elder Scipios, one part of their fleet, carrying a consular army. This made the voyage without serious loss, and the army established itself successfully north of the Ebro, on Hannibal's line of communications. At the same time another squadron, with an army commanded by the other consul, was sent to Sicily. The two together numbered two hundred and twenty ships. On its station each met and defeated a Carthaginian squadron with an ease which may be inferred from the slight mention made of the actions, and which indicates the actual superiority of the Roman fleet.

After the second year the war assumed the following shape: Hannibal, having entered Italy by the north, after a series of successes had passed southward around Rome and fixed himself in southern Italy, living off the country,—a condition which tended to alienate the people, and was especially precarious when in contact with the mighty political and military system of control which Rome had there established. It was therefore from the first urgently necessary that he should establish, between himself and some reliable base, that stream of supplies and reinforcements which in terms of modern war is called "communications." There were three friendly regions which might, each or all, serve as such a base,—Carthage itself, Macedonia, and Spain. With the first two, communication could be had only by sea. From Spain, where his firmest support was found, he could be reached by both land and sea, unless an enemy barred the passage; but the sea route was the shorter and easier.

In the first years of the war, Rome, by her sea power, controlled absolutely the basin between Italy, Sicily, and Spain, known as the Tyrrhenian and Sardinian Seas. The seacoast from the Ebro to the

Tiber was mostly friendly to her. In the fourth year, after the battle of Cannæ, Syracuse forsook the Roman alliance, the revolt spread through Sicily, and Macedonia also entered into an offensive league with Hannibal. These changes extended the necessary operations of the Roman fleet, and taxed its strength. What disposition was made of it, and how did it thereafter influence the struggle?

The indications are clear that Rome at no time ceased to control the Tyrrhenian Sea, for her squadrons passed unmolested from Italy to Spain. On the Spanish coast also she had full sway till the younger Scipio saw fit to lay up the fleet. In the Adriatic, a squadron and naval station were established at Brindisi to check Macedonia, which performed their task so well that not a soldier of the phalanxes ever set foot in Italy. "The want of a war fleet," says Mommsen, "paralyzed Philip in all his movements." Here the effect of Sea Power is not even a matter of inference.

In Sicily, the struggle centred about Syracuse. The fleets of Carthage and Rome met there, but the superiority evidently lay with the latter; for though the Carthaginians at times succeeded in throwing supplies into the city, they avoided meeting the Roman fleet in battle. With Lilybæum, Palermo, and Messina in its hands, the latter was well based in the north coast of the island. Access by the south was left open to the Carthaginians, and they were thus able to maintain the insurrection.

Putting these facts together, it is a reasonable inference, and supported by the whole tenor of the history, that the Roman sea power controlled the sea north of a line drawn from Tarragona in Spain to Lilybæum (the modern Marsala), at the west end of Sicily, thence round by the north side of the island through the straits of Messina down to Syracuse, and from there to Brindisi in the Adriatic. This control lasted, unshaken, throughout the war. It did not exclude maritime raids, large or small, such as have been spoken of; but it did forbid the sustained and secure communications of which Hannibal was in deadly need.

On the other hand, it seems equally plain that for the first ten years of the war the Roman fleet was not strong enough for sustained operations in the sea between Sicily and Carthage, nor indeed much to the south of the line indicated. When Hannibal started, he assigned such ships as he had to maintaining the communications between Spain and Africa, which the Romans did not then attempt to disturb.

The Roman sea power, therefore, threw Macedonia wholly out of the war. It did not keep Carthage from maintaining a useful and most harassing diversion in Sicily; but it did prevent her sending troops, when they would have been most useful, to her great general in Italy. How was it as to Spain?

Spain was the region upon which the father of Hannibal and Hannibal himself had based their intended invasion of Italy. For eighteen years before this began they had occupied the country, extending and consolidating their power, both political and military, with rare sagacity. They had raised, and trained in local wars, a large and now veteran army. Upon his own departure, Hannibal intrusted the government to his younger brother, Hasdrubal, who preserved toward him to the end a loyalty and devotion which he had no reason to hope from the faction-cursed mother-city in Africa.

At the time of his starting, the Carthaginian power in Spain was secured from Cadiz to the river Ebro. The region between this river and the Pyrenees was inhabited by tribes friendly to the Romans, but unable, in the absence of the latter, to oppose a successful resistance to Hannibal. He put them down, leaving eleven thousand soldiers under Hanno to keep military possession of the country, lest the Romans should establish themselves there, and thus disturb his communications with his base.

Cnæus Scipio, however, arrived on the spot by sea the same year with twenty thousand men, defeated Hanno, and occupied both the coast and interior north of the Ebro. The Romans thus held ground by which they entirely closed the road between Hannibal and reinforcements from Hasdrubal, and whence they could attack the Carthaginian power in Spain; while their own communications with Italy, being by water, were secured by their naval supremacy. They made a naval base at Tarragona, confronting that of Hasdrubal at Cartagena, and then invaded the Carthaginian dominions. The war in Spain went on under the elder Scipios, seemingly a side issue, with varying fortune for seven years; at the end of which time Hasdrubal inflicted upon them a crushing defeat, the two brothers were killed, and the Carthaginians nearly succeeded in breaking through to the Pyrenees with reinforcements for Hannibal. The attempt, however, was checked for the moment; and before it could be renewed, the fall of Capua released twelve thousand veteran Romans, who were sent to Spain under Claudius Nero, a man of exceptional ability, to whom was due later the most decisive military movement made by any Roman general during the Second Punic War. This seasonable reinforcement, which again assured the shaken grip on Hasdrubal's line of march, came by sea,—a way which, though most rapid and easy, was closed to the Carthaginians by the Roman navy.

Two years later the younger Publius Scipio, celebrated afterward as Africanus, received the command in Spain, and captured Cartagena by a combined military and naval attack; after which he took the most extraordinary step of breaking up his fleet and transferring the seamen to the army. Not contented to act merely as the "containing"[6] force against Hasdrubal by closing the passes of the Pyrenees, Scipio pushed forward into southern Spain, and fought a severe but indecisive battle on the Guadalquivir; after which Hasdrubal slipped away from him, hurried north, crossed the Pyrenees at their extreme west, and pressed on to Italy, where Hannibal's position was daily growing weaker, the natural waste of his army not being replaced.

The war had lasted ten years, when Hasdrubal, having met little loss on the way, entered Italy at the north. The troops he brought, could they be safely united with those under the command of the unrivalled Hannibal, might give a decisive turn to the war, for Rome herself was nearly exhausted; the iron links which bound her own colonies and the allied States to her were strained to the utmost, and some had already snapped. But the military position of the two brothers was also perilous in the extreme. One being at the river Metaurus, the other in Apulia, two hundred miles apart, each was confronted by a superior enemy, and both these Roman armies were between their separated opponents. This false situation, as well as the long delay of Hasdrubal's coming, was due to the Roman control of the sea, which throughout the war limited the mutual support of the Carthaginian brothers to the route through Gaul. At the very time that Hasdrubal was making his long and dangerous circuit by land, Scipio had sent eleven thousand men from Spain by sea to reinforce the army opposed to him. The upshot was that

[6] A "containing" force is one to which, in a military combination, is assigned the duty of stopping, or delaying the advance of a portion of the enemy, while the main effort of the army or armies is being exerted in a different quarter.

messengers from Hasdrubal to Hannibal, having to pass over so wide a belt of hostile country, fell into the hands of Claudius Nero, commanding the southern Roman army, who thus learned the route which Hasdrubal intended to take. Nero correctly appreciated the situation, and, escaping the vigilance of Hannibal, made a rapid march with eight thousand of his best troops to join the forces in the north. The junction being effected, the two consuls fell upon Hasdrubal in overwhelming numbers and destroyed his army; the Carthaginian leader himself falling in the battle. Hannibal's first news of the disaster was by the head of his brother being thrown into his camp. He is said to have exclaimed that Rome would now be mistress of the world; and the battle of Metaurus is generally accepted as decisive of the struggle between the two States.

The military situation which finally resulted in the battle of the Metaurus and the triumph of Rome may be summed up as follows: To overthrow Rome it was necessary to attack her in Italy at the heart of her power, and shatter the strongly linked confederacy of which she was the head. This was the objective. To reach it, the Carthaginians needed a solid base of operations and a secure line of communications. The former was established in Spain by the genius of the great Barca family; the latter was never achieved. There were two lines possible,—the one direct by sea, the other circuitous through Gaul. The first was blocked by the Roman sea power, the second imperilled and finally intercepted through the occupation of northern Spain by the Roman army. This occupation was made possible through the control of the sea, which the Carthaginians never endangered. With respect to Hannibal and his base, therefore, Rome occupied two central positions, Rome itself and northern Spain, joined by an easy interior line of communications, the sea; by which mutual support was continually given.

Had the Mediterranean been a level desert of land, in which the Romans held strong mountain ranges in Corsica and Sardinia, fortified posts at Tarragona, Lilybæum, and Messina, the Italian coast-line nearly to Genoa, and allied fortresses in Marseilles and other points; had they also possessed an armed force capable by its character of traversing that desert at will, but in which their opponents were very inferior and therefore compelled to a great circuit in order to concentrate their troops, the military situation would have been at once recognized, and no words would have been too strong to express the value and effect of that peculiar force. It would have been perceived, also, that the enemy's force of the same kind might, however inferior in strength, make an inroad, or raid, upon the territory thus held, might burn a village or waste a few miles of borderland, might even cut off a convoy at times, without, in a military sense, endangering the communications. Such predatory operations have been carried on in all ages by the weaker maritime belligerent, but they by no means warrant the inference, irreconcilable with the known facts, "that neither Rome nor Carthage could be said to have undisputed mastery of the sea," because "Roman fleets sometimes visited the coasts of Africa, and Carthaginian fleets in the same way appeared off the coast of Italy." In the case under consideration, the navy played the part of such a force upon the supposed desert; but as it acts on an element strange to most writers, as its members have been from time immemorial a strange race apart, without prophets of their own, neither themselves nor their calling understood, its immense determining influence upon the history of that era, and consequently upon the history of the world, has been overlooked. If the preceding argument is sound, it is as defective to omit sea power from the list of principal factors in the result, as it would be absurd to claim for it an exclusive influence.

Instances such as have been cited, drawn from widely separated periods of time, both before and after that specially treated in this work, serve to illustrate the intrinsic interest of the subject, and the character of the lessons which history has to teach. As before observed, these come more often under the head of strategy than of tactics; they bear rather upon the conduct of campaigns than of battles, and hence are fraught with more lasting value. To quote a great authority in this connection, Jomini says: "Happening to be in Paris near the end of 1851, a distinguished person did me the honor to ask my opinion as to whether recent improvements in fire-arms would cause any great modifications in the way of making war. I replied that they would probably have an influence upon the details of tactics, but that in great strategic operations and the grand combinations of battles, victory would, now as ever, result from the application of the principles which had led to the success of great generals in all ages; of Alexander and Cæsar, as well as of Frederick and Napoleon." This study has become more than ever

18

important now to navies, because of the great and steady power of movement possessed by the modern steamer. The best-planned schemes might fail through stress of weather in the days of the galley and the sailing-ship; but this difficulty has almost disappeared. The principles which should direct great naval combinations have been applicable to all ages, and are deducible from history; but the power to carry them out with little regard to the weather is a recent gain.

The definitions usually given of the word "strategy" confine it to military combinations embracing one or more fields of operations, either wholly distinct or mutually dependent, but always regarded as actual or immediate scenes of war. However this may be on shore, a recent French author is quite right in pointing out that such a definition is too narrow for naval strategy. "This," he says, "differs from military strategy in that it is as necessary in peace as in war. Indeed, in peace it may gain its most decisive victories by occupying in a country, either by purchase or treaty, excellent positions which would perhaps hardly be got by war. It learns to profit by all opportunities of settling on some chosen point of a coast, and to render definitive an occupation which at first was only transient." A generation that has seen England within ten years occupy successively Cyprus and Egypt, under terms and conditions on their face transient, but which have not yet led to the abandonment of the positions taken, can readily agree with this remark; which indeed receives constant illustration from the quiet persistency with which all the great sea powers are seeking position after position, less noted and less noteworthy than Cyprus and Egypt, in the different seas to which their people and their ships penetrate. "Naval strategy has indeed for its end to found, support, and increase, as well in peace as in war, the sea power of a country"; and therefore its study has an interest and value for all citizens of a free country, but especially for those who are charged with its foreign and military relations.

The general conditions that either are essential to or powerfully affect the greatness of a nation upon the sea will now be examined; after which a more particular consideration of the various maritime nations of Europe at the middle of the seventeenth century, where the historical survey begins, will serve at once to illustrate and give precision to the conclusions upon the general subject.

Note—The brilliancy of Nelson's fame, dimming as it does that of all his contemporaries, and the implicit trust felt by England in him as the one man able to save her from the schemes of Napoleon, should not of course obscure the fact that only one portion of the field was, or could be, occupied by him. Napoleon's aim, in the campaign which ended at Trafalgar, was to unite in the West Indies the French fleets of Brest, Toulon, and Rochefort, together with a strong body of Spanish ships, thus forming an overwhelming force which he intended should return together to the English Channel and cover the crossing of the French army. He naturally expected that, with England's interests scattered all over the world, confusion and distraction would arise from ignorance of the destination of the French squadrons, and the English navy be drawn away from his objective point. The portion of the field committed to Nelson was the Mediterranean, where he watched the great arsenal of Toulon and the highways alike to the East and to the Atlantic. This was inferior in consequence to no other, and assumed additional importance in the eyes of Nelson from his conviction that the former attempts on Egypt would be renewed. Owing to this persuasion he took at first a false step, which delayed his pursuit of the Toulon fleet when it sailed under the command of Villeneuve; and the latter was further favored by a long continuance of fair winds, while the English had head winds. But while all this is true, while the failure of Napoleon's combinations must be attributed to the tenacious grip of the English blockade off Brest, *as well as* to Nelson's energetic pursuit of the Toulon fleet when it escaped to the West Indies and again on its hasty return to Europe, the latter is fairly entitled to the eminent distinction which history has accorded it, and which is asserted in the text. Nelson did not, indeed, fathom the intentions of Napoleon. This may have been owing, as some have said, to lack of insight; but it may be more simply laid to the usual disadvantage under which the defence lies before the blow has fallen, of ignorance as to the point threatened by the offence. It is insight enough to fasten on the key of a situation; and this Nelson rightly saw was the fleet, not the station. Consequently, his action has afforded a striking instance of how tenacity of purpose and untiring energy in execution can repair a first mistake and baffle deeply laid plans. His Mediterranean command embraced many duties and cares; but amid and dominating them all, he saw clearly the Toulon fleet as the controlling factor there, and an important factor in any naval combination of the Emperor. Hence his attention was unwaveringly fixed upon it; so much so that he called it "his fleet," a phrase which has somewhat vexed the sensibilities of French critics. This simple and accurate view of the military situation strengthened him in taking the fearless resolution and bearing the immense responsibility of abandoning his station in order to follow "his fleet." Determined thus on a pursuit the undeniable wisdom of which should not obscure the greatness of mind that undertook it, he followed so vigorously as to reach Cadiz on his return a week before Villeneuve entered Ferrol, despite unavoidable delays arising from false information and uncertainty as to the enemy's movements. The same untiring ardor enabled him to bring up his own ships from Cadiz to Brest in time to make the fleet there superior to Villeneuve's, had the latter persisted in his attempt to reach the neighborhood. The English, very inferior in aggregate number of vessels to the allied fleets, were by this seasonable reinforcement of eight veteran ships put into the best possible position strategically, as will be pointed out in dealing with similar conditions in the war of the American Revolution. Their forces were united in one great fleet in the Bay of Biscay, interposed between the two divisions of the enemy in Brest and Ferrol, superior in number to either singly, and with a strong probability of being able to deal with one before the other could come up. This was due to able action all round on the part of the English authorities; but above all other factors in the result stands Nelson's single-minded pursuit of "his fleet."

This interesting series of strategic movements ended on the 14th of August, when Villeneuve, in despair of reaching Brest, headed for Cadiz, where he anchored on the 20th. As soon as Napoleon heard of this, after an outburst of rage against the admiral, he at once dictated the series of movements which resulted in Ulm and Austerlitz, abandoning his purposes against England. The battle of Trafalgar, fought October 21, was therefore separated by a space of two months from the extensive movements of which it was nevertheless the outcome. Isolated from them in point of time, it was none the less the seal of Nelson's genius, affixed later to the record he had made in the near past. With equal truth it is said that England was saved at Trafalgar, though the Emperor had then given up his intended invasion; the destruction there emphasized and sealed the strategic triumph which had noiselessly foiled Napoleon's plans.

1

Discussion of the Elements of Sea Power

The first and most obvious light in which the sea presents itself from the political and social point of view is that of a great highway; or better, perhaps, of a wide common, over which men may pass in all directions, but on which some well-worn paths show that controlling reasons have led them to choose certain lines of travel rather than others. These lines of travel are called trade routes; and the reasons which have determined them are to be sought in the history of the world.

Notwithstanding all the familiar and unfamiliar dangers of the sea, both travel and traffic by water have always been easier and cheaper than by land. The commercial greatness of Holland was due not only to her shipping at sea, but also to the numerous tranquil water-ways which gave such cheap and easy access to her own interior and to that of Germany. This advantage of carriage by water over that by land was yet more marked in a period when roads were few and very bad, wars frequent and society unsettled, as was the case two hundred years ago. Sea traffic then went in peril of robbers, but was nevertheless safer and quicker than that by land. A Dutch writer of that time, estimating the chances of his country in a war with England, notices among other things that the water-ways of England failed to penetrate the country sufficiently; therefore, the roads being bad, goods from one part of the kingdom to the other must go by sea, and be exposed to capture by the way. As regards purely internal trade, this danger has generally disappeared at the present day. In most civilized countries, now, the destruction or disappearance of the coasting trade would only be an inconvenience, although water transit is still the cheaper. Nevertheless, as late as the wars of the French Republic and the First Empire, those who are familiar with the history of the period, and the light naval literature that has grown up around it, know how constant is the mention of convoys stealing from point to point along the French coast, although the sea swarmed with English cruisers and there were good inland roads.

Under modern conditions, however, home trade is but a part of the business of a country bordering on the sea. Foreign necessaries or luxuries must be brought to its ports, either in its own or in foreign ships, which will return, bearing in exchange the products of the country, whether they be the fruits of the earth or the works of men's hands; and it is the wish of every nation that this shipping business should be done by its own vessels. The ships that thus sail to and fro must have secure ports to which to return, and must, as far as possible, be followed by the protection of their country throughout the voyage.

This protection in time of war must be extended by armed shipping. The necessity of a navy, in the restricted sense of the word, springs, therefore, from the existence of a peaceful shipping, and disappears with it, except in the case of a nation which has aggressive tendencies, and keeps up a navy merely as a branch of the military establishment. As the United States has at present no aggressive purposes, and as its merchant service has disappeared, the dwindling of the armed fleet and general lack of interest in it are strictly logical consequences. When for any reason sea trade is again found to pay, a large enough shipping interest will reappear to compel the revival of the war fleet. It is possible that when a canal route through the Central-American Isthmus is seen to be a near certainty, the aggressive impulse may be strong enough to lead to the same result. This is doubtful, however, because a peaceful, gain-loving nation is not far-sighted, and far-sightedness is needed for adequate military preparation, especially in these days.

As a nation, with its unarmed and armed shipping, launches forth from its own shores, the need is soon felt of points upon which the ships can rely for peaceful trading, for refuge and supplies. In the present day friendly, though foreign, ports are to be found all over the world; and their shelter is enough while peace prevails. It was not always so, nor does peace always endure, though the United States have been favored by so long a continuance of it. In earlier times the merchant seaman, seeking for trade in new and unexplored regions, made his gains at risk of life and liberty from suspicious or hostile nations, and was under great delays in collecting a full and profitable freight. He therefore intuitively sought at the far end of his trade route one or more stations, to be given to him by force or favor, where he could fix himself or his agents in reasonable security, where his ships could lie in safety, and where the merchantable products of the land could be continually collecting, awaiting the arrival of the home fleet, which should carry them to the mother-country. As there was immense gain, as well as much risk, in these early voyages, such establishments naturally multiplied and grew until they became colonies; whose ultimate development and success depended upon the genius and policy of the nation from which they sprang, and form a very great part of the history, and particularly of the sea history, of the world. All colonies had not the simple and natural birth and growth above described. Many were more formal, and purely political, in their conception and founding, the act of the rulers of the people rather than of private individuals; but the trading-station with its after expansion, the work simply of the adventurer seeking gain, was in its reasons and essence the same as the elaborately organized and chartered colony. In both cases the mother-country had won a foothold in a foreign land, seeking a new outlet for what it had to sell, a new sphere for its shipping, more employment for its people, more comfort and wealth for itself.

The needs of commerce, however, were not all provided for when safety had been secured at the far end of the road. The voyages were long and dangerous, the seas often beset with enemies. In the most active days of colonizing there prevailed on the sea a lawlessness the very memory of which is now almost lost, and the days of settled peace between maritime nations were few and far between. Thus arose the demand for stations along the road, like the Cape of Good Hope, St. Helena, and Mauritius, not primarily for trade, but for defence and war; the demand for the possession of posts like Gibraltar, Malta, Louisburg, at the entrance of the Gulf of St. Lawrence, —posts whose value was chiefly strategic, though not necessarily wholly so. Colonies and colonial posts were sometimes commercial, sometimes military in their character; and it was exceptional that the same position was equally important in both points of view, as New York was.

In these three things—production, with the necessity of exchanging products, shipping, whereby the exchange is carried on, and colonies, which facilitate and enlarge the operations of shipping and tend to protect it by multiplying points of safety—is to be found the key to much of the history, as well as of the policy, of nations bordering upon the sea. The policy has varied both with the spirit of the age and with the character and clear-sightedness of the rulers; but the history of the seaboard nations has been less determined by the shrewdness and foresight of governments than by conditions of position, extent, configuration, number and character of their people,—by what are called, in a word, natural conditions. It must however be admitted, and will be seen, that the wise or unwise action of individual men has at certain periods had a great modifying influence upon the growth of sea power in the broad sense, which includes not only the military strength afloat, that rules the sea or any part of it by force of arms, but also the peaceful commerce and shipping from which alone a military fleet naturally and healthfully springs, and on which it securely rests.

The principal conditions affecting the sea power of nations may be enumerated as follows: I. Geographical Position. II. Physical Conformation, including, as connected therewith, natural productions and climate. III. Extent of Territory. IV. Number of Population. V. Character of the People. VI. Character of the Government, including therein the national institutions.

I *Geographical Position*—It may be pointed out, in the first place, that if a nation be so situated that it is neither forced to defend itself by land nor induced to seek extension of its territory by way of the land, it has, by the very unity of its aim directed upon the sea, an advantage as compared with a people one of whose boundaries is continental. This has been a great advantage to England over both France and Holland as a sea power. The strength of the latter was early exhausted by the necessity of keeping up a large army and carrying on expensive wars to preserve her independence; while the policy of France was constantly diverted, sometimes wisely and sometimes most foolishly, from the sea to projects of continental extension. These military efforts expended wealth; whereas a wiser and consistent use of her geographical position would have added to it.

The geographical position may be such as of itself to promote a concentration, or to necessitate a dispersion, of the naval forces. Here again the British Islands have an advantage over France. The position of the latter, touching the Mediterranean as well as the ocean, while it has its advantages, is on the whole a source of military weakness at sea. The eastern and western French fleets have only been able to unite after passing through the Straits of Gibraltar, in attempting which they have often risked and sometimes suffered loss. The position of the United States upon the two oceans would be either a source of great weakness or a cause of enormous expense, had it a large sea commerce on both coasts.

England, by her immense colonial empire, has sacrificed much of this advantage of concentration of force around her own shores; but the sacrifice was wisely made, for the gain was greater than the loss, as the event proved. With the growth of her colonial system her war fleets also grew, but her merchant shipping and wealth grew yet faster. Still, in the wars of the American Revolution, and of the French Republic and Empire, to use the strong expression of a French author, "England, despite the immense development of her navy, seemed ever, in the midst of riches, to feel all the embarrassment of poverty." The might of England was sufficient to keep alive the heart and the members; whereas the equally extensive colonial empire of Spain, through her maritime weakness, but offered so many points for insult and injury.

The geographical position of a country may not only favor the concentration of its forces, but give the further strategic advantage of a central position and a good base for hostile operations against its probable enemies. This again is the case with England; on the one hand she faces Holland and the northern powers, on the other France and the Atlantic. When threatened with a coalition between France and the naval powers of the North Sea and the Baltic, as she at times was, her fleets in the Downs and in the Channel, and even that off Brest, occupied interior positions, and thus were readily able to interpose their united force against either one of the enemies which should seek to pass through the Channel to effect a junction with its ally. On either side, also, Nature gave her better ports and a safer coast to approach. Formerly this was a very serious element in the passage through the Channel; but of late, steam and the improvement of her harbors have lessened the disadvantage under which France once labored. In the days of sailing-ships, the English fleet operated against Brest making its base at Torbay and Plymouth. The plan was simply this: in easterly or moderate weather the blockading fleet kept its position without difficulty; but in westerly gales, when too severe, they bore up for English ports, knowing that the French fleet could not get out till the wind shifted, which equally served to bring them back to their station.

The advantage of geographical nearness to an enemy, or to the object of attack, is nowhere more apparent than in that form of warfare which has lately received the name of commerce-destroying, which the French call *guerre de course*. This operation of war, being directed against peaceful merchant vessels which are usually defenceless, calls for ships of small military force. Such ships, having little power to defend themselves, need a refuge or point of support near at hand; which will be found either in certain parts of the sea controlled by the fighting ships of their country, or in friendly harbors. The latter give the strongest support, because they are always in the same place, and the approaches to them are more familiar to the commerce-destroyer than to his enemy. The nearness of France to England has thus greatly facilitated her *guerre de course* directed against the latter. Having ports on the North Sea, on the Channel, and on the Atlantic, her cruisers started from points near the focus of English trade, both coming and going. The distance of these ports from each other, disadvantageous for regular military combinations, is an advantage for this irregular secondary operation; for the essence of the one is concentration of effort, whereas for commerce-destroying diffusion of effort is the rule. Commerce-destroyers scatter, that they may see and seize more prey. These truths receive illustration from the history of the great French privateers, whose bases and scenes of action were largely on the Channel and North Sea, or else were found in distant colonial regions, where islands like Guadeloupe and Martinique afforded similar near refuge. The necessity of renewing coal makes the cruiser of the present day even more dependent than of old on his port. Public opinion in the United States has great faith in war directed against an enemy's commerce; but it must be remembered that the Republic has no ports very near the great centres of trade abroad. Her geographical position is therefore singularly disadvantageous for carrying on successful commerce-destroying, unless she find bases in the ports of an ally.

If, in addition to facility for offence, Nature has so placed a country that it has easy access to the high sea itself, while at the same time it controls one of the great thoroughfares of the world's traffic, it is evident that the strategic value of its position is very high. Such again is, and to a greater degree was, the position of England. The trade of Holland, Sweden, Russia, Denmark, and that which went up the great rivers to the interior of Germany, had to pass through the Channel close by her doors; for sailing-ships hugged the English coast. This northern trade had, moreover, a peculiar bearing upon sea power; for naval stores, as they are commonly called, were mainly drawn from the Baltic countries.

But for the loss of Gibraltar, the position of Spain would have been closely analogous to that of England. Looking at once upon the Atlantic and the Mediterranean, with Cadiz on the one side and Cartagena on the other, the trade to the Levant must have passed under her hands, and that round the Cape of Good Hope not far from her doors. But Gibraltar not only deprived her of the control of the Straits, it also imposed an obstacle to the easy junction of the two divisions of her fleet.

At the present day, looking only at the geographical position of Italy, and not at the other conditions affecting her sea power, it would seem that with her extensive sea-coast and good ports she is very well placed for exerting a decisive influence on the trade route to the Levant and by the Isthmus of Suez. This is true in a degree, and would be much more so did Italy now hold all the islands naturally Italian; but with Malta in the hands of England, and Corsica in those of France, the advantages of her geographical position are largely neutralized. From race affinities and situation those two islands are as legitimately objects of desire to Italy as Gibraltar is to Spain. If the Adriatic were a great highway of commerce, Italy's position would be still more influential. These defects in her geographical completeness, combined with other causes injurious to a full and secure development of sea power, make it more than doubtful whether Italy can for some time be in the front rank among the sea nations.

As the aim here is not an exhaustive discussion, but merely an attempt to show, by illustration, how vitally the situation of a country may affect its career upon the sea, this division of the subject may be dismissed for the present; the more so as instances which will further bring out its importance will continually recur in the historical treatment. Two remarks, however, are here appropriate.

Circumstances have caused the Mediterranean Sea to play a greater part in the history of the world, both in a commercial and a military point of view, than any other sheet of water of the same size. Nation after nation has striven to control it, and the strife still goes on. Therefore a study of the conditions upon which preponderance in its waters has rested, and now rests, and of the relative military values of different points upon its coasts, will be more instructive than the same amount of effort expended in another field. Furthermore, it has at the present time a very marked analogy in many respects to the Caribbean Sea,—an analogy which will be still closer if a Panama canal-route ever be completed. A study of the strategic conditions of the Mediterranean, which have received ample illustration, will be an excellent prelude to a similar study of the Caribbean, which has comparatively little history.

The second remark bears upon the geographical position of the United States relatively to a Central-American canal. If one be made, and fulfil the hopes of its builders, the Caribbean will be changed from a terminus, and place of local traffic, or at best a broken and imperfect line of travel, as it now is, into one of the great highways of the world. Along this path a great commerce will travel, bringing the interests of the other great nations, the European nations, close along our shores, as they have never been before. With this it will not be so easy as heretofore to stand aloof from international complications. The position of the United States with reference to this route will resemble that of England to the Channel, and of the Mediterranean countries to the Suez route. As regards influence and control over it, depending upon geographical position, it is of course plain that the centre of the national power, the permanent base,[1] is much nearer than that of other great nations. The positions now or hereafter occupied by them on island or mainland, however strong, will be but outposts of their power; while in all the

[1] By a base of permanent operations "is understood a country whence come all the resources, where are united the great lines of communication by land and water, where are the arsenals and armed posts."

raw materials of military strength no nation is superior to the United States. She is, however, weak in a confessed unpreparedness for war; and her geographical nearness to the point of contention loses some of its value by the character of the Gulf coast, which is deficient in ports combining security from an enemy with facility for repairing war-ships of the first class, without which ships no country can pretend to control any part of the sea. In case of a contest for supremacy in the Caribbean, it seems evident from the depth of the South Pass of the Mississippi, the nearness of New Orleans, and the advantages of the Mississippi Valley for water transit, that the main effort of the country must pour down that valley, and its permanent base of operations be found there. The defence of the entrance to the Mississippi, however, presents peculiar difficulties; while the only two rival ports, Key West and Pensacola, have too little depth of water, and are much less advantageously placed with reference to the resources of the country To get the full benefit of superior geographical position, these defects must be overcome. Furthermore, as her distance from the Isthmus, though relatively less, is still considerable, the United States will have to obtain in the Caribbean stations fit for contingent, or secondary, bases of operations; which by their natural advantages, susceptibility of defence, and nearness to the central strategic issue, will enable her fleets to remain as near the scene as any opponent. With ingress and egress from the Mississippi sufficiently protected, with such outposts in her hands, and with the communications between them and the home base secured, in short, with proper military preparation, for which she has all necessary means, the preponderance of the United States on this field follows, from her geographical position and her power, with mathematical certainty.

II *Physical Conformation*—The peculiar features of the Gulf coast, just alluded to, come properly under the head of Physical Conformation of a country, which is placed second for discussion among the conditions which affect the development of sea power.

The seaboard of a country is one of its frontiers; and the easier the access offered by the frontier to the region beyond, in this case the sea, the greater will be the tendency of a people toward intercourse with the rest of the world by it. If a country be imagined having a long seaboard, but entirely without a harbor, such a country can have no sea trade of its own, no shipping, no navy. This was practically the case with Belgium when it was a Spanish and an Austrian province. The Dutch, in 1648, as a condition of peace after a successful war, exacted that the Scheldt should be closed to sea commerce. This closed the harbor of Antwerp and transferred the sea trade of Belgium to Holland. The Spanish Netherlands ceased to be a sea power.

Numerous and deep harbors are a source of strength and wealth, and doubly so if they are the outlets of navigable streams, which facilitate the concentration in them of a country's internal trade; but by their very accessibility they become a source of weakness in war, if not properly defended. The Dutch in 1667 found little difficulty in ascending the Thames and burning a large fraction of the English navy within sight of London; whereas a few years later the combined fleets of England and France, when attempting a landing in Holland, were foiled by the difficulties of the coast as much as by the valor of the Dutch fleet. In 1778 the harbor of New York, and with it undisputed control of the Hudson River, would have been lost to the English, who were caught at disadvantage, but for the hesitancy of the French admiral. With that control, New England would have been restored to close and safe communication with New York, New Jersey, and Pennsylvania; and this blow, following so closely on Burgoyne's disaster of the year before, would probably have led the English to make an earlier peace. The Mississippi is a mighty source of wealth and strength to the United States; but the feeble defences of its mouth and the number of its subsidiary streams penetrating the country made it a weakness and source of disaster to the Southern Confederacy. And lastly, in 1814, the occupation of the Chesapeake and the destruction of Washington gave a sharp lesson of the dangers incurred through the noblest water-ways, if their approaches be undefended; a lesson recent enough to be easily recalled, but which, from the present appearance of the coast defences, seems to be yet more easily forgotten. Nor should it be thought that conditions have changed; circumstances and details of offence and defence have been modified, in these days as before, but the great conditions remain the same.

Before and during the great Napoleonic wars, France had no port for ships-of-the-line east of Brest. How great the advantage to England, which in the same stretch has two great arsenals, at Plymouth and at Portsmouth, besides other harbors of refuge and supply. This defect of conformation has since been remedied by the works at Cherbourg.

Besides the contour of the coast, involving easy access to the sea, there are other physical conditions which lead people to the sea or turn them from it. Although France was deficient in military ports on the Channel, she had both there and on the ocean, as well as in the Mediterranean, excellent harbors, favorably situated for trade abroad, and at the outlet of large rivers, which would foster internal traffic. But when Richelieu had put an end to civil war, Frenchmen did not take to the sea with the eagerness and success of the English and Dutch. A principal reason for this has been plausibly found in the physical conditions which have made France a pleasant land, with a delightful climate, producing within itself more than its people needed. England, on the other hand, received from Nature but little, and, until her manufactures were developed, had little to export. Their many wants, combined with their restless activity and other conditions that favored maritime enterprise, led her people abroad; and they there found lands more pleasant and richer than their own. Their needs and genius made them merchants and colonists, then manufacturers and producers; and between products and colonies shipping is the inevitable link. So their sea power grew. But if England was drawn to the sea, Holland was driven to it; without the sea England languished, but Holland died. In the height of her greatness, when she was one of the chief factors in European politics, a competent native authority estimated that the soil of Holland could not support more than one eighth of her inhabitants. The manufactures of the country were then numerous and important, but they had been much later in their growth than the shipping interest. The poverty of the soil and the exposed nature of the coast drove the Dutch first to fishing. Then the discovery of the process of curing the fish gave them material for export as well as home consumption, and so laid the corner-stone of their wealth. Thus they had become traders at the time that the Italian republics, under the pressure of Turkish power and the discovery of the passage round the Cape of Good Hope, were beginning to decline, and they fell heirs to the great Italian trade of the Levant. Further favored by their geographical position, intermediate between the Baltic, France, and the Mediterranean, and at the mouth of the

German rivers, they quickly absorbed nearly all the carrying-trade of Europe. The wheat and naval stores of the Baltic, the trade of Spain with her colonies in the New World, the wines of France, and the French coasting-trade were, little more than two hundred years ago, transported in Dutch shipping. Much of the carrying-trade of England, even, was then done in Dutch bottoms. It will not be pretended that all this prosperity proceeded only from the poverty of Holland's natural resources. Something does not grow from nothing. What is true, is, that by the necessitous condition of her people they were driven to the sea, and were, from their mastery of the shipping business and the size of their fleets, in a position to profit by the sudden expansion of commerce and the spirit of exploration which followed on the discovery of America and of the passage round the Cape. Other causes concurred, but their whole prosperity stood on the sea power to which their poverty gave birth. Their food, their clothing, the raw material for their manufactures, the very timber and hemp with which they built and rigged their ships (and they built nearly as many as all Europe besides), were imported; and when a disastrous war with England in 1653 and 1654 had lasted eighteen months, and their shipping business was stopped, it is said "the sources of revenue which had always maintained the riches of the State, such as fisheries and commerce, were almost dry. Workshops were closed, work was suspended. The Zuyder Zee became a forest of masts; the country was full of beggars; grass grew in the streets, and in Amsterdam fifteen hundred houses were untenanted." A humiliating peace alone saved them from ruin.

This sorrowful result shows the weakness of a country depending wholly upon sources external to itself for the part it is playing in the world. With large deductions, owing to differences of conditions which need not here be spoken of, the case of Holland then has strong points of resemblance to that of Great Britain now; and they are true prophets, though they seem to be having small honor in their own country, who warn her that the continuance of her prosperity at home depends primarily upon maintaining her power abroad. Men may be discontented at the lack of political privilege; they will be yet more uneasy if they come to lack bread. It is of more interest to Americans to note that the result to France, regarded as a power of the sea, caused by the extent, delightfulness, and richness of the land, has been reproduced in the United States. In the beginning, their forefathers held a narrow strip of land upon the sea, fertile in parts though little developed, abounding in harbors and near rich fishing-grounds. These physical conditions combined with an inborn love of the sea, the pulse of that English blood which still beat in their veins, to keep alive all those tendencies and pursuits upon which a healthy sea power depends. Almost every one of the original colonies was on the sea or on one of its great tributaries. All export and import tended toward one coast. Interest in the sea and an intelligent appreciation of the part it played in the public welfare were easily and widely spread; and a motive more influential than care for the public interest was also active, for the abundance of ship-building materials and a relative fewness of other investments made shipping a profitable private interest. How changed the present condition is, all know. The centre of power is no longer on the seaboard. Books and newspapers vie with one another in describing the wonderful growth, and the still undeveloped riches, of the interior. Capital there finds its best investments, labor its largest opportunities. The frontiers are neglected and politically weak; the Gulf and Pacific coasts actually so, the Atlantic coast relatively to the central Mississippi Valley. When the day comes that shipping again pays, when the three sea frontiers find that they are not only militarily weak, but poorer for lack of national shipping, their united efforts may avail to lay again the foundations of our sea power. Till then, those who follow the limitations which lack of sea power placed upon the career of France may mourn that their own country is being led, by a like redundancy of home wealth, into the same neglect of that great instrument.

Among modifying physical conditions may be noted a form like that of Italy,—a long peninsula, with a central range of mountains dividing it into two narrow strips, along which the roads connecting the different ports necessarily run. Only an absolute control of the sea can wholly secure such communications, since it is impossible to know at what point an enemy coming from beyond the visible horizon may strike; but still, with an adequate naval force centrally posted, there will be good hope of attacking his fleet, which is at once his base and line of communications, before serious damage has been done. The long, narrow peninsula of Florida, with Key West at its extremity, though flat and thinly populated, presents at first sight conditions like those of Italy. The resemblance may be only superficial, but it seems probable that if the chief scene of a naval war were the Gulf of Mexico, the communications by land to the end of the peninsula might be a matter of consequence, and open to attack.

When the sea not only borders, or surrounds, but also separates a country into two or more parts, the control of it becomes not only desirable, but vitally necessary. Such a physical condition either gives birth and strength to sea power, or makes the country powerless. Such is the condition of the present kingdom of Italy, with its islands of Sardinia and Sicily; and hence in its youth and still existing financial weakness it is seen to put forth such vigorous and intelligent efforts to create a military navy. It has even been argued that, with a navy decidedly superior to her enemy's, Italy could better base her power upon her islands than upon her mainland; for the insecurity of the lines of communication in the peninsula, already pointed out, would most seriously embarrass an invading army surrounded by a hostile people and threatened from the sea.

The Irish Sea, separating the British Islands, rather resembles an estuary than an actual division; but history has shown the danger from it to the United Kingdom. In the days of Louis XIV., when the French navy nearly equalled the combined English and Dutch, the gravest complications existed in Ireland, which passed almost wholly under the control of the natives and the French. Nevertheless, the Irish Sea was rather a danger to the English—a weak point in their communications—than an advantage to the French. The latter did not venture their ships-of-the-line in its narrow waters, and expeditions intending to land were directed upon the ocean ports in the south and west. At the supreme moment the great French fleet was sent upon the south coast of England, where it decisively defeated the allies, and at the same time twenty-five frigates were sent to St. George's Channel, against the English communications. In the midst of a hostile people, the English army in Ireland was seriously imperilled, but was saved by the battle of the Boyne and flight of James II. This movement against the enemy's communications was strictly strategic, and would be just as dangerous to England now as in 1690.

Spain, in the same century, afforded an impressive lesson of the weakness caused by such separation when the parts are not knit together by a strong sea power. She then still retained, as remnants of her past greatness, the Netherlands (now Belgium), Sicily, and other Italian possessions, not to speak of her vast colonies in the New World. Yet so low had the Spanish sea power fallen, that a well-informed and sober-minded Hollander of the day could claim that "in Spain all the coast is navigated by a few Dutch ships; and since the peace of 1648 their ships and seamen are so few that they have publicly begun to hire our ships to sail to the Indies, whereas they were formerly careful to exclude all foreigners from there. . . . It is manifest," he goes on, "that the West Indies, being as the stomach to Spain (for from it nearly all the revenue is drawn), must be joined to the Spanish head by a sea force; and that Naples and the Netherlands, being like two arms, they cannot lay out their strength for Spain, nor receive anything thence but by shipping,— all which may easily be done by our shipping in peace, and by it obstructed in war." Half a century before, Sully, the great minister of Henry IV., had characterized Spain "as one of those States whose legs and arms are strong and powerful, but the heart infinitely weak and feeble." Since his day the Spanish navy had suffered not only disaster, but annihilation; not only humiliation, but degradation. The consequences briefly were that shipping was destroyed; manufactures perished with it. The government depended for its support, not upon a widespread healthy commerce and industry that could survive many a staggering blow, but upon a narrow stream of silver trickling through a few treasure-ships from America, easily and frequently intercepted by an enemy's cruisers. The loss of half a dozen galleons more than once paralyzed its movements for a year. While the war in the Netherlands lasted, the Dutch control of the sea forced Spain to send her troops by a long and costly journey overland instead of by sea; and the same cause reduced her to such straits for necessaries that, by a mutual arrangement which seems very odd to modern ideas, her wants were supplied by Dutch ships, which thus maintained the enemies of their country, but received in return specie which was welcome in the Amsterdam exchange. In America, the Spanish protected themselves as best they might behind masonry, unaided from home; while in the Mediterranean they escaped insult and injury mainly through the indifference of the Dutch, for the French and English had not yet begun to contend for mastery there. In the course of history the Netherlands, Naples, Sicily, Minorca, Havana, Manila, and Jamaica were wrenched away, at one time or another, from this empire without a shipping. In short, while Spain's maritime impotence may have been primarily a symptom of her general decay, it became a marked factor in precipitating her into the abyss from which she has not yet wholly emerged.

Except Alaska, the United States has no outlying possession,— no foot of ground inaccessible by land. Its contour is such as to present few points specially weak from their saliency, and all important parts of the frontiers can be readily attained,—cheaply by water, rapidly by rail. The weakest frontier, the Pacific, is far removed from the most dangerous of possible enemies. The internal resources are boundless as compared with present needs; we can live off ourselves indefinitely in "our little corner," to use the expression of a French officer to the author. Yet should that little corner be invaded by a new commercial route through the Isthmus, the United States in her turn may have the rude awakening of those who have abandoned their share in the common birthright of all people, the sea.

III *Extent of Territory*—The last of the conditions affecting the development of a nation as a sea power, and touching the country itself as distinguished from the people who dwell there, is Extent of Territory. This may be dismissed with comparatively few words.

As regards the development of sea power, it is not the total number of square miles which a country contains, but the length of its coast-line and the character if its harbors that are to be considered. As to these it is to be said that, the geographical and physical conditions being the same, extent of sea-coast is a source of strength or weakness according as the population is large or small. A country is in this like a fortress; the garrison must be proportioned to the *enceinte*. A recent familiar instance is found in the American War of Secession. Had the South had a people as numerous as it was warlike, and a navy commensurate to its other resources as a sea power, the great extent of its sea-coast and its numerous inlets would have been elements of great strength. The people of the United States and the Government of that day justly prided themselves on the effectiveness of the blockade of the whole

Southern coast. It was a great feat, a very great feat; but it would have been an impossible feat had the Southerners been more numerous, and a nation of seamen. What was there shown was not, as has been said, how such a blockade can be maintained, but that such a blockade is possible in the face of a population not only unused to the sea, but also scanty in numbers. Those who recall how the blockade was maintained, and the class of ships that blockaded during great part of the war, know that the plan, correct under the circumstances, could not have been carried out in the face of a real navy. Scattered unsupported along the coast, the United States ships kept their places, singly or in small detachments, in face of an extensive network of inland water communications which favored secret concentration of the enemy. Behind the first line of water communications were long estuaries, and here and there strong fortresses, upon either of which the enemy's ships could always fall back to elude pursuit or to receive protection. Had there been a Southern navy to profit by such advantages, or by the scattered condition of the United States ships, the latter could not have been distributed as they were; and being forced to concentrate for mutual support, many small but useful approaches would have been left open to commerce. But as the Southern coast, from its extent and many inlets, might have been a source of strength, so, from those very characteristics, it became a fruitful source of injury. The great story of the opening of the Mississippi is but the most striking illustration of an action that was going on incessantly all over the South. At every breach of the sea frontier, war-ships were entering. The streams that had carried the wealth and supported the trade of the seceding States turned against them, and admitted their enemies to their hearts. Dismay, insecurity, paralysis, prevailed in regions that might, under happier auspices, have kept a nation alive through the most exhausting war. Never did sea power play a greater or a more decisive part than in the contest which determined that the course of the world's history would be modified by the existence of one great nation, instead of several rival States, in the North American continent. But while just pride is felt in the well-earned glory of those days, and the greatness of the results due to naval preponderance is admitted, Americans who understand the facts should never fail to remind the over-confidence of their countrymen that the South not only had no navy, not only was not a seafaring people, but that also its population was not proportioned to the extent of the sea-coast which it had to defend.

IV *Number of Population*—After the consideration of the natural conditions of a country should follow an examination of the characteristics of its population as affecting the development of sea power; and first among these will be taken, because of its relations to the extent of the territory, which has just been discussed, the number of the people who live in it. It has been said that in respect of dimensions it is not merely the number of square miles, but the extent and character of the sea-coast that is to be considered with reference to sea power; and so, in point of population, it is not only the grand total, but the number following the sea, or at least readily available for employment on ship-board and for the creation of naval material, that must be counted.

For example, formerly and up to the end of the great wars following the French Revolution, the population of France was much greater than that of England; but in respect of sea power in general, peaceful commerce as well as military efficiency, France was much inferior to England. In the matter of military efficiency this fact is the more remarkable because at times, in point of military preparation at the outbreak of war, France had the advantage; but she was not able to keep it. Thus in 1778, when war broke out, France, through her maritime inscription, was able to man at once fifty ships-of-the-line. England, on the contrary, by reason of the dispersal over the globe of that very shipping on which her naval strength so securely rested, had much trouble in manning forty at home; but in 1782 she had one hundred and twenty in commission or ready for commission, while France had never been able to exceed seventy-one. Again, as late as 1840, when the two nations were on the verge of war in the Levant, a most accomplished French officer of the day, while extolling the high state of efficiency of the French fleet and the eminent qualities of its admiral, and expressing confidence in the results of an encounter with an equal enemy, goes on to say: "Behind the squadron of twenty-one ships-of-the-line which we could then assemble, there was no reserve; not another ship could have been commissioned within six months." And this was due not only to lack of ships and of proper equipments, though both were wanting. "Our maritime inscription," he continues, "was so exhausted by what we had done [in manning twenty-one ships], that the permanent levy established in all quarters did not supply reliefs for the men, who were already more than three years on cruise."

A contrast such as this shows a difference in what is called staying power, or reserve force, which is even greater than appears on the surface; for a great shipping afloat necessarily employs, besides the crews, a large number of people engaged in the various handicrafts which facilitate the making and repairing of naval material, or following other callings more or less closely connected with the water and with craft of all kinds. Such kindred callings give an undoubted aptitude for the sea from the outset. There is an anecdote showing curious insight into this matter on the part of one of England's distinguished seamen, Sir Edward Pellew. When the war broke out in 1793, the usual scarceness of seamen was met. Eager to get to sea and unable to fill his complement otherwise than with landsmen, he instructed his officers to seek for Cornish miners; reasoning from the conditions and dangers of their calling, of which he had personal knowledge, that they would quickly fit into the demands of sea life. The result showed his sagacity, for, thus escaping an otherwise unavoidable delay, he was fortunate enough to capture the first frigate taken in the war in single combat; and what is especially instructive is, that although but a few weeks in commission, while his opponent had been over a year, the losses, heavy on both sides, were nearly equal.

It may be urged that such reserve strength has now nearly lost the importance it once had, because modern ships and weapons take so long to make, and because modern States aim at developing the whole power of their armed force, on the outbreak of war, with such rapidity as to strike a disabling blow before the enemy can organize an equal effort. To use a familiar phrase, there will not be time for the whole resistance of the national fabric to come into play; the blow will fall on the organized military fleet, and if that yield, the solidity of the rest of the structure will avail nothing. To a certain extent this is true; but then it has always been true, though to a less extent formerly than now. Granted the meeting of two fleets which represent practically the whole present strength of their two nations, if one of them be destroyed, while the other remains fit for action, there will be much less hope now than formerly that the vanquished can restore his navy for that war; and the result will be disastrous just in proportion to the dependence of the nation upon her sea power. A Trafalgar would have been a much more fatal blow to England than it was to France, had the English fleet then represented, as the allied fleet did, the bulk of the nation's power. Trafalgar in such a case would have been to England what Austerlitz was to Austria, and Jena to Prussia; an empire would have been laid prostrate by the destruction or disorganization of its military forces, which, it is said, were the favorite objective of Napoleon.

But does the consideration of such exceptional disasters in the past justify the putting a low value upon that reserve strength, based upon the number of inhabitants fitted for a certain kind of military life, which is here being considered? The blows just mentioned were dealt by men of exceptional genius, at the head of armed bodies of exceptional training, *esprit-de-corps,* and prestige, and were, besides, inflicted upon opponents more or less demoralized by conscious inferiority and previous defeat. Austerlitz had been closely preceded by Ulm, where thirty thousand Austrians laid down their arms without a battle; and the history of the previous years had been one long record of Austrian reverse and French success. Trafalgar followed closely upon a cruise, justly called a campaign, of almost constant failure; and farther back, but still recent, were the memories of St. Vincent for the Spaniards, and of the Nile for the French, in the allied fleet. Except the case of Jena, these crushing overthrows were not single disasters, but final blows; and in the Jena campaign there was a disparity in numbers, equipment, and general preparation for war, which makes it less applicable in considering what may result from a single victory.

England is at the present time the greatest maritime nation in the world; in steam and iron she has kept the superiority she had in the days of sail and wood. France and England are the two powers that have the largest military navies; and it is so far an open question which of the two is the more powerful, that they may be regarded as practically of equal strength in material for a sea war. In the case of a collision can there be assumed such a difference of *personnel,* or of preparation, as to make it probable that a decisive inequality will result from one battle or one campaign?

If not, the reserve strength will begin to tell; organized reserve first, then reserve of seafaring population, reserve of mechanical skill, reserve of wealth. It seems to have been somewhat forgotten that England's leadership in mechanical arts gives her a reserve of mechanics, who can easily familiarize themselves with the appliances of modern iron-clads; and as her commerce and industries feel the burden of the war, the surplus of seamen and mechanics will go to the armed shipping.

The whole question of the value of a reserve, developed or undeveloped, amounts now to this: Have modern conditions of warfare made it probable that, of two nearly equal adversaries, one will be so prostrated in a single campaign that a decisive result will be reached in that time? Sea warfare has given no answer. The crushing successes of Prussia against Austria, and of Germany against France, appear to have been those of a stronger over a much weaker nation, whether the weakness were due to natural causes, or to official incompetency. How would a delay like that of Plevna have affected the fortune of war, had Turkey had any reserve of national power upon which to call?

If time be, as is everywhere admitted, a supreme factor in war, it behooves countries whose genius is essentially not military, whose people, like all free people, object to pay for large military establishments, to see to it that they are at least strong enough to gain the time necessary to turn the spirit and capacity of their subjects into the new activities which war calls for. If the existing force by land or sea is strong enough so to hold out, even though at a disadvantage, the country may rely upon its natural resources and strength coming into play for whatever they are worth,—its numbers, its wealth, its capacities of every kind. If, on the other hand, what force it has can be overthrown and crushed quickly, the most magnificent possibilities of natural power will not save it from humiliating conditions, nor, if its foe be wise, from guarantees which will postpone revenge to a distant future. The story is constantly repeated on the smaller fields of war: "If so-and-so can hold out a little longer, this can be saved or that can be done"; as in sickness it is often said: "If the patient can only hold out so long, the strength of his constitution may pull him through."

England to some extent is now such a country. Holland was such a country; she would not pay, and if she escaped, it was but by the skin of her teeth. "Never in time of peace and from fear of a rupture," wrote their great statesman, De Witt, "will they take resolutions strong enough to lead them to pecuniary sacrifices beforehand. The character of the Dutch is such that, unless danger stares them in the face, they are indisposed to lay out money for their own defence. I have to do with a people who, liberal to profusion where they ought to economize, are often sparing to avarice where they ought to spend."

That our own country is open to the same reproach, is patent to all the world. The United States has not that shield of defensive power behind which time can be gained to develop its reserve of strength. As for a seafaring population adequate to her possible needs, where is it? Such a resource, proportionate to her coast-line and population, is to be found only in a national merchant shipping and its related industries, which at present scarcely exist. It will matter little whether the crews of such ships are native or foreign born, provided they are attached to the flag, and her power at sea is sufficient to enable the most of them to get back in case of war. When foreigners by thousands are admitted to the ballot, it is of little moment that they are given fighting-room on board ship.

Though the treatment of the subject has been somewhat discursive, it may be admitted that a great population following callings related to the sea is, now as formerly, a great element of sea power; that the United States is deficient in that element; and that its foundations can be laid only in a large commerce under her own flag.

V *National Character*—The effect of national character and aptitudes upon the development of sea power will next be considered.

If sea power be really based upon a peaceful and extensive commerce, aptitude for commercial pursuits must be a distinguishing feature of the nations that have at one time or another been great upon the sea. History almost without exception affirms that this is true. Save the Romans, there is no marked instance to the contrary.

All men seek gain and, more or less, love money; but the way in which gain is sought will have a marked effect upon the commercial fortunes and the history of the people inhabiting a country.

If history may be believed, the way in which the Spaniards and their kindred nation, the Portuguese, sought wealth, not only brought a blot upon the national character, but was also fatal to the growth of a healthy commerce; and so to the industries upon which commerce lives, and ultimately to that national wealth which was sought by mistaken paths. The desire for gain rose in them to fierce avarice; so they sought in the new-found worlds which gave such an impetus to the commercial and maritime development of the countries of Europe, not new fields of industry, not even the healthy excitement of exploration and adventure, but gold and silver. They had many great qualities; they were bold, enterprising, temperate, patient of suffering, enthusiastic, and gifted with intense national feeling. When to these qualities are added the advantages of Spain's position and well-situated ports, the fact that she was first to occupy large and rich portions of the new worlds and long remained without a competitor, and that for a hundred years after the discovery of America she was the leading State in Europe, she might have been expected to take the foremost place among the sea powers. Exactly the contrary was the result, as all know. Since the battle of Lepanto in 1571, though engaged in many wars, no sea victory of any consequence shines on the pages of Spanish history; and the decay of her commerce sufficiently accounts for the painful and sometimes ludicrous inaptness shown on the decks of her ships of war. Doubtless such a result is not to be attributed to one cause only. Doubtless the government of Spain was in many ways such as to cramp and blight a free and healthy development of private enterprise; but the character of a great people breaks through and shapes the character of its government, and it can hardly be doubted that had the bent of the people been toward trade, the action of government would have been drawn into the same current. The great field of the colonies, also, was remote from the centre of that despotism which blighted the growth of old Spain. As it was, thousands of Spaniards, of the working as well as the upper classes, left Spain; and the occupations in which they engaged abroad sent home little but specie, or merchandise of small bulk, requiring but small tonnage. The mother-country herself produced little but wool, fruit, and iron; her manufactures were naught; her industries suffered; her population steadily decreased. Both she and her colonies depended upon the Dutch for so many of the necessaries of life, that the products of their scanty industries could not suffice to pay for them. "So that Holland merchants," writes a contemporary, "who carry money to most parts of the world to buy commodities, must out of this single country of Europe carry home money, which they receive in payment of their goods." Thus their eagerly sought emblem of wealth passed quickly from their hands. It has already been pointed out how weak, from a military point of view, Spain was from this decay of her shipping. Her wealth being in small bulk on a few ships, following more or less regular routes, was easily seized by an enemy, and the sinews of war paralyzed; whereas the wealth of England and Holland, scattered over thousands of ships in all parts of the world, received many bitter blows in many exhausting wars, without checking a growth which, though painful, was steady. The fortunes of Portugal, united to Spain during a most critical period of her history, followed the same downward path; although foremost in the beginning of the race for development by sea, she fell utterly behind. "The mines of Brazil were the ruin of Portugal, as those of Mexico and Peru had been of Spain; all manufactures fell into insane contempt; ere long the English supplied the Portuguese not only with clothes, but with all merchandise, all commodities, even to salt-fish and grain. After their gold, the Portuguese abandoned their very soil; the vineyards of Oporto were finally bought by the English with Brazilian gold, which had only passed through Portugal to be spread throughout England." We are assured that in fifty years, five hundred millions of dollars were extracted from "the mines of Brazil, and that at the end of the time Portugal had but twenty-five millions in specie,"—a striking example of the difference between real and fictitious wealth.

The English and Dutch were no less desirous of gain than the southern nations. Each in turn has been called "a nation of shopkeepers"; but the jeer, in so far as it is just, is to the credit of their wisdom and uprightness. They were no less bold, no less enterprising, no less patient. Indeed, they were more patient, in that they sought riches not by the sword but by labor, which is the reproach meant to be implied by the epithet; for thus they took the longest, instead of what seemed the shortest, road to wealth. But these two peoples, radically of the same race, had other qualities, no less important than those just named, which combined with their surroundings to favor their development by sea. They were by nature businessmen, traders, producers, negotiators. Therefore both in their native country and abroad, whether settled in the ports of civilized nations, or of barbarous eastern rulers, or in colonies of their own foundation, they everywhere strove to draw out all the resources of the land, to develop and increase them. The quick instinct of the born trader, shopkeeper if you will, sought continually new articles to exchange; and this search, combined with the industrious character evolved through generations of labor, made them necessarily producers. At home they became great as manufacturers; abroad, where they controlled, the land grew richer continually, products multiplied, and the necessary exchange between home and the settlements called for more ships. Their shipping therefore increased with these demands of trade, and nations with less aptitude for maritime enterprise, even France herself, great as she has been, called for their products and for the service of their ships. Thus in many ways they advanced to power at sea. This natural tendency and growth were indeed modified and seriously checked at times by the interference of other governments, jealous of a prosperity which their own people could invade only by the aid of artificial support,—a support which will be considered under the head of governmental action as affecting sea power.

The tendency to trade, involving of necessity the production of something to trade with, is the national characteristic most important to the development of sea power. Granting it and a good seaboard, it is not likely that the dangers of the sea, or any aversion to it, will deter a people from seeking wealth by the paths of ocean commerce. Where wealth is sought by other means, it may be found; but it will not necessarily lead to sea power. Take France. France has a fine country, an industrious people, an admirable position. The French navy has known periods of great glory, and in its lowest estate has never dishonored the military reputation so dear to the nation. Yet as a maritime State, securely resting upon a broad basis of sea commerce, France, as compared with other historical sea-peoples, has never held more than a respectable position. The chief reason for this, so far as national character goes, is the way in which wealth is sought. As Spain and Portugal sought it by digging gold out of the ground, the temper of the French people leads them to seek it by thrift, economy, hoarding. It is said to be harder to keep than to make a fortune. Possibly; but the adventurous temper, which risks what it has to gain more, has much in common with the adventurous spirit that conquers worlds for commerce. The tendency to save and put aside, to venture timidly and on a small scale, may lead to a general diffusion of wealth on a like small scale, but not to the risks and development of external trade and shipping interests. To illustrate,—and the incident is given only for what it is worth,—a French officer, speaking to the author about the Panama Canal, said: "I have two shares in it. In France we don't do as you, where a few people take a great many shares each. With us a large number of people take one share or a very few. When these were in the market my wife said to me, You take two shares, one for you and one for me.' " As regards the stability of a man's personal fortunes this kind of prudence is doubtless wise; but when excessive prudence or financial timidity becomes a national trait, it must tend to hamper the expansion of commerce and of the nation's shipping. The same caution in money matters, appearing in another relation of life, has checked the production of children, and keeps the population of France nearly stationary.

The noble classes of Europe inherited from the Middle Ages a supercilious contempt for peaceful trade, which has exercised a modifying influence upon its growth, according to the national character of different countries. The pride of the Spaniards fell easily in with this spirit of contempt, and co-operated with that disastrous unwillingness to work and wait for wealth which turned them away from commerce. In France, the vanity which is conceded even by Frenchmen to be a national trait led in the same direction. The numbers and brilliancy of the nobility, and the consideration enjoyed by them, set a seal of inferiority upon an occupation which they despised. Rich merchants and manufacturers sighed for the honors of nobility, and upon obtaining them, abandoned their lucrative professions. Therefore, while the industry of the people and the fruitfulness of the soil saved commerce from total decay, it was pursued under a sense of humiliation which caused its best representatives to escape from it as soon as they could. Louis XIV., under the influence of Colbert, put forth an ordinance "authorizing all noblemen to take an interest in merchant ships, goods and merchandise, without being considered as having derogated from nobility, provided they did not sell at retail"; and the reason given for this action was, "that it imports the good of our subjects and our own satisfaction, to efface the relic of a public opinion, universally prevalent, that maritime commerce is incompatible with nobility." But a prejudice involving conscious and open superiority is not readily effaced by ordinances, especially when vanity is a conspicuous trait in national character; and many years later Montesquieu taught that it is contrary to the spirit of monarchy that the nobility should engage in trade.

In Holland there was a nobility; but the State was republican in name, allowed large scope to personal freedom and enterprise, and the centres of power were in the great cities. The foundation of the national greatness was money—or rather wealth. Wealth, as a source of civic distinction, carried with it also power in the State; and with power there went social position and consideration. In England the same result obtained. The nobility were proud; but in a representative government the power of wealth could be neither put down nor overshadowed. It was patent to the eyes of all, it was honored by all; and in England, as well as Holland, the occupations which were the source of wealth shared in the honor given to wealth itself. Thus, in all the countries named, social sentiment, the outcome of national characteristics, had a marked influence upon the national attitude toward trade.

In yet another way does the national genius affect the growth of sea power in its broadest sense; and that is in so far as it possesses the capacity for planting healthy colonies. Of colonization, as of all other growths, it is true that it is most healthy when it is most natural. Therefore colonies that spring from the felt wants and natural impulses of a whole people will have the most solid foundations; and their subsequent growth will be surest when they are least trammelled from home, if the people have the genius for independent action. Men of the past three centuries have keenly felt the value to the mother-country of colonies as outlets for the home products and as a nursery for commerce and shipping; but efforts at colonization have not had the same general origin, nor have different systems all had the same success. The efforts of statesmen, however far-seeing and careful, have not been able to supply the lack of strong natural impulse; nor can the most minute regulation from home produce as good results as a happier neglect, when the germ of self-development is found in the national character. There has been no greater display of wisdom in the national administration of successful colonies than in that of unsuccessful. Perhaps there has been even less. If elaborate system and supervision, careful adaptation of means to ends, diligent nursing, could avail for colonial growth, the genius of England has less of this systematizing faculty than the genius of France; but England, not France, has been the great colonizer of the world. Successful colonization, with its consequent effect upon commerce and sea power, depends essentially upon national character; because colonies grow best when they grow of themselves, naturally. The character of the colonist, not the care of the home government, is the principle of the colony's growth.

This truth stands out the clearer because the general attitude of all the home governments toward their colonies was entirely selfish. However founded, as soon as it was recognized to be of consequence, the colony became to the home country a cow to be milked; to be cared for, of course, but chiefly as a piece of property valued for the returns it gave. Legislation was directed toward a monopoly of its external trade; the places in its government afforded posts of value for occupants from the mother-country; and the colony was looked upon, as the sea still so often is, as a fit place for those who were ungovernable or useless at home. The military administration, however, so long as it remains a colony, is the proper and necessary attribute of the home government.

The fact of England's unique and wonderful success as a great colonizing nation is too evident to be dwelt upon; and the reason for it appears to lie chiefly in two traits of the national character. The English colonist naturally and readily settles down in his new country, identifies his interest with it, and though keeping an affectionate remembrance of the home from which he came, has no restless eagerness to return. In the second place, the Englishman at once and instinctively seeks to develop the resources of the new country in the broadest sense. In the former particular he differs from the French, who were ever longingly looking back to the delights of their pleasant land; in the latter, from the Spaniards, whose range of interest and ambition was too narrow for the full evolution of the possibilities of a new country.

The character and the necessities of the Dutch led them naturally to plant colonies; and by the year 1650 they had in the East Indies, in Africa, and in America a large number, only to name which would be tedious. They were then far ahead of England in this matter. But though the origin of these colonies, purely commercial in its character, was natural, there seems to have been lacking to them a principle of growth. "In planting them they never sought an extension of empire, but merely an acquisition of trade and commerce. They attempted conquest only when forced by the pressure of circumstances. Generally they were content to trade under the protection of the sovereign of the country." This placid satisfaction with gain alone, unaccompanied by political ambition, tended, like the despotism of France and Spain, to keep the colonies mere commercial dependencies upon the mother-country, and so killed the natural principle of growth.

Before quitting this head of the inquiry, it is well to ask how far the national character of Americans is fitted to develop a great sea power, should other circumstances become favorable.

It seems scarcely necessary, however, to do more than appeal to a not very distant past to prove that, if legislative hindrances be removed, and more remunerative fields of enterprise filled up, the sea power will not long delay its appearance. The instinct for commerce, bold enterprise in the pursuit of gain, and a keen scent for the trails that lead to it, all exist; and if there be in the future any fields calling for colonization, it cannot be doubted that Americans will carry to them all their inherited aptitude for self-government and independent growth.

VI *Character of the Government*—In discussing the effects upon the development of a nation's sea power exerted by its government and institutions, it will be necessary to avoid a tendency to over-philosophizing, to confine attention to obvious and immediate causes and their plain results, without prying too far beneath the surface for remote and ultimate influences.

Nevertheless, it must be noted that particular forms of government with their accompanying institutions, and the character of rulers at one time or another, have exercised a very marked influence upon the development of sea power. The various traits of a country and its people which have so far been considered constitute the natural characteristics with which a nation, like a man, begins its career; the conduct of the government in turn corresponds to the exercise of the intelligent will-power, which, according as it is wise, energetic and persevering, or the reverse, causes success or failure in a man's life or a nation's history.

It would seem probable that a government in full accord with the natural bias of its people would most successfully advance its growth in every respect; and, in the matter of sea power, the most brilliant successes have followed where there has been intelligent direction by a government fully imbued with the spirit of the people and conscious of its true general bent. Such a government is most certainly secured when the will of the people, or of their best natural exponents, has some large share in making it; but such free governments have sometimes fallen short, while on the other hand despotic power, wielded with judgment and consistency, has created at times a great sea commerce and a brilliant navy with greater directness than can be reached by the slower processes of a free people. The difficulty in the latter case is to insure perseverance after the death of a particular despot.

England having undoubtedly reached the greatest height of sea power of any modern nation, the action of her government first claims attention. In general direction this action has been consistent, though often far from praiseworthy. It has aimed steadily at the control of the sea. One of its most arrogant expressions dates back as far as the reign of James I., when she had scarce any possessions outside her own islands; before Virginia or Massachusetts was settled. Here is Richelieu's account of it:—

"The Duke of Sully, minister of Henry IV. [one of the most chivalrous princes that ever lived], having embarked at Calais in a French ship wearing the French flag at the main, was no sooner in the Channel than, meeting an English despatch-boat which was there to receive him, the commander of the latter ordered the French ship to lower her flag. The Duke, considering that his quality freed him from such an affront, boldly refused; but this refusal was followed by three cannon-shot, which, piercing his ship, pierced the heart likewise of all good Frenchmen. Might forced him to yield what right forbade, and for all the complaints he made he could get no better reply from the English captain than this: 'That just as his duty obliged him to honor the ambassador's rank, it also obliged him to exact the honor due to the flag of his master as sovereign of the sea'. If the words of King James himself were more polite, they nevertheless had no other effect than to compel the Duke to take counsel of his prudence, feigning to be satisfied, while his wound was all the time smarting and incurable. Henry the Great had to practise moderation on this occasion; but with the resolve another time to sustain the rights of his crown by the force that, with the aid of time, he should be able to put upon the sea."

This act of unpardonable insolence, according to modern ideas, was not so much out of accord with the spirit of nations in that day. It is chiefly noteworthy as the most striking, as well as one of the earliest indications of the purpose of England to assert herself at all risks upon the sea; and the insult was offered under one of her most timid kings to an ambassador immediately representing the bravest and ablest of French sovereigns. This empty honor of the flag, a claim insignificant except as the outward manifestation of the purpose of a government, was as rigidly exacted under Cromwell as under the kings. It was one of the conditions of peace yielded by the Dutch after their disastrous war of 1654. Cromwell, a despot in everything but name, was keenly alive to all that concerned England's honor and strength, and did not stop at barren salutes to promote them. Hardly yet possessed of power, the English navy sprang rapidly into a new life and vigor under his stern rule. England's rights, or reparation for her wrongs, were demanded by her fleets throughout the world,—in the Baltic, in the Mediterranean, against the Barbary States, in the West Indies; and under him the conquest of Jamaica began that extension of her empire, by force of arms, which has gone on to our own days. Nor were equally strong peaceful measures for the growth of English trade and shipping forgotten. Cromwell's celebrated Navigation Act declared that all imports into England or her colonies must be conveyed exclusively in vessels belonging to England herself, or to the country in which the products carried were grown or manufactured. This decree, aimed specially at the Dutch, the common carriers of Europe, was resented throughout the commercial world; but the benefit to England, in those days of national strife and animosity, was so apparent that it lasted long under the monarchy. A century and a quarter later we find Nelson, before his famous career had begun, showing his zeal for the welfare of England's shipping by enforcing this same act in the West Indies against American merchant-ships. When Cromwell was dead, and Charles II. sat on the throne of his father, this king, false to the English people, was yet true to England's greatness and to the traditional policy of her government on the sea. In his treacherous intrigues with Louis XIV., by which he aimed to make himself independent of Parliament and people, he wrote to Louis: "There are two impediments to a perfect union. The first is the great care France is now taking to create a commerce and to be an imposing maritime power. This is so great a cause of suspicion with us, who can possess importance only by our commerce and our naval force, that every step which France takes in this direction will perpetuate the jealousy between the two nations." In the midst of the negotiations which preceded the detestable attack of the two kings upon the Dutch republic, a warm dispute arose as to who should command the united fleets of France and England. Charles was inflexible on this point. "It is the custom of the English," said he, "to command at sea"; and he told the French ambassador plainly that, were he to yield, his subjects would not obey him. In the projected partition of the United Provinces he reserved for England the maritime plunder in positions that controlled the mouths of the rivers Scheldt and Meuse. The navy under Charles preserved for some time the spirit and discipline impressed on it by Cromwell's iron rule; though later it shared in the general decay of *morale* which marked this evil reign. Monk, having by a great strategic blunder sent off a fourth of his fleet, found himself in 1666 in presence of a greatly superior Dutch force. Disregarding the odds, he attacked without hesitation, and for three days maintained the fight with honor, though with loss. Such conduct is not war; but in the single eye that looked to England's naval prestige and dictated his action, common as it was to England's people as well as to her government, has lain the secret of final success following many blunders through the centuries. Charles's successor, James II., was himself a seaman, and had commanded in two great sea-fights. When William III. came to the throne, the governments of England and Holland were under one hand, and continued united in one purpose against Louis XIV. until the Peace of Utrecht in 1713; that is, for a quarter of a century. The English government more and more steadily, and with conscious purpose, pushed on the extension of her sea dominion and fostered the growth of her sea power. While as an open enemy she struck at France upon the sea, so as an artful friend, many at least believed, she sapped the power of Holland afloat. The treaty between the two countries provided that of the

53

sea forces Holland should furnish three eighths, England five eighths, or nearly double. Such a provision, coupled with a further one which made Holland keep up an army of 102,000 against England's 40,000, virtually threw the land war on one and the sea war on the other. The tendency, whether designed or not, is evident; and at the peace, while Holland received compensation by land, England obtained, besides commercial privileges in France, Spain, and the Spanish West Indies, the important maritime concessions of Gibraltar and Port Mahon in the Mediterranean; of Newfoundland, Nova Scotia, and Hudson's Bay in North America. The naval power of France and Spain had disappeared; that of Holland thenceforth steadily declined. Posted thus in America, the West Indies, and the Mediterranean, the English government thenceforth moved firmly forward in the path which made of the English kingdom the British Empire. For the twenty-five years following the Peace of Utrecht, peace was the chief aim of the ministers who directed the policy of the two great seaboard nations, France and England; but amid all the fluctuations of continental politics in a most unsettled period, abounding in petty wars and shifty treaties, the eye of England was steadily fixed on the maintenance of her sea power. In the Baltic, her fleets checked the attempts of Peter the Great upon Sweden, and so maintained a balance of power in that sea, from which she drew not only a great trade but the chief part of her naval stores, and which the Czar aimed to make a Russian lake. Denmark endeavored to establish an East India company aided by foreign capital; England and Holland not only forbade their subjects to join it, but threatened Denmark, and thus stopped an enterprise they thought adverse to their sea interests. In the Netherlands, which by the Utrecht Treaty had passed to Austria, a similar East India company, having Ostend for its port, was formed, with the emperor's sanction. This step, meant to restore to the Low Countries the trade lost to them through their natural outlet of the Scheldt, was opposed by the sea powers England and Holland; and their greediness for the monopoly of trade, helped in this instance by France, stifled this company also after a few years of struggling life. In the Mediterranean, the Utrecht settlement was disturbed by the emperor of Austria, England's natural ally in the then existing state of European politics. Backed by England, he, having already Naples, claimed also Sicily in exchange for

Sardinia. Spain resisted; and her navy, just beginning to revive under a vigorous minister, Alberoni, was crushed and annihilated by the English fleet off Cape Passaro in 1718; while the following year a French army, at the bidding of England, crossed the Pyrenees and completed the work by destroying the Spanish dock-yards. Thus England, in addition to Gibraltar and Mahon in her own hands, saw Naples and Sicily in those of a friend, while an enemy was struck down. In Spanish America, the limited privileges to English trade, wrung from the necessities of Spain, were abused by an extensive and scarcely disguised smuggling system; and when the exasperated Spanish government gave way to excesses in the mode of suppression, both the minister who counselled peace and the opposition which urged war defended their opinions by alleging the effects of either upon England's sea power and honor. While England's policy thus steadily aimed at widening and strengthening the bases of her sway upon the ocean, the other governments of Europe seemed blind to the dangers to be feared from her sea growth. The miseries resulting from the overweening power of Spain in days long gone by seemed to be forgotten; forgotten also the more recent lesson of the bloody and costly wars provoked by the ambition and exaggerated power of Louis XIV. Under the eyes of the statesmen of Europe there was steadily and visibly being built up a third overwhelming power, destined to be used as selfishly, as aggressively, though not as cruelly, and much more successfully than any that had preceded it. This was the power of the sea, whose workings, because more silent than the clash of arms, are less often noted, though lying clearly enough on the surface. It can scarcely be denied that England's uncontrolled dominion of the seas, during almost the whole period chosen for our subject, was by long odds the chief among the military factors that determined the final issue.[2] So far, however, was this influence from being foreseen after Utrecht, that France for twelve years, moved by personal exigencies of her rulers, sided with England against Spain; and when Fleuri came into power in 1726, though his policy was reversed, the navy of France received no attention, and the only blow at England was the establishment of a Bourbon prince,

[2] An interesting proof of the weight attributed to the naval power of Great Britain by a great military authority will be found in the opening chapter of Jomini's "History of the Wars of the French Revolution." He lays down, as a fundamental principle of European policy, that an unlimited expansion of naval force should not be permitted to any nation which cannot be approached by land,—a description which can apply only to Great Britain.

a natural enemy to her, upon the throne of the two Sicilies in 1736. When war broke out with Spain in 1739, the navy of England was in numbers more than equal to the combined navies of Spain and France; and during the quarter of a century of nearly uninterrupted war that followed, this numerical disproportion increased. In these wars England, at first instinctively, afterward with conscious purpose under a government that recognized her opportunity and the possibilities of her great sea power, rapidly built up that mighty colonial empire whose foundations were already securely laid in the characteristics of her colonists and the strength of her fleets. In strictly European affairs her wealth, the outcome of her sea power, made her play a conspicuous part during the same period. The system of subsidies, which began half a century before in the wars of Marlborough and received its most extensive development half a century later in the Napoleonic wars, maintained the efforts of her allies, which would have been crippled, if not paralyzed, without them. Who can deny that the government which with one hand strengthened its fainting allies on the continent with the life-blood of money, and with the other drove its own enemies off the sea and out of their chief possessions, Canada, Martinique, Guadeloupe, Havana, Manila, gave to its country the foremost rôle in European politics; and who can fail to see that the power which dwelt in that government, with a land narrow in extent and poor in resources, sprang directly from the sea? The policy in which the English government carried on the war is shown by a speech of Pitt, the masterspirit during its course, though he lost office before bringing it to an end. Condemning the Peace of 1763, made by his political opponent, he said: "France is chiefly, if not exclusively, formidable to us as a maritime and commercial power. What we gain in this respect is valuable to us, above all, through the injury to her which results from it. You have left to France the possibility of reviving her navy." Yet England's gains were enormous; her rule in India was assured, and all North America east of the Mississippi in her hands. By this time the onward path of her government was clearly marked out, had assumed the force of a tradition, and was consistently followed. The war of the American Revolution was, it is true, a great mistake, looked at from the point of view of sea power; but the government was led into it insensibly by a series of natural blunders. Putting aside political and constitutional considerations, and looking at the question as purely military or naval, the case was this: The American colonies were large and growing communities at a great distance from England. So long as they remained attached to the mother-country, as they then were enthusiastically, they formed a solid base for her sea power in that part of the world; but their extent and population were too great, when coupled with the distance from England, to afford any hope of holding them by force, *if* any powerful nations were willing to help them. This "if," however, involved a notorious probability; the humiliation of France and Spain was so bitter and so recent that they were sure to seek revenge, and it was well known that France in particular had been carefully and rapidly building up her navy. Had the colonies been thirteen islands, the sea power of England would quickly have settled the question; but instead of such a physical barrier they were separated only by local jealousies which a common danger sufficiently overcame. To enter deliberately on such a contest, to try to hold by force so extensive a territory, with a large hostile population, so far from home, was to renew the Seven Years' War with France and Spain, and with the Americans, against, instead of for, England. The Seven Years' War had been so heavy a burden that a wise government would have known that the added weight could not be borne, and have seen it was necessary to conciliate the colonists. The government of the day was not wise, and a large element of England's sea power was sacrificed; but by mistake, not wilfully; through arrogance, not through weakness.

This steady keeping to a general line of policy was doubtless made specially easy for successive English governments by the clear indications of the country's conditions. Singleness of purpose was to some extent imposed. The firm maintenance of her sea power, the haughty determination to make it felt, the wise state of preparation in which its military element was kept, were yet more due to that feature of her political institutions which practically gave the government during the period in question, into the hands of a class,— a landed aristocracy. Such a class, whatever its defects otherwise, readily takes up and carries on a sound political tradition, is naturally proud of its country's glory, and comparatively insensible to the sufferings of the community by which that glory is maintained. It readily lays on the pecuniary burden necessary for preparation

57

and for endurance of war. Being as a body rich, it feels those burdens less. Not being commercial, the sources of its own wealth are not so immediately endangered, and it does not share that political timidity which characterizes those whose property is exposed and business threatened,—the proverbial timidity of capital. Yet in England this class was not insensible to anything that touched her trade for good or ill. Both houses of Parliament vied in careful watchfulness over its extension and protection, and to the frequency of their inquiries a naval historian attributes the increased efficiency of the executive power in its management of the navy. Such a class also naturally imbibes and keeps up a spirit of military honor, which is of the first importance in ages when military institutions have not yet provided the sufficient substitute in what is called *esprit-de-corps*. But although full of class feeling and class prejudice, which made themselves felt in the navy as well as elsewhere, their practical sense left open the way of promotion to its highest honors to the more humbly born; and every age saw admirals who had sprung from the lowest of the people. In this the temper of the English upper class differed markedly from that of the French. As late as 1789, at the outbreak of the Revolution, the French Navy List still bore the name of an official whose duty was to verify the proofs of noble birth on the part of those intending to enter the naval school.

Since 1815, and especially in our own day, the government of England has passed very much more into the hands of the people at large. Whether her sea power will suffer therefrom remains to be seen. Its broad basis still remains in a great trade, large mechanical industries, and an extensive colonial system. Whether a democratic government will have the foresight, the keen sensitiveness to national position and credit, the willingness to insure its prosperity by adequate outpouring of money in times of peace, all which are necessary for military preparation, is yet an open question. Popular governments are not generally favorable to military expenditure, however necessary, and there are signs that England tends to drop behind.

It has already been seen that the Dutch Republic, even more than the English nation, drew its prosperity and its very life from the sea. The character and policy of its government were far less favorable to a consistent support of sea power. Composed of seven provinces, with the political name of the United Provinces, the actual distribution of power may be roughly described to Americans as an exaggerated example of States Rights. Each of the maritime provinces had its own fleet and its own admiralty, with consequent jealousies. This disorganizing tendency was partly counteracted by the great preponderance of the Province of Holland, which alone contributed five-sixths of the fleet and fifty-eight per cent of the taxes, and consequently had a proportionate share in directing the national policy. Although intensely patriotic, and capable of making the last sacrifices for freedom, the commercial spirit of the people penetrated the government, which indeed might be called a commercial aristocracy, and made it averse to war, and to the expenditures which are necessary in preparing for war. As has before been said, it was not until danger stared them in the face that the burgomasters were willing to pay for their defences. While the republican government lasted, however, this economy was practised least of all upon the fleet; and until the death of John De Witt, in 1672, and the peace with England in 1674, the Dutch navy was in point of numbers and equipment able to make a fair show against the combined navies of England and France. Its efficiency at this time undoubtedly saved the country from the destruction planned by the two kings. With De Witt's death the republic passed away, and was followed by the practically monarchical government of William of Orange. The life-long policy of this prince, then only eighteen, was resistance to Louis XIV. and to the extension of French power. This resistance took shape upon the land rather than the sea,—a tendency promoted by England's withdrawal from the war. As early as 1676, Admiral De Ruyter found the force given him unequal to cope with the French alone. With the eyes of the government fixed on the land frontier, the navy rapidly declined. In 1688, when William of Orange needed a fleet to convoy him to England, the burgomasters of Amsterdam objected that the navy was incalculably decreased in strength, as well as deprived of its ablest commanders. When king of England, William still kept his position as *stadtholder,* and with it his general European policy. He found in England the sea power he needed, and used the resources of Holland for the land war. This Dutch prince consented that in the allied fleets, in councils of war, the Dutch admirals should sit below the junior English captain; and Dutch interests at sea were sacrificed as readily as Dutch pride to the demands of England. When William died, his policy was still followed by the government which succeeded him. Its aims were wholly centred upon the land, and at the Peace of Utrecht, which closed a series of wars extending over forty years, Holland, having established no sea claim, gained nothing in the way of sea resources, of colonial extension, or of commerce.

Of the last of these wars an English historian says: "The economy of the Dutch greatly hurt their reputation and their trade. Their men-of-war in the Mediterranean were always victualled short, and their convoys were so weak and ill-provided that for one ship that we lost, they lost five, which begat a general notion that we were the safer carriers, which certainly had a good effect. Hence it was that our trade rather increased than diminished in this war."

From that time Holland ceased to have a great sea power, and rapidly lost the leading position among the nations which that power had built up. It is only just to say that no policy could have saved from decline this small, though determined, nation, in face of the persistent enmity of Louis XIV. The friendship of France, insuring peace on her landward frontier, would have enabled her, at least for a longer time, to dispute with England the dominion of the seas; and as allies the navies of the two continental States might have checked the growth of the enormous sea power which has just been considered. Sea peace between England and Holland was only possible by the virtual subjection of one or the other, for both aimed at the same object. Between France and Holland it was otherwise; and the fall of Holland proceeded, not necessarily from her inferior size and numbers, but from faulty policy on the part of the two governments. It does not concern us to decide which was the more to blame.

France, admirably situated for the possession of sea power, received a definite policy for the guidance of her government from two great rulers, Henry IV. and Richelieu. With certain well-defined projects of extension eastward upon the land were combined a steady resistance to the House of Austria, which then ruled in both Austria and Spain, and an equal purpose of resistance to England upon the sea. To further this latter end, as well as for other reasons, Holland was to be courted as an ally. Commerce and fisheries as the basis of sea power were to be encouraged, and a military navy was to be built up. Richelieu left what he called his political will, in which he pointed out the opportunities of France for achieving sea power, based upon her position and resources; and French writers consider him the virtual founder of the navy, not merely because he equipped ships, but from the breadth of his views and his measures to insure sound institutions and steady growth. After his death, Mazarin inherited his views and general policy, but not his lofty and martial spirit, and during his rule the newly formed navy disappeared. When Louis XIV. took the government into his own hands, in 1661, there were but thirty ships of war, of which only three had as many as sixty guns. Then began a most astonishing manifestation of the work which can be done by absolute government ably and systematically wielded. That part of the administration which dealt with trade, manufactures, shipping, and colonies, was given to a man of great practical genius, Colbert, who had served with Richelieu and had drunk in fully his ideas and policy. He pursued his aims in a spirit thoroughly French. Everything was to be organized, the spring of everything was in the minister's cabinet. "To organize producers and merchants as a powerful army, subjected to an active and intelligent guidance, so as to secure an industrial victory for France by order and unity of efforts, and to obtain the best products by imposing on all workmen the processes recognized as best by competent men. . . . To organize seamen and distant commerce in large bodies like the manufactures and internal commerce, and to give as a support to the commercial power of France a navy established on a firm basis and of dimensions hitherto unknown,"— such, we are told, were the aims of Colbert as regards two of the three links in the chain of sea power. For the third, the colonies at the far end of the line, the same governmental direction and organization were evidently purposed; for the government began by buying back Canada, Newfoundland, Nova Scotia, and the French West India Islands from the parties who then owned them. Here, then, is seen pure, absolute, uncontrolled power gathering up into its hands all the reins for the guidance of a nation's course, and proposing so to direct it as to make, among other things, a great sea power.

To enter into the details of Colbert's action is beyond our purpose. It is enough to note the chief part played by the government in building up the sea power of the State, and that this very great man looked not to any one of the bases on which it rests to the exclusion of the others, but embraced them all in his wise and provident administration. Agriculture, which increases the products of the earth, and manufactures, which multiply the products of man's industry; internal trade routes and regulations, by which the exchange of products from the interior to the exterior is made easier; shipping and customs regulations tending to throw the carrying-trade into French hands, and so to encourage the building of French shipping, by which the home and colonial products should be carried back and forth; colonial administration and development, by which a far-off market might be continually growing up to be monopolized by the home trade; treaties with foreign States favoring French trade, and imposts on foreign ships and products tending to break down that of rival nations,—all these means, embracing countless details, were employed to build up for France (1) Production; (2) Shipping; (3) Colonies and Markets,—in a word, sea power. The study of such a work is simpler and easier when thus done by one man, sketched out by a kind of logical process, than when slowly wrought by conflicting interests in a more complex government. In the few years of Colbert's administration is seen the whole theory of sea power put into practice in the systematic, centralizing French way; while the illustration of the same theory in English and Dutch history is spread over generations. Such growth, however, was forced, and depended upon the endurance of the absolute power which watched over it; and as Colbert was not king, his control lasted only till he lost the king's favor. It is, however, most interesting to note the results of his labors in the proper field for governmental action—in the navy. It has been said that in 1661, when he took office, there were but thirty armed ships, of which three only had over sixty guns. In 1666 there were seventy, of which fifty were ships-of-the-line and twenty were fire-ships; in 1671, from seventy the number had increased to one hundred and ninety-six. In 1683 there were one hundred and seven ships of from twenty-four to one hundred and twenty guns, twelve of which carried over seventy-six guns, besides many smaller vessels. The order and system introduced into the dock-yards made them vastly more efficient than the English. An English captain, a prisoner in France while the effect of Colbert's work still lasted in the hands of his son, writes:—

"When I was first brought prisoner thither, I lay four months in a hospital at Brest for care of my wounds. While there I was astonished at the expedition used in manning and fitting out their ships, which till then I thought could be done nowhere sooner than in England, where we have ten times the shipping, and consequently ten times the seamen, they have in France; but there I saw twenty sail of ships, of about sixty guns each, got ready in twenty days' time; they were brought in and the men were discharged; and upon an order from Paris they were careened, keeled up, rigged, victualled, manned, and out again in the said time with the greatest ease imaginable. I likewise saw a ship of one hundred guns that had all her guns taken out in four or five hours' time; which I never saw done in England in twenty-four hours, and this with the greatest ease and less hazard than at home. This I saw under my hospital window."

A French naval historian cites certain performances which are simply incredible, such as that the keel of a galley was laid at four o'clock, and that at nine she left port, fully armed. These traditions may be accepted as pointing, with the more serious statements of the English officer, to a remarkable degree of system and order, and abundant facilities for work.

Yet all this wonderful growth, forced by the action of the government, withered away like Jonah's gourd when the government's favor was withdrawn. Time was not allowed for its roots to strike down deep into the life of the nation. Colbert's work was in the direct line of Richelieu's policy, and for a time it seemed there would continue the course of action which would make France great upon the sea as well as predominant upon the land. For reasons which it is not yet necessary to give, Louis came to have feelings of bitter enmity against Holland; and as these feelings were shared by Charles II., the two kings determined on the destruction of the United Provinces. This war, which broke out in 1672, though more contrary to natural feeling on the part of England, was less of a political mistake for her than for France, and especially as regards sea power. France was helping to destroy a probable, and certainly an indispensable, ally; England was assisting in the ruin of her greatest rival on the sea, at this time, indeed, still her commercial superior. France, staggering under debt and utter confusion in her finances when Louis mounted the throne, was just seeing her way clear in 1672, under Colbert's reforms and their happy results. The war, lasting six years, undid the greater part of his work. The agricultural classes, manufactures, commerce, and the colonies, all were smitten by it; the establishments of Colbert languished, and the order he had established in the finances was overthrown. Thus the action of Louis—and he alone was the directing government of France—struck at the roots of her sea power, and alienated her best sea ally.

The territory and the military power of France were increased, but the springs of commerce and of a peaceful shipping had been exhausted in the process; and although the military navy was for some years kept up with splendor and efficiency, it soon began to dwindle, and by the end of the reign had practically disappeared. The same false policy, as regards the sea, marked the rest of this reign of fifty-four years. Louis steadily turned his back upon the sea interests of France, except the fighting-ships, and either could not or would not see that the latter were of little use and uncertain life, if the peaceful shipping and the industries, by which they were supported, perished. His policy, aiming at supreme power in Europe by military strength and territorial extension, forced England and Holland into an alliance, which, as has before been said, directly drove France off the sea, and indirectly swamped Holland's power thereon. Colbert's navy perished, and for the last ten years of Louis' life no great French fleet put to sea, though there was constant war. The simplicity of form in an absolute monarchy thus brought out strongly how great the influence of government can be upon both the growth and the decay of sea power.

The latter part of Louis' life thus witnessed that power failing by the weakening of its foundations, of commerce, and of the wealth that commerce brings. The government that followed, likewise absolute, of set purpose and at the demand of England, gave up all pretence of maintaining an effective navy. The reason for this was that the new king was a minor; and the regent, being bitterly at enmity with the king of Spain, to injure him and preserve his own power, entered into alliance with England. He aided her to establish Austria, the hereditary enemy of France, in Naples and Sicily to the detriment of Spain, and in union with her destroyed the Spanish navy and dock-yards. Here again is found a personal ruler disregarding the sea interests of France, ruining a natural ally, and directly aiding, as Louis XIV. indirectly and unintentionally aided, the growth of a mistress of the seas. This transient phase of policy passed away with the death of the regent in 1726; but from that time until 1760 the government of France continued to disregard her maritime interests. It is said, indeed, that owing to some wise modifications of her fiscal regulations, mainly in the direction of free trade (and due to Law, a minister of Scotch birth), commerce with the East and West Indies wonderfully increased, and that the islands of Guadeloupe and Martinique became very rich and thriving; but both commerce and colonies lay at the mercy of England when war came, for the navy fell into decay. In 1756, when things were no longer at their worst, France had but forty-five ships-of-the-line, England nearly one hundred and thirty; and when the forty-five were to be armed and equipped, there was found to be neither material nor rigging nor supplies; not even enough artillery. Nor was this all.

"Lack of system in the government," says a French writer, "brought about indifference, and opened the door to disorder and lack of discipline. Never had unjust promotions been so frequent; so also never had more universal discontent been seen. Money and intrigue took the place of all else, and brought in their train commands and power. Nobles and upstarts, with influence at the capital and self-sufficiency in the seaports, thought themselves dispensed with merit. Waste of the revenues of the State and of the dock-yards knew no bounds. Honor and modesty were turned into ridicule. As if the evils were not thus great enough, the ministry took pains to efface the heroic traditions of the past which had escaped the general wreck. To the energetic fights of the great reign succeeded, by order of the court, 'affairs of circumspection.' To preserve to the wasted material a few armed ships, increased opportunity was given to the enemy. From this unhappy principle we were bound to a defensive as advantageous to the enemy as it was foreign to the genius of our people. This circumspection before the enemy, laid down for us by orders, betrayed in the long run the national temper; and the abuse of the system led to acts of indiscipline and defection under fire, of which a single instance would vainly be sought in the previous century."

A false policy of continental extension swallowed up the resources of the country, and was doubly injurious because, by leaving defence-less its colonies and commerce, it exposed the greatest source of wealth to be cut off, as in fact happened. The small squadrons that got to sea were destroyed by vastly superior force; the merchant shipping was swept away, and the colonies, Canada, Martinique, Guadeloupe, India, fell into England's hands. If it did not take too much space, interesting extracts might be made, showing the woful misery of France, the country that had abandoned the sea, and the growing wealth of England amid all her sacrifices and exertions. A contemporary writer has thus expressed his view of the policy of France at this period:—

"France, by engaging so heartily as she has done in the German war, has drawn away so much of her attention and her revenue from her navy that it enabled us to give such a blow to her maritime strength as possibly she may never be able to recover. Her engagement in the German war has likewise drawn her from the defence of her colonies, by which means we have conquered some of the most considerable she possessed. It has withdrawn her from the protection of her trade, by which it is entirely destroyed, while that of England has never, in the profoundest peace, been in so flourishing a condition. So that, by embarking in this German war, France has suffered herself to be undone, so far as regards her particular and immediate quarrel with England."

In the Seven Years' War France lost thirty-seven ships-of-the-line and fifty-six frigates,—a force three times as numerous as the whole navy of the United States at any time in the days of sailing-ships. "For the first time since the Middle Ages," says a French historian, speaking of the same war, "England had conquered France single-handed, almost without allies, France having powerful auxiliaries. She had conquered solely by the superiority of her government." Yes; but it was by the superiority of her government using the tremendous weapon of her sea power,—the reward of a consistent policy perseveringly directed to one aim.

The profound humiliation of France, which reached its depths between 1760 and 1763, at which latter date she made peace, has an instructive lesson for the United States in this our period of commercial and naval decadence. We have been spared her humiliation; let us hope to profit by her subsequent example. Between the same years (1760 and 1763) the French people rose, as afterward in 1793, and declared they would have a navy. "Popular feeling, skilfully directed by the government, took up the cry from one end of France to the other, 'The navy must be restored.' Gifts of ships were made by cities, by corporations, and by private subscriptions. A prodigious activity sprang up in the lately silent ports; everywhere ships were building or repairing." This activity was sustained; the arsenals were replenished, the material of every kind was put on a satisfactory footing, the artillery reorganized and ten thousand trained gunners drilled and maintained.

The tone and action of the naval officers of the day instantly felt the popular impulse, for which indeed some loftier spirits among them had been not only waiting but working. At no time was greater mental and professional activity found among French naval officers than just then, when their ships had been suffered to rot away by

66

governmental inaction. Thus a prominent French officer of our own day writes:—

"The sad condition of the navy in the reign of Louis XV., by closing to officers the brilliant career of bold enterprises and successful battles, forced them to fall back upon themselves. They drew from study the knowledge they were to put to the proof some years later, thus putting into practice that fine saying of Montesquieu, 'Adversity is our mother, Prosperity our step-mother. . . .' By the year 1769 was seen in all its splendor that brilliant galaxy of officers whose activity stretched to the ends of the earth, and who embraced in their works and in their investigations all the branches of human knowledge. The Académie de Marine, founded in 1752, was reorganized." [3]

The Académie's first director, a post-captain named Bigot de Morogues, wrote an elaborate treatise on naval tactics, the first original work on the subject since Paul Hoste's, which it was designed to supersede. Morogues must have been studying and formulating his problems in tactics in days when France had no fleet, and was unable so much as to raise her head at sea under the blows of her enemy. At the same time England had no similar book; and an English lieutenant, in 1762, was just translating a part of Hoste's great work, omitting by far the larger part. It was not until nearly twenty years later that Clerk, a Scotch private gentleman, published an ingenious study of naval tactics, in which he pointed out to English admirals the system by which the French had thwarted their thoughtless and ill-combined attacks.[4] "The researches of the Académie de Marine, and the energetic impulse which it gave to the labors of officers, were not, as we hope to show later, without influence upon the relatively prosperous condition in which the navy was at the beginning of the American war."

It has already been pointed out that the American War of Independence involved a departure from England's traditional and true policy, by committing her to a distant land war, while powerful enemies were waiting for an opportunity to attack her at sea. Like France in the then recent German wars, like Napoleon later in the Spanish war, England, through undue self-confidence, was about

[3] Gougeard: La Marine de Guerre; Richelieu et Colbert.
[4] Whatever may be thought of Clerk's claim to originality in constructing a system of naval tactics, and it has been seriously impugned, there can be no doubt that his criticisms on the past were sound. So far as the author knows, he in this respect deserves credit for an originality remarkable in one who had the training neither of a seaman nor of a military man.

to turn a friend into an enemy, and so expose the real basis of her power to a rude proof. The French government, on the other hand, avoided the snare into which it had so often fallen. Turning her back on the European continent, having the probability of neutrality there, and the certainty of alliance with Spain by her side, France advanced to the contest with a fine navy and a brilliant, though perhaps relatively inexperienced, body of officers. On the other side of the Atlantic she had the support of a friendly people, and of her own or allied ports, both in the West Indies and on the continent. The wisdom of this policy, the happy influence of this action of the government upon her sea power, is evident; but the details of the war do not belong to this part of the subject. To Americans, the chief interest of that war is found upon the land; but to naval officers, upon the sea, for it was essentially a sea war. The intelligent and systematic efforts of twenty years bore their due fruit; for though the warfare afloat ended with a great disaster, the combined efforts of the French and Spanish fleets undoubtedly bore down England's strength and robbed her of her colonies. In the various naval undertakings and battles the honor of France was upon the whole maintained; though it is difficult, upon consideration of the general subject, to avoid the conclusion that the inexperience of French seamen as compared with English, the narrow spirit of jealousy shown by the noble corps of officers toward those of different antecedents, and above all, the miserable traditions of three quarters of a century already alluded to, the miserable policy of a government which taught them first to save their ships, to economize the material, prevented French admirals from reaping, not the mere glory, but the positive advantages that more than once were within their grasp. When Monk said the nation that would rule upon the sea must always attack, he set the key-note to England's naval policy; and had the instructions of the French government consistently breathed the same spirit, the war of 1778 might have ended sooner and better than it did. It seems ungracious to criticise the conduct of a service to which, under God, our nation owes that its birth was not a miscarriage; but writers of its own country abundantly reflect the spirit of the remark. A French officer who served afloat during this war, in a work of calm and judicial tone, says:—

"What must the young officers have thought who were at Sandy Hook with D'Estaing, at St. Christopher with De Grasse, even those who arrived at Rhode Island with De Ternay, when they saw that these officers were not tried at their return?" [5]

Again, another French officer, of much later date, justifies the opinion expressed, when speaking of the war of the American Revolution in the following terms:—

"It was necessary to get rid of the unhappy prejudices of the days of the regency and of Louis XV.; but the mishaps of which they were full were too recent to be forgotten by our ministers. Thanks to a wretched hesitation, fleets, which had rightly alarmed England, became reduced to ordinary proportions. Intrenching themselves in a false economy, the ministry claimed that, by reason of the excessive expenses necessary to maintain the fleet, the admirals must be ordered to maintain the *'greatest circumspection,'* as though in war half measures have not always led to disasters. So, too, the orders given to our squadron chiefs were to keep the sea as long as possible, without engaging in actions which might cause the loss of vessels difficult to replace; so that more than once complete victories, which would have crowned the skill of our admirals and the courage of our captains, were changed into successes of little importance. A system which laid down as a principle that an admiral should not use the force in his hands, which sent him against the enemy with the foreordained purpose of receiving rather than making the attack, a system which sapped moral power to save material resources, must have unhappy results. . . . It is certain that this deplorable system was one of the causes of the lack of discipline and startling defections which marked the periods of Louis XVI., of the [first] Republic, and of the [first] Empire." [6]

Within ten years of the peace of 1783 came the French Revolution; but that great upheaval which shook the foundations of States, loosed the ties of social order, and drove out of the navy nearly all the trained officers of the monarchy who were attached to the old state of things, did not free the French navy from a false system. It was easier to overturn the form of government than to uproot a deep-seated tradition. Hear again a third French officer, of the highest rank and literary accomplishments, speaking of the inaction of Villeneuve, the admiral who commanded the French rear at the battle of the Nile, and who did not leave his anchors while the head of the column was being destroyed:—

"A day was to come [Trafalgar] in which Villeneuve in his turn, like De Grasse before him, and like Duchayla, would complain of being abandoned

[5] La Serre: Essais Hist. et Crit. sur la Marine Française.
[6] La Pérouse-Bonfils: Hist. de la Marine Française.

by part of his fleet. We have come to suspect some secret reason for this fatal coincidence. It is not natural that among so many honorable men there should so often be found admirals and captains incurring such a reproach. If the name of some of them is to this very day sadly associated with the memory of our disasters, we may be sure the fault is not wholly their own. We must rather blame the nature of the operations in which they were engaged, and that system of defensive war prescribed by the French government, which Pitt, in the English Parliament, proclaimed to be the forerunner of certain ruin. That system, when we wished to renounce it, had already penetrated our habits; it had, so to say, weakened our arms and paralyzed our self-reliance. Too often did our squadrons leave port with a special mission to fulfil, and with the intention of avoiding the enemy; to fall in with him was at once a piece of bad luck. It was thus that our ships went into action; they submitted to it instead of forcing it. . . . Fortune would have hesitated longer between the two fleets, and not have borne in the end so heavily against ours, if Brueys, meeting Nelson half way, could have gone out to fight him. This fettered and timid war, which Villaret and Martin had carried on, had lasted long, thanks to the circumspection of some English admirals and the traditions of the old tactics. It was with these traditions that the battle of the Nile had broken; the hour for decisive action had come." [7]

Some years later came Trafalgar, and again the government of France took up a new policy with the navy. The author last quoted speaks again:—

"The emperor, whose eagle glance traced plans of campaign for his fleets as for his armies, was wearied by these unexpected reverses. He turned his eyes from the one field of battle in which fortune was faithless to him, and decided to pursue England elsewhere than upon the seas; he undertook to rebuild his navy, but without giving it any part in the struggle which became more furious than ever. . . . Nevertheless, far from slackening, the activity of our dock-yards redoubled. Every year ships-of-the-line were either laid down or added to the fleet. Venice and Genoa, under his control, saw their old splendors rise again, and from the shores of the Elbe to the head of the Adriatic all the ports of the continent emulously seconded the creative thought of the emperor. Numerous squadrons were assembled in the Scheldt, in Brest Roads, and in Toulon. . . . But to the end the emperor refused to give this navy, full of ardor and self-reliance, an opportunity to measure its strength with the enemy. . . . Cast down by constant reverses, he had kept up our armed ships only to oblige our enemies to blockades whose enormous cost must end by exhausting their finances." [7]

When the empire fell, France had one hundred and three ships-of-the-line and fifty-five frigates.

[7] Jurien de la Gravière: Guerres Maritimes.

To turn now from the particular lessons drawn from the history of the past to the general question of the influence of government upon the sea career of its people, it is seen that that influence can work in two distinct but closely related ways.

First, in peace: The government by its policy can favor the natural growth of a people's industries and its tendencies to seek adventure and gain by way of the sea; or it can try to develop such industries and such sea-going bent, when they do not naturally exist; or, on the other hand, the government may by mistaken action check and fetter the progress which the people left to themselves would make. In any one of these ways the influence of the government will be felt, making or marring the sea power of the country in the matter of peaceful commerce; upon which alone, it cannot be too often insisted, a thoroughly strong navy can be based.

Secondly, for war: The influence of the government will be felt in its most legitimate manner in maintaining an armed navy, of a size commensurate with the growth of its shipping and the importance of the interests connected with it. More important even than the size of the navy is the question of its institutions, favoring a healthful spirit and activity, and providing for rapid development in time of war by an adequate reserve of men and of ships and by measures for drawing out that general reserve power which has before been pointed to, when considering the character and pursuits of the people. Undoubtedly under this second head of warlike preparation must come the maintenance of suitable naval stations, in those distant parts of the world to which the armed shipping must follow the peaceful vessels of commerce. The protection of such stations must depend either upon direct military force, as do Gibraltar and Malta, or upon a surrounding friendly population, such as the American colonists once were to England, and, it may be presumed, the Australian colonists now are. Such friendly surroundings and backing, joined to a reasonable military provision, are the best of defences, and when combined with decided preponderance at sea, make a scattered and extensive empire, like that of England, secure; for while it is true that an unexpected attack may cause disaster in some one quarter, the actual superiority of naval power prevents such disaster from being general or irremediable. History has sufficiently proved this. England's naval bases have been in all parts of the world; and her fleets have at once protected them, kept open the communications between them, and relied upon them for shelter.

Colonies attached to the mother-country afford, therefore, the surest means of supporting abroad the sea power of a country. In peace, the influence of the government should be felt in promoting by all means a warmth of attachment and a unity of interest which will make the welfare of one the welfare of all, and the quarrel of one the quarrel of all; and in war, or rather for war, by inducing such measures of organization and defence as shall be felt by all to be a fair distribution of a burden of which each reaps the benefit.

Such colonies the United States has not and is not likely to have. As regards purely military naval stations, the feeling of her people was probably accurately expressed by an historian of the English navy a hundred years ago, speaking then of Gibraltar and Port Mahon. "Military governments," said he, "agree so little with the industry of a trading people, and are in themselves so repugnant to the genius of the British people, that I do not wonder that men of good sense and of all parties have inclined to give up these, as Tangiers was given up." Having therefore no foreign establishments, either colonial or military, the ships of war of the United States, in war, will be like land birds, unable to fly far from their own shores. To provide resting-places for them, where they can coal and repair, would be one of the first duties of a government proposing to itself the development of the power of the nation at sea.

As the practical object of this inquiry is to draw from the lessons of history inferences applicable to one's own country and service, it is proper now to ask how far the conditions of the United States involve serious danger, and call for action on the part of the government, in order to build again her sea power. It will not be too much to say that the action of the government since the Civil War, and up to this day, has been effectively directed solely to what has been called the first link in the chain which makes sea power. Internal development, great production, with the accompanying aim and boast of self-sufficingness, such has been the object, such to some extent the result. In this the government has faithfully reflected the bent of the controlling elements of the country, though it is not always easy to feel that such controlling elements are truly representative, even in a free country. However that may be, there is no doubt that, besides having no colonies, the intermediate link of a peaceful shipping, and the interests involved in it, are now likewise lacking. In short, the United States has only one link of the three.

The circumstances of naval war have changed so much within the last hundred years, that it may be doubted whether such disastrous effects on the one hand, or such brilliant prosperity on the other, as were seen in the wars between England and France, could now recur. In her secure and haughty sway of the seas England imposed a yoke on neutrals which will never again be borne; and the principle that the "flag covers the goods" is forever secured. The commerce of a belligerent can therefore now be safely carried on in neutral ships, except when contraband of war or to blockaded ports; and as regards the latter, it is also certain that there will be no more paper blockades. Putting aside therefore the question of defending her seaports from capture or contribution, as to which there is practical unanimity in theory and entire indifference in practice, what need has the United States of sea power? Her commerce is even now carried on by others; why should her people desire that which, if possessed, must be defended at great cost? So far as this question is economical, it is outside the scope of this work; but conditions which may entail suffering and loss on the country by war are directly pertinent to it. Granting therefore that the foreign trade of the United States, going and coming, is on board ships which an enemy cannot touch except when bound to a blockaded port, what will constitute an efficient blockade? The present definition is, that it is such as to constitute a manifest danger to a vessel seeking to enter or leave the port. This is evidently very elastic. Many can remember that during the Civil War, after a night attack on the United States fleet off Charleston, the Confederates next morning sent out a steamer with some foreign consuls on board, who so far satisfied themselves that no blockading vessel was in sight that they issued a declaration to that effect. On the strength of this declaration some Southern authorities claimed that the blockade was technically broken, and could not be technically re-established without a new notification. Is it necessary, to constitute a real danger to blockade-runners, that the blockading fleet should be in sight? Half a dozen fast steamers, cruising twenty miles off-shore between the New Jersey and Long Island coast, would be a very real danger to ships seeking to go in or out by the principal entrance to New York; and similar positions might effectively blockade Boston, the Delaware, and the Chesapeake. The main body of the blockading fleet, prepared not only to capture merchant-ships but to resist military attempts to break the blockade, need not be within sight, nor in a position known to the shore. The bulk of Nelson's fleet was fifty miles from Cadiz two days before Trafalgar, with a small detachment watching close to the harbor. The allied fleet began to get under way at 7 A.M., and Nelson, even under the conditions of those days, knew it by 9.30. The English fleet at that distance was a very real danger to its enemy. It seems possible, in these days of submarine telegraphs, that the blockading forces in-shore and off-shore, and from one port to another, might be in telegraphic communication with one another along the whole coast of the United States, readily giving mutual support; and if, by some fortunate military combination, one detachment were attacked in force, it could warn the others and retreat upon them. Granting that such a blockade off one port were broken on one day, by fairly driving away the ships maintaining it, the notification of its being re-established could be cabled all over the world the next. To avoid such blockades there must be a military force afloat that will at all times so endanger a blockading fleet that it can by no means keep its place. Then neutral ships, except those laden with contraband of war, can come and go freely, and maintain the commercial relations of the country with the world outside.

It may be urged that, with the extensive sea-coast of the United States, a blockade of the whole line cannot be effectively kept up. No one will more readily concede this than officers who remember how the blockade of the Southern coast alone was maintained. But in the present condition of the navy, and, it may be added, with any additions not exceeding those so far proposed by the government,[8] the attempt to blockade Boston, New York, the Delaware, the Chesapeake, and the Mississippi, in other words, the great centres of export and import, would not entail upon one of the large maritime nations efforts greater than have been made before. England has at the same time blockaded Brest, the Biscay coast, Toulon, and Cadiz, when there were powerful squadrons lying within the harbors. It is true that commerce in neutral ships can then enter other ports of the United States than those named; but what a dislocation of the

[8] Since the above was written, the Secretary of the Navy, in his report for 1889, has recommended a fleet which would make such a blockade as here suggested very hazardous.

carrying traffic of the country, what failure of supplies at times, what inadequate means of transport by rail or water, of dockage, of lighterage, of warehousing, will be involved in such an enforced change of the ports of entry! Will there be no money loss, no suffering, consequent upon this? And when with much pain and expense these evils have been partially remedied, the enemy may be led to stop the new inlets as he did the old. The people of the United States will certainly not starve, but they may suffer grievously. As for supplies which are contraband of war, is there not reason to fear that the United States is not now able to go alone if an emergency should arise?

The question is eminently one in which the influence of the government should make itself felt, to build up for the nation a navy which, if not capable of reaching distant countries, shall at least be able to keep clear the chief approaches to its own. The eyes of the country have for a quarter of a century been turned from the sea; the results of such a policy and of its opposite will be shown in the instance of France and of England. Without asserting a narrow parallelism between the case of the United States and either of these, it may safely be said that it is essential to the welfare of the whole country that the conditions of trade and commerce should remain, as far as possible, unaffected by an external war. In order to do this, the enemy must be kept not only out of our ports, but far away from our coasts.[9]

Can this navy be had without restoring the merchant shipping? It is doubtful. History has proved that such a purely military sea

[9] The word "defence" in war involves two ideas, which for the sake of precision in thought should be kept separated in the mind. There is defence pure and simple, which strengthens itself and awaits attack. This may be called passive defence. On the other hand, there is a view of defence which asserts that safety for one's self, the real object of defensive preparation, is best secured by attacking the enemy. In the matter of sea-coast defence, the former method is exemplified by stationary fortifications, submarine mines, and generally all immobile works destined simply to stop an enemy if he tries to enter. The second method comprises all those means and weapons which do not wait for attack, but go to meet the enemy's fleet, whether it be but for a few miles, or whether to his own shores. Such a defence may seem to be really offensive war, but it is not; it becomes offensive only when its object of attack is changed from the enemy's fleet to the enemy's country. England defended her own coasts and colonies by stationing her fleets off the French ports, to fight the French fleet if it came out. The United States in the Civil War stationed her fleets off the Southern ports, not because she feared for her own, but to break down the Confederacy by isolation from the rest of the world, and ultimately by attacking the ports. The methods were the same; but the purpose in one case was defensive, in the other offensive.

The confusion of the two ideas leads to much unnecessary wrangling as to the proper sphere of army and navy in coast-defence. Passive defences belong to the army; everything that moves in the water to the navy, which has the prerogative of the offensive defence. If seamen are used to garrison forts, they become part of the land forces, as surely as troops, when embarked as part of the complement, become part of the sea forces.

power can be built up by a despot, as was done by Louis XIV.; but though so fair seeming, experience showed that his navy was like a growth which having no root soon withers away. But in a representative government any military expenditure must have a strongly represented interest behind it, convinced of its necessity. Such an interest in sea power does not exist, cannot exist here without action by the government. How such a merchant shipping should be built up, whether by subsidies or by free trade, by constant administration of tonics or by free movement in the open air, is not a military but an economical question. Even had the United States a great national shipping, it may be doubted whether a sufficient navy would follow; the distance which separates her from other great powers, in one way a protection, is also a snare. The motive, if any there be, which will give the United States a navy, is probably now quickening in the Central American Isthmus. Let us hope it will not come to the birth too late.

Here concludes the general discussion of the principal elements which affect, favorably or unfavorably, the growth of sea power in nations. The aim has been, first to consider those elements in their natural tendency for or against, and then to illustrate by particular examples and by the experience of the past. Such discussions, while undoubtedly embracing a wider field, yet fall mainly within the province of strategy, as distinguished from tactics. The considerations and principles which enter into them belong to the unchangeable, or unchanging, order of things, remaining the same, in cause and effect, from age to age. They belong, as it were, to the Order of Nature, of whose stability so much is heard in our day; whereas tactics, using as its instruments the weapons made by man, shares in the change and progress of the race from generation to generation. From time to time the superstructure of tactics has to be altered or wholly torn down; but the old foundations of strategy so far remain, as though laid upon a rock. There will next be examined the general history of Europe and America, with particular reference to the effect exercised upon that history, and upon the welfare of the people, by sea power in its broad sense. From time to time, as, occasion offers, the aim will be to recall and reinforce the general teaching, already elicited, by particular illustrations. The general tenor of the study will therefore be strategical, in that broad definition of naval strategy which has before been quoted and accepted:

"Naval strategy has for its end to found, support, and increase, as well in peace as in war, the sea power of a country." In the matter of particular battles, while freely admitting that the change of details has made obsolete much of their teaching, the attempt will be made to point out where the application or neglect of true general principles has produced decisive effects; and, other things being equal, those actions will be preferred which, from their association with the names of the most distinguished officers, may be presumed to show how far just tactical ideas obtained in a particular age or a particular service. It will also be desirable, where analogies between ancient and modern weapons appear on the surface, to derive such probable lessons as they offer, without laying undue stress upon the points of resemblance. Finally, it must be remembered that, among all changes, the nature of man remains much the same; the personal equation, though uncertain in quantity and quality in the particular instance, is sure always to be found.

2

State of Europe in 1660—Second Anglo-Dutch
War, 1665-1667—Sea Battles of Lowestoft and
of The Four Days

The period at which our historical survey is to begin has been loosely
stated as the middle of the seventeenth century. The year 1660 will
now be taken as the definite date at which to open. In May of that
year Charles II. was restored to the English throne amid the general
rejoicing of the people. In March of the following year, upon the
death of Cardinal Mazarin, Louis XIV. assembled his ministers and
said to them: "I have summoned you to tell you that it has pleased
me hitherto to permit my affairs to be governed by the late cardinal;
I shall in future be my own prime minister. I direct that no decree
be sealed except by my orders, and I order the secretaries of State
and the superintendent of the finances to sign nothing without my
command." The personal government thus assumed was maintained,
in fact as well as in name, for over half a century.

Within one twelvemonth then are seen, setting forward upon a
new stage of national life, after a period of confusion more or less
prolonged, the two States which, amid whatever inequalities, have
had the first places in the sea history of modern Europe and America,
indeed, of the world at large. Sea history, however, is but one factor
in that general advance and decay of nations which is called their
history; and if sight be lost of the other factors to which it is so
closely related, a distorted view, either exaggerated or the reverse,

of its importance will be formed. It is with the belief that that importance is vastly underrated, if not practically lost sight of, by people unconnected with the sea, and particularly by the people of the United States in our own day, that this study has been undertaken.

The date taken, 1660, followed closely another which marked a great settlement of European affairs, setting the seal of treaty upon the results of a general war, known to history as the Thirty Years' War. This other date was that of the Treaty of Westphalia, or Munster, in 1648. In this the independence of the Dutch United Provinces, long before practically assured, was formally acknowledged by Spain; and it being followed in 1659 by the Treaty of the Pyrenees between France and Spain, the two gave to Europe a state of general external peace, destined soon to be followed by a series of almost universal wars, which lasted as long as Louis XIV. lived,—wars which were to induce profound changes in the map of Europe; during which new States were to arise, others to decay, and all to undergo large modifications, either in extent of dominion or in political power. In these results maritime power, directly or indirectly, had a great share.

We must first look at the general condition of European States at the time from which the narrative starts. In the struggles, extending over nearly a century, whose end is marked by the Peace of Westphalia, the royal family known as the House of Austria had been the great overwhelming power which all others feared. During the long reign of the Emperor Charles V., who abdicated a century before, the head of that house had united in his own person the two crowns of Austria and Spain, which carried with them, among other possessions, the countries we now know as Holland and Belgium, together with a preponderating influence in Italy. After his abdication the two great monarchies of Austria and Spain were separated; but though ruled by different persons, they were still in the same family, and tended toward that unity of aim and sympathy which marked dynastic connections in tha and the following century. To this bond of union was added that ot a common religion. During the century before the Peace of Westphalia, the extension of family power, and the extension of the religion professed, were the two strongest motives of political action. This was the period of the great religious wars which arrayed nation against nation, principality against principality, and often, in the same nation, faction against faction. Religious persecution caused the revolt of the Protestant Dutch Provinces against Spain, which issued, after eighty years of more or less constant war, in the recognition of their independence. Religious discord, amounting to civil war at times, distracted France during the greater part of the same period, profoundly affecting not only her internal but her external policy. These were the days of St. Bartholomew, of the religious murder of Henry IV., of the siege of La Rochelle, of constant intriguing between Roman Catholic Spain and Roman Catholic Frenchmen. As the religious motive, acting in a sphere to which it did not naturally belong, and in which it had no rightful place, died away, the political necessities and interests of States began to have juster weight; not that they had been wholly lost sight of in the meantime, but the religious animosities had either blinded the eyes, or fettered the action, of statesmen. It was natural that in France, one of the greatest sufferers from religious passions, owing to the number and character of the Protestant minority, this reaction should first and most markedly be seen. Placed between Spain and the German States, among which Austria stood foremost without a rival, internal union and checks upon the power of the House of Austria were necessities of political existence. Happily, Providence raised up to her in close succession two great rulers, Henry IV. and Richelieu,—men in whom religion fell short of bigotry, and who, when forced to recognize it in the sphere of politics, did so as masters and not as slaves. Under them French statesmanship received a guidance, which Richelieu formulated as a tradition, and which moved on the following general lines,—(1) Internal union of the kingdom, appeasing or putting down religious strife and centralizing authority in the king; (2) Resistance to the power of the House of Austria, which actually and necessarily carried with it alliance with Protestant German States and with Holland; (3) Extension of the boundaries of France to the eastward, at the expense mainly of Spain, which then possessed not only the present Belgium, but other provinces long since incorporated with France; and (4) The creation and development of a great sea power, adding to the wealth of the kingdom, and intended specially to make head against France's hereditary enemy, England; for which end again the alliance with Holland was to be kept in view. Such were the broad outlines of policy laid down by statesmen in the front rank of genius for the guidance of that country whose people have, not without cause, claimed to be the most complete exponent of European civilization, foremost in the march of progress, combining political advance with individual development. This tradition, carried on by Mazarin, was received from him by Louis XIV.; it will be seen how far he was faithful to it, and what were the results to France of his action. Meanwhile it may be noted that of these four elements necessary to the greatness of France, sea power was one; and as the second and third were practically one in the means employed, it may be said that sea power was one of the two great means by which France's *external* greatness was to be maintained. England on the sea, Austria on the land, indicated the direction that French effort was to take.

As regards the condition of France in 1660, and her readiness to move onward in the road marked by Richelieu, it may be said that internal peace was secured, the power of the nobles wholly broken, religious discords at rest; the tolerant edict of Nantes was still in force, while the remaining Protestant discontent had been put down by the armed hand. All power was absolutely centred in the throne. In other respects, though the kingdom was at peace, the condition was less satisfactory. There was practically no navy; commerce, internal and external, was not prosperous; the finances were in disorder; the army small.

Spain, the nation before which all others had trembled less than a century before, was now long in decay and scarcely formidable; the central weakness had spread to all parts of the administration. In extent of territory, however, she was still great. The Spanish Netherlands still belonged to her; she held Naples, Sicily, and Sardinia; Gibraltar had not yet fallen into English hands; her vast possessions in America—with the exception of Jamaica, conquered by England a few years before—were still untouched. The condition of her sea power, both for peace and war, has been already alluded to.

Many years before, Richelieu had contracted a temporary alliance with Spain, by virtue of which she placed forty ships at his disposal; but the bad condition of the vessels, for the most part ill armed and ill commanded, compelled their withdrawal. The navy of Spain was then in full decay, and its weakness did not escape the piercing eye of the cardinal. An encounter which took place between the Spanish and Dutch fleets in 1639 shows most plainly the state of degradation into which this once proud navy had fallen.

"Her navy at this time," says the narrative quoted, "met one of those shocks, a succession of which during this war degraded her from her high station of mistress of the seas in both hemispheres, to a contemptible rank among maritime powers. The king was fitting out a powerful fleet to carry the war to the coasts of Sweden, and for its equipment had commanded a reinforcement of men and provisions to be sent from Dunkirk. A fleet accordingly set sail, but were attacked by Von Tromp, some captured, the remainder forced to retire within the harbor again. Soon after, Tromp seized three English [neutral] ships carrying 1070 Spanish soldiers from Cadiz to Dunkirk; he took the troops out, but let the ships go free. Leaving seventeen vessels to blockade Dunkirk, Tromp with the remaining twelve advanced to meet the enemy's fleet on its arrival. It was soon seen entering the Straits of Dover to the number of sixty-seven sail, and having two thousand troops. Being joined by De Witt with four more ships, Tromp with his small force made a resolute attack upon the enemy. The fight lasted till four P.M., when the Spanish admiral took refuge in the Downs. Tromp determined to engage if they should come out; but Oquendo with his powerful fleet, many of which carried from sixty to a hundred guns, suffered himself to be blockaded; and the English admiral told Tromp he was ordered to join the Spaniards if hostilities began. Tromp sent home for instructions, and the action of England only served to call out the vast maritime powers of the Dutch. Tromp was rapidly reinforced to ninety-six sail and twelve fire-ships, and ordered to attack. Leaving a detached squadron to observe the English, and to attack them if they helped the Spaniards, he began the fight embarrassed by a thick fog, under cover of which the Spaniards cut their cables to escape. Many running too close to shore went aground, and most of the remainder attempting to retreat were sunk, captured, or driven on the French coast. Never was victory more complete." [1]

When a navy submits to such a line of action, all tone and pride must have departed; but the navy only shared in the general decline which made Spain henceforward have an ever lessening weight in the policy of Europe.

"In the midst of the splendors of her court and language," says Guizot, "the Spanish government felt itself weak, and sought to hide its weakness under its immobility. Philip IV. and his minister, weary of striving only to be conquered, looked but for the security of peace, and only sought to put aside all questions which would call for efforts of which they felt themselves incapable. Divided and enervated, the house of Austria had even less ambition than power, and except when absolutely forced, a pompous inertia became the policy of the successors of Charles V." [2]

[1] Davies: History of Holland.
[2] République d'Angleterre.

Such was the Spain of that day. That part of the Spanish dominions which was then known as the Low Countries, or the Roman Catholic Netherlands (our modern Belgium), was about to be a fruitful source of variance between France and her natural ally, the Dutch Republic. This State, whose political name was the United Provinces, had now reached the summit of its influence and power, —a power based, as has already been explained, wholly upon the sea, and upon the use of that element made by the great maritime and commercial genius of the Dutch people. A recent French author thus describes the commercial and colonial conditions, at the accession of Louis XIV., of this people, which beyond any other in modern times, save only England, has shown how the harvest of the sea can lift up to wealth and power a country intrinsically weak and without resources:—

"Holland had become the Phœnicia of modern times. Mistresses of the Scheldt, the United Provinces closed the outlets of Antwerp to the sea, and inherited the commercial power of that rich city, which an ambassador of Venice in the fifteenth century had compared to Venice herself. They received besides in their principal cities the workingmen of the Low Countries who fled from Spanish tyranny of conscience. The manufactures of clothes, linen stuffs, etc., which employed six hundred thousand souls, opened new sources of gain to a people previously content with the trade in cheese and fish. Fisheries alone had already enriched them. The herring fishery supported nearly one fifth of the population of Holland, producing three hundred thousand tons of salt-fish, and bringing in more than eight million francs annually.

"The naval and commercial power of the republic developed rapidly. The merchant fleet of Holland alone numbered 10,000 sail, 168,000 seamen, and supported 260,000 inhabitants. She had taken possession of the greater part of the European carrying-trade, and had added thereto, since the peace, all the carriage of merchandise between America and Spain, did the same service for the French ports, and maintained an importation traffic of thirty-six million francs. The north countries, Brandenburg, Denmark, Sweden, Muscovy, Poland, access to which was opened by the Baltic to the Provinces, were for them an inexhaustible market of exchange. They fed it by the produce they sold there, and by purchase of the products of the North,—wheat, timber, copper, hemp, and furs. The total value of merchandise yearly shipped in Dutch bottoms, in all seas, exceeded a thousand million francs. The Dutch had made themselves, to use a contemporary phrase, the wagoners of all seas." [3]

[3] Lefèvre-Pontalis: Jean de Witt.

It was through its colonies that the republic had been able thus to develop its sea trade. It had the monopoly of all the products of the East. Produce and spices from Asia were by her brought to Europe of a yearly value of sixteen million francs. The powerful East India Company, founded in 1602, had built up in Asia an empire, with possessions taken from the Portuguese. Mistress in 1650 of the Cape of Good Hope, which guaranteed it a stopping-place for its ships, it reigned as a sovereign in Ceylon, and upon the coasts of Malabar and Coromandel. It had made Batavia its seat of government, and extended its traffic to China and Japan. Meanwhile the West India Company, of more rapid rise, but less durable, had manned eight hundred ships of war and trade. It had used them to seize the remnants of Portuguese power upon the shores of Guinea, as well as in Brazil.

The United Provinces had thus become the warehouse wherein were collected the products of all nations.

The colonies of the Dutch at this time were scattered throughout the eastern seas, in India, in Malacca, in Java, the Moluccas, and various parts of the vast archipelago lying to the northward of Australia. They had possessions on the west coast of Africa, and as yet the colony of New Amsterdam remained in their hands. In South America the Dutch West India Company had owned nearly three hundred leagues of coast from Bahia in Brazil northward; but much had recently escaped from their hands.

The United Provinces owed their consideration and power to their wealth and their fleets. The sea, which beats like an inveterate enemy against their shores, had been subdued and made a useful servant; the land was to prove their destruction. A long and fierce strife had been maintained with an enemy more cruel than the sea, —the Spanish kingdom; the successful ending, with its delusive promise of rest and peace, but sounded the knell of the Dutch Republic. So long as the power of Spain remained unimpaired, or at least great enough to keep up the terror that she had long inspired, it was to the interest of England and of France, both sufferers from Spanish menace and intrigue, that the United Provinces should be strong and independent. When Spain fell,—and repeated humiliations showed that her weakness was real and not seeming,—other motives took the place of fear. England coveted Holland's trade and sea dominion; France desired the Spanish Netherlands. The United Provinces had reason to oppose the latter as well as the former.

Under the combined assaults of the two rival nations, the intrinsic weakness of the United Provinces was soon to be felt and seen. Open to attack by the land, few in numbers, and with a government ill adapted to put forth the united strength of a people, above all unfitted to keep up adequate preparation for war, the decline of the republic and the nation was to be more striking and rapid than the rise. As yet, however, in 1660, no indications of the coming fall were remarked. The republic was still in the front rank of the great powers of Europe. If, in 1654, the war with England had shown a state of unreadiness wonderful in a navy that had so long humbled the pride of Spain on the seas, on the other hand the Provinces, in 1657, had effectually put a stop to the insults of France directed against her commerce; and a year later, "by their interference in the Baltic between Denmark and Sweden, they had hindered Sweden from establishing in the North a preponderance disastrous to them. They forced her to leave open the entrance to the Baltic, of which they remained masters, no other navy being able to dispute its control with them. The superiority of their fleet, the valor of their troops, the skill and firmness of their diplomacy, had caused the prestige of their government to be recognized. Weakened and humiliated by the last English war, they had replaced themselves in the rank of great powers. At this moment Charles II. was restored."

The general character of the government has been before mentioned, and need here only be recalled. It was a loosely knit confederacy, administered by what may not inaccurately be called a commercial aristocracy, with all the political timidity of that class, which has so much to risk in war. The effect of these two factors, sectional jealousy and commercial spirit, upon the military navy was disastrous. It was not kept up properly in peace, there were necessarily rivalries in a fleet which was rather a maritime coalition than a united navy, and there was too little of a true military spirit among the officers. A more heroic people than the Dutch never existed; the annals of Dutch sea-fights give instances of desperate enterprise and endurance certainly not excelled, perhaps never equalled, elsewhere; but they also exhibit instances of defection and misconduct which show a lack of military spirit, due evidently to lack of professional

85

pride and training. This professional training scarcely existed in any navy of that day, but its place was largely supplied in monarchical countries by the feeling of a military caste. It remains to be noted that the government, weak enough from the causes named, was yet weaker from the division of the people into two great factions bitterly hating each other. The one, which was the party of the merchants (burgomasters), and now in power, favored the confederate republic as described; the other desired a monarchical government under the House of Orange. The Republican party wished for a French alliance, if possible, and a strong navy; the Orange party favored England, to whose royal house the Prince of Orange was closely related, and a powerful army. Under these conditions of government, and weak in numbers, the United Provinces in 1660, with their vast wealth and external activities, resembled a man kept up by stimulants. Factitious strength cannot endure indefinitely; but it is wonderful to see this small State, weaker by far in numbers than either England or France, endure the onslaught of either singly, and for two years of both in alliance, not only without being destroyed, but without losing her place in Europe. She owed this astonishing result partly to the skill of one or two men, but mainly to her sea power.

The conditions of England, with reference to her fitness to enter upon the impending strife, differed from those of both Holland and France. Although monarchical in government, and with much real power in the king's hands, the latter was not able to direct the policy of the kingdom wholly at his will. He had to reckon, as Louis had not, with the temper and wishes of his people. What Louis gained for France, he gained for himself; the glory of France was his glory. Charles aimed first at his own advantage, then at that of England; but, with the memory of the past ever before him, he was determined above all not to incur his father's fate nor a repetition of his own exile. Therefore, when danger became imminent, he gave way before the feeling of the English nation. Charles himself hated Holland; he hated it as a republic; he hated the existing government because opposed in internal affairs to his connections, the House of Orange; and he hated it yet more because in the days of his exile, the republic, as one of the conditions of peace with Cromwell, had driven him from her borders. He was drawn to France by the political sympathy of a would-be absolute ruler, possibly by his Roman Catholic bias, and very largely by the money paid him by Louis, which partially freed him from the control of Parliament. In following these tendencies of his own, Charles had to take account of certain decided wishes of his people. The English, of the same race as the Dutch, and with similar conditions of situation, were declared rivals for the control of the sea and of commerce; and as the Dutch were now leading in the race, the English were the more eager and bitter. A special cause of grievance was found in the action of the Dutch East India Company, "which claimed the monopoly of trade in the East, and had obliged distant princes with whom it treated to close their States to foreign nations, who were thus excluded, not only from the Dutch colonies, but from all the territory of the Indies." Conscious of greater strength, the English also wished to control the action of Dutch politics, and in the days of the English Republic had even sought to impose a union of the two governments. At the first, therefore, popular rivalry and enmity seconded the king's wishes; the more so as France had not for some years been formidable on the continent. As soon, however, as the aggressive policy of Louis XIV. was generally recognized, the English people, both nobles and commons, felt the great danger to be there, as a century before it had been in Spain. The transfer of the Spanish Netherlands (Belgium) to France would tend toward the subjection of Europe, and especially would be a blow to the sea power both of the Dutch and English; for it was not to be supposed that Louis would allow the Scheldt and port of Antwerp to remain closed, as they then were, under a treaty wrung by the Dutch from the weakness of Spain. The reopening to commerce of that great city would be a blow alike to Amsterdam and to London. With the revival of inherited opposition to France the ties of kindred began to tell; the memory of past alliance against the tyranny of Spain was recalled; and similarity of religious faith, still a powerful motive, drew the two together. At the same time the great and systematic efforts of Colbert to build up the commerce and the navy of France excited the jealousy of both the sea powers; rivals themselves, they instinctively turned against a third party intruding upon their domain. Charles was unable to resist the pressure of his people under all these motives; wars between England and Holland ceased, and were followed, after Charles's death, by close alliance.

Although her commerce was less extensive, the navy of England in 1660 was superior to that of Holland, particularly in organization and efficiency. The stern, enthusiastic religious government of Cromwell, grounded on military strength, had made its mark both on the fleet and army. The names of several of the superior officers under the Protector, among which that of Monk stands foremost, appear in the narrative of the first of the Dutch wars under Charles. This superiority in tone and discipline gradually disappeared under the corrupting influence of court favor in a licentious government; and Holland, which upon the whole was worsted by England alone upon the sea in 1665, successfully resisted the combined navies of England and France in 1672. As regards the material of the three fleets, we are told that the French ships had greater displacement than the English relatively to the weight of artillery and stores; hence they could keep, when fully loaded, a greater height of battery. Their hulls also had better lines. These advantages would naturally follow from the thoughtful and systematic way in which the French navy at that time was restored from a state of decay, and has a lesson of hope for us in the present analogous condition of our own navy. The Dutch ships, from the character of their coast, were flatter-bottomed and of less draught, and thus were able, when pressed, to find a refuge among the shoals; but they were in consequence less weatherly and generally of lighter scantling than those of either of the other nations.

Thus as briefly as possible have been sketched the conditions, degree of power, and aims which shaped and controlled the policy of the four principal seaboard States of the day,—Spain, France, England, and Holland. From the point of view of this history, these will come most prominently and most often into notice; but as other States exercised a powerful influence upon the course of events, and our aim is not merely naval history but an appreciation of the effect of naval and commercial power upon the course of general history, it is necessary to state shortly the condition of the rest of Europe. America had not yet begun to play a prominent part in the pages of history or in the policies of cabinets.

Germany was then divided into many small governments, with the one great empire of Austria. The policy of the smaller States shifted, and it was the aim of France to combine as many of them as possible under her influence, in pursuance of her traditional opposition to Austria. With France thus working against her on the one side, Austria was in imminent peril on the other from the constant assaults of the Turkish Empire, still vigorous though decaying. The policy of France had long inclined to friendly relations with Turkey, not only as a check upon Austria, but also from her wish to engross the trade with the Levant. Colbert, in his extreme eagerness for the sea power of France, favored this alliance. It will be remembered that Greece and Egypt were then parts of the Turkish Empire.

Prussia as now known did not exist. The foundations of the future kingdom were then being prepared by the Elector of Brandenburg, a powerful minor State, which was not yet able to stand quite alone, but carefully avoided a formally dependent position. The kingdom of Poland still existed, a most disturbing and important factor in European politics, because of its weak and unsettled government, which kept every other State anxious lest some unforeseen turn of events there should tend to the advantage of a rival. It was the traditional policy of France to keep Poland upright and strong. Russia was still below the horizon; coming, but not yet come, within the circle of European States and their living interests. She and the other powers bordering upon the Baltic were naturally rivals for preponderance in that sea, in which the other States, and above all the maritime States, had a particular interest as the source from which naval stores of every kind were chiefly drawn. Sweden and Denmark were at this time in a state of constant enmity, and were to be found on opposite sides in the quarrels that prevailed. For many years past, and during the early wars of Louis XIV., Sweden was for the most part in alliance with France; her bias was that way.

The general state of Europe being as described, the spring that was to set the various wheels in motion was in the hands of Louis XIV. The weakness of his immediate neighbors, the great resources of his kingdom, only waiting for development, the unity of direction resulting from his absolute power, his own practical talent and untiring industry, aided during the first half of his reign by a combination of ministers of singular ability, all united to make every government in Europe hang more or less upon his action, and be determined by, if not follow, his lead. The greatness of France was his object, and he had the choice of advancing it by either of two roads, —by the land or by the sea; not that the one wholly forbade the other, but that France, overwhelmingly strong as she then was, had not power to move with equal steps on both paths.

Louis chose extension by land. He had married the eldest daughter of Philip IV., the then reigning king of Spain; and though by the treaty of marriage she had renounced all claim to her father's inheritance, it was not difficult to find reasons for disregarding this stipulation. Technical grounds were found for setting it aside as regarded certain portions of the Netherlands and Franche Comté, and negotiations were entered into with the court of Spain to annul it altogether. The matter was the more important because the male heir to the throne was so feeble that it was evident that the Austrian line of Spanish kings would end in him. The desire to put a French prince on the Spanish throne—either himself, thus uniting the two crowns, or else one of his family, thus putting the House of Bourbon in authority on both sides of the Pyrenees—was the false light which led Louis astray during the rest of his reign, to the final destruction of the sea power of France and the impoverishment and misery of his people. Louis failed to understand that he had to reckon with all Europe. The direct project on the Spanish throne had to wait for a vacancy; but he got ready at once to move upon the Spanish possessions to the east of France.

In order to do this more effectually, he cut off from Spain every possible ally by skilful diplomatic intrigues, the study of which would give a useful illustration of strategy in the realm of politics, but he made two serious mistakes to the injury of the sea power of France. Portugal had until twenty years before been united to the crown of Spain, and the claim to it had not been surrendered. Louis considered that were Spain to regain that kingdom she would be too strong for him easily to carry out his aims. Among other means of prevention he promoted a marriage between Charles II. and the Infanta of Portugal, in consequence of which Portugal ceded to England, Bombay in India, and Tangiers in the Straits of Gibraltar, which was reputed an excellent port. We see here a French king, in his eagerness for extension by land, inviting England to the Mediterranean, and forwarding her alliance with Portugal. The latter was the more curious, as Louis already foresaw the failure of the Spanish royal house, and should rather have wished the union of the peninsular kingdoms. As a matter of fact, Portugal became a dependent and outpost of England, by which she readily landed in the Peninsula down to the days of Napoleon. Indeed, if independent of Spain, she is too weak not to be under the control of the power that rules the sea and so has readiest access to her. Louis continued to support her against Spain, and secured her independence. He also interfered with the Dutch, and compelled them to restore Brazil, which they had taken from the Portuguese.

On the other hand, Louis obtained from Charles II. the cession of Dunkirk on the Channel, which had been seized and used by Cromwell. This surrender was made for money, and was inexcusable from the maritime point of view. Dunkirk was for the English a bridge-head into France. To France it became a haven for privateers, the bane of England's commerce in the Channel and the North Sea. As the French sea power waned, England in treaty after treaty exacted the dismantling of the works of Dunkirk, which it may be said in passing was the home port of the celebrated Jean Bart and other great French privateersmen.

Meanwhile the greatest and wisest of Louis' ministers, Colbert, was diligently building up that system of administration, which, by increasing and solidly basing the wealth of the State, should bring a surer greatness and prosperity than the king's more showy enterprises. With those details that concern the internal development of the kingdom this history has no concern, beyond the incidental mention that production, both agricultural and manufacturing, received his careful attention; but upon the sea a policy of skilful aggression upon the shipping and commerce of the Dutch and English quickly began, and was instantly resented. Great trading companies were formed, directing French enterprise to the Baltic, to the Levant, to the East and West Indies; customs regulations were amended to encourage French manufactures, and to allow goods to be stored in bond in the great ports, by which means it was hoped to make France take Holland's place as the great warehouse for Europe, a function for which her geographical position eminently fitted her; while tonnage duties on foreign shipping, direct premiums on home-built ships, and careful, rigorous colonial decrees giving French vessels the monopoly of trade to and from the colonies, combined to encourage the growth of her mercantile marine. England retaliated at once; the Dutch, more seriously threatened because their carrying-trade was greater and their home resources smaller, only remonstrated for a time; but after three years they also made reprisals. Colbert, relying on the great superiority of France as an actual, and still more as a possible producer, feared not to move steadily on the grasping path marked out; which, in building up a great merchant shipping, would lay the broad base for the military shipping, which was being yet more rapidly forced on by the measures of the State. Prosperity grew apace. At the end of twelve years everything was flourishing, everything rich in the State, which was in utter confusion when he took charge of the finances and marine.

"Under him," says a French historian, "France grew by peace as she had grown by war. . . . The warfare of tariffs and premiums skilfully conducted by him tended to reduce within just limits the exorbitant growth of commercial and maritime power which Holland had arrogated at the expense of other nations; and to restrain England, which was burning to wrest this supremacy from Holland in order to use it in a manner much more dangerous to Europe. The interest of France seemed to be peace in Europe and America; a mysterious voice, at once the voice of the past and of the future, called for her warlike activity on other shores." [4]

This voice found expression through the mouth of Leibnitz, one of the world's great men, who pointed out to Louis that to turn the arms of France against Egypt would give her, in the dominion of the Mediterranean and the control of Eastern trade, a victory over Holland greater than the most successful campaign on land; and while insuring a much needed peace within his kingdom, would build up a power on the sea that would insure preponderance in Europe. This memorial called Louis from the pursuit of glory on the land to seek the durable grandeur of France in the possession of a great sea power, the elements of which, thanks to the genius of Colbert, he had in his hands. A century later a greater man than Louis sought to exalt himself and France by the path pointed out by Leibnitz; but Napoleon did not have, as Louis had, a navy equal to the task proposed. This project of Leibnitz will be more fully referred to when the narrative reaches the momentous date at which it was broached; when Louis, with his kingdom and navy in the highest pitch of efficiency, stood at the point where the roads parted, and then took the one which settled that France should not be the power of the sea. This decision, which killed Colbert and ruined the prosperity of France, was felt

[4] Martin: History of France.

in its consequences from generation to generation afterward, as the great navy of England, in war after war, swept the seas, insured the growing wealth of the island kingdom through exhausting strifes, while drying up the external resources of French trade and inflicting consequent misery. The false line of policy that began with Louis XIV. also turned France away from a promising career in India, in the days of his successor.

Meanwhile the two maritime States, England and Holland, though eying France distrustfully, had greater and growing grudges against each other, which under the fostering care of Charles II. led to war. The true cause was doubtless commercial jealousy, and the conflict sprang immediately from collisions between the trading companies. Hostilities began on the west coast of Africa; and an English squadron, in 1664, after subduing several Dutch stations there, sailed to New Amsterdam (now New York), and seized it. All these affairs took place before the formal declaration of war in February, 1665. This war was undoubtedly popular in England; the instinct of the people found an expression by the lips of Monk, who is reported to have said, "What matters this or that reason? What we want is more of the trade which the Dutch now have." There is also little room to doubt that, despite the pretensions of the trading companies, the government of the United Provinces would gladly have avoided the war; the able man who was at their head saw too clearly the delicate position in which they stood between England and France. They claimed, however, the support of the latter in virtue of a defensive treaty made in 1662. Louis allowed the claim, but unwillingly; and the still young navy of France gave practically no help.

The war between the two sea States was wholly maritime, and had the general characteristics of all such wars. Three great battles were fought,—the first off Lowestoft, on the Norfolk coast, June 13, 1665; the second, known as the Four Days' Battle in the Straits of Dover, often spoken of by French writers as that of the Pas de Calais, lasting from the 11th to the 14th of June, 1666; and the third, off the North Foreland, August 4 of the same year. In the first and last of these the English had a decided success; in the second the advantage remained with the Dutch. This one only will be described at length, because of it alone has been found such a full, coherent account as will allow a clear and accurate tactical narrative to be given. There are in these fights points of interest more generally applicable to the present day than are the details of somewhat obsolete tactical movements.

In the first battle off Lowestoft, it appears that the Dutch commander, Opdam, who was not a seaman but a cavalry officer, had very positive orders to fight; the discretion proper to a commander-in-chief on the spot was not intrusted to him. To interfere thus with the commander in the field or afloat is one of the most common temptations to the government in the cabinet, and is generally disastrous. Tourville, the greatest of Louis XIV.'s admirals, was forced thus to risk the whole French navy against his own judgment; and a century later a great French fleet escaped from the English admiral Keith, through his obedience to imperative orders from his immediate superior, who was sick in port.

In the Lowestoft fight the Dutch van gave way; and a little later one of the junior admirals of the centre, Opdam's own squadron, being killed, the crew was seized with a panic, took command of the ship from her officers, and carried her out of action. This movement was followed by twelve or thirteen other ships, leaving a great gap in the Dutch line. The occurrence shows, what has before been pointed out, that the discipline of the Dutch fleet and the tone of the officers were not high, despite the fine fighting qualities of the nation, and although it is probably true that there were more good seamen among the Dutch than among the English captains. The natural steadfastness and heroism of the Hollanders could not wholly supply that professional pride and sense of military honor which it is the object of sound military institutions to encourage. Popular feeling in the United States is pretty much at sea in this matter; there is with it no intermediate step between personal courage with a gun in its hand and entire military efficiency.

Opdam, seeing the battle going against him, seems to have yielded to a feeling approaching despair. He sought to grapple the English commander-in-chief, who on this day was the Duke of York, the king's brother. He failed in this, and in the desperate struggle which followed, his ship blew up. Shortly after, three, or as one account says, four, Dutch ships ran foul of one another, and this group was burned by one fire-ship; three or four others singly met the same fate a little later. The Dutch fleet was now in disorder, and retreated under cover of the squadron of Von Tromp, son of the famous old admiral who in the days of the Commonwealth sailed through the Channel with a broom at his masthead.

Fire-ships are seen here to have played a very conspicuous part, more so certainly than in the war of 1653, though at both periods they formed an appendage to the fleet. There is on the surface an evident resemblance between the rôle of the fire-ship and the part assigned in modern warfare to the torpedo-cruiser. The terrible character of the attack, the comparative smallness of the vessel making it, and the large demands upon the nerve of the assailant, are the chief points of resemblance; the great points of difference are the comparative certainty with which the modern vessel can be handled, which is partly met by the same advantage in the iron-clad over the old ship-of-the-line, and the instantaneousness of the injury by torpedo, whose attack fails or succeeds at once, whereas that of the fire-ship required time for effecting the object, which in both cases is total destruction of the hostile ship, instead of crippling or otherwise reducing it. An appreciation of the character of fire-ships, of the circumstances under which they attained their greatest usefulness, and of the causes which led to their disappearance, may perhaps help in the decision to which nations must come as to whether the torpedo-cruiser, pure and simple, is a type of weapon destined to survive in fleets.

A French officer, who has been examining the records of the French navy, states that the fire-ship first appears, incorporated as an arm of the fleet, in 1636.

"Whether specially built for the purpose, or whether altered from other purposes to be fitted for their particular end, they received a special equipment. The command was given to officers not noble, with the grade of captain of fire-ship. Five subordinate officers and twenty-five seamen made up the crew. Easily known by grappling-irons which were always fitted to their yards, the fire-ship saw its rôle growing less in the early years of the eighteenth century. It was finally to disappear from the fleets *whose speed it delayed and whose evolutions were by it complicated.* As the ships-of-war grew larger, their action in concert with fire-ships became daily more difficult. On the other hand, there had already been abandoned the idea of combining them with the fighting-ships to form a few *groups, each* provided with all the means of attack and defence. The formation of the close-hauled line-of-battle, by assigning the fire-ships a place in a second line placed half a league on the side farthest from the enemy, made them more and more unfitted to fulfil their office. The official plan of the battle of Malaga (1704), drawn up immediately after the battle, shows the fire-ship in this position as laid down by Paul Hoste. Finally the use of shells, enabling ships to be set on fire more surely and quickly, and introduced on board at the period of which we are now treating, though the general use did not obtain until much later, was the last blow to the fire-ship." [5]

Those who are familiar with the theories and discussions of our own day on the subject of fleet tactics and weapons, will recognize in this short notice of a long obsolete type certain ideas which are not obsolete. The fire-ship disappeared from fleets "whose speed it delayed." In heavy weather small bulk must always mean comparatively small speed. In a moderate sea, we are now told, the speed of the torpedo-boat falls from twenty knots to fifteen or less, and the seventeen to nineteen knot cruiser can either run away from the pursuing boats, or else hold them at a distance under fire of machine and heavy guns. These boats are sea-going, "and it is thought can keep the sea in all weathers; but to be on board a 110-foot torpedo-boat, when the sea is lively, is said to be far from agreeable. The heat, noise, and rapid vibrations of the engines are intense. Cooking seems to be out of the question, and it is said that if food were well cooked few would be able to appreciate it. To obtain necessary rest under these conditions, added to the rapid motions of the boat, is most difficult." Larger boats are to be built; but the factor of loss of speed in rough weather will remain, unless the size of the torpedo-cruiser is increased to a point that will certainly lead to fitting them with something more than torpedoes. Like fire-ships, *small* torpedo-cruisers will delay the speed and complicate the evolutions of the fleet with which they are associated.[6] The disappearance of the fire-ship was also hastened, we are told, by the introduction of shell firing, or incendiary projectiles; and it is not improbable that for deep-sea fighting the transfer of the torpedo to a class of larger ships will put an end to the mere torpedo-cruiser. The fire-ship continued to be used against fleets at anchor down to the days of the American Civil War; and the torpedo-boat will always be useful within an easy distance of its port.

A third phase of naval practice two hundred years ago, mentioned

[5] Gougeard: Marine de Guerre.
[6] Since the above was written, the experience of the English autumn manœuvres of 1888 has verified this statement; not indeed that any such experiment was needed to establish a self-evident fact.

in the extract quoted, involves an idea very familiar to modern discussions; namely, the group formation. "The idea of combining fire-ships with the fighting-ships to form a few groups, each provided with all the means of attack and defence," was for a time embraced; for we are told that it was later on abandoned. The combining of the ships of a fleet into groups of two, three, or four meant to act specially together is now largely favored in England; less so in France, where it meets strong opposition. No question of this sort, ably advocated on either side, is to be settled by one man's judgment, nor until time and experience have applied their infallible tests. It may be remarked, however, that in a well-organized fleet there are two degrees of command which are in themselves both natural and necessary, that can be neither done away nor ignored; these are the command of the whole fleet as one unit, and the command of each ship as a unit in itself. When a fleet becomes too large to be handled by one man, it must be subdivided and in the heat of action become practically two fleets acting to one common end; as Nelson, in his noble order at Trafalgar, said, "The second in command will, *after* my intentions are made known to him" (mark the force of the "after," which so well protects the functions both of the commander-in-chief and the second), "have the entire direction of his line, to make the attack upon the enemy, and to follow up the blow until they are captured or destroyed."

The size and cost of the individual iron-clad of the present day makes it unlikely that fleets will be so numerous as to require subdivision; but whether they are or not does not affect the decision of the group question. Looking simply to the principle underlying the theory, and disregarding the seeming tactical clumsiness of the special groups proposed, the question is: Shall there be introduced between the natural commands of the admiral and of the captains of individual ships a third artificial contrivance, which on the one hand will in effect partly supersede the supreme authority, and on the other will partly fetter the discretion of commanders of ships? A further difficulty springing from the narrow principle of support specially due to particular ships, on which the group system rests, is this: that when signals can no longer be seen, the duty of the captain to his own ship and to the fleet at large will be complicated by his duty to observe certain relations to particular ships; which particular ships must in time come to have undue prominence in his views. The group formation had its day of trial in old times, and disappeared before the test of experience; whether in its restored form it will survive, time will show. It may be said, before quitting the subject, that as an order of sailing, corresponding to the route-step of an army in march, a loose group formation has some advantages; maintaining some order without requiring that rigid exactness of position, to observe which by day and night must be a severe strain on captain and deck-officers. Such a route-order should not, however, be permitted until a fleet has reached high tactical precision.

To return to the question of fire-ships and torpedo-boats, the rôle of the latter, it is often said, is to be found in that *mêlée* which is always to succeed a couple of headlong passes between the opposing fleets. In the smoke and confusion of that hour is the opportunity of the torpedo-boat. This certainly sounds plausible, and the torpedo vessel certainly has a power of movement not possessed by the fire-ship. A *mêlée* of the two fleets, however, was not the condition most favorable for the fire-ship. I shall quote here from another French officer, whose discussion of these Anglo-Dutch sea-fights, in a late periodical, is singularly clear and suggestive. He says:

"Far from impeding the direct action of the fire-ship, which was naught or nearly so during the confused battles of the war of 1652, the regularity and *ensemble* newly attained in the movements of squadrons seem rather to favor it. The fire-ships played a very important part at the battles of Lowestoft, Pas de Calais, and the North Foreland. Thanks to the good order preserved by the ships-of-the-line, these incendiary ships can indeed be better protected by the artillery; much more efficiently directed than before toward a distinct and determined end." [7]

In the midst of the confused *mêlées* of 1652 the fire-ship "acted, so to speak, alone, seeking by chance an enemy to grapple, running the risk of a mistake, without protection against the guns of the enemy, nearly sure to be sunk by him or else burned uselessly. All now, in 1665, has become different. Its prey is clearly pointed out; it knows it, follows it easily into the relatively fixed position had by it in the enemy's line. On the other hand, the ships of his own division do not lose sight of the fire-ship. They accompany it as

[7] Chabaud-Arnault, Revue Mar. et Col. 1885.

far as possible, cover it with their artillery to the end of its course, and disengage it before burning, if the fruitlessness of the attempt is seen soon enough. Evidently under such conditions its action, always uncertain (it cannot be otherwise), nevertheless acquires greater chances of success." These instructive comments need perhaps the qualifying, or additional, remark that confusion in the enemy's order at the time that your own remains good gives the best opening for a desperate attack. The writer goes on to trace the disappearance of the fire-ship:—

"Here then we see the fire-ship at the point of its highest importance. That importance will decrease, the fire-ship itself will end by disappearing from engagements in *the open sea,* when naval artillery becoming more perfect shall have greater range, be more accurate and more rapid;[8] when ships receiving better forms, greater steering power, more extensive and better balanced sail power, shall be able, thanks to quicker speed and handling, to avoid almost certainly the fire-ships sent against them; when, finally, fleets led on principles of tactics as skilful as they were timid, a tactics which will predominate a century later during the whole war of American Independence, when these fleets, in order not to jeopardize the perfect regularity of their order of battle, will avoid coming to close quarters, and will leave to the cannon alone to decide the fate of an action."

In this discussion the writer has in view the leading feature which, while aiding the action of the fire-ship, also gives this war of 1665 its peculiar interest in the history of naval tactics. In it is found for the first time the close-hauled line-of-battle undeniably adopted as the fighting order of the fleets. It is plain enough that when those fleets numbered, as they often did, from eighty to a hundred ships, such lines would be very imperfectly formed in every essential, both of line and interval; but the general aim is evident, amid whatever imperfections of execution. The credit for this development is generally given to the Duke of York, afterward James II.; but the question to whom the improvement is due is of little importance to sea-officers of the present day when compared with the instructive fact that so long a time elapsed between the appearance of the large sailing-ship, with its broadside battery, and the systematic adoption of the order which was best adapted to develop the full power of the fleet for mutual support. To us, having the

[8] The recent development of rapid-firing and machine guns, with the great increase of their calibre and consequent range and penetration, reproduces this same step in the cycle of progress.

elements of the problem in our hands, together with the result finally reached, that result seems simple enough, almost self-evident. Why did it take so long for the capable men of that day to reach it? The reason—and herein lies the lesson for the officer of today—was doubtless the same that leaves the order of battle so uncertain now; namely, that the necessity of war did not force men to make up their minds, until the Dutch at last met in the English their equals on the sea. The sequence of ideas which resulted in the line-of-battle is clear and logical. Though familiar enough to seamen, it will be here stated in the words of the writer last quoted, because they have a neatness and precision entirely French:—

"With the increase of power of the ship-of-war, and with the perfecting of its sea and warlike qualities, there has come an equal progress in the art of utilizing them. . . . As naval evolutions become more skilful, their importance grows from day to day. To these evolutions there is needed a base, a point from which they depart and to which they return. A fleet of war-ships must be always ready to meet an enemy; logically, therefore, this point of departure for naval evolutions must be the order of battle. Now, since the disappearance of galleys, almost all the artillery is found upon the sides of a ship of war. Hence it is the beam that must necessarily and always be turned toward the enemy. On the other hand, it is necessary that the sight of the latter must never be interrupted by a friendly ship. Only one formation allows the ships of the same fleet to satisfy fully these conditions. That formation is the line ahead [column]. This line, therefore, is imposed as the only order of battle, and consequently as the basis of all fleet tactics. In order that this order of battle, this long thin line of guns, may not be injured or broken at some point weaker than the rest, there is at the same time felt the necessity of putting in it only ships which, if not of equal force, have at least equally strong sides. Logically it follows, at the same moment in which the line ahead became definitively the order for battle, there was established the distinction between the ships 'of the line', alone destined for a place therein, and the lighter ships meant for other uses."

If to these we add the considerations which led to making the line-of-battle a close-hauled line, we have the problem fully worked out. But the chain of reasoning was as clear two hundred and fifty years ago as it is now; why then was it so long in being worked out? Partly, no doubt, because old traditions—in those days traditions of galley-fighting—had hold of and confused men's minds; chiefly because men are too indolent to seek out the foundation truths of the situation in their day, and develop the true theory of action from its base up. As a rare instance of clear-sightedness, recognizing such a fundamental change in conditions and predicting results, words of Admiral Labrousse of the French navy, written in 1840, are most instructive. "Thanks to steam," he wrote, "ships will be able to move in any direction with such speed that the effects of collision may, and indeed must, as they formerly did, take the place of projectile weapons and annul the calculations of the skilful manœuvrer. The ram will be favorable to speed, without destroying the nautical qualities of a ship. As soon as one power shall have adopted this terrible weapon, all others must accept it, under pain of evident inferiority, and thus combats will become combats of ram against ram." While forbearing the unconditional adhesion to the ram as the controlling weapon of the day, which the French navy has yielded, the above brief argument may well be taken as an instance of the way in which researches into the order of battle of the future should be worked out. A French writer, commenting on Labrousse's paper, says:—

"Twenty-seven years were scarce enough for our fathers, counting from 1638, the date of building the 'Couronne', to 1665, to pass from the tactical order of the line abreast, the order for galleys, to that of the line ahead. We ourselves needed twenty-nine years from 1830, when the first steamship was brought into our fleet, to 1859, when the application of the principle of ram-fighting was affirmed by laying down the 'Solferino' and the 'Magenta' to work a revolution in the contrary direction; so true it is that truth is always slow in getting to the light. . . . This transformation was not sudden, not only because the new material required time to be built and armed, but above all, it is sad to say, because the necessary consequences of the new motive power escaped most minds." [9]

We come now to the justly celebrated Four Days' Battle of June, 1666, which claims special notice, not only on account of the great number of ships engaged on either side, nor yet only for the extraordinary physical endurance of the men who kept up a hot naval action for so many successive days, but also because the commanders-in-chief on either side, Monk and De Ruyter, were the most distinguished seamen, or rather sea-commanders, brought forth by their respective countries in the seventeenth century. Monk was possibly inferior to Blake in the annals of the English navy; but there is a general agreement that De Ruyter is the foremost figure,

[9] Gougeard: Marine de Guerre.

not only in the Dutch service, but among all the naval officers of that age. The account about to be given is mainly taken from a recent number of the "Revue Maritime et Coloniale," [10] and is there published as a letter, recently discovered, from a Dutch gentleman serving as volunteer on board De Ruyter's ship, to a friend in France. The narrative is delightfully clear and probable,—qualities not generally found in the description of those long-ago fights; and the satisfaction it gave was increased by finding in the memoirs of the Count de Guiche, who also served as volunteer in the fleet, and was taken to De Ruyter after his own vessel had been destroyed by a fire-ship, an account confirming the former in its principal details.[11] This additional pleasure was unhappily marred by recognizing certain phrases as common to both stories; and a comparison showed that the two could not be accepted as independent narratives. There are, however, points of internal difference which make it possible that the two accounts are by different eye-witnesses, who compared and corrected their versions before sending them out to their friends or writing them in their journals.

The numbers of the two fleets were: English about eighty ships, the Dutch about one hundred; but the inequality in numbers was largely compensated by the greater size of many of the English. A great strategic blunder by the government in London immediately preceded the fight. The king was informed that a French squadron was on its way from the Atlantic to join the Dutch. He at once divided his fleet, sending twenty ships under Prince Rupert to the westward to meet the French, while the remainder under Monk were to go east and oppose the Dutch.

A position like that of the English fleet, threatened with an attack from two quarters, presents one of the subtlest temptations to a commander. The impulse is very strong to meet both by dividing his own numbers as Charles did; but unless in possession of overwhelming force it is an error, exposing both divisions to be beaten separately, which, as we are about to see, actually happened in this case. The result of the first two days was disastrous to the larger English division under Monk, which was then obliged to retreat toward Rupert; and probably the opportune return of the latter alone saved the English fleet from a very serious loss, or at the least

[10] Vol. lxxxii. p. 137.
[11] Mémoires du Cte. de Guiche. À Londres, chez P. Changuion. 1743, pp. 234-264.

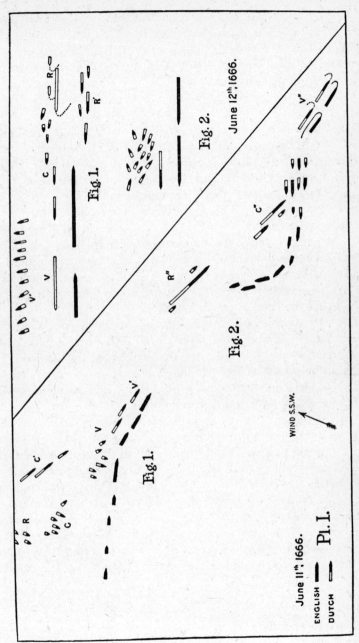

Fig. 1.

Fig. 2.

June 12ᵗʰ, 1666.

Fig. 2.

Fig. 1.

WIND S.S.W.

June 11ᵗʰ, 1666.

Pl. I.

ENGLISH

DUTCH

103

from being shut up in their own ports. A hundred and forty years later, in the exciting game of strategy that was played in the Bay of Biscay before Trafalgar, the English admiral Cornwallis made precisely the same blunder, dividing his fleet into two equal parts out of supporting distance, which Napoleon at the time characterized as a glaring piece of stupidity. The lesson is the same in all ages.

The Dutch had sailed for the English coast with a fair easterly wind, but it changed later to southwest with thick weather, and freshened, so that De Ruyter, to avoid being driven too far, came to anchor between Dunkirk and the Downs. The fleet then rode with its head to the south-southwest and the van on the right; while Tromp, who commanded the rear division in the natural order, was on the left. For some cause this left was most to windward, the centre squadron under Ruyter being to leeward, and the right, or van, to leeward again of the centre.[12] This was the position of the Dutch fleet at daylight of June 11, 1666; and although not expressly so stated, it is likely, from the whole tenor of the narratives, that it was not in good order.

The same morning Monk, who was also at anchor, made out the Dutch fleet to leeward, and although so inferior in numbers determined to attack at once, hoping that by keeping the advantage of the wind he would be able to commit himself only so far as might seem best. He therefore stood along the Dutch line on the starboard tack, leaving the right and centre out of cannon-shot, until he came abreast of the left, Tromp's squadron. Monk then had thirty-five ships well in hand; but the rear had opened and was straggling, as is apt to be the case with long columns. With the thirty-five he then put his helm up and ran down for Tromp, whose squadron cut their cables and made sail on the same tack (V′); the two engaged lines thus standing over toward the French coast, and the breeze heeling the ships so that the English could not use their lower-deck guns (Fig. 2, V″). The Dutch centre and rear also cut (Fig. 1, C′), and followed the movement, but being so far to leeward, could not for some time come into action. It was during this time that a large

---

[12] Plate I., June 11, 1666, Fig. 1. V, van; C, centre; R, rear: in this part of the action the Dutch order was inverted, so that the actual van was the proper rear. The great number of ships engaged in the fleet actions of these Anglo-Dutch wars make it impossible to represent each ship and at the same time preserve clearness in the plans. Each figure of a ship therefore represents a group, more or less numerous.

Dutch ship, becoming separated from her own fleet, was set on fire and burned, doubtless the ship in which was Count de Guiche.

As they drew near Dunkirk the English went about, probably all together; for in the return to the northward and westward the proper English van fell in with and was roughly handled by the Dutch centre under Ruyter himself (Fig. 2, C″). This fate would be more likely to befall the rear, and indicates that a simultaneous movement had reversed the order. The engaged ships had naturally lost to leeward, thus enabling Ruyter to fetch up with them. Two English flag-ships were here disabled and cut off; one, the "Swiftsure," hauled down her colors after the admiral, a young man of only twenty-seven, was killed. "Highly to be admired," says a contemporary writer, "was the resolution of Vice-Admiral Berkeley, who, though cut off from the line, surrounded by enemies, great numbers of his men killed, his ship disabled and boarded on all sides, yet continued fighting almost alone, killed several with his own hand, and would accept no quarter; till at length, being shot in the throat with a musket-ball, he retired into the captain's cabin, where he was found dead, extended at his full length upon a table, and almost covered with his own blood." Quite as heroic, but more fortunate in its issue, was the conduct of the other English admiral thus cut off; and the incidents of his struggle, though not specially instructive otherwise, are worth quoting, as giving a lively picture of the scenes which passed in the heat of the contests of those days, and afford coloring to otherwise dry details.

"Being in a short time completely disabled, one of the enemy's fire-ships grappled him on the starboard quarter; he was, however, freed by the almost incredible exertions of his lieutenant, who, having in the midst of the flames loosed the grappling-irons, swung back on board his own ship unhurt. The Dutch, bent on the destruction of this unfortunate ship, sent a second which grappled her on the larboard side, and with greater success than the former; for the sails instantly taking fire, the crew were so terrified that nearly fifty of them jumped overboard. The admiral, Sir John Harman, seeing this confusion, ran with his sword drawn among those who remained, and threatened with instant death the first man who should attempt to quit the ship, or should not exert himself to quench the flames. The crew then returned to their duty and got the fire under; but the rigging being a good deal burned, one of the topsail yards fell and broke Sir John's leg. In the midst of this accumulated distress, a third fire-ship prepared to grapple him, but was sunk by the guns before she could effect her purpose. The Dutch vice-admiral, Evertzen, now bore down to him and offered quarter; but Sir John replied, 'No, no, it is not come to that yet', and giving him a broadside, killed the Dutch commander; after which the other enemies sheered off." [13]

It is therefore not surprising that the account we have been following reported two English flag-ships lost, one by a fire-ship. "The English chief still continued on the port tack, and," says the writer, "as night fell we could see him proudly leading his line past the squadron of North Holland and Zealand [the actual rear, but proper van], which from noon up to that time had not been able to reach the enemy [Fig. 2, R"] from their leewardly position." The merit of Monk's attack as a piece of grand tactics is evident, and bears a strong resemblance to that of Nelson at the Nile. Discerning quickly the weakness of the Dutch order, he had attacked a vastly superior force in such a way that only part of it could come into action; and though the English actually lost more heavily, they carried off a brilliant prestige and must have left considerable depression and heart-burning among the Dutch. The eye-witness goes on: "The affair continued until ten P.M., friends and foes mixed together and as likely to receive injury from one as from the other. It will be remarked that the success of the day and the misfortunes of the English came from their being too much scattered, too extended in their line; but for which we could never have cut off a corner of them, as we did. The mistake of Monk was in not keeping his ships better together"; that is, closed up. The remark is just, the criticism scarcely so; the opening out of the line was almost unavoidable in so long a column of sailing-ships, and was one of the chances taken by Monk when he offered battle.

The English stood off on the port tack to the west or west-northwest, and next day returned to the fight. The Dutch were now on the port tack in natural order, the right leading, and were to windward; but the enemy, being more weatherly and better disciplined, soon gained the advantage of the wind. The English this day had forty-four ships in action, the Dutch about eighty; many of the English, as before said, larger. The two fleets passed on opposite tacks, the English to windward;[14] but Tromp, in the rear, seeing that the Dutch order of battle was badly formed, the ships in two

---

[13] Campbell: Lives of the Admirals.
[14] Plate I., June 12, Fig. 1, V, C, R.

or three lines, overlapping and so masking each other's fire, went about and gained to windward of the enemy's van (R′); which he was able to do from the length of the line, and because the English, running parallel to the Dutch order, were off the wind. "At this moment two flag-officers of the Dutch van kept broad off, presenting their sterns to the English (V′). Ruyter, greatly astonished, tried to stop them, but in vain, and therefore felt obliged to imitate the manœuvre in order to keep his squadron together; but he did so with some order, keeping some ships around him, and was joined by one of the van ships, disgusted with the conduct of his immediate superior. Tromp was now in great danger, separated [by his own act first and then by the conduct of the van] from his own fleet by the English, and would have been destroyed but for Ruyter, who, seeing the urgency of the case, hauled up for him," the van and centre thus standing back for the rear on the opposite tack to that on which they entered action. This prevented the English from keeping up the attack on Tromp, lest Ruyter should gain the wind of them, which they could not afford to yield because of their very inferior numbers. Both the action of Tromp and that of the junior flag-officers in the van, though showing very different degrees of warlike ardor, bring out strongly the lack of subordination and of military feeling which has been charged against the Dutch officers as a body; no signs of which appear among the English at this time.

How keenly Ruyter felt the conduct of his lieutenants was manifested when "Tromp, immediately after this partial action, went on board his flagship. The seamen cheered him; but Ruyter said, 'This is no time for rejoicing, but rather for tears'. Indeed, our position was bad, each squadron acting differently, in no line, and all the ships huddled together like a flock of sheep, so packed that the English might have surrounded all of them with their forty ships [June 12, Fig. 2]. The English were in admirable order, but did not push their advantage as they should, whatever the reason." The reason no doubt was the same that often prevented sailing-ships from pressing an advantage,—disability from crippled spars and rigging, added to the inexpediency of such inferior numbers risking a decisive action.

Ruyter was thus able to draw his fleet out into line again, although much maltreated by the English, and the two fleets passed again on opposite tacks, the Dutch to leeward, and Ruyter's ship the last in his column. As he passed the English rear, he lost his main-topmast and mainyard. After another partial rencounter the English drew away to the northwest toward their own shores, the Dutch following them; the wind being still from southwest, but light. The English were now fairly in retreat, and the pursuit continued all night, Ruyter's own ship dropping out of sight in the rear from her crippled state.

The third day Monk continued retreating to the westward. He burned, by the English accounts, three disabled ships, sent ahead those that were most crippled, and himself brought up the rear with those that were in fighting condition, which are variously stated, again by the English, at twenty-eight and sixteen in number (Plate II., June 13). One of the largest and finest of the English fleet, the "Royal Prince," of ninety guns, ran aground on the Galloper Shoal and was taken by Tromp (Plate II. A); but Monk's retreat was so steady and orderly that he was otherwise unmolested. This shows that the Dutch had suffered very severely. Toward evening Rupert's squadron was seen; and all the ships of the English fleet, except those crippled in action, were at last united.

The next day the wind came out again very fresh from the southwest, giving the Dutch the weather-gage. The English, instead of attempting to pass upon opposite tacks, came up from astern relying upon the speed and handiness of their ships. So doing, the battle engaged all along the line on the port tack, the English to leeward.[15] The Dutch fire-ships were badly handled and did no harm, whereas the English burned two of their enemies. The two fleets ran on thus, exchanging broadsides for two hours, at the end of which time the bulk of the English fleet had passed through the Dutch line.[16] All regularity of order was henceforward lost. "At this moment," says the eye-witness, "the lookout was extraordinary, for all were separated, the English as well as we. But luck would have it that the largest of our fractions surrounding the admiral remained to windward, and the largest fraction of the English, also with their admiral, remained to leeward [Figs. 1 and 2, C and C']. This was the cause of our victory and their ruin. Our admiral had with him

[15] Plate II., June 14, Fig. 1, E, D.
[16] Fig. 1, V, C, R. This result was probably due simply to the greater weatherliness of the English ships. It would perhaps be more accurate to say that the Dutch had sagged to leeward so that they drifted through the English line.

108

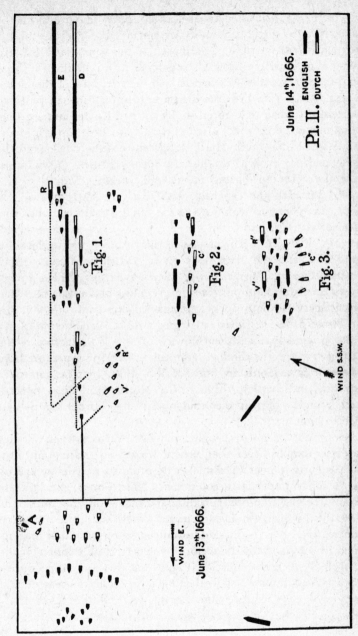

June 14th, 1666.

Pl. II.   ENGLISH   DUTCH

Fig. 1.

Fig. 2.

Fig. 3.

WIND S.S.W.

June 13th, 1666.

WIND E.

thirty-five or forty ships of his own and of other squadrons, for the squadrons were scattered and order much lost. The rest of the Dutch ships had left him. The leader of the van, Van Ness, had gone off with fourteen ships in chase of three or four English ships, which under a press of sail had gained to windward of the Dutch van [Fig. 1, V]. Van Tromp with the rear squadron had fallen to leeward, and so had to keep on [to leeward of Ruyter and the English main body, Fig. 1, R] after Van Ness, in order to rejoin the admiral by passing round the English centre." De Ruyter and the English main body kept up a sharp action, beating to windward all the time. Tromp, having carried sail, overtook Van Ness, and returned bringing the van back with him (V', R'); but owing to the constant plying to windward of the English main body he came up to leeward of it and could not rejoin Ruyter, who was to windward (Fig. 3, V'', R''). Ruyter, seeing this, made signal to the ships around him, and the main body of the Dutch kept away before the wind (Fig. 3, C''), which was then very strong. "Thus in less than no time we found ourselves in the midst of the English; who, being attacked on both sides, were thrown into confusion and saw their whole order destroyed, as well by dint of the action, as by the strong wind that was then blowing. This was the hottest of the fight [Fig. 3]. We saw the high admiral of England separated from his fleet, followed only by one fire-ship. With that he gained to windward, and passing through the North Holland squadron, placed himself again at the head of fifteen or twenty ships that rallied to him."

Thus ended this great sea-fight, the most remarkable, in some of its aspects, that has ever been fought upon the ocean. Amid conflicting reports it is not possible to do more than estimate the results. A fairly impartial account says: "The States lost in these actions three vice-admirals, two thousand men, and four ships. The loss of the English was five thousand killed and three thousand prisoners; and they lost besides seventeen ships, of which nine remained in the hands of the victors." [17] There is no doubt that the English had much the worst of it, and that this was owing wholly to the original blunder of weakening the fleet by a great detachment sent in another direction. Great detachments are sometimes necessary evils, but in this case no necessity existed. Granting the

[17] Lefèvre-Pontalis: Jean de Witt.

approach of the French, the proper course for the English was to fall with their whole fleet upon the Dutch before their allies could come up. This lesson is as applicable today as it ever was. A second lesson, likewise of present application, is the necessity of sound military institutions for implanting correct military feeling, pride, and discipline. Great as was the first blunder of the English, and serious as was the disaster, there can be no doubt that the consequences would have been much worse but for the high spirit and skill with which the plans of Monk were carried out by his subordinates, and the lack of similar support to Ruyter on the part of the Dutch subalterns. In the movements of the English, we hear nothing of two juniors turning tail at a critical moment, nor of a third, with misdirected ardor, getting on the wrong side of the enemy's fleet. Their drill also, their tactical precision, was remarked even then. The Frenchman De Guiche, after witnessing this Four Days' Fight, wrote:—

"Nothing equals the beautiful order of the English at sea. Never was a line drawn straighter than that formed by their ships; thus they bring all their fire to bear upon those who draw near them. . . . They fight like a line of cavalry which is handled according to rule, and applies itself solely to force back those who oppose; whereas the Dutch advance like cavalry whose squadrons leave their ranks and come separately to the charge." [18]

The Dutch government, averse to expense, unmilitary in its tone, and incautious from long and easy victory over the degenerate navy of Spain, had allowed its fleet to sink into a mere assembly of armed merchantmen. Things were at their worst in the days of Cromwell. Taught by the severe lessons of that war, the United Provinces, under an able ruler, had done much to mend matters, but full efficiency had not yet been gained.

"In 1666 as in 1653," says a French naval writer, "the fortune of war seemed to lean to the side of the English. Of the three great battles fought, two were decided victories; and the third, though adverse, had but increased the glory of her seamen. This was due to the intelligent boldness of Monk and Rupert, the talents of part of the admirals and captains, and the skill of the seamen and soldiers under them. The wise and vigorous efforts made by the government of the United Provinces, and the undeniable superiority of Ruyter in experience and genius over any one of his opponents, could not compensate for the weakness or incapacity of part

18 Mémoires, pp. 249, 251, 266, 267.

of the Dutch officers, and the manifest inferiority of the men under their orders." [19]

England, as has been said before, still felt the impress of Cromwell's iron hand upon her military institutions; but that impress was growing weaker. Before the next Dutch war Monk was dead, and was poorly replaced by the cavalier Rupert. Court extravagance cut down the equipment of the navy as did the burgomaster's parsimony, and court corruption undermined discipline as surely as commercial indifference. The effect was evident when the fleets of two countries met again, six years later.

There was one well-known feature of all the military navies of that day which calls for a passing comment; for its correct bearing and value is not always, perhaps not generally, seen. The command of fleets and of single vessels was often given to soldiers, to military men unaccustomed to the sea, and ignorant how to handle the ship, that duty being intrusted to another class of officer. Looking closely into the facts, it is seen that this made a clean division between the direction of the fighting and of the motive power of the ship. This is the essence of the matter; and the principle is the same whatever the motive power may be. The inconvenience and inefficiency of such a system was obvious then as it is now, and the logic of facts gradually threw the two functions into the hands of one corps of officers, the result being the modern naval officer, as that term is generally understood.[20] Unfortunately, in this process of blending, the less important function was allowed to get the upper hand; the naval officer came to feel more proud of his dexterity in managing the motive power of his ship than of his skill in developing her military efficiency. The bad effects of this lack of interest in military science became most evident when the point of handling fleets was reached, because for that military skill told most, and previous study was most necessary; but it was felt in the single ship as well. Hence it came to pass, and especially in the English navy, that the pride of the seaman took the place of the pride of the military man. The English naval officer thought more of that which likened him to the merchant captain than of that which made him

[19] Chabaud-Arnault: Revue Mar. et Col., 1885.
[20] The true significance of this change has often been misunderstood, and hence erroneous inferences as to the future have been drawn. It was not a case of the new displacing the old, but of the military element in a military organization asserting its necessary and inevitable control over all other functions.

akin to the soldier. In the French navy this result was less general, owing probably to the more military spirit of the government, and especially of the nobility, to whom the rank of officer was reserved. It was not possible that men whose whole association was military, all of whose friends looked upon arms as the one career for a gentleman, could think more of the sails and rigging than of the guns or the fleet. The English corps of officers was of different origin. There was more than the writer thought in Macaulay's well-known saying: "There were seamen and there were gentlemen in the navy of Charles II.; but the seamen were not gentlemen, and the gentlemen were not seamen." The trouble was not in the absence or presence of gentlemen as such, but in the fact that under the conditions of that day the gentleman was pre-eminently the military element of society; and that the seaman, after the Dutch wars, gradually edged the gentleman, and with him the military tone and spirit as distinguished from simple courage, out of the service. Even "such men of family as Herbert and Russell, William III.'s admirals," says the biographer of Lord Hawke, "were sailors indeed, but only able to hold their own by adopting the boisterous manners of the hardy tarpaulin." The same national traits which made the French inferior as seamen made them superior as military men; not in courage, but in skill. To this day the same tendency obtains; the direction of the motive power has no such consideration as the military functions in the navies of the Latin nations. The studious and systematic side of the French character also inclined the French officer, when not a trifler, to consider and develop tactical questions in a logical manner; to prepare himself to handle fleets, not merely as a seaman but as a military man. The result showed, in the American Revolutionary War, that despite a mournful history of governmental neglect, men who were first of all military men, inferior though they were in opportunities as seamen to their enemies, could meet them on more than equal terms as to tactical skill, and were practically their superiors in handling fleets. The false theory has already been pointed out, which directed the action of the French fleet not to crushing its enemy, but to some ulterior aim; but this does not affect the fact that in tactical skill the military men were superior to the mere seamen, though their tactical skill was applied to mistaken strategic ends. The source whence the Dutch mainly drew their officers does not certainly appear; for while the English naval historian in 1666 says that most of the captains of their fleet were sons of rich burgomasters, placed there for political reasons by the Grand Pensionary, and without experience, Duquesne, the ablest French admiral of the day, comments in 1676 on the precision and skill of the Dutch captains in terms very disparaging to his own. It is likely, from many indications, that they were generally merchant seamen, with little original military feeling; but the severity with which the delinquents were punished both by the State and by popular frenzy, seems to have driven these officers, who were far from lacking the highest personal courage, into a sense of what military loyalty and subordination required. They made a very different record in 1672 from that of 1666.

Before finally leaving the Four Days' Fight, the conclusions of another writer may well be quoted:—

"Such was that bloody Battle of the Four Days, or Straits of Calais, the most memorable sea-fight of modern days; not, indeed, by its results, but by the aspect of its different phases; by the fury of the combatants; by the boldness and skill of the leaders; and by the new character which it gave to sea warfare. More than any other this fight marks clearly the passage from former methods to the tactics of the end of the seventeenth century. For the first time we can follow, as though traced upon a plan, the principal movements of the contending fleets. It seems quite clear that to the Dutch as well as to the British have been given a tactical book and a code of signals; or, at the least, written instructions, extensive and precise, to serve instead of such a code. We feel that each admiral now has his squadron in hand, and that even the commander-in-chief disposes at his will, during the fight, of the various subdivisions of his fleet. Compare this action with those of 1652, and one plain fact stares you in the face,—that between the two dates naval tactics have undergone a revolution.

"Such were the changes that distinguish the war of 1665 from that of 1652. As in the latter epoch, the admiral still thinks the weather-gage an advantage for his fleet; but it is no longer, from the tactical point of view, the principal, we might almost say the sole, preoccupation. Now he wishes above all to keep his fleet in good order and compact as long as possible, so as to keep the power of *combining*, during the action, the movements of the different squadrons. Look at Ruyter, at the end of the Four Days' Fight; with great difficulty he has kept to windward of the English fleet, yet he does not hesitate to sacrifice this advantage in order to unite the two parts of his fleet, which are separated by the enemy. If at the later fight off the North Foreland great intervals exist between the Dutch squadrons, if the rear afterward continues to withdraw from the centre, Ruyter deplores such a fault as the chief cause of his defeat. He so deplores it in his official report; he even accuses Tromp [who was his personal enemy] of treason or cowardice,—an unjust accusation, but which none the less shows the enormous importance thenceforth attached, during action, to the reunion of the fleet into a whole strictly and regularly maintained." [21]

This commentary is justified in so far as it points out general aims and tendencies; but the results were not as complete as might be inferred from it.

The English, notwithstanding their heavy loss in the Four Days' Battle, were at sea again within two months, much to the surprise of the Dutch; and on the 4th of August another severe fight was fought off the North Foreland, ending in the complete defeat of the latter, who retired to their own coasts. The English followed, and effected an entrance into one of the Dutch harbors, where they destroyed a large fleet of merchantmen as well as a town of some importance. Toward the end of 1666 both sides were tired of the war, which was doing great harm to trade, and weakening both navies to the advantage of the growing sea power of France. Negotiations looking toward peace were opened; but Charles II., ill disposed to the United Provinces, confident that the growing pretensions of Louis XIV. to the Spanish Netherlands would break up the existing alliance between Holland and France, and relying also upon the severe reverses suffered at sea by the Dutch, was exacting and haughty in his demands. To justify and maintain this line of conduct he should have kept up his fleet, the prestige of which had been so advanced by its victories. Instead of that, poverty, the result of extravagance and of his home policy, led him to permit it to decline; ships in large numbers were laid up; and he readily adopted an opinion which chimed in with his penury, and which, as it has had advocates at all periods of sea history, should be noted and condemned here. This opinion, warmly opposed by Monk, was:—

"That as the Dutch were chiefly supported by trade, as the supply of their navy depended upon trade, and, as experience showed, nothing provoked the people so much as injuring their trade, his Majesty should therefore apply himself to this, which would effectually humble them, at the same time that it would less exhaust the English than fitting out such mighty fleets as had hitherto kept the sea every summer. . . . Upon these motives the king took a fatal resolution of laying up his great ships and keeping only a few frigates on the cruise." [22]

[21] Chaubaud-Arnault: Revue Mar. et Col., 1885.
[22] Campbell: Lives of the Admirals.

In consequence of this economical theory of carrying on a war, the Grand Pensionary of Holland, De Witt, who had the year before caused soundings of the Thames to be made, sent into the river, under De Ruyter, a force of sixty or seventy ships-of-the-line, which on the 14th of June, 1667, went up as high as Gravesend, destroying ships at Chatham and in the Medway, and taking possession of Sheerness. The light of the fires could be seen from London, and the Dutch fleet remained in possession of the mouth of the river until the end of the month. Under this blow, following as it did upon the great plague and the great fire of London, Charles consented to peace, which was signed July 31, 1667, and is known as the Peace of Breda. The most lasting result of the war was the transfer of New York and New Jersey to England, thus joining her northern and southern colonies in North America.

Before going on again with the general course of the history of the times, it will be well to consider for a moment the theory which worked so disastrously for England in 1667; that, namely, of maintaining a sea-war mainly by preying upon the enemy's commerce. This plan, which involves only the maintenance of a few swift cruisers and can be backed by the spirit of greed in a nation, fitting out privateers without direct expense to the State, possesses the specious attractions which economy always presents. The great injury done to the wealth and prosperity of the enemy is also undeniable; and although to some extent his merchant-ships can shelter themselves ignobly under a foreign flag while the war lasts, this *guerre de course,* as the French call it, this commerce-destroying, to use our own phrase, must, if in itself successful, greatly embarrass the foreign government and distress its people. Such a war, however, cannot stand alone; it must be *supported,* to use the military phrase; unsubstantial and evanescent in itself, it cannot reach far from its base. That base must be either home ports, or else some solid outpost of the national power, on the shore or the sea; a distant dependency or a powerful fleet. Failing such support, the cruiser can only dash out hurriedly a short distance from home, and its blows, though painful, cannot be fatal. It was not the policy of 1667, but Cromwell's powerful fleets of ships-of-the-line in 1652, that shut the Dutch merchantmen in their ports and caused the grass to grow in the streets of Amsterdam. When, instructed by the suffering of that time, the Dutch kept large fleets afloat through two exhausting wars, though their commerce suffered greatly, they bore up the burden of the strife against England and France united. Forty years later, Louis XIV. was driven, by exhaustion, to the policy adopted by Charles II. through parsimony. Then were the days of the great French privateers, Jean Bart, Forbin, Duguay-Trouin, Du Casse, and others. The regular fleets of the French navy were practically withdrawn from the ocean during the great War of the Spanish Succession (1702-1712). The French naval historian says:—

"Unable to renew the naval armaments, Louis XIV. increased the number of cruisers upon the more frequented seas, especially the Channel and the German Ocean [not far from home, it will be noticed]. In these different spots the cruisers were always in a position to intercept or hinder the movements of transports laden with troops, and of the numerous convoys carrying supplies of all kinds. In these seas, in the centre of the commercial and political world, there is always work for cruisers. Notwithstanding the difficulties they met, owing to the absence of large friendly fleets, they served advantageously the cause of the two peoples [French and Spanish]. These cruisers, in the face of the Anglo-Dutch power, needed good luck, boldness, and skill. These three conditions were not lacking to our seamen; but then, what chiefs and what captains they had!" [23]

The English historian, on the other hand, while admitting how severely the people and commerce of England suffered from the cruisers, bitterly reflecting at times upon the administration, yet refers over and over again to the increasing prosperity of the whole country, and especially of its commercial part. In the preceding war, on the contrary, from 1689 to 1697, when France sent great fleets to sea and disputed the supremacy of the ocean, how different the result! The same English writer says of that time:—

"With respect to our trade it is certain that we suffered infinitely more, not merely than the French, for that was to be expected from the greater number of our merchant-ships, but than we ever did in any former war. . . . This proceeded in great measure from the vigilance of the French, who carried on the war in a piratical way. It is out of all doubt that, taking all together, our traffic suffered excessively; our merchants were many of them ruined." [24]

Macaulay says of this period: "During many months of 1693 the English trade with the Mediterranean had been interrupted almost

23 La Pérouse-Bonfils: Hist. de la Marine Française.
24 Campbell: Lives of the Admirals.

entirely. There was no chance that a merchantman from London or Amsterdam would, if unprotected, reach the Pillars of Hercules without being boarded by a French privateer; and the protection of armed vessels was not easily obtained." Why? Because the vessels of England's navy were occupied watching the French navy, and this diversion of them from the cruisers and privateers constituted the support which a commerce-destroying war must have. A French historian, speaking of the same period in England (1696), says: "The state of the finances was deplorable; money was scarce, maritime insurance thirty per cent, the Navigation Act was virtually suspended, and the English shipping reduced to the necessity of sailing under the Swedish and Danish flags." [25] Half a century later the French government was again reduced, by long neglect of the navy, to a cruising warfare. With what results? First, the French historian says: "From June, 1756, to June, 1760, French privateers captured from the English more than twenty-five hundred merchantmen. In 1761, though France had not, so to speak, a single ship-of-the-line at sea, and though the English had taken two hundred and forty of our privateers, their comrades still took eight hundred and twelve vessels. But," he goes on to say, "the prodigious growth of the English shipping explains the number of these prizes." [26] In other words, the suffering involved to England in such numerous captures, which must have caused great individual injury and discontent, did not really prevent the growing prosperity of the State and of the community at large. The English naval historian, speaking of the same period, says: "While the commerce of France was nearly destroyed, the trading-fleet of England covered the seas. Every year her commerce was increasing; the money which the war carried out was returned by the produce of her industry. Eight thousand merchant vessels were employed by the English merchants." And again, summing up the results of the war, after stating the immense amount of specie brought into the kingdom by foreign conquests, he says: "The trade of England increased gradually every year, and such a scene of national prosperity, while waging a long, bloody, and costly war, was never before shown by any people in the world." On the other hand, the historian of the French navy, speaking of an earlier phase of the same wars, says: "The English fleets, having nothing

[25] Martin: History of France.
[26] Ibid.

to resist them, swept the seas. Our privateers and single cruisers, having no fleet to keep down the abundance of their enemies, ran short careers. Twenty thousand French seamen lay in English prisons." [27] When, on the other hand, in the War of the American Revolution France resumed the policy of Colbert and of the early reign of Louis XIV., and kept large battle-fleets afloat, the same result again followed as in the days of Tourville. "For the first time," says the Annual Register, forgetting or ignorant of the experience of 1693, and remembering only the glories of the later wars, "English merchant-ships were driven to take refuge under foreign flags." [28] Finally, in quitting this part of the subject, it may be remarked that in the island of Martinique the French had a powerful distant dependency upon which to base a cruising warfare; and during the Seven Years' War, as afterward during the First Empire, it, with Guadeloupe, was the refuge of numerous privateers. "The records of the English admiralty raise the losses of the English in the West Indies during the first years of the Seven Years' War to fourteen hundred merchantmen taken or destroyed." The English fleet was therefore directed against the islands, both of which fell, involving a loss to the trade of France greater than all the depredations of her cruisers on the English commerce, besides breaking up the system; but in the war of 1778 the great fleets protected the islands, which were not even threatened at any time.

So far we have been viewing the effect of a purely cruising warfare, not based upon powerful squadrons, only upon that particular part of the enemy's strength against which it is theoretically directed,— upon his commerce and general wealth; upon the sinews of war. The evidence seems to show that even for its own special ends such a mode of war is inconclusive, worrying but not deadly; it might almost be said that it causes needless suffering. What, however, is the effect of this policy upon the general ends of the war, to which it is one of the means, and to which it is subsidiary? How, again, does it react upon the people that practise it? As the historical evidences will come up in detail from time to time, it need here only be summarized. The result to England in the days of Charles II. has been seen,—her coast insulted, her shipping burned almost within sight of her capital. In the War of the Spanish Succession,

[27] La Pérouse-Bonfils.
[28] Annual Reg., vol. xxvii. p. 10.

when the control of Spain was the military object, while the French depended upon a cruising war against commerce, the navies of England and Holland, unopposed, guarded the coasts of the peninsula, blocked the port of Toulon, forced the French succors to cross the Pyrenees, and by keeping open the sea highway, neutralized the geographical nearness of France to the seat of war. Their fleets seized Gibraltar, Barcelona, and Minorca, and co-operating with the Austrian army failed by little of reducing Toulon. In the Seven Years' War the English fleets seized, or aided in seizing, all the most valuable colonies of France and Spain, and made frequent descents on the French coast. The War of the American Revolution affords no lesson, the fleets being nearly equal. The next most striking instance to Americans is the War of 1812. Everybody knows how our privateers swarmed over the seas, and that from the smallness of our navy the war was essentially, indeed solely, a cruising war. Except upon the lakes, it is doubtful if more than two of our ships at any time acted together. The injury done to English commerce, thus unexpectedly attacked by a distant foe which had been undervalued, may be fully conceded; but on the one hand, the American cruisers were powerfully supported by the French fleet, which being assembled in larger or smaller bodies in the many ports under the emperor's control from Antwerp to Venice, tied the fleets of England to blockade duty; and on the other hand, when the fall of the emperor released them, our coasts were insulted in every direction, the Chesapeake entered and controlled, its shores wasted, the Potomac ascended, and Washington burned. The Northern frontier was kept in a state of alarm, though there, squadrons, absolutely weak but relatively strong, sustained the general defence; while in the South the Mississippi was entered unopposed, and New Orleans barely saved. When negotiations for peace were opened, the bearing of the English toward the American envoys was not that of men who felt their country to be threatened with an unbearable evil. The late Civil War, with the cruises of the "Alabama" and "Sumter" and their consorts, revived the tradition of commerce-destroying. In so far as this is one means to a general end, and is based upon a navy otherwise powerful, it is well; but we need not expect to see the feats of those ships repeated in the face of a great sea power. In the first place, those cruises were powerfully supported by the determination of the United States to blockade, not only the chief centres of Southern trade, but every inlet of the coast, thus leaving few ships available for pursuit; in the second place, had there been ten of those cruisers where there was one, they would not have stopped the incursion in Southern waters of the Union fleet, which penetrated to every point accessible from the sea; and in the third place, the undeniable injury, direct and indirect, inflicted upon individuals and upon one branch of the nation's industry (and how high that shipping industry stands in the writer's estimation need not be repeated), did not in the least influence or retard the event of the war. Such injuries, unaccompanied by others, are more irritating than weakening. On the other hand, will any refuse to admit that the work of the great Union fleets powerfully modified and hastened an end which was probably inevitable in any case? As a sea power the South then occupied the place of France in the wars we have been considering, while the situation of the North resembled that of England; and, as in France, the sufferers in the Confederacy were not a class, but the government and the nation at large. It is not the taking of individual ships or convoys, be they few or many, that strikes down the money power of a nation; it is the possession of that overbearing power on the sea which drives the enemy's flag from it, or allows it to appear only as a fugitive; and which, by controlling the great common, closes the highways by which commerce moves to and from the enemy's shores. This overbearing power can only be exercised by great navies, and by them (on the broad sea) less efficiently now than in the days when the neutral flag had not its present immunity. It is not unlikely that, in the event of a war between maritime nations, an attempt may be made by the one having a great sea power and wishing to break down its enemy's commerce, to interpret the phrase "effective blockade" in the manner that best suits its interests at the time; to assert that the speed and disposal of its ships make the blockade effective at much greater distances and with fewer ships than formerly. The determination of such a question will depend, not upon the weaker belligerent, but upon neutral powers; it will raise the issue between belligerent and neutral rights; and if the belligerent have a vastly overpowering navy he may carry his point, just as England, when possessing the mastery of the seas, long refused to admit the doctrine of the neutral flag covering the goods.

3

War of England and France in Alliance against the United Provinces, 1672-1674—Finally, of France against Combined Europe, 1674-1678—Sea Battles of Solebay, the Texel, and Stromboli

Shortly before the conclusion of the Peace of Breda, Louis XIV. made his first step toward seizing parts of the Spanish Netherlands and Franche Comté. At the same time that his armies moved forward, he sent out a State paper setting forth his claims upon the territories in question. This paper showed unmistakably the ambitious character of the young king, roused the anxiety of Europe, and doubtless increased the strength of the peace party in England. Under the leadership of Holland, but with the hearty co-operation of the English minister, an alliance was formed between the two countries and Sweden, hitherto the friend of France, to check Louis' advance before his power became too great. The attack first on the Netherlands in 1667, and then on Franche Comté in 1668, showed the hopeless weakness of Spain to defend her possessions; they fell almost without a blow.

The policy of the United Provinces, relative to the claims of Louis at this time, was summed up in the phrase that "France was good as a friend, but not as a neighbor." They were unwilling to break their traditional alliance, but still more unwilling to have her on their border. The policy of the English people, though not of their king, turned toward the Dutch. In the increased greatness of Louis they saw danger to all Europe; to themselves more especially if, by a settled preponderance on the continent, his hands were free to develop his sea power. "Flanders once in the power of Louis XIV.," wrote the English ambassador Temple, "the Dutch feel that their country will be only a maritime province of France"; and sharing that opinion, "he advocated the policy of resistance to the latter country, whose domination in the Low Countries he considered as a threatened subjection of all Europe. He never ceased to represent to his government how dangerous to England would be the conquest of the sea provinces by France, and he urgently pointed out the need of a prompt understanding with the Dutch. 'This would be the best revenge,' said he, 'for the trick France has played us in involving us in the last war with the United Provinces'." These considerations brought the two countries together in that Triple Alliance with Sweden which has been mentioned, and which for a time checked the onward movement of Louis. But the wars between the two sea nations were too recent, the humiliation of England in the Thames too bitter, and the rivalries that still existed too real, too deeply seated in the nature of things, to make that alliance durable. It needed the dangerous power of Louis, and his persistence in a course threatening to both, to weld the union of these natural antagonists. This was not to be done without another bloody encounter.

Louis was deeply angered at the Triple Alliance, and his wrath was turned mainly upon Holland, in which from the necessities of her position he recognized his most steadfast opponent. For the time, however, he seemed to yield; the more readily because of the probable approaching failure of the Spanish royal line, and the ambition he had of getting more than merely the territory lying to the east of France, when the throne became vacant. But, though he dissembled and yielded, from that time he set his mind upon the destruction of the republic. This policy was directly contrary to that laid down by Richelieu, and to the true welfare of France. It was to England's interest, at least just then, that the United Provinces should not be trodden down by France; but it was much more to the interest of France that they should not be subjected to England. England, free from the continent, might stand alone upon the seas contending with France; but France, hampered by her continental politics, could not hope to wrest the control of the seas from England without an ally. This ally Louis proposed to destroy, and he asked England to help him. The final result is already known, but the outlines of the contest must now be followed.

Before the royal purpose had passed into action, and while there was still time to turn the energies of France into another channel, a different course was proposed to the king. This was the project of Leibnitz, before spoken of, which has special interest for our subject because, in proposing to reverse the lines which Louis then laid down, to make continental expansion secondary and growth beyond the sea the primary object of France, the tendency avowedly and necessarily was to base the greatness of the country upon the control of the sea and of commerce. The immediate object offered to the France of that day, with the attainment of which, however, she could not have stopped short, was the conquest of Egypt; that country which, facing both the Mediterranean and Eastern seas, gave control of the great commercial route which in our own day has been completed by the Suez Canal. That route had lost much of its value by the discovery of the way round the Cape of Good Hope, and yet more by the unsettled and piratical conditions of the seas through which it lay; but with a really strong naval power occupying the key of the position it might have been largely restored. Such a power posted in Egypt would, in the already decaying condition of the Ottoman Empire, have controlled the trade not only of India and the far East, but also of the Levant; but the enterprise could not have stopped there. The necessity of mastering the Mediterranean and opening the Red Sea, closed to Christian vessels by Mohammedan bigotry, would have compelled the occupation of stations on either side of Egypt; and France would have been led step by step, as England has been led by the possession of India, to the seizure of points like Malta, Cyprus, Aden, in short, to a great sea power. That is clear now; but it will be interesting to hear the arguments by which Leibnitz sought to convince the French king two hundred years ago.

After pointing out the weakness of the Turkish Empire, and the readiness with which it might be further embarrassed by stirring up Austria and Poland, the latter the traditional ally of France; after showing that France had no armed enemy in the Mediterranean, and that on the other side of Egypt she would meet the Portuguese colonies, longing to obtain protection against the Dutch in India, the memorial proceeds:—

"The conquest of Egypt, that Holland of the East, is infinitely easier than that of the United Provinces. France needs peace in the west, war at a distance. War with Holland will probably ruin the new Indian companies as well as the colonies and commerce lately revived by France, and will increase the burdens of the people while diminishing their resources. The Dutch will retire into their maritime towns, stand there on the defensive in perfect safety, and assume the offensive on the sea with great chance of success. If France does not obtain a complete victory over them, she loses all her influence in Europe, and by victory she endangers that influence. In Egypt, on the contrary, a repulse, almost impossible, will be of no great consequence, and victory will give the dominion of the seas, the commerce of the East and of India, the preponderance in Christendom, and even the empire of the East on the ruins of the Ottoman power. The possession of Egypt opens the way to conquests worthy of Alexander; the extreme weakness of the Orientals is no longer a secret. Whoever has Egypt will have all the coasts and islands of the Indian Ocean. It is in Egypt that Holland will be conquered; it is there she will be despoiled of what alone renders her prosperous, the treasures of the East. She will be struck without being able to ward off the blow. Should she wish to oppose the designs of France upon Egypt, she would be overwhelmed with the universal hatred of Christians; attacked at home, on the contrary, not only could she ward off the aggression, but she could avenge herself sustained by universal public opinion, which suspects the views of France of ambition." [1]

The memorial had no effect. "All that the efforts of ambition and human prudence could do to lay the foundations for the destruction of a nation, Louis XIV. now did. Diplomatic strategy on a vast scale was displayed in order to isolate and hem in Holland. Louis, who had been unable to make Europe accept the conquest of Belgium by France, now hoped to induce it to see without trembling the fall of Holland." His efforts were in the main successful. The Triple Alliance was broken; the King of England, though contrary to the wishes of his people, made an offensive alliance with Louis; and Holland, when the war began, found herself without an ally in Europe, except the worn-out kingdom of Spain and the Elector of Brandenburg, then by no means a first-class State. But in order to obtain the help of Charles II., Louis not only engaged to pay him large sums of money, but also to give to England, from the spoils of Holland and Belgium, Walcheren, Sluys, and Cadsand, and even the islands of Goree and Voorn; the control, that is, of the mouths of the great commercial rivers the Scheldt and the Meuse. With

[1] Martin: History of France.

regard to the united fleets of the two nations, it was agreed that the officer bearing the admiral's flag of England should command in chief. The question of naval precedence was reserved, by not sending the admiral of France afloat; but it was practically yielded. It is evident that in his eagerness for the ruin of Holland and his own continental aggrandizement Louis was playing directly into England's hand, as to power on the sea. A French historian is justified in saying: "These negotiations have been wrongly judged. It has been often repeated that Charles sold England to Louis XIV. This is true only of internal policy. Charles indeed plotted the political and religious subjugation of England with the help of a foreign power; but as to external interests, he did not sell them, for the greater share in the profit from the ruin of the Dutch was to go to England." [2]

During the years preceding the war the Dutch made every diplomatic effort to avert it, but the hatred of Charles and Louis prevented any concession being accepted as final. An English royal yacht was ordered to pass through the Dutch ships-of-war in the Channel, and to fire on them if they did not strike their flags. In January, 1672, England sent an ultimatum, summoning Holland to acknowledge the right of the English crown to the sovereignty of the British seas, and to order its fleets to lower their flags to the smallest English man-of-war; and demands such as these received the support of a French king. The Dutch continued to yield, but seeing at length that all concessions were useless, they in February ordered into commission seventy-five ships-of-the-line, besides smaller vessels. On the 23d of March the English, without declaration of war, attacked a fleet of Dutch merchantmen; and on the 29th the king declared war. This was followed, April 6th, by the declaration of Louis XIV.; and on the 28th of the same month he set out to take command in person of his army.

The war which now began, including the third and last of the great contests between the English and Dutch upon the ocean, was not, like those before it, purely a sea war; and it will be necessary to mention its leading outlines on the land also, not only in order to give a clear impression, but also to bring out the desperate straits to which the republic was reduced, and the final deliverance through its sea power in the hands of the great seaman De Ruyter.

The naval war differs from those that preceded it in more than

[2] Martin: History of France.

one respect; but its most distinctive feature is that the Dutch, except on one occasion at the very beginning, did not send out their fleet to meet the enemy, but made what may properly be called a strategic use of their dangerous coast and shoals, upon which were based their sea operations. To this course they were forced by the desperate odds under which they were fighting; but they did not use their shoals as a mere shelter,—the warfare they waged was the defensive-offensive. When the wind was fair for the allies to attack, Ruyter kept under cover of his islands, or at least on ground where the enemy dared not follow; but when the wind served so that he might attack in his own way, he turned and fell upon them. There are also apparent indications of tactical combinations, on his part, of a higher order than have yet been met; though it is possible that the particular acts referred to, consisting in partial attacks amounting to little more than demonstrations against the French contingent, may have sprung from political motives. This solution for the undoubted fact that the Dutch attacked the French lightly has not been met with elsewhere by the writer; but it seems possible that the rulers of the United Provinces may have wished not to increase the exasperation of their most dangerous enemy by humiliating his fleet, and so making it less easy to his pride to accept their offers. There is, however, an equally satisfactory military explanation in the supposition that, the French being yet inexperienced, Ruyter thought it only necessary to contain them while falling in force upon the English. The latter fought throughout with their old gallantry, but less than their old discipline; whereas the attacks of the Dutch were made with a sustained and unanimous vigor that showed a great military advance. The action of the French was at times suspicious; it has been alleged that Louis ordered his admiral to economize his fleet, and there is good reason to believe that toward the end of the two years that England remained in his alliance he did do so.

The authorities of the United Provinces, knowing that the French fleet at Brest was to join the English in the Thames, made great exertions to fit out their squadron so as to attack the latter before the junction was made; but the wretched lack of centralization in their naval administration caused this project to fail. The province of Zealand was so backward that its contingent, a large fraction of the whole, was not ready in time; and it has been charged that the delay was due, not merely to mismanagement, but to disaffection to the party in control of the government. A blow at the English fleet in its own waters, by a superior force, before its ally arrived, was a correct military conception; judging from the after-history of this war, it might well have produced a profound effect upon the whole course of the struggle. Ruyter finally got to sea and fell in with the allied fleets, but though fully intending to fight, fell back before them to his own coast. The allies did not follow him there, but retired, apparently in full security, to Southwold Bay, on the east coast of England, some ninety miles north of the mouth of the Thames. There they anchored in three divisions,—two English, the rear and centre of the allied line, to the northward, and the van, composed of French ships, to the southward. Ruyter followed them, and on the early morning of June 7, 1672, the Dutch fleet was signalled by a French lookout frigate in the northward and eastward; standing down before a northeast wind for the allied fleet, from which a large number of boats and men were ashore in watering parties. The Dutch order of battle was in two lines, the advanced one containing eighteen ships with fire-ships (Plate III., A). Their total force was ninety-one ships-of-the-line; that of the allies one hundred and one.

The wind was blowing toward the coast, which here trends nearly north and south, and the allies were in an awkward position. They had first to get under way, and they could not fall back to gain time or room to establish their order. Most of the ships cut their cables, and the English made sail on the starboard tack, heading about north-northwest, a course which forced them soon to go about; whereas the French took the other tack (Plate III., B). The battle began therefore by the separation of the allied fleet. Ruyter sent one division to attack the French, or rather to contain them; for these opponents exchanged only a distant cannonade, although the Dutch, being to windward, had the choice of closer action if they wished it. As their commander, Bankert, was not censured, it may be supposed he acted under orders; and he was certainly in command a year later, and acting with great judgment and gallantry at the battle of the Texel. Meanwhile Ruyter fell furiously upon the two English divisions, and apparently with superior forces; for the English naval historians claim that the Dutch were in the proportion of three to two.[3] If this can be accepted, it gives a marked evidence of Ruyter's

[3] Ledyard, vol. ii., p. 599; Campbell: Lives of the Admirals. See also letter of Sir Richard Haddock, Naval Chronicle, vol. xvii., p. 121.

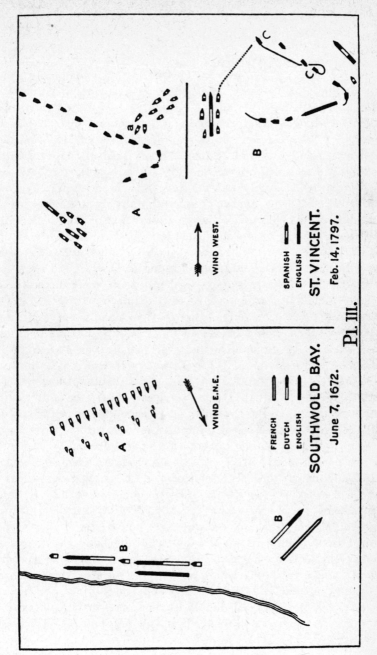

WIND WEST.

SPANISH
ENGLISH

ST. VINCENT.
Feb. 14, 1797.

SOUTHWOLD BAY.
June 7, 1672.

WIND E.N.E.

FRENCH
DUTCH
ENGLISH

Pl. III.

129

high qualities as a general officer, in advance of any other who appears in this century.

The results of the battle, considered simply as an engagement, were indecisive; both sides lost heavily, but the honors and the substantial advantages all belonged to the Dutch, or rather to De Ruyter. He had outgeneralled the allies by his apparent retreat, and then returning had surprised them wholly unprepared. The false move by which the English, two thirds of the whole, stood to the northward and westward, while the other third, the French, went off to the east and south, separated the allied fleet; Ruyter threw his whole force into the gap, showing front to the French with a division probably smaller in numbers, but which, from its position to windward, had the choice of coming to close action or not, while with the remainder he fell in much superior strength upon the English (Plate III., B). Paul Hoste says[4] that Vice-Admiral d'Estrées, commanding the French, had taken measures for tacking and breaking through the Dutch division opposed to him so to rejoin the Duke of York, the allied commander-in-chief. It may be so, for D'Estrées was a very brave man, and not enough of a seaman to appreciate the dangers of the attempt; but no such move was begun, and both the English and Ruyter thought that the French rather avoided than sought close action. Had D'Estrées, however, gone about, and attempted to break through the line of experienced Dutchmen to windward of him with the still raw seamen of France, the result would have been as disastrous as that which overtook the Spanish admiral at the battle of St. Vincent a hundred and twenty-five years later, when he tried to reunite his broken fleet by breaking through the close order of Jervis and Nelson. (See Plate III., A.) The truth, which gradually dawns through a mass of conflicting statements, is, that the Duke of York, though a fair seaman and a brave man, was not an able one; that his fleet was not in good order and was thus surprised; that his orders beforehand were not so precise as to make the French admiral technically disobedient in taking the opposite tack from the commander-in-chief, and so separating the squadrons; and that Ruyter profited most ably by the surprise which he had himself prepared, and by the further opportunity given him by the ineptness of his enemies. Unless for circumstances that are not stated, the French admiral took the right tack, with a northeast wind, for

4 Hoste: Naval Tactics.

it led out to sea and would give room for manœuvring; had the Duke of York chosen the same, the allied fleet would have gone out together, with only the disadvantage of the wind and bad order. In that case, however, Ruyter could, and probably would, have done just what he did at the Texel a year later,—check the van, the French, with a small containing force, and fall with the mass of his fleet upon the centre and rear. It is the similarity of his action in both cases, under very different conditions, that proves he intended at Southwold Bay merely to keep the French in check while he destroyed the English.

In this battle, called indifferently Southwold Bay and Solebay, Ruyter showed a degree of skill combined with vigor which did not appear upon the sea, after his death, until the days of Suffren and Nelson. His battles of the war of 1672 were no "affairs of circumspection," though they were fought circumspectly; his aim was no less than the enemy's total overthrow, by joining good combinations to fury of attack. At Solebay he was somewhat, though not greatly, inferior to his enemies; afterward much more so.

The substantial results of Solebay fight were wholly favorable to the Dutch. The allied fleets were to have assisted the operations of the French army by making a descent upon the coast of Zealand. Ruyter's attack had inflicted an amount of damage, and caused an expenditure of ammunition, which postponed the sailing of the fleet for a month; it was a diversion, not only important, but vital in the nearly desperate condition to which the United Provinces were reduced ashore. It may be added, as an instructive comment on the theory of commerce-destroying, that after this staggering check to the enemy's superior forces, Ruyter met and convoyed safely to port a fleet of Dutch merchantmen.

The progress of the land campaign must now be briefly described. Early in May the French army in several corps moved forward, passing through the outskirts of the Spanish Netherlands, and directing their attack upon Holland from the south and east. The republican party which was in power in Holland had neglected the army, and now made the mistake of scattering the force they had among many fortified towns, trusting that each would do something toward delaying the French. Louis, however, under the advice of Turenne, simply observed the more important places, while the second-rate towns surrendered nearly as fast as they were summoned; the army of the Provinces, as well as their territory, thus passing rapidly, by fractions, into the power of the enemy. Within a month the French were in the heart of the country, having carried all before them, and with no organized force remaining in their front sufficient of itself to stop them. In the fortnight following the battle of Solebay, terror and disorganization spread throughout the republic. On the 15th of June the Grand Pensionary obtained permission of the States-General to send a deputation to Louis XIV., begging him to name the terms on which he would grant them peace; any humiliation to the foreigner was better in the eyes of the politician than to see the opposite party, the House of Orange, come into power on his downfall. While negotiations were pending, the Dutch towns continued to surrender; and on the 20th of June a few French soldiers entered Muyden, the key to Amsterdam. They were only stragglers, though the large body to which they belonged was near at hand; and the burghers, who had admitted them under the influence of the panic prevailing throughout the land, seeing that they were alone, soon made them drunk and put them out. The nobler feeling that animated Amsterdam now made itself felt in Muyden; a body of troops hurried up from the capital, and the smaller city was saved. "Situated on the Zuyder Zee, two hours distant from Amsterdam, at the junction of a number of rivers and canals, Muyden not only held the key of the principal dykes by which Amsterdam could surround herself with a protecting inundation, it also held the key of the harbor of this great city, all the ships which went from the North Sea to Amsterdam by the Zuyder Zee being obliged to pass under its guns. Muyden saved and its dykes open, Amsterdam had time to breathe, and remained free to break off her communications by land and to maintain them by sea." [5] It was the turning-point of the invasion; but what would have been the effect upon the spirit of the Dutch, oppressed by defeat and distracted in council, if in that fateful fortnight which went before, the allied fleet had attacked their coasts? From this they were saved by the battle of Solebay.

Negotiations continued. The burgomasters—the party representing wealth and commerce—favored submission; they shrank from the destruction of their property and trade. New advances were

[5] Martin: History of France.

made; but while the envoys were still in the camp of Louis, the populace and the Orange party rose, and with them the spirit of resistance. On the 25th of June Amsterdam opened the dykes, and her example was followed by the other cities of Holland; immense loss was entailed, but the flooded country and the cities contained therein, standing like islands amid the waters, were safe from attack by land forces until freezing weather. The revolution continued. William of Orange, afterward William III. of England, was on the 8th of July made *stadtholder,* and head of the army and navy; and the two De Witts, the heads of the republican party, were murdered by a mob a few weeks later.

The resistance born of popular enthusiasm and pride of country was strengthened by the excessive demands of Louis XIV. It was plain that the Provinces must conquer or be destroyed. Meanwhile the other States of Europe were waking up to the danger, and the Emperor of Germany, the Elector of Brandenburg, and the King of Spain declared for Holland; while Sweden, though nominally in alliance with France, was unwilling to see the destruction of the Provinces, because that would be to the advantage of England's sea power. Nevertheless the next year, 1673, opened with promise for France, and the English king was prepared to fulfil his part of the compact on the seas; but the Dutch, under the firm leadership of William of Orange, and with their hold on the sea unshaken, now refused to accept conditions of peace which had been offered by themselves the year before.

Three naval battles were fought in 1673, all near the coast of the United Provinces; the first two, June 7 and June 14, off Schoneveldt, from which place they have taken their name; the third, known as the battle of the Texel, August 21. In all three Ruyter attacked, choosing his own time, and retiring when it suited him to the protection of his own shores. For the allies to carry out their objects and make any diversion upon the seaboard, or on the other hand to cripple the sea resources of the hard-pressed Provinces, it was necessary first to deal successfully with Ruyter's fleet. The great admiral and his government both felt this, and took the resolution that "the fleet should be posted in the passage of Schoneveldt, or a little farther south toward Ostend, to observe the enemy, and if attacked, or seeing the enemy's fleet disposed to make a descent upon the shores of the United Provinces, should resist vigorously, by opposing his designs and destroying his ships." [6] From this position, with good lookouts, any movement of the allies would be known.

The English and French put to sea about the 1st of June, under the command of Prince Rupert, first cousin to the king, the Duke of York having been obliged to resign his office on account of the passage of the Test Act, directed against persons of the Roman Catholic faith holding any public employment. The French were under Vice-Admiral d'Estrées, the same who had commanded them at Solebay. A force of six thousand English troops at Yarmouth was ready to embark if de Ruyter was worsted. On the 7th of June the Dutch were made out, riding within the sands at Schoneveldt. A detached squadron was sent to draw them out, but Ruyter needed no invitation; the wind served, and he followed the detached squadron with such impetuosity as to attack before the allied line was fairly formed. On this occasion the French occupied the centre. The affair was indecisive, if a battle can be called so in which an inferior force attacks a superior, inflicts an equal loss, and frustrates the main object of the enemy. A week later Ruyter again attacked, with results which, though indecisive as before as to the particular action, forced the allied fleet to return to the English coast to refit, and for supplies. The Dutch in these encounters had fifty-five ships-of-the-line; their enemies eighty-one, fifty-four of which were English.

The allied fleets did not go to sea again until the latter part of July, and this time they carried with them a body of troops meant for a landing. On the 20th of August the Dutch fleet was seen under way between the Texel and the Meuse. Rupert at once got ready to fight; but as the wind was from the northward and westward, giving the allies the weather-gage, and with it the choice of the method of attack, Ruyter availed himself of his local knowledge, keeping so close to the beach that the enemy dared not approach,—the more so as it was late in the day. During the night the wind shifted to east-southeast off the land, and at daybreak, to use the words of a French official narrative, the Dutch "made all sail and stood down boldly into action."

The allied fleet was to leeward on the port tack, heading about south,—the French in the van, Rupert in the centre, and Sir Edward Spragge commanding the rear. De Ruyter divided his fleet into three

[6] Brandt: Life of De Ruyter.

squadrons, the leading one of which, of ten or twelve ships only, he sent against the French; while with the rest of his force he attacked the English in the centre and rear (Plate IV., A, A', A''). If we accept the English estimate of the forces, which gives the English sixty ships, the French thirty, and the Dutch seventy, Ruyter's plan of attack, by simply holding the French in check as at Solebay, allowed him to engage the English on equal terms. The battle took on several distinct phases, which it is instructive to follow. M. de Martel, commanding the van of the French, and consequently the leading subdivision of the allied fleet, was ordered to stretch ahead, go about and gain to windward of the Dutch van, so as to place it between two fires. This he did (B); but as soon as Bankert—the same who had manœuvred so judiciously at Solebay the year before —saw the danger, he put his helm up and ran through the remaining twenty ships of D'Estrées' squadron with his own twelve (C),—a feat as creditable to him as it was discreditable to the French; and then wearing round stood down to De Ruyter, who was hotly engaged with Rupert (C'). He was not followed by D'Estrées, who suffered him to carry this important reinforcement to the Dutch main attack undisturbed. This practically ended the French share in the fight.

Rupert, during his action with De Ruyter, kept off continually, with the object of drawing the Dutch farther away from their coast, so that if the wind shifted they might not be able to regain its shelter. De Ruyter followed him, and the consequent separation of the centre from the van (B, B') was one of the reasons alleged by D'Estrées for his delay. It does not, however, seem to have prevented Bankert from joining his chief.

In the rear an extraordinary action on the part of Sir Edward Spragge increased the confusion in the allied fleet. For some reason this officer considered Tromp, who commanded the Dutch rear, as his personal antagonist, and in order to facilitate the latter's getting into action, he hove-to (stopped) the whole English rear to wait for him. This ill-timed point of honor on Spragge's part seems to have sprung from a promise he had made to the king that he would bring back Tromp alive or dead, or else lose his own life. The stoppage, which recalls the irresponsible and insubordinate action of the junior Dutch flag-officers in the former war, of course separated the rear (A'', B'', C''), which also drifted rapidly to leeward, Spragge and

Tromp carrying on a hot private action on their own account. These two junior admirals sought each other personally, and the battle between their flags was so severe that Spragge twice had to shift his own to another ship; on the second occasion the boat in which he was embarked was sunk by a shot, and he himself drowned.

Rupert, thus forsaken by his van and rear, found himself alone with Ruyter (B′); who, reinforced by his van, had the address further to cut off the rear subdivision of the allied centre, and to surround the remaining twenty ships with probably thirty or forty of his own (C′). It is not creditable to the gunnery of the day that more substantial results did not follow; but it is to be remembered that all Ruyter's skill could secure, except for probably a very short time, was an action on equal terms with the English; his total inferiority in numbers could not be quite overcome. The damage to the English and Dutch may therefore have been great, and was probably nearly equal.

Rupert finally disengaged himself, and seeing that the English rear (C″) was not replying well to its immediate opponents, ran down toward it, Ruyter following him; the two opposing centres steering parallel courses, and within cannon-shot, but by mutual consent, induced perhaps by ammunition running short, refraining from firing. At four P.M. the centres and rears united, and toward five a fresh engagement began, which continued till seven, when Ruyter withdrew, probably because of the approach of the French, who, by their own accounts, rejoined Rupert about that time. This ended the battle, which, like all that preceded it in this war, may be called a drawn fight, but as to which the verdict of the English naval historian is doubtless correct: "The consequences which the Dutch, through the prudence of their admiral, drew from this battle were exceedingly great; for they opened their ports, which were entirely blocked up, and put an end to all thoughts, by removing the possibility, of an invasion." [7]

The military features of the action have sufficiently appeared in the account that has been given,—the skill of De Ruyter; the firmness and promptness of Bankert, first in checking and then in passing through the French division; the apparent disloyalty or, at the best, inefficiency of the latter; the insubordination and military blundering of Spragge; the seeming lack of everything but hard fighting on

[7] Campbell: Lives of the Admirals.

136

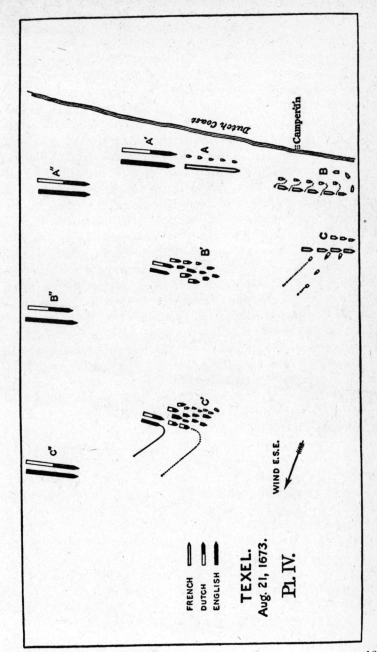

Dutch Coast

Camperdín

A'

A

A''

B

B'

C

B''

C'

C''

WIND E.S.E.

FRENCH
DUTCH
ENGLISH

TEXEL.
Aug. 21, 1673.

Pl. IV.

Rupert's part. The allies indulged in bitter mutual recriminations. Rupert blamed both D'Estrées and Spragge; D'Estrées found fault with Rupert for running to leeward; and D'Estrées' own second, Martel, roundly called his chief a coward, in a letter which earned him an imprisonment in the Bastille. The French king ordered an inquiry by the intendant of the navy at Brest, who made a report[8] upon which the account here given has mainly rested, and which leaves little doubt of the dishonor of the French arms in this battle. "M. d'Estrées gave it to be understood," says the French naval historian, "that the king wished his fleet spared, and that the English should not be trusted. Was he wrong in not relying upon the sincerity of the English alliance, when he was receiving from all quarters warnings that the people and the nobles were murmuring against it, and Charles II. was perhaps alone in his kingdom in wishing it?" [9] Possibly not; but he was surely wrong if he wished any military man, or body of men, to play the equivocal part assigned to the French admiral on this day; the loss of the fleet would have been a lighter disaster. So evident to eye-witnesses was the bad faith or cowardice (and the latter supposition is not admissible), that one of the Dutch seamen, as they discussed among themselves why the French did not come down, said: "You fools! they have hired the English to fight for them, and all their business here is to see that they earn their wages." A more sober-minded and significant utterance is that with which the intendant at Brest ends the official report before mentioned: "It would appear in all these sea-fights Ruyter has never cared to attack the French squadron, and that in this last action he had detached ten ships of the Zealand squadron to keep it in play." [10] No stronger testimony is needed to Ruyter's opinion of the inefficiency or faithlessness of that contingent to the allied forces.

Another chapter in the history of maritime coalitions was closed, on the 21st of August, 1673, by the battle of the Texel. In it, as in others, were amply justified the words with which a modern French naval officer has stamped them: "United by momentary political interests, but at bottom divided to the verge of hatred, never following the same path in counsel or in action, they have never produced good results, or at least results proportioned to the efforts of the powers allied against a common enemy. The navies of France, Spain,

---

[8] Troude: Batailles Navales de la France, year 1673.
[9] Ibid.
[10] Ibid.

and Holland seem, at several distinct times, to have joined only to make more complete the triumph of the British arms." [11] When to this well-ascertained tendency of coalitions is added the equally well known jealousy of every country over the increasing power of a neighbor, and the consequent unwillingness to see such increase obtained by crushing another member of the family of nations, an approach is made to the measure of naval strength required by a State. It is not necessary to be able to meet all others combined, as some Englishmen have seemed to think; it is necessary only to be able to meet the strongest on favorable terms, sure that the others will not join in destroying a factor in the political equilibrium, even if they hold aloof. England and Spain were allies in Toulon in 1793, when the excesses of Revolutionary France seemed to threaten the social order of Europe; but the Spanish admiral told the English flatly that the ruin of the French navy, a large part of which was there in their hands, could not fail to be injurious to the interests of Spain, and a part of the French ships was saved by his conduct, which has been justly characterized as not only full of firmness, but also as dictated by the highest political reason.[12]

The battle of the Texel, closing the long series of wars in which the Dutch and English contended on equal terms for the mastery of the seas, saw the Dutch navy in its highest efficiency, and its greatest ornament, De Ruyter, at the summit of his glory. Long since old in years, for he was now sixty-six, he had lost none of his martial vigor; his attack was as furious as eight years before, and his judgment apparently had ripened rapidly through the experience of the last war, for there is far more evidence of plan and military insight than before. To him, under the government of the great Pensionary De Witt, with whom he was in close sympathy, the increase of discipline and sound military tone now apparent in the Dutch navy must have been largely due. He went to this final strife of the two great sea-peoples in the fulness of his own genius, with an admirably tempered instrument in his hands, and with the glorious disadvantage of numbers, to save his country. The mission was fulfilled not by courage alone, but by courage, forethought, and skill. The attack at the Texel was, in its general lines, the same as that at Trafalgar, the enemy's van being neglected to fall on the centre and rear, and

[11] Chaubaud-Arnault: Revue Mar. et Col., July, 1885.
[12] Jurien de la Gravière: Guerres Maritimes.

as at Trafalgar the van, by failing to do its duty, more than justified the conception; but as the odds against De Ruyter were greater than those against Nelson, so was his success less. The part played by Bankert at Solebay was essentially the same as that of Nelson at St. Vincent, when he threw himself across the path of the Spanish division with his single ship (see Plate III., C, C′); but Nelson took his course without orders from Jervis, while Bankert was carrying out Ruyter's plan. Once more, still himself in his bearing, but under sadly altered surroundings, will this simple and heroic man come before us; and here, in contrast with his glory, seems a proper place to insert a little description by the Comte de Guiche[13] of his bearing in the Four Days' Fight, which brings out at once the homely and the heroic sides of his character.

"I never saw him [during those last three days] other than even-tempered; and when victory was assured, saying always it was the good God that gives it to us. Amid the disorders of the fleet and the appearance of loss, he seemed to be moved only by the misfortune to his country, but always submissive to the will of God. Finally, it may be said that he has something of the frankness and lack of polish of our patriarchs; and, to conclude what I have to say of him, I will relate that the day after the victory I found him sweeping his own room and feeding his chickens."

Nine days after the battle of the Texel, on the 30th of August, 1673, a formal alliance was made between Holland on the one hand, and Spain, Lorraine, and the emperor of Germany on the other, and the French ambassador was dismissed from Vienna. Louis almost immediately offered Holland comparatively moderate terms; but the United Provinces, with their new allies by their sides and with their backs borne firmly upon the sea which had favored and supported them, set their face steadily against him. In England the clamor of the people and Parliament became louder; the Protestant feeling and the old enmity to France were daily growing, as was the national distrust of the king. Charles, though he had himself lost none of his hatred of the republic, had to give way. Louis, seeing the gathering storm, made up his mind, by the counsel of Turenne, to withdraw from his dangerously advanced position by evacuating Holland, and to try to make peace with the Provinces separately while continuing the war with the House of Austria in Spain and Germany. Thus he

[13] Mémoires du Cte. de Guiche, 1743.

returned to Richelieu's policy, and Holland was saved. February 19, 1674, peace was signed between England and the Provinces. The latter recognized the absolute supremacy of the English flag from Cape Finisterre in Spain to Norway, and paid a war indemnity.

The withdrawal of England, which remained neutral during the remaining four years of the war, necessarily made it less maritime. The King of France did not think his navy, either in numbers or efficiency, able to contend alone with that of Holland; he therefore withdrew it from the ocean and confined his sea enterprises to the Mediterranean, with one or two half-privateering expeditions to the West Indies. The United Provinces for their part, being freed from danger on the side of the sea, and not having, except for a short time, any serious idea of operating against the French coast, diminished their own fleets. The war became more and more continental, and drew in more and more the other powers of Europe. Gradually the German States cast their lot with Austria, and on May 28, 1674, the Diet proclaimed war against France. The great work of French policy in the last generations was undone, Austria had resumed her supremacy in Germany, and Holland had not been destroyed. On the Baltic, Denmark, seeing Sweden inclining toward France, hastened to make common cause with the German Empire, sending fifteen thousand troops. There remained in Germany only Bavaria, Hanover, and Wurtemberg faithful still to their French alliance. The land war had thus drawn in nearly all the powers of Europe, and, from the nature of the case, the principal theatre of the conflict was beyond the eastern boundary of France, toward the Rhine, and in the Spanish Netherlands; but while this was raging, a maritime episode was introduced by the fact of Denmark and Sweden being engaged on opposite sides. Of this it will not be necessary to speak, beyond mentioning that the Dutch sent a squadron under Tromp to join the Danes, and that the united fleets won a great victory over the Swedes in 1676, taking from them ten ships. It is therefore evident that the sea superiority of Holland detracted greatly from Sweden's value as an ally to Louis XIV.

Another maritime strife arose in the Mediterranean by the revolt of the Sicilians against the Spanish rule. The help they asked from France was granted as a diversion against Spain, but the Sicilian enterprise never became more than a side issue. Its naval interest springs from bringing Ruyter once more on the scene, and that as the antagonist of Duquesne, the equal, and by some thought even the superior, of Tourville, whose name has always stood far above all others in the French navy of that day.

Messina revolted in July, 1674, and the French king at once took it under his protection. The Spanish navy throughout seems to have behaved badly, certainly inefficiently; and early in 1675 the French were safely established in the city. During the year their naval power in the Mediterranean was much increased, and Spain, unable to defend the island herself, applied to the United Provinces for a fleet, the expenses of which she would bear. The Provinces, "fatigued by the war, involved in debt, suffering cruelly in their commerce, exhausted by the necessity of paying the emperor and all the German princes, could no longer fit out the enormous fleets which they had once opposed to France and England." They however hearkened to Spain and sent De Ruyter, with a squadron of only eighteen ships and four fire-ships. The admiral, who had noted the growth of the French navy, said the force was too small, and departed oppressed in spirit, but with the calm resignation which was habitual to him. He reached Cadiz in September, and in the meantime the French had further strengthened themselves by the capture of Agosta, a port commanding the southeast of Sicily. De Ruyter was again delayed by the Spanish government, and did not reach the north coast of the island until the end of December, when head winds kept him from entering the Straits of Messina. He cruised between Messina and the Lipari Islands in a position to intercept the French fleet convoying troops and supplies, which was expected under Duquesne.

On the 7th of January, 1676, the French came in sight, twenty ships-of-the-line and six fire-ships; the Dutch had but nineteen ships, one of which was a Spaniard, and four fire-ships; and it must be remembered that, although there is no detailed account of the Dutch ships in this action, they were as a rule inferior to those of England, and yet more to those of France. The first day was spent in manœuvring, the Dutch having the weather-gage; but during that night, which was squally and drove the Spanish galleys accompanying the Dutch to take refuge under Lipari, the wind shifted, and coming out at west-southwest, gave the French the weather-gage and the power to attack. Duquesne resolved to use it, and sending the convoy ahead, formed his line on the starboard tack standing south; the Dutch did the same, and waited for him (Plate V., A, A, A).

An emotion of surprise must be felt at seeing the great Dutch admiral surrender the choice of attack on the 7th. At daybreak of that day he saw the enemy and steered for him; at three P.M., a French account says, he hauled his wind on the same tack as themselves, but out of cannon-shot to windward. How account for the seeming reluctance of the man who three years before had made the desperate attacks of Solebay and the Texel? His reasons have not been handed down; it may be that the defensive advantages of the lee-gage had been recognized by this thoughtful seaman, especially when preparing to meet, with inferior forces, an enemy of impetuous gallantry and imperfect seamanship. If any such ideas did influence him they were justified by the result. The battle of Stromboli presents a partial anticipation of the tactics of the French and English a hundred years later; but in this case it is the French who seek the weather-gage and attack with fury, while the Dutch take the defensive. The results were very much such as Clerk pointed out to the English in his celebrated work on naval tactics, the accounts here followed being entirely French.[14]

The two fleets being drawn up in line-of-battle on the starboard tack, heading south, as has been said, De Ruyter awaited the attack which he had refused to make. Being between the French and their port, he felt they must fight. At nine A.M. the French line kept away altogether and ran down obliquely upon the Dutch, a manœuvre difficult to be performed with accuracy, and during which the assailant receives his enemy's fire at disadvantage (A', A'', A'''). In doing this, two ships in the French van were seriously disabled. "M. de la Fayette, in the 'Prudente', began the action; but having rashly thrown himself into the midst of the enemy's van, he was dismantled and forced to haul off." (a). Confusion ensued in the French line, from the difficult character of the manœuvre. "Vice-Admiral de Preuilli, commanding the van, in keeping away took too little room, so that in coming to the wind again, the ships, in too close order, lapped and interfered with one another's fire [A']. The absence of M. de la Fayette from the line threw the 'Parfait' into peril. Attacked by two ships, she lost her maintopmast and had also to haul off for

14 La Pérouse-Bonfils: Hist. de la Marine Française.

repairs." Again, the French came into action in succession instead of all together, a usual and almost inevitable result of the manœuvre in question. "In the *midst* of a terrible cannonade," (that is, after part of his ships were engaged), "Duquesne, commanding the centre, took post on the beam of Ruyter's division." The French rear came into action still later, after the centre (A″, A‴). "Langeron and Bethune, commanding leading ships of the French center, are crushed by superior forces." How can this be, seeing the French had the more ships? It was because, as the narrative tells us, "the French had not yet repaired the disorder of the first movement." However, all at last got into action (B, B, B), and Duquesne gradually restored order. The Dutch, engaged all along the line, resisted everywhere, and there was not one of their ships which was not closely engaged; more cannot be said for the admiral and captains of the inferior fleet. The remaining part of the fight is not very clearly related. Ruyter is said to have given way continually with his two leading divisions; but whether this was a confession of weakness or a tactical move does not appear. The rear was separated (C′), in permitting which either Ruyter or the immediate commander was at fault; but the attempts made by the French to surround and isolate it failed, probably because of damaged spars, for one French ship did pass entirely around the separated division. The action ended at 4.30 P.M., except in the rear, and the Spanish galleys shortly after came up and towed the disabled Dutch ships away. Their escape shows how injured the French must have been. The positions, C, C′, are intended to show the Dutch rear far separated, and the disorder in which a fleet action under sail necessarily ended from loss of spars.

Those who are familiar with Clerk's work on naval tactics, published about 1780, will recognize in this account of the battle of Stromboli all the features to which he called the attention of English seamen in his thesis on the methods of action employed by them and their adversaries in and before his time. Clerk's thesis started from the postulate that English seamen and officers were superior in skill or spirit, or both, to the French, and their ships on the whole as fast; that they were conscious of this superiority and therefore eager to attack, while the French, equally conscious of inferiority, or for other reasons, were averse to decisive engagements. With these dispositions the latter, feeling they could rely on a blindly

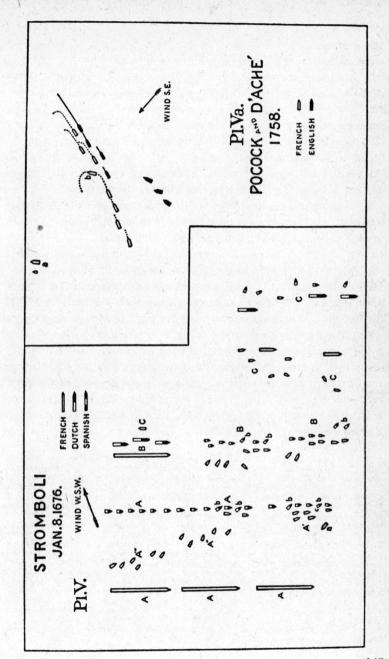

Pl.V.

STROMBOLI
JAN.8.1676.

WIND W.S.W.

FRENCH
DUTCH
SPANISH

Pl.Va.
POCOCK AND D'ACHÉ.
1758.

FRENCH
ENGLISH

WIND S.E.

145

furious attack by the English, had evolved a crafty plan by which, while seeming to fight, they really avoided doing so, and at the same time did the enemy much harm. This plan was to take the lee-gage, the characteristic of which, as has before been pointed out, is that it is a defensive position, and to await attack. The English error, according to Clerk, upon which the French had learned by experience that they could always count, was in drawing up their line parallel to the enemy, or nearly so, and then keeping away altogether to attack, ship for ship, each its opposite in the hostile line. By standing down in this manner the assailant lost the use of most of his artillery, while exposed to the full fire of his opponent, and invariably came up in confusion, because the order of attack was one difficult to maintain at any time, and much more so in the smoke under fire, with torn sails and falling masts. This was precisely the attack made by Duquesne at Stromboli, and it there had precisely the consequences Clerk points out,—confusion in the line, the van arriving first and getting the brunt of the fire of the defence, disabled ships in the van causing confusion in the rear, etc. Clerk further asserts, and he seems to be right, that as the action grew warm, the French, by running off to leeward, in their turn, led the English to repeat the same mode of attack;[15] and so we find, at Stromboli, Ruyter giving ground in the same way, though his motive does not appear. Clerk also points out that a necessary corollary of the lee-gage, assumed for tactical reasons, is to aim at the assailant's spars, his motive power, so that his attack cannot be pushed farther than the defendant chooses, and at Stromboli the

[15] This movement, according to Clerk, was not made by the whole of a French line together, but in a way much more scientific and military. A group of two or three ships withdrew at a time, being covered by the smoke and the continued fire of the rest of their line. In time a second line was partly formed, which in its turn protected the ships which had remained on the first, as they executed the somewhat exposed movement of falling back. In Plan V., Dutch ships at b, b, b, are represented as thus withdrawing. English official reports of the eighteenth century often speak of French ships acting thus; the English officers attributing to their superior valor a movement which Clerk more plausibly considers a skilful military manœuvre, well calculated to give the defence several opportunities of disabling the assailants as they bore down on a course which impeded the use of their artillery. In 1812 the frigate "United States," commanded by Decatur, employed the same tactics in her fight with the "Macedonian"; and the Confederate gunboats at Mobile by the same means inflicted on Farragut's flag-ship the greater part of the heavy loss which she sustained. In its essential features the same line of action can now be followed by a defendant, having greater speed, when the ardor of the attack, or the necessities of the case, force the assailant to a direct approach. An indirect cause of a lee line falling farther to leeward has never been noticed. When a ship in that line (as at c) found itself without an opponent abeam, and its next ahead perhaps heavily engaged, the natural impulse would be to put up the helm so as to bring the broadside to bear. This advantage would be gained by a loss of ground to leeward and consequent disorder in the line; which, if the act were repeated by several ships, could only be restored by the whole line keeping away.

crippled condition of the French is evident; for after Ruyter had fallen to leeward, and could no longer help his separated rear, it was practically unmolested by the French, although none of these had been sunk. While therefore there cannot with certainty be attributed to Ruyter the deliberate choice of the lee-gage, for which there was as yet no precedent, it is evident that he reaped all its benefits, and that the character of the French officers of his day, inexperienced as seamen and of impetuous valor, offered just the conditions that gave most advantage to an inferior force standing on the defensive. The qualities and characteristics of the enemy are among the principal factors which a man of genius considers, and it was to this as much as to any other one trait that Nelson owed his dazzling successes. On the other hand, the French admiral attacked in a wholly unscientific manner, ship against ship, without an attempt to concentrate on a part of the enemy, or even trying to keep him in play until the French squadron of eight ships-of-the-line in Messina, near by, could join. Such tactics cannot be named beside those of Solebay or the Texel; but as Duquesne was the best French officer of the century, with the possible exception of Tourville, this battle has a value of its own in the history of tactics, and may by no means be omitted. The standing of the commander-in-chief is the warrant that it marks the highest point to which French naval tactics has as yet attained. Before quitting this discussion, it may be noted that the remedy Clerk proposed was to attack the rear ships of the enemy's line, and preferably to leeward; the remainder of the fleet must then either abandon them or stand down for a general action, which according to his postulate was all that the English seamen desired.

After the fight De Ruyter sailed to Palermo, one of his ships sinking on the way. Duquesne was joined outside Messina by the French division that had been lying there. The remaining incidents of the Sicilian war are unimportant to the general subject. On the 22d of April, De Ruyter and Duquesne met again off Agosta. Duquesne had twenty-nine ships, the allied Spaniards and Dutch twenty-seven, of which ten were Spanish. Unfortunately the Spaniard commanded-in-chief, and took the centre of the line with the ships of his country, contrary to the advice of Ruyter, who, knowing how inefficient his allies were, wished to scatter them through the line and so support them better. Ruyter himself took the van, and the allies, having the wind, attacked; but the Spanish centre kept at long cannon range, leaving the brunt of the battle to fall on the Dutch van. The rear, following the commander-in-chief's motions, was also but slightly engaged. In this sorrowful yet still glorious fulfilment of hopeless duty, De Ruyter, who never before in his long career had been struck by an enemy's shot, received a mortal wound. He died a week later at Syracuse, and with him passed away the last hope of resistance on the sea. A month later the Spanish and Dutch fleets were attacked at anchor at Palermo, and many of them destroyed; while a division sent from Holland to reinforce the Mediterranean fleet was met by a French squadron in the Straits of Gibraltar and forced to take refuge in Cadiz.

The Sicilian enterprise continued to be only a diversion, and the slight importance attached to it shows clearly how entirely Louis XIV. was bent on the continental war. How differently would the value of Sicily have impressed him, had his eyes been fixed on Egypt and extension by sea. As the years passed, the temper of the English people became more and more excited against France; the trade rivalries with Holland seemed to fall into the shade, and it became likely that England, which had entered the war as the ally of Louis, would, before it closed, take up arms against him. In addition to other causes of jealousy she saw the French navy increased to a number superior to her own. Charles for a while resisted the pressure of Parliament, but in January, 1678, a treaty of alliance, offensive and defensive, was made between the two sea countries; the king recalled the English troops which until now had been serving as part of the French army, and when Parliament opened again in February, asked for money to equip ninety ships and thirty thousand soldiers. Louis, who was expecting this result, at once ordered the evacuation of Sicily. He did not fear England by land, but on the sea he could not yet hold his own against the union of the two sea powers. At the same time he redoubled his attacks on the Spanish Netherlands. As long as there was a hope of keeping the ships of England out of the fight, he had avoided touching the susceptibilities of the English people on the subject of the Belgian sea-coast; but now that they could no longer be conciliated, he thought best to terrify Holland by the sharpness of his attack in the quarter where she dreaded him most.

The United Provinces were in truth the mainspring of the coalition. Though among the smallest in extent of the countries arrayed against Louis, they were strongest in the character and purpose of their ruler, the Prince of Orange, and in the wealth which, while supporting the armies of the confederates, also kept the poor and greedy German princes faithful to their alliance. Almost alone, by dint of mighty sea power, by commercial and maritime ability, they bore the burden of the war; and though they staggered and complained, they still bore it. As in later centuries England, so at the time we are now speaking of Holland, the great sea power, supported the war against the ambition of France; but her sufferings were great. Her commerce, preyed upon by French privateers, lost heavily; and there was added an immense indirect loss in the transfer of the carrying-trade between foreign countries, which had contributed so much to the prosperity of the Dutch. When the flag of England became neutral, this rich business went to her ships, which crossed the seas the more securely because of the eager desire of Louis to conciliate the English nation. This desire led him also to make very large concessions to English exigencies in the matter of commercial treaties, undoing much of the work of protection upon which Colbert sought to nourish the yet feeble growth of French sea power. These sops, however, only stayed for a moment the passions which were driving England; it was not self-interest, but stronger motives, which impelled her to a break with France.

Still less was it to the interest of Holland to prolong the war, after Louis showed a wish for peace. A continental war could at best be but a necessary evil, and source of weakness to her. The money she spent on her own and the allied armies was lost to her navy, and the sources of her prosperity on the sea were being exhausted. How far the Prince of Orange was justified, by the aims of Louis XIV., in that unyielding attitude of opposition toward him which he always maintained, may be uncertain, and there is here no need to decide the question; but there can be no doubt that the strife sacrificed the sea power of Holland through sheer exhaustion, and with it destroyed her position among the nations of the world. "Situated between France and England," says a historian of Holland, "by one or other of them were the United Provinces, after they had achieved their independence of Spain, constantly engaged in wars, which exhausted their finances, annihilated their navy, and caused the rapid decline of their trade, manufactures, and commerce; and

149

thus a peace-loving nation found herself crushed by the weight of unprovoked and long-continued hostilities. Often, too, the friendship of England was scarcely less harmful to Holland than her enmity. As one increased and the other lessened, it became the alliance of the giant and the dwarf." [16] Hitherto we have seen Holland the open enemy or hearty rival of England; henceforward she appears as an ally—in both cases a sufferer from her smaller size, weaker numbers, and less favored situation.

The exhaustion of the United Provinces and the clamor of their merchants and peace party on the one hand, aided on the other by the sufferings of France, the embarrassment of her finances, and the threatened addition of England's navy to her already numerous enemies, inclined to peace the two principal parties to this long war. Louis had long been willing to make peace with Holland alone; but the States had been withheld, at first by fidelity to those who had joined them in their hour of trouble, and latterly by the firm purpose of William of Orange. Difficulties were gradually smoothed away, and the Peace of Nimeguen between the United Provinces and France was signed August 11, 1678. The other powers shortly afterward acceded to it. The principal sufferer, as was natural, was the overgrown but feeble monarchy whose centre was Spain, which gave up to France Franche Comté and a number of fortified towns in the Spanish Netherlands, thus extending the boundaries of France to the east and northeast. Holland, for whose destruction Louis began the war, lost not a foot of ground in Europe; and beyond the seas only her colonies on the west coast of Africa and in Guiana. She owed her safety at first, and the final successful issue, to her sea power. That delivered her in the hour of extreme danger, and enabled her afterward to keep alive the general war. It may be said to have been one of the chief factors, and inferior to no other one singly, in determining the event of the great war which was formally closed at Nimeguen.

The effort none the less sapped her strength, and being followed by many years of similar strain broke her down. But what was the effect upon the vastly greater state, the extreme ambition of whose king was the principal cause of the exhausting wars of this time? Among the many activities which illustrated the brilliant opening of the reign of the then youthful king of France, none was so im-

[16] Davies: History of Holland.

portant, none so intelligently directed, as those of Colbert, who aimed first at restoring the finances from the confusion into which they had fallen, and then at establishing them upon a firm foundation of national wealth. This wealth, at that time utterly beneath the possibilities of France, was to be developed on the lines of production encouraged, trade stimulated to healthful activity, a large merchant shipping, a great navy, and colonial extension. Some of these are sources, others the actual constituents, of sea power; which indeed may be said in a seaboard nation to be the invariable accompaniment, if it be not the chief source, of its strength. For nearly twelve years all went well; the development of the greatness of France in all these directions went forward rapidly, if not in all with equal strides, and the king's revenues increased by bounds. Then came the hour in which he had to decide whether the exertions which his ambition naturally, perhaps properly, prompted should take the direction which, while imposing great efforts, did nothing to sustain but rather hindered the natural activities of his people, and broke down commerce by making control of the sea uncertain; or whether he should launch out in pursuits which, while involving expense, would keep peace on his borders, lead to the control of the sea, and by the impulse given to trade, and all upon which trade depends, would bring in money nearly if not quite equal to that which the State spent. This is not a fanciful picture; by his attitude toward Holland, and its consequences, Louis gave the first impulse to England upon the path which realized to her, within his own day, the results which Colbert and Leibnitz had hoped for France. He drove the Dutch carrying-trade into the ships of England; allowed her to settle peacefully Pennsylvania and Carolina, and to seize New York and New Jersey; and he sacrificed, to gain her neutrality, the growing commerce of France. Not all at once, but very rapidly, England pressed into the front place as a sea power; and however great her sufferings and the sufferings of individual Englishmen, it remained true of her that even in war her prosperity was great. Doubtless France could not forget her continental position, nor wholly keep free from continental wars; but it may be believed that if she had chosen the path of sea power, she might both have escaped many conflicts and borne those that were unavoidable with greater ease. At the Peace of Nimeguen the injuries were not irreparable, but "the agricultural classes, commerce, manufactures, and the colonies had alike been smitten by the war; and the conditions of peace, so advantageous to the territorial and military power of France, were much less so to manufactures, the protective tariffs having been lowered in favor of England and Holland," [17] the two sea powers. The merchant shipping was stricken, and the splendid growth of the royal navy, that excited the jealousy of England, was like a tree without roots; it soon withered away under the blast of war.

Before finally quitting this war with Holland, a short notice of the Comte d'Estrées, to whom Louis committed the charge of the French contingent of the allied fleet, and who commanded it at Solebay and the Texel, will throw some light upon the qualifications of the French naval officers of the day before experience had made seamen of many of them. D'Estrées went to sea for the first time in 1667, being then a man of mature years; but in 1672 we find him in the chief command of an important squadron, having under him Duquesne, who was a seaman, and had been so for nearly forty years. In 1677, D'Estrées obtained from the king a body of eight ships which he undertook to maintain at his own expense, upon the condition of receiving half the prizes made. With this squadron he made an attack upon the then Dutch island of Tobago, with a recklessness which showed that no lack of courage prompted his equivocal conduct at the Texel. The next year he went out again and contrived to run the whole squadron ashore on the Aves Islands. The account given by the flag-captain of this transaction is amusing as well as instructive. In his report he says:—

"The day that the squadron was lost, the sun having been taken by the pilots, the vice-admiral as usual had them put down the position in his cabin. As I was entering to learn what was going on, I met the third pilot, Bourdaloue, who was going out crying. I asked him what the matter was, and he answered: 'Because I find more drift than the other pilots, the admiral is threatening me and abusing me, as usual; yet I am only a poor lad who does the best he can.' When I had entered the cabin, the admiral, who was very angry, said to me, 'That scoundrel of a Bourdaloue is always coming to me with some nonsense or other; I will drive him out of the ship. He makes us to be running a course, the devil knows where, I don't.' As I did not know which was right," says the captain of the ship, rather naïvely, "I did not dare to say anything for fear of bringing down a like storm on my own head." [18]

[17] Martin: History of France.
[18] Gougeard: Marine de Guerre.

Some hours after this scene, which, as the French officer from whom the extract is taken says, "appears now almost grotesque," but which is only an exact portrayal of the sea manners of the day, the whole squadron was lost on a group of rocks known as the Aves Islands. Such were the officers. The flag-captain, in another part of his report, says: "The shipwreck resulted from the general line of conduct held by Vice-Admiral d'Estrées. It was always the opinion of his servants, or others than the proper officers of the ship, which prevailed. This manner of acting may be understood in the Comte d'Estrées, who, without the necessary knowledge of a profession he had embraced so late, always had with him obscure counsellors, in order to appropriate the opinions they gave him so as to blind the ship's company as to his capacity." [19] D'Estrées had been made vice-admiral two years after he first went aboard ship.

[19] Troude: Batailles Navales.

4

English Revolution—War of the League of Augsburg, 1688-1697—Sea Battles of Beachy Head and La Hougue

The Peace of Nimeguen was followed by a period of ten years in which no extensive war broke out. They were, however, far from being years of political quiet. Louis XIV. was as intent upon pushing on his frontiers to the eastward in peace as in war, and grasped in quick succession fragments of territory which had not been given him by the peace. Claiming this and that in virtue of ancient feudal ties; this and that other as implicitly surrendered by the treaty, because dependent upon something else that had been explicitly surrendered; purchasing at one time, using bare force in other cases, and backing up all the so-called peaceful methods of obtaining his asserted rights by the presence of armed power, he carried on this process of extension between 1679 and 1682. The aggression most startling to Europe, and above all to the German Empire, was the seizure of the then imperial city of Strasburg on the 30th of September, 1681; and on the same day Casale, in Italy, was sold to him by the Duke of Mantua, showing that his ambitions were directed that way as well as to the north and east. Both of these were positions of great strategic importance, threatening, the one Germany, the other Italy, in case of war.

The excitement throughout Europe was very great; in every direction Louis, serenely trusting to his power, was making new enemies and alienating former friends. The king of Sweden, directly insulted, and injured in his duchy of Deux-Ponts, turned against him, as did the Italian States; and the Pope himself sided with the enemies of a king who was already showing his zeal for the conversion of the Protestants, and was preparing for the revocation of the Edict of Nantes. But the discontent, though deep and general, had to be organized and directed; the spirit necessary to give it form and final effective expression was found again in Holland, in William of Orange. Time, however, was needed to mature the work. "No one yet armed himself; but every one talked, wrote, agitated, from Stockholm to Madrid. . . . The war of the pen preceded by many years the war of the sword; incessant appeals were made to European opinion by indefatigable publicists; under all forms was diffused the terror of the New Universal Monarchy," which was seeking to take the place once filled by the House of Austria. It was known that Louis sought to make himself or his son emperor of Germany. But complications of different kinds, private interests, lack of money, all combined to delay action. The United Provinces, despite William's wishes, were yet unwilling to act again as banker for a coalition, and the emperor was so threatened on his eastern frontier by the rebel Hungarians and the Turks that he dared not risk a western war.

Meanwhile the armed navy of France was daily growing in strength and efficiency under Colbert's care, and acquiring the habit of war by attacks upon the Barbary pirates and their ports. During the same years the navies both of England and of Holland were declining in numbers and efficiency. It has already been said that in 1688, when William needed Dutch ships for his expedition to England, it was objected that the navy was in a far different condition from 1672, "being incalculably decreased in strength and deprived of its most able commanders." In England, the decline of discipline had been followed by an economical policy as to material, gradually lessening the numbers and injuring the condition of the fleet; and after the little flare-up and expected war with France in 1678, the king gave the care of the navy to a new body of men, concerning whom an English naval historian says: "This new administration lasted five years, and if it had continued five years longer would in all probability have remedied even the numerous and mighty evils it had introduced, by wearing out the whole royal navy, and so leaving no room for future mistakes. However, a just sense of this induced the king, in 1684, to resume the management of the fleet into his own hands, restoring most of the old officers; but before any great progress in the work of restoration could be made, his Majesty died," [1]—in 1685. The change of sovereigns was of vast importance, not merely to the English navy, but from the ultimate effect it was to have upon the designs of Louis XIV. and the fortune of the general war which his aggressions were preparing. James II. was peculiarly interested in the navy, being himself a seaman, and having commanded in chief at Lowestoft and South-wold Bay. He knew its actual depressed condition; and the measures he at once took to restore it, both in numbers and efficiency, were thoughtful and thorough. In the three years of his reign very much indeed was done to prepare a weapon which was first proved against himself and his best friend.

The accession of James II., which promised fairly for Louis, pre-cipitated the action of Europe against him. The House of Stuart, closely allied to the King of France, and sympathizing with his absolutist rule, had used the still great power of the sovereign to check the political and religious enmity of the English nation to France. James II. added to the same political sympathies a strength of Roman Catholic fervor which led him into acts peculiarly fitted to revolt the feeling of the English people, with the final result of driving him from the throne, and calling to it, by the voice of Parlia-ment, his daughter Mary, whose husband was William of Orange.

In the same year that James became king, a vast diplomatic com-bination against France began. This movement had two sides, religious and political. The Protestant States were enraged at the increasing persecutions of the French Protestants, and their feelings became stronger as the policy of James of England showed itself more and more bent toward Rome. The Protestant northern States, Holland, Sweden, and Brandenburg, drew together in alliances; and they counted for support upon the Emperor of Austria and Ger-many, upon Spain and other Roman Catholic States whose motives were political apprehension and anger. The emperor had latterly been successful against the Turks, thus freeing his hands for a move against France. July 9, 1686, there was signed at Augsburg a secret agreement between the emperor, the kings of Spain and Sweden,

[1] Campbell: Lives of the Admirals.

and a number of German princes. Its object was at first defensive only against France, but it could readily be turned into an offensive alliance. This compact took the name of the League of Augsburg, and from it the general war which followed two years later was called the War of the League of Augsburg.

The next year, 1687, saw yet greater successes of the Empire over the Turks and Hungarians. It was evident that France could expect no more from diversions in that quarter. At the same time the discontent of the English and the ambitions of the Prince of Orange, who hoped from his accession to the throne of England no ordinary personal aggrandizement, but the fulfilment of his strongest political wish and conviction, in curbing forever the power of Louis XIV., became more and more plain. But for his expedition into England, William needed ships, money, and men from the United Provinces; and they hung back, knowing that the result would be war with the French king, who proclaimed James his ally. Their action was at last decided by the course of Louis, who chose this moment to revoke concessions made at Nimeguen to Dutch trade. The serious injury thus done to Holland's material interests turned the wavering scale. "This violation of the conventions of Nimeguen," says a French historian,[2] "by giving a severe blow to Dutch commerce, reducing her European trade more than one fourth, removed the obstacle that religious passions still encountered in material interests, and put all Holland at the disposition of William, none having reason longer to conciliate France." This was in November, 1687. In the summer of the following year the birth of an heir to the English throne brought things to an issue. English loyalty might have put up with the reign of the father, now advanced in years, but could not endure the prospect of a continued Roman Catholic royalty.

Matters had at last reached the crisis to which they had been tending for years. Louis and William of Orange, long-standing enemies, and at the moment the two chief figures in European politics, alike from their own strong personalities and the cause which either represented, stood on the brink of great actions, whose effects were to be felt through many generations. William, despotic in temper himself, stood on the shores of Holland looking hopefully toward free England, from which he was separated by the narrow belt of water that was the defence of the island kingdom, and might yet

[2] Martin: History of France.

be an impassable barrier to his own high aims; for the French king at that moment could control the sea if he would. Louis, holding all the power of France in his single grasp, facing eastward as before, saw the continent gathering against him; while on his flank was England heartily hostile, longing to enter on the strife against him, but as yet without a leader. It still remained with him to decide whether he would leave the road open for the head to join the waiting body, and to bring Holland and England, the two sea powers, under one rule. If he attacked Holland by land, and sent his superior navy into the Channel, he might well keep William in his own country; the more so as the English navy, beloved and petted by the king, was likely to have more than the usual loyalty of seamen to their chief. Faithful to the bias of his life, perhaps unable to free himself from it, he turned toward the continent, and September 24, 1688, declared war against Germany and moved his armies toward the Rhine. William, overjoyed, saw removed the last obstacle to his ambition. Delayed for some weeks by contrary winds, he finally set sail from Holland on the 30th of October. More than five hundred transports, with fifteen thousand troops, escorted by fifty men-of-war, formed the expedition; and it is typical of its mingled political and religious character, that the larger part of the army officers were French Protestants who had been driven from France since the last war, the commander-in-chief under William being the Huguenot Schomberg, late a marshal of France. The first start was foiled by a violent storm; but sailing again on the 10th of November, a fresh, fair breeze carried the ships through the Straits and the Channel, and William landed on the 15th at Torbay. Before the end of the year, James had fled from his kingdom. On the 21st of the following April, William and Mary were proclaimed sovereigns of Great Britain, and England and Holland were united for the war, which Louis had declared against the United Provinces as soon as he heard of William's invasion. During all the weeks that the expedition was preparing and delayed, the French ambassador at the Hague and the minister of the navy were praying the king to stop it with his great sea power,—a power so great that the French fleet in the first years of the war outnumbered those of England and Holland combined; but Louis would not. Blindness seems to have struck the kings of England and France alike; for James, amid all his apprehensions, steadily refused any assistance from the French fleet, trusting to the fidelity of the English seamen to his person, although his attempts to have Mass celebrated on board the ships had occasioned an uproar and mutiny which nearly ended in the crews throwing the priests overboard.

France thus entered the War of the League of Augsburg without a single ally. "What her policy had most feared, what she had long averted, was come to pass. England and Holland were not only allied, but united under the same chief; and England entered the coalition with all the eagerness of passions long restrained by the Stuart policy." As regards the sea war, the different battles have much less tactical value than those of De Ruyter. The chief points of strategic interest are the failure of Louis, having a decided superiority at sea, properly to support James II. in Ireland, which remained faithful to him, and the gradual disappearance from the ocean of the great French fleets, which Louis XIV. could no longer maintain, owing to the expense of that continental policy which he had chosen for himself. A third point of rather minor interest is the peculiar character and large proportions taken on by the commerce-destroying and privateering warfare of the French, as their large fleets were disappearing. This, and the great effect produced by it, will appear at first to contradict what has been said as to the general inadequacy of such a warfare when not supported by fleets; but an examination of the conditions, which will be made later on, will show that the contradiction is rather apparent than real.

Taught by the experience of the last conflict, the chief effort of the French king, in the general war he had brought upon himself, should have been directed against the sea powers,—against William of Orange and the Anglo-Dutch alliance. The weakest point in William's position was Ireland; though in England itself not only were there many partisans of the exiled king, but even those who had called in William fenced his kingship about with jealous restrictions. His power was not secure so long as Ireland was not subdued. James, having fled from England in January, 1689, landed in Ireland in the following March, accompanied by French troops and a French squadron, and was enthusiastically welcomed everywhere but in the Protestant North. He made Dublin his capital, and remained in the country until July of the next year. During these fifteen months the French were much superior at sea; they landed troops in Ireland on more than one occasion; and the English, attempting to prevent this, were defeated in the naval battle of Bantry Bay. But although James was so well established, and it was of the utmost importance to sustain him; although it was equally important to keep William from getting a foothold till James was further strengthened and Londonderry, then passing through its famous siege, reduced; and although the French were superior to the united English and Dutch on the seas in 1689 and 1690; nevertheless, the English admiral Rooke was able, unmolested, to throw succors and troops into Londonderry, and afterward landed Marshal Schomberg, with a small army, near Carrickfergus. Rooke stopped intercourse between Ireland and Scotland, where were many Stuart partisans, and then with his small squadron passed along the east coast of Ireland, attempted to burn the shipping in Dublin harbor, failing only through lack of wind, and finally came off Cork, then occupied by James, took possession of an island in the harbor, and returned in safety to the Downs in October. These services, which raised the siege of Londonderry and kept open the communications between England and Ireland, extended throughout the summer months; nor was any attempt made by the French to stop them. There can be little doubt that an effective co-operation of the French fleet in the summer of 1689 would have broken down all opposition to James in Ireland, by isolating that country from England, with corresponding injury to William's power.

The following year the same strategic and political mistake was made. It is the nature of an enterprise such as James's, dependent upon a weaker people and foreign help, to lose strength if it does not progress; but the chances were still in his favor, provided France co-operated heartily, and above all, with her fleet. It is equally the nature of a merely military navy like that of France to be strongest at the beginning of hostilities; whereas that of the allied sea powers grew daily stronger, drawing upon the vast resources of their merchant shipping and their wealth. The disparity of force was still in favor of France in 1690, but it was not as great as the year before. The all-important question was where to direct it. There were two principal courses, involving two views of naval strategy. The one was to act against the allied fleet, whose defeat, if sufficiently severe, might involve the fall of William's throne in England; the other was to make the fleet subsidiary to the Irish campaign. The French king decided upon the former, which was undoubtedly the proper course; but there was no reason for neglecting, as he did, the important duty of cutting off the communications between the two islands. As early as March he had sent a large fleet with six thousand troops and supplies of war, which were landed without any trouble in the southern ports of Ireland; but after performing that service, the ships employed returned to Brest, and there remained inactive during May and June while the grand fleet under the Comte de Tourville was assembling. During those two months the English were gathering an army on their west coast, and on the 21st of June, William embarked his forces at Chester on board two hundred and eighty-eight transports, escorted by only six men-of-war. On the 24th he landed in Carrickfergus, and the ships-of-war were dismissed to join the English grand fleet, which, however, they were not able to do; Tourville's ships having in the meantime got to sea and occupied the channel to the eastward. There is nothing more striking than the carelessness shown by both the contending parties, during the time that Ireland was in dispute, as to the communications of their opponents with the island; but this was especially strange in the French, as they had the larger forces, and must have received pretty accurate information of what was going on from disaffected persons in England. It appears that a squadron of twenty-five frigates, to be supported by ships-of-the-line, were told off for duty in St. George's Channel; but they never reached their station, and only ten of the frigates had got as far as Kinsale by the time James had lost all at the battle of the Boyne. The English communications were not even threatened for an hour.

Tourville's fleet, complete in numbers, having seventy-eight ships, of which seventy were in the line-of-battle, with twenty-two fire-ships, got to sea June 22, the day after William embarked. On the 30th the French were off the Lizard, to the dismay of the English admiral, who was lying off the Isle of Wight in such an unprepared attitude that he had not even lookout ships to the westward. He got under way, standing off-shore to the southeast, and was joined from time to time, during the next ten days, by other English and Dutch ships. The two fleets continued moving to the eastward, sighting each other from time to time.

The political situation in England was critical. The Jacobites were growing more and more open in their demonstrations, Ireland had been in successful revolt for over a year, and William was now there, leaving only the queen in London. The urgency of the case was such that the council decided the French fleet must be fought, and orders to that effect were sent to the English admiral, Herbert. In obedience to his instructions he went out, and on the 10th of July, being to windward, with the wind at northeast, formed his line-of-battle, and then stood down to attack the French, who waited for him, with their foretopsails aback[3] on the starboard tack, heading to the northward and westward.

The fight that followed is known as the battle of Beachy Head. The ships engaged were, French seventy, English and Dutch according to their own account fifty-six, according to the French sixty. In the allied line of battle the Dutch were in the van; the English, commanded in person by Herbert, in the centre; and the rear was made up partly of English and partly of Dutch ships. The stages of the battle were as follows:—

1. The allies, being to windward, bore down together in line abreast. As usual, this manœuvre was ill performed, and as also generally happens, the van came under fire before the centre and rear, and bore the brunt of the injury.

2. Admiral Herbert, though commander-in-chief, failed to attack vigorously with the centre, keeping it at long range. The allied van and rear came to close action (Plate VI., A). Paul Hoste's[4] account of this manœuvre of the allies is that the admiral intended to fall mainly on the French rear. To that end he closed the centre to the rear and kept it to windward at long cannon-shot (refused it), so as to prevent the French from tacking and doubling on the rear. If that were his purpose, his plan, though tolerably conceived in the main, was faulty in detail, for this manœuvre of the centre left a great gap between it and the van. He should rather have attacked, as Ruyter did at the Texel, as many of the rear ships as he thought he could deal with, and refused his van, assigning to it the part of checking the French van. It may be conceded that an admiral who, from inferior numbers, cannot spread as long and close a line as his enemy, should not let the latter overlap the extremities of his fleet; but he should attain his end not, as Herbert did, by leaving a great opening in the centre, but by increasing each interval be-

<hr>

[3] That is—nearly motionless.
[4] Hoste: Naval Tactics.

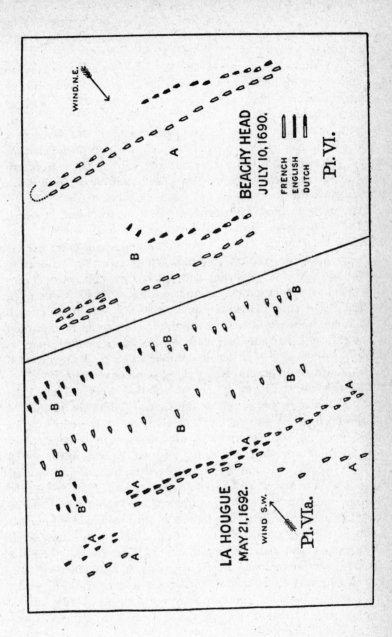

WIND.N.E.

BEACHY HEAD
JULY 10, 1690.

FRENCH
ENGLISH
DUTCH

Pl. VI.

A

B

LA HOUGUE
MAY 21, 1692.

WIND S.W.

Pl. VIa.

A

A

A

A

A

B

B

B

B

B

B

163

tween the ships refused. The allied fleet was thus exposed to be doubled on at two points, both van and centre; and both points were attacked.

3. The commander of the French van, seeing the Dutch close to his·line and more disabled than himself, pressed six of his leading ships ahead, where they went about, and so put the Dutch between two fires (Plate VI., B).

At the same time Tourville, finding himself without adversaries in the centre, having beaten off the leading division of the enemy's centre, pushed forward his own leading ships, which Herbert's dispositions had left without opponents; and these fresh ships strengthened the attack upon the Dutch in the van (B).

This brought about a *mêlée* at the head of the lines, in which the Dutch, being inferior, suffered heavily. Luckily for the allies the wind fell calm; and while Tourville himself and other French ships got out their boats to tow into action again, the allies were shrewd enough to drop anchor with all sail set, and before Tourville took in the situation the ebb-tide, setting southwest, had carried his fleet out of action. He finally anchored a league from his enemy.

At nine P.M., when the tide changed, the allies weighed and stood to the eastward. So badly had many of them been mauled, that, by English accounts, it was decided rather to destroy the disabled ships than to risk a general engagement to preserve them.

Tourville pursued; but instead of ordering a general chase, he kept the line-of-battle, reducing the speed of the fleet to that of the slower ships. The occasion was precisely one of those in which a *mêlée* is permissible, indeed, obligatory. An enemy beaten and in flight should be pursued with ardor, and with only so much regard to order as will prevent the chasing vessels from losing mutual support,—a condition which by no means implies such relative bearings and distances as are required in the beginning or middle of a well-contested action. The failure to order such general pursuit indicates the side on which Tourville's military character lacked completeness; and the failure showed itself, as is apt to be the case, at the supreme moment of his career. He never had such another opportunity as in this, the first great general action in which he commanded-in-chief, and which Hoste, who was on board the flag-ship, calls the most complete naval victory ever gained. It was indeed at that time,—the most complete, but not the most decisive, as it perhaps might have been. The French, according to Hoste, lost not even a boat, much less a ship, which, if true, makes yet more culpable the sluggishness of the pursuit; while the allies fled, casting sixteen of their ships ashore and burning them in sight of the enemy, who pursued as far as the Downs. The English indeed give the allied loss as only eight ships,—an estimate probably full as much out one way as the French the other. Herbert took his fleet to the Thames, and baffled the enemy's further pursuit by removing the buoys.[5]

Tourville's is the only great historical name among the seamen of this war, if we except the renowned privateersmen at whose head was Jean Bart. Among the English, extraordinary merit cannot be claimed for any one of the gallant and enterprising men who commanded squadrons. Tourville, who by this time had served afloat for nearly thirty years, was at once a seaman and a military man. With superb courage, of which he had given dazzling examples in his youth, he had seen service wherever the French fleets had fought, —in the Anglo-Dutch war, in the Mediterranean, and against the Barbary pirates. Reaching the rank of admiral, he commanded in person all the largest fleets sent out during the earlier years of this war, and he brought to the command a scientific knowledge of tactics, based upon both theory and experience, joined to that practical acquaintance with the seaman's business which is necessary in order to apply tactical principles upon the ocean to the best advantage. But with all these high qualities he seems to have failed, where so many warriors fail, in the ability to assume a great responsibility.[6] The caution in his pursuit of the allies after Beachy Head, though so different in appearance, came from the same trait which impelled him two years later to lead his fleet into almost certain destruction at La Hougue, because he had the king's order in his pocket. He was brave enough to do anything, but not strong enough to bear the heaviest burdens. Tourville was in fact the forerunner of the careful and skilful tacticians of the coming era, but with the savor still of the impetuous hard-fighting which characterized the sea commanders of the seventeenth century. He doubtless felt, after Beachy Head, that he had done very well and could be satisfied; but he

---

[5] Ledyard says the order to remove the buoys was not carried out (Naval History, vol. ii. p. 636).
[6] Seignelay, the French minister of marine of the day, called him "poltron de tête, mais pas de cœur."

could not have acted as he did had he felt, to use Nelson's words, that "if we had taken ten ships out of the enemy's eleven, and let the eleventh escape, being able to take her, I could never call such a good day."

The day after the sea fight off Beachy Head, with its great but still partial results, the cause of James II. was lost ashore in Ireland. The army which William had been allowed to transport there unmolested was superior in number and quality to that of James, as William himself was superior as a leader to the ex-king. The counsel of Louis XIV. was that James should avoid decisive action, retiring if necessary to the Shannon, in the midst of a country wholly devoted to him. It was, however, a good deal to ask, this abandonment of the capital after more than a year's occupancy, with all the consequent moral effect; it would have been much more to the purpose to stop William's landing. James undertook to cover Dublin, taking up the line of the river Boyne, and there on the 11th of July the two armies met, with the result that James was wholly defeated. The king himself fled to Kinsale, where he found ten of those frigates that had been meant to control St. George's Channel. He embarked, and again took refuge in France, begging Louis to improve the victory at Beachy Head by landing him with another French army in England itself. Louis angrily refused, and directed that the troops still remaining in Ireland should be at once withdrawn.

The chances of a rising in favor of James, at least upon the shores of the Channel, if they existed at all, were greatly exaggerated by his own imagination. After the safe retreat of the allied fleet to the Thames, Tourville, in accordance with his instructions, made several demonstrations in the south of England; but they were wholly fruitless in drawing out any show of attachment to the Stuart cause.

In Ireland it was different. The Irish army with its French contingent fell back, after the battle of the Boyne, to the Shannon, and there again made a stand; while Louis, receding from his first angry impulse, continued to send reinforcements and supplies. But the increasing urgency of the continental war kept him from affording enough support, and the war in Ireland came to a close a little over a year later, by the defeat at Aghrim and capitulation of Limerick. The battle of the Boyne, which from its peculiar religious coloring has obtained a somewhat factitious celebrity, may be taken as the date at which the English crown was firmly fixed on William's head.

Yet it would be more accurate to say that the success of William, and with it the success of Europe against Louis XIV. in the War of the League of Augsburg, was due to the mistakes and failure of the French naval campaign in 1690; though in that campaign was won the most conspicuous single success the French have ever gained at sea over the English. As regards the more striking military operations, it is curious to remark that Tourville sailed the day after William left Chester, and won Beachy Head the day before the battle of the Boyne; but the real failure lay in permitting William to transport that solid body of men without hindrance. It might have been favorable to French policy to let him get into Ireland, but not with such a force at his back. The result of the Irish campaign was to settle William safely on the English throne and establish the Anglo-Dutch alliance; and the union of the two sea peoples under one crown was the pledge, through their commercial and maritime ability, and the wealth they drew from the sea, of the successful prosecution of the war by their allies on the continent.

The year 1691 was distinguished by only one great maritime event. This was ever afterward known in France as Tourville's "deep-sea" or "off-shore" cruise; and the memory of it as a brilliant strategic and tactical display remains to this day in the French navy. That staying power, which has already been spoken of as distinctive of nations whose sea power is not a mere military institution, but based upon the character and pursuits of the people, had now come into play with the allies. Notwithstanding the defeat and loss of Beachy Head, the united fleets took the sea in 1691 with one hundred ships-of-the-line under the command of Admiral Russell. Tourville could only gather seventy-two, the same number as the year before. With these he left Brest June 25. As the enemy had not yet appeared upon the coasts of the Channel, he took up his cruising ground at the entrance, sending lookout ships in all directions. Informed that the allies had stationed themselves near the Scilly Islands to cover the passage of a convoy expected from the Levant, Tourville did not hesitate to steer for the English coasts, where the approaching arrival of another merchant fleet from Jamaica was equally expected. Deceiving the English cruisers by false courses, he reached the latter fleet, took from it several ships, and dispersed it before Russell could come up to fight him. When at last Tourville was in presence of the allied fleet, he manœuvred so skilfully, always keeping the weather-gage, that the enemy, drawn far out into the ocean, lost fifty days without finding an opportunity to engage. During this time French privateers, scattered throughout the Channel, harassed the enemy's commerce and protected convoys sent into Ireland. Worn out by fruitless efforts, Russell steered for the Irish coast. Tourville, after having protected the return of the French convoys, anchored again in Brest Roads.

The actual captures made by Tourville's own fleet were insignificant, but its service to the commerce-destroying warfare of the French, by occupying the allies, is obvious; nevertheless, the loss of English commerce was not as great this year as the next. The chief losses of the allies seem to have been in the Dutch North Sea trade.

The two wars, continental and maritime, that were being waged, though simultaneous, were as yet independent of each other. It is unnecessary in connection with our subject to mention the operations of the former. In 1692 there occurred the great disaster to the French fleet which is known as the battle of La Hougue. In itself, considered tactically, it possesses little importance, and the actual results have been much exaggerated; but popular report has made it one of the famous sea battles of the world, and therefore it cannot be wholly passed by.

Misled by reports from England, and still more by the representations of James, who fondly nursed his belief that the attachment of many English naval officers to his person was greater than their love of country or faithfulness to their trust, Louis XIV. determined to attempt an invasion of the south coast of England, led by James in person. As a first step thereto, Tourville, at the head of between fifty and sixty ships-of-the-line, thirteen of which were to come from Toulon, was to engage the English fleet; from which so many desertions were expected as would, with the consequent demoralization, yield the French an easy and total victory. The first hitch was in the failure of the Toulon fleet, delayed by contrary winds, to join; and Tourville went to sea with only forty-four ships, but with a preemptory order from the king to fight when he fell in with the enemy, were they few or many, and come what might.

On the 29th of May, Tourville saw the allies to the northward and eastward; they numbered ninety-nine sail-of-the-line. The wind being southwest, he had the choice of engaging, but first summoned all the flag-officers on board his own ship, and put the question to them whether he ought to fight. They all said not, and he then handed them the order of the king.[7] No one dared dispute that; though, had they known it, light vessels with contrary orders were even then searching for the fleet. The other officers then returned to their ships, and the whole fleet kept away together for the allies, who waited for them, on the starboard tack, heading south-southeast, the Dutch occupying the van, the English the centre and rear. When they were within easy range, the French hauled their wind on the same tack, keeping the weather-gage. Tourville, being so inferior in numbers, could not wholly avoid the enemy's line extending to the rear of his own, which was also necessarily weak from its extreme length; but he avoided Herbert's error at Beachy Head, keeping his van refused with long intervals between the ships, to check the enemy's van, and engaging closely with his centre and rear (Plate VIᵃ.-A, A, A). It is not necessary to follow the phases of this unequal fight; the extraordinary result was that when the firing ceased at night, in consequence of a thick fog and calm, not a single French ship had struck her colors nor been sunk. No higher proof of military spirit and efficiency could be given by any navy, and Tourville's seamanship and tactical ability contributed largely to the result, which it must also be confessed was not creditable to the allies. The two fleets anchored at nightfall (B, B, B), a body of English ships (B′) remaining to the southward and westward of the French. Later on, these cut their cables and allowed themselves to drift through the French line in order to rejoin their main body; in doing which they were roughly handled.

Having amply vindicated the honor of his fleet, and shown the uselessness of further fighting, Tourville now thought of retreat, which was begun at midnight with a light northeast wind and continued all the next day. The allies pursued, the movements of the French being much embarrassed by the crippled condition of the flag-ship "Royal Sun," the finest ship in the French navy, which the

[7] The author has followed in the text the traditional and generally accepted account of Tourville's orders and the motives of his action. A French writer, M. de Crisenoy, in a very interesting paper upon the secret history preceding and accompanying the event, traverses many of these traditional statements. According to him, Louis XIV. was not under any illusion as to the loyalty of the English officers to their flag; and the instructions given to Tourville, while peremptory under certain conditions, did not compel him to fight in the situation of the French fleet on the day of the battle. The tone of the instructions, however, implied dissatisfaction with the admiral's action in previous cruises, probably in the pursuit after Beachy Head, and a consequent doubt of his vigor in the campaign then beginning. Mortification therefore impelled him to the desperate attack on the allied fleet; and, according to M. de Crisenoy, the council of war in the admiral's cabin, and the dramatic production of the king's orders, had no existence in fact.

admiral could not make up his mind to destroy. The direction of the main retreat was toward the Channel Islands, thirty-five ships being with the admiral; of them twenty passed with the tidal current through the dangerous passage known as the Race of Alderney, between the island of that name and the mainland, and got safe to St. Malo. Before the remaining fifteen could follow, the tide changed; and the anchors which had been dropped dragging, these ships were carried to the eastward and to leeward of the enemy. Three sought refuge in Cherbourg, which had then neither breakwater nor port, the remaining twelve at Cape La Hougue; and they were all burned either by their own crews or by the allies. The French thus lost fifteen of the finest ships in their navy, the least of which carried sixty guns; but this was little more than the loss of the allies at Beachy Head. The impression made upon the public mind, accustomed to the glories and successes of Louis XIV., was out of all proportion to the results, and blotted out the memory of the splendid self-devotion of Tourville and his followers. La Hougue was also the last general action fought by the French fleet, which did rapidly dwindle away in the following years, so that this disaster seemed to be its death-blow. As a matter of fact, however, Tourville went to sea the next year with seventy ships, and the losses were at the time repaired. The decay of the French navy was not due to any one defeat, but to the exhaustion of France and the great cost of the continental war; and this war was mainly sustained by the two sea peoples whose union was secured by the success of William in the Irish campaign. Without asserting that the result would have been different had the naval operations of France been otherwise directed in 1690, it may safely be said that their misdirection was the immediate cause of things turning out as they did, and the first cause of the decay of the French navy.

The five remaining years of the War of the League of Augsburg, in which all Europe was in arms against France, are marked by no great sea battles, nor any single maritime event of the first importance. To appreciate the effect of the sea power of the allies, it is necessary to sum up and condense an account of the quiet, steady pressure which it brought to bear and maintained in all quarters against France. It is thus indeed that sea power usually acts, and just because so quiet in its working, it is the more likely to be unnoticed and must be somewhat carefully pointed out.

The head of the opposition to Louis XIV. was William III., and his tastes being military rather than naval combined with the direction of Louis' policy to make the active war continental rather than maritime; while the gradual withdrawal of the great French fleets, by leaving the allied navies without enemies on the sea, worked in the same way. Furthermore, the efficiency of the English navy, which was double in numbers that of the Dutch, was at this time at a low pitch; the demoralizing effects of the reign of Charles II. could not be wholly overcome during the three years of his brother's rule, and there was a yet more serious cause of trouble growing out of the political state of England. It has been said that James believed the naval officers and seamen to be attached to his person; and, whether justly or unjustly, this thought was also in the minds of the present rulers, causing doubts of the loyalty and trustworthiness of many officers, and tending to bring confusion into the naval administration. We are told that "the complaints made by the merchants were extremely well supported, and showed the folly of preferring unqualified men to that board which directed the naval power of England; and yet the mischief could not be amended, because the more experienced people who had been long in the service were thought disaffected, and it appeared the remedy might have proved worse than the disease."[8] Suspicion reigned in the cabinet and the city, factions and irresolution among the officers; and a man who was unfortunate or incapable in action knew that the yet more serious charge of treason might follow his misadventure.

After La Hougue, the direct military action of the allied navies was exerted in three principal ways, the first being in attacks upon the French ports, especially those in the Channel and near Brest. These had rarely in view more than local injury and the destruction of shipping, particularly in the ports whence the French privateers issued; and although on some occasions the number of troops embarked was large, William proposed to himself little more than the diversion which such threats caused, by forcing Louis to take troops from the field for coast defence. It may be said generally of all these enterprises against the French coast, in this and later wars, that they effected little, and even as a diversion did not weaken the French armies to any great extent. If the French ports had been less well defended, or French water-ways open into the heart of the country,

[8] Campbell: Lives of the Admirals.

like our own Chesapeake and Delaware bays and the Southern sounds, the result might have been different.

In the second place, the allied navies were of great direct military value, though they fought no battles, when Louis XIV. decided in 1694 to make his war against Spain offensive. Spain, though so weak in herself, was yet troublesome from her position in the rear of France; and Louis finally concluded to force her to peace by carrying the war into Catalonia, on the northeast coast. The movement of his armies was seconded by his fleet under Tourville; and the reduction of that difficult province went on rapidly until the approach of the allied navies in largely superior force caused Tourville to retire to Toulon. This saved Barcelona; and from that time until the two sea nations had determined to make peace, they kept their fleets on the Spanish coast and arrested the French advance. When, in 1697, William had become disposed to peace and Spain refused it, Louis again invaded, the allied fleet did not appear, and Barcelona fell. At the same time a French naval expedition was successfully directed against Cartagena in South America, and under the two blows, both of which depended upon the control of the sea, Spain yielded.

The third military function of the allied navies was the protection of their sea commerce; and herein, if history may be trusted, they greatly failed. At no time has war against commerce been conducted on a larger scale and with greater results than during this period; and its operations were widest and most devastating at the very time that the great French fleets were disappearing, in the years immediately after La Hougue, apparently contradicting the assertion that such a warfare must be based on powerful fleets or neighboring seaports. A somewhat full discussion is due, inasmuch as the distress to commerce wrought by the privateers was a large factor in bringing the sea nations to wish for peace; just as the subsidies, which their commerce enabled them to pay the continental armies, besides keeping up their own, were the chief means by which the war was prolonged and France brought to terms. The attack and defence of commerce is still a living question.

In the first place it is to be observed that the decay of the French fleet was gradual, and that the moral effect of its appearance in the Channel, its victory at Beachy Head, and gallant conduct at La Hougue remained for some time impressed on the minds of the allies.

This impression caused their ships to be kept together in fleets, instead of scattering in pursuit of the enemy's cruisers, and so brought to the latter a support almost equal to an active warfare on the seas. Again, the efficiency of the English navy, as has been said, was low, and its administration perhaps worse; while treason in England gave the French the advantage of better information. Thus in the year following La Hougue, the French, having received accurate information of a great convoy sailing for Smyrna, sent out Tourville in May, getting him to sea before the allies were ready to blockade him in Brest, as they had intended. This delay was due to bad administration, as was also the further misfortune that the English government did not learn of Tourville's departure until after its own fleet had sailed with the trade. Tourville surprised the convoy near the Straits, destroyed or captured one hundred out of four hundred ships, and scattered the rest. This is not a case of simple cruising warfare, for Tourville's fleet was of seventy-one ships; but it shows the incompetency of the English administration. In truth, it was immediately after La Hougue that the depredations of cruisers became most ruinous; and the reason was twofold: first, the allied fleet was kept together at Spithead for two months and more, gathering troops for a landing on the continent, thus leaving the cruisers unmolested; and in the second place, the French, not being able to send their fleet out again that summer, permitted the seamen to take service in private ships, thus largely increasing the numbers of the latter. The two causes working together gave an impunity and extension to commerce-destroying which caused a tremendous outcry in England. "It must be confessed," says the English naval chronicler, "that our commerce suffered far less the year before, when the French were masters at sea, than in this, when their grand fleet was blocked up in port." But the reason was that the French having little commerce and a comparatively large number of seamen, mainly employed in the fleet, were able, when this lay by, to release them to cruisers. As the pressure of the war became greater, and Louis continued to reduce the number of his ships in commission, another increase was given to the commerce-destroyers. "The ships and officers of the royal navy were loaned, under certain conditions, to private firms, or to companies who wished to undertake privateering enterprises, in which even the cabinet ministers did not disdain to take shares"; indeed, they were urged to do so to please the king. The conditions generally provided that a certain proportion of the profits should go to the king, in return for the use of the ships. Such employment would be demoralizing to any military service, but not necessarily all at once; and the conditions imparted for the time a tone and energy to privateering that it cannot always have. In truth, the public treasury, not being able to maintain the navy, associated with itself private capital, risking only material otherwise useless, and looking for returns to robbing the enemy. The commerce-destroying of this war, also, was no mere business of single cruisers; squadrons of three or four up to half a dozen ships acted together under one man, and it is only just to say that under seamen like Jean Bart, Forbin, and Duguay-Trouin, they were even more ready to fight than to pillage. The largest of these private expeditions, and the only one that went far from the French shores, was directed in 1697 against Cartagena, on the Spanish Main. It numbered seven ships-of-the-line and six frigates, besides smaller vessels, and carried twenty-eight hundred troops. The chief object was to lay a contribution on the city of Cartagena; but its effect on the policy of Spain was marked, and led to peace. Such a temper and concert of action went far to supply the place of supporting fleets, but could not wholly do so; and although the allies continued to keep their large fleets together, still, as the war went on and efficiency of administration improved, commerce-destroying was brought within bounds. At the same time, as an evidence of how much the unsupported cruisers suffered, even under these favorable conditions, it may be mentioned that the English report fifty-nine ships-of-war captured against eighteen admitted by the French during the war,—a difference which a French naval historian attributes, with much probability, to the English failing to distinguish between ships-of-war properly so called, and those loaned to private firms. Captures of actual privateers do not appear in the list quoted from. "The commerce-destroying of this war, therefore, was marked by the particular characteristics of cruisers acting together in squadron, not far from their base, while the enemy thought best to keep his fleet concentrated elsewhere; notwithstanding which, and the bad administration of the English navy, the cruisers were more and more controlled as the great French fleets disappeared." The results of the war of 1689-1697 do not therefore vitiate the general conclusion that "a cruising, commerce-destroying warfare, to be destructive, must be seconded by a squadron warfare, and by divisions of ships-of-the-line; which, forcing the enemy to unite his forces, permit the cruisers to make fortunate attempts upon his trade. Without such backing the result will be simply the capture of the cruisers." Toward the end of this war the real tendency was becoming manifest, and was still more plainly seen in the next, when the French navy had sunk to a yet lower state of weakness.

Notwithstanding their losses, the sea nations made good their cause. The war, which began with the French taking the offensive, ended by reducing them everywhere to the defensive, and forced Louis to do violence at once to his strongest prejudices and his most reasonable political wishes, by recognizing as king of England him whom he looked upon as a usurper as well as his own inveterate enemy. On its surface, and taken as a whole, this war will appear almost wholly a land struggle, extending from the Spanish Nether-lands down the line of the Rhine, to Savoy in Italy and Catalonia in Spain. The sea fights in the Channel, the Irish struggle receding in the distance, look like mere episodes; while the underlying action of trade and commerce is wholly disregarded, or noticed only as their outcries tell of their sufferings. Yet trade and shipping not only bore the burden of suffering, but in the main paid the armies that were fighting the French; and this turning of the stream of wealth from both sea nations into the coffers of their allies was per-haps determined, certainly hastened, by the misdirection of that naval supremacy with which France began the war. It was then possible, as it will usually be possible, for a really fine military navy of superior force to strike an overwhelming blow at a less ready rival; but the opportunity was allowed to slip, and the essentially stronger, better founded sea power of the allies had time to assert itself.

The peace signed at Ryswick in 1697 was most disadvantageous to France; she lost all that had been gained since the Peace of Nime-guen, nineteen years before, with the single important execption of Strasburg. All that Louis XIV. had gained by trick or force during the years of peace was given up. Immense restitutions were made to Germany and to Spain. In so far as the latter were made in the Netherlands, they were to the immediate advantage of the United Provinces, and indeed of all Europe as well as of Spain. To the two sea nations the terms of the treaty gave commercial benefits, which tended to the increase of their own sea power and to the consequent injury of that of France.

France had made a gigantic struggle; to stand alone as she did then, and as she has since done more than once, against all Europe is a great feat. Yet it may be said that as the United Provinces taught the lesson that a nation, however active and enterprising, cannot rest upon external resources alone, if intrinsically weak in numbers and territory, so France in its measure shows that a nation cannot subsist indefinitely off itself, however powerful in numbers and strong in internal resources.

It is said that a friend once found Colbert looking dreamily from his windows, and on questioning him as to the subject of his meditations, received this reply: "In contemplating the fertile fields before my eyes, I recall those which I have seen elsewhere; what a rich country is France!" This conviction supported him amid the many discouragements of his official life, when struggling to meet the financial difficulties arising from the extravagance and wars of the king; and it has been justified by the whole course of the nation's history since his days. France is rich in natural resources as well as in the industry and thrift of her people. But neither individual nations nor men can thrive when severed from natural intercourse with their kind; whatever the native vigor of constitution, it requires healthful surroundings, and freedom to draw to itself from near and from far all that is conducive to its growth and strength and general welfare. Not only must the internal organism work satisfactorily, the processes of decay and renewal, of movement and circulation, go on easily, but, from sources external to themselves, both mind and body must receive healthful and varied nourishment. With all her natural gifts France wasted away because of the want of that lively intercourse between the different parts of her own body and constant exchange with other people, which is known as commerce, internal or external. To say that war was the cause of these defects is to state at least a partial truth; but it does not exhaust the matter. War, with its many acknowledged sufferings, is above all harmful when it cuts a nation off from others and throws it back upon itself. There may indeed be periods when such rude shocks have a bracing effect, but they are exceptional, and of short duration, and they do not invalidate the general statement. Such isolation was the lot of

France during the later wars of Louis XIV., and it well-nigh destroyed her; whereas to save her from the possibility of such stagnation was the great aim of Colbert's life.

War alone could not entail it, if only war could be postponed until the processes of circulation within and without the kingdom were established and in vigorous operation. They did not exist when he took office; they had to be both created and firmly rooted in order to withstand the blast of war. Time was not given to accomplish this great work, nor did Louis XIV. support the schemes of his minister by turning the budding energies of his docile and devoted subjects into paths favorable to it. So when the great strain came upon the powers of the nation, instead of drawing strength from every quarter and through many channels, and laying the whole outside world under contribution by the energy of its merchants and seamen, as England has done in like straits, it was thrown back upon itself, cut off from the world by the navies of England and Holland, and the girdle of enemies which surrounded it upon the continent. The only escape from this process of gradual starvation was by an effectual control of the sea; the creation of a strong sea power which should insure free play for the wealth of the land and the industry of the people. For this, too, France had great natural advantages in her three seaboards, on the Channel, the Atlantic, and the Mediterranean; and politically she had had the fair opportunity of joining to her own maritime power that of the Dutch in friendly alliance, hostile or at least wary toward England. In the pride of his strength, conscious of absolute control in his kingdom, Louis cast away this strong reinforcement to his power, and proceeded to rouse Europe against him by repeated aggressions. In the period which we have just considered, France justified his confidence by a magnificent, and upon the whole successful, maintenance of his attitude against all Europe; she did not advance, but neither did she greatly recede. But this display of power was exhausting; it ate away the life of the nation, because it drew wholly upon itself and not upon the outside world, with which it could have been kept in contact by the sea. In the war that next followed, the same energy is seen, but not the same vitality; and France was everywhere beaten back and brought to the verge of ruin. The lesson of both is the same; nations, like men, however strong, decay when cut off from the external activities and resources which at once draw out and support their internal powers. A nation, as we have already shown, cannot live indefinitely off itself, and the easiest way by which it can communicate with other peoples and renew its own strength is the sea.

5

War of the Spanish Succession, 1702-1713—
Sea Battle of Malaga

During the last thirty years of the seventeenth century, amid all the strifes of arms and diplomacy, there had been clearly foreseen the coming of an event which would raise new and great issues. This was the failure of the direct royal line in that branch of the House of Austria which was then on the Spanish throne; and the issues to be determined when the present king, infirm both in body and mind, should die, were whether the new monarch was to be taken from the House of Bourbon or from the Austrian family in Germany; and whether, in either event, the sovereign thus raised to the throne should succeed to the entire inheritance, the Empire of Spain, or some partition of that vast inheritance be made in the interests of the balance of European power. But this balance of power was no longer understood in the narrow sense of continental possessions; the effect of the new arrangements upon commerce, shipping, and the control both of the ocean and the Mediterranean, was closely looked to. The influence of the two sea powers and the nature of their interests were becoming more evident.

It is necessary to recall the various countries that were ruled by Spain at that time in order to understand the strategic questions, as they may fairly be called, now to be settled. These were, in Europe, the Netherlands (now Belgium); Naples and the south of Italy; Milan and other provinces in the north; and, in the Mediterranean, Sicily, Sardinia, and the Balearic Isles. Corsica at that time belonged to

Genoa. In the western hemisphere, besides Cuba and Porto Rico, Spain then held all that part of the continent now divided among the Spanish American States, a region whose vast commercial possibilities were coming to be understood; and in the Asian archipelago, there were large possessions that entered less into the present dispute. The excessive weakness of this empire, owing to the decay of the central kingdom, had hitherto caused other nations, occupied as they were with more immediate interests, to regard with indifference its enormous extent. This indifference could not last when there was a prospect of a stronger administration, backed possibly by alliances with one of the great powers of Europe.

It would be foreign to our subject to enter into the details of diplomatic arrangement, which, by shifting about peoples and territories from one ruler to another, sought to reach a political balance peacefully. The cardinal points of each nation's policy may be shortly stated. The Spanish cabinet and people objected to any solution which dismembered the empire. The English and the Dutch objected to any extension of France in the Spanish Netherlands, and to the monopoly by the French of the trade with Spanish America, both which they feared as the results of placing a Bourbon on the Spanish throne. Louis XIV. wanted Naples and Sicily for one of his sons, in case of any partition; thus giving France a strong Mediterranean position, but one which would be at the mercy of the sea powers,—a fact which induced William III. to acquiesce in this demand. The Emperor of Austria particularly objected to these Mediterranean positions going away from his family, and refused to come into any of the partition treaties. Before any arrangement was perfected, the actual king of Spain died, but before his death was induced by his ministers to sign a will, bequeathing all his States to the grandson of Louis XIV., then Duke of Anjou, known afterward as Philip V. of Spain. By this step it was hoped to preserve the whole, by enlisting in its defence the nearest and one of the most powerful States in Europe,—nearest, if are excepted the powers ruling the sea, which are always near any country whose ports are open to their ships.

Louis XIV. accepted the bequest, and in so doing felt bound in honor to resist all attempts at partition. The union of the two kingdoms under one family promised important advantages to France, henceforth delivered from that old enemy in the rear, which had balked so many of her efforts to extend her frontiers eastward. As a matter of fact, from that time, with rare breaks, there existed between the two kingdoms an alliance, the result of family ties, which only the weakness of Spain kept from being dangerous to the rest of Europe. The other countries at once realized the situation, and nothing could have saved war but some backward step on the part of the French king. The statesmen of England and Holland, the two powers on whose wealth the threatened war must depend, proposed that the Italian States should be given to the son of the Austrian emperor, Belgium be occupied by themselves, and that the new king of Spain should grant no commercial privileges in the Indies to France above other nations. To the credit of their wisdom it must be said that this compromise was the one which after ten years of war was found, on the whole, best; and in it is seen the growing sense of the value of extension by sea. Louis, however, would not yield; on the contrary, he occupied, by connivance of the Spanish governors, towns in the Netherlands which had been held by Dutch troops under treaties with Spain. Soon after, in February, 1701, the English Parliament met, and denounced any treaty which promised France the dominion of the Mediterranean. Holland began to arm, and the Emperor of Austria pushed his troops into northern Italy, where a campaign followed, greatly to the disadvantage of Louis.

In September of the same year, 1701, the two sea powers and the Emperor of Austria signed a secret treaty, which laid down the chief lines of the coming war, with the exception of that waged in the Spanish peninsula itself. By it the allies undertook to conquer the Spanish Netherlands in order to place a barrier between France and the United Provinces; to conquer Milan as a security for the emperor's other provinces; and to conquer Naples and Sicily for the same security, and also for the security of the navigation and commerce of the subjects of his Britannic Majesty and of the United Provinces. The sea powers should have the right to conquer, for the utility of the said navigation and commerce, the countries and towns of the Spanish Indies; and all that they should be able to take there should be for them and remain theirs. The war begun, none of the allies could treat without the others, nor without having taken just measures—first, to prevent the kingdoms of France and Spain from ever being united under the same king; second, to prevent the French from ever making themselves masters of the Spanish Indies, or from sending ships thither to engage, directly or indirectly, in commerce; third, to secure to the subjects of his Britannic Majesty and of the United Provinces the commercial privileges which they enjoyed in all the Spanish States under the late king.

It will be noticed that in these conditions there is no suggestion of any intention to resist the accession of the Bourbon king, who was called to the throne by the Spanish government and at first acknowledged by England and Holland; but, on the other hand, the Emperor of Austria does not withdraw the Austrian claim, which centred in his own person. The voice of the sea powers was paramount in the coalition, as the terms of the treaty safeguarding their commercial interests show, though, as they were about to use German armies for the land war, German claims also had to be considered. As a French historian points out:—

"This was really a new treaty of partition. . . . William III., who had conducted all, had taken care not to exhaust England and Holland, in order to restore the Spanish monarchy, intact, to the emperor; his final condition was to reduce the new king, Philip V., to Spain proper, and to secure to England and Holland at once the commercial use of all the regions that had been under the Spanish monarchy, together with important military and maritime positions against France." [1]

But though war was imminent, the countries about to engage hesitated. Holland would not move without England, and despite the strong feeling of the latter country against France, the manufacturers and merchants still remembered the terrible sufferings of the last war. Just then, as the scales were wavering, James II. died. Louis, yielding to a sentiment of sympathy and urged by his nearest intimates, formally recognized the son of James as king of England; and the English people, enraged at what they looked on as a threat and an insult, threw aside all merely prudential considerations. The House of Lords declared that "there could be no security till the usurper of the Spanish monarchy was brought to reason"; and the House of Commons voted fifty thousand soldiers and thirty-five thousand seamen, besides subsidies for German and Danish auxiliaries. William III. died soon after, in March, 1702; but Queen Anne took up his policy, which had become that of the English and Dutch peoples.

[1] Martin: History of France.

Louis XIV. tried to break part of the on-coming storm by forming a league of neutrals among the other German States; but the emperor adroitly made use of the German feeling, and won to his side the Elector of Brandenburg by acknowledging him as king of Prussia, thus creating a North-German Protestant royal house, around which the other Protestant States naturally gathered, and which was in the future to prove a formidable rival to Austria. The immediate result was that France and Spain, whose cause was thenceforth known as that of the two crowns, went into the war without any ally save Bavaria. War was declared in May by Holland against the kings of France and Spain; by England against France and Spain, Anne refusing to recognize Philip V. even in declaring war, because he had recognized James III. as king of England; while the emperor was still more outspoken, declaring against the king of France and the Duke of Anjou. Thus began the great War of the Spanish Succession.

It is far from easy, in dealing with a war of such proportions, lasting for more than ten years, to disentangle from the general narrative that part which particularly touches our subject, without at the same time losing sight of the relation of the one part to the whole. Such a loss, however, is fatal to the end in view, which is not a mere chronicle of naval events, nor even a tactical or strategic discussion of certain naval problems divorced from their surroundings of cause and effect in general history, but an appreciation of the effect of sea power upon the general result of the war and upon the prosperity of nations. It will conduce to clearness, however, to point out again that the aim of William III. was not to dispute the claim of Philip V. to the throne,—a matter of comparative indifference to the sea powers,—but to seize, to the benefit of their commerce and colonial empire, such portions of the Spanish American possessions as he could, and at the same time to impose such conditions upon the new monarchy as would at least prevent any loss, to English and Dutch commerce, of the privileges they had had under the Austrian line. Such a policy would not direct the main effort of the sea nations upon the Spanish peninsula, but upon America; and the allied fleets might not have entered the Straits. Sicily and Naples were to go, not to England, but to Austria. Subsequent causes led to an entire change in this general plan. A new candidate, a son of the Emperor of Germany, was set up in 1703 by the coalition under the name of Carlos III., and the peninsula became the scene of a doubtful and bloody war, keeping the Anglo Dutch fleets hovering round the coasts; with the result, as regards the sea powers, that nothing of decisive importance was done in Spanish America, but that England issued from the strife with Gibraltar and Port Mahon in her hands, to be thenceforth a Mediterranean power. At the same time that Carlos III. was proclaimed, a treaty was negotiated with Portugal, known as the Methuen Treaty, which gave England the practical monopoly of Portuguese trade, and sent the gold of Brazil by way of Lisbon to London,—an advantage so great that it aided materially in keeping up the war on the continent as well as in maintaining the navy. At the same time the efficiency of the latter so increased that the losses by French cruisers, though still heavy, were at no time unendurable.

When the war broke out, in pursuance of the original policy, Sir George Rooke, with a fleet of fifty ships-of-the-line and transports carrying fourteen thousand troops, was sent against Cadiz, which was the great European centre of the Spanish-American trade; there came the specie and products of the West, and thence they were dispersed through Europe. It had been the purpose of William III. also to seize Cartagena, one of the principal centres of the same trade in the other hemisphere; and to that end, six months before his death, in September, 1701, he had despatched there a squadron under that traditional seaman of the olden time, Benbow. Benbow fell in with a French squadron sent to supply and strengthen the place, and brought it to action north of Cartagena; but though superior in force, the treason of several of his captains, who kept out of action, defeated his purpose, and after fighting till his ship was helpless and he himself had received a mortal wound, the French escaped and Cartagena was saved. Before his death Benbow received a letter from the French commodore to this effect: "Yesterday morning I had no hope but I should have supped in your cabin. As for those cowardly captains of yours, hang them up, for, by God! they deserve it." And hanged two of them were. Rooke's expedition against Cadiz also failed, as it was nearly certain to do; for his instructions were so to act as to conciliate the Spanish people and disincline them to the Bourbon king. Such doubtful orders tied his hands; but after failing there, he learned that the galleons from the West Indies, loaded with silver and merchandise. had put into Vigo Bay under escort of French ships-of-war. He went there at once, and found the enemy in a harbor whose entrance was but three quarters of a mile wide, defended by fortifications and a heavy boom; but a passage was forced through the boom under a hot fire, the place seized, and all the shipping, with much of the specie, either taken or sunk. This affair, which is known in history as that of the Vigo galleons, was a brilliant and interesting feat of arms, but has no military features calling for mention, except the blow it gave to the finances and prestige of the two crowns.

The affair at Vigo had, however, important political results, and helped to that change in the general plan of the sea powers which has been mentioned. The king of Portugal, moved by fear of the French, had acknowledged Philip V.; but his heart was against him, for he dreaded French influence and power brought so near his little and isolated kingdom. It had been a part of Rooke's mission to detach him from the alliance of the two crowns; and the affair of Vigo, happening so near his own frontiers, impressed him with a sense of the power of the allied navies. In truth, Portugal is nearer to the sea than to Spain, and must fall naturally under the influence of the power controlling the sea. Inducements were offered,—by the emperor of Austria a cession of Spanish territory, by the sea powers a subsidy; but the king was not willing to declare himself until the Austrian claimant should have landed at Lisbon, fairly committing the coalition to a peninsular as well as a continental war. The emperor transferred his claims to his second son, Charles; and the latter, after being proclaimed in Vienna and acknowledged by England and Holland, was taken by the allied fleets to Lisbon, where he landed in March, 1704. This necessitated the important change in the plans of the sea powers. Pledged to the support of Carlos, their fleets were thenceforth tied to the shores of the peninsula and the protection of commerce; while the war in the West Indies, becoming a side issue on a small scale, led to no results. From this time on, Portugal was the faithful ally of England, whose sea power during this war gained its vast preponderance over all rivals. Her ports were the refuge and support of English fleets, and on Portugal was based in later days the Peninsular war with Napoleon. In and through all, Portugal, for a hundred years, had more to gain and more to fear from England than from any other power.

Great as were the effects of the maritime supremacy of the two sea powers upon the general result of the war, and especially upon that undisputed empire of the seas which England held for a century after, the contest is marked by no one naval action of military interest. Once only did great fleets meet, and then with results that were indecisive; after which the French gave up the struggle at sea, confining themselves wholly to a commerce-destroying warfare. This feature of the War of the Spanish Succession characterizes nearly the whole of the eighteenth century, with the exception of the American Revolutionary struggle. The noiseless, steady, exhausting pressure with which sea power acts, cutting off the resources of the enemy while maintaining its own, supporting war in scenes where it does not appear itself, or appears only in the background, and striking open blows at rare intervals, though lost to most, is emphasized to the careful reader by the events of this war and of the half-century that followed. The overwhelming sea power of England was the determining factor in European history during the period mentioned, maintaining war abroad while keeping its own people in prosperity at home, and building up the great empire which is now seen; but from its very greatness its action, by escaping opposition, escapes attention. On the few occasions in which it is called to fight, its superiority is so marked that the affairs can scarcely be called battles; with the possible exceptions of Byng's action at Minorca and Hawke's at Quiberon, the latter one of the most brilliant pages in naval history, no decisive encounter between equal forces, possessing military interest, occurs between 1700 and 1778.

Owing to this characteristic, the War of the Spanish Succession, from the point of view of our subject, has to be blocked out in general outline, avoiding narrative and indicating general bearings, especially of the actions of the fleets. With the war in Flanders, in Germany, and in Italy the navies had naturally no concern; when they had so protected the commerce of the allies that there was no serious check to that flow of subsidies upon which the land war depended, their part toward it was done. In the Spanish peninsula it was different. Immediately after landing Carlos III. at Lisbon, Sir George Rooke sailed for Barcelona, which it was understood would be handed over when the fleets appeared; but the governor was faithful to his king and kept down the Austrian party. Rooke then sailed for Toulon, where a French fleet was at anchor. On his way he sighted another French fleet coming from Brest, which he chased but was unable to overtake; so that both the enemy's squadrons were united in the port. It is worth while to note here that the English navy did not as yet attempt to blockade the French ports in winter, as they did at a later date. At this period fleets, like armies, went into winter quarters. Another English admiral, Sir Cloudesley Shovel, had been sent in the spring to blockade Brest; but arriving too late, he found his bird flown, and at once kept on to the Mediterranean. Rooke, not thinking himself strong enough to resist the combined French squadrons, fell back toward the Straits; for at this time England had no ports, no base, in the Mediterranean, no useful ally; Lisbon was the nearest refuge. Rooke and Shovel met off Lagos, and there held a council of war, in which the former, who was senior, declared that his instructions forbade his undertaking anything without the consent of the kings of Spain and Portugal. This was indeed tying the hands of the sea powers; but Rooke at last, chafing at the humiliating inaction, and ashamed to go home without doing something, decided to attack Gibraltar for three reasons: because he heard it was insufficiently garrisoned, because it was of infinite importance as a port for the present war, and because its capture would reflect credit on the queen's arms. The place was attacked, bombarded, and then carried by an assault in boats. The English possession of Gibraltar dates from August 4, 1704, and the deed rightly keeps alive the name of Rooke, to whose judgment and fearlessness of responsibility England owes the key of the Mediterranean.

The Bourbon king of Spain at once undertook to retake the place, and called upon the French fleet in Toulon to support his attack. Tourville had died in 1701, and the fleet was commanded by the Count of Toulouse,—a natural son of Louis XIV., only twenty-six years old. Rooke also sailed eastward, and the two fleets met on the 24th of August off Velez Malaga. The allies were to windward with a northeast wind, both fleets on the port tack heading to the southward and eastward. There is some uncertainty as to the numbers; the French had fifty-two ships-of-the-line, their enemy probably half a dozen more. The allies kept away together, each ship for its opposite; there was apparently no attempt on Rooke's part at any tactical combination. The battle of Malaga possesses indeed no military interest, except that it is the first in which we find fully developed that wholly unscientific method of attack by the English which Clerk criticised, and which prevailed throughout the century. It is instructive to notice that the result in it was the same as in all others fought on the same principle. The van opened out from the centre, leaving quite an interval; and the attempt made to penetrate this gap and isolate the van was the only tactical move of the French. We find in them at Malaga no trace of the cautious, skilful tactics which Clerk rightly thought to recognize at a later day. The degeneracy from the able combinations of Monk, Ruyter, and Tourville to the epoch of mere seamanship is clearly marked by the battle of Malaga, and gives it its only historical importance. In it was realized that primitive mode of fighting which Macaulay has sung, and which remained for many years the ideal of the English navy:—

> "Then on both sides the leaders
>   Gave signal for the charge;
> And on both sides the footmen
>   Strode forth with lance and targe;
> And on both sides the horsemen
>   Struck their spurs deep in gore,
> And *front to front* the armies
>   Met with a mighty roar."

Human movement is not always advance; and there are traces of a somewhat similar ideal in the naval periodical literature of our own day. The fight was severe, lasting from ten in the morning till five in the afternoon, but was entirely indecisive. The next day the wind shifted, giving the weather-gage to the French, but they did not use the opportunity to attack; for which they were much to blame, if their claim of the advantage the day before is well founded. Rooke could not have fought; nearly half his fleet, twenty-five ships, it is said, had used up all their ammunition. Even during the battle itself several of the allied ships were towed out of line, because they had not powder and ball for a single broadside. This was doubtless due to the attack upon Gibraltar, in which fifteen thousand shot were expended, and to the lack of any port serving as a base of supplies,—a deficiency which the new possession would hereafter remove. Rooke, in seizing Gibraltar, had the same object in view that prompted the United States to seize Port Royal at the beginning of the Civil War, and which made the Duke of Parma urge upon his king, before sending the Spanish Great Armada, to seize Flushing on the coast of Holland,—advice which, had it been followed, would have made unnecessary that dreary and disastrous voyage to the north of England. The same reasons would doubtless lead any nation intending serious operations against our seaboard, to seize points remote from the great centres and susceptible of defence, like Gardiner's Bay or Port Royal, which in an inefficient condition of our navy they might hold with and for their fleets.

Rooke retired in peace to Lisbon, bestowing by the way on Gibraltar all the victuals and ammunition that could be spared from the fleet. Toulouse, instead of following up his victory, if it was one, went back to Toulon, sending only ten ships-of-the-line to support the attack on Gibraltar. All the attempts of the French against the place were carried on in a futile manner; the investing squadron was finally destroyed and the land attack converted into a blockade. "With this reverse," says a French naval officer, "began in the French people a regrettable reaction against the navy. The wonders to which it had given birth, its immense services, were forgotten. Its value was no longer believed. The army, more directly in contact with the nation, had all its favor, all its sympathy. The prevailing error, that the greatness or decay of France depended upon some Rhenish positions, could not but favor these ideas adverse to the sea service, which have made England's strength and our weakness." [2]

During this year, 1704, the battle of Blenheim was fought, in which the French and Bavarian troops were wholly overthrown by the English and German under Marlborough and Prince Eugene. The result of this battle was that Bavaria forsook the French alliance, and Germany became a secondary theatre of the general war, which was waged thereafter mainly in the Netherlands, Italy, and the Peninsula.

The following year, 1705, the allies moved against Philip V. by two roads,—from Lisbon upon Madrid, and by way of Barcelona. The former attack, though based upon the sea, was mainly by land, and resultless; the Spanish people in that quarter showed unmistakably that they would not welcome the king set up by foreign powers. It was different in Catalonia. Carlos III. went there in person with the allied fleet. The French navy, inferior in numbers,

[2] La Pérouse-Bonfils: Hist. de la Marine Française.

kept in port. The French army also did not appear. The allied troops invested the town, aided by three thousand seamen and supported by supplies landed from the fleet, which was to them both base of supplies and line of communications. Barcelona surrendered on the 9th of October; all Catalonia welcomed Carlos, and the movement spread to Aragon and Valencia, the capital of the latter province declaring for Carlos.

The following year, 1706, the French took the offensive in Spain on the borders of Catalonia, while defending the passes of the mountains toward Portugal. In the absence of the allied fleet, and of the succors which it brought and maintained, the resistance was weak, and Barcelona was again besieged, this time by the French party supported by a French fleet of thirty sail-of-the-line and numerous transports with supplies from the neighboring port of Toulon. The siege, begun April 5, was going on hopefully; the Austrian claimant himself was within the walls, the prize of success; but on the 10th of May the allied fleet appeared, the French ships retired, and the siege was raised in disorder. The Bourbon claimant dared not retreat into Aragon, and so passed by Roussillon into France, leaving his rival in possession. At the same time there moved forward from Portugal—that other base which the sea power of the English and Dutch at once controlled and utilized—another army maintained by the subsidies earned from the ocean. This time the western attack was more successful; many cities in Estremadura and Leon fell, and as soon as the allied generals learned the raising of the siege of Barcelona, they pressed on by way of Salamanca to Madrid. Philip V., after escaping into France, had returned to Spain by the western Pyrenees; but on the approach of the allies he had again to fly, leaving to them his capital. The Portuguese and allied troops entered Madrid, June 26, 1706. The allied fleet, after the fall of Barcelona, seized Alicante and Cartagena.

So far success had gone; but the inclinations of the Spanish people had been mistaken, and the strength of their purpose and pride, supported by the natural features of their country, was not yet understood. The national hatred to the Portuguese was aroused, as well as the religious dislike to heretics, the English general himself being a Huguenot refugee. Madrid and the surrounding country were disaffected, and the south sent the Bourbon king assurance of its fidelity. The allies were not able to remain in the hostile capital, particularly as the region around was empty of supplies and full of guerillas. They retired to the eastward, drawing toward the Austrian claimant in Aragon. Reverse followed reverse, and on the 25th of April, 1707, the allied army was disastrously overthrown at Almansa, losing fifteen thousand men. All Spain fell back again into the power of Philip V., except the province of Catalonia, part of which also was subdued. The next year 1708, the French made some progress in the same quarter, but were not able to attack Barcelona; Valencia and Alicante, however, were reduced.

The year 1707 was not marked by any naval event of importance. During the summer the allied fleets in the Mediterranean were diverted from the coast of Spain to support an attack upon Toulon made by the Austrians and Piedmontese. The latter moved from Italy along the coast of the Mediterranean, the fleet supporting the flank on the sea, and contributing supplies. The siege, however, failed, and the campaign was inconclusive. Returning home, the admiral, Sir Cloudesley Shovel, with several ships-of-the-line, was lost on the Scilly Islands, in one of those shipwrecks which have become historical.

In 1708 the allied fleets seized Sardinia, which from its fruitfulness and nearness to Barcelona became a rich storehouse to the Austrian claimant, so long as by the allied help he controlled the sea. The same year Minorca, with its valuable harbor, Port Mahon, was also taken, and from that time for fifty years remained in English hands. Blocking Cadiz and Cartagena by the possession of Gibraltar, and facing Toulon with Port Mahon, Great Britain was now as strongly based in the Mediterranean as either France or Spain; while, with Portugal as an ally, she controlled the two stations of Lisbon and Gibraltar, watching the trade routes both of the ocean and of the inland sea. By the end of 1708 the disasters of France by land and sea, the frightful sufferings of the kingdom, and the almost hopelessness of carrying on a strife which was destroying France, and easily borne by England, led Louis XIV. to offer most humiliating concessions to obtain peace. He undertook to surrender the whole Spanish monarchy, reserving only Naples for the Bourbon king. The allies refused; they demanded the abandonment of the whole Spanish Empire without exception by the Duke of Anjou, refusing to call him king, and added thereto ruinous conditions for France herself. Louis would not yield these, and the war went on.

During the remaining years the strenuous action of the sea power of the allies, which had by this time come to be that of Great Britain alone, with little help from Holland, was less than ever obtrusive, but the reality of its effect remained. The Austrian claimant, confined to Catalonia for the most part, was kept in communication with Sardinia and the Italian provinces of Germany by the English fleet; but the entire disappearance of the French navy and the evident intention on the part of Louis to keep no squadrons at sea, allowed some diminution of the Mediterranean fleet, with the result of greater protection to trade. In the years 1710 and 1711 expeditions were also made against the French colonies in North America. Nova Scotia was taken, but an attempt on Quebec failed.

During the winter of 1709 and 1710 Louis withdrew all the French troops from Spain, thus abandoning the cause of his grandson. But when the cause of France was at the very lowest, and it seemed as though she might be driven to concessions which would reduce her to a second-class power, the existence of the coalition was threatened by the disgrace of Marlborough, who represented England in it. His loss of favor with the queen was followed by the accession to power of the party opposed to the war, or rather to its further continuance. This change took place in the summer of 1710, and the inclination toward peace was strengthened both by the favorable position in which England then stood for treating, and by the heavy burden she was bearing; which it became evident could bring in no further advantages commensurate to its weight. The weaker ally, Holland, had gradually ceased to contribute her stipulated share to the sea forces; and although far-sighted Englishmen might see with complacency the disappearance of a rival sea power, the immediate increase of expense was more looked to and felt by the men of the day. The cost both of the continental and Spanish wars was also largely defrayed by England's subsidies; and while that on the continent could bring her no further gain, it was seen that the sympathies of the Spanish people could not be overborne in favor of Carlos III. without paying more than the game was worth. Secret negotiations between England and France soon began, and received an additional impulse by the unexpected death of the Emperor of

Germany, the brother of the Austrian claimant of the Spanish throne. There being no other male heir, Carlos became at once emperor of Austria, and was soon after elected emperor of Germany. England had no more wish to see two crowns on an Austrian head than on that of a Bourbon.

The demands made by England, as conditions of peace in 1711, showed her to have become a sea power in the purest sense of the word, not only in fact, but also in her own consciousness, She required that the same person should never be king both of France and Spain; that a barrier of fortified towns should be granted her allies, Holland and Germany, as a defensive line against France; that French conquests from her allies should be restored; and for herself she demanded the formal cession of Gibraltar and Port Mahon, whose strategic and maritime value has been pointed out, the destruction of the port of Dunkirk, the home nest of the privateers that preyed on English commerce, the cession of the French colonies of Newfoundland, Hudson's Bay, and Nova Scotia, the last of which she held at that time, and finally, treaties of commerce with France and Spain, and the concession of the monopoly of the slave trade with Spanish America, known as the Asiento, which Spain had given to France in 1701.

Negotiations continued, though hostilities did not cease; and in June, 1712, a four months' truce between Great Britain and France removed the English troops from the allied armies on the continent, their great leader Marlborough having been taken from their head the year before. The campaign of 1712 was favorable to France; but in almost any event the withdrawal of Great Britain made the end of the war a question of but a short time. The remonstrances of Holland were met by the reply that since 1707 the Dutch had not furnished more than one third their quota of ships, and taking the war through, not over one half. The House of Commons in an address to the throne in 1712 complained that—

"The service at sea hath been carried on through the whole course of the war in a manner highly disadvantageous to your Majesty's kingdom, for the necessity requiring that great fleets should be fitted out every year for maintaining a superiority in the Mediterranean and for opposing any force which the enemy might prepare either at Dunkirk or in the ports of west France; your Majesty's readiness, in fitting out your proportion of ships for all parts of that service, hath not prevailed with Holland, which has been greatly deficient every year in proportion to what your Majesty hath furnished. . . . Hence your Majesty hath been obliged to supply those deficiencies with additional reinforcements of your own ships, and your Majesty's ships have been forced in greater numbers to continue in remote seas, and at unseasonable times of the year, to the great damage of the navy. This also hath straitened the convoys for trade; the coasts have been exposed for want of cruisers; and you have been disabled from annoying the enemy in their most beneficial commerce with the West Indies, whence they received those vast supplies of treasure, without which they could not have supported the expenses of the war."

In fact, between 1701 and 1716 the commerce of Spanish America had brought into France forty million dollars in specie. To these complaints the Dutch envoy to England could only reply that Holland was not in a condition to fulfil her compacts. The reverses of 1712, added to Great Britain's fixed purpose to have peace, decided the Dutch to the same; and the English still kept, amid their dissatisfaction with their allies, so much of their old feeling against France as to support all the reasonable claims of Holland. April 11, 1713, an almost general peace, known as the Peace of Utrecht, one of the landmarks of history, was signed between France on the one hand, and England, Holland, Prussia, Portugal, and Savoy on the other. The emperor still held out, but the loss of British subsidies fettered the movements of his armies, and with the withdrawal of the sea powers the continental war might have fallen of itself; but France with her hands freed carried on during 1713 a brilliant and successful campaign in Germany. On the 7th of March, 1714, peace was signed between France and Austria. Some embers of the war continued to burn in Catalonia and the Balearic Islands, which persisted in their rebellion against Philip V.; but the revolt was stifled as soon as the arms of France were turned against them. Barcelona was taken by storm in September, 1714; the islands submitted in the following summer.

The changes effected by this long war and sanctioned by the peace, neglecting details of lesser or passing importance, may be stated as follows: 1. The House of Bourbon was settled on the Spanish throne, and the Spanish empire retained its West Indian and American possessions; the purpose of William III. against her dominion there was frustrated when England undertook to support the Austrian prince, and so fastened the greater part of her naval force to the Mediterranean. 2. The Spanish empire lost its possessions in the Netherlands, Gelderland going to the new kingdom of Prussia and Belgium to the emperor; the Spanish Netherlands thus became the Austrian Netherlands. 3. Spain lost also the principal islands of the Mediterranean; Sardinia being given to Austria, Minorca with its fine harbor to Great Britain, and Sicily to the Duke of Savoy. 4. Spain lost also her Italian possessions, Milan and Naples going to the emperor. Such, in the main, were the results to Spain of the fight over the succession to her throne.

France, the backer of the successful claimant, came out of the strife worn out, and with considerable loss of territory. She had succeeded in placing a king of her own royal house on a neighboring throne, but her sea strength was exhausted, her population diminished, her financial condition ruined. The European territory surrendered was on her northern and eastern boundaries; and she abandoned the use of the port of Dunkirk, the centre of that privateering warfare so dreaded by English merchants. In America, the cession of Nova Scotia and Newfoundland was the first step toward that entire loss of Canada which befell half a century later; but for the present she retained Cape Breton Island, with its port Louisburg, the key to the Gulf and River St. Lawrence.

The gains of England, by the treaty and the war, corresponded very nearly to the losses of France and Spain, and were all in the direction of extending and strengthening her sea power. Gibraltar and Port Mahon in the Mediterranean, and the colonies already mentioned in North America, afforded new bases to that power, extending and protecting her trade. Second only to the expansion of her own was the injury to the sea power of France and Holland, by the decay of their navies in consequence of the immense drain of the land warfare; further indications of that decay will be given later. The very neglect of Holland to fill up her quota of ships, and the bad condition of those sent, while imposing extra burdens upon England, may be considered a benefit, forcing the British navy to greater development and effort. The disproportion in military power on the sea was further increased by the destruction of the works at Dunkirk; for though not in itself a first-class port, nor of much depth of water, it had great artificial military strength, and its position was peculiarly adapted to annoy English trade. It was but forty miles from the South Foreland and the Downs, and the Channel abreast it is but twenty miles wide. Dunkirk was one of Louis' earliest acquisitions, and in its development was as his own child; the dismantling of the works and filling-in of the port show the depth of his humiliation at this time. But it was the wisdom of England not to base her sea power solely on military positions nor even on fighting-ships, and the commercial advantages she had now gained by the war and the peace were very great. The grant of the slave trade with Spanish America, in itself lucrative, became yet more so as the basis for an immense smuggling intercourse with those countries, which gave the English a partial recompense for their failure to obtain actual possession; while the cessions made to Portugal by France in South America were mainly to the advantage of England, which had obtained the control of Portuguese trade by the treaty of 1703. The North American colonies ceded were valuable, not merely nor chiefly as military stations, but commercially; and treaties of commerce on favorable terms were made both with France and Spain. A minister of the day, defending the treaty in Parliament, said: "The advantages from this peace appear in the addition made to our wealth; in the great quantities of bullion lately coined in our mint; by the vast increase in our shipping employed since the peace, in the fisheries, and in merchandise; and by the remarkable growth of the customs upon imports, and of our manufactures, and the growth of our country upon export"; in a word, by the impetus to trade in all its branches.

While England thus came out from the war in good running condition, and fairly placed in that position of maritime supremacy which she has so long maintained, her old rival in trade and fighting was left hopelessly behind. As the result of the war Holland obtained nothing at sea,—no colony, no station. The commercial treaty with France placed her on the same terms as England, but she received no concessions giving her a footing in Spanish America like that obtained by her ally. Indeed, some years before the peace, while the coalition was still maintaining Carlos, a treaty was made with the latter by the British minister, unknown to the Dutch, practically giving the British monopoly of Spanish trade in America; sharing it only with Spaniards, which was pretty much the same as not sharing it at all. This treaty accidentally became known, and made a great impression on the Dutch; but England was then so necessary to the coalition that she ran no risk of being left out by its other members. The gain which Holland made by land was that of military occupation only, of certain fortified places in the Austrian Netherlands, known to history as the "barrier towns"; nothing was added by them to her revenue, population, or resources; nothing to that national strength which must underlie military institutions. Holland had forsaken, perhaps unavoidably, the path by which she had advanced to wealth and to leadership among nations. The exigencies of her continental position had led to the neglect of her navy, which in those days of war and privateering involved a loss of carrying-trade and commerce; and although she held her head high through the war, the symptoms of weakness were apparent in her failing armaments. Therefore, though the United Provinces attained the great object for which they began the war, and saved the Spanish Netherlands from the hands of France, the success was not worth the cost. Thenceforth they withdrew for a long period from the wars and diplomacy of Europe; partly, perhaps, because they saw how little they had gained, but yet more from actual weakness and inability. After the strenuous exertions of the war came a reaction, which showed painfully the inherent weakness of a State narrow in territory and small in the number of its people. The visible decline of the Provinces dates from the Peace of Utrecht; the real decline began earlier. Holland ceased to be numbered among the great powers of Europe, her navy was no longer a military factor in diplomacy, and her commerce also shared in the general decline of the State.

It remains only to notice briefly the results to Austria, and to Germany generally. France yielded the barrier of the Rhine, with fortified places on the east bank of the river. Austria received, as has been mentioned, Belgium, Sardinia, Naples, and the Spanish possessions in northern Italy; dissatisfied in other respects, Austria was especially discontented at her failure to obtain Sicily, and did not cease negotiating afterward, until she had secured that island. A circumstance more important to Germany and to all Europe than this transitory acquisition of distant and alien countries by Austria was the rise of Prussia, which dates from this war as a Protestant and military kingdom destined to weigh in the balance against Austria.

Such were the leading results of the War of the Spanish Succession, "the vastest yet witnessed by Europe since the Crusades." It was a war whose chief military interest was on the land,—a war in which fought two of the greatest generals of all times, Marlborough and Prince Eugene, the names of whose battles, Blenheim, Ramillies, Malplaquet, Turin, are familiar to the most casual reader of history;

while a multitude of able men distinguished themselves on the other theatres of the strife, in Flanders, in Germany, in Italy, in Spain. On the sea only one great battle, and that scarcely worthy of the name, took place. Yet looking only, for the moment, to immediate and evident results, who reaped the benefit? Was it France, whose only gain was to seat a Bourbon on the Spanish throne? Was it Spain, whose only gain was to have a Bourbon king instead of an Austrian, and thus a closer alliance with France? Was it Holland, with its barrier of fortified towns, its ruined navy, and its exhausted people? Was it, lastly, Austria, even though she had fought with the money of the sea powers, and gained such maritime States as the Netherlands and Naples? Was it with these, who had waged war more and more exclusively by land, and set their eyes more and more on gains on the land, or was it not rather with England, who had indeed paid for that continental war and even backed it with her troops, but who meanwhile was building up her navy, strengthening, extending, and protecting her commerce, seizing maritime positions,—in a word, founding and rearing her sea power upon the ruins of that of her rivals, friend and foe alike? It is not to depreciate the gains of others that the eye fixes on England's naval growth; their gains but bring out more clearly the immenseness of hers. It was a gain to France to have a friend rather than an enemy in her rear, though her navy and shipping were ruined. It was a gain to Spain to be brought in close intercourse with a living country like France after a century of political death, and she had saved the greater part of her threatened possessions. It was a gain to Holland to be definitively freed from French aggression, with Belgium in the hands of a strong instead of a weak State. And it doubtless was a gain to Austria not only to have checked, chiefly at the expense of others, the progress of her hereditary enemy, but also to have received provinces like Sicily and Naples, which, under wise government, might become the foundation of a respectable sea power. But not one of these gains, nor all together, compared in greatness, and much less in solidity, with the gain to England of that unequalled sea power which started ahead during the War of the League of Augsburg, and received its completeness and seal during that of the Spanish Succession. By it she controlled the great commerce of the open sea with a military shipping that had no rival, and in the exhausted condition of the other nations could have none; and that shipping was now securely based on strong positions in all the disputed quarters of the world. Although her Indian empire was not yet begun, the vast superiority of her navy would enable her to control the communications of other nations with those rich and distant regions, and to assert her will in any disputes arising among the trading-stations of the different nationalities. The commerce which had sustained her in prosperity, and her allies in military efficiency, during the war, though checked and harassed by the enemy's cruisers (to which she could pay only partial attention amid the many claims upon her), started with a bound into new life when the war was over. All over the world, exhausted by their share of the common suffering, people were longing for the return of prosperity and peaceful commerce; and there was no country ready as England was in wealth, capital, and shipping to forward and reap the advantages of every enterprise by which the interchange of commodities was promoted, either by lawful or unlawful means. In the War of the Spanish Succession, by her own wise management and through the exhaustion of other nations, not only her navy but her trade was steadily built up; and indeed, in that dangerous condition of the seas, traversed by some of the most reckless and restless cruisers France ever sent out, the efficiency of the navy meant safer voyages, and so more employment for the merchant-ships. The British merchant-ships, being better protected than those of the Dutch, gained the reputation of being far safer carriers, and the carrying-trade naturally passed more and more into their hands; while the habit of employing them in preference, once established, was likely to continue.

"Taking all things together," says an historian of the British navy, "I doubt whether the credit of the English nation ever stood higher than at this period, or the spirit of the people higher. The success of our arms at sea, the necessity of protecting our trade, and the popularity of every step taken to increase our maritime power, occasioned such measures to be pursued as annually added to our force. Hence arose that mighty difference which at the close of the year 1706 appeared in the Royal Navy; this, not only in the number but in the quality of the ships, was much superior to what it had been at the time of the Revolution or even before. Hence it was that our trade rather increased than diminished during the last war, and that we gained so signally by our strict intercourse with Portugal." [3]

_____
[3] Campbell: Lives of the Admirals.

The sea power of England therefore was not merely in the great navy, with which we too commonly and exclusively associate it; France had had such a navy in 1688, and it shrivelled away like a leaf in the fire. Neither was it in a prosperous commerce alone; a few years after the date at which we have arrived, the commerce of France took on fair proportions, but the first blast of war swept it off the seas as the navy of Cromwell had once swept that of Holland. It was in the union of the two, carefully fostered, that England made the gain of sea power over and beyond all other States; and this gain is distinctly associated with and dates from the War of the Spanish Succession. Before that war England was one of the sea powers; after it she was *the* sea power, without any second. This power also she held alone, unshared by friend and unchecked by foe. She alone was rich, and in her control of the sea and her extensive shipping had the sources of wealth so much in her hands that there was no present danger of a rival on the ocean. Thus her gain of sea power and wealth was not only great but solid, being wholly in her own hands; while the gains of the other States were not merely inferior in degree, but weaker in kind, in that they depended more or less upon the good will of other peoples.

Is it meant, it may be asked, to attribute to sea power alone the greatness or wealth of any State? Certainly not. The due use and control of the sea is but one link in the chain of exchange by which wealth accumulates; but it is the central link, which lays under contribution other nations for the benefit of the one holding it, and which, history seems to assert, most surely of all gathers to itself riches. In England, this control and use of the sea seems to arise naturally, from the concurrence of many circumstances; the years immediately preceding the War of the Spanish Succession had, moreover, furthered the advance of her prosperity by a series of fiscal measures, which Macaulay speaks of as "the deep and solid foundation on which was to rise the most gigantic fabric of commercial prosperity which the world had ever seen." It may be questioned, however, whether the genius of the people, inclined to and developed by trade, did not make easier the taking of such measures; whether their adoption did not at least partially spring from, as well as add to, the sea power of the nation. However that may be, there is seen, on the opposite side of the Channel, a nation which started ahead of England in the race,—a nation peculiarly well fitted, by situation and resources, for the control of the sea both by war and commerce. The position of France is in this peculiar, that of all the great powers she alone had a free choice; the others were more or less constrained to the land chiefly, or to the sea chiefly, for any movement outside their own borders, but she to her long continental frontier added a seaboard on three seas. In 1672 she definitely chose expansion by land. At that time Colbert had administered her finances for twelve years, and from a state of terrible confusion had so restored them that the revenue of the king of France was more than double that of the king of England. In those days France paid the subsidies of Europe; but Colbert's plans and hopes for France rested upon making her powerful on the sea. The war with Holland arrested these plans, the onward movement of prosperity ceased, the nation was thrown back upon itself, shut off from the outside world. Many causes doubtless worked together to the disastrous result which marked the end of the reign of Louis XIV.: constant wars, bad administration in the latter half of the period, extravagance throughout; but France was practically never invaded, the war was kept at or beyond her own frontiers with slight exceptions, her home industries could suffer little from direct hostilities. In these respects she was nearly equal to England, and under better conditions than her other enemies. What made the difference in the results? Why was France miserable and exhausted, while England was smiling and prosperous? Why did England dictate, and France accept, terms of peace? The reason apparently was the difference in wealth and credit. France stood alone against many enemies; but those enemies were raised and kept moving by English subsidies. The Lord Treasurer of England, writing in 1706 to Marlborough, says:—

"Though the land and trade of both England and Holland have excessive burthens upon them, yet the credit continues good both of them and us; whereas the finances of France are so much more exhausted that they are forced to give twenty and twenty-five per cent for every penny they send out of the kingdom, unless they send it in specie."

In 1712 the expenditure of France was 240,000,000 francs, while the taxes brought in only 113,000,000 gross, of which, after deducting losses and necessary expenses, only 37,000,000 remained in the treasury; the deficit was sought to be met by anticipating parts of the revenue for years ahead, and by a series of extraordinary transactions tedious to name or to understand.

"In the summer of 1715 [two years after the peace] it seemed as if the situation could not grow worse,—no more public nor private credit; no more clear revenue for the State; the portions of the revenue not pledged, anticipated on the following years. Neither labor nor consumption could be resumed for want of circulation; usury reigned on the ruins of society. The alternations of high prices and the depreciation of commodities finally crushed the people. Provision riots broke out among them, and even in the army. Manufactures were languishing or suspended; forced mendicity was preying upon the cities. The fields were deserted, the lands fallow for lack of instruments, for lack of manure, for lack of cattle; the houses were falling to ruin. Monarchical France seemed ready to expire with its aged king." [4]

Thus it was in France, with a population of nineteen millions at that time to the eight millions of all the British Islands; with a land vastly more fertile and productive; before the great days, too, of coal and iron. "In England, on the contrary, the immense grants of Parliament in 1710 struck the French prodigiously; for while their credit was low, or in a manner quite gone, ours was at its zenith." During that same war "there appeared that mighty spirit among our merchants which enabled them to carry on all their schemes with a vigor that kept a constant circulation of money throughout the kingdom, and afforded such mighty encouragement to all manufactures as has made the remembrance of those times grateful in worse."

"By the treaty with Portugal we were prodigious gainers. . . . The Portuguese began to feel the comfortable effects of their Brazil gold mines, and the prodigious commerce that followed with us made their good fortune in great measure ours; and so it has been ever since; otherwise I know not how the expenses of the war had been borne. . . . The running cash in the kingdom increased very considerably, which must be attributed in great measure to our Portuguese trade; and this, as I have made manifest, we owed wholly to our power at sea [which took Portugal from the alliance of the two crowns, and threw her upon the protection of the maritime powers]. Our trade with the Spanish West Indies by way of Cadiz was certainly much interrupted at the beginning of this war; but afterward it was in great measure restored, as well by direct communication with several provinces when under the Archduke, as through Portugal, by which a very great though contraband trade was carried on. We were at the same time very great gainers by our commerce with the Spaniards in the West Indies [also contraband]. . . . Our colonies, though complaining of neglect, grew richer, more populous, and carried their trade farther than

[4] Martin: History of France.

in former times. . . . Our national end with respect to England was in this war particularly in great measure answered,—I mean the destruction of the French power at sea, for, after the battle of Malaga, we hear no more of their great fleets; and though by this the number of their privateers was very much increased, yet the losses of our merchants were far less in the latter than in the former reign. . . . It is certainly a matter of great satisfaction that . . . setting out at first with the sight of so great a naval power as the French king had assembled in 1688, while we struggled under such difficulties, and when we got out of that troublesome war, in 1697, found ourselves loaded with a debt too heavy to be shaken off in the short interval of peace, yet by 1706, instead of seeing the navy of France riding upon our coast, we sent every year a powerful fleet to insult theirs, superior to them not only in the ocean, but in the Mediterranean, forcing them entirely out of that sea by the mere sight of our flag. . . . By this we not only secured our trade with the Levant, and strengthened our interests with all the Italian princes, but struck the States of Barbary with terror, and awed the Sultan from listening to any proposals from France. Such were the fruits of the increase of our naval power, and of the manner in which it was employed. . . . Such fleets were necessary; they at once protected our flag and our allies, and attached them to our interest; and, what is of greater importance than all the rest, they established our reputation for maritime force so effectually that we feel even to this day [1740] the happy effects of the fame thus acquired." [5]

It is needless to add more. Thus stood the Power of the Seas during the years in which the French historians tell us that their cruisers were battening on her commerce. The English writer admits heavy losses. In 1707, that is, in the space of five years, the returns, according to the report of a committee of the House of Lords, "show that since the beginning of the war England had lost 30 ships-of-war and 1146 merchant-ships, of which 300 were retaken; whereas we had taken from them, or destroyed, 80 ships-of-war, and 1346 merchantmen; 175 privateers also were taken." The greater number of the ships-of-war were probably on private venture, as has been explained. But, be the relative numbers what they may, no argument is needed beyond the statements just given, to show the inability of a mere cruising warfare, not based upon large fleets, to break down a great sea power. Jean Bart died in 1702; but in Forbin, Du Casse, and others, and above all in Duguay-Trouin, he left worthy successors, the equals of any commerce-destroyers the world has ever seen.

The name of Duguay-Trouin suggests the mention, before finally leaving the War of the Spanish Succession, of his greatest privateer-

[5] Campbell: Lives of the Admirals.

ing expedition, carried to a distance from home rarely reached by the seamen of his occupation, and which illustrates curiously the spirit of such enterprises in that day, and the shifts to which the French government was reduced. A small French squadron had attacked Rio Janeiro in 1710, but being repulsed, had lost some prisoners, who were said to have been put to death. Duguay-Trouin sought permission to avenge the insult to France. The king, consenting, advanced the ships and furnished the crews; and a regular contract was drawn up between the king on the one hand and the company employing Duguay-Trouin on the other, stipulating the expenses to be borne and supplies furnished on either hand; among which we find the odd, business-like provision that for every one of the troops embarked who shall die, be killed, or desert during the cruise, the company should pay a forfeit of thirty francs. The king was to receive one fifth of the net profits, and was to bear the loss of any one of the vessels that should be wrecked, or destroyed in action. Under these provisions, enumerated in full in a long contract, Duguay-Trouin received a force of six ships-of-the-line, seven frigates, and over two thousand troops, with which he sailed to Rio Janeiro in 1711; captured the place after a series of operations, and allowed it to be ransomed at the price of something under four hundred thousand dollars, probably nearly equal to a million in the present day, besides five hundred cases of sugar. The privateering company cleared about ninety-two per cent on their venture. As two of the ships-of-the-line were never heard from after sailing on the return voyage, the king's profits were probably small.

While the War of the Spanish Succession was engaging all western Europe, a strife which might have had a profound influence upon its issue was going on in the east. Sweden and Russia were at war, the Hungarians had revolted against Austria, and Turkey was finally drawn in, though not till the end of the year 1710. Had Turkey helped the Hungarians, she would have made a powerful diversion, not for the first time in history, in favor of France. The English historian suggests that she was deterred by fear of the English fleet; at all events she did not move, and Hungary was reduced to obedience. The war between Sweden and Russia was to result in the preponderance of the latter upon the Baltic, the subsidence of Sweden, the old ally of France, into a second-rate State, and the entrance of Russia definitively into European politics.

6

The Regency in France—Alberoni in Spain—
Policies of Walpole and Fleuri—War of the
Polish Succession—English Contraband Trade
in Spanish America—Great Britain Declares
War against Spain—1715-1739

The Peace of Utrecht was soon followed by the deaths of the rulers
of the two countries which had played the foremost part in the War
of the Spanish Succession. Queen Anne died August 1, 1714; Louis
XIV. on the 1st of September, 1715.

The successor to the English throne, the German George I.,
though undoubtedly the choice of the English people, was far from
being their favorite, and was rather endured as a necessary evil, giving them a Protestant instead of a Roman Catholic king. Along with
the coldness and dislike of his own partisans, he found a very considerable body of disaffected men, who wished to see the son of
James II. on the throne. There was therefore a lack of solidity, more
apparent than real, but still real, in his position. In France, on the
contrary, the succession to the throne was undisputed; but the heir
was a child of five years, and there was much jealousy as to the possession of the regency, a power more absolute than that of the king
of England. The regency was obtained and exercised by the next
in succession to the throne, Philip, Duke of Orleans; but he had to
apprehend, not only attempts on the part of rivals in France to

shake his hold, but also the active enmity of the Bourbon king of Spain, Philip V.,—an enmity which seems to have dated from an intrigue of Orleans, during the late war, to supplant Philip on the Spanish throne. There was therefore a feeling of instability, of apprehension, in the governments of England and France, which influenced the policy of both. As regards the relations of France and Spain, the mutual hatred of the actual rulers stood for a while in the way of the friendly accord Louis XIV. had hoped from family ties, and was injurious to the true interests of both nations.

The Regent Orleans, under the advice of the most able and celebrated French statesman of that day, the Abbé Dubois, made overtures of alliance to the king of Great Britain. He began first by commercial concessions of the kind generally acceptable to the English, forbidding French shipping to trade to the South Seas under penalty of death, and lowering the duties on the importation of English coal. England at first received these advances warily; but the regent would not be discouraged, and offered, further, to compel the Pretender, James III., to withdraw beyond the Alps. He also undertook to fill up the port at Mardyck, a new excavation by which the French government was trying to indemnify itself for the loss of Dunkirk. These concessions, all of which but one, it will be noted, were at the expense of the sea power or commercial interests of France, induced England to sign a treaty by which the two countries mutually guaranteed the execution of the treaties of Utrecht as far as their respective interests were concerned; especially the clause by which the House of Orleans was to succeed to the French throne, if Louis XV. died childless. The Protestant succession in England was likewise guaranteed. Holland, exhausted by the war, was unwilling to enter upon new engagements, but was at last brought over to this by the remission of certain dues on her merchandise entering France. The treaty, signed in January, 1717, was known as the Triple Alliance, and bound France to England for some years to come.

While France was thus making overtures to England, Spain, under the guidance of another able churchman, was seeking the same alliance and at the same time developing her national strength with the hope of recovering her lost Italian States. The new minister, Cardinal Alberoni, promised Philip V. to put him in a position to reconquer Sicily and Naples, if granted five years of peace. He worked hard to bring up the revenues, rebuild the navy, and re-establish the army, while at the same time promoting manufactures, commerce, and shipping, and the advance made in all these was remarkable; but the more legitimate ambition of Spain to recover her lost possessions, and with them to establish her power in the Mediterranean, so grievously wounded by the loss of Gibraltar, was hampered by the ill-timed purpose of Philip to overthrow the regency of Orleans in France. Alberoni was compelled to alienate France, whose sea power, as well as that of Spain, was concerned in seeing Sicily in friendly hands, and, instead of that natural ally, had to conciliate the maritime powers, England and Holland. This he also sought to do by commercial concessions; promising promptly to put the English in possession of the privileges granted at Utrecht, concerning which Spain had so far delayed. In return, he asked favorable action from them in Italy. George I., who was at heart German, received coldly advances which were unfriendly to the German emperor in his Italian dominions; and Alberoni, offended, withdrew them. The Triple Alliance, by guaranteeing the existing arrangement of succession to the French throne, gave further offence to Philip V., who dreamed of asserting his own claim. The result of all these negotiations was to bind England and France together against Spain,—a blind policy for the two Bourbon kingdoms.

The gist of the situation created by these different aims and feelings was that the emperor of Austria and the king of Spain both wanted Sicily, which at Utrecht had been given to the Duke of Savoy; and that France and England both wished for peace in western Europe, because war would give an opportunity to the malcontents in either kingdom. The position of George, however, being more secure than that of Orleans, the policy of the latter tended to yield to that of the former, and this tendency was increased by the active ill-will of the king of Spain. George, as a German, wished the emperor's success; and the English statesmen naturally preferred to see Sicily in the hands of their late ally and well-assured friend rather than in Spain's. France, contrary to her true policy, but under the urgency of the regent's position, entertained the same views, and it was proposed to modify the Treaty of Utrecht by transferring Sicily from Savoy to Austria, giving the former Sardinia instead. It was necessary, however, to consider Spain, which under Alberoni had already gained a degree of military power astounding to those who had known her weakness during the last war. She was not yet ready to fight, for only half of the five years asked by the cardinal had passed; but still less was she ready to forego her ambitions. A trifling incident precipitated an outbreak. A high Spanish official, travelling from Rome to Spain by land, and so passing through the Italian States of the emperor, was arrested as a rebellious subject by order of the latter, who still styled himself king of Spain. At this insult, Alberoni could not hold Philip back. An expedition of twelve ships-of-war and eighty-six hundred soldiers was sent against Sardinia, the transfer to Savoy not having yet taken effect, and reduced the island in a few months. This happened in 1717.

Doubtless the Spaniards would at once have moved on against Sicily; but France and England now intervened more actively to prevent the general war that seemed threatening. England sent a fleet to the Mediterranean, and negotiations began at Paris, Vienna, and Madrid. The outcome of these conferences was an agreement between England and France to effect the exchange of Sardinia and Sicily just mentioned, recompensing Spain by giving her Parma and Tuscany in northern Italy, and stipulating that the emperor should renounce forever his absurd but irritating claim to the Spanish crown. This arrangement was to be enforced by arms, if necessary. The emperor at first refused consent; but the increasing greatness of Alberoni's preparations at last decided him to accept so advantageous an offer, and the accession of Holland to the compact gave it the historical title of the Quadruple Alliance. Spain was obstinate; and it is significant of Alberoni's achievements in developing her power, and the eagerness, not to say anxiety, of George I., that the offer was made to purchase her consent by ceding Gibraltar. If the Regent Orleans knew this, it would partly justify his forwarding the negotiations.

Alberoni tried to back up his military power by diplomatic efforts extending all over Europe. Russia and Sweden were brought together in a project for invading England in the interest of the Stuarts; the signing of the Quadruple Alliance in Holland was delayed by his agents; a conspiracy was started in France against the regent; the Turks were stirred up against the emperor; discontent was fomented throughout Great Britain; and an attempt was made to gain over the Duke of Savoy, outraged by being deprived of Sicily. On the 1st of July, 1718, a Spanish army of thirty thousand troops, escorted by twenty-two ships-of-the-line, appeared at Palermo. The troops of Savoy evacuated the city and pretty nearly the whole island, resistance being concentrated in the citadel of Messina. Anxiety was felt in Naples itself, until the English admiral, Byng,[1] anchored there the day after the investment of Messina. The king of Sicily having now consented to the terms of the Quadruple Alliance, Byng received on board two thousand Austrian troops to be landed at Messina. When he appeared before the place, finding it besieged, he wrote to the Spanish general suggesting a suspension of arms for two months. This was of course refused; so the Austrians were landed again at Reggio, in Italy, and Byng passed through the Straits of Messina to seek the Spanish fleet, which had gone to the southward.

The engagement which ensued can scarcely be called a battle, and, as is apt to happen in such affairs, when the parties are on the verge of war but war has not actually been declared, there is some doubt as to how far the attack was morally justifiable on the part of the English. It seems pretty sure that Byng was determined beforehand to seize or destroy the Spanish fleet, and that as a military man he was justified by his orders. The Spanish naval officers had not made up their minds to any line of conduct; they were much inferior in numbers, and, as must always be the case, Alberoni's hastily revived navy had not within the same period reached nearly the efficiency of his army. The English approached threateningly near, one or more Spanish ships opened fire, whereupon the English, being to windward, stood down and made an end of them; a few only escaped into Valetta harbor. The Spanish navy was practically annihilated. It is difficult to understand the importance attached by some writers to Byng's action at this time in attacking without regard to the line-of-battle. He had before him a disorderly force, much inferior both in numbers and discipline. His merit seems rather to lie in the readiness to assume a responsibility from which a more scrupulous man might have shrunk; but in this and throughout the campaign he rendered good service to England, whose sea power was again strengthened by the destruction not of an actual but a possible rival, and his services were rewarded by a peerage. In connection with this day's work was written a despatch which has great favor with English historians. One of the senior captains was detached with a division against some escaping ships of the enemy. His report to the

[1] Afterward Lord Torrington; father of Admiral John Byng, shot in 1757.

admiral ran thus: "SIR,—We have taken or destroyed all the Spanish ships upon this coast, the number as per margin. Respectfully, etc., G. Walton." One English writer makes, and another indorses, the uncalled-for but characteristic fling at the French, that the ships thus thrust into the margin would have filled some pages of a French narration.[2] It may be granted that the so-called "battle" of Cape Passaro did not merit a long description, and Captain Walton possibly felt so; but if all reports of naval transactions were modelled upon his, the writing of naval history would not depend on official papers.

Thus the Spanish navy was struck down on the 11th of August, 1718, off Cape Passaro. This settled the fate of Sicily, if it had been doubtful before. The English fleet cruised round the island, supporting the Austrians and isolating the Spaniards, none of whom were permitted to withdraw before peace was made. Alberoni's diplomatic projects failed one after the other, with a strange fatality. In the following year the French, in pursuance of the terms of the alliance, invaded the north of Spain and destroyed the dockyards: burning nine large ships on the stocks, besides the materials for seven more, at the instigation of an English *attaché* accompanying the French headquarters. Thus was completed the destruction of the Spanish navy, which, says an English historian, was ascribed to the maritime jealousy of England. "This was done," wrote the French commander, the Duke of Berwick, a bastard of the house of Stuart, "in order that the English government may be able to show the next Parliament that nothing has been neglected to diminish the navy of Spain." The acts of Sir George Byng, as given by the English naval historian, make yet more manifest the purpose of England at this time. While the city and citadel of Messina were being besieged by the Austrians, English, and Sardinians, a dispute arose as to the possession of the Spanish men-of-war within the mole. Byng, "reflecting within himself that possibly the garrison might capitulate for the safe return of those ships into Spain, which he was determined not to suffer; that on the other hand the right of possession might breed an inconvenient dispute at a critical juncture among the princes concerned, and if it should at length be determined that they did not belong to England it were better they belonged to no one else, proposed to Count de Merci, the Austrian

[2] Campbell: Lives of the Admirals; quoted by Lord Mahon in his History of England.

general, to erect a battery and destroy them as they lay." [3] After some demur on the part of the other leaders, this was done. If constant care and watchfulness deserve success, England certainly deserved her sea power; but what shall be said of the folly of France at this time and in this connection?

The steady stream of reverses, and the hopelessness of contending for distant maritime possessions when without a navy, broke down the resistance of Spain. England and France insisted upon the dismissal of Alberoni, and Philip yielded to the terms of the Quadruple Alliance. The Austrian power, necessarily friendly to England, was thus firmly settled in the central Mediterranean, in Naples and Sicily, as England herself was in Gibraltar and Port Mahon. Sir Robert Walpole, the minister now coming into power in England, failed at a later day to support this favorable conjunction, and so far betrayed the traditional policy of his country. The dominion of the House of Savoy in Sardinia, which then began, has lasted; it is only within our own day that the title king of Sardinia has merged in the broader one of king of Italy.

Contemporaneously with and for some time after the short episode of Alberoni's ministry and Spain's ambition, a struggle was going on around the shores of the Baltic which must be mentioned, because it gave rise to another effectual illustration of the sea power of England, manifested alike in the north and south with a slightness of exertion which calls to mind the stories of the tap of a tiger's paw. The long contest between Sweden and Russia was for a moment interrupted in 1718 by negotiations looking to peace and to an alliance between the two for the settlement of the succession in Poland and the restoration of the Stuarts in England. This project, on which had rested many of Alberoni's hopes, was finally stopped by the death in battle of the Swedish king. The war went on; and the czar, seeing the exhaustion of Sweden, purposed its entire subjugation. This destruction of the balance of power in the Baltic, making it a Russian lake, suited neither England nor France; especially the former, whose sea power both for peace and war depended upon the naval stores chiefly drawn from those regions. The two western kingdoms interfered, both by diplomacy, while England besides sent her fleet. Denmark, which was also at war with her traditional enemy Sweden, readily yielded; but Peter the Great chafed

[3] Campbell: Lives of the Admirals.

heavily under the implied coercion, until at last orders were sent to the English admiral to join his fleet to that of the Swedes and repeat in the Baltic the history of Cape Passaro. The czar in alarm withdrew his fleet. This happened in 1719; but Peter, though baffled, was not yet subdued. The following year the interposition of England was repeated with greater effect, although not in time to save the Swedish coasts from serious injury; but the czar, recognizing the fixed purpose with which he had to deal, and knowing from personal observation and practical experience the efficiency of England's sea power, consented finally to peace. The French claim much for their own diplomacy in this happy result, and say that England supported Sweden feebly; being willing that she should lose her provinces on the eastern shore of the Baltic because Russia, thus brought down to the sea-shore, could more easily open to English trade the vast resources of her interior. This may very possibly be true, and certainty can be felt that British interests, especially as to commerce and sea power, were looked after; but the character of Peter the Great is the guarantee that the argument which weighed most heavily with him was the military efficiency of the British fleet and its ability to move up to his very doors. By this Peace of Nystadt, August 30, 1721, Sweden abandoned Livonia, Esthonia, and other provinces on the east side of the Baltic. This result was inevitable; it was yearly becoming less possible for small States to hold their own.

It can readily be understood that Spain was utterly discontented with the terms wrung from her by the Quadruple Alliance. The twelve years which followed are called years of peace, but the peace was very uncertain, and fraught with elements of future wars. The three great grievances rankling with Spain were—Sicily and Naples in the possession of Austria, Gibraltar and Mahon in the hands of England, and lastly, the vast contraband trade carried on by English merchants and ships in Spanish America. It will be seen that England was the active supporter of all these injuries; England therefore was the special enemy of Spain, but Spain was not the only enemy of England.

The quiet, such as it was, that succeeded the fall of Alberoni was due mainly to the character and policy of the two ministers of France and England, who agreed in wishing a general peace. The policy and reasons of the French regent are already known. Moved by the same reasons, and to remove an accidental offence taken by England,

Dubois obtained for her the further concession from Spain, additional to the commercial advantages granted at Utrecht, of sending a ship every year to trade in the West Indies. It is said that this ship, after being anchored, was kept continually supplied by others, so that fresh cargo came in over one side as fast as the old was sent ashore from the other. Dubois and the regent both died in the latter half of 1723, after an administration of eight years, in which they had reversed the policy of Richelieu by alliance with England and Austria and sacrificing to them the interests of France.

The regency and the nominal government of France passed to another member of the royal family; but the real ruler was Cardinal Fleuri, the preceptor of the young king, who was now thirteen years of age. Efforts to displace the preceptor resulted only in giving him the title, as well as the power, of minister in 1726. At this time Sir Robert Walpole had become prime minister of England, with an influence and power which gave him practically the entire guidance of the policy of the State. The chief wish of both Walpole and Fleuri was peace, above all in western Europe. France and England therefore continued to act together for that purpose, and though they could not entirely stifle every murmur, they were for several years successful in preventing outbreaks. But while the aims of the two ministers were thus agreed, the motives which inspired them were different. Walpole desired peace because of the still unsettled condition of the English succession; for the peaceful growth of English commerce, which he had ever before his eyes; and probably also because his spirit, impatient of equals in the government, shrank from war which would raise up stronger men around him. Fleuri, reasonably secure as to the throne and his own power, wished like Walpole the peaceful development of his country, and shrank from war with the love of repose natural to old age; for he was seventy-three when he took office, and ninety when he laid it down in death. Under his mild administration the prosperity of France revived; the passing traveller could note the change in the face of the country and of the people; yet it may be doubted whether this change was due to the government of the quiet old man, or merely to the natural elasticity of the people, no longer drained by war nor isolated from the rest of the world. French authorities say that agriculture did not revive throughout the country. It is certain, however, that the maritime prosperity of France advanced wonderfully, owing mainly to the removal of commercial restrictions in the years immediately following the death of Louis XIV. The West India islands in particular throve greatly, and their welfare was naturally shared by the home ports that traded with them. The tropical climate of Martinique, Guadeloupe, and Louisiana, and cultivation by slaves, lent themselves readily to the paternal, semi-military government which marks all French colonies, but which produced less happy results in the bitter weather of Canada. In the West Indies, France at this time obtained a decided preponderance over England; the value of the French half of Hayti was alone equal to that of all the English West Indies, and French coffee and sugar were driving those of England out of European markets. A like advantage over England in the Mediterranean and Levant trade is asserted by French historians. At the same time the East India Company was revived, and its French depot, whose name tells its association with the East, the Breton town of L'Orient, quickly became a splendid city. Pondicherry on the Coromandel coast, and Chandernagore on the Ganges, the chief seats of French power and commerce in India, grew rapidly; the Isle of Bourbon and the Isle of France, now the Mauritius, whose position is so well suited for the control of the Indian Ocean, became, the one a rich agricultural colony, the other a powerful naval station. The monopoly of the great company was confined to the trade between home and the chief Indian stations; the traffic throughout the Indian seas was open to private enterprise and grew more rapidly. This great movement, wholly spontaneous, and even looked on with distrust by the government, was personified in two men, Dupleix and La Bourdonnais; who, the former at Chandernagore and the latter at the Isle of France, pointed out and led the way in all these undertakings, which were building up the power and renown of the French in the Eastern seas. The movement was begun which, after making France the rival of England in the Hindustan peninsula, and giving her for a moment the promise of that great empire which has bestowed a new title on the queen of Great Britain, was destined finally to falter and perish before the sea power of England. The extent of this expansion of French trade, consequent upon peace and the removal of restrictions, and not due in any sense to government protection, is evidenced by the growth of French merchant shipping from only three hundred vessels at the death of Louis XIV., to eighteen hundred, twenty years later.

This, a French historian claims, refutes "the deplorable prejudices, born of our misfortunes, that France is not fitted for sea commerce, the only commerce that indefinitely extends the power of a nation with its sphere of activity." [4]

This free and happy movement of the people was far from acceptable to Fleuri, who seems to have seen it with the distrust of a hen that has hatched ducklings. Walpole and himself were agreed to love peace; but Walpole was obliged to reckon with the English people, and these were prompt to resent rivalry upon the sea and in trade, however obtained. Moreover, Fleuri had inherited the unfortunate policy of Louis XIV.; his eyes were fixed on the continent. He did not indeed wish to follow the course of the regency in quarrelling with Spain, but rather to draw near to her; and although he was not able for a time to do so without sacrificing his peace policy, because of Spain's restless enmity to England, yet his mind was chiefly bent upon strengthening the position of France on the land, by establishing Bourbon princes where he could, and drawing them together by family alliances. The navy was allowed to decay more and more. "The French government abandoned the sea at the very moment that the nation, through the activity of private individuals, was making an effort to regain it." The material force fell to fifty-four ships-of-the-line and frigates, mostly in bad condition; and even when war with England had been imminent for five years, France had but forty-five ships-of-the-line to England's ninety. This difference foreshadowed the results which followed a quarter of a century of war.

During the same period Walpole, relying upon Fleuri's co-operation, resolutely set his face against open war between England and Spain. The difficulties caused by the threatening and exasperating action of the latter country, and of such allies as she from time to time could raise, were met, and for a while successfully met, by naval demonstrations,—reminders of that sea power which one nation after another had felt and yielded to. In 1725, the Spanish king and the emperor agreed to sink their long-standing feud, and signed a treaty at Vienna, in which there was a secret clause providing that the emperor would support the claim of Spain to Gibraltar and Port Mahon, by arms if necessary. Russia also showed a disposition to join this confederacy. A counter-alliance was formed between

4 Martin: History of France.

England, France, and Prussia; and English fleets were sent, one to the Baltic to awe the czarina, another to the coast of Spain to check that government and protect Gibraltar, and a third to Porto Bello, on the Spanish Main, to blockade the fleet of galleons there assembled, and by cutting off the supplies remind the Spanish king at once of his dependence upon the specie of America, and of England's control of the highway by which it reached him. Walpole's aversion to war was marked by giving the admiral at Porto Bello the strictest orders not to fight, only to blockade; the consequence of which, through the long delay of the squadron upon the sickly coast, was a mortality among the crews that shocked the nation, and led, among other causes, to the minister's overthrow many years later. Between three and four thousand officers and men, including Admiral Hosier himself, died there. Walpole's aim, however, was reached; though Spain made a foolish attack by land upon Gibraltar, the presence of the English fleet assured its supplies and provisions and averted the formal outbreak of war. The emperor withdrew from the alliance, and under English pressure also revoked the charter of an East India company which he had authorized in the Austrian Netherlands, and which took its name from the port of Ostend. English merchants demanded the removal of this competitor, and also of a similar rival established in Denmark; both which concessions the English ministry, backed by Holland, obtained. So long as commerce was not seriously disturbed, Walpole's peace policy, accompanied as it naturally was by years of plenty and general content, was easily maintained, even though Spain continued threatening and arrogant in her demands for Gibraltar; but unfortunately she now entered more deeply upon a course of annoyance to English trade. The concessions of the Asiento, or slave-trade, and of the annual ship to South America have been mentioned; but these privileges were but a part of the English commerce in those regions. The system of Spain with regard to the trade of her colonies was of the narrowest and most exclusive character; but, while attempting to shut them out from foreign traffic, she neglected to provide for their wants herself. The consequence was that a great smuggling or contraband trade arose throughout her American possessions, carried on mainly by the English, who made their lawful traffic by the Asiento and their yearly ship subserve also the unlawful, or at least unauthorized, trade. This system was doubtless advantageous to the great body of the Spanish colonists, and was encouraged by them, while colonial governors connived at it, sometimes for money, sometimes swayed by local public opinion and their own knowledge of the hardships of the case; but there were Spanish subjects who saw their own business injured by the use and abuse of English privileges, and the national government suffered both in pocket and in pride by these evasions of the revenue. It now began to pull the strings tighter. Obsolete regulations were revived and enforced. Words in which the action of Spain in this old controversy have been described are curiously applicable to certain recent disputes to which the United States has been a party. "The letter of the treaty was now followed, though the spirit which dictated it was abandoned. Although English ships still enjoyed the liberty of putting into Spanish harbors for the purpose of refitting and provisioning, yet they were far from enjoying the same advantages of carrying on a friendly and commercial intercourse. They were now watched with a scrupulous jealousy, strictly visited by *guarda-costas,* and every efficient means adopted to prevent any commerce with the colonies, except what was allowed by the annual ship." If Spain could have confined herself to closer watchfulness and to enforcing in her own waters vexatious customs regulations, not essentially different from those sanctioned by the general commercial ideas of that day, perhaps no further harm would have resulted; but the condition of things and the temper of her government would not let her stop there. It was not possible to guard and effectually seal a sea-coast extending over hundreds of miles, with innumerable inlets; nor would traders and seamen, in pursuit of gain which they had come to consider their right, be deterred by fears of penalties nor consideration for Spanish susceptibilities. The power of Spain was not great enough to enforce on the English ministry any regulation of their shipping, or stoppage of the abuse of the treaty privileges, in face of the feelings of the merchants; and so the weaker State, wronged and harassed, was goaded into the use of wholly unlawful means. Ships-of-war and *guarda-costas* were instructed, or at least permitted, to stop and search English ships on the high seas, outside of Spanish jurisdiction; and the arrogant Spanish temper, unrestrained by the weak central government, made many of these visits, both the lawful and the unlawful, scenes of insult and even violence. Somewhat similar results, springing from causes not entirely different, have occurred in the relations of Spanish officials to the United States and American merchant-ships in our own day. The stories of these acts of violence coming back to England, coupled with cases of loss by confiscation and by the embarrassment of trade, of course stirred up the people. In 1737 the West India merchants petitioned the House of Commons, saying,—

"For many years past their ships have not only frequently been stopped and searched, but also forcibly and arbitrarily seized upon the high seas, by Spanish ships fitted out to cruise, under the plausible pretext of guarding their own coasts; that the commanders thereof, with their crews, have been inhumanly treated, and their ships carried into some of the Spanish ports and there condemned with their cargoes, in manifest violation of the treaties subsisting between the two crowns; that the remonstrances of his Majesty's ministers at Madrid receive no attention, and that insults and plunder must soon destroy their trade."

Walpole struggled hard, during the ten years following 1729, to keep off war. In that year a treaty signed at Seville professed to regulate matters, restoring the conditions of trade to what they had been four years before, and providing that six thousand Spanish troops should at once occupy the territory of Tuscany and Parma. Walpole argued with his own people that war would lose them the commercial privileges they already enjoyed in Spanish dominions; while with Spain he carried on constant negotiations, seeking concessions and indemnities that might silence the home clamor. In the midst of this period a war broke out concerning the succession to the Polish throne. The father-in-law of the French king was one claimant; Austria supported his opponent. A common hostility to Austria once more drew France and Spain together, and they were joined by the king of Sardinia, who hoped through this alliance to wrest Milan from Austria and add it to his own territory of Piedmont. The neutrality of England and Holland was secured by a promise not to attack the Austrian Netherlands, the possession of any part of which by France was considered to be dangerous to England's sea power. The allied States declared war against Austria in October, 1733, and their armies entered Italy together; but the Spaniards, intent on their long-cherished projects against Naples and Sicily, left the others and turned southward. The two kingdoms were easily and quickly conquered, the invaders having command of the sea and the favor of the population. The second son of the king of

Spain was proclaimed king under the title of Carlos III., and the Bourbon Kingdom of the Two Sicilies thus came into existence. Walpole's aversion to war, leading him to abandon a long-standing ally, thus resulted in the transfer of the central Mediterranean to a control necessarily unfriendly to Great Britain.

But while Walpole thus forsook the emperor, he was himself betrayed by his friend Fleuri. While making the open alliance with Spain against Austria, the French government agreed to a secret clause directed against England. This engagement ran as follows: "Whenever it seems good to both nations alike, the abuses which have crept into commerce, especially through the English, shall be abolished; and if the English make objection, France will ward off their hostility with all its strength by land and sea." "And this compact was made," as the biographer of Lord Hawke points out, "during a period of intimate and ostentatious alliance with England itself." [5] Thus the policy against which William III. had called on England and Europe to arm, at last came into existence. Had Walpole known of this secret agreement, it might have seemed to him an additional argument in favor of peace; for, his keen political sagacity warning him of the existence of a danger which he yet could not see, he told the House of Commons that "if the Spaniards had not private encouragement from powers more considerable than themselves, they would never have ventured on the insults and injuries which have been proved at your bar"; and he expressed the opinion that "England was not a match for the French and Spaniards too."

Fleuri had indeed given his old friend and fellow-statesman an ugly fall. The particular question which excited the two years' War of the Polish Succession, the choice of a ruler for a distracted kingdom fated soon to disappear from the list of European States, seems a small matter; but the turn imparted to European politics by the action of the powers engaged gives it a very different importance. France and Austria came to an arrangement in October, 1735, upon terms to which Sardinia and Spain afterward acceded, the principal points of which were as follows: The French claimant to the Polish throne gave up his claim to it, and received instead the duchies of Bar and Lorraine on the east of France, with the provision that upon his death they were to go to his son-in-law, the king of France, in full sovereignty; the two kingdoms of Sicily and Naples were con-

5 Burrows: Life of Lord Hawke.

firmed to the Spanish Bourbon prince, Don Carlos; and Austria received back Parma. The Sardinian monarchy also got an increase to its Italian territory. France thus, under the peace-loving Fleuri, obtained in Bar and Lorraine an accession of strength which more warlike rulers had coveted in vain; and at the same time her external position was fortified at the expense of England, by the transfer of controlling positions in the central Mediterranean to an ally. Yet the heart of Fleuri might well have failed him as he remembered the secret agreement to check the commerce of England, and thought of her mighty sea power alongside of the decayed navy of France. That compact between France and Spain, to which the Two Sicilies acceded later, bore within it, in the then strained relations between England and Spain, the germ of the great wars between England and the House of Bourbon which issued in the creation of the British Empire and the independence of the United States.

The clamor in England over Spanish outrages continued, and was carefully nursed by the opposition to Walpole. The minister was now over sixty years of age, and scarcely able to change the settled convictions and policy of his prime. He was face to face with one of those irrepressible conflicts between nations and races toward which a policy of repression and compromise can be employed but for a short time. The English were bent upon opening the West Indies and Spanish America, the Spanish government equally bent upon obstructing them. Unfortunately for their policy of obstruction, they strengthened Walpole's enemies by unlawful search of English ships on the open sea, and possibly also by outrages to English seamen. Some of the latter were brought before the bar of the House of Commons, and testified that they had been not merely plundered, but tortured, shut up in prison, and compelled to live and work under loathsome conditions. The most celebrated case was that of a certain Jenkins, the master of a merchant-brig, who told that a Spanish officer had torn off one of his ears, bidding him carry it to the king his master, and say that if he had been there he would have been served likewise. Being asked what were his feelings at such a moment of danger and suffering, he was said to have replied, "I commended my soul to God and my cause to my country." This well-turned dramatic utterance from the mouth of a man of his class throws a suspicion of high coloring over the whole story; but it can be readily imagined what a capital campaign-cry it would be in the heat of a popular movement. The tide of feeling swept away Walpole's patchwork of compromise, and war was declared against Spain by Great Britain on the 19th of October, 1739. The English ultimatum insisted upon a formal renunciation of the right of search as claimed and exercised by the Spaniards, and upon an express acknowledgment of the British claims in North America. Among these claims was one relating to the limits of Georgia, then a recently established colony, touching the Spanish territory of Florida.

How far the war thus urged on and begun by England, against the judgment of her able minister, was morally justifiable has been warmly argued on either side by English writers. The laws of Spain with regard to the trade of her colonies did not differ in spirit from those of England herself as shown by her Navigation Act, and Spanish naval officers found themselves in a position nearly identical with that of Nelson when captain of a frigate in the West Indies half a century later. American ships and merchants then, after the separation from the mother-country, continued the trade which they had enjoyed as colonists; Nelson, zealous for the commercial advantage of England as then understood, undertook to enforce the act, and in so doing found against him the feeling of the West Indians and of the colonial authorities. It does not seem that he or those supporting him searched unlawfully, for the power of England was great enough to protect her shipping interests without using irregular means; whereas Spain between 1730 and 1740, being weak, was tempted, as she has since been, to seize those whom she knew to have injured her wherever she could find them, even outside her lawful jurisdiction.

After reading the entirely sympathetic presentation of the case of Walpole's opponents, urging war, which is given by Professor Burrows in his Life of Lord Hawke, a foreigner can scarcely fail to conclude that the Spaniards were grievously wronged, according to the rights of the mother-country over colonies as commonly admitted in that day; though no nation could tolerate the right of search as claimed by them. It chiefly concerns our subject to notice that the dispute was radically a maritime question, that it grew out of the uncontrollable impulse of the English people to extend their trade and colonial interests. It is possible that France was acting under a similar impulse, as English writers have asserted; but the character and general policy of Fleuri, as well as the genius of the French people, make this unlikely. There was no Parliament and no opposition to make known popular opinion in the France of that day, and very different estimates of Fleuri's character and administration have found voice since then. The English look rather at the ability which obtained Lorraine for France and the Sicilies for the House of Bourbon, and blame Walpole for being overreached. The French say of Fleuri that "he lived from day to day seeking only to have quiet in his old age. He had stupefied France with opiates, instead of laboring to cure her. He could not even prolong this silent sleep until his own death." [6] When the war broke out between England and Spain, "the latter claimed the advantage of her defensive alliance with France. Fleuri, grievously against his will, was forced to fit out a squadron; he did so in niggardly fashion." This squadron, of twenty-two ships, convoyed to America the Spanish fleet assembled at Ferrol, and the reinforcement prevented the English from attacking.[7] "Still, Fleuri made explanations to Walpole and hoped for compromise,—an ill-founded hope, which had disastrous results for our sea interests, and prevented measures which would have given France, from the beginning of the war, the superiority in eastern seas." But "upon Walpole's overthrow," says another Frenchman, "Fleuri perceived his mistake in letting the navy decay. Its importance had lately struck him. He knew that the kings of Naples and Sardinia forsook the French alliance merely because an English squadron threatened to bombard Naples and Genoa and to bring an army into Italy. For lack of this element of greatness, France silently swallowed the greatest humiliations, and could only complain of the violence of English cruisers, which pillaged our commerce, in violation of the law of nations," [8] during the years of

[6] Martin: History of France.

[7] The peculiar political relation which France bore toward England between 1739 and 1744, while the latter country was at war with Spain, needs to be explained, as it depended upon views of international duties which are practically obsolete. By her defensive alliance with Spain, France had bound herself to furnish a contingent of specified force to the Spanish fleet when that country was involved in war of a certain kind. She claimed, however, that her sending these succors was not such an act of hostility to England as involved a breach of the peace existing between the two nations. The French ships-of-war, while thus serving with the Spanish fleet under the terms of the treaty, were enemies; but the French nation and all other armed forces of France, on sea and land, were neutrals, with all the privileges of neutrality. Of course England was not bound to accept this view of the matter, and could make the action of France a *casus belli;* but France claimed it was not justly so, and England practically conceded the claim, though the relation was likely to lead to formal war, as it did in 1744. A few years later the Dutch will be found claiming the same privilege of neutrality toward France while furnishing a large contingent to the Austrian army acting against her.

[8] La Pérouse-Bonfils: Hist. de la Marine Française.

nominal peace that elapsed between the time when the French fleet was confined to protecting the Spanish against the English and the outbreak of formal war. The explanation of these differing views seems not very hard. The two ministers had tacitly agreed to follow lines which apparently could not cross. France was left free to expand by land, provided she did not excite the jealousy of the English people, and Walpole's own sense of English interests, by rivalry at sea. This course suited Fleuri's views and wishes. The one sought power by sea, the other by land. Which had been wiser, war was to show; for, with Spain as an ally to one party, war had to come, and that on the sea. Neither minister lived to see the result of his policy. Walpole was driven from power in 1742, and died in March, 1745. Fleuri died in office, January 29, 1743.

7

War between Great Britain and Spain, 1739—
War of the Austrian Succession, 1740—France
Joins Spain against Great Britain, 1744—Sea
Battles of Matthews, Anson, and Hawke—
Peace of Aix-la-Chapelle, 1748

We have now reached the opening of a series of great wars, destined to last with short intervals of peace for nearly half a century, and having, amid many misleading details, one broad characteristic distinguishing them from previous, and from many subsequent, wars. This strife embraced the four quarters of the world, and that not only as side issues here and there, the main struggle being in Europe; for the great questions to be determined by it, concerning the world's history, were the dominion of the sea and the control of distant countries, the possession of colonies, and, dependent upon these, the increase of wealth. Singularly enough it is not till nearly the end of the long contest that great fleets are found engaging, and the struggle transferred to its proper field, the sea. The action of sea power is evident enough, the issue plainly indicated from the beginning; but for a long time there is no naval warfare of any consequence, because the truth is not recognized by the French government. The movement toward colonial extension by France is wholly popular, though illustrated by a few great names; the attitude of the rulers is cold and mistrustful: hence came neglect of the navy, a foregone conclusion of defeat on the main question, and destruction for the time of her sea power.

Such being the character of the coming wars, it is important to realize the relative positions of the three great powers in those quarters of the world, outside of Europe, where the strife was to engage.

In North America, England now held the thirteen colonies, the original United States, from Maine to Georgia. In these colonies was to be found the highest development of that form of colonization peculiar to England, bodies of free men essentially self-governing and self-dependent, still enthusiastically loyal, and by occupation at once agricultural, commercial, and sea-faring. In the character of their country and its productions, in its long sea-coast and sheltered harbors, and in their own selves, they had all the elements of sea power, which had already received large development. On such a country and such a people the royal navy and army were securely based in the western hemisphere. The English colonists were intensely jealous of the French and Canadians.

France held Canada and Louisiana, a name much more extensive in its application then than now, and claimed the entire valley of the Ohio and Mississippi, by right of prior discovery, and as a necessary link between the St. Lawrence and the Gulf of Mexico. There was as yet no adequate occupation of this intermediate country, nor was the claim admitted by England, whose colonists asserted the right to extend indefinitely westward. The strength of the French position was in Canada; the St. Lawrence gave them access to the heart of the country, and though Newfoundland and Nova Scotia had been lost, in Cape Breton Island they still held the key of the gulf and river. Canada had the characteristics of the French colonial system planted in a climate least suited to it. A government paternal, military, and monkish discouraged the development of individual enterprise and of free association for common ends. The colonists abandoned commerce and agriculture, raising only food enough for immediate consumption, and were given to arms and hunting. Their chief traffic was in furs. There was so little mechanical art among them that they bought of the English colonies part of the vessels for their interior navigation. The chief element of strength was the military, arms-bearing character of the population; each man was a soldier.

Besides the hostility inherited from the mother-countries, there was a necessary antagonism between two social and political systems, so directly opposed, and lying one alongside the other. The remoteness of Canada from the West Indies, and the inhospitable winter climate, made it, from the naval point of view, of much less value to France than the English colonies to England; besides which the resources and population were greatly inferior. In 1750 the population of Canada was eighty thousand, that of the English colonies twelve hundred thousand. With such disparity of strength and resources, the only chance for Canada lay in the support of the sea power of France, either by direct control of the neighboring seas, or by such powerful diversion elsewhere as would relieve the pressure upon her.

On the continent of North America, in addition to Mexico and the countries south of it, Spain held Florida; under which name were embraced extensive regions beyond the peninsula, not accurately defined, and having little importance at any period of these long wars.

In the West Indies and South America, Spain held mainly what are still known as Spanish American countries, besides Cuba, Porto Rico, and port of Hayti; France had Guadeloupe, Martinique, and the western half of Hayti; England, Jamaica, Barbadoes, and some of the smaller islands. The fertile character of the soil, the commercial productions, and the less rigorous climate would seem to make these islands objects of particular ambition in a colonial war; but as a matter of fact no attempt was made, nor, except as to Jamaica, which Spain wished to recover, was any intention entertained of conquering any of the larger islands. The reason probably was that England, whose sea power made her the principal aggressor, was influenced in the direction of her efforts by the wishes of the great body of Englishmen on the North American continent. The smaller West India islands are singly too small to be strongly held except by a power controlling the sea. They had a twofold value in war: one as offering military positions for such a power; the other a commercial value, either as adding to one's own resources or diminishing those of the enemy. War directed against them may be considered as a war upon commerce, and the islands themselves as ships or convoys loaded with enemy's wealth. They will be found therefore changing hands like counters, and usually restored when peace comes; though the final result was to leave most of them in the hands of England. Nevertheless, the fact of each of the great powers having a share in this focus of commerce drew thither both large fleets and small squadrons, a tendency aided by the unfavorable seasons for military operations on the continent; and in the West Indies took place the greater number of the fleet-actions that illustrated this long series of wars.

In yet another remote region was the strife between England and France to be waged, and there, as in North America, finally decided by these wars. In India, the rival nations were represented by their East India companies, who directly administered both government and commerce. Back of them, of course, were the mother-countries; but in immediate contact with the native rulers were the presidents and officers appointed by the companies. At this time the principal settlements of the English were,—on the west coast, Bombay; on the east, Calcutta upon the Ganges, at some distance from the sea, and Madras; while a little south of Madras another town and station, known generally to the English as Fort St. David, though sometimes called Cuddalore, had been established later. The three presidencies of Bombay, Calcutta, and Madras were at this time mutually independent, and responsible only to the Court of Directors in England.

France was established at Chandernagore, on the Ganges, above Calcutta; at Pondicherry, on the east coast, eighty miles south of Madras; and on the west coast, far to the south of Bombay, she had a third station of inferior importance, called Mahé. The French, however, had a great advantage in the possession of the intermediate station already pointed out in the Indian Ocean, the neighboring islands of France and Bourbon. They were yet more fortunate in the personal character of the two men who were at this time at the head of their affairs, in the Indian peninsula and the islands, Dupleix and La Bourdonnais,—men to whom no rivals in ability or force of character had as yet appeared among the English Indian officials. Yet in these two men, whose cordial fellow-working might have ruined the English settlement in India, there appeared again that singular conflict of ideas, that hesitation between the land and the sea as the stay of power, a prophecy of which seems to be contained in the geographical position of France itself. The mind of Dupleix, though not inattentive to commercial interests, was fixed on building up a great empire in which France should rule over a multitude of vassal native princes. In the pursuit of this end he displayed great tact and untiring activity, perhaps also a somewhat soaring and fantastic imagination; but when he met La Bourdonnais, whose simpler and sounder views aimed at sea supremacy, at a dominion based upon free and certain communication with the home country instead of the shifting sands of Eastern intrigues and alliances, discord at once arose. "Naval inferiority," says a French historian who considers Dupleix to have had the higher aims, "was the principal cause that arrested his progress";[1] but naval superiority was precisely the point at which La Bourdonnais, himself a seaman and the governor of an island, aimed. It may be that with the weakness of Canada, compared to the English colonies, sea power could not there have changed the actual issue; but in the condition of the rival nations in India everything depended upon controlling the sea.

Such were the relative situations of the three countries in the principal foreign theatres of war. No mention has been made of the colonies on the west coast of Africa, because they were mere trading stations having no military importance. The Cape of Good Hope was in possession of the Dutch, who took no active part in the earlier wars, but long maintained toward England a benevolent neutrality, surviving from the alliance in the former wars of the century. It is necessary to mention briefly the condition of the military navies, which were to have an importance as yet unrealized. Neither precise numbers nor an exact account of condition of the ships, can be given; but the relative efficiency can be fairly estimated. Campbell, the English contemporary naval historian, says that in 1727 the English navy had eighty-four ships-of-the-line, from sixty guns up; forty 50-gun ships, and fifty-four frigates and smaller vessels. In 1734 this number had fallen to seventy ships-of-the-line and nineteen 50-gun ships. In 1744, after four years of war with Spain alone, the number was ninety ships-of-the-line and eighty-four frigates. The French navy at the same time he estimates at forty-five ships-of-the-line and sixty-seven frigates. In 1747, near the end of the first war, he says that the royal navy of Spain was reduced to twenty-two ships-of-the-line, that of France to thirty-one, while the English had risen to one hundred and twenty-six. The French

[1] Martin: History of France.

writers consulted are less precise in their figures, but agree in representing not only that the navy was reduced to a pitiful number of ships, but that these were in bad condition and the dock-yards destitute of materials. This neglect of the navy lasted more or less throughout these wars, until 1760, when the sense of the nation was aroused to the importance of restoring it; too late, however, to prevent the most serious of the French losses. In England as well as in France discipline and administration had been sapped by the long peace; the inefficiency of the armaments sent out was notorious, and recalls the scandals that marked the outbreak of the Crimean War; while the very disappearance of the French ships led, by the necessity of replacing them, to putting afloat vessels superior singly, because more modern and scientific, to the older ships of the same class in England. Care must be had, however, in accepting too easily the complaints of individual writers; French authors will be found asserting that English ships are faster, while at the same period Englishmen complain that they are slower. It may be accepted as generally true that the French ships built between 1740 and 1800 were better designed and larger, class for class, than the English. The latter had the undoubted superiority both in the number and quality of the seamen and officers. Keeping some fleets always afloat, whether better or worse, the officers could not quite lose touch with their profession; whereas in France it is said that not one fifth of the officers were, in 1744, employed. This superiority was kept and increased by the practice, which henceforth obtained, of blockading the French military ports with superior force; the enemy's squadrons when they put to sea found themselves at once at a disadvantage in point of practical skill. On the other hand, large as was the number of English seamen, the demands of commerce were so great that war found them scattered all over the world, and part of the fleet was always paralyzed for lack of crews. This constant employment assured good seamanship, but the absence of so many men had to be supplied by an indiscriminate press, which dragged in a class of miserable and sickly men, sadly diluting the quality of the whole. To realize the condition of ships' companies of that day, it will be necessary only to read the accounts of those sent to Anson starting for a cruise round the world, or to Hawke when fitting out for war service; the statements are now almost incredible, and the results most deplorable. It was not a question of sanitation only; the material sent was entirely unfit to meet the conditions of sea life under the most favorable circumstances. In both the French and English service a great deal of weeding among the officers was necessary. Those were the palmy days of court and political influence; and, moreover, it is not possible, after a long peace, at once to pick out from among the fairest-seeming the men who will best stand the tests of time and exposure to the responsibilities of war. There was in both nations a tendency to depend upon officers who had been in their prime a generation before, and the results were not fortunate.

War having been declared against Spain by England in October, 1739, the first attempts of the latter power were naturally directed against the Spanish-American colonies, the cause of the dispute, in which it was expected to find an easy and rich prey. The first expedition sailed under Admiral Vernon in November of the same year, and took Porto Bello by a sudden and audacious stroke, but found only the insignificant sum of ten thousand dollars in the port whence the galleons sailed. Returning to Jamaica, Vernon received large reinforcements of ships, and was joined by a land force of twelve thousand troops. With this increased force, attempts were made upon both Cartagena and Santiago de Cuba, in the years 1741 and 1742, but in both wretched failures resulted; the admiral and the general quarrelled, as was not uncommon in days when neither had an intelligent comprehension of the other's business. Marryat, when characterizing such misunderstandings by a humorous exaggeration, seems to have had in view this attempt on Cartagena: "The army thought that the navy might have beaten down stone ramparts ten feet thick; and the navy wondered why the army had not walked up the same ramparts, which were thirty feet perpendicular."

Another expedition, justly celebrated for the endurance and perseverance shown by its leader, and famous both for the hardships borne and singular final success, was sent out in 1740 under Anson. Its mission was to pass round Cape Horn and attack the Spanish colonies on the west coast of South America. After many delays, due apparently to bad administration, the squadron finally got away toward the end of 1740. Passing the Cape at the worst season of the year, the ships met a series of tempests of the most violent kind; the squadron was scattered, never all to meet again, and

Anson, after infinite peril, succeeded in rallying a part of it at Juan Fernandez. Two ships had put back to England, a third was lost to the southward of Chiloe. With the three left to him he cruised along the South American coast, taking some prizes and pillaging the town of Payta, intending to touch near Panama and join hands with Vernon for the capture of that place and the possession of the isthmus, if possible. Learning of the disaster at Cartagena, he then determined to cross the Pacific and waylay the two galleons that sailed yearly from Acapulco to Manila. In the passage across, one of the two ships now left to him was found in such bad condition that she had to be destroyed. With the other he succeeded in his last undertaking, capturing the great galleon with a million and a half dollars in specie. The expedition, from its many misfortunes, had no military result beyond the terror and consequent embarrassment caused to the Spanish settlements; but its very misfortunes, and the calm persistency which worked out a great success from them all, have given it a well-deserved renown.

During the year 1740 happened two events which led to a general European war breaking in upon that in which Spain and England were already engaged. In May of that year Frederick the Great became king of Prussia, and in October the emperor Charles VI., formerly the Austrian claimant of the Spanish throne, died. He had no son, and left by will the sovereignty of his estates to his eldest daughter, the celebrated Maria Theresa, to secure whose succession the efforts of his diplomacy had been directed for many years. This succession had been guaranteed by the European powers; but the apparent weakness of her position excited the ambitions of other sovereigns. The Elector of Bavaria laid claim to the whole inheritance, in which he was supported by France; while the Prussian king claimed and seized the province of Silesia. Other powers, large and small, threw in their lot with one or the other; while the position of England was complicated by her king being also elector of Hanover, and in that capacity hurriedly contracting an obligation of neutrality for the electorate, although English feeling was strongly in favor of Austria. Meanwhile the failure of the Spanish-American expeditions and the severe losses of English commerce increased the general outcry against Walpole, who resigned early in 1742. England under the new ministry became the open ally of Austria; and Parliament voted not only a subsidy to the empress-queen, but also a body of troops to be sent as auxiliaries to the Austrian Netherlands. At the same time Holland, under English influence, and bound like England by previous treaties to support the succession of Maria Theresa, also voted a subsidy. Here occurs again that curious view of international relations before mentioned. Both of these powers thus entered the war against France, but only as auxiliaries to the empress, not as principals; as nations, except the troops actually in the field, they were considered to be still at peace. Such an equivocal situation could in the end have only one result. On the sea France had already assumed the same position of auxiliary to Spain, in virtue of the defensive alliance between the two kingdoms, while affecting still to be at peace with England; and it is curious to see the gravity with which French writers complain of assaults upon French by English ships, upon the plea that there was no open war between the two States. It has already been mentioned that in 1740 a French squadron supported a division of Spanish ships on their way to America. In 1741, Spain, having now entered the continental war as an enemy of Austria, sent a body of fifteen thousand troops from Barcelona to attack the Austrian possessions in Italy. The English admiral Haddock, in the Mediterranean, sought and found the Spanish fleet; but with it was a division of twelve French sail-of-the-line, whose commander informed Haddock that he was engaged in the same expedition and had orders to fight, if the Spaniards, though formally at war with England, were attacked. As the allies were nearly double his force, the English admiral was obliged to go back to Port Mahon. He was soon after relieved; and the new admiral, Matthews, held at once the two positions of commander-in-chief in the Mediterranean and English minister at Turin, the capital of the king of Sardinia. In the course of the year 1742 an English captain in his fleet, chasing some Spanish galleys, drove them into the French port of St. Tropez, and following them into the harbor, burned them, in spite of the so-called neutrality of France. In the same year Matthews sent a division of ships under Commodore Martin to Naples, to compel the Bourbon king to withdraw his contingent of twenty thousand troops serving with the Spanish army in northern Italy against the Austrians. To the attempts to negotiate, Martin replied only by pulling out his watch and giving the government an hour to come to terms. There was nothing for it but submission; and the English fleet left the harbor after a stay of twenty-four hours, having relieved the empress of a dangerous enemy. Henceforward it was evident that the Spanish war in Italy could only be maintained by sending troops through France; England controlled the sea and the action of Naples. These two last incidents, at St. Tropez and Naples, deeply impressed the aged Fleuri, who recognized too late the scope and importance of a well-founded sea power. Causes of complaint were multiplying on both sides, and the moment was fast approaching when both France and England must quit the pretence of being only auxiliaries in the war. Before it came to that, however, the controlling sea power and wealth of England again made itself felt by attaching the king of Sardinia to the Austrian cause. Between the dangers and advantages of the French or English alliance the king's action was determined by a subsidy and the promise of a strong English fleet in the Mediterranean; in return he engaged to enter the war with an army of forty-five thousand men. This compact was signed in September, 1743. In October, Fleuri being now dead, Louis XV. made with Spain a treaty, by which he engaged to declare war against England and Sardinia, and to support the Spanish claims in Italy, as also to Gibraltar, Mahon, and Georgia. Open war was thus near at hand, but the declaration was still deferred. The greatest sea fight that took place occurred while nominal peace yet existed.

In the latter part of 1743 the Infante Philip of Spain had sought to land on the coast of the Genoese Republic, which was unfriendly to the Austrians; but the attempt had been frustrated by the English fleet, and the Spanish ships forced to retreat into Toulon. They lay there for four months, unable to go out on account of the English superiority. In this dilemma the court of Spain applied to Louis XV. and obtained an order for the French fleet, under the command of Admiral de Court,—an old man of eighty years, a veteran of the days of Louis XIV.,—to escort the Spaniards either to the Gulf of Genoa or to their own ports, it does not clearly appear which. The French admiral was ordered not to fire unless he was attacked. In order to secure the best co-operation of the Spaniards, whose efficiency he probably distrusted, De Court proposed, as Ruyter had done in days long gone by, to scatter their ships among his own; but as the Spanish admiral, Navarro, refused, the line-of-battle was formed with nine French ships in the van, in the centre six French and three Spaniards, in the rear nine Spanish ships; in all, twenty-seven. In this order the combined fleets sailed from Toulon February 19, 1744. The English fleet, which had been cruising off Hyères in observation, chased, and on the 22d its van and centre came up with the allies; but the rear division was then several miles to windward and astern, quite out of supporting distance (Plate VII., r). The wind was easterly, both fleets heading to the southward, and the English had the weather-gage. The numbers were nearly equal, the English having twenty-nine to the allied twenty-seven; but this advantage was reversed by the failure of the English rear to join. The course of the rear-admiral has been generally attributed to ill-will toward Matthews; for although he proved that in his separated position he made all sail to join, he did not attack later on when he could, on the plea that the signal for the line-of-battle was flying at the same time as the signal to engage; meaning that he could not leave the line to fight without disobeying the order to form line. This technical excuse was, however, accepted by the subsequent courtmartial. Under the actual conditions Matthews, mortified and harassed by the inaction of his lieutenant, and fearing that the enemy would escape if he delayed longer, made the signal to engage when his own van was abreast the enemy's centre, and at once bore down himself out of the line and attacked with his flag-ship of ninety guns the largest ship in the enemy's line, the "Royal Philip," of one hundred and ten guns, carrying the flag of the Spanish admiral (a). In doing this he was bravely supported by his next ahead and astern. The moment of attack seems to have been judiciously chosen; five Spanish ships had straggled far to the rear, leaving their admiral with the support only of his next ahead and astern, while three other Spaniards continued on with the French. The English van stood on, engaging the allied centre, while the allied van was without antagonists. Being thus disengaged, the latter was desirous of tacking to windward of the head of the English line, thus putting it between two fires, but was checked by the intelligent action of the three leading English captains, who, disregarding the signal to bear down, kept their commanding position and stopped the enemy's attempts to double. For this they were cashiered by the court-martial, but afterward restored. This circumspect but justifiable disregard of signals was imitated without any justification by all the English captains of the centre, save the admiral's seconds

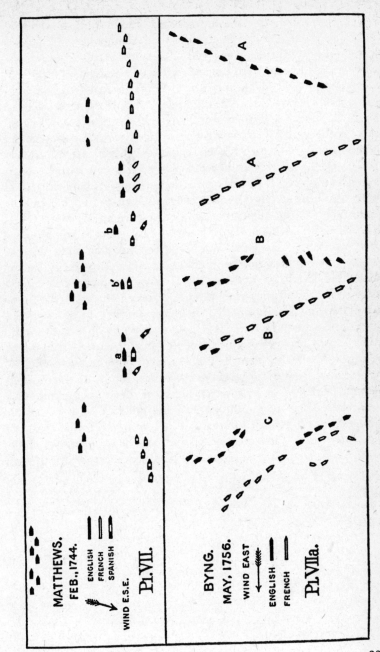

MATTHEWS.
FEB., 1744.

ENGLISH
FRENCH
SPANISH

WIND E.S.E.

Pl. VII.

BYNG.
MAY, 1756.

WIND EAST

ENGLISH
FRENCH

Pl. VIIa.

already mentioned, as well as by some of those in the van, who kept up a cannonade at long range while their commander-in-chief was closely and even furiously engaged. The one marked exception was Captain Hawke, afterward the distinguished admiral, who imitated the example of his chief, and after driving his first antagonist out of action, quitted his place in the van (b), brought to close quarters (b') a fine Spanish ship that had kept at bay five other English ships, and took her,—the only prize made that day. The commander of the English van, with his seconds, also behaved with spirit and came to close action. It is unnecessary to describe the battle further; as a military affair it deserves no attention, and its most important result was to bring out the merit of Hawke, whom the king and the government always remembered for his share in it. The general inefficiency and wide-spread misbehavior of the English captains, after five years of declared war, will partly explain the failure of England to obtain from her undoubted naval superiority the results she might have expected in this war—the first act in a forty years' drama—and they give military officers a lesson on the necessity of having their minds prepared and stocked, by study of the conditions of war in their own day, if they would not be found unready and perhaps disgraced in the hour of battle.[2] It is not to be supposed that so many English seamen misbehaved through so vulgar and rare a defect as mere cowardice; it was unpreparedness of mind and lack of military efficiency in the captains, combined with bad leadership on the part of the admiral, with a possible taint of ill will toward him as a rude and domineering superior, that caused this fiasco. Attention may here fitly be drawn to the effect of a certain cordiality and good-will on the part of superiors

[2] There is not in modern naval history a more striking warning to the officers of every era, than this battle of Toulon. Coming as it did after a generation of comparative naval inactivity, it tried men's reputation as by fire. The lesson, in the judgment of the author, is the danger of disgraceful failure to men who have neglected to keep themselves prepared, not only in knowledge of their profession, but in the sentiment of what war requires. The average man is not a coward; but neither is he endowed by nature only with the rare faculty of seizing intuitively the proper course at a critical moment. He gains it, some more, some less, by experience or by reflection. If both have been lacking to him, indecision will follow; either from not knowing what to do, or from failure to realize that utter self-devotion of himself and his command are required. Of one of the captains cashiered it is said: "No man had ever lived with a fairer or more honorable character previous to the unfortunate event which did such irreparable injury to his reputation. Many of his contemporaries, men in the highest popular estimation, who knew him well, could scarcely credit what were indisputably established as facts, and declared, with the utmost astonishment, 'they believed it next to impossible for Captain Burrish to behave otherwise than as a man of gallantry and intrepidity'." He had been twenty-five years in service, and eleven afloat as a captain (Charnock's Biographia Nevalis). Others of the condemned men bore fair characters; and even Richard Norris, who absconded to avoid trial, had been of respectable repute.

toward their subordinates. It is not perhaps essential to military success, but it undoubtedly contributes to the other elements of that success a spirit, a breath of life, which makes possible what would otherwise be impossible; which reaches heights of devotion and achievement that the strictest discipline, not so enkindled, cannot attain. Doubtless it is a natural gift. The highest example of it possibly ever known among seamen was Nelson. When he joined the fleet just before Trafalgar, the captains who gathered on board the flag-ship seemed to forget the rank of their admiral in their desire to testify their joy at meeting him. "This Nelson," wrote Captain Duff, who fell in the battle, "is so lovable and excellent a man, so kindly a leader, that we all wish to exceed his desires and anticipate his orders." He himself was conscious of this fascination and its value, when writing of the battle of the Nile to Lord Howe, he said, "I had the happiness to command a band of brothers."

The celebrity attained by Matthews's action off Toulon, certainly not due to the skill with which it was managed, nor to its results, sprang from the clamor at home, and chiefly from the number and findings of the courts-martial that followed. Both the admiral and his second, and also eleven captains out of the twenty-nine, had charges preferred against them. The admiral was cashiered because he had broken the line; that is, because his captains did not follow him when he left it to get at the enemy,—a decision that smacks more of the Irish bull than of the Irish love of fighting. The second was acquitted on the technical grounds already given; he avoided the fault of breaking the line by keeping far enough away. Of the eleven captains one died, one deserted, seven were dismissed or suspended, two only were acquitted. Nor were the French and Spaniards better pleased; mutual recriminations passed. Admiral de Court was relieved from his command, while the Spanish admiral was decorated by his government with the title of Marquis de la Victoria, a most extraordinary reward for what was at best a drawn fight. The French, on the other hand, assert that he left the deck on the plea of a very slight wound, and that the ship was really fought by a French captain who happened to be on board.

To use a common expression, this battle, the first general action since that off Malaga forty years before, "woke up" the English people and brought about a healthful reaction. The sifting process begun by the battle itself was continued, but the result was reached too late to have its proper effect on the current war. It is rather by its deficient action, than by such conspicuous successes as were attained in earlier and later times, that the general value of England's sea power is now shown; like some precious faculty, scarcely valued when possessed, but keenly missed when withdrawn. Mistress now of the seas rather by the weakness of her enemies than by her own disciplined strength, she drew from that mastery on adequate results; the most solid success, the capture of Cape Breton Island, in 1745, was achieved by the colonial forces of New England, to which indeed the royal navy lent valuable aid, for to troops so situated the fleet is the one line of communication. The misconduct off Toulon was repeated by officers high in command in the West and East Indies, resulting in the latter case in the loss of Madras. Other causes concurred with the effete condition of the naval officers to hamper the action of that sea power which launches out far from home. The condition of England itself was insecure; the cause of the Stuarts was still alive, and though a formidable invasion by fifteen thousand troops under Marshal Saxe, in 1744, was foiled, partly by the English Channel fleet, and party by a storm which wrecked several of the transports assembled off Dunkirk, with the loss of many lives, yet the reality of the danger was shown in the following year, when the Pretender landed in Scotland with only a few man at his back and the northern kingdom rose with him. His successful invasion was carried well down into England itself; and sober historians have thought that at one time the chances of ultimate success were rather with than against him. Another serious fetter upon the full use of England's power was the direction given to the French operations on land and the mistaken means used to oppose them. Neglecting Germany, France turned upon the Austrian Netherlands, a country which England, out of regard to her sea interests, was not willing to see conquered. Her commercial preponderance would be directly threatened by the passing of Antwerp, Ostend, and the Scheldt into the hands of her great rival; and though her best check against this would have been to seize valuable French possessions elsewhere and hold them as a pledge, the weakness of her government and the present inefficiency of the navy prevented her doing so. The position of Hanover, again, controlled the action of England; for though united only by the tie of a common sovereign, the love of that sovereign for his continental dominion, his native country, made itself strongly felt in the councils of a weak and time-serving ministry. It was the disregard of Hanover by the first William Pitt, consequent upon his strong English feeling, that incensed the king and led him so long to resist the demands of the nation that he should be put at the head of affairs. These different causes—dissension at home, interest in the Netherlands, regard for Hanover—combined to prevent a subservient and second-rate ministry, divided also among themselves, from giving a proper direction and infusing a proper spirit into the naval war; but a better condition of the navy itself, more satisfactory results from it, might have modified even their action. As it was, the outcome of the war was almost nothing as regards the disputes between England and her special enemies. On the continent, the questions after 1745 reduced themselves to two,—what part of the Austrian possessions should be given to Prussia, Spain, and Sardinia, and how peace was to be wrenched by France from England and Holland. The sea countries still, as of old, bore the expenses of the war, which however new fell chiefly upon England. Marshal Saxe, who commanded the French in Flanders throughout this war, summed up the situation in half a dozen words to his king. "Sire," said he, "peace is within the walls of Maestricht." This strong city opened the course of the Meuse and the way for the French army into the United Provinces from the rear; for the English fleet, in conjunction with that of Holland, prevented an attack from the sea. By the end of 1746, despite the efforts of the allies, nearly all Belgium was in the hands of the French; but up to this time, although Dutch subsidies were supporting the Austrian government, and Dutch troops in the Netherlands were fighting for it, there was nominal peace between the United Provinces and France. In April, 1747, "the King of France invaded Dutch Flanders, announcing that he was obliged to send his army into the territory of the republic, to arrest the protection granted by the States-General to the Austrian and English troops; but that he had no intention of breaking with it, and that the places and provinces occupied would be restored to the United Provinces as soon as they gave proof that they had ceased to succor the enemies of France." This was actual, but not formal, war. Numerous places fell during the year, and the successes of the French inclined both Holland and England to come to terms. Negotiations went on during the winter;

but in April, 1748, Saxe invested Maestricht. This forced a peace.

Meanwhile, though languishing, the sea war was not wholly uneventful. Two encounters between English and French squadrons happened during the year 1747, completing the destruction of the French fighting navy. In both cases the English were decidedly superior; and though there was given opportunity for some brilliant fighting by particular captains, and for the display of heroic endurance on the part of the French, greatly outnumbered but resisting to the last, only one tactical lesson is afforded. This lesson is, that when an enemy, either as the result of battle or from original inequality, is greatly inferior in force, obliged to fly without standing on the order of his flying, the regard otherwise due to order must be in a measure at least dismissed, and a general chase ordered. The mistake of Tourville in this respect after Beachy Head has already been noted. In the first of the cases now under discussion, the English admiral Anson had fourteen ships against eight French, weaker individually as well as in total number; in the second, Sir Edward Hawke had fourteen against nine, the latter being somewhat larger, ship for ship, than the English. In both cases the signal was made for a general chase, and the action which resulted was a *mêlée*. There was no opportunity for anything else; the one thing necessary was to overtake the running enemy, and that can only certainly be done by letting the fleetest or best situated ships get ahead, sure that the speed of the fastest pursuers is better than that of the slowest of the pursued, and that therefore either the latter must be abandoned or the whole force brought to bay. In the second case the French commander, Commodore L'Étenduère, did not have to be followed far. He had with him a convoy of two hundred and fifty merchant-ships; detaching one ship-of-the-line to continue the voyage with the convoy, he placed himself with the other eight between it and the enemy, awaiting the attack under his topsails. As the English came up one after another they divided on either side of the French column, which was thus engaged on both sides. After an obstinate resistance, six of the French ships were taken, but the convoy was saved. The English had been so roughly handled that the two remaining French men-of-war got back safely to France. If, therefore, Sir Edward Hawke showed in his attack the judgment and dash which always distinguished that remarkable officer, it may be claimed for Commodore L'Étenduère that fortune, in assigning him the glorious disadvantage of numbers, gave him also the leading part in the drama, and that he filled it nobly. A French officer justly remarks that "he defended his convoy as on shore a position is defended, when the aim is to save an army corps or to assure an evolution; he gave himself to be crushed. After an action that lasted from mid-day till eight P.M. the convoy was saved, thanks to the obstinacy of the defence; two hundred and fifty ships were saved to their owners by the devotion of L'Étenduère and of the captains under his orders. This devotion cannot be questioned, for eight ships had but few chances of surviving an action with fourteen; and not only did the commander of the eight accept an action which he might possibly have avoided, but he knew how to inspire his lieutenants with trust in him; for all supported the strife with honor, and yielded at last, showing the most indisputable proofs of their fine and energetic defence. Four ships were entirely dismasted, two had only the foremast standing." [3] The whole affair, as conducted on both sides, affords an admirable study of how to follow up an advantage, original or acquired, and of the results that may be obtained by a gallant, even hopeless defence, for the furtherance of a particular object. It may be added that Hawke, disabled from further pursuit himself, sent a sloop of war express to the West Indies, with information of the approach of the convoy,— a step which led to the capture of part of it, and gives a touch of completeness to the entire transaction, which cannot fail to be gratifying to a military student interested in seeing the actors in history fully alive to and discharging to the utmost their important tasks.

Before bringing to a close the story of this war and mentioning the peace settlement, an account must be given of the transactions in India, where France and England were then on equal terms. It has been said that affairs there were controlled by the East India companies of either nation; and that the French were represented in the peninsula by Dupleix, in the islands by La Bourdonnais. The latter was appointed to his post in 1735, and his untiring genius had been felt in all the details of administration, but especially in converting the Isle of France into a great naval station,—a work which had to be built up from the foundations. Everything was wanting; everything was by him in greater or less measure supplied,—storehouses, dock-yards, fortifications, seamen. In 1740, when war between France

[3] Troude: Batailles Navales de la France.

and England became probable, he obtained from the East India Company a squadron, though smaller than he asked, with which he proposed to ruin the English commerce and shipping; but when war actually began in 1744, he received orders not to attack the English, the French company hoping that neutrality might exist between the companies in that distant region, though the nations were at war. The proposition does not seem absurd in view of the curious relations of Holland to France, nominally at peace while sending troops to the Austrian army; but it was much to the advantage of the English, who were inferior in the Indian seas. Their company accepted the proffer, while saying that it of course could bind neither the home government nor the royal navy. The advantage won by the forethought of La Bourdonnais was thus lost; though first, and long alone, on the field, his hand was stayed. Meanwhile the English admiralty sent out a squadron and began to seize French ships between India and China; not till then did the company awake from its illusion. Having done this part of its work, the English squadron sailed to the coast of India, and in July, 1745, appeared off Pondicherry, the political capital of French India, prepared to sustain an attack which the governor of Madras was about to make by land. La Bourdonnais' time was now come.

Meanwhile, on the mainland of the Indian peninsula, Dupleix had been forming wide views and laying broad foundations for the establishment of French preponderance. Having entered the service of their company at first in a subordinate clerical position, his ability had raised him by rapid steps to be head of the commercial establishments at Chandernagore, to which he gave a very great enlargement, seriously affecting, it is said even destroying, parts of the English trade. In 1742 he was made governor-general, and as such removed to Pondicherry. Here he began to develop his policy, which aimed at bringing India under the power of France. He saw that through the progress and extension of the European races over the seas of the whole world the time had come when the Eastern peoples must be brought into ever-increasing contact with them; and he judged that India, so often conquered before, was now about to be conquered by Europeans. He meant that France should win the prize, and saw in England the only rival. His plan was to meddle in Indian politics: first, as head of a foreign and independent colony, which he already was; and second, as a vassal of the Great Mogul, which he intended to become. To divide and conquer, to advance the French lines and influence by judicious alliances, to turn wavering scales by throwing in on one side or the other the weight of French courage and skill,—such were his aims. Pondicherry, though a poor harbor, was well adapted for his political plans; being far distant from Delhi, the capital of the Mogul, aggressive extension might go on unmarked, until strong enough to bear the light. Dupleix's present aim, therefore, was to build up a great French principality in southeast India, around Pondicherry, while maintaining the present positions in Bengal.

Let it be noted, however,—and the remark is necessary in order to justify the narration of these plans in connection with our subject, a connection perhaps not at first evident,—that the kernel of the question now before Dupleix was not how to build up an empire out of the Indian provinces and races, but how to get rid of the English, and that finally. The wildest dreams of sovereignty he may have entertained could not have surpassed the actual performance of England a few years later. European qualities were bound to tell, if not offset by the opposition of other Europeans; and such opposition on the one side or the other depended upon the control of the sea. In a climate so deadly to the white races, the small numbers whose heroism bore up the war against fearful odds on many a field must be continually renewed. As everywhere and always, the action of sea power was here quiet and unperceived; but it will not be necessary to belittle in the least the qualities and career of Clive, the English hero of this time and the founder of their empire, in order to prove the decisive influence which it exerted, despite the inefficiency of the English naval officers first engaged, and the lack of conclusive results in such naval battles as were fought.[4] If, during the twenty years following 1743, French fleets instead of English had controlled the coasts of the peninsula and the seas between it and Europe, can it be believed that the schemes of Dupleix would

[4] "Notwithstanding the extraordinary effort made by the French in sending out M. Lally with a considerable force last year, I am confident before the end of this [1759] they will be near their last gasp in the Carnatic unless some very unforeseen event interpose in their favor. The *superiority of our squadron* and the plenty of money and supplies of all kinds which our friends on that coast will be furnished with from this province [Bengal], while the enemy are in total want of everything, without any visible means of redress, are such advantages as, if properly attended to, cannot fail of wholly effecting their ruin in that as well as in every other part of India" (Letter of Clive to Pitt, Calcutta, January 7, 1759; Gleig's Life of Lord Clive). It will be remembered that the control and use of Bengal, upon which Clive here counts, had only lately been acquired by the English; in the days of Dupleix they did not possess them. As will be seen later, Clive's predictions in this letter were wholly fulfilled.

have utterly failed? "Naval inferiority," justly says a French historian, "was the principal cause that arrested the progress of Dupleix. The French royal navy did not make its appearance in the East Indies" in his day. It remains to tell the story briefly.

The English, in 1745, made preparations to besiege Pondicherry, in which the royal navy was to support the land forces; but the effects of Dupleix's political schemes were at once seen. The Nabob of the Carnatic threatened to attack Madras, and the English desisted. The following year La Bourdonnais appeared on the scene, and an action took place between his squadron and that under Commodore Peyton; after which, although it had been a drawn fight, the English officer deserted the coast, taking refuge in Ceylon, and leaving the control at sea with the French. La Bourdonnais anchored at Pondicherry, where quarrels between him and Dupleix soon arose, and were aggravated by the conflicting tone of their instructions from home. In September he went to Madras, attacked by land and sea, and took the place, but made with the governor the stipulation that it might be ransomed; and a ransom of two million dollars was accordingly paid. When Dupleix heard of this he was very angry, and claimed to annul the terms of capitulation on the ground that, once taken, the place was within his jurisdiction. La Bourdonnais resented this attempt as dishonorable to him after the promise given. While the quarrel was going on, a violent cyclone wrecked two of his ships and dismasted the rest. He soon after returned to France, where his activity and zeal were repaid by three years' imprisonment under charges, from the effects of which treatment he died. After his departure Dupleix broke the capitulation, seized and kept Madras, drove out the English settlers, and went on to strengthen the fortifications. From Madras he turned against Fort St. David, but the approach of an English squadron compelled him to raise the siege in March, 1747.

During this year the disasters to the French navy in the Atlantic, already related, left the English undisturbed masters of the sea. In the following winter they sent to India the greatest European fleet yet seen in the East, with a large land force, the whole under the command of Admiral Boscawen, who bore a general's commission in addition to his naval rank. The fleet appeared off the Coromandel coast in August, 1748. Pondicherry was attacked by land and sea, but Dupleix made a successful resistance. The English fleet in its turn suffered from a hurricane, and the siege was raised in October. Shortly after came the news of the Peace of Aix-la-Chapelle, which ended the European war. Dupleix, with his home communications restored, could now resume his subtle and persevering efforts to secure a territorial base which should, as far as possible, shelter him from the chances of sea war. Pity that so much genius and patience should have been spent in an effort wholly vain; nothing could protect against that sea attack but a naval aid, which the home government could not give. One of the conditions of the peace was that Madras should be restored to the English in exchange for Louisburg, the prize won by the North American colonists and released by them as reluctantly as Madras was by Dupleix. This was indeed illustrating Napoleon's boast that he would reconquer Pondicherry on the bank of the Vistula; yet, although the maritime supremacy of England made Louisburg in her hands much stronger than Madras, or any other position in India, when held by the French, the gain by the exchange was decidedly on the side of Great Britain. The English colonists were not men to be contented with this action; but they knew the naval power of England, and that they could do again what they had done once, at a point not far distant from their own shores. They understood the state of the case. Not so with Madras. How profound must have been the surprise of the native princes at this surrender, how injurious to the personality of Dupleix and the influence he had gained among them, to see him, in the very hour of victory, forced, by a power they could not understand, to relinquish his spoil! They were quite right; the mysterious power which they recognized by its working, though they saw it not, was not in this or that man, king or statesman, but in that control of the sea which the French government knew forbade the hope of maintaining that distant dependency against the fleets of England. Dupleix himself saw it not; for some years more he continued building, on the sand of Oriental intrigues and lies, a house which he vainly hoped would stand against the storms that must descend upon it.

The Treaty of Aix-la-Chapelle, ending this general war, was signed April 30, 1748, by England, France, and Holland, and finally by all the powers in October of the same year. With the exception of certain portions shorn off the Austrian Empire,—Silesia for Prussia, Parma for the Infante Philip of Spain, and some Italian territory to the east of Piedmont for the king of Sardinia,—the general tenor of the terms was a return to the status before the war. "Never, perhaps, did any war, after so many great events, and so large a loss of blood and treasure, end in replacing the nations engaged in it so nearly in the same situation as they held at first." In truth, as regarded France, England, and Spain, the affair of the Austrian succession, supervening so soon upon the outbreak of war between the two latter, had wholly turned hostilities aside from their true direction and postponed for fifteen years the settlement of disputes which concerned them much more nearly than the accession of Maria Theresa. In the distress of her old enemy, the House of Austria, France was easily led to renew her attacks upon it, and England as easily drawn to oppose the attempts of the French to influence or dictate in German affairs,—a course the more readily followed from the German interests of the king. It may be questioned whether the true policy for France was to direct the war upon the heart of the Austrian Empire, by way of the Rhine and Germany, or, as she finally did, upon the remote possessions of the Netherlands. In the former case she rested on friendly territory in Bavaria, and gave a hand to Prussia, whose military power was now first felt. Such was the first theatre of the war. On the other hand, in the Netherlands, whither the chief scene of hostilities shifted later, France struck not only at Austria, but also at the sea powers, always jealous of her intrusion there. They were the soul of the war against her, by their subsidies to her other enemies and by the losses inflicted on her commerce and that of Spain. The misery of France was alleged to the king of Spain by Louis XV., as forcing him to conclude peace; and it is evident that the suffering must have been great to induce him to yield such easy terms as he did, when he already held the Netherlands and parts of Holland itself by force of arms. But while so successful on the continent, his navy was annihilated and communication with the colonies thus cut off; and though it may be doubted whether the French government of that day cherished the colonial ambitions ascribed to it by some, it is certain French commerce was suffering enormously.

While this was the condition of France, impelling her to peace, England in 1747 found that, from disputes about trade in Spanish America and through the inefficient action of her navy, she had been led away into a continental war, in which she had met with disaster,

246

incurred nearly £80,000,000 of debt, and now saw her ally Holland threatened with invasion. The peace itself was signed under a threat by the French envoy that the slightest delay would be the signal for the French to destroy the fortifications of the captured towns and at once begin the invasion. At the same time her own resources were drained, and Holland, exhausted, was seeking to borrow from her. "Money," we are told, "was never so scarce in the city, and cannot be had at twelve per cent." Had France, therefore, at this time had a navy able to make head against that of England, even though somewhat inferior in strength, she might, with her grip on the Netherlands and Maestricht, have exacted her own conditions. England, on the other hand, though driven to the wall on the continent, was nevertheless able to obtain peace on equal terms, through the control of the sea by her navy.

The commerce of all three nations had suffered enormously, but the balance of prizes in favor of Great Britain was estimated at £2,000,000. Stated in another way, it is said that the combined losses of French and Spanish commerce amounted during the war to 3,434 ships, the English to 3,238; but in considering such figures, the relation they bear to the total merchant shipping of either nation must not be forgotten. A thousand vessels were a very much larger fraction of French shipping than of English, and meant more grievous loss.

"After the disaster to the squadron of L'Étenduère," says a French writer, "the French flag did not appear at sea. Twenty-two ships-of-the-line composed the navy of France, which sixty years before had one hundred and twenty. Privateers made few prizes; followed everywhere, unprotected, they almost always fell a prey to the English. The British naval forces, without any rivals, passed unmolested over the seas. In one year they are said to have taken from French commerce £7,000,000 sterling. Yet this sea power, which might have seized French and Spanish colonies, made few conquests from want of unity and persistence in the direction given them." [5]

To sum up, France was forced to give up her conquests for want of a navy, and England saved her position by her sea power, though she had failed to use it to the best advantage.

[5] La Pérouse-Bonfils: Hist. de la Marine Française.

8

Seven Years' War, 1756-1763—England's Overwhelming Power and Conquests on the Seas
in North America, Europe, and East and West
Indies—Sea Battles: Byng off Minorca; Hawke
and Conflans; Pocock and D'Aché in East Indies

The urgency with which peace was desired by the principal parties
to the War of the Austrian Succession may perhaps be inferred from
the neglect to settle definitely and conclusively many of the questions
outstanding between them, and notably the very disputes about
which the war between England and Spain began. It seems as though
the powers feared to treat thoroughly matters that contained the
germs of future quarrels, lest the discussion should prolong the war
that then existed. England made peace because the fall of Holland
was otherwise inevitable, not because she had enforced, or surrendered, her claims of 1739 against Spain. The right of uninterrupted navigation in West Indian seas, free from any search, was
left undetermined, as were other kindred matters. Not only so, but
the boundaries between the English and French colonies in the
valley of the Ohio, toward Canada, and on the land side of the Nova
Scotian peninsula, remained as vague as they had before been. It
was plain that peace could not last; and by it, if she had saved Holland, England surrendered the control of the sea which she had
won. The true character of the strife, shrouded for a moment by the

continental war, was revealed by the so-called peace; though formally allayed, the contention continued in every part of the world.

In India, Dupleix, no longer able to attack the English openly, sought to undermine their power by the line of policy already described. Mingling adroitly in the quarrels of surrounding princes, and advancing his own power while so doing, he attained by rapid steps to the political control, in 1751, of the southern extremity of India,—a country nearly as large as France. Given the title of Nabob, he now had a place among the princes of the land. "A merely commercial policy was in his eyes a delusion; there could be no middle course between conquest and abandonment." In the course of the same year further grants extended the French power through extensive regions to the north and east, embracing all the coast of Orissa, and made Dupleix ruler of a third of India. To celebrate his triumphs, perhaps also in accordance with his policy of impressing the native mind, he now founded a town and put up a pillar setting forth his successes. But his doings caused the directors of the company only disquietude; instead of the reinforcements he asked for they sent him exhortations to peace; and at about this time Robert Clive, then but twenty-six years old, began to show his genius. The success of Dupleix and his allies became checkered with reverses; the English under Clive's leadership supported the native opponents of the French. The company at home was but little interested in his political schemes, and was annoyed at the failure of dividends. Negotiations were opened at London for a settlement of difficulties, and Dupleix was summoned home; the English government, it is said, making his recall an absolute condition of continued peace. Two days after his departure, in 1754, his successor signed a treaty with the English governor, wholly abandoning his policy, stipulating that neither company should interfere in the internal politics of India, and that all possessions acquired during the war in the Carnatic should be given back to the Mogul. What France thus surrendered was in extent and population an empire, and the mortification of French historians has branded the concession as ignominious; but how could the country have been held, with the English navy cutting off the eagerly desired reinforcements?

In North America, the declaration of peace was followed by renewed agitation, which sprang from and betokened the deep feeling and keen sense of the situation had by the colonists and local authorities on either side. The Americans held to their points with the stubbornness of their race. "There is no repose for our thirteen colonies," wrote Franklin, "so long as the French are masters of Canada." The rival claims to the central unsettled region, which may accurately enough be called the valley of the Ohio, involved, if the English were successful, the military separation of Canada from Louisiana; while on the other hand, occupation by the French, linking the two extremes of their acknowledged possessions, would shut up the English colonists between the Allegheny Mountains and the sea. The issues were apparent enough to leading Americans of that day, though they were more far-reaching than the wisest of them could have foreseen; there is room for curious speculation as to the effect, not only upon America, but upon the whole world, if the French government had had the will, and the French people the genius, effectively to settle and hold the northern and western regions which they then claimed. But while Frenchmen upon the spot saw clearly enough the coming contest and the terrible disadvantage of unequal numbers and inferior navy under which Canada must labor, the home government was blind alike to the value of the colony and to the fact that it must be fought for; while the character and habits of the French settlers, lacking in political activity and unused to begin and carry through measures for the protection of their own interests, did not remedy the neglect of the mother-country. The paternal centralizing system of French rule had taught the colonists to look to the mother-country, and then failed to take care of them. The governors of Canada of that day acted as careful and able military men, doing what they could to supply defects and weaknesses; it is possible that their action was more consistent and well-planned than that of the English governors; but with the carelessness of both home governments, nothing in the end could take the place of the capacity of the English colonists to look out for themselves. It is odd and amusing to read the conflicting statements of English and French historians as to the purposes and aims of the opposing statesmen in these years when the first murmurings of the storm were heard; the simple truth seems to be that one of those conflicts familiarly known to us as irrepressible was at hand, and that both governments would gladly have avoided it. The boundaries might be undetermined; the English colonists were not.

The French governors established posts where they could on the debatable ground, and it was in the course of a dispute over one of these, in 1754, that the name of Washington first appears in history. Other troubles occurred in Nova Scotia, and both home governments then began to awake. In 1755 Braddock's disastrous expedition was directed against Fort Duquesne, now Pittsburg, where Washington had surrendered the year before. Later in the year another collision between the English and French colonists happened near Lake George. Although Braddock's expedition had been first to start, the French government was also moving. In May of the same year a large squadron of ships-of-war, mostly armed *en flûte*,[1] sailed from Brest with three thousand troops, and a new governor, De Vaudreuil, for Canada. Admiral Boscawen had already preceded this fleet, and lay in wait for it off the mouth of the St. Lawrence. There was as yet no open war, and the French were certainly within their rights in sending a garrison to their own colonies; but Boscawen's orders were to stop them. A fog which scattered the French squadron also covered its passage; but two of the ships were seen by the English fleet and captured, June 8, 1755. As soon as this news reached Europe, the French ambassador to London was recalled, but still no declaration of war followed. In July, Sir Edward Hawke was sent to sea with orders to cruise between Ushant and Cape Finisterre, and to seize any French ships-of-the-line he might see; to which were added in August further orders to take all French ships of every kind, men-of-war, privateers, and merchantmen, and to send them into English ports. Before the end of the year, three hundred trading vessels, valued at six million dollars, had been captured, and six thousand French seamen were imprisoned in England,—enough to man nearly ten ships-of-the-line. All this was done while nominal peace still existed. War was not declared until six months later.

France still seemed to submit, but she was biding her time, and preparing warily a severe stroke for which she had now ample provocation. Small squadrons, or detachments of ships, continued to be sent to the West Indies and to Canada, while noisy preparations were made in the dock-yard of Brest, and troops assembled upon the shores of the Channel. England saw herself threatened with invasion,—a menace to which her people have been peculiarly susceptible. The government of the day, weak at best, was singularly

---

[1] That is—with the guns on board, but for the most part not mounted on their carriages, in order to give increased accommodation for troops. When the troops were landed, the guns were mounted.

unfit for waging war, and easily misled as to the real danger. Besides, England was embarrassed, as always at the beginning of a war, not only by the numerous points she had to protect in addition to her commerce, but also by the absence of a large number of her seamen in trading-vessels all over the world. The Mediterranean was therefore neglected; and the French, while making loud demonstrations on the Channel, quietly equipped at Toulon twelve ships-of-the-line, which sailed on the 10th of April, 1756, under Admiral La Galissonière, convoying one hundred and fifty transports with fifteen thousand troops, commanded by the Duke of Richelieu. A week later the army was safely landed in Minorca, and Port Mahon invested, while the fleet established itself in blockade before the harbor.

Practically this was a complete surprise; for though the suspicions of the English government had been at last aroused, its action came too late. The garrison had not been reinforced, and numbered a scant three thousand men, from which thirty-five officers were absent on leave, among them the governor and the colonels of all the regiments. Admiral Byng sailed from Portsmouth with ten ships-of-the-line only three days before the French left Toulon. Six weeks later, when he reached the neighborhood of Port Mahon, his fleet had been increased to thirteen ships-of-the-line, and he had with him four thousand troops. It was already late; a practicable breach had been made in the fortress a week before. When the English fleet came in sight, La Galissonière stood out to meet it and bar the entrance to the harbor.

The battle that followed owes its historical celebrity wholly to the singular and tragic event which arose from it. Unlike Matthews's battle off Toulon, it does afford some tactical instruction, though mainly applicable to the obsolete conditions of warfare under sail; but it is especially linked to the earlier action through the effect produced upon the mind of the unfortunate Byng by the sentence of the court-martial upon Matthews. During the course of the engagement he repeatedly alluded to the censure upon that admiral for leaving the line, and seems to have accepted the judgment as justifying, if not determining, his own course. Briefly, it may be said that the two fleets, having sighted each other on the morning of the 20th of May, were found after a series of manœuvres both on the port tack, with an easterly wind, heading southerly, the French to leeward, between the English and the harbor. Byng ran down in line ahead of the wind, the French remaining by it, so that when the former made the signal to engage, the fleets were not parallel, but formed an angle of from thirty to forty degrees (Plate VIIa., A, A). The attack which Byng by his own account meant to make, each ship against its opposite in the enemy's line, difficult to carry out under any circumstances, was here further impeded by the distance between the two rears being much greater than that between the vans; so that his whole line could not come into action at the same moment. When the signal was made, the van ships kept away in obedience to it, and ran down for the French so nearly head-on (B, B) as to sacrifice their artillery fire in great measure; they received three raking broadsides, and were seriously dismantled aloft. The sixth English ship, counting from the van, had her foretopmast shot away, flew up into the wind, and came aback, stopping and doubling up the rear of the line. Then undoubtedly was the time for Byng, having committed himself to the fight, to have set the example and borne down, just as Farragut did at Mobile when his line was confused by the stopping of the next ahead; but according to the testimony of the flag-captain, Matthews's sentence deterred him. "You see, Captain Gardiner, that the signal for the line is out, and that I am ahead of the ships 'Louisa' and 'Trident'—" [which in the order should have been ahead of him]. "You would not have me, as the admiral of the fleet, run down as if I were going to engage a single ship. It was Mr. Matthews's misfortune to be prejudiced by not carrying down his force together, which I shall endeavor to avoid." The affair thus became entirely indecisive; the English van was separated from the rear and got the brunt of the fight (C). One French authority blames Galissonière for not tacking to windward of the enemy's van and crushing it. Another says he ordered the movement, but that it could not be made from the damage to the rigging; but this seems improbable, as the only injury the French squadron underwent aloft was the loss of one topsail yard, whereas the English suffered very badly. The true reason is probably that given and approved by one of the French authorities on naval warfare. Galissonière considered the support of the land attack on Mahon paramount to any destruction of the English fleet, if he thereby exposed his own. "The French navy has always preferred the glory of assuring or preserving a conquest to that more brilliant perhaps, but actually less real, of taking some ships, and therein has approached more nearly the true end that has been proposed in war." [2] The justice of this conclusion depends upon the view that is taken of the true end of naval war. If it is merely to assure one or more positions ashore, the navy becomes simply a branch of the army for a particular occasion, and subordinates its action accordingly; but if the true end is to preponderate over the enemy's navy and so control the sea, then the enemy's ships and fleets are the true objects to be assailed on all occasions. A glimmer of this view seems to have been present to Morogues when he wrote that at sea there is no field of battle to be held, nor places to be won. If naval warfare is a war of posts, then the action of the fleets must be subordinate to the attack and defence of the posts; if its object is to break up the enemy's power on the sea, cutting off his communications with the rest of his possessions, drying up the sources of his wealth in his commerce, and making possible a closure of his ports, then the object of attack must be his organized military forces afloat; in short, his navy. It is to the latter course, for whatever reason adopted, that England owed a control of the sea that forced the restitution of Minorca at the end of this war. It is to the former that France owed the lack of prestige in her navy. Take this very case of Minorca; had Galissonière been beaten, Richelieu and his fifteen thousand troops must have been lost to France, cooped up in Minorca, as the Spaniards, in 1718, were confined to Sicily. The French navy therefore assured the capture of the island; but so slight was the impression on the ministry and the public, that a French naval officer tells us: "Incredible as it may seem, the minister of marine, after the glorious affair off Mahon, instead of yielding to the zeal of an enlightened patriotism and profiting by the impulse which this victory gave to France to build up the navy, saw fit to sell the ships and rigging which we still had in our ports. We shall soon see the deplorable consequences of this cowardly conduct on the part of our statesmen." [3] Neither the glory nor the victory is very apparent; but it is quite conceivable that had the French admiral thought less of Mahon and used the great advantage luck had given him to take, or sink, four or five of the enemy, the French people would have anticipated the outbreak of naval enthusiasm which appeared too late, in 1760. During the remainder of this war the French fleets,

[2] Ramatuelle: Tactique Navale.
[3] La Pérouse-Bonfils: Hist. de la Marine.

except in the East Indies, appear only as the pursued in a general chase.

The action imposed upon the French fleets was, however, consistent with the general policy of the French government; and John Clerk was probably right in saying that there is apparent in this action off Minorca a tactics too well defined to be merely accidental, —a tactics essentially defensive in its scope and aim.[4] In assuming the lee-gage the French admiral not only covered Mahon, but took a good defensive position, imposing upon his enemy the necessity of attacking with all the consequent risks. Clerk seems to bring evidence enough to prove that the leading French ships did, after roughly handling their assailants, astutely withdraw (C) thus forcing the latter to attack again with like results. The same policy was repeatedly followed during the American war twenty years later, and with pretty uniform success; so much so that, although formal avowal of the policy is wanting, it may be concluded that circumspection, economy, defensive war, remained the fixed purpose of the French authorities, based doubtless upon the reasons given by Admiral Grivel, of that navy:—

"If two maritime powers are at strife, the one that has the fewest ships must always avoid doubtful engagements; it must run only those risks necessary for carrying out its missions, avoid action by manœuvring, or at worst, if forced to engage, assure itself of favorable conditions. The attitude to be taken should depend radically upon the power of your opponent. Let us not tire of repeating, according as she has to do with an inferior or superior power, France has before her two distinct strategies, radically opposite both in means and ends, — Grand War and Cruising War."

Such a formal utterance by an officer of rank must be received with respect, and the more so when it expresses a consistent policy followed by a great and warlike nation; yet it may be questioned whether a sea power worthy of the name can thus be secured. Logically, it follows from the position assumed, that combats between equal forces are to be discouraged, because the loss to you is greater than the loss to your opponent. "In fact," says Ramatuelle, upholding the French policy, "of what consequence to the English would be the loss of a few ships?" But the next inevitable step in the argu-

[4] Clerk: Naval Tactics.

ment is that it is better not to meet the enemy. As another Frenchman,[5] previously quoted, says, it was considered a mishap to their ships to fall in with a hostile force, and, if one was met, their duty was to avoid action if possible to do so honorably. They had ulterior objects of more importance than fighting the enemy's navy. Such a course cannot be consistently followed for years without affecting the spirit and tone of the officers charged with it; and it led directly to as brave a man as ever commanded a fleet, the Comte de Grasse, failing to crush the English under Rodney when he had the chance, in 1782. On the 9th of April of that year, being chased by the English among the Windward Islands, it happened to him to have sixteen of their fleet under his lee while the main body was becalmed under Dominica. Though greatly superior to the separated ships, during the three hours that this state of things lasted, De Grasse left them undisturbed, except by a distant cannonade by his own van; and his action was justified by the court which tried him, in which were many officers of high rank and doubtless of distinction, as being "an act of prudence on the part of the admiral, dictated to him by the ulterior projects of the cruise." Three days later he was signally beaten by the fleet he had failed to attack at disadvantage, and all the ulterior projects of the cruise went down with him.

To return to Minorca; after the action of the 20th, Byng called a council of war, which decided that nothing more could be done, and that the English fleet should go to Gibraltar and cover that place from an attack. At Gibraltar, Byng was relieved by Hawke and sent home to be tried. The court-martial, while expressly clearing him of cowardice or disaffection, found him guilty of not doing his utmost either to defeat the French fleet or to relieve the garrison at Mahon; and, as the article of war prescribed death with no alternative punishment for this offence, it felt compelled to sentence him to death. The king refused to pardon, and Byng was accordingly shot.

The expedition against Minorca was begun while nominal peace still lasted. On the 17th of May, three days before Byng's battle, England declared war, and France replied on the 20th of June. On the 28th, Port Mahon surrendered, and Minorca passed into the hands of France.

The nature of the troubles between the two nations, and the scenes where they occurred, pointed out clearly enough the proper

[5] Jurien de la Gravière: Guerres Maritimes.

theatre of the strife, and we should by rights now be at the opening of a sea war, illustrated by great naval actions and attended with great modifications in the colonial and foreign possessions of the two powers. Of the two, England alone recognized the truth; France was again turned aside from the sea by causes which will shortly be given. Her fleets scarcely appeared; and losing the control of the sea, she surrendered one by one her colonies and all her hopes in India. Later in the struggle she drew in Spain as her ally, but it was only to involve that country in her own external ruin. England, on the other hand, defended and nourished by the sea, rode it everywhere in triumph. Secure and prosperous at home, she supported with her money the enemies of France. At the end of seven years the kingdom of Great Britain had become the British Empire.

It is far from certain that France could have successfully contended with England on the sea, without an ally. In 1756 the French navy had sixty-three ships-of-the-line, of which forty-five were in fair condition; but equipments and artillery were deficient. Spain had forty-six ships-of-the-line; but from the previous and subsequent performances of the Spanish navy, it may well be doubted if its worth were equal to its numbers. England at this time had one hundred and thirty ships-of-the-line; four years later she had one hundred and twenty actually in commission. Of course when a nation allows its inferiority, whether on land or sea, to become as great as that of France now was, it cannot hope for success.

Nevertheless, she obtained advantages at first. The conquest of Minorca was followed in November of the same year by the acquisition of Corsica. The republic of Genoa surrendered to France all the fortified harbors of the island. With Toulon, Corsica, and Port Mahon, she now had a strong grip on the Mediterranean. In Canada, the operations of 1756, under Montcalm, were successful despite the inferiority of numbers. At the same time an attack by a native prince in India took from the English Calcutta, and gave an opportunity to the French.

Yet another incident offered a handle for French statesmanship to strengthen her position on the ocean. The Dutch had promised France not to renew their alliance with England, but to remain neutral. England retaliated by declaring "all the ports of France in a state of blockade, and all vessels bound to those ports liable to seizure as lawful prize." Such a violation of the rights of neutrals can only be undertaken by a nation that feels it has nothing to fear from their rising against it. The aggressiveness, born of the sense of power, which characterized England might have been used by France to draw Spain and possibly other States into alliance against her.

Instead of concentrating against England, France began another continental war, this time with a new and extraordinary alliance. The empress of Austria, working on the religious superstitions of the king and upon the anger of the king's mistress, who was piqued at sarcasms uttered against her by Frederick the Great, drew France into an alliance with Austria against Prussia. This alliance was further joined by Russia, Sweden, and Poland. The empress urged that the two Roman Catholic powers should unite to take Silesia away from a Protestant king, and expressed her willingness to give to France a part of her possessions in the Netherlands, which France had always desired.

Frederick the Great, learning the combination against him, instead of waiting for it to develop, put his armies in motion and invaded Saxony, whose ruler was also king of Poland. This movement, in October, 1756, began the Seven Years' War; which, like the War of the Austrian Succession, but not to the same extent, drew some of the contestants off from the original cause of difference. But while France, having already on hand one large quarrel with her neighbor across the Channel, was thus needlessly entering upon another struggle, with the avowed end of building up that Austrian empire which a wiser policy had long striven to humble, England this time saw clearly where her true interests lay. Making the continental war wholly subsidiary, she turned her efforts upon the sea and the colonies; at the same time supporting Frederick both with money and cordial sympathy in the war for the defence of his kingdom, which so seriously diverted and divided the efforts of France. England thus had really but one war on hand. In the same year the direction of the struggle was taken from the hands of a weak ministry and given into those of the bold and ardent William Pitt, who retained his office till 1761, by which time the ends of the war had practically been secured.

In the attack upon Canada there were two principal lines to be chosen,—that by the way of Lake Champlain, and that by the way of the St. Lawrence. The former was entirely inland, and as such does not concern our subject, beyond noting that not till after the fall of

Quebec, in 1759, was it fairly opened to the English. In 1757 the attempt against Louisburg failed; the English admiral being unwilling to engage sixteen ships-of-the-line he found there, with the fifteen under his own command, which were also, he said, of inferior metal. Whether he was right in his decision or not, the indignation felt in England clearly shows the difference of policy underlying the action of the French and English governments. The following year an admiral of a higher spirit, Boscawen, was sent out accompanied with twelve thousand troops, and, it must in fairness be said, found only five ships in the port. The troops were landed, while the fleet covered the siege from the only molestation it could fear, and cut off from the besieged the only line by which they could look for supplies. The island fell in 1758, opening the way by the St. Lawrence to the heart of Canada, and giving the English a new base both for the fleet and army.

The next year the expedition under Wolfe was sent against Quebec. All his operations were based upon the fleet, which not only carried his army to the spot, but moved up and down the river as the various feints required. The landing which led to the decisive action was made directly from the ships. Montcalm, whose skill and determination had blocked the attacks by way of Lake Champlain the two previous years, had written urgently for reinforcements; but they were refused by the minister of war, who replied that in addition to other reasons it was too probable that the English would intercept them on the way, and that the more France sent, the more England would be moved to send. In a word, the possession of Canada depended upon sea power.

Montcalm, therefore, in view of the certain attack upon Quebec by the river, was compelled to weaken his resistance on the Champlain route; nevertheless, the English did not get farther than the foot of the lake that year, and their operations, though creditable, had no effect upon the result at Quebec.

In 1760, the English, holding the course of the St. Lawrence, with Louisburg at one end and Quebec at the other, seemed firmly seated. Nevertheless, the French governor, De Vaudreuil, still held out at Montreal, and the colonists still hoped for help from France. The English garrison at Quebec, though inferior in numbers to the forces of the Canadians, was imprudent enough to leave the city and meet them in the open field. Defeated there, and pursued by the enemy, the latter nearly entered Quebec pell-mell with the English troops, and trenches were opened against the city. A few days later an English squadron came in sight, and the place was relieved. "Thus," says the old English chronicler of the navy, "the enemy saw what it was to be inferior at sea; for, had a French squadron got the start of the English in sailing up the river, Quebec must have fallen." Wholly cut off now, the little body of Frenchmen that remained in Montreal was surrounded by three English armies, which had come, one by way of Lake Champlain, the others from Oswego and from Quebec. The surrender of the city on the 8th of September, 1760, put an end forever to the French possession of Canada.

In all other quarters of the world, after the accession of Pitt to power, the same good fortune followed the English arms, checkered only at the first by some slight reverses. It was not so on the continent, where the heroism and skill of Frederick the Great maintained with difficulty his brilliant struggle against France, Austria, and Russia. The study of the difficulties of his position, of the military and political combinations attending it, do not belong to our subject. Sea power does not appear directly in its effects upon the struggle, but indirectly it was felt in two ways,—first, by the subsidies which the abundant wealth and credit of England enabled her to give Frederick, in whose thrifty and able hands they went far; and second, in the embarrassment caused to France by the attacks of England upon her colonies and her own seacoast, in the destruction of her commerce, and in the money—all too little, it is true, and grudgingly given—which France was forced to bestow on her navy. Stung by the constant lashing of the Power of the Sea, France, despite the blindness and unwillingness of the rulers, was driven to undertake something against it. With a navy much inferior, unable to cope in all quarters of the world, it was rightly decided to concentrate upon one object; and the object chosen was Great Britain itself, whose shores were to be invaded. This decision, soon apprehended by the fears of the English nation, caused the great naval operations to centre for some years around the coast of France and in the Channel. Before describing them, it will be well to sum up the general plan by which England was guided in the use of her overwhelming sea power.

Besides the operations on the North American continent already described, this plan was fourfold:—

1. The French Atlantic ports were watched in force, especially Brest, so as to keep the great fleets or small squadrons from getting out without fighting.

2. Attacks were made upon the Atlantic and Channel coasts with flying squadrons, followed at times by the descent of small bodies of troops. These attacks, the direction of which could not be foreseen by the enemy, were chiefly intended to compel him to keep on hand forces at many points, and so to diminish the army acting against the King of Prussia. While the tendency would certainly be that way, it may be doubted whether the actual diversion in favor of Frederick was of much consequence. No particular mention will be made of these operations, which had but little visible effect upon the general course of the war.

3. A fleet was kept in the Mediterranean and near Gibraltar to prevent the French Toulon fleet from getting round to the Atlantic. It does not appear that any attempt was seriously made to stop communications between France and Minorca. The action of the Mediterranean fleet, though an independent command, was subsidiary to that in the Atlantic.

4. Distant foreign expeditions were sent against the French colonies in the West India Islands and on the coast of Africa, and a squadron was maintained in the East Indies to secure the control of those seas, thereby supporting the English in the Peninsula, and cutting off the communications of the French. These operations in distant waters, never intermitted, assumed greater activity and larger proportions after the destruction of the French navy had relieved England from the fear of invasion, and when the ill-advised entrance of Spain into the war, in 1762 offered yet richer prizes to her enterprise.

The close blockade of the enemy's fleet in Brest, which was first systematically carried out during this war, may be considered rather a defensive than an offensive operation; for though the intention certainly was to fight if opportunity offered, the chief object was to neutralize an offensive weapon in the enemy's hands; the destruction of the weapon was secondary. The truth of this remark is shown by the outburst of fear and anger which swept over England when an unavoidable absence of the blockading fleet in 1759 allowed the French to escape. The effect of the blockade in this and after wars was to keep the French in a state of constant inferiority in the practical handling of their ships, however fair-showing their outward appearance or equal their numerical force. The position of the port of Brest was such that a blockaded fleet could not get out during the heavy westerly gales that endangered the blockaders; the latter, therefore, had the habit of running away from them to Torbay or Plymouth, sure, with care, of getting back to their station with an east wind before a large and ill-handled fleet could get much start of them.

In the latter part of 1758, France, depressed by the sense of failure upon the continent, mortified and harassed by English descents upon her coasts, which had been particularly annoying that year, and seeing that it was not possible to carry on both the continental and sea wars with her money resources, determined to strike directly at England. Her commerce was annihilated while the enemy's throve. It was the boast of London merchants that under Pitt commerce was united with and made to flourish by war;[6] and this thriving commerce was the soul also of the land struggle, by the money it lavished on the enemy of France.

At this time a new and active-minded minister, Choiseul, was called into power by Louis XV. From the beginning of 1759, preparations were made in the ocean and Channel ports. Flat-boats to transport troops were built at Havre, Dunkirk, Brest, and Rochefort. It was intended to embark as many as fifty thousand men for the invasion of England, while twelve thousand were to be directed upon Scotland. Two squadrons were fitted out, each of respectable strength, one at Toulon, the other at Brest. The junction of these two squadrons at Brest was the first step in the great enterprise.

It was just here that it broke down, through the possession of Gibraltar by the English, and their naval superiority. It seems incredible that even the stern and confident William Pitt should, as late as 1757, have offered to surrender to Spain the watch-tower from which England overlooks the road between the Mediterranean and the Atlantic, as the price of her help to recover Minorca. Happily for England, Spain refused. In 1759, Admiral Boscawen commanded the English Mediterranean fleet. In making an attack upon French frigates in Toulon roads, some of his ships were so damaged that he sailed with his whole squadron to Gibraltar to refit; taking the precaution, however, to station lookout frigates at

[6] Mahon: History of England.

intervals, and to arrange signals by guns to notify him betimes of the enemy's approach. Taking advantage of his absence. and in obedience to orders, the French commodore, De la Clue, left Toulon with twelve ships-of-the-line on the 5th of August, and on the 7th found himself at the Straits of Gibraltar, with a brisk east wind carrying him out into the Atlantic. Everything seemed propitious, a thick haze and falling night concealing the French ships from the land, while not preventing their sight of each other, when an English frigate loomed up in the near distance. As soon as she saw the fleet, knowing they must be enemies, she hauled in for the land and began firing signal-guns. Pursuit was useless; flight alone remained. Hoping to elude the chase he knew must follow, the French commodore steered west-northwest for the open sea, putting out all lights; but either from carelessness or disaffection,—for the latter is hinted by one French naval officer,—five out of the twelve ships headed to the northward and put into Cadiz when on the following morning they could not see the commodore. The latter was dismayed when at daylight he saw his forces thus diminished. At eight o'clock some sails made their appearance, and for a few minutes he hoped they were the missing ships. Instead of that, they were the lookouts of Boscawen's fleet, which, numbering fourteen ships-of-the-line, was in full pursuit. The French formed their order on one of the close-hauled lines, and fled; but of course their fleet-speed was less than that of the fastest English ships. The general rule for all chases where the pursuer is decidedly superior, namely, that order must be observed only so far as to keep the leading ships within reasonable supporting distance of the slower ones, so that they may not be singly overpowered before the latter can come up, was by this time well understood in the English navy, and that is certainly the fitting time for a *mêlée*. Boscawen acted accordingly. The rear ship of the French, on the other hand, nobly emulated the example of L'Étenduère when he saved his convoy. Overtaken at two o'clock by the leading English ship, and soon after surrounded by four others, her captain made for five hours a desperate resistance, from which he could hope, not to save himself, but to delay the enemies long enough for the better sailers to escape. He so far succeeded that—thanks to the injury done by him and their better speed—they did that day escape action at close quarters, which could only have ended in their capture. When he hauled down his flag, his three topmasts were gone, the mizzen-mast fell immediately after, and the hull was so full of water that the ship was with difficulty kept afloat. M. de Sabran—his name is worthy to be remembered—had received eleven wounds in this gallant resistance, by which he illustrated so signally the duty and service of a rearguard in retarding pursuit. That night two of the French ships hauled off to the westward, and so escaped. The other four continued their flight as before; but the next morning the commodore, despairing of escape, headed for the Portuguese coast, and ran them all ashore between Lagos and Cape St. Vincent. The English admiral followed and attacked them, taking two and burning the others, without regard to the neutrality of Portugal. For this insult no amend was made beyond a formal apology; Portugal was too dependent upon England to be seriously considered. Pitt, writing to the English minister to Portugal about the affair, told him that while soothing the susceptibilities of the Portuguese government he must not allow it to suppose that either the ships would be given up or the distinguished admiral censured.[7]

The destruction or dispersal of the Toulon fleet stopped the invasion of England, though the five ships that got into Cadiz remained a matter of anxiety to Sir Edward Hawke, who cruised before Brest. Choiseul, balked of his main object, still clung to the invasion of Scotland. The French fleet at Brest, under Marshal de Conflans, a sea officer despite his title, numbered twenty sail-of-the-line, besides frigates. The troops to be embarked are variously stated at fifteen to twenty thousand. The original purpose was to escort the transports with only five ships-of-the-line, besides smaller vessels. Conflans insisted that the whole fleet ought to go. The minister of the navy thought that the admiral was not a sufficiently skilful tactician to be able to check the advance of an enemy, and so insure the safe arrival of the convoy at its destination near the Clyde without risking a decisive encounter. Believing therefore that there would be a general action, he considered that it would be better to fight it before the troops sailed; for if disastrous, the convoy would not be sacrificed, and if decisively victorious, the road would then be clear. The transports were assembled, not at Brest, but in the ports to the southward as far as the mouth of the Loire. The French fleet therefore put to sea with the expectation and purpose of fighting the enemy; but it is not easy to reconcile its subsequent course with that purpose, nor

[7] Mahon: History of England.

with the elaborate fighting instructions[8] issued by the admiral before sailing.

About the 5th or 6th of November there came on a tremendous westerly gale. After buffeting it for three days, Hawke bore up and ran into Torbay, where he waited for the wind to shift, keeping his fleet in readiness to sail at once. The same gale, while keeping back the French already in Brest, gave the chance to a small squadron under M. Bompart, which was expected from the West Indies, to slip in during Hawke's absence. Conflans made his preparations with activity, distributed Bompart's crews among his own ships, which were not very well manned, and got to sea with an easterly wind on the 14th. He stood at once to the southward, flattering himself that he had escaped Hawke. The latter, however, had sailed from Torbay on the 12th; and though again driven back, sailed a second time on the 14th, the same day that Conflans left Brest. He soon reached his station, learned that the enemy had been seen to the southward steering east, and easily concluding that they were bound to Quiberon Bay, shaped his own course for the same place under a press of sail. At eleven P.M. of the 19th the French admiral estimated his position to be seventy miles southwest by west from Belle Isle;[9] and the wind springing up fresh from the westward, he stood for it under short sail, the wind continuing to increase and hauling to west-northwest. At daybreak several ships were seen ahead, which proved to be the English squadron of Commodore Duff, blockading Quiberon. The signal was made to chase; and the English, taking flight, separated into two divisions,—one going off before the wind, the other hauling up to the southward. The greater part of the French fleet continued its course after the former division, that is, toward the coast; but one ship hauled up for the second. Immediately after, the rear French ships made signal of sails to windward, which were also visible from aloft on board the flag-ship. It must have been about the same moment that the lookout frigate in advance of the English fleet informed her admiral of sails to leeward. Hawke's diligence had brought him up with Conflans, who, in his official reports, says he had considered it impossible that the enemy could have in that neighborhood forces superior or even equal to his own. Conflans now ordered his rear division to haul its wind

[8] For these, see Troude: Batailles Navales.
[9] See Plate VIII., p. 267.

in support of the ship chasing to the southward and eastward. In a few moments more it was discovered that the fleet to windward numbered twenty-three ships-of-the-line to the French twenty-one, and among them some three-deckers. Conflans then called in the chasing ships and got ready for action. It remained to settle his course under circumstances which he had not foreseen. It was now blowing hard from the west-northwest, with every appearance of heavy weather, the fleet not far from a lee shore, with an enemy considerably superior in numbers; for besides Hawke's twenty-three of the line, Duff had four fifty-gun ships. Conflans therefore determined to run for it and lead his squadron into Quiberon Bay, trusting and believing that Hawke would not dare to follow, under the conditions of the weather, into a bay which French authorities describe as containing banks and shoals, and lined with reefs which the navigator rarely sees without fright and never passes without emotion. It was in the midst of these ghastly dangers that forty-four large ships were about to engage pell-mell; for the space was too contracted for fleet manœuvres. Conflans flattered himself that he would get in first and be able to haul up close under the western shore of the bay, forcing the enemy, if he followed, to take position between him and the beach, six miles to leeward. None of his expectations were fulfilled. In the retreat he took the head of his fleet; a step not unjustifiable, since only by leading in person could he have shown just what he wanted to do, but unfortunate for his reputation with the public, as it placed the admiral foremost in the flight. Hawke was not in the least, nor for one moment, deterred by the dangers before him, whose full extent he, as a skilful seaman, entirely realized; but his was a calm and steadfast as well as a gallant temper, that weighed risks justly, neither dissembling nor exaggerating. He has not left us his reasoning, but he doubtless felt that the French, leading, would serve partially as pilots, and must take the ground before him; he believed the temper and experience of his officers, tried by the severe school of the blockade, to be superior to those of the French; and he knew that both the government and the country demanded that the enemy's fleet should not reach another friendly port in safety. On the very day that he was thus following the French, amid dangers and under conditions that have made this one of the most dramatic of sea fights, he was being burnt in effigy in England for allowing them to escape. As Conflans, leading his

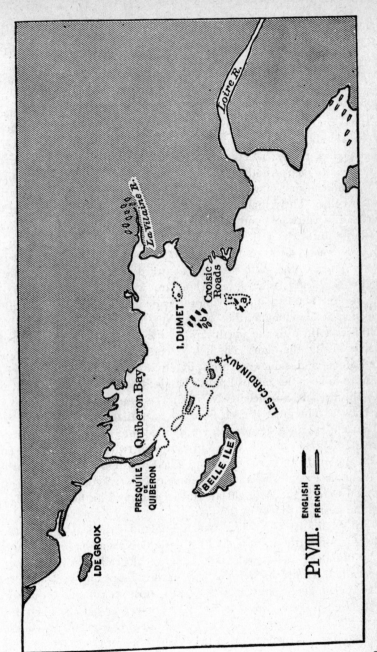

Loire R.

La Vilaine R.

Croisic Roads

I. DUMET

LES CARDINAUX

Quiberon Bay

PRESQU'ILE
DE
QUIBERON

BELLE ILE

I. DE GROIX

Pl. VIII.

ENGLISH

FRENCH

267

fleet, was rounding the Cardinals,—as the southernmost rocks at the entrance of Quiberon Bay are called,—the leading English ships brought the French rear to action. It was another case of a general chase ending in a *mêlée*, but under conditions of exceptional interest and grandeur from the surrounding circumstances of the gale of wind, the heavy sea, the lee shore, the headlong speed, shortened canvas, and the great number of ships engaged. One French seventy-four, closely pressed and out-numbered, ventured to open her lower-deck ports; the sea sweeping in carried her down with all on board but twenty men. Another was sunk by the fire of Hawke's flag-ship. Two others, one of which carried a commodore's pennant, struck their colors. The remainder were dispersed. Seven fled to the northward and eastward, and anchored off the mouth of the little river Vilaine, into which they succeeded in entering at the top of high water in two tides,—a feat never before performed. Seven others took refuge to the southward and eastward in Rochefort. One, after being very badly injured, ran ashore and was lost near the mouth of the Loire. The flag-ship bearing the same name as that of Tourville burned at La Hougue, the "Royal Sun," anchored at nightfall off Croisic, a little to the northward of the Loire, where she rode in safety during the night. The next morning the admiral found himself alone, and, somewhat precipitately it would seem, ran the ship ashore to keep her out of English hands. This step has been blamed by the French, but needlessly, as Hawke would never have let her get away. The great French fleet was annihilated; for the fourteen ships not taken or destroyed were divided into two parts, and those in the Vilaine only succeeded in escaping, two at a time, between fifteen months and two years later. The English lost two ships which ran upon a shoal (a), and were hopelessly wrecked; their losses in action were slight. At nightfall Hawke anchored his fleet and prizes in the position shown in the plate (b).

All possibility of an invasion of England passed away with the destruction of the Brest fleet. The battle of November 20, 1759, was the Trafalgar of this war; and though a blockade was maintained over the fractions that were laid up in the Vilaine and at Rochefort, the English fleets were now free to act against the colonies of France, and later of Spain, on a grander scale than ever before. The same year that saw this great sea fight and the fall of Quebec witnessed also the capture of Guadeloupe in the West Indies, of Goree on the west coast of Africa, and the abandonment of the East Indian seas by the French flag after three indecisive actions between their commodore, D'Aché, and Admiral Pocock,—an abandonment which necessarily led to the fall of the French power in India, never again to rise. In this year also the King of Spain died, and his brother succeeded, under the title of Charles III. This Charles had been king of Naples at the time when an English commodore had allowed one hour for the court to determine to withdraw the Neapolitan troops from the Spanish army. He had never forgotten this humiliation, and brought to his new throne a heart unfriendly to England. With such feelings on his part, France and Spain drew more readily together. Charles's first step was to propose mediation, but Pitt was averse to it. Looking upon France as the chief enemy of England, and upon the sea and the colonies as the chief source of power and wealth, he wished, now that he had her down, to weaken her thoroughly for the future as well as the present, and to establish England's greatness more firmly upon the wreck. Later on he offered certain conditions; but the influence of Louis's mistress, attached to the Empress of Austria, prevailed to except Prussia from the negotiations, and England would not allow the exception. Pitt, indeed, was not yet ready for peace. A year later, October 25, 1760, George II. died, and Pitt's influence then began to wane, the new king being less bent on war. During these years, 1759 and 1760, Frederick the Great still continued the deadly and exhausting strife of his small kingdom against the great States joined against him. At one moment his case seemed so hopeless that he got ready to kill himself; but the continuance of the war diverted the efforts of France from England and the sea.

The hour was fast approaching for the great colonial expeditions, which made the last year of the war illustrious by the triumph of the sea power of England over France and Spain united. It is first necessary to tell the entirely kindred story of the effect of that sea power in the East Indian peninsula.

The recall of Dupleix and the entire abandonment of his policy, which resulted in placing the two East India companies on equal terms, have already been told. The treaty stipulations of 1754 had not, however, been fully carried out. The Marquis de Bussy, a brave and capable soldier who had been a second to Dupleix, and was wholly in accord with his policy and ambitions, remained in the Deccan,—a large region in the southern central part of the peninsula, over which Dupleix had once ruled. In 1756, troubles arose between the English and the native prince in Bengal. The nabob of that province had died, and his successor, a young man of nineteen, attacked Calcutta. The place fell, after a weak resistance, in June, and the surrender was followed by the famous tragedy known as that of the Black Hole of Calcutta. The news reached Madras in August, and Clive, whose name has already been mentioned, sailed with the fleet of Admiral Watson, after a long and vexatious delay. The fleet entered the river in December and appeared before Calcutta in January, when the place fell into English hands again as easily as it had been lost.

The nabob was very angry, and marched against the English; sending meanwhile an invitation to the French at Chandernagore to join him. Although it was now known that England and France were at war, the French company, despite the experience of 1744, weakly hoped that peace might be kept between it and the English. The native invitation was therefore refused, and offers of neutrality made to the other company. Clive marched out, met the Indian forces and defeated them, and the nabob at once asked for peace, and sought the English alliance, yielding all the claims on the strength of which he had first attacked Calcutta. After some demur his offers were accepted. Clive and Watson then turned upon Chandernagore and compelled the surrender of the French settlement.

The nabob, who had not meant to allow this, took umbrage, and entered into correspondence with Bussy in the Deccan. Clive had full knowledge of his various intrigues, which were carried on with the vacillation of a character as weak as it was treacherous; and seeing no hope of settled peace or trade under the rule of this man, entered into an extensive conspiracy for his dethronement, the details of which need not be given. The result was that war broke out again, and that Clive with three thousand men, one third of whom were English, met the nabob at the head of fifteen thousand horse and thirty-five thousand foot. The disproportion in artillery was nearly as great. Against these odds was fought and won the battle of Plassey, on the 23d of June, 1757,—the date from which, by common consent, the British empire in India is said to begin. The overthrow of the nabob was followed by placing in power one of the conspirators against him, a creature of the English, and dependent upon them for support. Bengal thus passed under their control, the first-fruits of India. "Clive," says a French historian, "had understood and applied the system of Dupleix."

This was true; yet even so it may be said that the foundation thus laid could never have been kept nor built upon, had the English nation not controlled the sea. The conditions of India were such that a few Europeans, headed by men of nerve and shrewdness, dividing that they might conquer, and advancing their fortunes by judicious alliances, were able to hold their own, and more too, amidst overwhelming numerical odds; but it was necessary that they should not be opposed by men of their own kind, a few of whom could turn the wavering balance the other way. At the very time that Clive was acting in Bengal, Bussy invaded Orissa, seized the English factories, and made himself master of much of the coast regions between Madras and Calcutta; while a French squadron of nine ships, most of which, however, belonged to the East India Company and were not first-rate men-of-war, was on its way to Pondicherry with twelve hundred regular troops,—an enormous European army for Indian operations of that day. The English naval force on the coast, though fewer in numbers, may be considered about equal to the approaching French squadron. It is scarcely too much to say that the future of India was still uncertain, and the first operations showed it.

The French division appeared off the Coromandel coast to the southward of Pondicherry on the 26th of April, 1758, and anchored on the 28th before the English station called Fort St. David. Two ships kept on to Pondicherry, having on board the new governor, Comte de Lally, who wished to go at once to his seat of government. Meanwhile, the English admiral, Pocock, having news of the enemy's coming, and fearing specially for this post, was on his way to it, and appeared on the 29th of April, before the two ships with the governor were out of sight. The French at once got under way and stood out to sea on the starboard tack (Plate Va.), heading to the northward and eastward, the wind being south-east, and signals were made to recall the ship and frigate (a) escorting Lally; but they were disregarded by the latter's order, an act which must have increased, if it did not originate, the ill-will between him and Commodore d'Aché, through which the French campaign in India miscarried. The English, having formed to windward on the same tack as the French, made their attack in the then usual way, and with the usual results. The seven English ships were ordered to keep away together for the French eight, and the four leading ships, including the admiral's, came into action handsomely; the last three, whether by their own fault or not, were late in doing so, but it will be remembered that this was almost always the case in such attacks. The French commodore, seeing this interval between the van and the rear, formed the plan of separating them, and made signal to wear together, but in his impatience did not wait for an answer. Putting his own helm up, he wore round, and was followed in succession by the rear ships, while the van stood on. The English admiral, who had good reason to know, gives D'Aché more credit than the French writers, for he describes this movement thus:—

"At half-past four P.M. the rear of the French line had drawn pretty close up to their flag-ship. Our three rear ships were signalled to engage closer. Soon after, M. d'Aché broke the line, and put before the wind; his second astern, who had kept on the 'Yarmouth's' [English flag-ship] quarter most part of the action, then came up alongside, gave his fire, and then bore away; and a few minutes after, the enemy's van bore away also."

By this account, which is by no means irreconcilable with the French, the latter effected upon the principal English ship a movement of concentration by defiling past her. The French now stood down to their two separated ships, while the English vessels that had been engaged were too much crippled to follow. This battle prevented the English fleet from relieving Fort St. David, which surrendered on the 2d of June.

After the fall of this place, the two opposing squadrons having refitted at their respective ports and resumed their station, a second action was fought in August, under nearly the same conditions and in much the same fashion. The French flag-ship met with a series of untoward accidents, which determined the commodore to withdraw from action; but the statement of his further reasons is most suggestive of the necessary final overthrow of the French cause. "Prudence," a writer of his own country says, "commanded him not to prolong a contest from which his ships could not but come out with injuries very difficult to repair in a region where it was impossible to supply the almost entire lack of spare stores." This want of so absolute a requisite for naval efficiency shows in a strong light the fatal tendency of that economy which always characterized French operations at sea, and was at once significant and ominous.

Returning to Pondicherry, D'Aché found that, though the injuries to the masts and rigging could for this time be repaired, there was lack of provisions, and that the ships needed calking. Although his orders were to remain on the coast until October 15, he backed himself with the opinion of a council of war which decided that the ships could not remain there longer, because, in case of a third battle, there was neither rigging nor supplies remaining in Pondicherry; and disregarding the protests of the governor, Lally, he sailed on the 2d of September for the Isle of France. The underlying motive of D'Aché, it is known, was hostility to the governor, with whom he quarrelled continually. Lally, deprived of the help of the squadron, turned his arms inland instead of against Madras.

Upon arriving at the islands, D'Aché found a state of things which again singularly illustrates the impotence and short-sightedness characteristic of the general naval policy of the French at this time. His arrival there was as unwelcome as his departure from India had been to Lally. The islands were then in a state of the most complete destitution. The naval division, increased by the arrival of three ships-of-the-line from home, so exhausted them that its immediate departure was requested of the commodore. Repairs were pushed ahead rapidly, and in November several of the ships sailed to the Cape of Good Hope, then a Dutch colony, to seek provisions; but these were consumed soon after being received, and the pressure for the departure of the squadron was renewed. The situation of the ships was no less precarious than that of the colony; and accordingly the commodore replied by urging his entire lack of food and supplies. The condition was such that, a little later, it was necessary to make running rigging out of the cables, and to put some of the ships on the bottom, so as to give their materials to others. Before returning to India, D'Aché wrote to the minister of the navy that he "was about to leave, only to save the crews from dying of hunger, and that nothing need be expected from the squadron if supplies were not sent, for both men and things were in a deplorable state."

Under these circumstances D'Aché sailed from the islands in July, 1759, and arrived off the Coromandel coast in September. During his year of absence Lally had besieged Madras for two months, during the northeast monsoon. Both squadrons were absent, that season being unfit for naval operations on this coast; but the English returned first, and are said by the French to have caused, by the English to have hastened, the raising of the siege. D'Aché, upon his return, was much superior in both number and size of ships; but when the fleets met, Pocock did not hesitate to attack with nine against eleven. This action, fought September 10, 1759, was as indecisive as the two former; but D'Aché retreated, after a very bloody contest. Upon it Campbell, in his "Lives of the Admirals," makes a droll, but seemingly serious, comment: "Pocock had reduced the French ships to a very shattered condition, and killed a great many of their men; but what shows the singular talents of both admirals, they had fought three pitched battles in eighteen months without the loss of a ship on either side." The fruits of victory, however, were with the weaker fleet; for D'Aché returned to Pondicherry and thence sailed on the 1st of the next month for the islands, leaving India to its fate. From that time the result was certain. The English continued to receive reinforcements from home, while the French did not; the men opposed to Lally were superior in ability; place after place fell, and in January, 1761, Pondicherry itself surrendered, surrounded by land and cut off from the sea. This was the end of the French power in India; for though Pondicherry and other possessions were restored at the peace, the English tenure there was never again shaken, even under the attacks of the skilful and bold Suffren, who twenty years later met difficulties as great as D'Aché's with a vigor and conduct which the latter at a more hopeful moment failed to show.

France having thus lost both Canada and India by the evident failure of her power to act at a distance by sea, it would seem scarcely possible that Spain, with her own weak navy and widely scattered possessions, would choose this moment for entering the war. Yet so it was. The maritime exhaustion of France was plain to all, and is abundantly testified to by her naval historians. "The resources of France were exhausted," says one; "the year 1761 saw only a few single ships leave her ports, and all of them were captured. The alliance with Spain came too late. The occasional ships that went to sea in 1762 were taken, and the colonies still remaining to France could not be saved." [10] Even as early as 1758, another

---

[10] Troude: Batailles Navales de la France.

Frenchman writes, "want of money, the depression of commerce given over to English cruisers, the lack of good ships, the lack of supplies, etc., compelled the French ministry, unable to raise large forces, to resort to stratagems, to replace the only rational system of war, Grand War, by the smallest of petty wars,—by a sort of game in which the great aim is not to be caught. Even then, the arrival of four ships-of-the-line at Louisburg, by avoiding the enemy, was looked on as a very fortunate event. . . . In 1759 the lucky arrival of the West India convoy caused as much surprise as joy to the merchants. We see how rare had become such a chance in seas ploughed by the squadrons of England." [11] This was before the disasters of La Clue and Conflans. The destruction of French commerce, beginning by the capture of its merchant-ships, was consummated by the reduction of the colonies. It can hardly, therefore, be conceded that the Family Compact now made between the two courts, containing, as it did, not only an agreement to support each other in any future war, but also a secret clause binding Spain to declare war against England within a year, if peace were not made, "was honorable to the wisdom of the two governments." It is hard to pardon, not only the Spanish government, but even France for alluring a kindred people into such a bad bargain. It was hoped, however, to revive the French navy and to promote an alliance of neutral powers; many of which, besides Spain, had causes of complaint against England. "During the war with France," confesses an English historian, "the Spanish flag had not always been respected by British cruisers." [12] "During 1758," says another, "not less than one hundred and seventy-six neutral vessels, laden with the rich produce of the French colonies or with military or naval stores, fell into the hands of the English." [13] The causes were already at work which twenty years later gave rise to the "armed neutrality" of the Baltic powers, directed against the claims of England on the sea. The possession of unlimited power, as the sea power of England then really was, is seldom accompanied by a profound respect for the rights of others. Without a rival upon the ocean, it suited England to maintain that enemy's property was liable to capture on board neutral ships, thus subjecting these nations not only to

---

[11] La Pérouse-Bonfils.
[12] Mahon: History of England.
[13] Campbell: Lives of the Admirals.

vexatious detentions, but to loss of valuable trade; just as it had suited her earlier in the war to establish a paper blockade of French ports. Neutrals of course chafed under the exactions; but the year 1761 was ill-chosen for an armed protest, and of all powers Spain risked most by a war. England had then one hundred and twenty ships-of-the-line in commission, besides those in reserve, manned by seventy thousand seamen trained and hardened by five years of constant warfare afloat, and flushed with victory. The navy of France, which numbered seventy-seven ships-of-the-line in 1758, lost as prizes to the English in 1759 twenty-seven, besides eight destroyed and many frigates lost; indeed, as has been seen, their own writers confess that the navy was ruined, root and branch. The Spanish navy contained about fifty ships; but the personnel, unless very different from the days before and after, must have been very inferior. The weakness of her empire, in the absence of an efficient navy, has before been pointed out. Neutrality, too, though at times outraged, had been of great advantage to her, permitting her to restore her finances and trade and to re-establish her internal resources; but she needed a still longer period of it. Nevertheless, the king, influenced by family feeling and resentment against England, allowed himself to be drawn on by the astute Choiseul, and the Family Compact between the two crowns was signed on the 15th of August, 1761. This compact, into which the king of Naples was also to enter, guaranteed their mutual possessions by the whole power of both kingdoms. This in itself was a weighty undertaking; but the secret clause further stipulated that Spain should declare war against England on the 1st of May, 1762, if peace with France had not then been made. Negotiations of this character could not be kept wholly secret, and Pitt learned enough to convince him that Spain was becoming hostile in intention. With his usual haughty resolve, he determined to forestall her by declaring war; but the influence against him in the councils of the new king was too strong. Failing to carry the ministry with him, he resigned on the 5th of October, 1761. His prevision was quickly justified; Spain had been eager in professing good-will until the treasure-ships from America should arrive laden with the specie so needed for carrying on war. On the 21st of September the flota of galleons anchored safely in Cadiz; and on the 2d of November the British ambassador announced to his government that "two ships had safely arrived with very extraordinary rich cargoes from the West Indies, so that all the wealth that was expected from Spanish America is now safe in old Spain," and in the same despatch reports a surprising change in the words of the Spanish minister, and the haughty language now used.[14] The grievances and claims of Spain were urged peremptorily, and the quarrel grew so fast that even the new English ministry, though ardently desiring peace, recalled their ambassador before the end of the year, and declared war on the 4th of January, 1762; thus adopting Pitt's policy, but too late to reap the advantages at which he had aimed.

However, no such delay on the part of England could alter the essential inequality, in strength and preparation, between the two nations. The plans formed by Pitt were in the main adopted by his successor, and carried out with a speed which the readiness of the English navy permitted. On the 5th of March, Pocock, who had returned from the East Indies, sailed from Portsmouth, convoying a fleet of transports to act against Havana; in the West Indies he was reinforced from the forces in that quarter, so that his command contained nineteen ships-of-the-line besides smaller vessels, and ten thousand soldiers.

In the previous January, the West India fleet, under the well-known Rodney, had acted with the land forces in the reduction of Martinique, the gem and tower of the French islands and the harbor of an extensive privateering system. It is said that fourteen hundred English merchantmen were taken during this war in the West Indian seas by cruisers whose principal port was Fort Royal in Martinique. With this necessary base fell also the privateering system resting upon it. Martinique was surrendered February 12, and the loss of this chief commercial and military centre was immediately followed by that of the smaller islands, Grenada, Sta. Lucia, St. Vincent. By these acquisitions the English colonies at Antigua, St. Kitts, and Nevis as well as the ships trading to those islands, were secured against the enemy, the commerce of England received large additions, and all the Lesser Antilles, or Windward Islands, became British possessions.

Admiral Pocock was joined off Cape St. Nicholas by the West Indian reinforcement on the 27th of May, and as the season was so far advanced, he took his great fleet through the old Bahama chan-

[14] Mahon: History of England.

nel instead of the usual route around the south side of Cuba. This was justly considered a great feat in those days of poor surveys, and was accomplished without an accident. Lookout and sounding vessels went first, frigates followed, and boats or sloops were anchored on shoals with carefully arranged signals for day or night. Having good weather, the fleet got through in a week and appeared before Havana. The operations will not be given in detail. After a forty days' siege the Moro Castle was taken on the 30th of July, and the city surrendered on the 10th of August. The Spaniards lost not only the city and port, but twelve ships-of-the-line, besides £3,000,000 in money and merchandise belonging to the Spanish king. The importance of Havana was not to be measured only by its own size, or its position as centre of a large and richly cultivated district; it was also the port commanding the only passage by which the treasure and other ships could sail from the Gulf of Mexico to Europe in those days. With Havana in an enemy's hands it would be necessary to assemble them at Cartagena and from there beat up against the trade-winds,—an operation always difficult, and which would keep ships long in waters where they were exposed to capture by English cruisers. Not even an attack upon the isthmus would have been so serious a blow to Spain. This important result could only be achieved by a nation confident of controlling the communications by its sea power, to which the happy issue must wholly be ascribed, and which had another signal illustration in the timely conveying of four thousand American troops to reinforce the English ranks, terribly wasted by battle and fever. It is said that only twenty-five hundred serviceable fighting men remained on foot when the city fell.

While the long reach and vigor of England's sea power was thus felt in the West Indies, it was receiving further illustration in Portugal and in the far East. The allied crowns in the beginning had invited Portugal to join their alliance against those whom they had taken to calling the "tyrants of the seas," reminding her how the English monopoly of her trade was draining the country of gold, and recalling the deliberate violation of her neutrality by the fleet under Boscawen. The Portuguese minister of the day well knew all this, and keenly felt it; but though the invitation was accompanied by the plain statement that Portugal would not be allowed to continue a neutrality she could not enforce, he judged rightly that the country had more to fear from England and her fleet than from the Spanish army. The allies declared war and invaded Portugal. They were for a time successful; but the "tyrants of the seas" answered Portugal's call, sent a fleet and landed at Lisbon eight thousand soldiers, who drove the Spaniards over the frontiers, and even carried the war into Spain itself.

Simultaneous with these significant events, Manila was attacked. With so much already on hand, it was found impossible to spare troops or ships from England. The successes in India and the absolute security of the establishments there, with the control of the sea, allowed the Indian officials themselves to undertake this colonial expedition. It sailed in August, 1762, and reaching Malacca on the 19th, was supplied at that neutral port with all that was needed for the siege about to be undertaken; the Dutch, though jealous of the English advance, not venturing to refuse their demands. The expedition, which depended entirely upon the fleet, resulted in the whole group of Philippine Islands surrendering in October and paying a ransom of four million dollars. At about the same time the fleet captured the Acapulco galleon having three million dollars on board, and an English squadron in the Atlantic took a treasure-ship from Lima with four million dollars in silver for the Spanish government.

"Never had the colonial empire of Spain received such blows. Spain, whose opportune intervention might have modified the fate of the war, entered it too late to help France, but in time to share her misfortunes. There was reason to fear yet more. Panama and San Domingo were threatened, and the Anglo-Americans were preparing for the invasion of Florida and Louisiana. . . . The conquest of Havana had in great measure interrupted the communications between the wealthy American colonies of Spain and Europe. The reduction of the Philippine Islands now excluded her from Asia. The two together severed all the avenues of Spanish trade and cut off all intercourse between the parts of their vast but disconnected empire." [15]

The selection of the points of attack, due to the ministry of Pitt, was strategically good, cutting effectually the sinews of the enemy's strength; and if his plans had been fully carried out and Panama also seized, the success would have been yet more decisive. England had lost also the advantage of the surprise she would have

[15] Martin: History of France.

effected by anticipating Spain's declaration of war; but her arms were triumphant during this short contest, through the rapidity with which her projects were carried into execution, due to the state of efficiency to which her naval forces and administration had been brought.

With the conquest of Manila ended the military operations of the war. Nine months, counting from the formal declaration by England in January, had been sufficient to shatter the last hope of France, and to bring Spain to a peace in which was conceded every point on which she had based her hostile attitude and demands. It seems scarcely necessary, after even the brief summary of events that has been given, to point out that the speed and thoroughness with which England's work was done was due wholly to her sea power, which allowed her forces to act on distant points, widely apart as Cuba, Portugal, India, and the Philippines, without a fear of serious break in their communications.

Before giving the terms of peace which ought to summarize the results of the war, but do so imperfectly, owing to the weak eagerness of the English ministry to conclude it, it is necessary to trace in outline the effect of the war upon commerce, upon the foundations of sea power and national prosperity.

One prominent feature of this war may be more strongly impressed upon the mind by a startling, because paradoxical, statement that the prosperity of the English is shown by the magnitude of their losses.

"From 1756 to 1760," states a French historian, "French privateers captured from the English more than twenty-five hundred merchantmen. In 1761, though France had not, so to speak, a single ship-of-the-line at sea, and though the English had taken two hundred and forty of our privateers, their comrades still took eight hundred and twelve English vessels. The explanation of the number of these prizes lies in the prodigious growth of the English shipping. In 1760 it is claimed that the English had at sea eight thousand sail; of these the French captured nearly one tenth, despite escorts and cruisers. In the four years from 1756 to 1760 the French lost only nine hundred and fifty vessels." [16]

But this discrepancy is justly attributed by an English writer "to the diminution of the French commerce and the dread of falling into

[16] Martin: History of France.

280

the hands of the English, which kept many of their trading-vessels from going to sea"; and he goes on to point out that the capture of vessels was not the principal benefit resulting from the efficiency of England's fleets. "Captures like Duquesne, Louisburg, Prince Edward's Island, the reduction of Senegal, and later on of Guadeloupe and Martinique, were events no less destructive to French commerce and colonies than advantageous to those of England." [17] The multiplication of French privateers was indeed a sad token to an instructed eye, showing behind them merchant shipping in enforced idleness, whose crews and whose owners were driven to speculative pillage in order to live. Nor was this risk wholly in vain. The same Englishman confesses that in 1759 the losses of merchantmen showed a worse balance than the ships-of-war. While the French were striving in vain to regain equality upon the sea and repair their losses, but to no purpose, for "in building and arming vessels they labored only for the English fleet," yet, "notwithstanding the courage and vigilance of English cruisers, French privateers so swarmed that in this year they took two hundred and forty British vessels, chiefly coasters and small craft." In 1760 the same authority gives the British loss in trading-vessels at over three hundred, and in 1761 at over eight hundred, three times that of the French; but he adds: "It would not have been wonderful had they taken more and richer ships. While their commerce was nearly destroyed, and they had few merchant-ships at sea, the trading-fleets of England covered the seas. Every year her commerce was increasing; the money which the war carried out was returned by the produce of her industry. Eight thousand vessels were employed by the traders of Great Britain." The extent of her losses is attributed to three causes, of which the first only was preventable: (1) The inattention of merchant-ships to the orders of the convoying vessels; (2) The immense number of English ships in all seas; (3) The enemy's venturing the whole remains of his strength in privateering. During the same year, 1761, the navy lost one ship-of-the-line, which was retaken, and one cutter. At the same time, notwithstanding the various exchanges, the English still held twenty-five thousand French prisoners, while the English prisoners in France were but twelve hundred. These were the results of the sea war.

[17] Campbell: Lives of the Admirals.

Finally, in summing up the commercial condition of the kingdom at the end of the war, after mentioning the enormous sums of specie taken from Spain, the writer says:—

"These strengthened trade and fostered industry. The remittances for foreign subsidies were in great part paid by bills on merchants settled abroad, who had the value of the drafts in British manufactures. The trade of England increased gradually every year, and such a scene of national prosperity while waging a long, costly, and bloody war, was never before shown by any people in the world."

No wonder, with such results to her commerce and such unvarying success attending her arms, and seeing the practical annihilation of the French navy, that the union of France and Spain, which was then lowering on her future and had once excited the fears of all Europe, was now beheld by Great Britain alone without the smallest fear or despondency. Spain was by her constitution and the distribution of her empire peculiarly open to the attack of a great sea people; and whatever the views of the government of the day, Pitt and the nation saw that the hour had come, which had been hoped for in vain in 1739, because then years of peace and the obstinate bias of a great minister had relaxed the muscles of her fleet. Now she but reached forth her hand and seized what she wished; nor could there have been any limit to her prey, had not the ministry again been untrue to the interests of the country.

The position of Portugal with reference to Great Britain has been alluded to, but merits some special attention as instancing an element of sea power obtained not by colonies, but by alliance, whether necessary or prudential. The commercial connection before spoken of "was strengthened by the strongest political ties. The two kingdoms were so situated as to have little to fear from each other, while they might impart many mutual advantages. The harbors of Portugal gave shelter as well as supplies to the English fleet, while the latter defended the rich trade of Portugal with Brazil. The antipathy between Portugal and Spain made it necessary for the former to have an ally, strong yet distant. None is so advantageous in that way as England, which in her turn might, and always has, derived great advantages from Portugal in a war with any of the southern powers of Europe."

This is an English view of a matter which to others looks somewhat like an alliance between a lion and a lamb. To call a country with a fleet like England's "distant" from a small maritime nation like Portugal is an absurdity. England is, and yet more in those days was, wherever her fleet could go. The opposite view of the matter, showing equally the value of the alliance, was well set forth in the memorial by which, under the civil name of an invitation, the crowns of France and Spain ordered Portugal to declare against England.

The grounds of that memorial—namely, the unequal benefit to Portugal from the connection and the disregard of Portuguese neutrality—have already been given. The king of Portugal refused to abandon the alliance, for the professed reason that it was ancient and wholly defensive. To this the two crowns replied:—

"The defensive alliance is actually an offensive one by the situation of the Portuguese dominions and the nature of the English power. The English squadrons cannot in all seasons keep the sea, nor cruise on the principal coasts of France and Spain for cutting off the navigation of the two countries, without the ports and assistance of Portugal; and these islanders could not insult all maritime Europe, if the whole riches of Portugal did not pass through their hands, which furnishes them with the means to make war and renders the alliance truly and properly offensive."

Between the two arguments the logic of situation and power prevailed. Portugal found England nearer and more dangerous than Spain, and remained for generations of trial true to the alliance. This relationship was as useful to England as any of her colonial possessions, depending of course upon the scene of the principal operations at any particular time.

The preliminaries of peace were signed at Fontainebleau, November 3, 1762; the definitive treaty on the 10th of the following February, at Paris, whence the peace takes its name.

By its terms France renounced all claims to Canada, Nova Scotia, and all the islands of the St. Lawrence; along with Canada she ceded the valley of the Ohio and all her territory on the east side of the Mississippi, except the city of New Orleans. At the same time Spain, as an equivalent for Havana, which England restored, yielded Florida, under which name were comprised all her continental possessions east of the Mississippi. Thus England obtained a colonial empire embracing Canada, from Hudson's Bay, and all of the present United States east of the Mississippi. The possibilities of this vast region were then only partially foreseen, and as yet there was no foreshadowing of the revolt of the thirteen colonies.

In the West Indies, England gave back to France the important islands of Guadeloupe and Martinique. The four so-called neutral islands of the Lesser Antilles were divided between the two powers; Sta. Lucia going to France, St. Vincent, Tobago, and Dominica to England, which also retained Grenada.

Minorca was given back to England; and as the restoration of the island to Spain had been one of the conditions of the alliance with the latter, France, unable to fulfil her stipulation, ceded to Spain Louisiana west of the Mississippi.

In India, France recovered the possessions she had held before Dupleix began his schemes of aggrandizement; but she gave up the right of erecting fortifications or keeping troops in Bengal, and so left the station at Chandernagore defenceless. In a word, France resumed her facilities for trading, but practically abandoned her pretensions to political influence. It was tacitly understood that the English company would keep all its conquests.

The right of fishing upon the coasts of Newfoundland and in parts of the Gulf of St. Lawrence, which France had previously enjoyed, was conceded to her by this treaty; but it was denied to Spain, who had claimed it for her fishermen. This concession was among those most attacked by the English opposition.

The nation at large and Pitt, the favorite of the nation, were bitterly opposed to the terms of the treaty. "France," said Pitt, "is chiefly formidable to us as a maritime and commercial power. What we gain in this respect is valuable to us above all through the injury to her which results from it. You leave to France the possibility of reviving her navy." In truth, from the point of view of sea power and of the national jealousies which the spirit of that age sanctioned, these words, though illiberal, were strictly justifiable. The restoration to France of her colonies in the West Indies and her stations in India, together with the valuable right of fishery in her former American possessions, put before her the possibility and the inducement to restore her shipping, her commerce, and her navy, and thus tended to recall her from the path of continental ambition which had been so fatal to her interests, and in the same proportion favorable to the unprecedented growth of England's power upon the ocean. The opposition, and indeed some of the ministry, also thought that so commanding and important a position as Havana was poorly paid for by the cession of the yet desolate and unproductive region called Florida. Porto Rico was suggested, Florida accepted. There were other minor points of difference, into which it is unnecessary to enter. It could scarcely be denied that with the commanding military control of the sea held by England, grasping as she now did so many important positions, with her navy overwhelmingly superior in numbers, and her commerce and internal condition very thriving, more rigorous terms might easily have been exacted and would have been prudent. The ministry defended their eagerness and spirit of concession on the ground of the enormous growth of the debt, which then amounted to £122,000,000, a sum in every point of view much greater then than now; but while this draft upon the future was fully justified by the success of the war, it also imperatively demanded that the utmost advantages which the military situation made attainable should be exacted. This the ministry failed to do. As regards the debt, it is well observed by a French writer that "in this war, and for years afterward, England had in view nothing less than the conquest of America and the progress of her East India Company. By these two countries her manufactures and commerce acquired more than sufficient outlets, and repaid her for the numerous sacrifices she had made. Seeing the maritime decay of Europe,—its commerce annihilated, its manufactures so little advanced,—how could the English nation feel afraid of a future which offered so vast a perspective?" Unfortunately the nation needed an exponent in the government; and its chosen mouthpiece, the only man, perhaps, able to rise to the level of the great opportunity, was out of favor at court.

Nevertheless, the gains of England were very great, not only in territorial increase, nor yet in maritime preponderance, but in the prestige and position achieved in the eyes of the nations, now fully opened to her great resources and mighty power. To these results, won by the sea, the issue of the continental war offered a singular and suggestive contrast. France had already withdrawn, along with England, from all share in that strife, and peace between the other parties to it was signed five days after the Peace of Paris. The terms of the peace were simply the *status quo ante bellum*. By the estimate of the king of Prussia, one hundred and eighty thousand of his soldiers had fallen or died in this war, out of a kingdom of five million souls; while the losses of Russia, Austria, and France aggregated four hundred and sixty thousand men. The result was simply that things remained as they were.[18] To attribute this only to a difference between the possibilities of land and sea war is of course absurd. The genius of Frederick, backed by the money of England, had proved an equal match for the mismanaged and not always hearty efforts of a coalition numerically overwhelming. What does seem a fair conclusion is, that States having a good seaboard, or even ready access to the ocean by one or two outlets, will find it to their advantage to seek prosperity and extension by the way of the sea and of commerce, rather than in attempts to unsettle and modify existing political arrangements in countries where a more or less long possession of power has conferred acknowledged rights, and created national allegiance or political ties. Since the Treaty of Paris in 1763, the waste places of the world have been rapidly filled; witness our own continent, Australia, and even South America. A nominal and more or less clearly defined political possession now generally exists in the most forsaken regions, though to this statement there are some marked exceptions; but in many places this political possession is little more than nominal, and in others of a character so feeble that it cannot rely upon itself alone for support or protection. The familiar and notorious example of the Turkish Empire, kept erect only by the forces pressing upon it from opposing sides, by the mutual jealousies of powers that have no sympathy with it, is an instance of such weak political tenure; and though the question is wholly European, all know enough of it to be aware that the interest and control of the sea powers is among the chief, if not the first, of the elements that now fix the situation; and that they, if intelligently used, will direct the future inevitable changes. Upon the western continents the political condition of the Central American and tropical South American States is so unstable as to cause constant anxiety about the maintenance of internal order, and seriously to interfere with commerce and with the peaceful development of their resources. So long as—to use a familiar expression—they hurt no one but themselves, this may go on; but for a long time the citizens of more stable governments

[18] See Annual Register, 1762, p. 63.

have been seeking to exploit their resources, and have borne the losses arising from their distracted condition. North America and Australia still offer large openings to immigration and enterprise; but they are filling up rapidly, and as the opportunities there diminish, the demand must arise for a more settled government in those disordered States, for security to life and for reasonable stability of institutions enabling merchants and others to count upon the future. There is certainly no present hope that such a demand can be fulfilled from the existing native materials; if the same be true when the demand arises, no theoretical positions, like the Monroe Doctrine, will prevent interested nations from attempting to remedy the evil by some measure, which, whatever it may be called, will be a political interference. Such interferences must produce collisions, which may be at times settled by arbitration, but can scarcely fail at other times to cause war. Even for a peaceful solution, that nation will have the strongest arguments which has the strongest organized force. It need scarcely be said that the successful piercing of the Central American Isthmus at any point may precipitate the moment that is sure to come sooner or later. The profound modification of commercial routes expected from this enterprise, the political importance to the United States of such a channel of communication between her Atlantic and Pacific seaboards, are not, however, the whole nor even the principal part of the question. As far as can be seen, the time will come when stable governments for the American tropical States must be assured by the now existing powerful and stable States of America or Europe. The geographical position of those States, the climatic conditions, make it plain at once that sea power will there, even more than in the case of Turkey, determine what foreign State shall predominate,—if not by actual possession, by its influence over the native governments. The geographical position of the United States and her intrinsic power give her an undeniable advantage; but that advantage will not avail if there is a great inferiority of organized brute-force, which still remains the last argument of republics as of kings. Herein lies to us the great and still living interest of the Seven Years' War. In it we have seen and followed England, with an army small as compared with other States, as is still her case to-day, first successfully defending her own shores, then carrying her arms in every direction, spreading her rule and influence over remote regions, and not only binding them to her obedience, but making them tributary to her wealth, her strength, and her reputation. As she loosens the grasp and neutralizes the influence of France and Spain in regions beyond the sea, there is perhaps seen the prophecy of some other great nation in days yet to come, that will incline the balance of power in some future sea war, whose scope will be recognized afterward, if not by contemporaries, to have been the political future and the economical development of regions before lost to civilization; but that nation will not be the United States if the moment find her indifferent, as now, to the empire of the seas.

The direction then given to England's efforts, by the instinct of the nation and the fiery genius of Pitt, continued after the war, and has profoundly influenced her subsequent policy. Mistress now of North America, lording it in India, through the company whose territorial conquests had been ratified by native princes, over twenty millions of inhabitants,—a population larger than that of Great Britain and having a revenue respectable alongside of that of the home government,—England, with yet other rich possessions scattered far and wide over the globe, had ever before her eyes, as a salutary lesson, the severe chastisement which the weakness of Spain had allowed her to inflict upon that huge disjointed empire. The words of the English naval historian of that war, speaking about Spain, apply with slight modifications to England in our own day:

"Spain is precisely that power against which England can always contend with the fairest prospect of advantage and honor. That extensive monarchy is exhausted at heart, her resources lie at a great distance, and whatever power commands the sea, may command the wealth and commerce of Spain. The dominions from which she draws her resources, lying at an immense distance from the capital and from one another, make it more necessary for her than for any other State to temporize, until she can inspire with activity all parts of her enormous but disjointed empire." [19]

It would be untrue to say that England is exhausted at heart; but her dependence upon the outside world is such as to give a certain suggestiveness to the phrase.

This analogy of positions was not overlooked by England. From that time forward up to our own day, the possessions won for her by her sea power have combined with that sea power itself to control

[19] Campbell: Lives of the Admirals.

her policy. The road to India—in the days of Clive a distant and perilous voyage on which she had not a stopping-place of her own—was reinforced as opportunity offered by the acquisition of St. Helena, of the Cape of Good Hope, of the Mauritius. When steam made the Red Sea and Mediterranean route practicable, she acquired Aden, and yet later has established herself at Socotra. Malta had already fallen into her hands during the wars of the French Revolution; and her commanding position, as the corner-stone upon which the coalitions against Napoleon rested, enabled her to claim it at the Peace of 1815. Being but a short thousand miles from Gibraltar, the circles of military command exercised by these two places intersect. The present day has seen the stretch from Malta to the Isthmus of Suez, formerly without a station, guarded by the cession to her of Cyprus. Egypt, despite the jealousy of France, has passed under English control. The importance of that position to India, understood by Napoleon and Nelson, led the latter at once to send an officer overland to Bombay with the news of the battle of the Nile and the downfall of Bonaparte's hopes. Even now, the jealousy with which England views the advance of Russia in Central Asia is the result of those days in which her sea power and resources triumphed over the weakness of D'Aché and the genius of Suffren, and wrenched the peninsula of India from the ambition of the French.

"For the first time since the Middle Ages," says M. Martin, speaking of the Seven Years' War, "England had conquered France single-handed almost without allies, France having powerful auxiliaries. She had conquered solely by the superiority of her government."

Yes! but by the superiority of her government using the tremendous weapon of her sea power. This made her rich, and in turn protected the trade by which she had her wealth. With her money she upheld her few auxiliaries, mainly Prussia and Hanover, in their desperate strife. Her power was everywhere that her ships could reach, and there was none to dispute the sea to her. Where she would she went, and with her went her guns and her troops. By this mobility her forces were multiplied, those of her enemies distracted. Ruler of the seas, she everywhere obstructed its highways. The enemies' fleets could not join; no great fleet could get out, or if it did, it was only to meet at once, with uninured officers and crews, those who were veterans in gales and warfare. Save in the case of Minorca, she carefully held her own sea-bases and eagerly seized those of the enemy. What a lion in the path was Gibraltar to the French squadrons of Toulon and Brest! What hope for French succor to Canada, when the English fleet had Louisburg under its lee?

The one nation that gained in this war was that which used the sea in peace to earn its wealth, and ruled it in war by the extent of its navy, by the number of its subjects who lived on the sea or by the sea, and by its numerous bases of operations scattered over the globe. Yet it must be observed that these bases themselves would have lost their value if their communications remained obstructed. Therefore the French lost Louisburg, Martinique, Pondicherry; so England herself lost Minorca. The service between the bases and the mobile force between the ports and the fleets is mutual.[20] In this respect the navy is essentially a light corps; it keeps open the communications between its own ports, it obstructs those of the enemy; but it sweeps the sea for the service of the land, it controls the desert that man may live and thrive on the habitable globe.

[20] These remarks, always true, are doubly so now since the introduction of steam. The renewal of coal is a want more frequent, more urgent, more peremptory, than any known to the sailing-ship. It is vain to look for energetic naval operations distant from coal stations. It is equally vain to acquire distant coaling stations without maintaining a powerful navy; they will but fall into the hands of the enemy. But the vainest of all delusions is the expectation of bringing down an enemy by commerce-destroying alone, with no coaling stations outside the national boundaries.

9

Course of Events from the Peace of Paris to 1778—Maritime War consequent upon the American Revolution—Sea Battle off Ushant

If England had reason to complain that she had not reaped from the Treaty of Paris all the advantages that her military achievements and position entitled her to expect, France had every cause for discontent at the position in which the war left her. The gain of England was nearly measured by her losses; even the cession of Florida, made to the conqueror by Spain, had been bought by France at the price of Louisiana. Naturally the thoughts of her statesmen and of her people, as they bent under the present necessity to bear the burden of the vanquished, turned to the future with its possibilities of revenge and compensation. The Duc de Choiseul, able though imperious, remained for many years more at the head of affairs, and worked persistently to restore the power of France from the effects of the treaty. The Austrian alliance had been none of his seeking; it was already made and working when he came to office in 1758; but he had even at the first recognized that the chief enemy was England, and tried as far as could be to direct the forces of the nation against her. The defeat of Conflans having thwarted his projects of invasion, he next sought, in entire consistency with his main purpose, to stir up Spain and gain her alliance. The united efforts of the two kingdoms with their fine seaboards could, under good administration and with time for preparation, put afloat a navy that would be a fair counterpoise to that of England. It was also doubtless true that weaker maritime States, if they saw such a combination successfully made and working efficiently, would pluck up heart to declare against a government whose greatness excited envy and fear, and which acted with the disregard to the rights and welfare of others common to all uncontrolled power. Unhappily for both France and Spain, the alliance came too late. The virtual annihilation of the French fleet in 1759 was indeed followed by an outburst of national enthusiasm for the navy, skilfully fostered and guided by Choiseul. "Popular feeling took up the cry, from one end of France to the other, 'The navy must be restored.' Gifts of cities, corporations, and private individuals raised funds. A prodigious activity sprang up in the lately silent ports; everywhere ships were building and repairing." The minister also recognized the need of restoring the discipline and tone, as well as the material of the navy. The hour, however, was too late; the middle of a great and unsuccessful war is no time to begin preparations. "Better late than never" is not so safe a proverb as "In time of peace prepare for war." The condition of Spain was better. When war broke out, the English naval historian estimates that she had one hundred ships of all sizes; of these, probably sixty were of the line. Nevertheless, although the addition of Spain to her numerous enemies might make the position of England seem critical, the combination in her favor of numbers, skill, experience, and prestige, was irresistible. With seventy thousand veteran seamen, she had only to maintain a position already won. The results we know.

After the peace, Choiseul wisely remained faithful to his own first ideas. The restoration of the navy continued, and was accompanied and furthered by a spirit of professional ambition and of desire to excel, among the officers of the navy, which has been before mentioned, and which, in the peculiar condition of the United States navy at the present day, may be commended as a model. The building of ships-of-war continued with great activity and on a large scale. At the end of the war, thanks to the movement begun in 1761, there were forty ships-of-the-line in good condition. In 1770, when Choiseul was dismissed, the royal navy numbered sixty-four of the line and fifty frigates afloat. The arsenals and store-houses were filled, and a stock of ship-timber laid up. At the same time the minister tried to improve the efficiency of the officers by repressing the arrogant spirit of those of noble birth, which showed itself both toward superiors and toward another order of officers, not of the nobility, whose abilities made them desired on board the fleet. This class-feeling carried with it a curious sentiment of equality among officers of very different grades, which injuriously affected the spirit of subordination. Members, all, of a privileged social order, their equality as such was more clearly recognized than their inequality as junior and senior. The droll story told by Marryat of the midshipman, who represented to his captain that a certain statement had been made in confidence, seems to have had a realization on the French quarter-deck of that day. "Confidence!" cried the captain; "who ever heard of confidence between a post-captain and a midshipman!" "No sir," replied the youngster, "not between a captain and a midshipman, but between two gentlemen." Disputes, arguments, suggestions, between two gentlemen, forgetful of their relative rank, would break out at critical moments, and the feeling of equality, which wild democratic notions spread throughout the fleets of the republic, was curiously forestalled by that existing among the members of a most haughty aristocracy. "I saw by his face," says one of Marryat's heroes, "that the first lieutenant did not agree with the captain; but he was too good an officer to say so at such a moment." The phrase expresses one of the deepest-rooted merits of the English system, the want of which is owned by French writers:—

"Under Louis XVI. the intimacy and fellowship existing between the chief and the subordinate led the latter to discuss the orders which were given him. . . . The relaxation of discipline and the spirit of independence were due also to another cause than that pointed out; they can be partly attributed to the regulation of the officers' messes. Admiral, captain, officers, midshipmen, ate together; everything was in common. They thee-and-thou'd each other like chums. In handling the ship, the inferior gave his opinion, argued, and the chief, irritated, often preferred to yield rather than make enemies. Facts of this kind are asserted by witnesses whose truthfulness is above suspicion." [1]

Insubordination of this character, to which weaker men gave way, dashed in vain against the resolute and fiery temper of Suffren; but the spirit of discontent rose almost to the height of mutiny, causing him to say in his despatches to the minister of the navy, after his fourth battle: "My heart is pierced by the most general defection.

[1] Troude: Batailles Navales.

It is frightful to think that I might four times have destroyed the English fleet, and that it still exists." Choiseul's reforms broke against this rock, which only the uprising of the whole nation finally removed; but in the personnel of the crews a great improvement was made. In 1767 he reorganized the artillery of the fleet, forming a body of ten thousand gunners, who were systematically drilled once a week during the ten years still to intervene before the next war with England.

Losing sight of no part of his plans, Choiseul, while promoting the naval and military power of France, paid special attention to the alliance with Spain and judiciously encouraged and furthered the efforts of that country in the path of progress under Charles III., the best of her kings of the Bourbon line. The Austrian alliance still existing was maintained, but his hopes were chiefly fixed upon Spain. The wisdom and insight which had at once fastened upon England as the centre of enmity to France had been justified and further enlightened by the whole course of the Seven Years' War. In Spain was the surest, and, with good administration, the most powerful ally. The close proximity of the two countries, the relative positions of their ports, made the naval situation particularly strong; and the alliance which was dictated by sound policy, by family ties, and by just fear of England's sea power, was further assured to France by recent and still existing injuries that must continue to rankle with Spain. Gibraltar, Minorca, and Florida were still in the hands of England; no Spaniard could be easy till this reproach was wiped out.

It may be readily believed, as is asserted by French historians, that England viewed with disquietude the growth of the French navy, and would gladly have nipped it betimes; but it is more doubtful whether she would have been willing to force a war for that purpose. During the years succeeding the Peace of Paris a succession of short ministries, turning mainly upon questions of internal policy or unimportant party arrangement, caused her foreign policy to present a marked contrast to the vigorous, overbearing, but straightforward path followed by Pitt. Internal commotions, such as are apt to follow great wars, and above all the controversy with the North American colonies, which began as early as 1765 with the well-known Stamp Act, conspired with other causes to stay the hand of England. Twice at least during the years of Choiseul's ministry there occurred opportunities which a resolute, ready, and not too scrupulous government might easily have converted into a cause of war; the more so as they involved that sea power which is to England above all other nations the object of just and jealous concern. In 1764 the Genoese, weary of their unsuccessful attempts to control Corsica, again asked France to renew the occupation of the ports which had been garrisoned by her in 1756. The Corsicans also sent an ambassador to France in order to solicit recognition of the independence of the island, in consideration of a tribute equivalent to that which they had formerly paid to Genoa. The latter, feeling its inability to reconquer the island, at length decided practically to cede it. The transaction took the shape of a formal permission for the king of France to exercise all the rights of sovereignty over all the places and harbors of Corsica, as security for debts owing to him by the republic. This cession, disguised under the form of a security in order to palliate the aggrandizement of France in the eyes of Austria and England, recalls the conditional and thinly veiled surrender of Cyprus to England nine years ago,—a transfer likely to be as final and far-reaching as that of Corsica. England then remonstrated and talked angrily; but though Burke said, "Corsica as a province of France is terrible to me," only one member of the House of Commons, the veteran admiral Sir Charles Saunders, was found to say "that it would be better to go to war with France than consent to her taking possession of Corsica." [2] Having in view the then well-recognized interests of England in the Mediterranean, it is evident that an island so well situated as Corsica for influencing the shores of Italy and checking the naval station at Minorca, would not have been allowed to go into the hands of a strong master, if the nation had felt ready and willing for war.

Again, in 1770, a dispute arose between England and Spain relative to the possession of the Falkland Islands. It is not material to state the nature of either claim to what was then but a collection of barren islands, destitute of military as well as of natural advantages. Both England and Spain had had a settlement, on which the national colors were flying; and at the English station a captain in the navy commanded. Before this settlement, called Port Egmont, there suddenly appeared, in June, 1770, a Spanish expedition, fitted out in Buenos Ayres, of five frigates and sixteen hundred soldiers. To

[2] Mahon: History of England.

such a force the handful of Englishmen could make no serious resistance; so after a few shots, exchanged for the honor of the flag, they capitulated.

The news of this transaction, which reached England in the following October, showed by its reception how much more serious is an insult than an injury, and how much more bitterly resented. The transfer of Corsica had scarcely occasioned a stir outside the offices of statesmen; the attack on Port Egmont roused the people and Parliament. The minister to Madrid was ordered to demand the immediate restoration of the islands, with a disavowal of the action of the officer who had ordered the attack. Without waiting for a reply, ships were ordered into commission, press-gangs swept the streets, and in a short time a powerful fleet was ready at Spithead to revenge the insult. Spain, relying upon the Bourbon family compact and the support of France, was disposed to stand firm; but the old king, Louis XV., was averse to war, and Choiseul, among whose enemies at court was the last mistress, was dismissed. With his fall disappeared the hopes of Spain, which at once complied with the demands of England, reserving, however, the question as to the rights of sovereignty. This conclusion shows clearly that England, though still wielding an effective sea power able to control Spain, was not eager for a war merely in order to break down the rival navies.

It is not wholly alien to the question of sea power to note, without dwelling upon it, a great event which now happened, seemingly utterly removed from all relation to the sea. The first partition of Poland between Prussia, Russia, and Austria, carried out in 1772, was made easier by the preoccupation of Choiseul with his naval policy and the Spanish alliance. The friendship and support of Poland and Turkey, as checks upon the House of Austria, were part of the tradition received from Henry IV. and Richelieu; the destruction of the former was a direct blow to the pride and interest of France. What Choiseul would have done had he been in office, cannot be known; but if the result of the Seven Years' War had been different, France might have interfered to some purpose.

On the 10th of May, 1774, Louis XV. died, at the time when the troubles in the North American colonies were fast coming to a head. Under his youthful successor, Louis XVI., the policy of peace on the continent, of friendly alliance with Spain, and of building up the navy in numbers and efficiency, was continued. This was the foreign policy of Choiseul, directed against the sea power of England as the chief enemy, and toward the sea power of France as the chief support, of the nation. The instructions which, according to a French naval author, the new king gave to his ministers show the spirit with which his reign up to the Revolution was inspired, whether or not they originated with the king himself:—

"To watch all indications of approaching danger; to observe by cruisers the approaches to our islands and the entrance to the Gulf of Mexico; to keep track of what was passing on the banks of Newfoundland, and to follow the tendencies of English commerce; to observe in England the state of the troops and armaments, the public credit and the ministry; to meddle adroitly in the affairs of the British colonies; to give the insurgent colonists the means of obtaining supplies of war, while maintaining the strictest neutrality; to develop actively, but noiselessly, the navy; to repair our ships of war; to fill our storehouses and to keep on hand the means for rapidly equipping a fleet at Brest and at Toulon, while Spain should be fitting one at Ferrol; finally, at the first serious fear of rupture, to assemble numerous troops upon the shores of Brittany and Normandy, and get everything ready for an invasion of England, so as to force her to concentrate her forces, and thus restrict her means of resistance at the extremities of the empire." [3]

Such instructions, whether given all at once as a symmetrical, well-thought-out plan, or from time to time, as occasion arose, showed that an accurate forecast of the situation had been made, and breathed a conviction which, if earlier felt, would have greatly modified the history of the two countries. The execution was less thorough than the conception.

In the matter of developing the navy, however, fifteen years of peace and steady work showed good results. When war openly broke out in 1778, France had eighty ships-of-the-line in good condition, and sixty-seven thousand seamen were borne on the rolls of the maritime conscription. Spain, when she entered the war in 1779 as the ally of France, had in her ports nearly sixty ships-of-the-line. To this combination England opposed a total number of two hundred and twenty-eight ships of all classes, of which about one hundred and fifty were of the line. The apparent equality in material which would result from these numbers was affected, to the disadvantage of England, by the superior size and artillery of the French and Spaniards;

[3] La Pérouse-Bonfils, vol. iii, p. 5.

but on the other hand her strength was increased by the unity of aim imparted by belonging to one nation. The allies were destined to feel the proverbial weakness of naval coalitions, as well as the degenerate administration of Spain, and the lack of habit—may it not even be said without injustice, of aptitude for the sea—of both nations. The naval policy with which Louis XVI. began his reign was kept up to the end; in 1791, two years after the assembly of the States-General, the French navy numbered eighty-six ships-of-the-line, generally superior, both in dimensions and model, to English ships of the same class.

We have come, therefore, to the beginning of a truly maritime war; which, as will be granted by those who have followed this narrative, had not been seen since the days of De Ruyter and Tourville. The magnificence of sea power and its value had perhaps been more clearly shown by the uncontrolled sway, and consequent exaltation, of one belligerent; but the lesson thus given, if more striking, is less vividly interesting than the spectacle of that sea power meeting a foe worthy of its steel, and excited to exertion by a strife which endangered, not only its most valuable colonies, but even its own shores. Waged, from the extended character of the British Empire, in all quarters of the world at once, the attention of the student is called now to the East Indies and now to the West; now to the shores of the United States and thence to those of England; from New York and Chesapeake Bay to Gibraltar and Minorca, to the Cape Verde Islands, the Cape of Good Hope, and Ceylon. Fleets now meet fleets of equal size, and the general chase and the *mêlée*, which marked the actions of Hawke, Boscawen, and Anson, though they still occur at times, are for the most part succeeded by wary and complicated manœuvres, too often barren of decisive results as naval battles, which are the prevailing characteristic of this coming war. The superior tactical science of the French succeeded in imparting to this conflict that peculiar feature of their naval policy, which subordinated the control of the sea by the destruction of the enemy's fleets, of his organized naval forces, to the success of particular operations, the retention of particular points, the carrying out of particular ulterior strategic ends. It is not necessary to endeavor to force upon others the conviction of the present writer that such a policy, however applicable as an exception, is faulty as a rule; but

298

it is most desirable that all persons responsible for the conduct of naval affairs should recognize that the two lines of policy, in direct contradiction to each other, do exist. In the one there is a strict analogy to a war of posts; while in the other the objective is that force whose destruction leaves the posts unsupported and therefore sure to fall in due time. These opposing policies being recognized, consideration should also be had of the results of the two as exemplified in the history of England and France.

It was not, however, with such cautious views that the new king at first sought to impress his admirals. In the instructions addressed to the Count d'Orvilliers, commanding the first fleet sent out from Brest, the minister, speaking in the name of the king, says:—-

"Your duty now is to restore to the French flag the lustre with which it once shone; past misfortunes and faults must be buried out of sight; only by the most illustrious actions can the navy hope to succeed in doing this. His Majesty has the right to expect the greatest efforts from his officers. . . . Under whatever circumstances the king's fleet may be placed, his Majesty's orders, which he expressly charges me to impress upon you, as well as upon all officers in command, are that his ships attack with the greatest vigor, and defend themselves, on all occasions, to the last extremity."

More follows to the same effect; upon which a French officer, who has not before been quoted in connection with this phase of French naval policy, says:—

"How different this language from that held to our admirals during the last war; for it would be an error to believe that they followed by choice and temper the timid and defensive system which predominated in the tactics of the navy. The government, always finding the expenses exacted by the employment of the navy excessive, too often prescribed to its admirals to keep the sea as long as possible without coming to pitched battles, or even to brushes, generally very expensive, and from which might follow the loss of ships difficult to replace. Often they were enjoined, if driven to accept action, carefully to avoid compromising the fate of their squadron by too decisive encounters. They thought themselves, therefore, obliged to retreat as soon as an engagement took too serious a turn. Thus they acquired the unhappy habit of voluntarily yielding the field of battle as soon as an enemy, even inferior, boldly disputed it with them. Thus to send a fleet to meet the enemy, only to retire shamefully from his presence; to receive action instead of offering it; to begin battles only to end them with the semblance of defeat; to ruin moral force in order to save physical force,—that was the spirit which, as has been very judiciously said by M. Charles Dupin, guided the French ministry of that epoch. The results are known." [4]

The brave words of Louis XVI. were followed almost immediately by others, of different and qualifying tenor, to Admiral d'Orvilliers before he sailed. He was informed that the king, having learned the strength of the English fleet, relied upon his prudence as to the conduct to be followed at a moment when he had under his orders all the naval force of which France could dispose. As a matter of fact the two fleets were nearly equal; it would be impossible to decide which was the stronger, without detailed information as to the armament of every ship. D'Orvilliers found himself, as many a responsible man has before, with two sets of orders, on one or the other of which he was sure to be impaled, if unlucky; while the government, in the same event, was sure of a scape-goat.

The consideration of the relative force of the two navies, material and moral, has necessarily carried us beyond the date of the opening of the American Revolutionary War. Before beginning with that struggle, it may be well to supplement the rough estimate of England's total naval force, given, in lack of more precise information, by the statement of the First Lord of the Admiralty made in the House of Lords in November, 1777, a very few months before the war with France began. Replying to a complaint of the opposition as to the smallness of the Channel fleet, he said:—

"We have now forty-two ships-of-the-line in commission in Great Britain (without counting those on foreign service), thirty-five of which are completely manned, and ready for sea at a moment's warning. . . . I do not believe that either France or Spain entertains any hostile disposition toward us; but from what I have now submitted to you, I am authorized to affirm that our navy is more than a match for that of the whole House of Bourbon." [5]

It must, however, be said that this pleasing prospect was not realized by Admiral Keppel when appointed to command in the following March, and looking at his fleet with (to use his own apt expression) "a seaman's eye"; [6] and in June he went to sea with only twenty ships.

[4] Troude, vol. ii, pp. 3-5. For other quotations from French authors to the same effect, see *ante*, pages 67, 69, 70.
[5] Mahon: History of England; Gentleman's Magazine, 1777, p. 553.
[6] Keppel's Defence.

It is plainly undesirable to insert in a narrative of this character any account of the political questions which led to the separation of the United States from the British Empire. It has already been remarked that the separation followed upon a succession of blunders by the English ministry,—not unnatural in view of the ideas generally prevalent at that day as to the relations of colonies to the mother-country. It needed a man of commanding genius to recognize, not only the substantial justice of the American claims,—many did that,—but also the military strength of their situation, as before indicated. This lay in the distance of the colonies from home, their nearness to each other independently of the command of the sea, the character of the colonists,—mainly of English and Dutch stock, —and the probable hostility of France and Spain. Unfortunately for England, the men most able to cope with the situation were in the minority and out of office.

It has been said before that, had the thirteen colonies been islands, the sea power of Great Britain would have so completely isolated them that their fall, one after the other, must have ensued. To this it may be added that the narrowness of the strip then occupied by civilized man, and the manner in which it was intersected by estuaries of the sea and navigable rivers, practically reduced to the condition of islands, so far as mutual support went, great sections of the insurgent country, which were not large enough to stand alone, yet too large for their fall not to have been a fatal blow to the common cause. The most familiar case is that of the line of the Hudson, where the Bay of New York was held from the first by the British, who also took the city in September, 1776, two months after the Declaration of Independence. The difficulties in the way of moving up and down such a stream were doubtless much greater to sailing vessels than they now are to steamers; yet it seems impossible to doubt that active and capable men wielding the great sea power of England could so have held that river and Lake Champlain with ships-of-war at intervals and accompanying galleys as to have supported a sufficient army moving between the head-waters of the Hudson and the lake, while themselves preventing any intercourse by water between New England and the States west of the river. This operation would have closely resembled that by which in the Civil War the United States fleets and armies gradually cut in twain the Southern Confederacy by mastering the course of the Mississippi, and the political results would have been even more important than the military; for at that early stage of the war the spirit of independence was far more general and bitter in the section that would have been cut off,—in New England,—than in New York and New Jersey, perhaps than anywhere except in South Carolina.[7]

In 1777 the British attempted to accomplish this object by sending General Burgoyne from Canada to force his way by Lake Champlain to the Hudson. At the same time Sir Henry Clinton moved north from New York with three thousand men, and reached West Point, whence he sent by shipping a part of his force up the river to within forty miles of Albany. Here the officer in command learned of the surrender of Burgoyne at Saratoga, and returned; but what he did at the head of a detachment from a main body of only three thousand, shows what might have been done under a better system. While this was happening on the Hudson, the English commander-in-chief of the troops acting in America had curiously enough made use of the sea power of his nation to transport the bulk of his army— fourteen thousand men—from New York to the head of Chesapeake Bay, so as to take Philadelphia in the rear. This eccentric movement was successful as regarded its objective, Philadelphia; but it was determined by political considerations, because Philadelphia was the seat of Congress, and was contrary to sound military policy. The conquest therefore was early lost; but it was yet more dearly won, for by this diversion of the British forces the different corps were placed out of mutual support, and the control of the water-line of the Hudson was abandoned. While Burgoyne, with seven thousand regular troops, besides auxiliaries, was moving down to seize the head-waters of the river, fourteen thousand men were removed from its mouth to the Chesapeake. The eight thousand left in or near New York were consequently tied to the city by the presence of the American army in New Jersey. This disastrous step was taken in August; in October Burgoyne, isolated and hemmed in, surrendered.

[7] "A candid view of our affairs, which I am going to exhibit, will make you a judge of the difficulties under which we labor. Almost all our supplies of flour and no inconsiderable part of our meat are drawn from the States westward of Hudson's River. This renders a secure communication across that river indispensably necessary, both to the support of your squadron and the army. The enemy, being masters of that navigation, would interrupt this essential intercourse between the States. They have been sensible of these advantages. . . . If they could by any demonstration in another part draw our attention and strength from this important point, and by anticipating our return possess themselves of it, the consequences would be fatal. Our dispositions must therefore have equal regard to co-operating with you [at Boston] in a defensive plan, and securing the North River, which the remoteness of the two objects from each other renders peculiarly difficult."—WASHINGTON to D'ESTAING, Sept. 11, 1778.

In the following May the English evacuated Philadelphia, and after a painful and perilous march through New Jersey, with Washington's army in close pursuit, regained New York.

This taking of the British fleet to the head of the Chesapeake, coupled with the ascent of the Potomac in 1814 by English sailing-frigates, shows another weak line in the chain of the American colonies; but it was not, like that of the Hudson and Champlain, a line both ends of which rested in the enemy's power,—in Canada on the one hand, on the sea on the other.

As to the sea warfare in general, it is needless to enlarge upon the fact that the colonists could make no head against the fleets of Great Britain, and were consequently forced to abandon the sea to them, resorting only to a cruising warfare, mainly by privateers, for which their seamanship and enterprise well fitted them, and by which they did much injury to English commerce. By the end of 1778 the English naval historian estimates that American privateers had taken nearly a thousand merchant-ships, valued at nearly £2,000,000; he claims, however, that the losses of the Americans were heavier. They should have been; for the English cruisers were both better supported and individually more powerful, while the extension of American commerce had come to be the wonder of the statesmen of the mother-country. When the war broke out, it was as great as that of England herself at the beginning of the century.

An interesting indication of the number of the seafaring population of North America at that time is given by the statement in Parliament by the First Lord of the Admiralty, "that the navy had lost eighteen thousand of the seamen employed in the last war by not having America," [8]—no inconsiderable loss to a sea power, particularly if carried over to the ranks of the enemy.

The course of warfare on the sea gave rise, as always, to grievances of neutrals against the English for the seizures of their ships in the American trade. Such provocation, however, was not necessary to excite the enmity and the hopes of France in the harassed state of the British government. The hour of reckoning, of vengeance, at which the policy of Choiseul had aimed, seemed now at hand. The question was early entertained at Paris what attitude should be assumed, what advantage drawn from the revolt of the colonies. It was decided that the latter should receive all possible support short

[8] Annual Register, 1778, p. 201.

of an actual break with England; and to this end a Frenchman named Beaumarchais was furnished with money to establish a business house which should supply the colonists with warlike stores. France gave a million francs, to which Spain added an equal sum, and Beaumarchais was allowed to buy from government arsenals. Meanwhile agents were received from the United States, and French officers passed into its service with little real hindrance from their government. Beaumarchais' house was started in 1776; in December of that year Benjamin Franklin landed in France, and in May, 1777, Lafayette came to America. Meanwhile the preparations for war, especially for a sea war, were pushed on; the navy was steadily increased, and arrangements were made for threatening an invasion from the Channel, while the real scene of the war was to be in the colonies. There France was in the position of a man who has little to lose. Already despoiled of Canada, she had every reason to believe that a renewal of war, with Europe neutral and the Americans friends instead of enemies, would not rob her of her islands. Recognizing that the Americans, who less than twenty years before had insisted upon the conquest of Canada, would not consent to her regaining it, she expressly stipulated that she would have no such hopes, but exacted that in the coming war she should retain any English West Indian possessions which she could seize. Spain was differently situated. Hating England, wanting to regain Gibraltar, Minorca, and Jamaica,—no mere jewels in her crown, but foundation-stones of her sea power,—she nevertheless saw that the successful rebellion of the English colonists against the hitherto unrivalled sea power of the mother-country would be a dangerous example to her own enormous colonial system, from which she yearly drew so great subsidies. If England with her navy should fail, what could Spain achieve? In the introductory chapter it was pointed out that the income of the Spanish government was drawn, not as a light tax upon a wealthy sea power, built upon the industry and commerce of the kingdom, but from a narrow stream of gold and silver trickling through a few treasureships loaded with the spoils of colonies administered upon the narrowest system. Spain had much to lose, as well as to gain. It was true still, as in 1760, that she was the power with which England could war to the greatest advantage. Nevertheless, existing injuries and dynastic sympathy carried the day. Spain entered upon the secretly hostile course pursued by France.

To this explosive condition of things the news of Burgoyne's surrender acted as a spark. The experience of former wars had taught France the worth of the Americans as enemies, and she was expecting to find in them valuable helpers in her schemes of revenge; now it seemed that even alone they might be able to take care of themselves, and reject any alliance. The tidings reached Europe on the 2d of December, 1777; on the 16th the French foreign minister informed the commissioners of Congress that the king was ready to recognize the independence of the United States, and to make with them a commercial treaty and contingent defensive alliance. The speed with which the business was done shows that France had made up her mind; and the treaty, so momentous in its necessary consequences, was signed on the 6th of February, 1778.

It is not necessary to give the detailed terms of the treaty; but it is important to observe, first, that the express renunciation of Canada and Nova Scotia by France foreshadowed that political theory which is now known as the Monroe Doctrine, the claims of which can scarcely be made good without an adequate sea-force; and next, that the alliance with France, and subsequently with Spain, brought to the Americans that which they above all needed,—a sea power to counterbalance that of England. Will it be too much for American pride to admit that, had France refused to contest the control of the sea with England, the latter would have been able to reduce the Atlantic seaboard? Let us not kick down the ladder by which we mounted, nor refuse to acknowledge what our fathers felt in their hour of trial.

Before going on with the story of this maritime war, the military situation as it existed in the different parts of the world should be stated.

The three features which cause it to differ markedly from that at the opening of the Seven Years' War, in 1756, are—(1) the hostile relation of America to England; (2) the early appearance of Spain as the ally of France; and (3) the neutrality of the other continental States, which left France without preoccupation on the land side.

On the North American continent the Americans had held Boston for two years. Narragansett Bay and Rhode Island were occupied by the English, who also held New York and Philadelphia. Chesapeake Bay and its entrance, being without strong posts, were in the power of any fleet that appeared against them. In the South, since the unsuccessful attack upon Charlestown in 1776, no movement of importance had been made by the English; up to the declaration of war by France the chief events of the war had been north of the Chesapeake (of Baltimore). In Canada, on the other hand, the Americans had failed, and it remained to the end a firm base to the English power.

In Europe the most significant element to be noted is the state of preparedness of the French navy, and to some extent of the Spanish, as compared with previous wars. England stood wholly on the defensive, and without allies; while the Bourbon kings aimed at the conquest of Gibraltar and Port Mahon, and the invasion of England. The first two, however, were the dear objects of Spain, the last of France; and this divergence of aims was fatal to the success of this maritime coalition. In the introductory chapter allusion was made to the strategic question raised by these two policies.

In the West Indies the grip of the two combatants on the land was in fact about equal, though it should not have been so. Both France and England were strongly posted in the Windward Islands,—the one at Martinique, the other at Barbadoes. It must be noted that the position of the latter, to windward of all others of the group, was a decided strategic advantage in the days of sail. As it happened, the fighting was pretty nearly confined to the neighborhood of the Lesser Antilles. Here, at the opening of the struggle, the English island of Dominica lay between the French Martinique and Guadeloupe; it was therefore coveted and seized. Next south of Martinique lay Sta. Lucia, a French colony. Its strong harbor on the lee side, known as Gros Ilot Bay, was a capital place from which to watch the proceedings of the French navy in Fort Royal, Martinique. The English captured the island, and from that safe anchorage Rodney watched and pursued the French fleet before his famous action in 1782. The islands to the southward were of inferior military consequence. In the greater islands, Spain should have outweighed England, holding as she did Cuba, Porto Rico, and, with France, Hayti, as against Jamaica alone. Spain, however, counted here for nothing but a deadweight; and England had elsewhere too much on her hands to attack her. The only point in America where the Spanish arms made themselves felt was in the great region east of the Mississippi, then known as Florida, which, though at that time an English possession, did not join the revolt of the colonies.

In the East Indies it will be remembered that France had received back her stations at the peace of 1763; but the political predominance of the English in Bengal was not offset by similar control of the French in any part of the peninsula. During the ensuing years the English had extended and strengthened their power, favored in so doing by the character of their chief representatives, Clive and Warren Hastings. Powerful native enemies had, however, risen against them in the south of the peninsula, both on the east and west, affording an excellent opportunity for France to regain her influence when the war broke out; but her government and people remained blind to the possibilities of that vast region. Not so England. The very day the news of the outbreak of war reached Calcutta, July 7, 1778, Hastings sent orders to the governor of Madras to attack Pondicherry, and set the example by seizing Chandernagore. The naval force of each nation was insignificant; but the French commodore, after a brief action, forsook Pondicherry, which surrendered after a siege by land and sea of seventy days. The following March, 1779, Mahé, the last French settlement, fell, and the French flag again disappeared; while at the same time there arrived a strong English squadron of six ships-of-the-line under Admiral Hughes. The absence of any similar French force gave the entire control of the sea to the English until the arrival of Suffren, nearly three years later. In the meanwhile Holland had been drawn into the war, and her stations, Negapatam on the Coromandel coast, and the very important harbor of Trincomalee in Ceylon, were both captured, the latter in January, 1782, by the joint forces of the army and navy. The successful accomplishment of these two enterprises completed the military situation in Hindostan at the time when the arrival of Suffren, just one month later, turned the nominal war into a desperate and bloody contest. Suffren found himself with a decidedly stronger squadron, but without a port, either French or allied, on which to base his operations against the English.

Of these four chief theatres of the war, two, North America and the West Indies, as might be expected from their nearness, blend and directly affect each other. This is not so obviously the case with the struggles in Europe and India. The narrative therefore naturally falls into three principal divisions, which may to some extent be treated separately. After such separate consideration their mutual influence will be pointed out, together with any useful lessons to be gathered from the goodness or badness, the success or failure, of the grand combinations, and from the part played by sea power.

On the 13th of March, 1778, the French ambassador at London notified the English government that France had acknowledged the independence of the United States, and made with them a treaty of commerce and defensive alliance. England at once recalled her ambassador; but though war was imminent and England at disadvantage, the Spanish king offered mediation, and France wrongly delayed to strike. In June, Admiral Keppel sailed from Portsmouth, with twenty ships, on a cruise. Falling in with two French frigates, his guns, to bring them to, opened the war. Finding from their papers that thirty-two French ships lay in Brest, he at once returned for reinforcements. Sailing again with thirty ships, he fell in with the French fleet under D'Orvilliers to the westward of Ushant, and to windward, with a westerly wind. On the 27th of July was fought the first fleet action of the war, generally known as the Battle of Ushant.

This battle, in which thirty ships-of-the-line fought on either side, was wholly indecisive in its results. No ship was taken or sunk; both fleets, after separating, returned to their respective ports. The action nevertheless obtained great celebrity in England from the public indignation at its lack of result, and from the storm of naval and political controversy which followed. The admiral and the officer third in command belonged to different political parties; they made charges, one against the other, and in the following courts-martial all England divided, chiefly on party lines. Public and naval sentiment generally favored the commander-in-chief, Keppel.

Tactically, the battle presents some interesting features, and involves one issue which is still living today. Keppel was to leeward and wished to force an action; in order to do this he signalled a general chase to windward, so that his fastest ships might overtake the slower ones of the enemy. Granting equal original fleet-speed, this was quite correct. D'Orvilliers, to windward, had no intention of fighting except on his own terms. As will generally be the case, the fleet acting on the offensive obtained its wish. At daybreak of the 27th both fleets were on the port tack, heading west-northwest, with a steady breeze at southwest (Plate IX., A, A, A).[9] The English rear

[9] In this plate the plan followed in every other instance, of showing only the characteristic phases of a battle, in succession but disconnected, has been abandoned, and the attempt is to indicate *continuously* the series of manœuvres and the tracks by which the fleets at last came into contact (from A to C). As the *battle* consisted merely in the passage

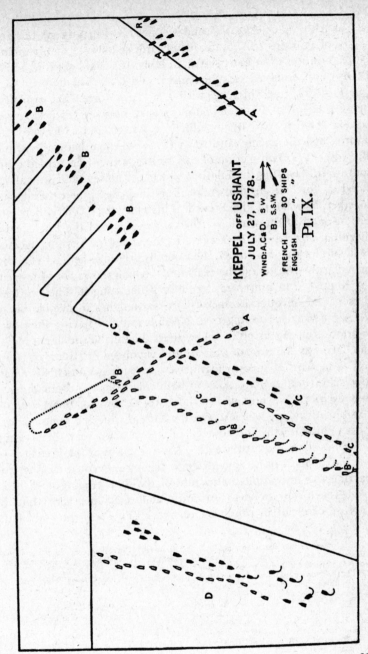

KEPPEL off USHANT
JULY 27, 1778.
WIND: A. C&D. S W
B. S.S.W.
FRENCH ⟹ 30 SHIPS
ENGLISH " "
Pl. IX.

(R) had fallen to leeward,[10] and Keppel consequently made signal to six of its ships to chase to windward, so as to place them in a better position to support the main body if it could get into action. D'Orvilliers observed this movement, and construed it to show an intention to attack his rear with a superior force. The two fleets being then from six to eight miles apart, he wore his fleet in succession (French A to B), by which he lost ground to leeward, but approached the enemy, and was able to see them better (Positions B, B, B). At the completion of this evolution the wind hauled to the southward, favoring the English; so Keppel, instead of going about, stood on for half an hour more (English B to C), and then tacked together in wake of the French. This confirmed D'Orvilliers' suspicions, and as the wind, which certainly favored the English that morning, now hauled back again to the westward, permitting them to lay up for the French rear, he wore his fleet together (B to C), thus bringing the rest to aid the rear, now become the van, and preventing Keppel from concentrating on or penetrating it. The two fleets thus passed on opposite tacks (C),[11] exchanging ineffective broadsides, the French running free to windward and having the power to attack, but not using it. D'Orvilliers then made the signal for his van, formerly the rear, to wear to leeward of the English rear, which was to leeward of its own main body, intending himself to remain to windward and so attack it on both sides; but the commander of that division, a prince of the blood royal, did not obey, and the possible advantage was lost. On the English side the same manœuvre was attempted. The admiral of the van and some of his ships tacked, as soon as out of fire (D),[12] and stood after the French rear; but for the most part the damage to rigging prevented tacking, and wearing was impossible on account of the ships coming up behind. The French now stood to leeward and formed line again, but the English were not in condition to attack. This was the end of the battle.

by each other of two fleets, moving in opposite parallel directions, an encounter always indecisive and futile, the previous manœuvres constitute the chief interest in an affair whose historical importance is due to other than tactical reasons.

[10] The line drawn through the centre of the English fleet at A shows the close-hauled line (south-southeast) on which, by strict tactical requirement, the English ships should have borne from each other.

[11] The leading ships of the two fleets diverged from each other (C), which is, by the French, attributed to the English van keeping away; by the English, it is said that the French van luffed. The latter account is followed in the diagrams.

[12] The position D, separated from the rest of the plan, shows the end of the passage by, which began at C. It could not be shown in connection with the other tracks without producing confusion.

It has been said that there are some interesting points about this resultless engagement. One is, that Keppel's conduct was approved throughout, on oath before the court-martial, by one of the most distinguished admirals England has brought forth, Sir John Jervis, who commanded a ship in the fleet. It does not indeed appear what he could have done more; but his lack of tactical understanding is shown by a curious remark in his defence. "If the French admiral really meant to come to action," says he, "I apprehend he would never have put his fleet on the contrary tack to that on which the British fleet was approaching." This remark can only proceed from ignorance or thoughtlessness of the danger to which the rear of the French fleet would have been exposed, and is more curious as he himself had said the English were lying up for it. Keppel's idea seems to have been that the French should have waited for him to come up abreast, and then go at it, ship for ship, in what was to him the good old style; D'Orvilliers was too highly trained to be capable of such action.

The failure of the Duc de Chartres,[13] commanding the French van during the firing, to wear in obedience to orders, whether due to misunderstanding or misconduct, raises the question, which is still debated, as to the proper position for a naval commander-in-chief in action. Had D'Orvilliers been in the van, he could have insured the evolution he wished. From the centre the admiral has the extremities of his fleet equally visible, or invisible, as it may be. At the head he enforces his orders by his example. The French toward the end of this war solved the question by taking him out of the line altogether and putting him on board a frigate, for the avowed reasons that he could thus better see the movements of his fleet and of the enemy without being blinded by smoke or distracted by the occurrences on board his own ship, and that his signals could be better seen.[14] This position, resembling somewhat that of a general on shore, being remote from personal risk, was also assumed by Lord Howe in 1778; but both that officer and the French abandoned the practice later. Nelson at Trafalgar, the end of his career, led his column; but it may be doubted whether he had any other motive than his ardor for battle. The two other great attacks in which he commanded in chief

13 Afterward Duc d'Orleans; the Philippe Égalité of the French Revolution, and father of Louis Philippe.
14 The capture of the French commander-in-chief on board his flag-ship, in the battle of April 12, 1782, was also a motive for this new order.

were directed against ships at anchor, and in neither did he take the head of the column; for the good reason that, his knowledge of the ground being imperfect, the leading ship was in most danger of grounding. The common practice in the days of broadside sailing-ships, except when a general chase was ordered, was for the admiral to be in the line, and in the centre of it. The departure from this custom on the part of both Nelson and Collingwood, each of whom led his own columns at Trafalgar, may have had some reason, and an ordinary man rather shrinks from criticising the action of officers of their eminence. The danger to which were exposed the two senior officers of the fleet, upon whom so much depended, is obvious; and had any serious injury befallen their persons, or the head of their columns, the lack of their influence would have been seriously felt. As it was, they were speedily obliterated, as admirals, in the smoke of the battle, leaving to those who came after them no guidance or control except the brilliancy of their courage and example. A French admiral has pointed out that the practical effect of the mode of attack at Trafalgar, two columns bearing down upon a line at right angles to them, was to sacrifice the head of the columns in making two breaches in the enemy's line. So far, very well; the sacrifice was well worth while; and into these breaches came up the rear ships of each column, nearly fresh, forming in fact a *reserve* which fell upon the shattered ships of the enemy on either side of the breaks. Now this idea of a reserve prompts a thought as to the commander-in-chief. The size of his ship was such as precluded its being out of the order; but would it not have been well had the admiral of each column been with this reserve, keeping in his hands the power of directing it according to the chances of the action, making him a reality as well as a name for some time longer, and to a very useful purpose? The difficulty of arranging any system of signals or light despatch-boats which could take the place of the aids or messengers of a general, coupled with the fact that ships cannot stand still, as divisions of men do, waiting orders, but that they must have steerage-way, precludes the idea of putting an admiral of a fleet under way in a light vessel. By so doing he becomes simply a spectator; whereas by being in the most powerful ship of the fleet he retains the utmost weight possible after action is once engaged, and, if this ship be in the reserve, the admiral keeps to the latest possible moment the power of commander-in-chief in his own hands. "Half a loaf is better than no bread"; if the admiral cannot, from the conditions of sea warfare, occupy the calmly watchful position of his brother on shore, let there be secured for him as much as may be. The practice of Farragut after New Orleans and Vicksburg, that is to say, in the latter part of his career, when it may be believed experience had determined his views, was to lead in person. It is known that he very reluctantly, at the solicitation of various officers, yielded his convictions in this matter at Mobile so far as to take the second place, and afterward freely expressed his regrets for having done so. It may, however, be argued that the character of all the actions in which Farragut commanded had a peculiarity, differentiating them from battles in the strict sense of the word. At New Orleans, at Vicksburg, at Port Hudson, and at Mobile, the task was not to engage, but to pass fortifications which the fleet confessedly could not stand up to; and the passage was to be made under conditions mainly of pilotage upon ground as to which, unlike Nelson, he had good knowledge. There was thus imposed upon the commander-in-chief the duty of leadership in the literal, as well as the military, sense of the term. So leading, he not only pointed out to the fleet the safe road, but, drawing continually ahead of the smoke, was better able to see and judge the path ahead, and to assume the responsibility of a course which he may have prescribed and intended throughout, but from which a subordinate might shrink. It has not perhaps been commonly noted, that at Mobile the leaders, not only of one but of both columns, at the critical point of the road hesitated and doubted as to the admiral's purpose; not that they had not received it clearly, but because circumstances seemed to them to be different from what he had supposed. Not only Alden in the "Brooklyn," but Craven also in the "Tecumseh," departed from the admiral's orders and left the course dictated to them, with disastrous results. There is no necessity to condemn either captain; but the irresistible inference is that Farragut was unqualifiedly right in his opinion that the man who alone has the highest responsibility should, under the conditions of his battles, be in the front. And here it must be remarked that at such critical moments of doubt any but the highest order of mind tends to throw off the responsibility of decision upon the superior, though from the instancy of the case hesitation or delay may be fatal. A man who as the commissioned chief would act intelligently, as the mere subordinate will balk. Nelson's action at

313

St. Vincent will rarely be emulated, a truth which is strongly shown by the fact that Collingwood was immediately in his rear that day, and did not imitate his action till signalled by the commander-in-chief; yet after receiving the authority of the signal, he particularly distinguished himself by his judgment and daring.[15] It will be re-called, also, in connection with this question of pilot-ground battles, that a central position nearly lost the flag-ship at New Orleans, ow-ing to the darkness and to the smoke from the preceding ships; the United States fleet came near finding itself without its leader after the passage of the forts. Now as the mention of a reserve prompted one set of considerations, so the name of pilotage suggests certain ideas, broader than itself, which modify what has been said of keep-ing the admiral with the reserve. The ease and quickness with which a steam fleet can change its formation make it very probable that a fleet bearing down to attack may find itself, almost at the very moment of collision, threatened with some unlooked-for combina-tion; then where would be the happiest position for an admiral? Doubtless in that part of his own order where he could most readily pilot his ships into the new disposition, or direction, by which he would meet the changed conditions; that is, in the position of lead-ing. It would seem that there are always two moments of greatest importance in a sea-fight; one which determines the method of the main attack, the other the bringing up and directing the effort of the reserve. If the first is more important, the second perhaps re-quires the higher order of ability; for the former may and should proceed on a before-determined plan, while the latter may, and often

[15] The following incident, occurring during Rodney's chase of De Grasse, in April, 1782, shows how far subordination may be carried. Hood was one of the finest of the British officers; nor does the author undertake to criticise his action. He was some miles from Rodney at the time. "The separated French ship in the N.W., having got the breeze at the same time as our van division, boldly stood for and endeavored to weather the British advanced ships; that being the only way to regain her own fleet, then to windward. To such a length did she carry her audacity that she compelled the Alfred, the headmost ship of Sir Samuel Hood's division, to bear up in order to allow her to pass. Every eye was fixed upon the bold Frenchman, excepting those who were anxiously looking out on the commander-in-chief to make the signal to engage, but who, most likely from not supposing it could be an enemy, did not throw out the ardently looked-for signal, and therefore not a gun was fired. This is mentioned to show the state of discipline on board the ships composing Sir Samuel Hood's division, and that he, though second in command, would not fire a single shot until directed to do so by his commander-in-chief. 'It is more than probable that Sir S. Hood's reason for having waited for the signal to engage from his commander-in-chief, ere he would fire, arose from the supposition that had he been the occasion of prematurely bringing on an action under the above circumstances, he would have been responsible for the results.'" (White's Naval Researches, p. 97.)

Hood may have been influenced by Rodney's bearing toward inferiors whose initiative displeased him. The relations of the two seem to have been strained.

must, be shaped to meet unforeseen exigencies. The conditions of sea-battles of the future contain one element that land battles cannot have,—the extreme rapidity with which encounters and changes of order can take place. However troops may be moved by steam to the field of battle, they will there fight on foot or on horseback, and with a gradual development of their plan, which will allow the commander-in-chief time to make his wishes known (as a rule, of course), in case of a change in the enemy's attack. On the other hand, a fleet, comparatively small in numbers and with its component units clearly defined, may be meditating an important change of which no sign can appear until it begins, and which will occupy but a few minutes. So far as these remarks are sound, they show the need of a second in command thoroughly conversant with not only the plans, but with the leading principles of action of his chief,— a need plain enough from the fact that the two extremities of the order-of-battle may be necessarily remote, and that you want the spirit of the leader at both extremities. As he cannot be there in person, the best thing is to have an efficient second at one end. As regards Nelson's position at Trafalgar, mentioned at the beginning of this discussion, it is to be noted that the "Victory" did nothing that another ship could not have done as well, and that the lightness of the wind forbade the expectation of any sudden change in the enemy's order. The enormous risk run by the person of the admiral, on whose ship was concentrated the fire of the enemy's line, and which led several captains to implore a change, was condemned long before by Nelson himself in one of his letters after the battle of the Nile:—

"I think, if it had pleased God I had not been wounded, not a boat would have escaped to have told the tale; but do not believe that any individual in the fleet is to blame. . . . I only mean to say that if my experience could in person have directed those individuals, there was every appearance that Almighty God would have continued to bless my endeavors," etc.[16]

Yet, notwithstanding such an expression of opinion based upon experience, he took the most exposed position at Trafalgar, and upon the loss of the leader there followed a curious exemplification

[16] Sir N. H. Nicholas: Despatches and Letters of Lord Nelson.

of its effects. Collingwood at once, rightly or wrongly, avoidably or unavoidably, reversed Nelson's plans, urged with his last breath. "Anchor! Hardy, do you anchor!" said the dying chief. "Anchor!" said Collingwood. "It is the last thing I should have thought of."

10

Maritime War in North America and West
Indies, 1778-1781—Its Influence upon the
Course of the American Revolution—Fleet
Actions off Grenada, Dominica, and
Chesapeake Bay

On the 15th of April, 1778, Admiral Comte d'Estaing sailed from
Toulon for the American continent, having under his command
twelve ships-of-the-line and five frigates. With him went as a passen-
ger a minister accredited to Congress, who was instructed to decline
all requests for subsidies and to avoid explicit engagements relative
to the conquest of Canada and other British possessions. "The
Cabinet of Versailles," says a French historian, "was not sorry for the
United States to have near them a cause of anxiety, which would
make them feel the value of the French alliance." [1] While acknowledging the generous sympathy of many Frenchmen for their struggle,
Americans need not blind themselves to the self-interestedness of the
French government. Neither should they find fault; for its duty was
to consider French interests first.

D'Estaing's progress was very slow. It is said that he wasted much
time in drills, and even uselessly. However that may be, he did not
reach his destination, the Capes of the Delaware, until the 8th of
July,—making a passage of twelve weeks, four of which were spent
in reaching the Atlantic. The English government had news of his

[1] Martin: History of France.

intended sailing; and in fact, as soon as they recalled their ambassador at Paris, orders were sent to America to evacuate Philadelphia, and concentrate upon New York. Fortunately for them, Lord Howe's movements were marked by a vigor and system other than D'Estaing's. First assembling his fleet and transports in Delaware Bay, and then hastening the embarkation of stores and supplies, he left Philadelphia as soon as the army had marched from there for New York. Ten days were taken up in reaching the mouth of the bay;[2] but he sailed from it the 28th of June, ten days before D'Estaing arrived, though more than ten weeks after he had sailed. Once outside, a favoring wind took the whole fleet to Sandy Hook in two days. War is unforgiving; the prey that D'Estaing had missed by delays foiled him in his attempts upon both New York and Rhode Island.

The day after Howe's arrival at Sandy Hook the English army reached the heights of Navesink, after an harassing march through New Jersey, with Washington's troops hanging upon its rear. By the active co-operation of the navy it was carried up to New York by the 5th of July; and Howe then went back to bar the entrance to the port against the French fleet. As no battle followed, the details of his arrangements will not be given; but a very full and interesting account by an officer of the fleet can be found in Ekins's *Naval Battles*. Attention, however, may well be called to the combination of energy, thought, skill, and determination shown by the admiral. The problem before him was to defend a practicable pass with six sixty-four-gun ships and three of fifty, against eight of seventy-four guns or over, three sixty-fours, and one fifty,—it may be said against nearly double his own force.

D'Estaing anchored outside, south of the Hook, on the 11th of July, and there remained until the 22nd, engaged in sounding the bar, and with every apparent determination to enter. On the 22nd a high northeast wind, coinciding with a spring tide, raised the water on the bar to thirty feet. The French fleet got under way, and worked up to windward to a point fair for crossing the bar. Then D'Estaing's heart failed him under the discouragement of the pilots; he gave up the attack and stood away to the southward.

Naval officers cannot but sympathize with the hesitation of a seaman to disregard the advice of pilots, especially on a coast foreign

---

[2] This delay was due to calms. Howe's Despatch, Gentleman's Magazine, 1778.

to him; but such sympathy should not close their eyes to the highest type of character. Let anyone compare the action of D'Estaing at New York with that of Nelson at Copenhagen and the Nile, or that of Farragut at Mobile and Port Hudson, and the inferiority of the Frenchman as a military leader, guided only by military considerations, is painfully apparent. New York was the very centre of the British power; its fall could not but have shortened the war. In fairness to D'Estaing, however, it must be remembered that other than military considerations had to weigh with him. The French admiral doubtless had instructions similar to those of the French minister, and he probably reasoned that France had nothing to gain by the fall of New York, which might have led to peace between America and England, and left the latter free to turn all her power against his own country. Less than that would have been enough to decide his wavering mind as to risking his fleet over the bar.

Howe was more fortunate than D'Estaing, in having no divided purposes. Having escaped from Philadelphia and saved New York by his diligence, he had in store the further honor of saving Rhode Island by the like rapid movements. Scattered ships-of-war from a fleet despatched from England now began to arrive. On the 28th of July Howe was informed that the French fleet, which had disappeared to the southward, had been seen heading for Rhode Island. In four days his fleet was ready for sea, but owing to contrary winds did not reach Point Judith till the 9th of August. There he anchored, and learned that D'Estaing had run the batteries the day before and anchored between Gould and Canonicut Islands;[3] the Seakonnet and Western passages had also been occupied by French ships, and the fleet was prepared to sustain the American army in an attack upon the British works.

The arrival of Howe, although his reinforcements did not raise the English fleet to over two thirds the strength of the French, upset D'Estaing's plans. With the prevailing summer southwest breezes blowing straight into the bay, he was exposed to any attempts his adversary might make. That same night the wind shifted unexpect-

[3] Most accounts say between Goat Island and Canonicut; but the position given seems more probable. The names "Goat" and "Gould" (often written "Gold") are easily confused. Since writing the above, the author has been favored with the sight of a contemporary manuscript map obtained in Paris, which shows the anchorage as near Canonicut and abreast Coaster's Harbor Island; the latter being marked "L'Isle d'Or ou Golde Isle." The sketch, while accurate in its main details, seems the more authentic from its mistakes being such as a foreigner, during a hurried and exciting stay of twenty-four hours, might readily make.

edly to the northward, and D'Estaing at once got under way and stood out to sea. Howe, though surprised by this unlooked-for act, —for he had not felt himself strong enough to attack,—also made sail to keep the weather-gage. The next twenty-four hours passed in manœuvring for the advantage; but on the night of the 11th of August a violent gale of wind dispersed the fleets. Great injury was done to the vessels of both, and among others the French flag-ship "Languedoc," of ninety guns, lost all her masts and her rudder. Immediately after the gale two different English fifty-gun ships, in fighting order, fell in, the one with the "Languedoc," the other with the "Tonnant," of eighty guns, having only one mast standing. Under such conditions both English ships attacked; but night coming on, they ceased action, intending to begin again in the morning. When morning came, other French ships also came, and the opportunity was lost. It is suggestive to note that one of the captains was Hotham, who as admiral of the Mediterranean fleet, seventeen years later, so annoyed Nelson by his cool satisfaction in having taken only two ships: "We must be contented; we have done very well." This was the immediate occasion of Nelson's characteristic saying, "Had we taken ten sail, and allowed the eleventh to escape, being able to get at her, I could never have called it well done."

The English fell back on New York. The French rallied again off the entrance of Narragansett Bay; but D'Estaing decided that he could not remain on account of the damage to the squadron, and accordingly sailed for Boston on the 21st of August. Rhode Island was thus left to the English, who retained it for a year longer, evacuating then for strategic reasons. Howe on his part diligently repaired his ships, and sailed again for Rhode Island when he heard of the French being there; but meeting on the way a vessel with word of their going to Boston, he followed them to that harbor, in which they were too strongly placed to be attacked. Taking into consideration his enforced return to New York, the necessary repairs, and the fact that he was only four days behind the French at Boston, it may be believed that Howe showed to the end the activity which characterized the beginning of his operations.

Scarcely a shot had been exchanged between the two fleets, yet the weaker had thoroughly outgeneralled the stronger. With the exception of the manœuvres for the weather-gage after D'Estaing left Newport, which have not been preserved, and of Howe's dispositions to receive the expected attack in New York Bay, the lessons are not tactical, but strategic, and of present application. Chief among them undoubtedly stands the value of celerity and watchfulness, combined with knowledge of one's profession. Howe learned of his danger by advices from home three weeks after D'Estaing sailed from Toulon. He had to gather in his cruisers from the Chesapeake and outside, get his ships-of-the-line from New York and Rhode Island, embark the supplies of an army of ten thousand men, move down the Delaware,—which unavoidably took ten days,—and round to New York again. D'Estaing was ten days behind him at the Delaware, twelve days at Sandy Hook, and only one day ahead of him in entering Newport, outside which harbor he had lain ten days before sailing in. An English narrator in the fleet, speaking of the untiring labor between June 30, when the English army reached Navesink, and the arrival of the French fleet on the 11th of July, says: "Lord Howe attended in person as usual, and by his presence animated the zeal and quickened the industry of officers and men." In this quality he was a marked contrast to his amiable but indolent brother, General Howe.

The same industry and watchfulness marked his remaining operations. As soon as the French ships hauled off to the southward, look-out vessels followed them, and preparations continued (notably of fire-ships) for pursuit. The last ship that joined from England crossed the bar at New York on the 30th of July. On the 1st of August the fleet was ready for sea, with four fire-ships. The accident of the wind delayed his next movements; but, as has been seen, he came up only one day after the entrance of the enemy into Newport, which his inferior force could not have prevented. But the object of the enemy, which he could not oppose, was frustrated by his presence. D'Estaing was no sooner in Newport than he wished himself out. Howe's position was strategically excellent. With his weatherly position in reference to the prevailing winds, the difficulty of beating a fleet out through the narrow entrance to the harbor would expose the French ships trying it to be attacked in detail; while if the wind unluckily came fair, the admiral relied upon his own skill to save his squadron.

Cooper, in one of his novels, *The Two Admirals,* makes his hero say to a cavilling friend that if he had not been in the way of good luck, he could not have profited by it. The sortie of the French, the subsequent gale, and the resulting damage were all what is commonly called luck; but if it had not been for Howe's presence off Point Judith threatening them, they would have ridden out the gale at their anchors inside. Howe's energy and his confidence in himself as a seaman had put him in the way of good luck, and it is not fair to deny his active share in bringing it about. But for him the gale would not have saved the British force in Newport.[4]

D'Estaing, having repaired his ships, sailed with his whole force for Martinique on the 4th of November; on the same day Commodore Hotham left New York for Barbadoes, with five sixty-four and fifty-gun ships and a convoy of five thousand troops, destined for the conquest of Sta. Lucia Island. On the way a heavy gale of wind injured the French fleet more than the English, the French flag-ship losing her main and mizzen topmasts. The loss of these spars, and the fact that twelve unencumbered ships-of-war reached Martinique only one day before the convoy of fifty-nine English transports reached Barbadoes, a hundred miles farther on, tells badly for the professional skill which then and now is a determining feature in naval war.

Admiral Barrington, commanding at Barbadoes, showed the same energy as Howe. The transports arrived on the 10th; the troops were kept on board; sailed on the morning of the 12th for Sta. Lucia and anchored there at three P.M. the 13th. The same afternoon half the troops were landed, and the rest the next morning. They seized at once a better port, to which the admiral was about to move the transports when the appearance of D'Estaing prevented him. All that night the transports were being warped inside the ships-of-war,

---

[4] "The arrival of the French fleet upon the coast of America is a great and striking event; but the operations of it have been injured by a number of unforeseen and unfavorable circumstances, which, though they ought not to detract from the merit and good intention of our great ally, have nevertheless lessened the importance of its services in a great degree. The length of the passage, in the first instance, was a capital misfortune; for had even one of common length taken place, Lord Howe, with the British ships-of-war and all the transports in the river Delaware, must inevitably have fallen; and Sir Henry Clinton must have had better luck than is commonly dispensed to men of his profession under such circumstances, if he and his troops had not shared at least the fate of Burgoyne. The long passage of Count d'Estaing was succeeded by an unfavorable discovery at the Hook, which hurt us in two respects,—first, in a defeat of the enterprise upon New York and the shipping and troops at that place, and next in the delay occasioned in ascertaining the depth of water over the bar, which was essential to their entrance into the harbor of New York. And, moreover, after the enterprise upon Rhode Island had been planned and was in the moment of execution, that Lord Howe with the British ships should interpose merely to create a diversion and draw the French fleet from the island was again unlucky, as the Count had not returned on the 17th to the island, though drawn off from it on the 10th; by which means the land operations were retarded, and the whole subjected to a miscarriage in case of the arrival of Byron's squadron."—WASHINGTON's Letter, Aug. 20, 1778.

and the latter anchored across the entrance to the bay, especial care being taken to strengthen the two extremities of the line, and to prevent the enemy from passing inside the weather end, as the English ships in after years did at the battle of the Nile. The French was much more than double the English fleet; and if the latter were destroyed, the transports and troops would be trapped.

D'Estaing stood down along the English order twice from north to south, cannonading at long range, but did not anchor. Abandoning then his intentions against the fleet, he moved to another bay, landed some French soldiers, and assaulted the position of the English troops. Failing here also, he retired to Martinique; and the French garrison, which had been driven into the interior of the island, surrendered.

It seems scarcely necessary to point out the admirable diligence of Admiral Barrington, to which and to the skill of his dispositions he owed this valuable strategic success; for such it was. Sta. Lucia was the island next south of Martinique, and the harbor of Gros Ilot at its northern end was especially adapted to the work of watching the French depot at Fort Royal, their principal station in the West Indies. Thence Rodney pursued them before his great action in 1782.

The absence of precise information causes hesitation in condemning D'Estaing for this mortifying failure. His responsibility depends upon the wind, which may have been light under the land, and upon his power to anchor. The fact, however, remains that he passed twice along the enemy's line within cannon-shot, yet did not force a decisive action. His course was unfavorably criticized by the great Suffren, then one of his captains.[5]

The English had thus retrieved the capture of Dominica, which had been taken on the 8th of September by the French governor of the West India Islands. There being no English squadron there, no difficulty had been met. The value of Dominica to the French has been pointed out; and it is necessary here to use the example of both Dominica and Sta. Lucia to enforce what has before been said, that the possession of these smaller islands depended solely upon the naval preponderance. Upon the grasp of this principle held by anyone will depend his criticism upon the next action of D'Estaing, to be immediately related.

Six months of almost entire quiet followed the affair of Sta. Lucia.

[5] See page 378.

The English were reinforced by the fleet of Byron, who took chief command; but the French, being joined by ten more ships-of-the-line, remained superior in numbers. About the middle of June, Byron sailed with his fleet to protect a large convoy of merchant-ships, bound for England, till they were clear of the islands. D'Estaing then sent a very small expedition which seized St. Vincent, June 16, 1779, without difficulty; and on the 30th of June he sailed with his whole fleet to attack Grenada. Anchoring off Georgetown on the 2nd of July, he landed his soldiers, and on the 4th the garrison of seven hundred men surrendered the island. Meanwhile Byron, hearing of the loss of St. Vincent and probable attack on Grenada, sailed with a large convoy of vessels carrying troops, and with twenty-one ships-of-the-line, to regain the one and relieve the other. Receiving on the way definite information that the French were before Grenada, he kept on for it, rounding the north-west point of the island at daybreak of July 6. His approach had been reported the day before to D'Estaing, who remained at anchor,[6] fearing lest with the currents and light winds he might drop too far to leeward if he let go the bottom. When the English came in sight, the French got under way; but the confused massing of their ships prevented Byron from recognizing at once the disparity of numbers, they having twenty-five ships-of-the-line. He made signal for a general chase, and as the disorder of the French fleet forced it to form on the leewardmost ships, the English easily retained the advantage of the wind with which they approached. As the action began, therefore, the French were to the westward with a partly formed line, on the starboard tack, heading north, the rear in disorder, and to windward of the van and centre (Plate X., A). The English stood down with a fair wind, steering south by west on the port tack (A), between the island and the enemy, their leading ships approaching at a slight angle, but heading more directly for his yet unformed rear; while the English convoy was between its own fleet and the island, under special charge of three ships (A, a), which were now called in. As the signal so far commanded a general chase, the three fastest of the English, among which was the flag of the second in command, Admiral Barrington, came under fire of the French centre and rear, apparently unsupported (b), and suffered much from the consequent concentration of fire upon them.

[6] D'Estaing's position at anchor is marked by the anchor in Plate X.

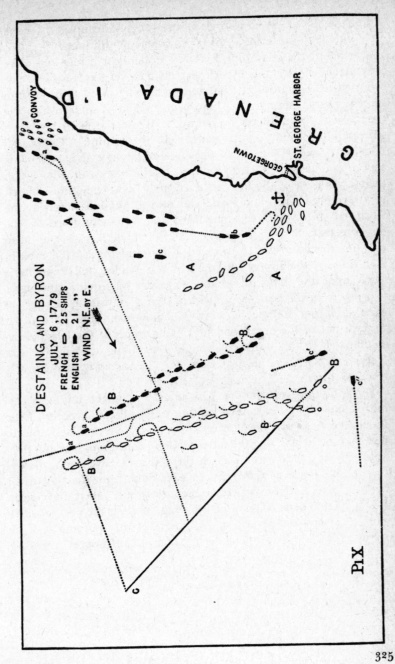

GRENADA I'D

CONVOY

ST. GEORGE HARBOR

GEORGETOWN

D'ESTAING AND BYRON

JULY 6, 1779
FRENCH ➡ 25 SHIPS
ENGLISH ➡ 21 ,,
WIND N.E. BY E.

PiX

325

When they reached the sternmost ships they wore upon the same tack with them and stood north, after and to windward of them; and at about the same time Byron, who had not before known of the surrender, saw the French flag flying over the forts. Signals followed to wear in succession, and for the advanced ships to form line for mutual support, ceasing the general chase under which the engagement had hitherto been fought. While the main body was still standing south on the port tack, three ships,—"Cornwall," "Grafton," and "Lion" (c),—obeying literally the signal for close action, had passed much to leeward of the others, drawing upon themselves most of the fire of the enemy's line. They thus suffered very severely in men and spars; and though finally relieved by the advanced ships, as these approached from the southward on the opposite tack, they were unable, after wearing (B, c′, c″), to keep up with the fleet, and so dropped astern and toward the French. The bulk of the injury sustained by the English fell upon these three, upon the three advanced ships under Barrington, and upon two others in the rear (A, a), which, seeing the van so heavily engaged, did not follow the successive movement, but bore down straight out of the order, and took their places at the head of the column (B, a, a′),—an act strongly resembling that which won Nelson such high renown at Cape St. Vincent, but involving less responsibility.[7]

So far Byron had conducted his attack, using the initiative permitted him by the advantage of the wind and the disorder of the French rear. It will be observed that, though it was desirable to lose no time in assailing the latter while in confusion, it is questionable whether Barrington's three ships should have been allowed to separate as far as they seem to have done from the rest of the fleet. A general chase is permissible and proper when, from superiority of numbers, original or acquired, or from the general situation, the ships first in action will not be greatly outnumbered, or subjected to overpowering concentration before support comes up,

[7] Of one of these, the "Monmouth," sixty-four (a′), it is said that the officers of the French flag-ship drank to the health of the captain of the "little black ship." Ships' names, like those of families, often have a marked career. A former "Monmouth," twenty years before, had attacked and taken, practically single-handed, the "Foudroyant," eighty-four, one of the finest ships in the French navy. She was then commanded by a Captain Gardiner, who, having commanded Byng's ship in the battle which led to his execution, was moved by his mortification at the result of that affair to dare such desperate odds, and thereby lost his life. The same ship, here punished so severely off Grenada, will be found in like sturdy fight, under another captain, three years later in India.

or when there is probability that the enemy may escape unless promptly struck. This was not so here. Nor should the "Cornwall," "Grafton," and "Lion" have been permitted to take a course which allowed, almost compelled, the enemy to concentrate rather than diffuse his fire. The details of the affair are not precise enough to warrant more comment than naming these mistakes, without necessarily attributing them to fault on the part of the admiral.

The French had up to this time remained strictly on the defensive, in accordance with their usual policy. There was now offered an opportunity for offensive action which tested D'Estaing's professional qualities, and to appreciate which the situation at the moment must be understood. Both fleets were by this time on the starboard tack, heading north (B, B, B), the French to leeward. The latter had received little injury in their motive power, though their line was not in perfect order; but the English, owing to the faulty attack, had seven ships seriously crippled, four of which—the "Monmouth" (a') "Grafton," and "Cornwall" (c'), and "Lion" (c'')—were disabled. The last three, by three P.M., were a league astern and much to leeward of their line, being in fact nearer the French than the English; while the speed of the English fleet was necessarily reduced to that of the crippled ships remaining in line. These conditions bring out strongly the embarrassments of a fleet whose injuries are concentrated upon a few ships, instead of being distributed among all; the ten or twelve which were practically untouched had to conform to the capabilities of the others. D'Estaing, with twenty-five ships, now had Byron to windward of him with seventeen or eighteen capable of holding together, but slower and less handy than their enemies, and saw him tactically embarrassed by the care of a convoy to windward and three disabled ships to leeward. Under these circumstances three courses were open to the French admiral: (1) He might stretch ahead, and, tacking in succession, place himself between Byron and the convoy, throwing his frigates among the latter; (2) He might tack his fleet together and stand up to the English line to bring on a general action; or (3) He could, after going about, cut off the three disabled ships, which might bring on a general action with less exposure.

None of these did he do. As regards the first, he, knowing the criticisms of the fleet, wrote home that his line was too much disordered to allow it. Whatever the technical irregularity, it is difficult to believe that, with the relative power of motion in the two fleets, the attempt was hopeless. The third alternative probably presented the greatest advantage, for it insured the separation between the enemy's main body and the crippled ships, and might very probably exasperate the British admiral into an attack under most hazardous conditions. It is stated by English authorities that Byron said he would have borne down again, had any attack been made on them. At three P.M. D'Estaing tacked all together, forming line on the lee ship,[8] and stood to the southward again. The English imitated this movement, except the van ship "Monmouth" (a′), which being too badly hurt to manœuvre kept on to the northward, and the three separated ships. Two of these (c′) kept on north and passed once more under the French broadsides; but the "Lion" (c″), unable to keep to the wind, kept broad off before it across the bows of the enemy, for Jamaica, a thousand miles away. She was not pursued; a single transport was the sole maritime trophy of the French. "Had the admiral's seamanship equalled his courage," wrote the celebrated Suffren, who commanded the French van ship, "we would not have suffered four dismasted vessels to escape." "D'Estaing, at the age of thirty, had been transferred from the army to the navy with the premature rank of rear-admiral. The navy did not credit him with nautical ability when the war broke out, and it is safe to say that its opinion was justified by his conduct during it." [9] "Brave as his sword, D'Estaing was always the idol of the soldier, the idol of the seaman; but moral authority over his officers failed him on several occasions, notwithstanding the marked protection extended to him by the king." [10]

Another cause than incapacity as a seaman has usually been assigned by French historians for the impotent action of D'Estaing on this occasion. He looked upon Grenada, they say, as the real objective of his efforts, and considered the English fleet a very secondary concern. Ramatuelle, a naval tactician who served actively in this war and wrote under the Empire, cites this case, which he couples with that of Yorktown and others, as exemplifying the true

[8] The line BC shows the final direction of the French line-of-battle; the lee ship (o) having tacked and standing to o′, while the other ships took position in her wake. Though not expressly stated, Byron doubtless formed in the same way on a parallel line. Into this new line the disabled ships (c′), which could scarcely have made good the course they were heading, would be easily received.

[9] Chevalier: Hist. de la Marine Française.

[10] Guérin: Hist. Maritime.

policy of naval war. His words, which probably reflect the current opinion of his service in that day, as they certainly do the policy of French governments, call for more than passing mention, as they involve principles worthy of most serious discussion:—

"The French navy has always preferred the glory of assuring or preserving a conquest to that, more brilliant perhaps, but actually less real, of taking a few ships; and in that it has approached more nearly the true end to be proposed in war. What in fact would the loss of a few ships matter to the English? The essential point is to attack them in their possessions, the immediate source of their commercial wealth and of their maritime power. The war of 1778 furnishes examples which prove the devotion of the French admirals to the true interests of the country. The preservation of the island of Grenada, the reduction of Yorktown where the English army surrendered, the conquest of the island of St. Christopher, were the result of great battles in which the enemy was allowed to retreat undisturbed, rather than risk giving him a chance to succor the points attacked."

The issue could not be more squarely raised than in the case of Grenada. No one will deny that there are moments when a probable military success is to be foregone, or postponed, in favor of one greater or more decisive. The position of De Grasse at the Chesapeake, in 1781, with the fate of Yorktown hanging in the balance, is in point; and it is here coupled with that of D'Estaing at Grenada, as though both stood on the same grounds. Both are justified alike; not on their respective merits as fitting the particular cases, but upon a general principle. Is that principle sound? The bias of the writer quoted betrays itself unconsciously, in saying "a few ships." A whole navy is not usually to be crushed at a blow; a few ships mean an ordinary naval victory. In Rodney's famous battle only five ships were taken, though Jamaica was saved thereby.

In order to determine the soundness of the principle, which is claimed as being illustrated by these two cases (St. Christopher will be discussed later on), it is necessary to examine what was the advantage sought, and what the determining factor of success in either case. At Yorktown the advantage sought was the capture of Cornwallis's army; the objective was the destruction of the enemy's organized military force on shore. At Grenada the chosen objective was the possession of a piece of territory of no great military value; for it must be remarked that all these smaller Antilles, if held in force at all, multiplied large detachments, whose mutual support depended wholly upon the navy. These large detachments were liable to be crushed separately, if not supported by the navy; and if naval superiority is to be maintained, the enemy's navy must be crushed. Grenada, near and to leeward of Barbadoes and Sta. Lucia, both held strongly by the English, was peculiarly weak to the French; but sound military policy for all these islands demanded one or two strongly fortified and garrisoned naval bases, and dependence for the rest upon the fleet. Beyond this, security against attacks by single cruisers and privateers alone was needed.

Such were the objectives in dispute. What was the determining factor in this strife? Surely the navy, the organized military force afloat. Cornwallis's fate depended absolutely upon the sea. It is useless to speculate upon the result, had the odds on the 5th of September, 1781, in favor of De Grasse, been reversed; if the French, instead of five ships more, had had five ships less than the English. As it was, De Grasse, when that fight began, had a superiority over the English equal to the result of a hard-won fight. The question then was, should he risk the almost certain decisive victory over the organized enemy's force ashore, for the sake of a much more doubtful advantage over the organized force afloat? This was not a question of Yorktown, but of Cornwallis and his army; there is a great deal in the way things are put.

So stated,—and the statement needs no modifications,—there can to be but one answer. Let it be remarked clearly, however, that *both* De Grasse's alternatives brought before him the organized forces as the objective.

Not so with D'Estaing at Grenada. His superiority in numbers over the English was nearly as great as that of De Grasse; his alternative objectives were the organized force afloat and a small island, fertile, but militarily unimportant. Grenada is said to have been a strong position for defence; but intrinsic strength does not give importance, if the position has not strategic value. To save the island, he refused to use an enormous advantage fortune had given him over the fleet. Yet upon the strife between the two navies depended the tenure of the islands. Seriously to hold the West India Islands required, first, a powerful seaport, which the French had; second, the control of the sea. For the latter it was necessary, not to multiply detachments in the islands, but to destroy the enemy's navy, which may be accurately called the army in the field. The islands were but rich towns; and not more than one or two fortified towns, or posts, were needed.

It may safely be said that the principle which led to D'Estaing's action was not, to say the least, unqualifiedly correct; for it led him wrong. In the case of Yorktown, the principle as stated by Ramatuelle is not the *justifying* reason of De Grasse's conduct, though it likely enough was the *real* reason. What justified De Grasse was that, the event depending upon the unshaken control of the sea, for a short time only, he already had it by his greater numbers. Had the numbers been equal, loyalty to the military duty of the hour must have forced him to fight, to stop the attempt which the English admiral would certainly have made. The destruction of a few ships, as Ramatuelle slightingly puts it, gives just that superiority to which the happy result at Yorktown was due. As a general principle, this is undoubtedly a better objective than that pursued by the French. Of course, exceptions will be found; but those exceptions will probably be where, as at Yorktown, the military force is struck at directly elsewhere, or, as at Port Mahon, a desirable and powerful base of that force is at stake; though even at Mahon it is doubtful whether the prudence was not misplaced. Had Hawke or Boscawen met with Byng's disaster, they would not have gone to Gibraltar to repair it, unless the French admiral had followed up his first blow with others, increasing their disability.

Grenada was no doubt very dear in the eyes of D'Estaing, because it was his only success. After making the failures at the Delaware, at New York, and at Rhode Island, with the mortifying affair at Sta. Lucia, it is difficult to understand the confidence in him expressed by some French writers. Gifted with a brilliant and contagious personal daring, he distinguished himself most highly, when an admiral, by leading in person assaults upon intrenchments at Sta. Lucia and Grenada, and a few months later in the unsuccessful attack upon Savannah.

During the absence of the French navy in the winter of 1778-79, the English, controlling now the sea with a few of their ships that had not gone to the West Indies, determined to shift the scene of the continental war to the Southern States, where there was believed to be a large number of loyalists. The expedition was directed upon Georgia, and was so far successful that Savannah fell into their hands in the last days of 1778. The whole State speedily submitted.

Operations were thence extended into South Carolina, but failed to bring about the capture of Charleston.

Word of these events was sent to D'Estaing in the West Indies, accompanied by urgent representations of the danger to the Carolinas, and the murmurings of the people against the French, who were accused of forsaking their allies, having rendered them no service, but on the contrary having profited by the cordial help of the Bostonians to refit their crippled fleet. There was a sting of truth in the alleged failure to help, which impelled D'Estaing to disregard the orders actually in his hands to return at once to Europe with certain ships. Instead of obeying them he sailed for the American coast with twenty-two ships-of-the-line, having in view two objects,—the relief of the Southern States and an attack upon New York in conjunction with Washington's army.

Arriving off the coast of Georgia on the 1st of September, D'Estaing took the English wholly at unawares; but the fatal lack of promptness, which had previously marked the command of this very daring man, again betrayed his good fortune. Dallying at first before Savannah, the fleeting of precious days again brought on a change of conditions, and the approach of the bad-weather season impelled him, too slow at first, into a premature assault. In it he displayed his accustomed gallantry, fighting at the head of his column, as did the American general; but the result was a bloody repulse. The siege was raised, and D'Estaing sailed at once for France, not only giving up his project upon New York, but abandoning the Southern States to the enemy. The value of this help from the great sea power of France, thus cruelly dangled before the eyes of the Americans only to be withdrawn, was shown by the action of the English, who abandoned Newport in the utmost haste when they learned the presence of the French fleet. Withdrawal had been before decided upon, but D'Estaing's coming converted it into flight.

After the departure of D'Estaing, which involved that of the whole French fleet,—for the ships which did not go back to France returned to the West Indies,—the English resumed the attack upon the Southern States, which had for a moment been suspended. The fleet and army left New York for Georgia in the last weeks of 1779, and after assembling at Tybee, moved upon Charleston by way of Edisto. The powerlessness of the Americans upon the sea left this movement unembarrassed save by single cruisers, which picked up some stragglers,—affording another lesson of the petty results of a merely cruising warfare. The siege of Charleston began at the end of March,—the English ships soon after passing the bar and Fort Moultrie without serious damage, and anchoring within gunshot of the place. Fort Moultrie was soon and easily reduced by land approaches, and the city itself was surrendered on the 12th of May, after a siege of forty days. The whole State was then quickly overrun and brought into military subjection.

The fragments of D'Estaing's late fleet were joined by a reinforcement from France under the Comte de Guichen, who assumed chief command in the West Indian seas March 22, 1780. The next day he sailed for Sta. Lucia, which he hoped to find unprepared; but a crusty, hard-fighting old admiral of the traditional English type, Sir Hyde Parker, had so settled himself at the anchorage, with sixteen ships, that Guichen with his twenty-two would not attack. The opportunity, if it were one, did not recur. De Guichen, returning to Martinique, anchored there on the 27th; and the same day Parker at Sta. Lucia was joined by the new English commander-in-chief, Rodney.

This since celebrated, but then only distinguished, admiral was sixty-two years old at the time of assuming a command where he was to win an undying fame. Of distinguished courage and professional skill, but with extravagant if not irregular habits, money embarrassments had detained him in exile in France at the time the war began. A boast of his ability to deal with the French fleet, if circumstances enabled him to go back to England, led a French nobleman who heard it to assume his debts, moved by feelings in which chivalry and national pique probably bore equal shares. Upon his return he was given a command, and sailed, in January, 1780, with a fleet of twenty ships-of-the-line, to relieve Gibraltar, then closely invested. Off Cadiz, with a good luck for which he was proverbial, he fell in with a Spanish fleet of eleven ships-of-the-line, which awkwardly held their ground until too late to fly.[11] Throwing out the signal for a general chase, and cutting in to leeward of the enemy, between them and their port, Rodney, despite a dark and stormy night, succeeded in blowing up one ship and taking six. Hastening on, he relieved Gibraltar, placing it out of all danger

[11] Drinkwater, in his history of the siege of Gibraltar, explains that the Spanish admiral believed that Rodney would not accompany the convoy to the Straits, but had separated from it. He did not detect his mistake until too late.

from want; and then, leaving the prizes and the bulk of his fleet, sailed with the rest for his station.

Despite his brilliant personal courage and professional skill, which in the matter of tactics was far in advance of his contemporaries in England, Rodney, as a commander-in-chief, belongs rather to the wary, cautious school of the French tacticians than to the impetuous, unbounded eagerness of Nelson. As in Tourville we have seen the desperate fighting of the seventeenth century, unwilling to leave its enemy, merging into the formal, artificial—we may almost say trifling—parade tactics of the eighteenth, so in Rodney we shall see the transition from those ceremonious duels to an action which, while skilful in conception, aimed at serious results. For it would be unjust to Rodney to press the comparison to the French admirals of his day. With a skill that De Guichen recognized as soon as they crossed swords, Rodney meant mischief, not idle flourishes. Whatever incidental favors fortune might bestow by the way, the objective from which his eye never wandered was the French fleet,— the organized military force of the enemy on the sea. And on the day when Fortune forsook the opponent who had neglected her offers, when the conqueror of Cornwallis failed to strike while he had Rodney at a disadvantage, the latter won a victory which redeemed England from the depths of anxiety, and restored to her by one blow all those islands which the cautious tactics of the allies had for a moment gained, save only Tobago.

De Guichen and Rodney met for the first time on the 17th of April, 1780, three weeks after the arrival of the latter. The French fleet was beating to windward in the Channel between Martinique and Dominica, when the enemy was made in the southeast. A day was spent in manœuvring for the weather-gage, which Rodney got. The two fleets being now well to leeward of the islands[12] (Plate XI.), both on the starboard tack heading to the northward and the French on the lee bow of the English, Rodney, who was carrying a press of sail, signalled to his fleet that he meant to attack the enemy's rear and centre with his whole force; and when he had reached the position he thought suitable, ordered them to keep away eight points (90°) together (A, A, A). De Guichen, seeing the danger of the rear, wore his fleet all together and stood down to succor it. Rodney, finding himself foiled, hauled up again on the same tack

---

[12] The place where the battle was fought is shown by the crossed flags.

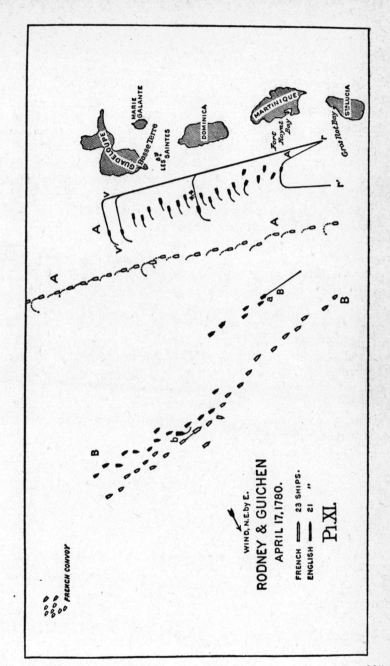

MARIE GALANTE

GUADELOUPE

BASSE TERRE

LES SAINTES

DOMINICA

MARTINIQUE

Fort Royal Bay

St. LUCIA

Gros Ilot Bay

FRENCH CONVOY

WIND, N.E. by E.

RODNEY & GUICHEN

APRIL 17, 1780.

FRENCH ———— 23 SHIPS.

ENGLISH ———— 21 "

Pl. XI.

as the enemy, both fleets now heading to the southward and east-ward.[13] Later, he again made signal for battle, followed an hour after, just at noon, by the order (quoting his own despatch), "for every ship to bear down and steer for her opposite in the enemy's line." This, which sounds like the old story of ship to ship, Rodney explains to have meant her opposite at the moment, not her opposite in numerical order. His own words are: "In a slanting position, that my leading ships might attack the van ships of the enemy's centre division, and the whole British fleet be opposed to only two thirds of the enemy" (B, B). The difficulty and misunderstanding which followed seem to have sprung mainly from the defective character of the signal book. Instead of doing as the admiral wished, the lead-ing ships (a) carried sail so as to reach their supposed station abreast their numerical opposite in the order. Rodney stated afterward that when he bore down the second time, the French fleet was in a very extended line of battle; and that, had his orders been obeyed, the centre and rear must have been disabled before the van could have joined.

There seems every reason to believe that Rodney's intentions throughout were to double on the French, as asserted. The failure sprang from the signal-book and tactical inefficiency of the fleet; for which he, having lately joined, was not answerable. But the ugliness of his fence was so apparent to De Guichen, that he ex-claimed, when the English fleet kept away the first time, that six or seven of his ships were gone; and sent word to Rodney that if his signals had been obeyed he would have had him for his pris-oner.[14] A more convincing proof that he recognized the dangerous-ness of his enemy is to be found in the fact that he took care not to have the lee-gage in their subsequent encounters. Rodney's care-

[13] The black ships, in position A, represent the English ships bearing down upon the French centre and rear. The line v r is the line-of-battle from van to rear before bearing down. The positions v', r', are those of the van and rear ships after hauling up on the port tack, when the French wore.

[14] In a severe reprimand addressed to Captain Carkett, commanding the leading ship of the English line, by Rodney, he says: "Your leading in the manner you did, induced others to follow so bad an example; and thereby, forgetting that the signal for the line was at only two cables' length distance from each other, the van division was led by you to *more than two leagues distance* from the centre division, which was thereby exposed to the greatest strength of the enemy and not properly supported." (Life, vol. i, p. 351). By all rules of tactical common-sense it would seem that the other ships should have taken their distance from their next astern, that is, should have closed toward the centre. In conversation with Sir Gilbert Blane, who was not in this action, Rodney stated that the French line extended four leagues in length, "as if De Guichen thought we meant to run away from him." (Naval Chronicle, vol. xxv. p. 402).

ful plans being upset, he showed that with them he carried all the stubborn courage of the most downright fighter; taking his own ship close to the enemy and ceasing only when the latter hauled off, her foremast and mainyard gone, and her hull so damaged that she could hardly be kept afloat.

An incident of this battle mentioned by French writers and by Botta,[15] who probably drew upon French authorities, but not found in the English accounts, shows the critical nature of the attack in the apprehension of the French. According to them, Rodney, marking a gap in their order due to a ship in rear of the French admiral being out of station, tried to break through (b); but the captain of the "Destin," seventy-four, pressed up under more sail and threw himself across the path of the English ninety-gun ship.

"The action of the 'Destin' was justly praised," says La Pérouse-Bonfils. "The fleet ran the danger of almost certain defeat, but for the bravery of M. de Goimpy. Such, after the affair, was the opinion of the whole French squadron. Yet, admitting that our line was broken, what disasters then would necessarily threaten the fleet? Would it not always have been easy for our rear to remedy the accident by promptly standing on to fill the place of the vessels cut off? That movement would necessarily have brought about a *mêlée*, which would have turned to the advantage of the fleet having the bravest and most devoted captains. But then, as under the empire, it was an acknowledged principle that ships cut off were ships taken, and the belief wrought its own fulfilment."

The effect of breaking an enemy's line, or order-of-battle, depends upon several conditions. The essential idea is to divide the opposing force by penetrating through an interval found, or made, in it, and then to concentrate upon that one of the fractions which can be least easily helped by the other. In a column of ships this will usually be the rear. The compactness of the order attacked, the number of the ships cut off, the length of time during which they can be isolated and outnumbered, will all affect the results. A very great factor in the issue will be the moral effect, the confusion introduced into a line thus broken. Ships coming up toward the break are stopped, the rear doubles up, while the ships ahead continue their course. Such a moment is critical, and calls for instant action; but the men are rare who in an unforeseen emergency can see, and at once take the right course, especially if, being subordinates, they

[15] History of the American Revolution.

incur responsibility. In such a scene of confusion the English, without presumption, hoped to profit by their better seamanship; for it is not only "courage and devotion," but skill, which then tells. All these effects of "breaking the line" received illustration in Rodney's great battle in 1782.

De Guichen and Rodney met twice again in the following month, but on neither occasion did the French admiral take the favorite lee-gage of his nation. Meanwhile a Spanish fleet of twelve ships-of-the-line was on its way to join the French. Rodney cruised to windward of Martinique to intercept them; but the Spanish admiral kept a northerly course, sighted Guadeloupe, and thence sent a despatch to De Guichen, who joined his allies and escorted them into port. The great preponderance of the coalition, in numbers, raised the fears of the English islands; but lack of harmony led to delays and hesitations, a terrible epidemic raged in the Spanish squadron, and the intended operations came to nothing. In August De Guichen sailed for France with fifteen ships. Rodney, ignorant of his destination, and anxious about both North America and Jamaica, divided his fleet, leaving one half in the islands, and with the remainder sailing for New York, where he arrived on the 12th of September. The risk thus run was very great, and scarcely justifiable; but no ill effect followed the dispersal of forces.[16] Had De Guichen intended to turn upon Jamaica, or, as was expected by Washington, upon New York, neither part of Rodney's fleet could well have withstood him. Two chances of disaster, instead of one, were run, by being in small force on two fields instead of in full force on one.

Rodney's anxiety about North America was well grounded. On the 12th of July of this year the long expected French succor arrived,—five thousand French troops under Rochambeau and seven ships-of-the-line under De Ternay. Hence the English, though still superior at sea, felt forced to concentrate at New York, and were unable to strengthen their operations in Carolina. The difficulty and distance of movements by land gave such an advantage to sea power that Lafayette urged the French government further to increase the fleet; but it was still naturally and properly attentive to its own immediate interests in the Antilles. It was not yet time to deliver America.

[16] For Rodney's reasons, see his Life, vol. i, pp. 365, 367.

Rodney, having escaped the great hurricane of October, 1780, by his absence, returned to the West Indies later in the year, and soon after heard of the war between England and Holland; which, proceeding from causes which will be mentioned later, was declared December 20, 1780. The admiral at once seized the Dutch islands of St. Eustatius and St. Martin, besides numerous merchant-ships, with property amounting in all to fifteen million dollars. These islands, while still neutral, had played a rôle similar to that of Nassau during the American Civil War, and had become a great depot of contraband goods, immense quantities of which now fell into the English hands.

The year 1780 had been gloomy for the cause of the United States. The battle of Camden had seemed to settle the English yoke on South Carolina, and the enemy formed high hopes of controlling both North Carolina and Virginia. The treason of Arnold following had increased the depression, which was but partially relieved by the victory at King's Mountain. The substantial aid of French troops was the most cheerful spot in the situation. Yet even that had a checkered light, the second division of the intended help being blocked in Brest by the English fleet; while the final failure of De Guichen to appear, and Rodney coming in his stead, made the hopes of the campaign fruitless.

A period of vehement and decisive action was, however, at hand. At the end of March, 1781, the Comte de Grasse sailed from Brest with twenty-six ships-of-the-line and a large convoy. When off the Azores, five ships parted company for the East Indies, under Suffren, of whom more will be heard later on. De Grasse came in sight of Martinique on the 28th of April. Admiral Hood (Rodney having remained behind at St. Eustatius) was blockading before Fort Royal, the French port and arsenal on the lee side of the island, in which were four ships-of-the-line, when his lookouts reported the enemy's fleet. Hood had two objects before him,—one to prevent the junction of the four blockaded ships with the approaching fleet, the other to keep the latter from getting between him and Gros Ilot Bay in Sta. Lucia. Instead of effecting this in the next twenty-four hours, by beating to windward of the Diamond Rock, his fleet got so far to leeward that De Grasse, passing through the channel on the 29th, headed up for Fort Royal, keeping his convoy between the fleet and the island. For this false position Hood was severely blamed by Rodney, but it may have been due to light winds and the lee current. However that be, the four ships in Fort Royal got under way and joined the main body. The English had now only eighteen ships to the French twenty-four, and the latter were to windward; but though thus in the proportion of four to three, and having the power to attack, De Grasse would not do it. The fear of exposing his convoy prevented him from running the chance of a serious engagement. Great must have been his distrust of his forces, one would say. When is a navy to fight, if this was not a time? He carried on a distant cannonade, with results so far against the English as to make his backwardness yet more extraordinary. Can a policy or a tradition which justifies such a line of conduct be good?

The following day, April 30, De Grasse, having thrown away his chance, attempted to follow Hood; but the latter had no longer any reason for fighting, and his original inferiority was increased by the severe injuries of some ships on the 29th. De Grasse could not overtake him, owing to the inferior speed of his fleet, many of the ships not being coppered,—a fact worthy of note, as French vessels by model and size were generally faster than English; but this superiority was sacrificed through the delay of the government in adopting the new improvement.

Hood rejoined Rodney at Antigua, and De Grasse, after remaining a short time at Fort Royal, made an attempt upon Gros Ilot Bay, the possession of which by the English kept all the movements of his fleet under surveillance. Foiled here, he moved against Tobago, which surrendered June 2, 1781. Sailing thence, after some minor operations, he anchored on the 26th of July at Cap Français (now Cape Haytien), in the island of Hayti. Here he found awaiting him a French frigate from the United States, bearing despatches from Washington and Rochambeau, upon which he was to take the most momentous action that fell to any French admiral during the war.

The invasion of the Southern States by the English, beginning in Georgia and followed by the taking of Charleston and the military control of the two extreme States, had been pressed on to the northward by way of Camden into North Carolina. On the 16th of August, 1780, General Gates was totally defeated at Camden; and during the following nine months the English under Cornwallis persisted in their attempts to overrun North Carolina. These operations, the narration of which is foreign to our immediate subject, had ended by forcing Cornwallis, despite many successes in actual encounter, to fall back exhausted toward the seaboard, and finally upon Wilmington, in which place depots for such a contingency had been established. His opponent, General Greene, then turned the American troops toward South Carolina. Cornwallis, too weak to dream of controlling, or even penetrating, into the interior of an unfriendly country, had now to choose between returning to Charleston, to assure there and in South Carolina the shaken British power, and moving northward again into Virginia, there to join hands with a small expeditionary force operating on the James River under Generals Phillips and Arnold. To fall back would be a confession that the weary marching and fighting of months past had been without results, and the general readily convinced himself that the Chesapeake was the proper seat of war, even if New York itself had to be abandoned. The commander-in-chief, Sir Henry Clinton, by no means shared this opinion, upon which was justified a step taken without asking him. "Operations in the Chesapeake," he wrote, "are attended with great risk unless we are sure of a permanent superiority at sea. I tremble for the fatal consequences that may ensue." For Cornwallis, taking the matter into his own hands, had marched from Wilmington on the 25th of April, 1781, joining the British already at Petersburg on the 20th of May. The forces thus united numbered seven thousand men. Driven back from the open country of South Carolina into Charleston, there now remained two centres of British power,—at New York and in the Chesapeake. With New Jersey and Pennsylvania in the hands of the Americans, communication between the two depended wholly upon the sea.

Despite his unfavorable criticism of Cornwallis's action, Clinton had himself already risked a large detachment in the Chesapeake. A body of sixteen hundred men under Benedict Arnold had ravaged the country of the James and burned Richmond in January of this same year. In the hopes of capturing Arnold, Lafayette had been sent to Virginia with a nucleus of twelve hundred troops, and on the evening of the 8th of March the French squadron at Newport sailed, in concerted movement, to control the waters of the bay.

'Admiral Arbuthnot, commanding the English fleet lying in Gardiner's Bay,[17] learned the departure by his lookouts, and started in pursuit on the morning of the 10th, thirty-six hours later. Favored either by diligence or luck, he made such good time that when the two fleets came in sight of each other, a little outside of the capes of the Chesapeake, the English were leading[18] (Plate XII., A, A). They at once went about to meet their enemy, who, on his part, formed a line-of-battle. The wind at this time was west, so that neither could head directly into the bay.

The two fleets were nearly equal in strength, there being eight ships on each side; but the English had one ninety-gun ship, while of the French one was only a heavy frigate, which was put into the line. Nevertheless, the case was eminently one for the general French policy to have determined the action of a vigorous chief, and the failure to see the matter through must fall upon the good-will of Commodore Destouches, or upon some other cause than that preference for the ulterior objects of the operations, of which the reader of French naval history hears so much. The weather was boisterous and threatening, and the wind, after hauling once or twice, settled down to northeast, with a big sea, but was then fair for entering the bay. The two fleets were by this time both on the port tack standing out to sea, The French leading, and about a point on the weather bow of the English (B, B). From this position they wore in succession (c) ahead of the latter, taking the lee-gage, and thus gaining the use of their lower batteries, which the heavy sea forbade to the weather-gage. The English stood on till abreast the enemy's line (a, b), when they wore together, and soon after attacked in the usual manner, and with the usual results (C). The three van ships were very badly injured aloft, but in their turn, throwing their force mainly on the two leaders of the enemy, crippled them seriously in hulls and rigging. The French van then kept away, and Arbuthnot, in perplexity, ordered his van to haul the wind again. M. Destouches now executed a very neat movement by defiling. Signalling his van to haul up on the other tack (e), he led the rest of his squadron by the disabled English ships, and after giving them the successive broadsides of his comparatively fresh ships, wore (d), and out to

[17] At the eastern end of Long Island.
[18] The French ascribe this disadvantage to the fact that some of their ships were not coppered.

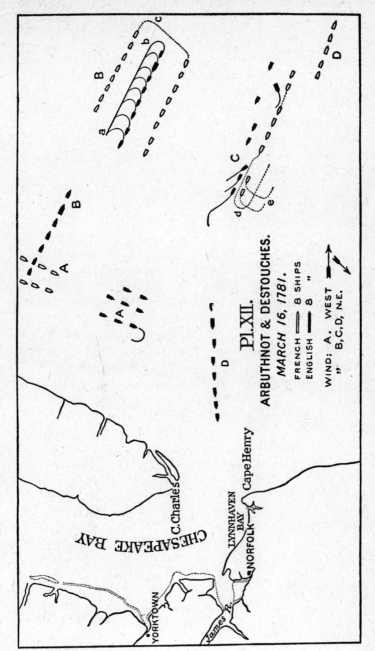

Pl. XII.

ARBUTHNOT & DESTOUCHES.

MARCH 16, 1781.

FRENCH ━━━ 8 SHIPS
ENGLISH ━━━ 8 "

WIND: A. WEST
     " B,C,D, N.E.

CHESAPEAKE BAY

C. Charles

LYNNHAVEN BAY

Cape Henry

NORFOLK

YORKTOWN

James

sea (D). This was the end of the battle, in which the English certainly got the worst; but with their usual tenacity of purpose, being unable to pursue their enemy afloat, they steered for the bay (D), made the junction with Arnold, and thus broke up the plans of the French and Americans, from which so much had been hoped by Washington. There can be no doubt, after careful reading of the accounts, that after the fighting the French were in better force than the English, and they in fact claimed the victory; yet the ulterior objects of the expedition did not tempt them again to try the issue with a fleet of about their own size.[19]

The way of the sea being thus open and held in force, two thousand more English troops sailing from New York reached Virginia on the 26th of March, and the subsequent arrival of Cornwallis in May raised the number to seven thousand. The operations of the contending forces during the spring and summer months, in which Lafayette commanded the Americans, do not concern our subject. Early in August, Cornwallis, acting under orders from Clinton, withdrew his troops into the peninsula between the York and James rivers, and occupied Yorktown.

Washington and Rochambeau had met on the 21st of May, and decided that the situation demanded that the effort of the French West Indian fleet, when it came, should be directed against either New York or the Chesapeake. This was the tenor of the despatch found by De Grasse at Cap Français, and meantime the allied generals drew their troops toward New York, where they would be on hand for the furtherance of one object, and nearer the second if they had to make for it.

In either case the result, in the opinion both of Washington and of the French government, depended upon superior sea power; but Rochambeau had privately notified the admiral that his own preference was for the Chesapeake as the scene of the intended operations, and moreover the French government had declined to furnish the means for a formal siege of New York.[20] The enterprise therefore assumed the form of an extensive military combination, dependent

[19] That the French government was not satisfied with M. Destouches's action can be safely inferred from its delay to reward the officers of the squadron, which called forth much feeling and very lively remonstrances. The French asserted that Arbuthnot was hooted in the streets of New York and recalled by his government. The latter is a mistake, as he went home by his own request; but the former is likely enough. Both commanders reversed in this case the usual naval policy of their nations.

[20] Bancroft: History of the United States.

upon ease and rapidity of movement, and upon blinding the eyes of the enemy to the real objective,—purposes to which the peculiar qualities of a navy admirably lent themselves. The shorter distance to be traversed, the greater depth of water and easier pilotage of the Chesapeake, were further reasons which would commend the scheme to the judgment of a seaman; and De Grasse readily accepted it, without making difficulties or demanding modifications which would have involved discussion and delay.

Having made his decision, the French admiral acted with great good judgment, promptitude, and vigor. The same frigate that brought despatches from Washington was sent back, so that by August 15th the allied generals knew of the intended coming of the fleet. Thirty-five hundred soldiers were spared by the governor of Cap Français, upon the condition of a Spanish squadron anchoring at the place, which De Grasse procured. He also raised from the governor of Havana the money urgently needed by the Americans; and finally, instead of weakening his force by sending convoys to France, as the court had wished, he took every available ship to the Chesapeake. To conceal his coming as long as possible, he passed through the Bahama Channel, as a less frequented route, and on the 30th of August anchored in Lynnhaven Bay, just within the capes of the Chesapeake, with twenty-eight ships-of-the-line. Three days before, August 27, the French squadron at Newport, eight ships-of-the-line with four frigates and eighteen transports under M. de Barras, sailed for the rendezvous; making, however, a wide circuit out to sea to avoid the English. This course was the more necessary as the French siege-artillery was with it. The troops under Washington and Rochambeau had crossed the Hudson on the 24th of August, moving toward the head of Chesapeake Bay. Thus the different armed forces, both land and sea, were converging toward their objective, Cornwallis.

The English were unfortunate in all directions. Rodney, learning of De Grasse's departure, sent fourteen ships-of-the-line under Admiral Hood to North America, and himself sailed for England in August, on account of ill health. Hood, going by the direct route, reached the Chesapeake three days before De Grasse, looked into the bay, and finding it empty went on to New York. There he met five ships-of-the-line under Admiral Graves, who, being senior officer, took command of the whole force and sailed on the 31st of August for the Chesapeake, hoping to intercept De Barras before he could join De Grasse. It was not till two days later that Sir Henry Clinton was persuaded that the allied armies had gone against Cornwallis, and had too far the start to be overtaken.

Admiral Graves was painfully surprised, on making the Chesapeake, to find anchored there a fleet which from its numbers could only be an enemy's. Nevertheless, he stood in to meet it, and as De Grasse got under way, allowing his ships to be counted, the sense of numerical inferiority—nineteen to twenty-four—did not deter the English admiral from attacking. The clumsiness of his method, however, betrayed his gallantry; many of his ships were roughly handled, without any advantage being gained. De Grasse, expecting De Barras, remained outside five days, keeping the English fleet in play without coming to action; then returning to port he found De Barras safely at anchor. Graves went back to New York, and with him disappeared the last hope of succor that was to gladden Cornwallis's eyes. The siege was steadily endured, but the control of the sea made only one issue possible, and the English forces were surrendered October 19, 1781. With this disaster the hope of subduing the colonies died in England. The conflict flickered through a year longer, but no serious operations were undertaken.

In the conduct of the English operations, which ended thus unfortunately, there was both bad management and ill fortune. Hood's detachment might have been strengthened by several ships from Jamaica, had Rodney's orders been carried out.[21] The despatch-ship, also, sent by him to Admiral Graves commanding in New York, found that officer absent on a cruise to the eastward, with a view to intercept certain very important supplies which had been forwarded by the American agent in France. The English Court had laid great stress upon cutting off this convoy; but, with the knowledge that he had of the force accompanying it, the admiral was probably ill-advised in leaving his headquarters himself, with all his fleet, at the time when the approach of the hurricane season in the West Indies directed the active operations of the navies toward the continent. In consequence of his absence, although Rodney's despatches were at once sent on by the senior officer in New York, the vessel carrying them being driven ashore by enemy's cruisers, Graves did not learn their contents until his return to port, August 16. The information

[21] Life of Rodney, vol. ii, p. 152; Clerk: Naval Tactics, p. 84.

sent by Hood of his coming was also intercepted. After Hood's arrival, it does not appear that there was avoidable delay in going to sea; but there does seem to have been misjudgment in the direction given to the fleet. It was known that De Barras had sailed from Newport with eight ships, bound probably for the Chesapeake, certainly to effect a junction with De Grasse; and it has been judiciously pointed out that if Graves had taken up his cruising-ground near the Capes, but out of sight of land, he could hardly have failed to fall in with him in overwhelming force. Knowing what is now known, this would undoubtedly have been the proper thing to do; but the English admiral had imperfect information. It was nowhere expected that the French would bring nearly the force they did; and Graves lost information, which he ought to have received, as to their numbers, by the carelessness of his cruisers stationed off the Chesapeake. These had been ordered to keep under way, but were both at anchor under Cape Henry when De Grasse's appearance cut off their escape. One was captured, the other driven up York River. No single circumstance contributed more to the general result than the neglect of these two subordinate officers, by which Graves lost that all-important information. It can readily be conceived how his movements might have been affected, had he known two days earlier that De Grasse had brought twenty-seven or twenty-eight sail of the line; how natural would have been the conclusion, first, to waylay De Barras, with whom his own nineteen could more than cope. "Had Admiral Graves succeeded in capturing that squadron, it would have greatly paralyzed the besieging army [it had the siege train on board], if it would not have prevented its operations altogether; it would have put the two fleets nearly on an equality in point of numbers, would have arrested the progress of the French arms for the ensuing year in the West Indies, and might possibly have created such a spirit of discord between the French and Americans[22] as would have sunk the latter into the lowest depths of despair, from which they were only extricated by the arrival of the forces under De Grasse." [23] These are true and sober comments upon the naval strategy.

In regard to the admiral's tactics, it will be enough to say that the

---

[22] De Barras had been unwilling to go to the Chesapeake, fearing to be intercepted by a superior force, and had only yielded to the solicitation of Washington and Rochambeau.

[23] Capt. Thomas White, R. N.: Naval Researches.

fleet was taken into battle nearly as Byng took his; that very similar mishaps resulted; and that, when attacking twenty-four ships with nineteen, seven, under that capable officer Hood, were not able to get into action, owing to the dispositions made.

On the French side De Grasse must be credited with a degree of energy, foresight, and determination surprising in view of his failures at other times. The decision to take every ship with him, which made him independent of any failure on the part of De Barras; the passage through the Bahama Channel to conceal his movements; the address with which he obtained the money and troops required, from the Spanish and the French military authorities; the prevision which led him, as early as March 29, shortly after leaving Brest, to write to Rochambeau that American coast pilots should be sent to Cap Français; the coolness with which he kept Graves amused until De Barras's squadron had slipped in, are all points worthy of admiration. The French were also helped by the admiral's power to detain the two hundred merchant-ships, the "West India trade," awaiting convoy at Cap Français, where they remained from July till November, when the close of operations left him at liberty to convoy them with ships-of-war. The incident illustrates one weakness of a mercantile country with representative government, compared with a purely military nation. "If the British government," wrote an officer of that day, "had sanctioned, or a British admiral had adopted, such a measure, the one would have been turned out and the other hanged." [24] Rodney at the same time had felt it necessary to detach five ships-of-the-line with convoys, while half a dozen more went home with the trade from Jamaica.

It is easier to criticise the division of the English fleet between the West Indies and North America in the successive years 1780 and 1781, than to realize the embarrassment of the situation. This embarrassment was but the reflection of the military difficulty of England's position, all over the world, in this great and unequal war. England was everywhere outmatched and embarrassed, as she has always been as an empire, by the number of her exposed points. In Europe the Channel fleet was more than once driven into its ports by overwhelming forces. Gibraltar, closely blockaded by land and sea, was only kept alive in its desperate resistance by the skill of English seamen triumphing over the inaptness and discords of

[24] White: Naval Researches.

their combined enemies. In the East Indies, Sir Edward Hughes met in Suffren an opponent as superior to him in numbers as was De Grasse to Hood, and of far greater ability. Minorca, abandoned by the home government, fell before superior strength, as has been seen to fall, one by one, the less important of the English Antilles. The position of England from the time that France and Spain opened their maritime war was everywhere defensive, except in North America; and was therefore, from the military point of view, essentially false. She everywhere awaited attacks which the enemies, superior in every case, could make at their own choice and their own time. North America was really no exception to this rule, despite some offensive operations which in no way injured her real, that is her naval, foes.

Thus situated, and putting aside questions of national pride or sensitiveness, what did military wisdom prescribe to England? The question would afford an admirable study to a military inquirer, and is not to be answered off-hand, but certain evident truths may be pointed out. In the first place, it should have been determined what part of the assailed empire was most necessary to be preserved. After the British islands themselves, the North American colonies were the most valuable possessions in the eyes of the England of that day. Next should have been decided what others by their natural importance were best worth preserving, and by their own inherent strength, or that of the empire, which was mainly naval strength, could most surely be held. In the Mediterranean, for instance, Gibraltar and Mahon were both very valuable positions. Could both be held? Which was more easily to be reached and supported by the fleet? If both could not probably be held, one should have been frankly abandoned, and the force and efforts necessary to its defence carried elsewhere. So in the West Indies the evident strategic advantages of Barbadoes and Sta. Lucia prescribed the abandonment of the other small islands by garrisons as soon as the fleet was fairly outnumbered, if not before. The case of so large an island as Jamaica must be studied separately, as well as with reference to the general question. Such an island may be so far self-supporting as to defy any attack but one in great force and numbers, and that would rightly draw to it the whole English force from the windward stations at Barbadoes and Sta. Lucia.

With the defence thus concentrated, England's great weapon, the navy, should have been vigorously used on the offensive. Experience has taught that free nations, popular governments, will seldom dare wholly to remove the force that lies between an invader and its shores or capital. Whatever the military wisdom, therefore, of sending the Channel fleet to seek the enemy before it united, the step may not have been possible. But at points less vital the attack of the English should have anticipated that of the allies. This was most especially true of that theatre of the war which has so far been considered. If North America was the first object, Jamaica and the other islands should have been boldly risked. It is due to Rodney to say that he claims that his orders to the admirals at Jamaica and New York were disobeyed in 1781, and that to this was owing the inferiority in number of Graves's fleet.

But why, in 1780, when the departure of De Guichen for Europe left Rodney markedly superior in numbers during his short visit to North America, from September 14 to November 14, should no attempt have been made to destroy the French detachment of seven ships-of-the-line in Newport? These ships had arrived there in July; but although they had at once strengthened their position by earthworks, great alarm was excited by the news of Rodney's appearance off the coast. A fortnight passed by Rodney in New York and by the French in busy work, placed the latter, in their own opinion, in a position to brave all the naval force of England. "We twice feared, and above all at the time of Rodney's arrival," wrote the chief of staff of the French squadron, "that the English might attack us in the road itself; and there was a space of time during which such an undertaking would not have been an act of rashness. Now [October 20], the anchorage is fortified so that we can there brave all the naval force of England." [25]

The position thus taken by the French was undoubtedly very strong.[26] It formed a re-entrant angle of a little over ninety degrees, contained by lines drawn from Goat Island to what was then called Brenton's Point, the site of the present Fort Adams on the one side, and to Rose Island on the other. On the right flank of the position, Rose Island received a battery of thirty-six 24-pounders; while twelve

[25] Bouclon: La Marine de Louis XVI., p. 281. Under a rather misleading title this work is really a lengthy biography of Liberge de Granchain, chief of staff to the French squadron under Ternay.

[26] Diary of a French officer, 1781; Magazine of American History for March, 1880. The works at the time of Rodney's visit to New York were doubtless less complete than in 1781. This authority, a year later, gives the work on Rose Island twenty 36-pounders.

guns of the same size were placed on the left flank at Brenton's Point. Between Rose and Goat islands four ships, drawn up on a west-northwest line, bore upon the entrance and raked an approaching fleet; while three others, between Goat Island and Brenton's Point, crossed their fire at right angles with the former four.

On the other hand, the summer winds blow directly up the entrance, often with great force. There could be no question even of a considerably crippled attacking ship reaching her destined position, and when once confused with the enemy's line, the shore batteries would be neutralized. The work on Rose Island certainly, that on Brenton's Point probably, had less height than the two upper batteries of a ship-of-the-line, and could be vastly outnumbered. They could not have been casemated, and might indisputably have been silenced by the grapeshot of the ships that could have been brought against them. Rose Island could be approached on the front and on the west flank within two hundred yards, and on the north within half a mile. There was nothing to prevent this right flank of the French, including the line of ships, being enfiladed and crushed by the English ships taking position west of Rose Island. The essential points of close range and superior height were thus possible to the English fleet, which numbered twenty to the enemy's seven. If successful in destroying the shipping and reducing Rose Island, it could find anchorage farther up the bay and await a favorable wind to retire. In the opinion of a distinguished English naval officer of the day,[27] closely familiar with the ground, there was no doubt of the success of an attack; and he urged it frequently upon Rodney, offering himself to pilot the leading ship. The security felt by the French in this position, and the acquiescence of the English in that security, mark clearly the difference in spirit between this war and the wars of Nelson and Napoleon.

It is not, however, merely as an isolated operation, but in relation to the universal war, that such an attempt is here considered. England stood everywhere on the defensive, with inferior numbers. From such a position there is no salvation except by action vigorous almost to desperation. "It is impossible for us," wrote with great truth the First Lord of the Admiralty to Rodney, "to have a superior fleet in every part; and unless our commanders-in-chief will take the

[27] Sir Thomas Graves, afterward second in command to Nelson in the attack at Copenhagen in 1801,—an enterprise fully as desperate and encompassed with greater difficulties of pilotage than the one here advocated. See biographical memoir, Naval Chronicle, vol. viii.

great line, as you do, and consider the king's whole dominions under their care, our enemies must find us unprepared somewhere, and carry their point against us." [28] Attacks which considered in themselves alone might be thought unjustifiable were imposed upon English commanders. The allied navy was the key of the situation, and its large detachments, as at Newport, should have been crushed at any risk. The effect of such a line of action upon the policy of the French government is a matter of speculation, as to which the present writer has no doubts; but no English officer in chief command rose to the level of the situation, with the exception of Hood, and possibly of Howe. Rodney was now old, infirm, and though of great ability, a careful tactician rather than a great admiral.

The defeat of Graves and subsequent surrender of Cornwallis did not end the naval operations in the western hemisphere. On the contrary, one of the most interesting tactical feats and the most brilliant victory of the whole war were yet to grace the English flag in the West Indies; but with the events at Yorktown the patriotic interest for Americans closes. Before quitting that struggle for independence, it must again be affirmed that its successful ending, at least at so early a date, was due to the control of the sea,—to sea power in the hands of the French, and its improper distribution by the English authorities. This assertion may be safely rested on the authority of the one man who, above all others, thoroughly knew the resources of the country, the temper of the people, the difficulties of the struggle, and whose name is still the highest warrant for sound, quiet, unfluttered good-sense and patriotism.

The keynote to all Washington's utterances is set in the "Memorandum for concerting a plan of operations with the French army," dated July 15, 1780, and sent by the hands of Lafayette:—

"The Marquis de Lafayette will be pleased to communicate the following general ideas to Count de Rochambeau and the Chevalier de Ternay, as the sentiments of the underwritten:

"I. *In any operation, and under all circumstances, a decisive naval superiority is to be considered as a fundamental principle, and the basis upon which every hope of success must ultimately depend.*"

This, however, though the most formal and decisive expression of Washington's views, is but one among many others equally distinct. Thus, writing to Franklin, December 20, 1780, he says:—

[28] Rodney's Life, vol. i, p. 402.

"Disappointed of the second division of French troops [blockaded in Brest], but more especially in the expected naval superiority, which was the pivot upon which everything turned, we have been compelled to spend an inactive campaign after a flattering prospect at the opening of it. . . . Latterly we have been obliged to become spectators of a succession of detachments from the army at New York in aid of Lord Cornwallis; while our naval weakness, and the political dissolution of a large part of our army, put it out of our power to counteract them at the southward, or to take advantage of them here."

A month later, January 15, 1781, in a memorandum letter to Colonel Laurens, sent on a special mission to France, he says:—

"Next to a loan of money, a constant naval superiority upon these coasts is the object most interesting. This would instantly reduce the enemy to a difficult defensive. . . . Indeed, it is not to be conceived how they could subsist a large force in this country, if we had the command of the seas to interrupt the regular transmission of supplies from Europe. This superiority, with an aid in money, would enable us to convert the war into a vigorous offensive. With respect to us it seems to be one of two deciding points."

In another letter to the same person, then in Paris, dated April 9, he writes:—

"If France delays a timely and powerful aid in the critical posture of our affairs, it will avail us nothing, should she attempt it hereafter. . . . Why need I run into detail, when it may be declared in a word that we are at the end of our tether, and that now or never our deliverance must come? How easy would it be to retort the enemy's own game upon them, if it could be made to comport with the general plan of the war to keep a superior fleet always in these seas, and France would put us in condition to be active by advancing us money."

Ships and money are the burden of his cry. May 23, 1781, he writes to the Chevalier de la Luzerne: "I do not see how it is possible to give effectual support to the Southern States, and avert the evils which threaten, while we are inferior in naval force in these seas." As the season for active operations advances, his utterances are more frequent and urgent. To Major General Greene, struggling with his difficulties in South Carolina, he writes, June 1, 1781: "Our affairs have been attentively considered in every point of view, and it was finally determined to make an attempt upon New York, in preference to a Southern operation, as we had not decided command of the water." To Jefferson, June 8: "Should I be supported in the manner I expect, by the neighboring States, the enemy will, I hope, be reduced to the necessity of recalling part of their force from the southward to support New York, or they will run the most imminent risk of being expelled from that post, which is to them invaluable; and should we, by a lucky coincidence of circumstances, gain a naval superiority, their ruin would be inevitable. . . . While we remain inferior at sea . . . policy dictates that relief should be attempted by diversion rather than by sending reinforcements immediately to the point in distress," that is, to the South. To Rochambeau, June 13: "Your Excellency will recollect that New York was looked upon by us as the only practicable object under present circumstances; but should we be able to secure a naval superiority, we may perhaps find others more practicable and equally advisable." By the 15th of August the letters of De Grasse announcing his sailing for the Chesapeake were received, and the correspondence of Washington is thenceforth filled with busy preparations for the campaign in Virginia, based upon the long-delayed fleet. The discouragement of De Grasse, and his purpose to go to sea, upon learning that the English fleet in New York had been reinforced, drew forth an appealing letter dated September 25, which is too long for quotation; but the danger passed, Washington's confidence returns. The day after the capitulation he writes to De Grasse: "The surrender of York . . . *the honor of which belongs to your Excellency,* has greatly anticipated [in time] our most sanguine anticipations." He then goes on to urge further operations in the South, seeing so much of the good season was still left: "The general naval superiority of the British, previous to your arrival, gave them decisive advantages in the South, in the rapid transport of their troops and supplies; while the immense land marches of our succors, too tardy and expensive in every point of view, subjected us to be beaten in detail. It will depend upon your Excellency, therefore, to terminate the war." De Grasse refusing this request, but intimating an intention to co-operate in the next year's campaign, Washington instantly accepts: "With your Excellency I need not insist upon the indispensable necessity of a maritime force capable of giving you an absolute ascendency in these seas. . . . You will have observed that, whatever efforts are made by the land armies, the navy must have the casting vote in the present contest." A fortnight later, November 15, he writes to Lafayette, who is on the point of sailing for France:—

"As you expressed a desire to know my sentiments respecting the operations of the next campaign, I will, without a tedious display of reasoning, declare in one word that it must depend absolutely upon the naval force which is employed in these seas, and the time of its appearance next year. No land force can act decisively unless accompanied by a maritime superiority. . . . A doubt did not exist, nor does it at this moment, in any man's mind, of the total extirpation of the British force in the Carolinas and Georgia, if Count de Grasse could have extended his co-operation two months longer."

Such, in the opinion of the revered commander-in-chief of the American armies, was the influence of sea power upon the contest which he directed with so much skill and such infinite patience, and which, amidst countless trials and discouragements, he brought to a glorious close.

It will be observed that the American cause was reduced to these straits, notwithstanding the great and admitted losses of British commerce by the cruisers of the allies and by American privateers. This fact, and the small results from the general war, dominated as it was by the idea of commerce-destroying, show strongly the secondary and indecisive effect of such a policy upon the great issues of war.

11

Maritime War in Europe, 1779-1782

The last chapter closed with the opinions of Washington, expressed in many ways and at many times, as to the effect of sea power upon the struggle for American independence. If space allowed, these opinions could be amply strengthened by similar statements of Sir Henry Clinton, the English commander-in-chief.[1] In Europe the results turned yet more entirely upon the same factor. There the allies had three several objectives, at each of which England stood strictly upon the defensive. The first of these was England herself, involving, as a preliminary to an invasion, the destruction of the Channel fleet,—a project which, if seriously entertained, can scarcely be said to have been seriously attempted; the second was the reduction of Gibraltar; the third, the capture of Minorca. The last alone met with success. Thrice was England threatened by a largely superior fleet, thrice the threat fell harmless. Thrice was Gibraltar reduced to straits; thrice was it relieved by the address and fortune of English seamen, despite overpowering odds.

After Keppel's action off Ushant, no general encounter took place between fleets in European seas during the year 1778 and the first half of 1779. Meantime Spain was drawing toward a rupture with England and an active alliance with France. War was declared by her on the 16th of June, 1779; but as early as April 12, a treaty between the two Bourbon kingdoms, involving active war upon England, had been signed. By its terms the invasion of Great Britain or Ire-

---

[1] The curious reader can consult Clinton's letters and notes, in the "Clinton-Cornwallis Controversy," by B. F. Stevens. London, 1888.

land was to be undertaken, every effort made to recover for Spain, Minorca, Pensacola, and Mobile, and the two courts bound themselves to grant neither peace, nor truce, nor suspension of hostilities, until Gibraltar should be restored.[2]

The declaration of war was withheld until ready to strike; but the English government, doubtless, should have been upon its guard in the strained relations of the two countries, and prepared to prevent a junction of the two fleets. As it was, no efficient blockade of Brest was established, and twenty-eight French sail-of-the-line went out unopposed [3] June 3, 1779, under D'Orvilliers, Keppel's opponent of the year before. The fleet steered for the coasts of Spain, where it was to find the Spanish ships; but it was not till the 22nd of July that the full contingent joined. Seven precious summer weeks thus slipped by unimproved, but that was not all the loss; the French had been provisioned for only thirteen weeks, and this truly great armada of sixty-six ships-of-the-line and fourteen frigates had not more than forty working-days before it. Sickness, moreover, ravaged the fleet; and although it was fortunate enough to enter the Channel while the English were at sea, the latter, numbering little more than half their enemies, succeeded in passing within them. The flabbiness of coalitions increased the weakness due to inefficient preparation; a great and not unnatural panic on the English Channel coast, and the capture of one ship-of-the-line, were the sole results of a cruise extending, for the French, over fifteen weeks.[4] The disappointment,

[2] Bancroft: History of the United States, vol. x, p. 191.
[3] Although the English thus culpably failed to use their superiority to the French alone, the Channel fleet numbering over forty of the line, the fear that it might prevent the junction caused the Brest fleet to sail in haste and undermanned,—a fact which had an important effect upon the issue of the cruise. (Chevalier, p. 159.)
[4] The details of the mismanagement of this huge mob of ships are so numerous as to confuse a narrative, and are therefore thrown into a foot-note. The French fleet was hurried to sea four thousand men short. The Spaniards were seven weeks in joining. When they met, no common system of signals had been arranged; five fair summer days were spent in remedying this defect. Not till a week after the junction could the fleet sail for England. No steps were taken to supply the provisions consumed by the French during the seven weeks. The original orders to D'Orvilliers contemplated a landing at Portsmouth, or the seizure of the Isle of Wight, for which a large army was assembled on the coast of Normandy. Upon reaching the Channel, these orders were suddenly changed, and Falmouth indicated as the point of landing. By this time, August 16, summer was nearly over; and Falmouth, if taken, would offer no shelter to a great fleet. Then an easterly gale drove the fleet out of the Channel. By this time the sickness which raged had so reduced the crews that many ships could be neither handled nor fought. Ships companies of eight hundred or a thousand men could muster only from three to five hundred. Thus—bad administration crippled the fighting powers of the fleet; while the unaccountable military blunder of changing the objective from a safe and accessible roadstead to a fourth-rate and exposed harbor completed the disaster by taking away the only hope of a secure base of operations during the fall and winter months. France then had no first-class port on the Channel; hence the violent westerly gales which prevail in the autumn and winter would have driven the allies into the North Sea.

due to bad preparation, mainly on the part of Spain, though the French ministry utterly failed to meet the pressing wants of its fleet, fell, of course, upon the innocent Admiral d'Orvilliers. That brave and accomplished but unfortunate officer, whose only son, a lieutenant, had died of the pestilence which scourged the allies, could not support the odium. Being of a deeply religious character, the refuge which Villeneuve after Trafalgar found in suicide was denied him; but he threw up his command and retired into a religious house.

The scanty maritime interest of the year 1780, in Europe, centres round Cadiz and Gibraltar. This fortress was invested by Spain immediately upon the outbreak of war, and, while successfully resisting direct attack, the supply of provisions and ammunition was a matter of serious concern to England, and involved both difficulty and danger. For this purpose, Rodney sailed on the 29th of December, 1779, having under his command twenty ships-of-the-line with a large convoy and reinforcements for Gibraltar and Minorca, as well as the West India trade. The latter parted company on the 7th of January, under the care of four frigates, and the following morning the fleet fell in with and captured a Spanish squadron of seven ships-of-war and sixteen supply-ships. Twelve of the latter being laden with provisions were carried on to Gibraltar. A week later, at one P.M. of the 16th, a Spanish fleet of eleven sail-of-the-line was seen in the southeast. They held their ground, supposing the approaching vessels to be only supply-ships for Gibraltar, without a strong force of men-of-war,—an unfortunate error from which they did not awake until too late to escape, owing to the yet more unfortunate oversight of having no lookout frigates thrown out. When the Spanish admiral, Don Juan de Langara, recognized his mistake, he attempted to escape; but the English ships were copper-bottomed, and Rodney making the signal for a general chase overtook the enemy, cut in between him and his port, regardless of a blowy night, lee shore, and dangerous shoals, and succeeded in capturing the commander-in-chief with six ships-of-the-line. A seventh was blown up. The weather continuing very tempestuous, one of the prizes was wrecked, and one forced into Cadiz; several of the English ships were also in great danger, but happily escaped, and within a few days the entire force entered Gibraltar Bay. The convoy for Minorca was at once despatched, and immediately after the return of the ships-of-war guarding it, on the 13th of February, Rodney sailed for the West Indies with four ships-of-the-line, sending the rest of his force, with the prizes, to England under Admiral Digby.

The state of politics and parties in England at this time was such that, combined with the unavoidable inferiority of the Channel fleet, it was difficult to find an admiral willing to accept the chief command. An admirable officer, Barrington, the captor of Sta. Lucia, refused the first place, though willing to serve as second, even to a junior.[5] The allied fleet, to the number of thirty-six sail-of-the-line, assembled at Cadiz. Their cruises, however, were confined to the Portuguese coast; and their only service, a most important one, was the capture of an entire convoy, largely laden with military stores, for the East and West Indies. The entrance of sixty English prizes, with nearly three thousand prisoners, into Cadiz, was a source of great rejoicing to Spain. On the 24th of October, De Guichen, returning from his contest with Rodney, came into the same port with his West Indian squadron, of nineteen ships-of-the-line; but the immense armament thus assembled did nothing. The French ships returned to Brest in January, 1781.

While thus unproductive of military results in Europe, the war in 1780 gave rise to an event which cannot wholly be passed over by any history of sea power. This was the Armed Neutrality, at the head of which stood Russia, joined by Sweden and Denmark. The claim of England to seize enemy's goods in neutral ships bore hard upon neutral powers, and especially upon those of the Baltic and upon Holland, into whose hands, and those of the Austrian Netherlands, the war had thrown much of the European carrying-trade; while the products of the Baltic, naval stores and grain, were those which England was particularly interested in forbidding to her enemies. The declarations finally put forth by Russia, and signed by Sweden and Denmark, were four in number:

1. That neutral vessels had a right, not only to sail to unblockaded ports, but also from port to port of a belligerent nation; in other words, to maintain the coasting trade of a belligerent.

2. That property belonging to the subjects of a power at war should be safe on board neutral vessels. This was the principle involved in the now familiar maxim, "Free ships make free goods."

---

[5] Life of Admiral Keppel, vol. ii, pp. 72, 346, 403. See also Barrow: Life of Lord Howe, pp. 123-126.

3. That no articles are contraband, except arms, equipments, and munitions of war. This ruled out naval stores and provisions unless belonging to the government of a belligerent.

4. That blockades, to be binding, must have an adequate naval force stationed in close proximity to the blockaded port.

The contracting parties being neutral in the present war, but binding themselves to support these principles by a combined armed fleet of a fixed minimum number, the agreement received the name of the Armed Neutrality. The discussion of the propriety of the various declarations belongs to international law; but it is evident that no great maritime State, situated as England then was, would submit to the first and third as a matter of right. Policy only could induce her to do so. Without meeting the declarations by a direct contradiction, the ministry and the king determined to disregard them,—a course which was sustained in principle even by prominent members of the bitter opposition of that day. The undecided attitude of the United Provinces, divided as in the days of Louis XIV. between the partisans of England and France, despite a century of alliance with the former, drew the especial attention of Great Britain. They had been asked to join the Armed Neutrality; they hesitated, but the majority of the provinces favored it. A British officer had already gone so far as to fire upon a Dutch man-of-war which had resisted the search of merchant-ships under its convoy; an act which, whether right or wrong, tended to incense the Dutch generally against England. It was determined by the latter that if the United Provinces acceded to the coalition of neutrals, war should be declared. On the 16th of December, 1780, the English ministry was informed that the States-General had resolved to sign the declarations of the Armed Neutrality without delay. Orders were at once sent out to Rodney to seize the Dutch West India and South American possessions; similar orders to the East Indies; and the ambassador at the Hague was recalled. England declared war four days later. The principal effect, therefore, of the Armed Neutrality upon the war was to add the colonies and commerce of Holland to the prey of English cruisers. The additional enemy was of small account to Great Britain, whose geographical position effectually blocked the junction of the Dutch fleet with those of her other enemies. The possessions of Holland fell everywhere, except when saved by the French; while a bloody but wholly uninstructive battle between

English and Dutch squadrons in the North Sea, in August, 1781, was the only feat of arms illustrative of the old Dutch courage and obstinacy.

The year 1781, decisive of the question of the independence of the United States, was marked in the European seas by imposing movements of great fleets followed by puny results. At the end of March De Grasse sailed from Brest with twenty-six ships-of-the-line. On the 29th he detached five under Suffren to the East Indies, and himself continued on to meet success at Yorktown and disaster in the West Indies. On the 23d of June De Guichen sailed from Brest with eighteen ships-of-the-line for Cadiz, where he joined thirty Spanish ships. This immense armament sailed on the 22nd of July for the Mediterranean, landed fourteen thousand troops at Minorca, and then moved upon the English Channel.

The English had this year first to provide against the danger to Gibraltar. That beset fortress had had no supplies since Rodney's visit, in January of the year before, and was now in sore want, the provisions being scanty and bad, the biscuits weevilly, and the meat tainted. Amid the horrors and uproar of one of the longest and most exciting sieges of history, the sufferings of the combatants were intensified by the presence of many peaceful inhabitants, including the wives and families of soldiers as well as of officers. A great fleet of twenty-eight ships-of-the-line sailed from Portsmouth on the 13th of March, convoying three hundred merchant-ships for the East and West Indies, besides ninety-seven transports and supply-ships for the Rock. A delay on the Irish coast prevented its falling in with De Grasse, who had sailed nine days after it. Arriving off Cape St. Vincent, it met no enemy, and looking into Cadiz saw the great Spanish fleet at anchor. The latter made no move, and the English admiral, Derby, threw his supplies into Gibraltar on the 12th of April, undisturbed. At the same time he, like De Grasse, detached to the East Indies a small squadron, which was destined before long to fall in with Suffren. The inaction of the Spanish fleet, considering the eagerness of its government about Gibraltar and its equal if not superior numbers, shows scanty reliance of the Spanish admiral upon himself or his command. Derby, having relieved Gibraltar and Minorca, returned to the Channel in May.

Upon the approach of the combined fleet of nearly fifty sail in August following, Derby fell back upon Torbay and there anchored his fleet, numbering thirty ships. De Guichen, who held chief command, and whose caution when engaged with Rodney has been before remarked, was in favor of fighting; but the almost unanimous opposition of the Spaniards, backed by some of his own officers, overruled him in a council of war,[6] and again the great Bourbon coalition fell back, foiled by their own discord and the unity of their enemy. Gibraltar relieved, England untouched, were the results of these gigantic gatherings; they can scarcely be called efforts. A mortifying disaster closed the year for the allies. De Guichen sailed from Brest with seventeen sail, protecting a large convoy of merchantmen and ships with military supplies. The fleet was pursued by twelve English ships under Admiral Kempenfeldt, an officer whose high professional abilities have not earned the immortality with which poetry has graced his tragical death. Falling in with the French one hundred and fifty miles west of Ushant, he cut off a part of the convoy, despite his inferior numbers.[7] A few days later a tempest dispersed the French fleet. Only two ships-of-the-line and five merchantmen out of one hundred and fifty reached the West Indies.

The year 1782 opened with the loss to the English of Port Mahon, which surrendered on the 5th of February, after a siege of six months,—a surrender induced by the ravages of scurvy, consequent upon the lack of vegetables, and confinement in the foul air of bombproofs and casemates, under the heavy fire of an enemy. On the last night of the defence the call for necessary guards was four hundred and fifteen, while only six hundred and sixty men were fit for duty, thus leaving no reliefs.

[6] Beatson gives quite at length (vol. v, p. 395) the debate in the allied council of war. The customary hesitation of such councils, in face of the difficulties of the situation, was increased by an appeal to the delusion of commerce-destroying as a decisive mode of warfare. M. de Beausset urged that "the allied fleets should direct their whole attention to that great and attainable object, the intercepting of the British homeward-bound West India fleets. This was a measure which, as they were now masters of the sea, could scarcely fail of success; and it would prove a blow so fatal to that nation, that she could not recover it during the whole course of the war." The French account of La Pérouse-Bonfils is essentially the same. Chevalier, who is silent as to details, justly remarks: "The cruise just made by the allied fleet was such as to injure the reputation of France and Spain. These two powers had made a great display of force which had produced no result." The English trade also received little injury. Guichen wrote home: "I have returned from a cruise fatiguing but not glorious."

[7] This mishap of the French was largely due to mismanagement by De Guichen, a skilful and usually a careful admiral. When Kempenfeldt fell in with him, all the French ships-of-war were to leeward of their convoy, while the English were to windward of it. The former, therefore, were unable to interpose in time; and the alternative remedy, of the convoy running down to leeward of their escort, could not be applied by all the merchant-ships in so large a body.

The allied fleets assembled this year in Cadiz, to the number of forty ships-of-the-line. It was expected that this force would be increased by Dutch ships, but a squadron under Lord Howe drove the latter back to their ports. It does not certainly appear that any active enterprise was intended against the English coast; but the allies cruised off the mouth of the Channel and in the Bay of Biscay during the summer months. Their presence insured the safe arrival and departure of the homeward and outward bound merchantmen, and likewise threatened English commerce; notwithstanding which, Howe, with twenty-two ships, not only kept the sea and avoided an engagement, but also succeeded in bringing the Jamaica fleet safe into port. The injury to trade and to military transportation by sea may be said to have been about equal on either side; and the credit for successful use of sea power for these most important ends must therefore be given to the weaker party.

Having carried out their orders for the summer cruise, the combined fleets returned to Cadiz. On the 10th of September they sailed thence for Algeciras, on the opposite side of the bay from Gibraltar, to support a grand combined attack by land and sea, which, it was hoped, would reduce to submission the key to the Mediterranean. With the ships already there, the total rose to nearly fifty ships-of-the-line. The details of the mighty onslaught scarcely belong to our subject, yet cannot be wholly passed by, without at least such mention as may recognize and draw attention to their interest.

The three years' siege which was now drawing to its end had been productive of many brilliant feats of arms, as well as of less striking but more trying proofs of steadfast endurance, on the part of the garrison. How long the latter might have held out cannot be said, seeing the success with which the English sea power defied the efforts of the allies to cut off the communications of the fortress; but it was seemingly certain that the place must be subdued by main force or not at all, while the growing exhaustion of the belligerents foretold the near end of the war. Accordingly Spain multiplied her efforts of preparation and military ingenuity; while the report of them and of the approaching decisive contest drew to the scene volunteers and men of eminence from other countries of Europe. Two French Bourbon princes added, by their coming, to the theatrical interest with which the approaching drama was invested. The presence of royalty was needed adequately to grace the sublime catastrophe;

for the sanguine confidence of the besiegers had determined a satisfactory *dénouement* with all the security of a playwright.

Besides the works on the isthmus which joins the Rock to the mainland, where three hundred pieces of artillery were now mounted, the chief reliance of the assailants was upon ten floating batteries elaborately contrived to be shot-and-fire proof, and carrying one hundred and fifty-four heavy guns. These were to anchor in a close north-and-south line along the west face of the works, at about nine hundred yards' distance. They were to be supported by forty gunboats and as many bomb vessels, besides the efforts of the ships-of-the-line to cover the attack and distract the garrison. Twelve thousand French troops were brought to reinforce the Spaniards in the grand assault, which was to be made when the bombardment had sufficiently injured and demoralized the defenders. At this time the latter numbered seven thousand, their land opponents thirty-three thousand men.

The final act was opened by the English. At seven o'clock on the morning of September 8, 1782, the commanding general, Elliott, began a severe and most injurious fire upon the works on the isthmus. Having effected his purpose, he stopped; but the enemy took up the glove the next morning, and for four days successively poured in a fire from the isthmus alone of six thousand five hundred cannon-balls and one thousand one hundred bombs every twenty-four hours. So approached the great closing scene of September 13. At seven A.M. of that day the ten battering-ships unmoored from the head of the bay and stood down to their station. Between nine and ten they anchored, and the general fire at once began. The besieged replied with equal fury. The battering-ships seem in the main, and for some hours, to have justified the hopes formed of them; cold shot glanced or failed to get through their sides, while the self-acting apparatus for extinguishing fires balked the hot shot.

About two o'clock, however, smoke was seen to issue from the ship of the commander-in-chief, and though controlled for some time, the fire continued to gain. The same misfortune befell others; by evening, the fire of the besieged gained a marked superiority, and by one o'clock in the morning the greater part of the battering-ships were in flames. Their distress was increased by the action of the naval officer commanding the English gunboats, who now took post upon the flank of the line and raked it effectually,—a service which the Spanish gunboats should have prevented. In the end, nine of the ten blew up at their anchors, with a loss estimated at fifteen hundred men, four hundred being saved from the midst of the fire by the English seamen. The tenth ship was boarded and burned by the English boats. The hopes of the assailants perished with the failure of the battering-ships.

There remained only the hope of starving out the garrison. To this end the allied fleets now gave themselves. It was known that Lord Howe was on his way out with a great fleet, numbering thirty-four ships-of-the-line, besides supply vessels. On the 10th of October a violent westerly gale injured the combined ships, driving one ashore under the batteries of Gibraltar, where she was surrendered. The next day Howe's force came in sight, and the transports had a fine chance to make the anchorage, which, through carelessness, was missed by all but four. The rest, with the men-of-war, drove eastward into the Mediterranean. The allies followed on the 13th; but though thus placed between the port and the relieving force, and not encumbered, like the latter, with supply-ships, they yet contrived to let the transports, with scarcely an exception, slip in and anchor safely. Not only provisions and ammunition, but also bodies of troops carried by the ships-of-war, were landed without molestation. On the 19th the English fleet repassed the straits with an easterly wind, having within a week's time fulfilled its mission, and made Gibraltar safe for another year. The allied fleet followed, and on the 20th an action took place at long range, the allies to windward, but not pressing their attack close. The number of ships engaged in this magnificent spectacle, the closing scene of the great drama in Europe, the after-piece to the successful defence of Gibraltar, was eighty-three of the line,—forty-nine allies and thirty-four English. Of the former, thirty-three only got into action; but as the duller sailers would have come up to a general engagement, Lord Howe was probably right in declining, so far as in him lay, a trial which the allies did not too eagerly court.

Such were the results of this great contest in the European seas, marked on the part of the allies by efforts gigantic in size, but loose-jointed and flabby in execution. By England, so heavily overmatched in mere numbers, were shown firmness of purpose, high courage, and seamanship; but it can scarcely be said that the military conceptions of her councils, or the cabinet management of her sea forces, were worthy of the skill and devotion of her seamen. The odds against her were not so great—not nearly so great—as the formidable lists of guns and ships seemed to show; and while allowance must justly be made for early hesitations, the passing years of indecision and inefficiency on the part of the allies should have betrayed to her their weakness. The reluctance of the French to risk their ships, so plainly shown by D'Estaing, De Grasse, and De Guichen, the sluggishness and inefficiency of the Spaniards, should have encouraged England to pursue her old policy, to strike at the organized forces of the enemy afloat. As a matter of fact, and probably from the necessities of the case, the opening of every campaign found the enemies separated,—the Spaniards in Cadiz, the French in Brest.[8] To blockade the latter in full force before they could get out, England should have strained every effort; thus she would have stopped at its head the main stream of the allied strength, and, by knowing exactly where this great body was, would have removed that uncertainty as to its action which fettered her own movements as soon as it had gained the freedom of the open sea. Before Brest she was interposed between the allies; by her lookouts she would have known the approach of the Spaniards long before the French could know it; she would have kept in her hands the power of bringing against each, singly, ships more numerous and individually more effective. A wind that was fair to bring on the Spaniards would have locked their allies in the port. The most glaring instances of failure on the part of England to do this were when De Grasse was permitted to get out unopposed in March, 1781; for an English fleet of superior force had sailed from Portsmouth nine days before him, but was delayed by the admiralty on the Irish coast;[9] and again at the end of that year,

[8] "In the spring of 1780 the British admiralty had assembled in the Channel ports forty-five ships-of-the-line. The squadron at Brest was reduced to twelve or fifteen. . . . To please Spain, twenty French ships-of-the-line had joined the flag of Admiral Cordova in Cadiz. In consequence of these dispositions, the English with their Channel fleet held in check the forces which we had in Brest and in Cadiz. Enemy's cruisers traversed freely the space between the Lizard and the Straits of Gibraltar." (Chevalier, p. 202.)

In 1781 "the Cabinet of Versailles called the attention of Holland and Spain to the necessity of assembling at Brest a fleet strong enough to impose upon the ships which Great Britain kept in the Channel. The Dutch remained in the Texel, and the Spaniards did not leave Cadiz. From this state of things it resulted that the English, with forty ships-of-the-line, blocked seventy belonging to the allied powers." (p. 265.)

[9] "A question was very much agitated both in and out of Parliament; namely, Whether the intercepting of the French fleet under the Count de Grasse should not have been the first object of the British fleet under Vice-Admiral Darby, instead of losing time in going to Ireland, by which that opportunity was missed. The defeat of the French fleet would certainly have totally disconcerted the great plans which the enemies had formed in the East and West Indies. It would have insured the safety of the British West India islands; the Cape of Good Hope must have fallen into the hands of Britain; and the campaign in North

when Kempenfeldt was sent to intercept De Guichen with an inferior force, while ships enou~h to change the odds were kept at home. Several of the ships which were to accompany Rodney to the West Indies were ready when Kempenfeldt sailed, yet they were not associated with an enterprise so nearly affecting the objects of Rodney's campaign. The two forces united would have made an end of De Guichen's seventeen ships and his invaluable convoy.

Gibraltar was indeed a heavy weight upon the English operations, but the national instinct which clung to it was correct. The fault of the English policy was in attempting to hold so many other points of land, while neglecting, by rapidity of concentration, to fall upon any of the detachments of the allied fleets. The key of the situation was upon the ocean; a great victory there would have solved all the other points in dispute. But it was not possible to win a great victory while trying to maintain a show of force everywhere.[10]

North America was a yet heavier clog, and there undoubtedly the feeling of the nation was mistaken; pride, not wisdom, maintained that struggle. Whatever the sympathies of individuals and classes in the allied nations, by their governments American rebellion was valued only as a weakening of England's arm. The operations there depended, as has been shown, upon the control of the sea; and to maintain that, large detachments of English ships were absorbed from the contest with France and Spain. Could a successful war have made America again what it once was, a warmly attached dependency of Great Britain, a firm base for her sea power, it would have been worth much greater sacrifices; but that had become impossible. But although she had lost, by her own mistakes, the affection of the colonists, which would have supported and secured her hold upon their ports and seacoast, there nevertheless remained to the mother-country, in Halifax, Bermuda, and the West Indies, enough strong military stations, inferior, as naval bases, only to those strong ports which are surrounded by a friendly country, great in its resources and population. The abandonment of the contest in North America would have strengthened England very much more than the allies. As it was, her large naval detachments there were always liable to be

America might have had a very different termination." (Beatson's Memoirs, vol. v. p. 341, where the contrary arguments are also stated.)

[10] This is one of the most common and flagrant violations of the principles of war,—stretching a thin line, everywhere inadequate, over an immense frontier. The clamors of trade and local interests make popular governments especially liable to it.

overpowered by a sudden move of the enemy from the sea, as happened in 1778 and 1781.

To the abandonment of America as hopelessly lost, because no military subjection could have brought back the old loyalty, should have been added the giving up, for the time, all military occupancy which fettered concentration, while not adding to military strength. Most of the Antilles fell under this head, and the ultimate possession of them would depend upon the naval campaign. Garrisons could have been spared for Barbadoes and Sta. Lucia, for Gibraltar and perhaps for Mahon, that could have effectually maintained them until the empire of the seas was decided; and to them could have been added one or two vital positions in America, like New York and Charleston, to be held only till guarantees were given for such treatment of the loyalists among the inhabitants as good faith required England to exact.

Having thus stripped herself of every weight, rapid concentration with offensive purpose should have followed. Sixty ships-of-the-line on the coast of Europe, half before Cadiz and half before Brest, with a reserve at home to replace injured ships, would not have exhausted by a great deal the roll of the English navy; and that such fleets would not have had to fight, may not only be said by us, who have the whole history before us, but might have been inferred by those who had watched the tactics of D'Estaing and De Guichen, and later on of De Grasse. Or, had even so much dispersal been thought unadvisable, forty ships before Brest would have left the sea open to the Spanish fleet to try conclusions with the rest of the English navy when the question of controlling Gibraltar and Mahon came up for decision. Knowing what we do of the efficiency of the two services, there can be little question of the result; and Gibraltar, instead of a weight, would, as often before and since those days, have been an element of strength to Great Britain.

The conclusion continually recurs. Whatever may be the determining factors in strifes between neighboring continental States, when a question arises of control over distant regions, politically weak,—whether they be crumbling empires, anarchical republics, colonies, isolated military posts, or islands below a certain size,—it must ultimately be decided by naval power, by the organized military force afloat, which represents the communications that form so prominent a feature in all strategy. The magnificent defence of

368

Gibraltar hinged upon this; upon this depended the military results of the war in America; upon this the final fate of the West India Islands; upon this certainly the possession of India. Upon this will depend the control of the Central American Isthmus, if that question take a military coloring; and though modified by the continental position and surroundings of Turkey, the same sea power must be a weighty factor in shaping the outcome of the Eastern Question in Europe.

If this be true, military wisdom and economy, both of time and money, dictate bringing matters to an issue as soon as possible upon the broad sea, with the certainty that the power which achieves military preponderance there will win in the end. In the war of the American Revolution the numerical preponderance was very great against England; the actual odds were less, though still against her. Military considerations would have ordered the abandonment of the colonies; but if the national pride could not stoop to this, the right course was to blockade the hostile arsenals. If not strong enough to be in superior force before both, that of the more powerful nation should have been closed. Here was the first fault of the English admiralty; the statement of the First Lord as to the available force at the outbreak of the war was not borne out by facts. The first fleet, under Keppel, barely equalled the French; and at the same time Howe's force in America was inferior to the fleet under D'Estaing. In 1779 and 1781, on the contrary, the English fleet was superior to that of the French alone; yet the allies joined unopposed, while in the latter year De Grasse got away to the West Indies, and Suffren to the East. In Kempenfeldt's affair with De Guichen, the admiralty knew that the French convoy was of the utmost importance to the campaign in the West Indies, yet they sent out their admiral with only twelve ships; while at that time, besides the reinforcement destined for the West Indies, a number of others were stationed in the Downs, for what Fox justly called "the paltry purpose" of distressing the Dutch trade. The various charges made by Fox in the speech quoted from, and which, as regarded the Franco-Spanish War, were founded mainly on the expediency of attacking the allies before they got away into the ocean wilderness, were supported by the high professional opinion of Lord Howe, who of the Kempenfeldt affair said: "Not only the fate of the West India Islands, but perhaps the whole future fortune of the war, might have been decided, almost without a risk, in the Bay of Biscay." [11] Not without a risk, but with strong probabilities of success, the whole fortune of the war should at the first have been staked on a concentration of the English fleet between Brest and Cadiz. No relief for Gibraltar would have been more efficacious; no diversion surer for the West India Islands; and the Americans would have appealed in vain for the help, scantily given as it was, of the French fleet. For the great results that flowed from the coming of De Grasse must not obscure the fact that he came on the 31st of August, and announced from the beginning that he must be in the West Indies again by the middle of October. Only a providential combination of circumstances prevented a repetition to Washington, in 1781, of the painful disappointments by D'Estaing and De Guichen in 1778 and 1780.

[11] Annual Register, 1782.

12

Events in the East Indies, 1778-1781—Suffren
Sails from Brest, 1781—His Brilliant Naval
Campaign in the Indian Seas, 1782-1783

The very interesting and instructive campaign of Suffren in the
East Indies, although in itself by far the most noteworthy and
meritorious naval performance of the war of 1778, failed, through
no fault of his, to affect the general issue. It was not till 1781 that
the French Court felt able to direct upon the East naval forces
adequate to the importance of the issue. Yet the conditions of the
peninsula at that time were such as to give an unusual opportunity
for shaking the English power. Hyder Ali, the most skilful and daring of all the enemies against whom the English had yet fought in
India, was then ruling over the kingdom of Mysore, which, from its
position in the southern part of the peninsula, threatened both the
Carnatic and the Malabar coast. Hyder, ten years before, had maintained alone a most successful war against the intruding foreigners,
concluding with a peace upon the terms of a mutual restoration of
conquests; and he was now angered by the capture of Mahé. On the
other hand, a number of warlike tribes, known by the name of the
Mahrattas, of the same race and loosely knit together in a kind of
feudal system, had become involved in war with the English. The
territory occupied by these tribes, whose chief capital was at Poonah,
near Bombay, extended northward from Mysore to the Ganges. With
boundaries thus conterminous, and placed centrally with reference
to the three English presidencies of Bombay, Calcutta, and Madras,

Hyder and the Mahrattas were in a position of advantage for mutual support and for offensive operations against the common enemy. At the beginning of the war between England and France, a French agent appeared at Poonah. It was reported to Warren Hastings, the Governor-General, that the tribes had agreed to terms and ceded to the French a seaport on the Malabar coast. With his usual promptness, Hastings at once determined on war, and sent a division of the Bengal army across the Jumna and into Berar. Another body of four thousand English troops also marched from Bombay; but being badly led, was surrounded and forced to surrender in January, 1779. This unusual reverse quickened the hopes and increased the strength of the enemies of the English; and although the material injury was soon remedied by substantial successes under able leaders, the loss of prestige remained. The anger of Hyder Ali, roused by the capture of Mahé, was increased by imprudent thwarting on the part of the governor of Madras. Seeing the English entangled with the Mahrattas, and hearing that a French armament was expected on the Coromandel coast, he quietly prepared for war. In the summer of 1780 swarms of his horsemen descended without warning from the hills, and appeared near the gates of Madras. In September one body of English troops, three thousand strong, was cut to pieces, and another of five thousand was only saved by a rapid retreat upon Madras, losing its artillery and trains. Unable to attack Madras, Hyder turned upon the scattered posts separated from each other and the capital by the open country, which was now wholly in his control.

Such was the state of affairs when, in January, 1781, a French squadron of six ships-of-the-line and three frigates appeared on the coast. The English fleet under Sir Edward Hughes had gone to Bombay. To the French commodore, Count d'Orves, Hyder appealed for aid in an attack upon Cuddalore. Deprived of support by sea, and surrounded by the myriads of natives, the place must have fallen. D'Orves, however, refused, and returned to the Isle of France. At the same time one of the most skilful of the English Indian soldiers, Sir Eyre Coote, took the field against Hyder. The latter at once raised the siege of the beleaguered posts, and after a series of operations extending through the spring months, was brought to battle on the 1st of July, 1781. His total defeat restored to the English the open country, saved the Carnatic, and put an end to the hopes of the partisans of the French in their late possession of Pondicherry. A great opportunity had been lost.

Meanwhile a French officer of very different temper from his predecessors was on his way to the East Indies. It will be remembered that when De Grasse sailed from Brest, March 22, 1781, for the West Indies, there went with his fleet a division of five ships-of-the-line under Suffren. The latter separated from the main body on the 29th of the month, taking with him a few transports destined for the Cape of Good Hope, then a Dutch colony. The French government had learned that an expedition from England was destined to seize this important halting-place on the road to India, and Suffren's first mission was to secure it. In fact, the squadron under Commodore Johnstone[1] had got away first, and had anchored at Porto Praya, in the Cape Verde Islands, a Portuguese colony, on the 11th of April. It numbered two ships-of-the-line, and three of fifty guns, with frigates and smaller vessels, besides thirty-five transports, mostly armed. Without apprehension of attack, not because he trusted to the neutrality of the port but because he thought his destination secret, the English commodore had not anchored with a view to battle.

It so happened that at the moment of sailing from Brest one of the ships intended for the West Indies was transferred to Suffren's squadron. She consequently had not water enough for the longer voyage, and this with other reasons determined Suffren also to anchor at Porto Praya. On the 16th of April, five days after Johnstone, he made the island early in the morning and stood for the anchorage, sending a coppered ship ahead to reconnoitre. Approaching from the eastward, the land for some time hid the English squadron; but at quarter before nine the advance ship, the "Artésien," signalled that enemy's ships were anchored in the bay. The latter is open to the southward, and extends from east to west about a mile and a half; the conditions are such that ships usually lie in the northeast part, near the shore (Plate XIII.).[2] The English were there, stretching irregularly in a west-northwest line. Both Suffren and

---

[1] This Commodore Johnstone, more commonly known as Governor Johnstone, was one of the three commissioners sent by Lord North in 1778 to promote a reconciliation with America. Owing to certain suspicious proceedings on his part, Congress declared it was incompatible with their honor to hold any manner of correspondence or intercourse with him. His title of Governor arose from his being at one time governor of Pensacola. He had a most unenviable reputation in the English navy. (See Charnock's Biog. Navalis.)

[2] This plate is taken almost wholly from Cunat's "Vie de Suffren."

Johnstone were surprised, but the latter more so; and the initiative remained with the French officer. Few men were fitter, by natural temper and the teaching of experience, for the prompt decision required. Of ardent disposition and inborn military genius, Suffren had learned, in the conduct of Boscawen toward the squadron of De la Clue, in which he had served, not to lay weight upon the power of Portugal to enforce respect for her neutrality. He knew that this must be the squadron meant for the Cape of Good Hope. The only question for him was whether to press on to the Cape with the chance of getting there first, or to attack the English at their anchors, in the hope of so crippling them as to prevent their further progress. He decided for the latter; and although the ships of his squadron, not sailing equally well, were scattered, he also determined to stand in at once, rather than lose the advantage of a surprise. Making signal to prepare for action at anchor, he took the lead in his flag-ship, the "Héros," of seventy-four guns, hauled close round the southeast point of the bay, and stood for the English flag-ship (f). He was closely followed by the "Hannibal," seventy-four (line a b); the advance ship "Artésien" (c), a sixty-four, also stood on with him; but the two rear ships were still far astern.

The English commodore got ready for battle as soon as he made out the enemy, but had no time to rectify his order. Suffren anchored five hundred feet from the flag-ship's starboard beam (by a singular coincidence the English flag-ship was also called "Hero"), thus having enemy's ships on both sides, and opened fire. The "Hannibal" anchored ahead of her commodore (b), and so close that the latter had to veer cable and drop astern (a); but her captain, ignorant of Suffren's intention to disregard the neutrality of the port, had not obeyed the order to clear for action, and was wholly unprepared,—his decks lumbered with water-casks which had been got up to expedite watering, and the guns not cast loose. He did not add to this fault by any hesitation, but followed the flag-ship boldly, receiving passively the fire, to which for a time he was unable to reply. Luffing to the wind, he passed to windward of his chief, chose his position with skill, and atoned by his death for his first fault. These two ships were so placed as to use both broadsides. The "Artésien" in the smoke, mistook an East India ship for a man-of-war. Running alongside (c'), her captain was struck dead at the

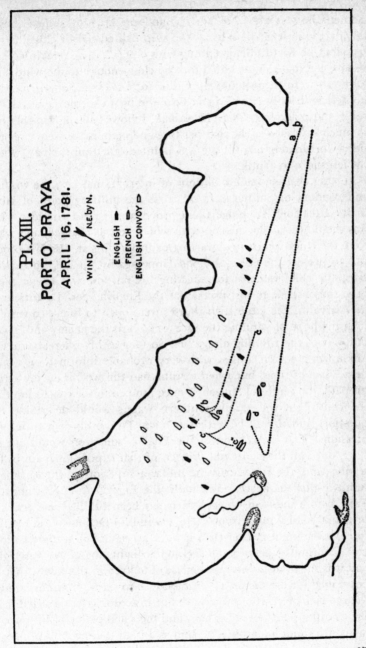

PL.XIII.

PORTO PRAYA

APRIL 16, 1781.

WIND N.E.by N.

ENGLISH ━━
FRENCH ━━
ENGLISH CONVOY ▷

moment he was about to anchor, and the critical moment being lost by the absence of a head, the ship drifted out of close action, carrying the East-Indiaman along with her (c''). The remaining two vessels, coming up late, failed to keep close enough to the wind, and they too were thrown out of action (d, e). Then Suffren, finding himself with only two ships to bear the brunt of the fight, cut his cable and made sail. The "Hannibal" followed his movement; but so much injured was she that her fore and main masts went over the side,—fortunately not till she was pointed out from the bay, which she left shorn to a hulk.

Putting entirely aside questions of international law, the wisdom and conduct of Suffren's attack, from the military point of view, invite attention. To judge them properly, we must consider what was the object of the mission with which he was charged, and what were the chief factors in thwarting or forwarding it. His first object was to protect the Cape of Good Hope against an English expedition; the chief reliance for effecting his purpose was to get there first; the obstacle to his success was the English fleet. To anticipate the arrival of the latter, two courses were open to him,—to run for it in the hope of winning the race, or to beat the enemy and so put him out of the running altogether. So long as his whereabouts was unknown, a search, unless with very probable information, would be a waste of time; but when fortune had thrown his enemy across his path, the genius of Suffren at once jumped to the conclusion that the control of the sea in southern waters would determine the question, and should be settled at once. To use his own strong expression, "The destruction of the English squadron would *cut off the root* of all the plans and projects of that expedition, gain us for a long time the superiority in India, a superiority whence might result a glorious peace, and hinder the English from reaching the Cape before me,—an object which has been fulfilled and was the principal aim of my mission." He was ill-informed as to the English force, believing it greater than it was; but he had it at disadvantage and surprised. The prompt decision to fight, therefore, was right, and it is the most pronounced merit of Suffren in this affair, that he postponed for the moment—dismissed, so to speak, from his mind—the ulterior projects of the cruise; but in so doing he departed from the traditions of the French navy and the usual policy of his government. It cannot be imputed to him as a fault that he did not receive from his captains the support he was fairly entitled to expect. The accidents and negligence which led to their failure have been mentioned; but having his three best ships in hand, there can be little doubt he was right in profiting by the surprise, and trusting that the two in reserve would come up in time.

The position taken by his own ship and by the "Hannibal," enabling them to use both broadsides,—in other words, to develop their utmost force,—was excellently judged. He thus availed himself to the full of the advantage given by the surprise and by the lack of order in the enemy's squadron. This lack of order, according to English accounts, threw out of action two of their fifty-gun ships,— a circumstance which, while discreditable to Johnstone, confirmed Suffren's judgment in precipitating his attack. Had he received the aid upon which, after all deductions, he was justified in counting, he would have destroyed the English squadron; as it was, he saved the Cape Colony at Porto Praya. It is not surprising, therefore, that the French Court, notwithstanding its traditional sea policy and the diplomatic embarrassment caused by the violation of Portuguese neutrality, should have heartily and generously acknowledged a vigor of action to which it was unused in its admirals.

It has been said that Suffren, who had watched the cautious movements of D'Estaing in America, and had served in the Seven Years' War, attributed in part the reverses suffered by the French at sea to the introduction of Tactics, which he stigmatized as the veil of timidity; but that the results of the fight at Porto Praya, necessarily engaged without previous arrangement, convinced him that system and method had their use.[4] Certainly his tactical combinations afterward were of a high order, especially in his earlier actions in the East (for he seems again to have abandoned them in the later fights under the disappointment caused by his captains' disaffection or blundering). But his great and transcendent merit lay in the clearness with which he recognized in the English fleets, the exponent of the British sea power, the proper enemy of the French fleet, to be attacked first and always when with any show of equality. Far from blind to the importance of those ulterior objects to which the action of the French navy was so constantly subordinated, he yet saw plainly that the way to assure those objects was not by economizing his own ships, but by destroying those of the enemy. At-

[4] La Serre: Essais Hist. et Critiques sur la Marine Française.

tack, not defence, was the road to sea power in his eyes; and sea power meant control of the issues upon the land, at least in regions distant from Europe. This view out of the English policy he had the courage to take, after forty years of service in a navy sacrificed to the opposite system; but he brought to its practical application a method not to be found in any English admiral of the day, except perhaps Rodney, and a fire superior to the latter. Yet the course thus followed was no mere inspiration of the moment; it was the result of clear views previously held and expressed. However informed by natural ardor, it had the tenacity of an intellectual conviction. Thus he wrote to D'Estaing, after the failure to destroy Barrington's squadron at Sta. Lucia, remonstrating upon the half-manned condition of his own and other ships, from which men had been landed to attack the English troops:—

"Notwithstanding the small results of the two cannonades of the 15th of December [directed against Barrington's squadron], and the unhappy check our land forces have undergone, we may yet hope for success. But the only means to have it is to attack vigorously the squadron, which, with our superiority, cannot resist, notwithstanding its land batteries, whose effects will be neutralized if we run them aboard, or anchor upon their buoys. If we delay, they may escape. . . . Besides, our fleet being unmanned, it is in condition neither to sail nor to fight. What would happen if Admiral Byron's fleet should arrive? What would become of ships having neither crews nor admiral? Their defeat would cause the loss of the army and the colony. Let us destroy that squadron; their army, lacking everything and in a bad country, would soon be obliged to surrender. Then let Byron come, we shall be pleased to see him. I think it is not necessary to point out that for this attack we need men and plans well concerted with those who are to execute them."

Equally did he condemn the failure of D'Estaing to capture the four crippled ships of Byron's squadron, after the action off Grenada.

Owing to a combination of misfortunes, the attack at Porto Praya had not the decisive result it deserved. Commodore Johnstone got under way and followed Suffren; but he thought his force was not adequate to attack in face of the resolute bearing of the French, and feared the loss of time consequent upon chasing to leeward of his port. He succeeded, however, in retaking the East India ship which the "Artésien" had carried out. Suffren continued his course and anchored at the Cape, in Simon's Bay, on the 21st of June. Johnstone followed him a fortnight later; but learning by an advance ship that the French troops had been landed, he gave up the enterprise against the colony, made a successful commerce-destroying attack upon five Dutch India ships in Saldanha Bay, which poorly repaid the failure of the military undertaking, and then went back himself to England, after sending the ships-of-the-line on to join Sir Edward Hughes in the East Indies.

Having seen the Cape secured, Suffren sailed for the Isle of France, arriving there on the 25th of October, 1781. Count d'Orves, being senior, took command of the united squadron. The necessary repairs were made, and the fleet sailed for India, December 17. On the 22nd of January, 1782, an English fifty-gun ship, the "Hannibal," was taken. On the 9th of February Count d'Orves died, and Suffren became commander-in-chief, with the rank of commodore. A few days later the land was seen to the northward of Madras; but owing to head-winds the city was not sighted until February 15. Nine large ships-of-war were found anchored in order under the guns of the forts. They were the fleet of Sir Edward Hughes, not in confusion like that of Johnstone.[5]

Here, at the meeting point between these two redoubtable champions, each curiously representative of the characteristics of his own race,—the one of the stubborn tenacity and seamanship of the English, the other of the ardor and tactical science of the French too long checked and betrayed by a false system,—is the place to give an accurate statement of the material forces. The French fleet had three seventy-fours, seven sixty-fours, and two fifty-gun ships, one of which was the lately captured English "Hannibal." To these Sir Edward Hughes opposed two seventy-fours, one seventy, one sixty-eight, four sixty-fours, and one fifty-gun ship. The odds, therefore, twelve to nine, were decidedly against the English; and it is likely that the advantage in single-ship power, class for class, was also against them.

It must be recalled that at the time of his arrival Suffren found no friendly port or roadstead, no base of supplies or repair. The French posts had all fallen by 1779; and his rapid movement, which

[5] The question of attacking the English squadron at its anchors was debated in a council of war. Its opinion confirmed Suffren's decision not to do so. In contrasting this with the failure of the English to attack the French detachment in Newport (p. 350), it must be borne in mind that in the latter case there was no means of forcing the ships to leave their strong position; whereas by threatening Trincomalee, or other less important points, Suffren could rely upon drawing Hughes out. He was therefore right in not attacking, while the English before Newport were probably wrong.

saved the Cape, did not bring him up in time to prevent the capture of the Dutch Indian possessions. The invaluable harbor of Trinco-malee, in Ceylon, was taken just one month before Suffren saw the English fleet at Madras. But if he thus had everything to gain, Hughes had as much to lose. To Suffren, at the moment of first meeting, belonged superiority of numbers and the power of taking the offensive, with all its advantages in choice of initiative. Upon Hughes fell the anxiety of the defensive, with inferior numbers, many assailable points, and uncertainty as to the place where the blow would fall.

It was still true, though not so absolutely as thirty years before, that control in India depended upon control of the sea. The passing years had greatly strengthened the grip of England, and proportion-ately loosened that of France. Relatively, therefore, the need of Suffren to destroy his enemy was greater than that of his predeces-sors, D'Aché and others; whereas Hughes could count upon a greater strength in the English possessions, and so bore a somewhat less responsibility than the admirals who went before him.

Nevertheless, the sea was still by far the most important factor in the coming strife, and for its proper control it was necessary to disable more or less completely the enemy's fleet, and to have some reasonably secure base. For the latter purpose, Trincomalee, though unhealthy, was by far the best harbor on the east coast; but it had not been long enough in the hands of England to be well supplied. Hughes, therefore, inevitably fell back on Madras for repairs after an action, and was forced to leave Trincomalee to its own resources until ready to take the sea again. Suffren, on the other hand, found all ports alike destitute of naval supplies, while the natural ad-vantages of Trincomalee made its possession an evident object of importance to him; and Hughes so understood it.

Independently, therefore, of the tradition of the English navy impelling Hughes to attack, the influence of which appears plainly between the lines of his letters, Suffren had, in moving toward Trincomalee, a threat which was bound to draw his adversary out of his port. Nor did Trincomalee stand alone; the existing war be-tween Hyder Ali and the English made it imperative for Suffren to seize a port upon the mainland, at which to land the three thou-sand troops carried by the squadron to co-operate on shore against the common enemy, and from which supplies, at least of food, might be had. Everything, therefore, concurred to draw Hughes out, and make him seek to cripple or hinder the French fleet.

The method of his action would depend upon his own and his adversary's skill, and upon the uncertain element of the weather. It was plainly desirable for him not to be brought to battle except on his own terms; in other words, without some advantage of situation to make up for his weaker force. As a fleet upon the open sea cannot secure any advantages of ground, the position favoring the weaker was that to windward, giving choice of time and some choice as to method of attack, the offensive position used defensively, with the intention to make an offensive movement if circumstances warrant. The leeward position left the weaker no choice but to run, or to accept action on its adversary's terms.

Whatever may be thought of Hughes's skill, it must be conceded that his task was difficult. Still, it can be clearly thought down to two requisites. The first was to get in a blow at the French fleet, so as to reduce the present inequality; the second, to keep Suffren from getting Trincomalee, which depended wholly on the fleet.[6] Suffren, on the other hand, if he could do Hughes, in an action, more injury than he himself received, would be free to turn in any direction he chose.

Suffren having sighted Hughes's fleet at Madras, February 15, anchored his own four miles to the northward. Considering the enemy's line, supported by the batteries, to be too strong for attack, he again got under way at four P.M., and stood south. Hughes also weighed, standing to the southward all that night under easy sail, and at daylight found that the enemy's squadron had separated from the convoy, the ships of war being about twelve miles east, while the transports were nine miles southwest, from him (Plate XIV. A, A). This dispersal is said to have been due to the carelessness of the French frigates, which did not keep touch of the English. Hughes at once profited by it, chasing the convoy (c), knowing that the line-of-battle ships must follow. His copper-bottomed ships came up with and captured six of the enemy, five of which were English

[6] The dependence of Trincomalee upon the English fleet in this campaign affords an excellent illustration of the embarrassment and false position in which a navy finds itself when the defence of its seaports rests upon it. This bears upon a much debated point of the present day, and is worthy the study of those who maintain, too unqualifiedly, that the best coast defence is a navy. In one sense this is doubtless true,—to attack the enemy abroad is the best of defences; but in the narrow sense of the word "defence" it is not true. Trincomalee unfortified was simply a centre round which Hughes had to revolve like a tethered animal; and the same will always happen under like conditions.

prizes. The sixth carried three hundred troops with military stores. Hughes had scored a point.

Suffren of course followed in a general chase, and by three P.M. four of his best sailers were two or three miles from the sternmost English ships. Hughes's ships were now much scattered, but not injudiciously so, for they joined by signal at seven P.M. Both squadrons stood to the southeast during the night, under easy sail.

At daylight of the 17th—the date of the first of four actions fought between these two chiefs within seven months—the fleets were six or eight miles apart, the French bearing north-northeast from the English (B, B). The latter formed line-ahead on the port tack (a), with difficulty, owing to the light winds and frequent calms. Admiral Hughes explains that he hoped to weather the enemy by this course so as to engage closely, counting probably on finding himself to windward when the sea-breeze made. The wind continuing light, but with frequent squalls, from north-northeast, the French, running before it, kept the puffs longer and neared the English rapidly, Suffren's intention to attack the rear being aided by Hughes's course. The latter finding his rear straggling, bore up to line abreast (b), retreating to gain time for the ships to close on the centre. These movements in line abreast continued till twenty minutes before four P.M., when, finding he could not escape attack on the enemy's terms, Hughes hauled his wind on the port tack and awaited it (C). Whether by his own fault or not, he was now in the worst possible position, waiting for an attack by a superior force at its pleasure. The rear ship of his line, the "Exeter," was not closed up; and there appears no reason why she should not have been made the van, by forming on the starboard tack, and thus bringing the other ships up to her.

The method of Suffren's attack (C) is differently stated by him and by Hughes, but the difference is in detail only; the main facts are certain. Hughes says the enemy "steered down on the rear of our line in an irregular double-line abreast," in which formation they continued till the moment of collision, when "three of the enemy's ships in the first line bore right down upon the 'Exeter,' while four more of their second line, headed by the 'Héros,' in which M. de Suffren had his flag, hauled *along the outside of the first line* toward our centre. At five minutes past four the enemy's three ships began their fire upon the 'Exeter,' which was returned by her and her

382

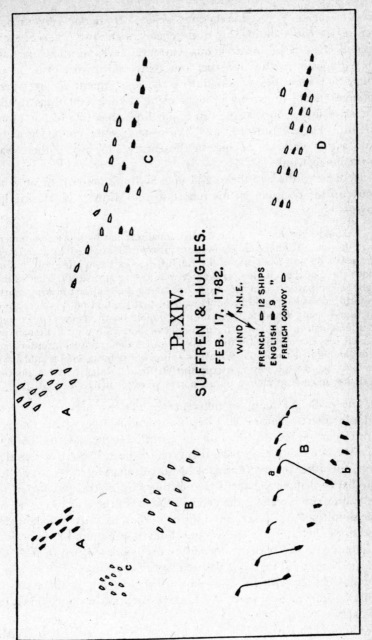

Pl. XIV.

SUFFREN & HUGHES.

FEB. 17, 1782.

WIND N.N.E.

FRENCH 12 SHIPS
ENGLISH 9 "
FRENCH CONVOY

second ahead; the action became general from our rear to our centre, the commanding ship of the enemy, with three others of their second line, leading down on our centre, yet never advancing farther than opposite to the 'Superbe,' our centre ship, with little or no wind and some heavy rain during the engagement. Under these circumstances, the enemy brought eight of their best ships to the attack of five of ours, as the van of our line, consisting of the 'Monmouth,' 'Eagle,' 'Burford,' and 'Worcester,' could not be brought into action without tacking on the enemy," for which there was not enough wind.

Here we will leave them, and give Suffren's account of how he took up his position. In his report to the Minister of Marine he says:—

"I should have destroyed the English squadron, less by superior numbers than by the advantageous disposition in which I attacked it. I attacked the rear ship and stood along the English line as far as the sixth. I thus made three of them useless, so that we were twelve against six. I began the fight at half-past three in the afternoon, taking the lead and making signal to form line as best could be done; without that I would not have engaged. At four I made signal to three ships to double on the enemy's rear, and to the squadron to approach within pistol-shot. This signal, though repeated, was not executed. I did not *myself* give the example, in order that I might hold in check the three van ships, which by tacking would have doubled on me. However, except the 'Brilliant,' which doubled on the rear, no ship was as close as mine, nor received as many shots."

The principal point of difference in the two accounts is, that Suffren asserts that his flag-ship passed along the whole English line, from the rear to the sixth ship; while Hughes says the French divided into two lines, which, upon coming near, steered, one on the rear, the other on the centre, of his squadron. The latter would be the better manœuvre; for if the leading ship of the attack passed, as Suffren asserts, along the enemy's line from the rear to the sixth, she should receive in succession the first fire of six ships, which ought to cripple her and confuse her line. Suffren also notes the intention to double on the rear by placing three ships to leeward of it. Two of the French did take this position. Suffren further gives his reason for not closing with his own ship, which led; but as those which followed him went no nearer, Hughes's attention was not drawn to his action.

The French commodore was seriously, and it would seem justly, angered by the inaction of several of his captains. Of the second in command he complained to the minister: "Being at the head, I could not well see what was going on in the rear. I had directed M. de Tromelin to make signals to ships which might be near him; he only repeated my own without having them carried out." This complaint was wholly justified. On the 6th of February, ten days before the fight, he had written to his second as follows:—

"If we are so fortunate as to be to windward, as the English are not more than eight, or at most nine, my intention is to double on their rear. Supposing your division to be in the rear, you will see by your position what number of ships will overlap the enemy's line, and you will make signal to them to double[7] [that is, to engage on the lee side]. . . . In any case, I beg you to order to your division the manœuvres which you shall think best fitted to assure the success of the action. The capture of Trincomalee and that of Negapatam, and perhaps of all Ceylon, should make us wish for a general action."

The last two sentences reveal Suffren's own appreciation of the military situation in the Indian seas, which demanded, first, the disabling of the hostile fleet, next, the capture of certain strategic ports. That this diagnosis was correct is as certain as that it reversed the common French maxims, which would have put the port first and the fleet second as objectives. A general action was the first desideratum of Suffren, and it is therefore safe to say that to avoid such action should have been the first object of Hughes. The attempt of the latter to gain the windward position was consequently correct; and as in the month of February the sea-breeze at Madras sets in from the eastward and southward about eleven A.M., he probably did well to steer in that general direction, though the result disappointed him. De Guichen in one of his engagements with Rodney shaped the course of his fleet with reference to being to windward when the afternoon breeze made, and was successful. What use Hughes would have made of the advantage of the wind can only be inferred from his own words,—that he sought it in order to engage more closely. There is not in this the certain promise of any skilful use of a tactical advantage.

Suffren also illustrates, in his words to Tromelin, his conception

---

[7] Plate XIV., Fig. D, shows the order of battle Suffren intended in this action. The five rear ships of the enemy would each have two opponents close aboard. The leading French ship on the weather side was to be kept farther off, so that while attacking the sixth Englishman she could "contain" the van ships if they attempted to reinforce the rear by tacking.

of the duties of a second in command, which may fairly be paralleled with that of Nelson in his celebrated order before Trafalgar. In this first action he led the main attack himself, leaving the direction of what may be called the reserve—at any rate, of the second half of the assault—to his lieutenant, who, unluckily for him, was not a Collingwood, and utterly failed to support him. It is probable that Suffren's leading was due not to any particular theory, but to the fact that his ship was the best sailer in the fleet, and that the lateness of the hour and lightness of the wind made it necessary to bring the enemy to action speedily. But here appears a fault on the part of Suffren. Leading as he did involves, not necessarily but very naturally, the idea of example; and holding his own ship outside of close range, for excellent tactical reasons, led the captains in his wake naturally, almost excusably, to keep at the same distance, notwithstanding his signals. The conflict between orders and example, which cropped out so singularly at Vicksburg in our Civil War, causing the misunderstanding and estrangement of two gallant officers, should not be permitted to occur. It is the business of a chief to provide against such misapprehensions by most careful previous explanation of both the letter and spirit of his plans. Especially is this so at sea, where smoke, slack wind, and intervening rigging make signals hard to read, though they are almost the only means of communication. This was Nelson's practice; nor was Suffren a stranger to the idea. "Dispositions well concerted with those who are to carry them out are needed," he wrote to D'Estaing, three years before. The excuse which may be pleaded for those who followed him, and engaged, cannot avail for the rear ships, and especially not for the second in command, who knew Suffren's plans. He should have compelled the rear ships to take position to leeward, leading himself, if necessary. There was wind enough; for two captains actually engaged to leeward, one of them without orders, acting, through the impulse of his own good will and courage, on Nelson's saying, "No captain can do very wrong who places his ship alongside that of an enemy." He received the special commendation of Suffren, in itself an honor and a reward. Whether the failure of so many of his fellows was due to inefficiency, or to a spirit of faction and disloyalty, is unimportant to the general military writer, however interesting to French officers jealous for the honor of their service. Suffren's complaints, after several disappointments, became vehement.

"My heart," wrote he, "is wrung by the most general defection. I have just lost the opportunity of destroying the English squadron. . . . All—yes, all—might have got near, since we were to windward and ahead, and none did so. Several among them had behaved bravely in other combats. I can only attribute this horror to the wish to bring the cruise to an end, to ill-will, and to ignorance; for I dare not suspect anything worse. The result has been terrible. I must tell you, Monseigneur, that officers who have been long at the Isle of France are neither seamen nor military men. Not seamen, for they have not been at sea; and the trading temper, independent and insubordinate, is absolutely opposed to the military spirit."

This letter, written after his fourth battle with Hughes, must be taken with allowance. Not only does it appear that Suffren himself, hurried away on this last occasion by his eagerness, was partly responsible for the disorder of his fleet, but there were other circumstances, and above all the character of some of the officers blamed, which made the charge of a general disaffection excessive. On the other hand, it remains true that after four general actions, with superior numbers on the part of the French, under a chief of the skill and ardor of Suffren, the English squadron, to use his own plaintive expression, "still existed"; not only so, but had not lost a single ship. The only conclusion that can be drawn is that of a French naval writer: "Quantity disappeared before quality." [8] It is immaterial whether the defect was due to inefficiency or disaffection.

The inefficiency which showed itself on the field of battle disappeared in the general conduct of the campaign where the qualities of the chief alone told. The battle of February 17th ended with a shift of wind to the southeast at six P.M., after two hours action. The English were thus brought to windward, and their van ships enabled to share in the fight. Night falling, Suffren, at half-past six, hauled his squadron by the wind on the starboard tack, heading northeast, while Hughes steered south under easy sail. It is said by Captain Chevalier, of the French navy, that Suffren intended to renew the fight next day. In that case he should have taken measures to keep within reach. It was too plainly Hughes's policy not to fight without some advantage,—to allow the supposition that with one

[8] Troude: Batailles Navales.

ship, the "Exeter," lost to him through the concentration of so many enemies upon her, he would quietly await an attack. This is so plain as to make it probable that Suffren saw sufficient reason, in the results to his fleet and the misconduct of his officers, not to wish to renew action at once. The next morning the two fleets were out of sight of each other. The continuance of the north wind, and the crippled state of two of his ships, forced Hughes to go to Trincomalee, where the sheltered harbor allowed them to repair. Suffren, anxious about his transports, went to Pondicherry, where he anchored in their company. It was his wish then to proceed against Negapatam; but the commander of the troops chose to act against Cuddalore. After negotiations and arrangements with Hyder Ali the army landed south of Porto Novo, and marched against Cuddalore, which surrendered on the 4th of April.

Meanwhile Suffren, anxious to act against his principal objective, had sailed again on the 23rd of March. It was his hope to cut off two ships-of-the-line which were expected from England. For this he was too late; the two seventy-fours joined the main body at Madras, March 30th. Hughes had refitted at Trincomalee in a fortnight, and reached Madras again on the 12th of March. Soon after the reinforcement had joined him, he sailed again for Trincomalee with troops and military stores for the garrison. On the 8th of April Suffren's squadron was seen to the northeast, also standing to the southward. Hughes kept on, through that and the two following days, with light northerly winds. On the 11th he made the coast of Ceylon, fifty miles north of Trincomalee, and bore away for the port. On the morning of the 12th the French squadron in the northeast was seen crowding sail in pursuit. It was the day on which Rodney and De Grasse met in the West Indies, but the parts were reversed; here the French, not the English, sought action.

The speed of the ships in both squadrons was very unequal; each had some coppered ships and some not coppered. Hughes found that his slow sailers could not escape the fastest of his enemy,—a condition which will always compel a retreating force to hazard an action, unless it can resolve to give up the rear ships, and which makes it imperative for the safety, as well as the efficiency, of a squadron that vessels of the same class should all have a certain minimum speed. The same cause—the danger of a separated ship— led the unwilling De Grasse, the same day, in another scene, to a

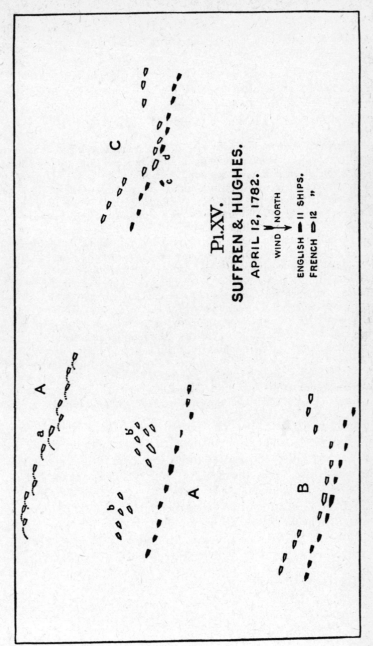

Pl.XV.
SUFFREN & HUGHES.
APRIL 12, 1782.

WIND NORTH

ENGLISH ■—— 11 SHIPS.
FRENCH ▷—— 12 "

risky manœuvre and a great mishap. Hughes, with better reason, resolved to fight; and at nine A.M. formed his line on the starboard tack, standing in-shore (Plate XV., A), the squadron in good order, with intervals of two cables between the ships.[9] His account, which again varies from that of Suffren, giving a radically different idea of the tactics used by the French commodore, and more to the credit of the latter's skill, will first be followed. He says:—

"The enemy, bearing north by east, distant six miles, with wind at north by east, continued manœuvring their ships and changing their positions in line, till fifteen minutes past noon, when they bore away (a) to engage us, five sail of their van stretching along (b) to engage the ships of our van, and the other seven sail (b′) steering directly on our three centre ships, the 'Superbe,' the 'Monmouth,' her second ahead, and the 'Monarca,' her second astern. At half-past one the engagement began in the van of both squadrons; three minutes after, I made the signal for battle. The French admiral in the 'Héros' and his second astern in 'L'Orient' (both seventy-fours) bore down on the 'Superbe'[10] within pistol-shot. The 'Héros' continued in her position, giving and receiving a severe fire for nine minutes, and then stood on, greatly damaged, to attack the 'Monmouth,' at that time engaged with another of the enemy's ships, making room for the ships in his rear to come up to the attack of our centre, where the engagement was hottest. At three the 'Monmouth' had her mizzen-mast shot away, and in a few minutes her mainmast, and bore out of the line to leeward (C, c); and at forty minutes past three the wind unexpectedly continuing far northerly without any sea-breeze, and being careful not to entangle our ships with the land, I made signal to wear and haul by the wind in a line-of-battle on the larboard tack, still engaging the enemy."

Now here, practically, was concentration with a vengeance. In this, the hardest fight between these two hard fighters, the English loss was 137 killed and 430 wounded in eleven ships. Of this total, the two centre ships, the flag-ship and her next ahead, lost 104 killed and 198 wounded,—fifty-three per cent of the entire loss of the squadron, of which they formed eighteen per cent. The casualties were very much heavier, in proportion to the size of the ships, than those of the leaders of the two columns at Trafalgar.[11] The material injury to hulls, spars, etc., was yet more serious. The English

[9] Between four and five hundred yards.
[10] The English and French flag-ships are denoted in the plan by their exceptional size.
[11] The "Victory," Nelson's ship at Trafalgar, a 100-gun ship, lost 57 killed and 102 wounded; Hughes's ship, a 74, lost 59 killed and 96 wounded. Collingwood's ship, the "Royal Sovereign," also of 100 guns, lost 47 killed and 94 wounded; the "Monmouth," a 64, in Hughes's action lost 45 killed and 102 wounded.

squadron, by this concentration of the enemy upon a small fraction of it, was entirely crippled. Inferior when the action began, its inferiority was yet more decisive by the substraction of two ships, and Suffren's freedom to move was increased.

But how far was this concentration intended by Suffren? For this we must go to the pages of two French writers,[12] who base their narratives upon his own despatches on record in the French Marine Office. The practical advantage gained by the French must also be tested by comparing the lists of casualties, and the injuries received by their individual ships; for it is evident that if both the squadrons received the same total amount of injury, but that with the English it fell on two ships, so that they could not be ready for action for a month or more, while with the French the damage was divided among the twelve, allowing them to be ready again in a few days, the victory tactically and strategically would rest with the latter.[13]

As regards Suffren's purpose, there is nothing to indicate that he meant to make such an attack as Hughes describes. Having twelve ships to the English eleven, his intention seems to have been to pursue the usual English practice,—form line parallel to the enemy, bear down together, and engage ship to ship. To this he added one simple combination; the twelfth French ship, being unprovided with an opponent, was to engage the rear English ship on her lee side, placing her thus between two fires. In truth, a concentration upon the van and centre, such as Hughes describes, is tactically inferior to a like effort upon the centre and rear of a column. This is true of steamers even, which, though less liable to loss of motive power, must still turn round to get from van to rear, losing many valuable seconds; but it is specially true of sailing vessels, and above all in the light, baffling airs which are apt to mark the change of monsoon at the season when this fight was fought. Nelson emphasized his contempt of the Russians of his day by saying he would not hesitate to attack their van, counting upon throwing the whole line in confusion from their want of seamanship; but though entertaining a not much better opinion of the Spaniards, he threw the weight of attack on the rear of the allied fleets at Trafalgar. In dealing with

---

[12] Troude: Batailles Navales; Chevalier: Hist. de la Marine Française.
[13] This remark seems too self-evident to need emphasis; yet it may be questioned whether naval men generally carry it in their stock of axioms.

such seamen as the captains of Hughes's fleet, it would have been an error to assail the van instead of the rear. Only a dead calm could have kept the latter out of action.

Suffren's attack is thus described by Captain Chevalier. After mentioning Hughes's forming line on the starboard tack, he says:—

"This manœuvre was imitated by the French, and the two squadrons ran on parallel lines, heading about west-northwest (A, A). At eleven, our line being well formed, Suffren made signal to keep away to west-southwest, by a movement all together. Our ships did not keep their bearing upon the prescribed line, and the van, composed of the best sailers, came first within range of the enemy.[14] At one, the leading ships of the English fleet opened fire upon the 'Vengeur' and 'Artésien' [French van]. These two ships, having luffed [15] to return the fire, were at once ordered to keep away again. Suffren, who wished for a decisive action, kept his course, receiving without reply the shots directed upon his ship by the enemy. When at pistol-range of the 'Superbe,' he hauled to the wind (B), and the signal to open fire appeared at his mainmast head. Admiral Hughes having only eleven ships, the 'Bizarre,' according to the dispositions taken by the commander-in-chief, was to attack on the quarter the rear ship of the English fleet and double on it to leeward. At the moment when the first cannon-shots were heard, our worst sailers were not up with their stations. Breathing the letter, and not the spirit, of the commodore's orders, the captains of these ships luffed at the same time as those which preceded them. Hence it resulted that the French line formed a curve (B), whose extremities were represented in the van by the 'Artésien' and 'Vengeur,' and in the rear by the 'Bizarre,' 'Ajax,' and 'Sévère.' In consequence, these ships were very far from those which corresponded to them in the enemy's line."

It is evident from all this, written by a warm admirer of Suffren, who has had full access to the official papers, that the French chief intended an attack elementary in conception and difficult of execution. To keep a fleet on a line of bearing, sailing free, requires much drill, especially when the ships have different rates of speed, as had Suffren's. The extreme injury suffered by the "Superbe" and "Monmouth," undeniably due to a concentration, cannot be attributed to Suffren's dispositions. "The injuries which the 'Héros' received at the beginning of the action did not allow her to remain by the 'Superbe'. Not being able to back her topsails in time, the braces having been cut, she passed ahead, and was only stopped on the

---

[14] As always.
[15] That is—turned their side to the enemy instead of approaching him.

beam of the 'Monmouth.'" [16] This accounts for the suffering of the latter ship, already injured, and now contending with a much larger opponent. The "Superbe" was freed from Suffren only to be engaged by the next Frenchman, an equally heavy ship; and when the "Monmouth" drifted or bore up, to leeward, the French flag-ship also drifted so that for a few moments she fired her stern guns into the "Superbe's" bow (C, d). The latter at the same time was engaged on the beam and quarter by two French ships, who, either with or without signal, came up to shield their commodore.

An examination of the list of casualties shows that the loss of the French was much more distributed among their ships than was the case with the English. No less than three of the latter escaped without a man killed, while of the French only one. The kernel of the action seems to have been in the somewhat fortuitous concentration of two French seventy-fours and one sixty-four on an English seventy-four and sixty-four. Assuming the ships to have been actually of the same force as their rates, the French brought, counting broadside only, one hundred and six guns against sixty-nine.

Some unfavorable criticism was excited by the management of Admiral Hughes during the three days preceding the fight, because he refrained from attacking the French, although they were for much of the time to leeward with only one ship more than the English, and much separated at that. It was thought that he had the opportunity of beating them in detail.[17] The accounts accessible are too meagre to permit an accurate judgment upon this opinion, which probably reflected the mess-table and quarter-deck talk of the subordinate officers of the fleet. Hughes's own report of the position of the two fleets is vague, and in one important particular directly contradictory to the French. If the alleged opportunity offered, the English admiral in declining to use it adhered to the resolve, with which he sailed, neither to seek nor shun the enemy, but to go directly to Trincomalee and land the troops and supplies he had on board. In other words, he was governed in his action by the French rather than the English naval policy, of subordinating the attack of the enemy's fleet to the particular mission in hand. If for this reason he did allow a favorable chance of fighting to slip,

[16] Chevalier: Hist. de la Marine Française.
[17] Annual Register, 1782.

he certainly had reason bitterly to regret his neglect, in the results of the battle which followed; but in the lack of precise information the most interesting point to be noted is the impression made upon public and professional opinion, indicating how strongly the English held that the attack on the enemy's fleet was the first duty of an English admiral. It may also be said that he could hardly have fared worse by attacking than he did by allowing the enemy to become the assailant; and certainly not worse than he would have fared had Suffren's captains been as good as his own.

After the action, towards sunset, both squadrons anchored in fifteen fathoms of water, irregular soundings, three of the French ships taking the bottom on coral patches. Here they lay for a week two miles apart, refitting. Hughes, from the ruined condition of the "Monmouth," expected an attack; but when Suffren had finished his repairs on the 19th, he got under way and remained outside for twenty-four hours, inviting a battle which he would not begin. He realized the condition of the enemy so keenly as to feel the necessity of justifying his action to the Minister of Marine, which he did for eight reasons unnecessary to particularize here. The last was the lack of efficiency and hearty support on the part of his captains.

It is not likely that Suffren erred on the side of excessive caution. On the contrary, his most marked defect as a commander-in-chief was an ardor which, when in sight of the enemy, became impatience, and carried him at times into action hastily and in disorder. But if, in the details and execution of his battles, in his tactical combinations, Suffren was at times foiled by his own impetuosity and the short-comings of most of his captains, in the general conduct of the campaign, in strategy, where the personal qualities of the commander-in-chief mainly told, his superiority was manifest, and achieved brilliant success. Then ardor showed itself in energy, untiring and infectious. The eagerness of his hot Provençal blood overrode difficulty, created resources out of destitution, and made itself felt through every vessel under his orders. No military lesson is more instructive nor of more enduring value than the rapidity and ingenuity with which he, without a port or supplies, continually refitted his fleet and took the field, while his slower enemy was dawdling over his repairs.

The battle forced the English to remain inactive for six weeks, till the "Monmouth" was repaired. Unfortunately, Suffren's situation did not allow him to assume the offensive at once. He was short of men, provisions, and especially of spare spars and rigging. In an official letter after the action her wrote: "I have no spare stores to repair rigging; the squadron lacks at least twelve spare topmasts." A convoy of supply-ships was expected at Point de Galles, which, with the rest of Ceylon, except Trincomalee, was still Dutch. He therefore anchored at Batacalo, south of Trincomalee, a position in which he was between Hughes and outward-bound English ships, and was favorably placed to protect his own convoys, which joined him there. On the 3d of June he sailed for Tranquebar, a Danish possession, where he remained two or three weeks, harassing the English communications between Madras and the fleet at Trincomalee. Leaving there, he sailed for Cuddalore, to communicate with the commander of the land forces and Hyder Ali. The latter was found to be much discontented with the scanty co-operation of the French general. Suffren, however, had won his favor, and he expressed a wish to see him on his return from the expedition then in contemplation; for, true to his accurate instinct, the commodore was bent upon again seeking out the English fleet, *after* beating which he intended to attack Negapatam. There was not in him any narrowness of professional prejudice; he kept always in view the necessity, both political and strategic, of nursing the alliance with the Sultan and establishing control upon the seaboard and in the interior; but he clearly recognized that the first step thereto was the control of the sea, by disabling the English fleet. The tenacity and vigor with which he followed this aim, amid great obstacles, joined to the clear-sightedness with which he saw it, are the distinguishing merits of Suffren amid the crowd of French fleet-commanders,—his equals in courage, but trammelled by the bonds of a false tradition and the perception of a false objective.

Hughes meantime, having rigged jury-masts to the "Monmouth," had gone to Trincomalee, where his squadron refitted and the sick were landed for treatment; but it is evident, as has before been mentioned, that the English had not held the port long enough to make an arsenal or supply port, for he says, "I will be able to remast the 'Monmouth' from the spare stores on board the several ships." His resources were nevertheless superior to those of his adversary. During the time that Suffren was at Tranquebar, worrying the English communications between Madras and Trincomalee, Hughes still stayed quietly in the latter port, sailing for Negapatam on the 23rd of June, the day after Suffren reached Cuddalore. The two squadrons had thus again approached each other, and Suffren hastened his preparations for attack as soon as he heard that his enemy was where he could get at him. Hughes awaited his movement.

Before sailing, however, Suffren took occasion to say in writing home: "Since my arrival in Ceylon, partly by the help of the Dutch, partly through the prizes we have taken, the squadron has been equipped for six months' service, and I have rations of wheat and rice assured for more than a year." This achievement was indeed a just source of pride and self-congratulation. Without a port, and destitute of resources, the French commodore had lived off the enemy; the store ships and commerce of the latter had supplied his wants. To his fertility of resource and the activity of his cruisers, inspired by himself, this result was due. Yet he had but two frigates, the class of vessel upon which an admiral must mainly depend for this predatory warfare. On the 23rd of March, both provisions and stores had been nearly exhausted. Six thousand dollars in money, and the provisions in the convoy, were then his sole resources. Since then he had fought a severe action, most expensive in rigging and men, as well as in ammunition. After that fight of April 12 he had left only powder and shot enough for one other battle of equal severity. Three months later he was able to report as above, that he could keep the sea on his station for six months without further supplies. This result was due wholly to himself,—to his self-reliance, and what may without exaggeration be called his greatness of soul. It was not expected at Paris; on the contrary, it was expected there that the squadron would return to the Isle of France to refit. It was not thought possible that it could remain on a hostile coast, so far from its nearest base, and be kept in efficient condition. Suffren thought otherwise; he considered, with true military insight and a proper sense of the value of his own profession, that the success of the operations in India depended upon the control of the sea, and therefore upon the uninterrupted presence of his squadron. He did not shrink from attempting that which had always been thought impossible. This firmness of spirit, bearing the stamp of genius, must, to be justly appreciated, be considered with reference to the

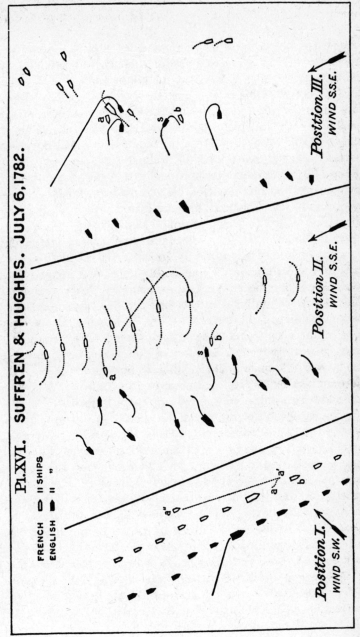

Pl. XVI.   SUFFREN & HUGHES. JULY 6, 1782.

FRENCH ◗ 11 SHIPS
ENGLISH ◆ 11 "

Position I.
WIND S.W.

Position II.
WIND S.S.E.

Position III.
WIND S.S.E.

397

circumstances of his own time, and of the preceding generations in which he grew up.

Suffren was born July 17, 1729, and served during the wars of 1739 and 1756. He was first under fire at Matthews's action off Toulon, February 22, 1744. He was the contemporary of D'Estaing, De Guichen, and De Grasse, before the days of the French Revolution, when the uprising of a people had taught men how often impossibilities are not impossible; before Napoleon and Nelson had made a mock of the word. His attitude and action had therefore at the time the additional merit of originality, but his lofty temper was capable of yet higher proof. Convinced of the necessity of keeping the squadron on its station, he ventured to disregard not only the murmurs of his officers but the express orders of the Court. When he reached Batacalo, he found despatches directing him to return to the Isle of France. Instead of taking them as a release from the great burden of responsibility, he disobeyed, giving his reasons, and asserting that he on the spot could judge better than a minister in Europe what the circumstances demanded. Such a leader deserved better subordinates, and a better colleague than he had in the commander of the forces on shore. Whether or no the conditions of the general maritime struggle would have permitted the overthrow of the English East Indian power may be doubtful; but it is certain that among all the admirals of the three nations there was none so fitted to accomplish that result as Suffren. We shall find him enduring severer tests, and always equal to them.

In the afternoon of the 5th of July Suffren's squadron came in sight of the English, anchored off Cuddalore. An hour later, a sudden squall carried away the main and mizzen topmasts of one of the French ships. Admiral Hughes got under way, and the two fleets manœuvred during the night. The following day the wind favored the English, and the opponents found themselves in line of battle on the starboard tack, heading south-southeast, with the wind at southwest. The disabled French ship having by unpardonable inactivity failed to repair her injuries, the numbers about to engage were equal,—eleven on each side. At eleven A.M. the English bore down together and engaged ship against ship; but as was usual under those conditions, the rear ships did not come to as close action as those ahead of them (Plate XVI., Position I.). Captain Chevalier carefully points out that their failure was a fair offset to the failure of the French rear on the 12th of April,[18] but fails to note in this connection that the French van, both on that occasion and again on the 3rd of September, bungled as well as the rear. There can remain little doubt, in the mind of the careful reader, that most of the French captains were inferior, as seamen, to their opponents. During this part of the engagement the fourth ship in the French order, the "Brilliant" (a), lost her mainmast, bore up out of the line (a'), and dropped gradually astern and to leeward (a'').

At one P.M., when the action was hottest, the wind suddenly shifted to south-southeast, taking the ships on the port bow (Position II.). Four English ships, the "Burford," "Sultan" (s), "Worcester," and "Eagle," seeing the breeze coming kept off to port toward the French line; the others were taken aback and paid off to starboard. The French ships, on the other hand, with two exceptions, the "Brilliant" (a) and "Sévère" (b), paid off from the English. The effect of the change of wind was therefore to separate the main parts of the two squadrons, but to bring together between the lines four English and two French ships. Technical order was destroyed. The "Brilliant," having dropped far astern of her position, came under the fire of two of the English rear, the "Worcester" and the "Eagle," who had kept off in time and so neared the French. Suffren in person came to her assistance (Position III., a) and drove off the English, who were also threatened by the approach of two other French ships that had worn to the westward in obedience to signal. While this partial action was taking place, the other endangered French ship, the "Sévère" (b), was engaged by the English "Sultan" (s), and, if the French captain M. de Cillart can be believed, by two other English ships. It is probable, from her place in the line, that the "Burford" also assailed her. However this may be, the "Sévère" hauled down her flag; but while the "Sultan" was wearing away from her, she resumed her fire, raking the English ship. The order to surrender, given by the French captain and carried into execution by the formal well-established token of submission, was disregarded by his subordinates, who fired upon their enemy while the flag was

[18] The British account differs materially as to the cause of the distance separating the two rears. "In this action it did not fall to the 'Monmouth's' lot to sustain a very considerable share, the enemy's rear being so far to leeward that the ships of the British rear could not, even whilst the wind was favorable, close with them without considerably breaking the order of their own line" (Memoir of Captain Alms, Naval Chronicle, vol. ii.). Such contradictions are common, and, except for a particular purpose, need not to be reconciled. Alms seems to have been not only a first-rate seaman, but an officer capable of resolute and independent action; his account is probably correct.

down. In effect, the action of the French ship amounted to using an infamous *ruse de guerre;* but it would be unjust to say that this was intended. The positions of the different vessels were such that the "Sultan" could not have secured her prize; other French ships were approaching and must have retaken it. The indignation of the French juniors at the weakness of their captain was therefore justified; their refusal to be bound by it may be excused to men face to face with an unexpected question of propriety, in the heat of battle and under the sting of shame. Nevertheless, scrupulous good faith would seem to demand that their deliverance should be awaited from other hands, not bound by the action of their commander; or at least that the forebearing assailant should not have suffered from them. The captain, suspended and sent home by Suffren, and cashiered by the king, utterly condemned himself by his attempted defence: "When Captain de Cillart saw the French squadron drawing off,—for all the ships except the 'Brilliant' had fallen off on the other tack,—he thought it useless to prolong his defence, and had the flag hauled down. *The ships engaged with him immediately ceased their fire,* and the one on the starboard side moved away. At this moment the 'Sévère' fell off to starboard and her sails filled; Captain de Cillart then ordered the fire to be resumed by his lower-deck guns, the only ones still manned, and he rejoined his squadron." [19]

This action was the only one of the five fought by Suffren on the coast of India, in which the English admiral was the assailant. There can be found in it no indication of military conceptions, of tactical combinations; but on the other hand Hughes is continually showing the aptitudes, habits of thought, and foresight of the skilful seaman, as well as a courage beyond all proof. He was in truth an admirable representative of the average English naval officer of the middle of the eighteenth century; and while it is impossible not to condemn the general ignorance of the most important part of the profession, it is yet useful to remark how far thorough mastery of its other details, and dogged determination not to yield, made up for so signal a defect. As the Roman legions often redeemed the

[19] Troude: Batailles Navales. It was seen from Suffren's ship that the "Sévère's" flag was down; but it was supposed that the ensign halliards had been shot away. The next day Hughes sent the captain of the "Sultan" to demand the delivery to him of the ship which had struck. The demand, of course, could not be complied with. "The 'Sultan,'" Troude says, "which had hove-to to take possession of the 'Sévère,' was the victim of this action; she received during some time, without replying, the whole fire of the French ship."

blunders of their generals, so did English captains and seamen often save that which had been lost by the errors of their admirals,—errors which neither captain nor seamen recognized, nor would probably have admitted. Nowhere were these solid qualities so clearly shown as in Suffren's battles, because nowhere else were such demands made upon them. No more magnificent instances of desperate yet useful resistance to overwhelming odds are to be found in naval annals, than that of the "Monmouth" on April 12, and of the "Exeter" on February 17. An incident told of the latter ship is worth quoting. "At the heel of the action, when the 'Exeter' was already in the state of a wreck, the master came to Commodore King to ask him what he should do with the ship, as two of the enemy were again bearing down upon her. He laconically answered, 'there is nothing to be done but to fight her till she sinks.'"[20] She was saved.

Suffren, on the contrary, was by this time incensed beyond endurance by the misbehavior of his captains. Cillart was sent home; but besides him two others, both of them men of influential connections, and one a relative of Suffren himself, were dispossessed of their commands. However necessary and proper this step, few but Suffren would have had the resolution to take it; for, so far as he then knew, he was only a captain in rank, and it was not permitted even to admirals to deal thus with their juniors. "You may perhaps be angry, Monseigneur," he wrote, "that I have not used rigor sooner; but I beg you to remember that the regulations do not give this power even to a general officer, which I am not."

It is immediately after the action of the 6th of July that Suffren's superior energy and military capacity begin markedly to influence the issue between himself and Hughes. The tussle had been severe; but military qualities began to tell, as they surely must. The losses of the two squadrons in men, in the last action, had been as one to three in favor of the English; on the other hand, the latter had apparently suffered more in sails and spars,—in motive power. Both fleets anchored in the evening, the English off Negapatam, the French to leeward, off Cuddalore. On the 18th of July Suffren was again ready for sea; whereas on the same day Hughes had but just decided to go to Madras to finish his repairs. Suffren was further delayed by the political necessity of an official visit to Hyder Ali, after which he sailed to Batacalo, arriving there on the 9th of Au-

[20] Annual Register, 1782.

gust, to await reinforcements and supplies from France. On the 21st, these joined him; and two days later he sailed, now with fourteen ships-of-the-line, for Trincomalee, anchoring off the town on the 25th. The following night the troops were landed, batteries thrown up, and the attack pressed with vigor. On the 30th and 31st the two forts which made the defensive strength of the place surrendered, and this all-important port passed into the hands of the French. Convinced that Hughes would soon appear, Suffren granted readily all the honors of war demanded by the governor of the place, contenting himself with the substantial gain. Two days later, on the evening of September 2nd, the English fleet was sighted by the French lookout frigates.

During the six weeks in which Suffren had been so actively and profitably employed, the English admiral had remained quietly at anchor, repairing and refitting. No precise information is available for deciding how far this delay was unavoidable; but having in view the well-known aptitude of English seamen of that age, it can scarcely be doubted that, had Hughes possessed the untiring energy of his great rival, he could have gained the few days which decided the fate of Trincomalee, and fought a battle to save the place. In fact, this conclusion is supported by his own reports, which state that on the 12th of August the ships were nearly fitted; and yet, though apprehending an attack on Trincomalee, he did not sail until the 20th. The loss of this harbor forced him to abandon the east coast, which was made unsafe by the approach of the northeast monsoon, and conferred an important strategic advantage upon Suffren, not to speak of the political effect upon the native rulers in India.

To appreciate thoroughly this contrast between the two admirals, it is necessary also to note how differently they were situated with regard to material for repairs. After the action of the 6th, Hughes found at Madras spars, cordage, stores, provisions, and material. Suffren at Cuddalore found nothing. To put his squadron in good fighting condition, nineteen new topmasts were needed, besides lower masts, yards, rigging, sails, and so on. To take the sea at all, the masts were removed from the frigates and smaller vessels, and given to the ships-of-the-line, while English prizes were stripped to equip the frigates. Ships were sent off to the Straits of Malacca to procure other spars and timber. Houses were torn down on shore to find lumber for repairing the hulls. The difficulties were increased by the character of the anchorage, on open roadstead with frequent heavy sea, and by the near presence of the English fleet; but the work was driven on under the eyes of the commander-in-chief, who, like Lord Howe at New York, inspired the working parties by his constant appearance among them. "Notwithstanding his prodigious obesity, Suffren displayed the fiery ardor of youth; he was everywhere where work was going on. Under his powerful impulse, the most difficult tasks were done with incredible rapidity. Nevertheless, his officers represented to him the bad state of the fleet, and the need of a port for the ships-of-the-line. 'Until we have taken Trincomalee,' he replied, 'the open roadsteads of the Coromandel coast will answer.' " [21] It was indeed to this activity on the Coromandel coast that the success at Trincomalee was due. The weapons with which Suffren fought are obsolete; but the results wrought by his tenacity and fertility in resources are among the undying lessons of history.

While the characters of the two chiefs were thus telling upon the strife in India, other no less lasting lessons were being afforded by the respective governments at home, who did much to restore the balance between them. While the English ministry, after the news of the battle of Porto Praya, fitted out in November, 1781, a large and compact expedition, convoyed by a powerful squadron of six ships-of-the-line, under the command of an active officer, to reinforce Hughes, the French despatched comparatively scanty succors in small detached bodies, relying apparently upon secrecy rather than upon force to assure their safety. Thus Suffren, while struggling with his innumerable embarrassments, had the mortification of learning that now one and now another of the small detachments sent to his relief were captured, or driven back to France, before they were clear of European waters. There was in truth little safety for small divisions north of the Straits of Gibraltar. Thus the advantages gained by his activity were in the end sacrificed. Up to the fall of Trincomalee the French were superior at sea; but in the six months which followed, the balance turned the other way, by the arrival of the English reinforcements under Sir Richard Bickerton.

With his usual promptness the French commodore had prepared

[21] Cunat: Vie de Suffren.

for further immediate action as soon as Trincomalee surrendered The cannon and men landed from the ships were at once re embarked, and the port secured by a garrison strong enough to relieve him of any anxiety about holding it. This great seaman, who had done as much in proportion to the means intrusted to him as any known to history, and had so signally illustrated the sphere and influence of naval power, had no intention of fettering the movements of his fleet, or risking his important conquest, by needlessly taking upon the shoulders of the ships the burden of defending a seaport. When Hughes appeared, it was past the power of the English fleet by a single battle to reduce the now properly garrisoned post. Doubtless a successful campaign, by destroying or driving away the French sea power, would achieve this result; but Suffren might well believe that, whatever mishaps might arise on a single day, he could in the long run more than hold his own with his opponent.

Seaports should defend themselves; the sphere of the fleet is on the open sea, its object offence rather than defence, its objective the enemy's shipping wherever it can be found. Suffren now saw again before him the squadron on which depended the English control of the sea; he knew that powerful reinforcements to it must arrive before the next season, and he hastened to attack. Hughes, mortified by his failure to arrive in time,—for a drawn battle beforehand would have saved what a successful battle afterward could not regain,—was in no humor to balk him. Still, with sound judgment, he retreated to the southeast, flying in good order, to use Suffren's expression; regulating speed by the slowest ships, and steering many different courses, so that the chase which began at daybreak overtook the enemy only at two in the afternoon. The object of the English was to draw Suffren so far to leeward of the port that, if his ships were disabled, he could not easily regain it.

The French numbered fourteen ships-of-the-line to twelve English. This superiority, together with his sound appreciation of the military situation in India, increased Suffren's natural eagerness for action; but his ships sailed badly, and were poorly handled by indifferent and dissatisfied men. These circumstances, during the long and vexatious pursuit, chafed and fretted the hot temper of the commodore, which still felt the spur of urgency that for two months had quickened the operations of the squadron. Signal followed sig-

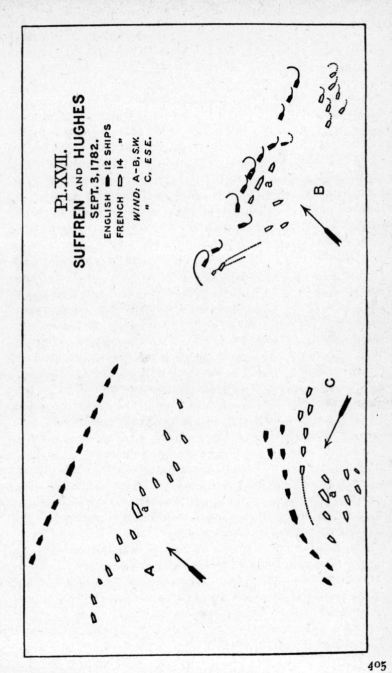

Pl. XVII.
SUFFREN and HUGHES
SEPT. 3, 1782.
ENGLISH ◣ 12 SHIPS
FRENCH ▷ 14 "
WIND: A–B, S.W.
" C, ESE.

nal, manœuvre succeeded manœuvre, to bring his disordered vessels into position. "Sometimes they edged down, sometimes they brought to," says the English admiral, who was carefully watching their approach, "in no regular order, as if undetermined what to do." Still, Suffren continued on, and at two P.M., having been carried twenty-five miles away from his port, his line being then partly formed and within striking distance of the enemy, the signal was made to come to the wind to correct the order before finally bearing down. A number of blunders in executing this made matters worse rather than better; and the commodore, at last losing patience, made signal thirty minutes later to attack (Plate XVII., A), following it with another for close action at pistol range. This being slowly and clumsily obeyed, he ordered a gun fired, as is customary at sea to emphasize a signal; unluckily this was understood by his own crew to be the opening of the action, and the flag-ship discharged all her battery. This example was followed by the other ships, though yet at the distance of half cannon-shot, which, under the gunnery conditions of that day, meant indecisive action. Thus at the end as the result of a mortifying series of blunders and bad seamanship, the battle began greatly to the disadvantage of the French, despite their superior numbers. The English, who had been retreating under short and handy sail, were in good order and quietly ready; whereas their enemies were in no order (B). Seven ships had forereached in rounding to,[22] and now formed an irregular group ahead of the English van, as well as far from it, where they were of little service; while in the centre a second confused group was formed, the ships overlapping and masking each other's fire. Under the circumstances the entire brunt of the action fell upon Suffren's flag-ship (a) and two others which supported him; while at the extreme rear a small ship-of-the-line, backed by a large frigate, alone engaged the English rear; but these, being wholly over-matched, were soon forced to retire.

A military operation could scarcely be worse carried out. The French ships in the battle did not support each other; they were so grouped as to hamper their own fire and needlessly increase the target offered to the enemy; so far from concentrating their own effort, three ships were left, almost unsupported, to a concentrated

[22] The curves in (B) represent the movements of the ships *after* the shift of wind, which practically ended the battle. The ships themselves show the order in fighting.

fire from the English line.[23] "Time passed on, and our three ships [B, a], engaged on the beam by the centre of the English fleet and raked [enfiladed] by van and rear, suffered greatly. After two hours the 'Héros's' sails were in rags, all her running rigging cut, and she could no longer steer. The 'Illustre' had lost her mizzen-mast and maintopmast." In this disorder such gaps existed as to offer a great opportunity to a more active opponent. "Had the enemy tacked now," wrote the chief-of-staff in his journal, "we would have been cut off and probably destroyed." The faults of an action in which every proper distribution was wanting are summed up in the results. The French had fourteen ships engaged. They lost eighty-two killed and two hundred and fifty-five wounded. Of this total, sixty-four killed and one hundred and seventy-eight wounded, or three fourths, fell to three ships. Two of these three lost their main and mizzen masts and foretopmast; in other words, were helpless.

This was a repetition on a larger scale of the disaster to two of Hughes's ships on the 12th of April; but on that day the English admiral, being to leeward and in smaller force, had to accept action on the adversary's terms, while here the loss fell on the assailant, who, to the advantage of the wind and choice of his mode of attack, added superiority in numbers. Full credit must in this action be allowed to Hughes, who, though lacking in enterprise and giving no token of tactical skill or *coup d'œil,* showed both judgment and good management in the direction of his retreat and in keeping his ships so well in hand. It is not easy to apportion the blame which rests upon his enemies. Suffren laid it freely upon his captains.[24] It has been rightly pointed out, however, that many of the officers thus condemned in mass had conducted themselves well before, both under Suffren and other admirals; that the order of pursuit was irregular, and Suffren's signals followed each other with confusing rapidity; and finally that chance, for which something must always be allowed, was against the French, as was also the inexperience of several captains. It is pretty certain that some of the mishap must be laid to the fiery and inconsiderate haste of Suffren, who had the defects of his great qualities, upon which his coy and wary antagonist unwittingly played.

[23] "The enemy formed a semicircle around us and raked us ahead and astern, as the ship came up and fell off, with the helm to leeward."—Journal de Bord du Bailli de Suffren.

[24] See page 387. He added: "It is frightful to have had four times in our power to destroy the English squadron, and that it still exists."

It is noteworthy that no complaints of his captains are to be found in Hughes's reports. Six fell in action, and of each he speaks in terms of simple but evidently sincere appreciation, while on the survivors he often bestows particular as well as general commendation. The marked contrast between the two leaders, and between the individual ship-commanders, on either side, makes this singularly instructive among naval campaigns; and the ultimate lesson taught is in entire accordance with the experience of all military history from the beginning. Suffren had genius, energy, great tenacity, sound military ideas, and was also an accomplished seaman. Hughes had apparently all the technical acquirements of the latter profession, would probably have commanded a ship equally well with any of his captains, but shows no trace of the qualities needed by a general officer. On the other hand, without insisting again upon the skill and fidelity of the English subordinates, it is evident that, to whatever it be attributed, the French single ships were as a rule incomparably worse-handled than those of their opponents. Four times, Suffren claims, certainly thrice, the English squadron was saved from overwhelming disaster by the difference in quality of the under officers. Good troops have often made amends for bad generalship; but in the end the better leader will prevail. This was conspicuously the case in the Indian seas in 1782 and 1783. War cut short the strife, but not before the issue was clearly indicated.

The action of September 3, like that of July 6, was brought to a close by a shift of wind to the southwest. When it came, the English line wore, and formed again on the other tack. The French also wore; and their van ships, being now to windward, stood down between their crippled ships and the enemy's line (C). Toward sundown Hughes hauled off to the northward, abandoning the hope of regaining Trincomalee, but with the satisfaction of having inflicted this severe retaliation upon his successful opponent.

That firmness of mind which was not the least of Suffren's qualities was severely tried soon after the action off Trincomalee. In returning to port, a seventy-four, the "Orient," was run ashore and lost by mismanagement, the only consolation being that her spars were saved for the two dismasted ships. Other crippled masts were replaced as before by robbing the frigates, whose crews also were needed to replace the losses in battle. Repairs were pushed on with the usual energy, the defence of the port was fully provided for, and on the 30th of September the squadron sailed for the Coromandel coast, where the state of French interests urgently called for it. Cuddalore was reached in four days; and here another incapable officer wrecked the "Bizarre," of sixty-four guns, in picking up his anchorage. In consequence of the loss of these two ships, Suffren, when he next met the enemy, could oppose only fifteen to eighteen ships-of-the-line; so much do general results depend upon individual ability and care. Hughes was at Madras, ninety miles north, whither he had gone at once after the late action. He reports his ships badly damaged; but the loss was so evenly distributed among them that it is difficult to justify his failure to follow up the injuries done to the French.

At this season the monsoon wind, which has come for four or five months from southwest, changes to northeast, blowing upon the east coast of the peninsula, where are no good harbors. The consequent swell made the shore often unapproachable, and so forbade support from fleet to army. The change of the monsoon is also frequently marked by violent hurricanes. The two commanders, therefore, had to quit a region where their stay might be dangerous as well as use-less. Had Trincomalee not been lost, Hughes, in the condition of his squadron, might have awaited there the reinforcements and supplies expected soon from England; for although the port is not healthy, it is secure and well situated. Bickerton had already reached Bombay, and was on his way now to Madras with five ships-of-the-line. As things were, Hughes thought necessary to go to Bombay for the season, sailing or rather being driven to sea by a hurricane, on the 17th of October. Four days later Bickerton reached Madras, not having fallen in with the admiral. With an activity which charac-terized him he sailed at once, and was again in Bombay on the 28th of November. Hughes's ships, scattered and crippled by tempest, dropped in one by one, a few days later.

Suffren held Trincomalee, yet his decision was not easy. The port was safe, he had not to fear an attack by the English fleet; and on the other hand, besides being sickly during the approaching monsoon, it was doubtful whether the provisions needed for the health of the crews could be had there. In short, though of strategic value from its strength and position, the port was deficient in resources. Opposed to Trincomalee there was an alternative in Achem, a harbor on the other side of the Bay of Bengal, at the west end of the island of Sumatra. This was healthy, could supply provisions, and, from its position with reference to the northeast monsoon, would permit ships to regain the Coromandel coast sooner than those in Bombay, when the milder ending of the season made landing more practicable.

These simple considerations were not, however, the only elements in the really difficult problem before Suffren. The small results that followed this campaign must not hide the fact that great issues were possible, and that much might depend upon his decision. Owing to the French policy of sending out reinforcements in several small bodies, not only was there much loss, but great uncertainty prevailed among the scattered commands as to conditions elsewhere. This uncertainty, loss, and delay profoundly affected the political situation in India. When Suffren first reached the coast, the English had on their hands not only Hyder Ali, but the Mahrattas as well. Peace with the latter was signed on the 17th of May, 1782; but, owing probably to an opposition party among them, the ratifications were not exchanged until December. Both there and in the court of Hyder Ali there was division of interest; and representations were made from both to the French, who, though suspicious, could obtain no certain information of the treaty, that everything depended upon the relative military strength of themselves and the English. The presence and the actions of Suffren were all that France had to show,—the prestige of his genius, the capture of Trincomalee, his success in battle. The French army, cooped up in Cuddalore, was dependent upon the sultan for money, for food, and for reinforcements; even the fleet called on him for money, for masts, for ammunition, for grain. The English, on the other hand, maintained their ground; though on the whole worsted, they lost no ships; and Bickerton's powerful squadron was known to have reached Bombay. Above all, while the French asked for money, the English lavished it.

It was impossible for the French to make head against their enemy without native allies; it was essential to keep Hyder from also making peace. Here the inadequate support and faulty dispositions of the home government made themselves felt. The command in India, both by land and sea, was intrusted to General de Bussy, once the brilliant fellow-worker with Dupleix, now a gouty invalid of sixty-four. With a view to secrecy, Bussy sailed from Cadiz in November, 1781, with two ships-of-the-line, for Teneriffe, where he was to be joined by a convoy leaving Brest in December. This convoy was captured by the English, only two of the vessels escaping to Bussy. The latter pursued his journey, and learning at the Cape of Good Hope that Bickerton's strong force was on the way, felt compelled to land there a great part of his troops. He reached the Isle of France on the 31st of May. The next convoy of eighteen transports, sailing in April for India, was also intercepted. Two of the four ships-of-war were taken, as also ten of the transports; the remainder returned to Brest. A third detachment was more fortunate, reaching the Cape in May; but it was delayed there two months by the wretched condition of the ships and crews. These disappointments decided Bussy to remain at the Island until joined by the expected ships from the Cape, and Suffren at this critical moment did not know what the state of things there was. The general had only written him that, as he could not reach the coast before the bad season, he should rendezvous at Achem. These uncertainties made a painful impression upon Hyder Ali, who had been led to expect Bussy in September, and had instead received news of Bickerton's arrival and the defection of his old allies, the Mahrattas. Suffren was forced to pretend a confidence which he did not feel, but which, with the influence of his own character and achievements, determined the sultan to continue the war. This settled, the squadron sailed for Achem on the 15th of October, anchoring there the 2nd of November.

Three weeks afterward a vessel arrived from Bussy, with word that his departure was indefinitely delayed by an epidemic raging among the troops. Suffren therefore determined to hasten his own return to the coast, and sailed on the 20th of December. January 8, 1783, he anchored off Ganjam, five hundred miles northeast of Cuddalore, whence he would have a fair wind to proceed when he wished. It was his purpose to attack not only the coasting vessels but the English factories on shore as well, the surf being now often moderate; but learning on the 12th, from an English prize, the important and discouraging news of Hyder Ali's death, he gave up all minor operations, and sailed at once for Cuddalore, hoping to secure by his presence the continuance of the alliance as well as the safety of the garrison. He reached the place on the 6th of February.

During his four months' absence the failure of Bussy to appear with his troops, and the arrival of Bickerton, who had shown himself on both coasts, had seriously injured the French cause. The treaty of peace between the English and the Mahrattas had been ratified; and the former, released from this war and reinforced, had attacked the sultan on the west, or Malabar, coast. The effect of this diversion was of course felt on the east coast, despite the efforts of the French to keep the new sultan there. The sickness among the troops at the Isle of France had, however, ceased early in November; and had Bussy then started without delay, he and Suffren would now have met in the Carnatic, with full command of the sea and large odds in their favor ashore. Hughes did not arrive till two months later.

Being thus alone, Suffren, after communicating with Tippoo-Saib, the new sultan of Mysore, went to Trincomalee; and there he was at last joined, on the 10th of March, by Bussy, accompanied by three ships-of-the-line and numerous transports. Eager to bring the troops into the field, Suffren sailed on the 15th with his fastest ships, and landed them the next day at Porto Novo. He returned to Trincomalee on the 11th of April, and fell in with Hughes's fleet of seventeen ships-of-the-line off the harbor's mouth. Having only part of his force with him, no fight ensued, and the English went on to Madras. The southwest monsoon was now blowing.

It is not necessary to follow the trivial operations of the next two months. Tippoo being engaged on the other side of the peninsula and Bussy displaying little vigor, while Hughes was in superior force off the coast, the affairs of the French on shore went from bad to worse. Suffren, having but fifteen ships to eighteen English, was unwilling to go to leeward of Trincomalee, lest it should fall before he could return to it. Under these conditions the English troops advanced from Madras, passing near but around Cuddalore, and encamped to the southward of it, by the sea. The supply-ships and light cruisers were stationed off the shore near the army; while Admiral Hughes, with the heavy ships, anchored some twenty miles south, where, being to windward, he covered the others.

In order to assure to Suffren the full credit of his subsequent course, it is necessary to emphasize the fact that Bussy, though commander-in-chief both by land and sea, did not venture to order him to leave Trincomalee and come to his support. Allowing him to feel the extremity of the danger, he told him not to leave port unless he heard that the army was shut up in Cuddalore, and blockaded by the English squadron. This letter was received on the 10th of June. Suffren waited for no more. The next day he sailed, and forty-eight hours later his frigates saw the English fleet. The same day, the 13th, after a sharp action, the French army was shut up in the town, behind very weak walls. Everything now depended on the action of the fleets.

Upon Suffren's appearance, Hughes moved away and anchored four or five miles from the town. Baffling winds prevailed for three days; but the monsoon resuming on the 16th, Suffren approached. The English admiral not liking to accept action at anchor, and to leeward, in which he was right, got under way; but attaching more importance to the weather-gage than to preventing a junction between the enemy's land and sea forces, he stood out into the offing with a southerly, or south-southeast wind, notwithstanding his superior numbers. Suffren formed on the same tack, and some manœuvring ensued during that night and the next day. At eight P.M. of the 17th the French squadron, which had refused to be drawn to sea, anchored off Cuddalore and communicated with the commander-in-chief. Twelve hundred of the garrison were hastily embarked to fill the numerous vacancies at the guns of the fleet.

Until the 20th the wind, holding unexpectedly at west, denied Hughes the advantage which he sought; and finally on that day he decided to accept action and await the attack. It was made by Suffren with fifteen ships to eighteen, the fire opening at quarter-past four P.M. and lasting until half-past six. The loss on both sides was nearly equal; but the English ships, abandoning both the field of battle and their army, returned to Madras. Suffren anchored before Cuddalore.

The embarrassment of the British army was now very great. The supply-ships on which it had depended fled before the action of the 20th, and the result of course made it impossible for them to return. The sultan's light cavalry harassed their communications by land. On the 25th, the general commanding wrote that his "mind was on the rack without a moment's rest since the departure of the fleet, considering the character of M. de Suffren, and the infinite superiority on the part of the French now that we are left to ourselves." From this anxiety he was relieved by the news of the conclusion of peace, which reached Cuddalore on the 29th by flag-of-truce from Madras.

If any doubt had remained as to the relative merits of the two sea-commanders, the last few days of their campaign would have removed them. Hughes alleges the number of his sick and shortness of water as his reasons for abandoning the contest. Suffren's difficulties, however, were as great as his own;[25] and if he had an advantage at Trincomalee, that only shifts the dispute a step back, for he owed its possession to superior generalship and activity. The simple facts that with fifteen ships he forced eighteen to abandon a blockade, relieved the invested army, strengthened his own crews, and fought a decisive action, make an impression which does not need to be diminished in the interests of truth.[26] It is probable that Hughes's self-reliance had been badly shaken by his various meetings with Suffren.

Although the tidings of peace sent by Hughes to Bussy rested only upon unofficial letters, they were too positive to justify a continuance of bloodshed. An arrangement was entered into by the authorities of the two nations in India, and hostilities ceased on the 8th of July. Two months later, at Pondicherry, the official despatches reached Suffren. His own words upon them are worth quoting, for they show the depressing convictions under which he had acted so noble a part: "God be praised for the peace! for it was clear that in India, though we had the means to impose the law, all would have been lost. I await your orders with impatience, and heartily pray they may permit me to leave. War alone can make bearable the weariness of certain things."

On the 6th of October, 1783, Suffren finally sailed from Trincomalee for France, stopping at the Isle of France and the Cape of Good Hope. The homeward voyage was a continued and spontaneous ovation. In each port visited the most flattering attentions were paid by men of every degree and of every nation. What especially gratified him was the homage of the English captains. It might well be so; none had so clearly established a right to his esteem as a warrior.

[25] There was not a single ship of Suffren's which had more than three-fourths of her regular complement of men. It must be added that soldiers and sepoys made up half of these reduced crews.—Chevalier, p. 463.

[26] "You will have learned my promotion to commodore and rear-admiral. Now, I tell you in the sincerity of my heart and for your own ear alone, that what I have done since then is worth infinitely more than what I had done before. You know the capture and battle of Trincomalee; but the end of the campaign, and that which took place between the month of March and the end of June, is far above anything that has been done in the navy since I entered it. The result has been very advantageous to the State, for the squadron was endangered and the army lost."—Private Letter of Suffren, Sept. 13, 1783; Journal de Bord du Bailli de Suffren.

414

On no occasion when Hughes and Suffren met, save the last, did the English number over twelve ships; but six English captains had laid down their lives, obstinately opposing his efforts. While he was at the Cape, a division of nine of Hughes's ships, returning from the war, anchored in the harbor. Their captains called eagerly upon the admiral, the stout Commodore King of the "Exeter" at their head. "The good Dutchmen have received me as their savior," wrote Suffren, "but among the tributes which have most flattered me, none has given me more pleasure than the esteem and consideration testified by the English who are here." On reaching home, rewards were heaped upon him. Having left France as a captain, he came back a rear-admiral; and immediately after his return the king created a fourth vice-admiralship, a special post to be filled by Suffren, and to lapse at his death. These honors were won by himself alone; they were the tribute paid to his unyielding energy and genius, shown not only in actual fight but in the steadfastness which held to his station through every discouragement, and rose equal to every demand made by recurring want and misfortune.

Alike in the general conduct of his operations and on the battle-field under the fire of the enemy, this lofty resolve was the distinguishing merit of Suffren; and when there is coupled with it the clear and absolute conviction which he held of the necessity to seek and crush the enemy's fleet, we have probably the leading traits of his military character. The latter was the light that led him, the former the spirit that sustained him. As a tactician, in the sense of a driller of ships, imparting to them uniformity of action and manœuvring, he seems to have been deficient, and would probably himself have admitted, with some contempt, the justice of the criticism made upon him in these respects. Whether or no he ever actually characterized tactics—meaning thereby, elementary or evolutionary tactics —as the veil of timidity, there was that in his actions which makes the *mot* probable. Such a contempt, however, is unsafe even in the case of genius. The faculty of moving together with uniformity and precision is too necessary to the development of the full power of a body of ships to be lightly esteemed; it is essential to that concentration of effort at which Suffren rightly aimed, but which he was not always careful to secure by previous dispositions. Paradoxical though it sounds, it is true that only fleets which are able to perform regular movements can afford at times to cast them aside; only captains whom the habit of the drill-ground has familiarized with the shifting phases it presents, can be expected to seize readily the opportunities for independent action presented by the field of battle. Howe and Jervis must make ready the way for the successes of Nelson. Suffren expected too much of his captains. He had the right to expect more than he got, but not that ready perception of the situation and that firmness of nerve which, except to a few favorites of Nature, are the result only of practice and experience.

Still, he was a very great man. When every deduction has been made, there must still remain his heroic constancy, his fearlessness of responsibility as of danger, the rapidity of his action, and the genius whose unerring intuition led him to break through the traditions of his service and assert for the navy that principal part which befits it, that offensive action which secures the control of the sea by the destruction of the enemy's fleet. Had he met in his lieutenants such ready instruments as Nelson found prepared for him, there can be little doubt that Hughes's squadron would have been destroyed while inferior to Suffren's, before reinforcements could have arrived; and with the English fleet it could scarcely have failed that the Coromandel coast also would have fallen. What effect this would have had upon the fate of the peninsula, or upon the terms of the peace, can only be surmised. His own hope was that, by acquiring the superiority in India, a glorious peace might result.

No further opportunities of distinction in war were given to Suffren. The remaining years of his life were spent in honored positions ashore. In 1788, upon an appearance of trouble with England, he was appointed to the command of a great fleet arming at Brest; but before he could leave Paris he died suddenly on the 8th of December, in the sixtieth year of his age. There seems to have been no suspicion at the time of other than natural causes of death, he being exceedingly stout and of apoplectic temperament; but many years after, a story, apparently well-founded, became current that he was killed in a duel arising out of his official action in India. His old antagonist on the battlefield, Sir Edward Hughes, died at a great age in 1794.

13

Events in the West Indies after the Surrender of Yorktown—Encounters of de Grasse with Hood—The Sea Battle of the Saints—
1781, 1782

The surrender of Cornwallis marked the end of the active war upon the American continent. The issue of the struggle was indeed assured upon the day when France devoted her sea power to the support of the colonists; but, as not uncommonly happens, the determining characteristics of a period were summed up in one striking event. From the beginning, the military question, owing to the physical characteristics of the country, a long seaboard with estuaries penetrating deep into the interior, and the consequent greater ease of movement by water than by land, had hinged upon the control of the sea and the use made of that control. Its misdirection by Sir William Howe in 1777, when he moved his army to the Chesapeake instead of supporting Burgoyne's advance, opened the way to the startling success at Saratoga, when amazed Europe saw six thousand regular troops surrendering to a body of provincials. During the four years that followed, until the surrender of York-town, the scales rose and fell according as the one navy or the other appeared on the scene, or as English commanders kept touch with the sea or pushed their operations far from its support. Finally, at the great crisis, all is found depending upon the question whether the French or the English fleet should first appear, and upon their relative force.

The maritime struggle was at once transferred to the West Indies. The events which followed there were antecedent in time both to Suffren's battles and to the final relief of Gibraltar; but they stand so much by themselves as to call for separate treatment, and have such close relation to the conclusion of the war and the conditions of peace, as to form the dramatic finale of the one and the stepping-stone of transition to the other. It is fitting indeed that a brilliant though indecisive naval victory should close the story of an essentially naval war.

The capitulation of Yorktown was completed on the 19th of October, 1781, and on the 5th of November, De Grasse, resisting the suggestions of Lafayette and Washington that the fleet should aid in carrying the war farther south, sailed from the Chesapeake. He reached Martinique on the 26th, the day after the Marquis de Bouillé commanding the French troops in the West Indies, had regained by a bold surprise the Dutch island of St. Eustatius. The two commanders now concerted a joint expedition against Barbadoes, which was frustrated by the violence of the trade winds.

Foiled here, the French proceeded against the island of St. Christopher, or St. Kitt's (Plate XVIII.). On the 11th of January, 1782, the fleet, carrying six thousand troops, anchored on the west coast off Basse Terre, the chief town. No opposition was met, the small garrison of six hundred men retiring to a fortified post ten miles to the northwest, on Brimstone Hill, a solitary precipitous height overlooking the lee shore of the island. The French troops landed and pursued, but the position being found too strong for assault, siege operations were begun.

The French fleet remained at anchor in Basse Terre road. Meanwhile, news of the attack was carried to Sir Samuel Hood, who had followed De Grasse from the continent, and, in the continued absence of Rodney, was naval commander-in-chief on the station. He sailed from Barbadoes on the 14th, anchored at Antigua on the 21st, and there embarked all the troops that could be spared,—about seven hundred men. On the afternoon of the 23rd the fleet started for St. Kitt's, carrying such sail as would bring it within striking distance of the enemy at daylight next morning.

The English having but twenty-two ships to the French twenty-

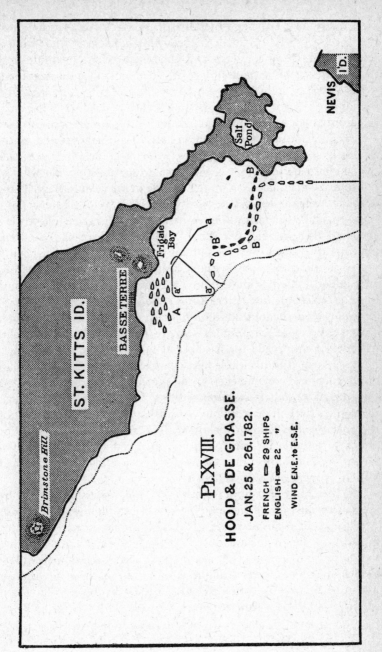

Pl. XVIII.
HOOD & DE GRASSE.
JAN. 25 & 26, 1782.
FRENCH ⊂⊃ 29 SHIPS
ENGLISH ⊂⊃ 22 "

WIND E.N.E. to E.S.E.

ST. KITTS ID.

BASSE TERRE

Brimstone Hill

Frigate
Bay

Salt
Pond

NEVIS

I'D.

419

nine, and the latter being generally superior in force, class for class, it is necessary to mark closely the lay of the land in order to understand Hood's original plans and their subsequent modifications; for, resultless as his attempt proved, his conduct during the next three weeks forms the most brilliant military effort of the whole war. The islands of St. Kitt's and Nevis (Plates XVIII. and XIX.) being separated only by a narrow channel, impracticable for ships-of-the-line, are in effect one, and their common axis lying northwest and southeast, it is necessary for sailing-ships, with the trade wind, to round the southern extremity of Nevis, from which position the wind is fair to reach all anchorages on the lee side of the islands. Basse Terre is about twelve miles distant from the western point of Nevis (Fort Charles), and its roadstead lies east and west. The French fleet were anchored there in disorder (Plate XVIII., A), three or four deep, not expecting attack, and the ships at the west end of the road could not reach those at the east without beating to windward,—a tedious and, under fire, a perilous process. A further most important point to note is that all the eastern ships were so placed that vessels approaching from the southward could reach them with the usual wind.

Hood, therefore, we are told, intended to appear at early daylight, in order of and ready for battle, and fall upon the eastern ships, filing by them with his whole fleet (a, a′), thus concentrating the fire of all upon a few of the enemy; then turning away, so as to escape the guns of the others, he proposed, first wearing and then tacking, to keep his fleet circling in long procession (a′, a″) past that part of the enemy's ships chosen for attack. The plan was audacious, but undeniably sound in principle; some good could hardly fail to follow, and unless De Grasse showed more readiness than he had hitherto done, even decisive results might be hoped for.[1]

The best-laid plans, however, may fail, and Hood's was balked by the awkwardness of a lieutenant of the watch, who hove-to (stopped) a frigate at night ahead of the fleet, and was consequently run down by a ship-of-the-line. The latter also received such injury as delayed the movement, several hours being lost in repairing damages. The French were thus warned of the enemy's approach, and although not suspecting his intention to attack, De Grasse feared that Hood would pass down to leeward of him and disturb the siege of Brim-

[1] The curve, a, a′, a″, represents the line which Hood proposed to follow with his fleet, the wind being supposed east-southeast. The positions B, B, B, refer to the proceedings of a subsequent day and have nothing to do with the diagram at A.

stone Hill,—an undertaking so rash for an inferior force that it is as difficult to conceive how he could have supposed it, as to account for his overlooking the weakness of his own position at anchor.

At one P.M. of the 24th the English fleet was seen rounding the south end of Nevis; at three De Grasse got under way and stood to the southward. Toward sundown Hood also went about and stood south, as though retreating; but he was well to windward of his opponent, and maintained this advantage through the night. At daybreak both fleets were to leeward of Nevis,—the English near the island, the French about nine miles distant (Plate XIX.). Some time was spent in manœuvring, with the object on Hood's part of getting the French admiral yet more to leeward; for, having failed in his first attempt, he had formed the yet bolder intention of seizing the anchorage his unskilful opponent had left, and establishing himself there in an impregnable manner. In this he succeeded, as will be shown; but to understand the justification for a movement confessedly hazardous, it must be pointed out that he thus would place himself between the besiegers of Brimstone Hill and their fleet; or, if the latter anchored near the hill, the English fleet would be between it and its base in Martinique, ready to intercept supplies or detachments approaching from the southward. In short, the position in which Hood hoped to establish himself was on the flank of the enemy's communications, a position the more advantageous because the island alone could not long support the large body of troops so suddenly thrown upon it. Moreover, both fleets were expecting reinforcements; Rodney was on his way and might arrive first, which he did, and in time to save St. Kitt's, which he did not. It was also but four months since Yorktown; the affairs of England were going badly; something must be done, something left to chance, and Hood knew himself and his officers. It may be added that he knew his opponent.

At noon, when the hillsides of Nevis were covered with expectant and interested sightseers, the English fleet rapidly formed its line on the starboard tack and headed north for Basse Terre (Plate XIX., A, A′). The French, at the moment, were in column steering south, but went about at once and stood for the enemy in a bow-and-quarter line[2] (A, A). At two the British had got far enough for Hood to make

[2] When a fleet is in line ahead, close to the wind, on one tack, and the ships go about together, they will, on the other tack, be on the same line, but not one ahead of the other. This formation was called bow-and-quarter line.

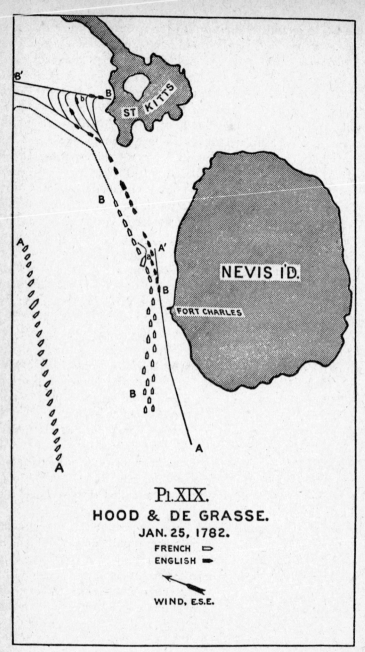

B'

B

b

ST KITTS

B

A

A'

a

B

NEVIS I'D.

FORT CHARLES

B

B

A

A

Pl. XIX.

HOOD & DE GRASSE.

JAN. 25, 1782.

FRENCH ⇨
ENGLISH ➡

WIND, E.S.E.

signal to anchor. At twenty minutes past two the van of the French came within gunshot of the English centre (B, B, B), and shortly afterward the firing began, the assailants very properly directing their main effort upon the English rear ships, which, as happens with most long columns, had opened out, a tendency increased in this case by the slowness of the fourth ship from the rear, the "Prudent." The French flag-ship, "Ville de Paris," of one hundred and twenty guns, bearing De Grasse's flag, pushed for the gap thus made, but was foiled by the "Canada," seventy-four, whose captain, Cornwallis, the brother of Lord Cornwallis, threw all his sails aback, and dropped down in front of the huge enemy to the support of the rear, —an example nobly followed by the "Resolution" and the "Bedford" immediately ahead of him (a). The scene was now varied and animated in the extreme. The English van, which had escaped attack, was rapidly anchoring (b) in its appointed position. The commander-in-chief in the centre, proudly reliant upon the skill and conduct of his captains, made signal for the ships ahead to carry a press of sail, and gain their positions regardless of the danger to the threatened rear. The latter, closely pressed and outnumbered, stood on unswervingly, shortened sail, and came to anchor, one by one, in a line ahead (B, B′), under the roar of the guns of their baffled enemies. The latter filed by, delivered their fire, and bore off again to the southward, leaving their former berths to their weaker but clever antagonists.

The anchorage thus brilliantly taken by Hood was not exactly the same as that held by De Grasse the day before; but as it covered and controlled it, his claim that he took up the place the other had left is substantially correct. The following night and morning were spent in changing and strengthening the order, which was finally established as follows (Plate XVIII., B, B′). The van ship was anchored about four miles southeast from Basse Terre, so close to the shore that a ship could not pass inside her, nor, with the prevailing wind, even reach her, because of a point and shoal just outside, covering her position. From this point the line extended in a west-northwest direction to the twelfth or thirteenth ship (from a mile and a quarter to a mile and a half), where it turned gradually but rapidly to north, the last six ships being on a north and south line. Hood's flag-ship, the "Barfleur," of ninety guns, was at the apex of the salient angle thus formed.

It would not have been impossible for the French fleet to take the anchorage they formerly held; but it and all others to leeward were forbidden by the considerations already stated, so long as Hood remained where he was. It became necessary therefore to dislodge him, but this was rendered exceedingly difficult by the careful tactical dispositions that have been described. His left flank was covered by the shore. Any attempt to enfilade his front by passing along the other flank was met by the broadsides of the six or eight ships drawn up *en potence* to the rear. The front commanded the approaches to Basse Terre. To attack him in the rear, from the northwest, was forbidden by the trade-wind. To these difficulties was to be added that the attack must be made under sail against ships at anchor, to whom loss of spars would be of no immediate concern; and which, having springs[3] out, could train their broadsides over a large area with great ease.

Nevertheless, both sound policy and mortification impelled De Grasse to fight, which he did the next day, January 26. The method of attack, in single column of twenty-nine ships against a line so carefully arranged, was faulty in the extreme; but it may be doubted whether any commander of that day would have broken through the traditional fighting order.[4] Hood had intended the same, but he hoped a surprise on an ill-ordered enemy, and at the original French anchorage it was possible to reach their eastern ships, with but slight exposure to concentrated fire. Not so now. The French formed to the southward and steered for the eastern flank of Hood's line. As their van ship drew up with the point already mentioned, the wind headed her, so that she could only reach the third in the English order, the first four ships of which, using their springs, concentrated their guns upon her. This vessel was supposed by the English to be the "Pluton," and if so, her captain was D'Albert de Rions, in Suffren's opinion the foremost officer of the French navy. "The crash occasioned by their destructive broadsides," wrote an English officer who was present, "was so tremendous that whole

---

[3] A spring is a rope taken from the stern or quarter of a ship at anchor, to an anchor properly placed, by which means the ship can be turned in a desired direction.

[4] In the council of war of the allied fleets on the expediency of attacking the English squadron anchored at Torbay (p. 361) an opponent of the measure urged "that the whole of the combined fleets could not bear down upon the English in a line-of-battle abreast, that of course they must form the line-of-battle ahead, and go down upon the enemy singly, by which they would run the greatest risk of being shattered and torn to pieces," etc. (Beatson, vol. v. p. 396).

pieces of plank were seen flying from her off side ere she could escape the cool, concentrated fire of her determined adversaries. As she proceeded along the British line, she received the first fire of every ship in passing. She was indeed in so shattered a state as to be compelled to bear away for St. Eustatius." And so ship after ship passed by, running the length of the line (Plate XVIII., B, B), distributing their successive fires in gallant but dreary, ineffectual monotony over the whole extent. A second time that day De Grasse attacked in the same order, but neglecting the English van, directed his effort upon the rear and centre. This was equally fruitless, and seems to have been done with little spirit.

From that time until the 14th of February, Hood maintained his position in sight of the French fleet, which remained cruising in the offing and to the southward. On the 1st a despatch vessel arrived from Kempenfeldt, informing him of the dispersal of the French reinforcements for the West Indies, which must have renewed his hopes that his bold attempt would be successful through Rodney's arrival. It was not, however, to be so. Brimstone Hill surrendered on the 12th, after a creditable defence. On the 13th De Grasse took his fleet, now amounting to thirty-three ships-of-the-line, to Nevis, and anchored there. On the night of the 14th Hood summoned all his captains on board, had them set their watches by his, and at eleven P.M., one after another, without noise or signal, cut their cables and made sail to the northward, passing round that end of the island unnoticed, or at least unmolested, by the French.

Both strategically and tactically Hood's conceptions and dispositions were excellent, and their execution was most honorable to the skill and steadiness of himself and his captains. Regarded as a single military operation, this was brilliant throughout; but when considered with reference to the general situation of England at the time, a much higher estimate must be formed of the admiral's qualities.[5] St. Kitt's in itself might not be worth a great risk; but it

[5] In war, as in cards, the state of the score must at times dictate the play; and the chief who never takes into consideration the effect which his particular action will have on the general result, nor what is demanded of him by the condition of things elsewhere, both political and military, lacks an essential quality of a great general. "The audacious manner in which Wellington stormed the redoubt of Francisco [at Ciudad Rodrigo], and broke ground on the first night of the investment, the more audacious manner in which he assaulted the place before the fire of the defence had in any way lessened, and before the counter-scarp had been blown in, were the true causes of the sudden fall of the place. *Both the military and political state of affairs warranted this neglect of rules.* When the general terminated his order for the assault with this sentence, 'Ciudad Rodrigo *must* be stormed this evening,' he knew well that it would be nobly understood." (Napier's Peninsular War). "Judg-

was of the first importance that energy and audacity should be carried into the conduct of England's naval war, that some great success should light upon her flag. Material success was not obtained. The chances, though fair enough, turned against Hood; but every man in that fleet must have felt the glow of daring achievement, the assured confidence which follows a great deed nobly done. Had this man been in chief command when greater issues were at stake, had he been first instead of second at the Chesapeake, Cornwallis might have been saved. The operation—seizing an anchorage left by the enemy—would have been nearly the same; and both situations may be instructively compared with Suffren's relief of Cuddalore.

The action of De Grasse, also, should be considered not only with reference to the particular occasion, but to the general condition of the war as well, and when thus weighed, and further compared with other very similar opportunities neglected by this general officer, a fair estimate of his military capacity can be reached. This comparison, however, is better deferred to the now not very distant close of the campaign. The most useful comment to be made here is, that his action in failing to crush Hood at his anchors, with a force at least fifty per cent greater, was in strict accordance with the general French principle of subordinating the action of the fleet to so-called particular operations; for nothing is more instructive than to note how an unsound principle results in disastrous action. Hood's inferiority was such as to weaken, for offensive purposes, his commanding position. So long as De Grasse kept to windward, he maintained his communications with Martinique, and he was strong enough, too, to force communication when necessary with the troops before Brimstone Hill. It was probable, as the event showed, that the particular operation, the reduction of St. Kitt's, would succeed despite the presence of the English fleet; and "the French navy has always preferred the glory of assuring a conquest to that, more brilliant perhaps but less real, of taking a few ships."

So far De Grasse may be acquitted of any error beyond that of not rising above the traditions of his service. Some days, however, before the surrender of the island and the departure of the English fleet, he was joined by two ships-of-the-line which brought him

ing that the honour of his Majesty's arms, *and the circumstances of the war in these seas*, required a considerable degree of enterprise, I felt myself justified in departing from the regular system." (Sir John Jervis's Report of the Battle of Cape St. Vincent).

word of the dispersal of the expected convoy and reinforcements from Europe.[6] He then knew that he himself could not be strengthened before Rodney's arrival, and that by that event the English would be superior to him. He had actually thirty-three ships-of-the-line in hand, and a few miles off lay twenty-two English in a position where he knew they would await his attack; yet he let them escape. His own explanation implies clearly that he had no intention of attacking them at anchor:—

"The day after the capitulation of Brimstone Hill was the moment to watch Hood closely, and to fight him *as soon as he got under way* from the conquered island. But our provisions were exhausted; we had only enough for thirty-six hours. Some supply-ships had arrived at Nevis, and you will admit one must live before fighting. I went to Nevis, always to windward and in sight of the enemy, a league and a half from him, in order to take on board the necessary supplies as rapidly as possible. Hood decamped at night without signals, and the next morning I found only the sick whom he left behind." [7]

In other words, Hood having held his ground with consummate audacity and skill, when he had some chance of successful resistance, declined to await his adversary's attack under conditions overwhelmingly unfavorable. What shall be said of this talk about provisions? Did not the Comte de Grasse know a month before how long, to a day, the supplies on board would last? Did he not know, four days before Hood sailed, that he had with him every ship he could probably count on for the approaching campaign, while the English would surely be reinforced? And if the English position was as strong as good judgment, professional skill, and bold hearts could make it, had it not weak points? Were not the lee ships to leeward? If they did attempt to beat to windward, had he not ships to "contain" them? If the van ship could not be reached, had he not force enough to double and treble on the third and following ships, as far down the line as he chose? A letter of Suffren's, referring to a similar condition of things at Santa Lucia,[8] but written three years before these events, seems almost a prophetic description of them:—

[6] By Kempenfeldt's attack upon De Guichen's convoy, and the following gale in December, 1781. See p. 362.
[7] Kerguelen: Guerre Maritime de 1778. Letter of De Grasse to Kerguelen, dated Paris, January 8, 1783: p. 263.
[8] See pp. 323, 378.

"Notwithstanding the slight results of the two cannonades of December 15 [1778], we can yet expect success; but the only way to attain it is to attack vigorously the squadron, which in consequence of our superiority cannot hold out, despite their land works, which will become of no effect *if we lay them on board, or anchor upon their buoys.* If we delay, a thousand circumstances may save them. *They may profit by the night to depart.*"

There can be no doubt that the English would have sold their defeat dearly; but results in war must be paid for, and the best are in the long run the cheapest. A tight grip of a few simple principles —that the enemy's fleet was the controlling factor in the coming campaign, that it was therefore his true objective, that one fraction of it must be crushed without delay when caught thus separated—would have saved De Grasse a great blunder; but it is only fair to note that it would have made him an exception to the practice of the French navy.

The hour was now close at hand when the French admiral should feel, even if he did not admit, the consequences of this mistake, by which he had won a paltry island and lost an English fleet. Rodney had sailed from Europe on the 15th of January, with twelve ships-of-the-line. On the 19th of February he anchored at Barbadoes, and the same day Hood reached Antigua from St. Kitt's. On the 25th the squadrons of Rodney and Hood met to windward of Antigua, forming a united fleet of thirty-four ships-of-the-line. The next day De Grasse anchored in Fort Royal, thus escaping the pursuit which Rodney at once began. The English admiral then returned to Sta. Lucia, where he was joined by three more ships-of-the-line from England, raising his force to thirty-seven. Knowing that a large convoy was expected from France, before the arrival of which nothing could be attempted, Rodney sent a part of his fleet to cruise to windward and as far north as Guadeloupe; but the officer in charge of the French convoy, suspecting this action, kept well north of that island, and reached Fort Royal, Martinique, on the 20th of March. The ships-of-war with him raised De Grasse's fleet to thirty-three effective sail-of-the-line and two fifty-gun ships.

The object of the united efforts of France and Spain this year was the conquest of Jamaica. It was expected to unite at Cap Français (now Cap Haïtien), in Hayti, fifty ships-of-the-line and twenty thousand troops. Part of the latter were already at the rendezvous; and De Grasse, appointed to command the combined fleets, was to collect in Martinique all the available troops and supplies in the French islands, and convoy them to the rendezvous. It was this junction that Rodney was charged to prevent.

The region within which occurred the important operations of the next few days covers a distance of one hundred and fifty miles, from south to north, including the islands of Sta. Lucia, Martinique, Dominica, and Guadeloupe, in the order named. (See Plate XI., p. 335.) At this time the first was in English, the others in French, hands. The final, and for the moment decisive, encounter took place between, and a little to westward of Dominica and Guadeloupe. These are twenty-three miles apart; but the channel is narrowed to thirteen by three islets called the Saints, lying ten miles south of Guadeloupe. It is said to have been De Grasse's intention, instead of sailing direct for Cap Français, to take a circuitous course near the islands, which, being friendly or neutral, would give refuge to the convoy if pressed. The close pursuit of the English, who came up with him off Dominica, led him to forsake this plan, sending the convoy into Basse Terre at the south end of Guadeloupe, while with the fleet he tried to beat through the channel and pass east of the island, thus drawing the English away from the transports and ridding himself of the tactical embarrassment due to the latter's presence. Accidents to various ships thwarted this attempt, and brought about a battle disastrous to him and fatal to the joint enterprise.

The anchorages of the two fleets, in Martinique and Sta. Lucia, were thirty miles apart. The prevailing east wind is generally fair to pass from one to the other; but a strong westerly current, and the frequency of calms and light airs, tend to throw to leeward sailing-ships leaving Sta. Lucia for the northern island. A chain of frigates connected the English lookout ships off Martinique, by signal, with Rodney's flag-ship in Gros Ilot Bay. Everything was astir at the two stations, the French busy with the multitudinous arrangements necessitated by a great military undertaking, the English with less to do, yet maintaining themselves in a state of expectancy and preparation for instant action, that entails constant alertness and mental activity.

On the 5th of April Rodney was informed that the soldiers were being embarked, and on the 8th, soon after daylight, the lookout frigates were seen making signal that the enemy was leaving port. The English fleet at once began to get under way, and by noon was clear of the harbor to the number of thirty-six of the line. At half-past two P.M. the advanced frigates were in sight of the French fleet, which was seen from the mastheads of the main body just before sundown. The English stood to the northward all night, and at day-break of the 9th were abreast Dominica, but for the most part becalmed. In-shore of them, to the northward and eastward, were seen the French fleet and convoy: the men-of-war numbering thirty-three of the line, besides smaller vessels; the convoy a hundred and fifty sail, under special charge of the two fifty-gun ships. The irregular and uncertain winds, common to the night and early hours of the day near the land, had scattered these unwieldy numbers. Fifteen sail-of-the-line were in the channel between Dominica and the Saints, with a fresh trade-wind, apparently beating to windward; the remainder of the ships-of-war and most of the convoy were still becalmed close under Dominica (Plate XX., Position I, b). Gradually, however, one by one, the French ships were catching light airs off the land; and by favor of these, which did not reach so far as the English in the offing, drew out from the island and entered the more steady breeze of the channel, reinforcing the group which was thus possessed of that prime element of naval power, mobility. At the same time light airs from the southeast crept out to the English van under Hood, fanning it gently north from the main body of the fleet toward two isolated French ships (i), which, having fallen to leeward during the night, had shared the calms that left the English motionless, with their heads all round the compass. They had come nearly within gunshot, when a light puff from the northwest enabled the Frenchmen to draw away and approach their own ships in the channel.

The farther the English van advanced, the fresher grew their wind, until they fairly opened the channel of the Saints and felt the trade-wind. De Grasse signalled to the convoy to put into Guadeloupe, which order was so well carried out that they were all out of sight to the northward by two in the afternoon, and will appear no more in the sequel. The two French ships, already spoken of as fallen to leeward, not being yet out of danger from the English van, which had now a commanding breeze, and the latter being much separated from their rear and centre, De Grasse ordered his van to bear down

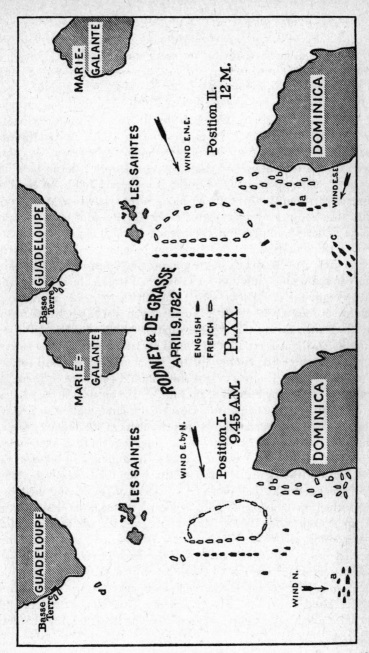

RODNEY & DE GRASSE.
APRIL 9, 1782.

ENGLISH
FRENCH

Pl. XX.

Position II. 12 M.

WIND E.N.E.

Position I. 9.45 AM.

WIND E. by N.

MARIE-GALANTE

GUADELOUPE

Basse Terre

LES SAINTES

DOMINICA

WIND S.E.

WIND N.

and engage. This was obeyed by the ships signalled and by three others, in all by fourteen or fifteen, the action beginning at half-past nine A.M., and lasting with intermissions until quarter-past one P.M. Hood was soon forced to heave-to, in order not to increase too much his separation from the main fleet; the French kept under way, approaching from the rear and passing in succession at half cannon-shot to windward (Plate XX., Position I.) As each ship drew ahead of the English division, she tacked, standing back to the southward until in position to resume her place in the order of attack, thus describing a continuous irregular curve of elliptical form, to wind-ward of their opponents. The brunt of the attack fell upon eight or nine of the English, this number being successively increased as one ship after another, as the baffling airs served, drew out from the calm space under Dominica; but the French received similar accessions. While this engagement was going on, part of the English centre, eight ships with Rodney's flag among them (Position I., a), by care-fully watching the puffs and cat's-paws, had worked in with the land and caught the sea breeze, which was felt there sooner than in the offing. As soon as they had it, about eleven A.M., they stood to the north, being now on the weather quarter[10] both of the English van and its assailants (Position II., a). The latter, seeing this, tacked, and abandoning the contest for the moment, steered south to join their centre, lest Rodney's eight ships should get between them. At half-past eleven the French again formed line on the starboard tack, most of their ships being now clear of the land, while the English rear was still becalmed. The greater numbers of the French enabled them to extend from north to south along the length of the English line, whereas the latter was still broken by a great gap between the van and centre (Position II.). The attack upon Hood was therefore hotly renewed; but the French centre and rear (b), having the wind, kept their distance, and held Rodney's division at long range. At quarter-past one the French, finding that the whole British line was coming up with the wind, ceased firing, and at two Rodney hauled down the signal for battle, the enemy having withdrawn.

This action of the 9th of April amounted actually to no more than an artillery duel. One French ship, the "Caton," a sixty-four (d), received injuries which sent her into Guadeloupe; two English were disabled, but repaired their injuries without leaving the fleet.

[10] Weather quarter is behind, but on the windward side.

The material advantage, therefore, lay with the latter. Opinions differ as to the generalship of the Comte de Grasse on this day, but they divide on the same basis of principle as to whether ulterior operations, or the chances of beating the enemy's fleet, are to determine an admiral's action. The facts of the case are these: Sixteen of the English fleet, all the rear and four of the centre (Position II., c), were not able at any time to fire a shot. Apparently every French ship, first and last, might have been brought into action. At the beginning, eight or nine English were opposed to fifteen French. At the end there were twenty English to thirty-three French, and these general proportions doubtless obtained throughout the four hours. De Grasse therefore found himself in the presence of a fleet superior to his own, in numbers at least, and by the favor of Providence that fleet so divided that nearly half of it was powerless to act. He had the wind, he had a fine body of captains; what was to prevent him from attacking Hood's nine ships with fifteen, putting one on each side of the six in the rear? Had those nine been thoroughly beaten, Rodney's further movements must have been hopelessly crippled. The French lost only five in their defeat three days later. The subsequent court-martial, however, laid down the French doctrine thus: "The decision to persist in engaging with only a part of our fleet may be considered as an act of prudence on the part of the admiral, which might be dictated by the ulterior projects of the campaign." On this a French professional writer naturally remarks, that if an attack were made at all, it would be more prudent to make it in force; less injury would fall on individual ships, while in the end the whole fleet would inevitably be drawn in to support any which, by losing spars, could not return to windward.

Three times in one year had Fortune thrown before De Grasse the opportunity of attacking English fleets with decisive odds on his side.[11] Her favors were now exhausted. Three days more were to show how decidedly the ulterior projects of a campaign may be affected by a battle and the loss of a few ships. From the 9th to the morning of the 12th the French fleet continued beating to windward between Dominica and the Saints, in no regular order. On the night of the 9th the English hove-to to repair damages. The next day the chase to windward was resumed, but the French gained

---

[11] April 29, 1781, off Martinique, twenty-four ships to eighteen; January, 1782, thirty to twenty-two; April 9, 1782, thirty to twenty.

very decidedly upon their pursuers. On the night of the 10th two ships, the "Jason" and "Zélé," collided. The "Zélé" was the bane of the French fleet during these days. She was one of those that were nearly caught by the enemy on the 9th, and was also the cause of the final disaster. The injuries to the "Jason" forced her to put into Guadeloupe. On the 11th the main body was to windward of the Saints, but the "Zélé" and another had fallen so far to leeward that De Grasse bore down to cover them, thus losing much of the ground gained. On the night following, the "Zélé" was again in collision, this time with De Grasse's flag-ship; the latter lost some sails, but the other, which had not the right of way and was wholly at fault, carried away both foremast and bowsprit. The admiral sent word to the frigate "Astrée" to take the "Zélé" in tow; and here flits across the page of our story a celebrated and tragical figure, for the captain of the "Astrée" was the ill-fated explorer La Pérouse, the mystery of whose disappearance with two ships and their entire crews remained so long unsolved. Two hours were consumed in getting the ship under way in tow of the frigate,—not very smart work under the conditions of weather and urgency; but by five A.M. the two were standing away for Basse Terre, where the "Caton" and "Jason," as well as the convoy, had already arrived. The French fleet had thus lost three from its line-of-battle since leaving Martinique.

The disabled ship had not long been headed for Basse Terre, when the faint streaks of dawn announced the approach of the 12th of April, a day doubly celebrated in naval annals. The sun had not quite set upon the exhausted squadrons of Suffren and Hughes, anchoring after their fiercest battle off Ceylon, when his early rays shone upon the opening strife between Rodney and De Grasse.[12] The latter was at the time the greatest naval battle in its results that had been fought in a century; its influence on the course of events was very great, though far from as decisive as it might have been; it was attended with circumstances of unusual though somewhat factitious brilliancy, and particularly was marked by a manœuvre that was then looked upon as exceptionally daring and decisive,— "breaking the line." It must be added that it has given rise to a storm of controversy; and the mass of details, as given by witnesses who should be reliable, are so confused and contradictory, owing mainly to the uncertainties of the wind, that it is impossible now to

[12] The difference of time from Trincomalee to the Saints is nine hours and a half.

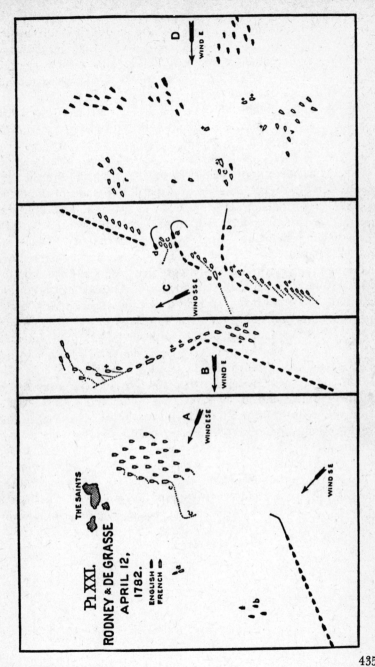

Pl. XXI.
RODNEY & DE GRASSE
APRIL 12,
1782.

ENGLISH ━━
FRENCH ⇨

THE SAINTS

WIND SE

A
WIND ESE

B
WIND E

C
WIND SSE

D
WIND E

do more than attempt to reconcile them in a full account. Nevertheless, the leading features can be presented with sufficient accuracy, and this will first be done briefly and barely; the outline thus presented can afterward be clothed with the details which give color, life, and interest to the great scene.

At daylight[13] (about half-past five) the English fleet, which had gone about at two A.M., was standing on the starboard tack, with the wind at southeast,[14] an unusual amount of southing for that hour (Plate XXI., A). It was then about fifteen miles from the Saints, which bore north-northeast, and ten from the French fleet, which bore northeast. The latter, owing to the events of the night, was greatly scattered, as much as eight or ten miles separating the weather, or easternmost, ships from the lee,[15] the flag-ship "Ville de Paris" being among the latter. Anxiety for the "Zélé" kept the French admiral, with the ships in his company, under short canvas, standing to the southward on the port tack (A). The English on the starboard tack, with the wind as they had it,[16] headed east-northeast, and thus, as soon as there was light to see, found the French "broad on the lee bow, and one of M. de Grasse's ships (the "Zélé") towed by a frigate, square under our lee (a), with his bowsprit and foremast prostrate across his forecastle." To draw the French farther to leeward, Rodney detached four ships (b) to chase the "Zélé." As soon as De Grasse saw this he signalled his fleet to keep away (c), as Rodney wished, and at the same time to form the line-of-battle, thus calling down to him the ships to windward. The English line was also formed rapidly, and the chasing ships recalled at seven A.M. De Grasse, seeing that if he stood on he would lose the weather-gage altogether, hauled up again on the port tack (c'); and the breeze changing to east-southeast and east in his favor and knocking the English off, the race of the two fleets on opposite tacks, for the advantage of the wind, became nearly equal. The French, however,

---

[13] The account of the transactions from April 9 to April 12 is based mainly upon the contemporary plates and descriptions of Lieutenant Matthews, R. N., and the much later Naval Researches of Capt. Thomas White, also of the British Navy, who were eye-witnesses, both being checked by French and other English narratives. Matthews and White are at variance with Rodney's official report as to the tack on which the English were at daybreak; but the latter is explicitly confirmed by private letters of Sir Charles Douglas, sent immediately after the battle to prominent persons, and is followed in the text.

[14] Letter of Sir Charles Douglas, Rodney's chief-of-staff: United Service Journal, 1833, Part I. p. 515.

[15] De Grasse calls this distance three leagues, while some of his captains estimated it to be as great as five.

[16] The French, in mid-channel, had the wind more to the eastward.

won, thanks to a superiority in sailing which had enabled them to draw so far to windward of the English on the previous days, and, but for the awkwardness of the "Zélé," might have cleared them altogether (Plate XXI., B). Their leading ships first reached and passed the point where the rapidly converging tracks intersected, while the English leader, the "Marlborough," struck the French line between the sixth and tenth ships (variously stated). The battle, of course, had by this time begun, the ninth ship in the French line, the "Brave," opening fire at twenty minutes before eight A.M. upon the "Marlborough." As there was no previous intention of breaking the line, the English leader kept away, in obedience to a signal from Rodney, and ran close along under the enemy's lee, followed in succession by all the ships as they reached her wake. The battle thus assumed the common and indecisive phase of two fleets passing on opposite tacks, the wind very light, however, and so allowing a more heavy engagement than common under these circumstances, the ships "sliding by" at the rate of three to four knots. Since the hostile lines diverged again south of their point of meeting, De Grasse made signal to keep away four points to south-southwest, thus bringing his van (B, a) to action with the English rear, and not permitting the latter to reach his rear unscathed. There were, however, two dangers threatening the French if they continued their course. Its direction, south or south-southwest, carried them into the calms that hung round the north end of Dominica; and the uncertainty of the wind made it possible that by its hauling to the southward the enemy could pass through their line and gain the wind, and with it the possibility of forcing the decisive battle which the French policy had shunned; and this was in fact what happened. De Grasse therefore made signal at half-past eight to wear *together* and take the same tack as the English. This, however, was impossible; the two fleets were too close together to admit the evolution. He then signalled to haul close to the wind and wear *in succession,* which also failed to be done, and at five minutes past nine the dreaded contingency arose; the wind hauled to the southward, knocking off all the French ships that had not yet kept away; that is, all who had English ships close under their lee (Plate XXI., C). Rodney, in the "Formidable," was at this time just drawing up with the fourth ship astern of De Grasse's flag. Luffing to the new wind, he passed through the French line, followed by the five ships next astern of him (C, a), while nearly at the same moment, and from the same causes, his sixth astern (C, b) led through the interval abreast him, followed by the whole English rear. The French line-of-battle was thus broken in two places by columns of enemies' ships in such close order as to force its vessels aside, even if the wind had not conspired to embarrass their action. Every principle upon which a line-of-battle was constituted, for mutual support and for the clear field of fire of each ship, was thus overthrown for the French, and preserved for the English divisions which filed through; and the French were forced off to leeward by the interposition of the enemy's columns, besides being broken up. Compelled thus to forsake the line upon which they had been ranged, it was necessary to re-form upon another, and unite the three groups into which they were divided,—a difficult piece of tactics under any circumstances, but doubly so under the moral impression of disaster, and in presence of a superior enemy, who, though himself disordered, was in better shape, and already felt the glow of victory.

It does not appear that any substantial attempt to re-form was made by the French. To reunite, yes; but only as a flying, disordered mass. The various shifts of wind and movements of the divisions left their fleet, at midday (Plate XXI., D), with the centre (c) two miles northwest of and to leeward of the van (v), the rear (r) yet farther from the centre and to leeward of it. Calms and short puffs of wind prevailed now through both fleets. At half-past one P.M. a light breeze from the east sprang up, and De Grasse made signal to form the line again on the port tack; between three and four, not having succeeded in this, he made signal to form on the starboard tack. The two signals and the general tenor of the accounts show that at no time were the French re-formed after their line was broken; and all the manœuvres tended toward, even if they did not necessitate, taking the whole fleet as far down as the most leewardly of its parts (D). In such a movement, it followed of course that the most crippled ships were left behind, and these were picked up, one by one, by the English, who pursued without any regular order, for which there was no need, as mutual support was assured without it. Shortly after six P.M. De Grasse's flag-ship, the "Ville de Paris," struck her colors to the "Barfleur," carrying the flag of Sir Samuel Hood. The French accounts state that nine of the enemy's ships then surrounded her, and there is no doubt that she had been fought to the bitter end. Her name, commemorating the great city whose gift she had been to the king, her unusual size, and the fact that no French naval commander-in-chief had before been taken prisoner in battle, conspired to bestow a peculiar brilliancy upon Rodney's victory. Four other ships-of-the-line were taken,[17] and, singularly enough, upon these particular ships was found the whole train of artillery intended for the reduction of Jamaica.

Such were the leading features of the Battle of the Saints, or, as it is sometimes styled, of the 12th of April, known to the French as the Battle of Dominica. Certain points which have so far been omitted for the sake of clearness, but which affect the issue, must now be given. When the day opened, the French fleet was greatly scattered and without order.[18] De Grasse, under the influence of his fears for the "Zélé," so precipitated his movements that his line was not properly formed at the moment of engaging. The van ships had not yet come into position (B, a), and the remainder were so far from having reached their places that De Vaudreuil, commanding the rear division and last engaged, states that the line was formed under the fire of musketry. The English, on the contrary, were in good order, the only change made being to shorten the interval between ships from two to one cable's length (seven hundred feet). The celebrated stroke of breaking through the French line was due, not to previous intention, but to a shift of wind throwing their ships out of order and so increasing the spaces between them; while the gap through which Rodney's group penetrated was widened by the "Diadème" on its north side being taken aback and paying round on the other tack (C, c). Sir Charles Douglas says the immediate effect, where the flag-ship broke through, was "the bringing together, almost if not quite in contact with each other, the four ships of the enemy which were nearest," (on the north) "to the point alluded to (c), and coming up in succession. This unfortunate group, composing now only one large single object at which to fire, was attacked by the 'Duke,' 'Namur,' and 'Formidable' (ninety-gun ships) all at once, receiving several broadsides from each, not a single shot missing; and great must have been the slaughter." The

[17] The positions of the French ships captured are shown by a cross in each of the three successive stages of the battle, B, C, D.
[18] The distance of the weathermost French ships from the "Ville de Paris," when the signal to form line-of-battle was made, is variously stated at from six to nine miles.

"Duke" (C, d), being next ahead of the flag-ship, had followed her leader under the French lee; but as soon as her captain saw that the "Formidable" had traversed the enemy's order, he did the same, passing north of this confused group and so bringing it under a fire from both sides. The log of the "Magnanime," one of the group, mentions passing under the fire of two three-deckers, one on either side.

As soon as the order was thus broken, Rodney hauled down the signal for the line, keeping flying that for close action, and at the same time ordered his van, which had now passed beyond and north of the enemy's rear, to go about and rejoin the English centre. This was greatly delayed through the injuries to spars and sails received in passing under the enemy's fire. His own flag-ship and the ships with her went about. The rear, under Hood, instead of keeping north again to join the centre, stood to windward for a time, and were then becalmed at a considerable distance from the rest of the fleet.

Much discussion took place at a later day as to the wisdom of Rodney's action in breaking through his enemy's order, and to whom the credit, if any, should be ascribed. The latter point is of little concern; but it may be said that the son of Sir Charles Douglas, Rodney's chief-of-staff, brought forward an amount of positive evidence, the only kind that could be accepted to diminish the credit of the person wholly responsible for the results, which proves that the suggestion came from Douglas, and Rodney's consent was with difficulty obtained. The value of the manœuvre itself is of more consequence than any question of personal reputation. It has been argued by some that, so far from being a meritorious act, it was unfortunate, and for Rodney's credit should rather be attributed to the force of circumstances than to choice. It had been better, these say, to have continued along under the lee of the French rear, thus inflicting upon it the fire of the whole English line, and that the latter should have tacked and doubled on the French rear. This argument conveniently forgets that tacking, or turning round in any way, after a brush of this kind, was possible to only a part of the ships engaged; and that these would have much difficulty in overtaking the enemies who had passed on, unless the latter were very seriously crippled. Therefore this suggested attack, the precise reproduction of the battle of Ushant, really reduces itself to the fleets passing on opposite tacks, each distributing its fire over the whole of the enemy's line without attempting any concentration on a part of it. It may, and must, be conceded at once, that Rodney's change of course permitted the eleven rear ships of the French (D, r) to run off to leeward, having received the fire of only part of their enemy, while the English van had undergone that of nearly the whole French fleet. These ships, however, were thus thrown entirely out of action for a measurable and important time by being driven to leeward, and would have been still more out of position to help any of their fleet, had not De Grasse himself been sent to leeward by Hood's division cutting the line three ships ahead of him. The thirteen leading French ships, obeying the last signal they had seen, were hugging the wind; the group of six with De Grasse (C, e) would have done the same had they not been headed off by Hood's division. The result of Rodney's own action alone, therefore, would have been to divide the French fleet into two parts, separated by a space of six miles, and one of them hopelessly to leeward. The English, having gained the wind, would have been in position easily to "contain" the eleven lee ships, and to surround the nineteen weather ones in overwhelming force. The actual condition, owing to the *two* breaches in the line, was slightly different; the group of six with De Grasse being placed between his weather and lee divisions, two miles from the former, four from the latter (D). It seems scarcely necessary to insist upon the tactical advantages of such a situation for the English, even disregarding the moral effect of the confusion through which the French had passed. In addition to this, a very striking lesson is deducible from the immediate effects of the English guns in passing through. Of the five ships taken, three were those under whose sterns the English divisions pierced.[19] Instead of giving and taking, as the parallel lines ran by, on equal terms, each ship having the support of those ahead and astern, the French ships near which the penetrating columns passed received each the successive fire of all the enemy's division. Thus Hood's thirteen ships filed by the two rear ones of the French van, the "César" and "Hector," fairly crushing them under this concentra-

[19] The other two French ships taken were the "Ville de Paris," which, in her isolated condition, and bearing the flag of the commander-in-chief, became the quarry around which the enemy's ships naturally gathered, and the "Ardent," of sixty-four guns, which appears to have been intercepted in a gallant attempt to pass from the van to the side of her admiral in his extremity. The latter was the solitary prize taken by the allied Great Armada in the English Channel, in 1779.

tion of fire; while in like manner, and with like results, Rodney's six passed by the "Glorieux." This "concentration by defiling" past the extremity of a column corresponds quite accurately to the concentration upon the flank of a line, and has a special interest, because if successfully carried out it would be as powerful an attack now as it ever has been. If quick to seize their advantage, the English might have fired upon the ships on both sides of the gaps through which they passed, as the "Formidable" actually did; but they were using the starboard broadsides, and many doubtless did not realize their opportunity until too late. The natural results of Rodney's act, therefore, were: (1) The gain of the wind, with the power of offensive action; (2) Concentration of fire upon a part of the enemy's order; and (3) The introduction into the latter of confusion and division, which might, and did, become very great, offering the opportunity of further tactical advantage. It is not a valid reply to say that, had the French been more apt, they could have united sooner. A manœuvre that presents a good chance of advantage does not lose its merit because it can be met by a prompt movement of the enemy, any more than a particular lunge of the sword becomes worthless because it has its appropriate parry. The chances were that by heading off the rear ships, while the van stood on, the French fleet would be badly divided; and the move was none the less sagacious because the two fragments could have united sooner than they did, had they been well handled. With the alternative action suggested, of tacking after passing the enemy's rear, the pursuit became a stern chase, in which both parties having been equally engaged would presumably be equally crippled. Signals of disability, in fact, were numerous in both fleets.

Independently of the tactical handling of the two fleets, there were certain differences of equipment which conferred tactical advantage, and are therefore worth noting. The French appear to have had finer ships, and class for class, heavier armaments. Sir Charles Douglas, an eminent officer of active and ingenious turn of mind, who paid particular attention to gunnery details, estimated that in weight of battery the thirty-three French were superior to the thirty-six English by the force of four 84-gun ships; and that after the loss of the "Zélé," "Jason," and "Caton" there still remained an advantage equal to two seventy-fours. The French admiral La Gravière admits the generally heavier calibre of French cannon at this era. The better construction of the French ships and their greater draught caused them to sail and beat better, and accounts in part for the success of De Grasse in gaining to windward; for in the afternoon of the 11th only three or four of the body of his fleet were visible *from the mast-head* of the English flag-ship, which had been within gunshot of them on the 9th. It was the awkwardness of the unlucky "Zélé" and of the "Magnanime," which drew down De Grasse from his position of vantage, and justified Rodney's perseverance in relying upon the chapter of accidents to effect his purpose. The greater speed of the French as a body is somewhat hard to account for, because, though undoubtedly with far better lines, the practice of coppering the bottom had not become so general in France as in England, and among the French there were several uncoppered and worm-eaten ships.[20] The better sailing of the French was, however, remarked by the English officers, though the great gain mentioned must have been in part owing to Rodney's lying-by, after the action of the 9th, to refit, due probably to the greater injury received by the small body of his vessels, which had been warmly engaged, with greatly superior numbers. It was stated, in narrating that action, that the French kept at half cannon-range; this was to neutralize a tactical advantage the English had in the large number of carronades and other guns of light weight but large calibre, which in close action told heavily, but were useless at greater distances. The second in command, De Vaudreuil, to whom was intrusted the conduct of that attack, expressly states that if he had come within reach of the carronades his ships would have been quickly unrigged. Whatever judgment is passed upon the military policy of refusing to crush an enemy situated as the English division was, there can be no question that, if the object was to prevent pursuit, the tactics of De Vaudreuil on the 9th was in all respects excellent. He inflicted the utmost injury with the least exposure of his own force. On the 12th, De Grasse, by allowing himself to be lured within reach of carronades, yielded this advantage, besides sacrificing to an impulse his whole previous strategic policy. Rapidly handled from their lightness, firing grape and shot of large diameter, these guns were peculiarly harmful in close action and useless at long range. In a later despatch De Vaudreuil says: "The effect of these new arms is most deadly within musket range; it is

[20] Official letter of the Marquis de Vaudreuil. Guérin: Histoire de la Marine Française, vol. v. p. 513.

they which so badly crippled us on the 12th of April." There were other gunnery innovations, in some at least of the English ships, which by increasing the accuracy, the rapidity, and the field of fire, greatly augmented the power of their batteries. These were the introduction of locks, by which the man who aimed also fired; and the fitting to the gun-carriages of breast-pieces and sweeps, so that the guns could be pointed farther ahead or astern,—that is, over a larger field than had been usual. In fights between single ships, not controlled in their movements by their relations to a fleet, this improvement would at times allow the possessor to take a position whence he could train upon his enemy without the latter being able to reply, and some striking instances of such tactical advantage are given. In a fleet fight, such as is now being considered, the gain was that the guns could be brought to bear farther forward, and could follow the opponent longer as he passed astern, thus doubling, or more, the number of shots he might receive, and lessening for him the interval of immunity enjoyed between two successive antagonists.[21] These matters of antiquated and now obsolete detail carry with them lessons that are never obsolete; they differ in no respect from the more modern experiences with the needle-gun and the torpedo.

And indeed this whole action of April 12, 1782, is fraught with sound military teaching. Perseverance in pursuit, gaining advantage of position, concentration of one's own effort, dispersal of the enemy's force, the efficient tactical bearing of small but important improvements in the material of war, have been dwelt on. To insist further upon the necessity of not letting slip a chance to beat the enemy in detail, would be thrown away on anyone not already convinced by the bearing of April 9 on April 12. The abandonment of the attack upon Jamaica, after the defeat of the French fleet, shows conclusively that the true way to secure ulterior objects is to defeat the force which threatens them. There remains at least one criticism, delicate in its character, but essential to draw out the full teachings of these events; that is, upon the manner in which the victory was followed up, and the consequent effects upon the war in general.

The liability of sailing-ships to injury in spars and sails, in other words, in that mobility which is the prime characteristic of naval

[21] See United Service Journal, 1834, Part II, pp. 109 and following.

444

strength, makes it difficult to say, after a lapse of time, what might or might not have been done. It is not only a question of actual damage received, which logbooks may record, but also of the means for repair, the energy and aptitude of the officers and seamen, which differ from ship to ship. As to the ability of the English fleet, however, to follow up its advantages by a more vigorous pursuit on the 12th of April, we have the authority of two most distinguished officers,—Sir Samuel Hood, the second in command, and Sir Charles Douglas, the captain of the fleet, or chief-of-staff to the admiral. The former expressed the opinion that twenty ships might have been taken, and said so to Rodney the next day; while the chief-of-staff was so much mortified by the failure, and by the manner in which the admiral received his suggestions, as seriously to contemplate resigning his position.[22]

Advice and criticism are easy, nor can the full weight of a responsibility be felt, except by the man on whom it is laid; but great results cannot often be reached in war without risk and effort. The accuracy of the judgment of these two officers, however, is confirmed by inference from the French reports. Rodney justifies his failure to pursue by alleging the crippled condition of many ships, and other matters incident to the conclusion of a hard-fought battle, and then goes on to suggest what might have been done that night, had he pursued, by the French fleet, which "went off in a body of twenty-six ships-of-the-line." [23] These possibilities are rather creditable to his imagination, considering what the French fleet had done by day; but as regards the body of twenty-six[24] ships, De Vaudreuil, who, after De Grasse's surrender, made the signal for the ships to rally round his flag, found only ten with him next morning, and was not joined by any more before the 14th. During the following days five more joined him at intervals.[25] With these he went to the rendezvous at Cap Français, where he found others, bringing the whole number who repaired thither to twenty. The five remaining, of those that had been in the action, fled to Curaçao, six hundred miles distant, and did not rejoin until May. The "body of twenty-six ships," therefore, had no existence in fact; on

[22] See letter of Sir Howard Douglas in United Service Journal, 1834, Part II, p. 97; also Naval Evolutions, by same author. The letters of Sir Samuel Hood have not come under the author's eye.
[23] Rodney's Life, vol. ii, p. 248.
[24] There were only twenty-five in all.
[25] Guérin, vol. v, p. 511.

the contrary, the French fleet was very badly broken up, and several of its ships isolated. As regards the crippled condition, there seems no reason to think the English had suffered more, but rather less, than their enemy; and a curious statement, bearing upon this, appears in a letter from Sir Gilbert Blane:—

"It was with difficulty we could make the French officers believe that the returns of killed and wounded, made by our ships to the admiral, were true; and one of them flatly contradicted me, saying we always gave the world a false account of our loss. I then walked with him over the decks of the 'Formidable', and bid him remark what number of shot-holes there were, and *also how little her rigging had suffered,* and asked if that degree of damage was likely to be connected with the loss of more than fourteen men, which was our number killed, and *the greatest of any in the fleet,* except the 'Royal Oak' and 'Monarch'. He . . . owned our fire must have been much better kept up and directed than theirs." [26]

There can remain little doubt, therefore, that the advantage was not followed up with all possible vigor. Not till five days after the battle was Hood's division sent toward San Domingo, where they picked up in the Mona Passage the "Jason" and the "Caton," which had separated before the battle and were on their way to Cap Français. These, and two small vessels with them, were the sole after-fruits of the victory. Under the conditions of England's war this cautious failure is a serious blot on Rodney's military reputation, and goes far to fix his place among successful admirals. He had saved Jamaica for the time; but he had not, having the opportunity, crushed the French fleet. He too, like De Grasse, had allowed the immediate objective to blind him to the general military situation, and to the factor which controlled it.

To appreciate the consequences of this neglect, and the real indecisiveness of this celebrated battle, we must go forward a year and listen to the debates in Parliament on the conditions of peace, in February, 1783. The approval or censure of the terms negotiated by the existing ministry involved the discussion of many considerations; but the gist of the dispute was, whether the conditions were such as the comparative financial and military situations of the belligerents justified, or whether it would have been better for England to continue the war rather than submit to the sacrifices she had made. As regards the financial condition, despite the gloomy

[26] Rodney's Life, vol. ii, p. 246.

picture drawn by the advocates of the peace, there was probably no more doubt then than there is now about the comparative resources of the different countries. The question of military strength was really that of naval power. The ministry argued that the whole British force hardly numbered one hundred sail-of-the-line, while the navies of France and Spain amounted to one hundred and forty, not to speak of that of Holland.

"With so glaring an inferiority, what hopes of success could we derive, either from the experience of the last campaign, or from any new distribution of our force in that which would have followed? In the West Indies we could not have had more than forty-six sail to oppose to forty, which on the day that peace was signed lay in Cadiz Bay, with sixteen thousand troops on board, ready to sail for that quarter of the world, where they would have joined by twelve of the line from Havana and ten from San Domingo. . . . Might we not too reasonably apprehend that the campaign in the West Indies would have closed with the loss of Jamaica itself, the avowed object of this immense armament?" [27]

These are certainly the reasonings of an avowed partisan, for which large allowances must be made. The accuracy of the statement of comparative numbers was denied by Lord Keppel, a member of the same party, and but lately at the head of the Admiralty, a post which he had resigned because he disapproved the treaty.[28] English statesmen, too, as well as English seamen, must by this time have learned to discount largely the apparent, when estimating the real, power of the other navies. Nevertheless, how different would have been the appreciation of the situation, both moral and material, had Rodney reaped the full fruits of the victory which he owed rather to chance than to his own merit, great as that undeniably was.

A letter published in 1809, anonymous, but bearing strong internal evidence of being written by Sir Gilbert Blane, the physician of the fleet and long on intimate terms with Rodney, who was a constant sufferer during his last cruise, states that the admiral "thought little of his victory on the 12th of April, 1782." He would have preferred to rest his reputation upon his combinations against De Guichen, April 17, 1780, and "looked upon that opportunity of beating, with an inferior fleet, such an officer, whom he considered the best in

[27] Annual Register, 1783, p. 151.
[28] Annual Register, 1783, p. 157; Life of Admiral Keppel, vol. ii, p. 403.

the French service, as one by which, but for the disobedience of his captains, he might have gained immortal renown." [29] Few students will be inclined to question this estimate of Rodney's merit on the two occasions. Fortune, however, decreed that his glory should depend upon a battle, brilliant in itself, to which his own qualities least contributed, and denied him success when he most deserved it. The chief action of his life in which merit and success met, the destruction of Langara's fleet off Cape St. Vincent, has almost passed into oblivion; yet it called for the highest qualities of a seaman, and is not unworthy of comparison with Hawke's pursuit of Conflans. [30]

Within the two years and a half which had elapsed since Rodney was appointed to his command he had gained several important successes, and, as was remarked, had taken a French, a Spanish, and a Dutch admiral. "In that time he had added twelve line-of-battle ships, all taken from the enemy, to the British navy, and destroyed five more; and to render the whole still more singularly remarkable, the 'Ville de Paris' was said to be the only first-rate man-of-war that ever was taken and carried into port by any commander of any nation." Notwithstanding his services, the party spirit that was then so strong in England, penetrating even the army and navy, obtained his recall [31] upon the fall of Lord North's ministry, and his successor, a man unknown to fame, had already sailed when news arrived of the victory. In the fallen and discouraging state of English affairs at the time, it excited the utmost exultation, and silenced the strictures which certain parts of the admiral's previous conduct had drawn forth. The people were not in a humor to be critical, and amid the exaggerated notions that prevailed of the results achieved, no one thought of the failure to obtain greater. This impression long prevailed. As late as 1830, when Rodney's *Life* was first published, it was asserted "that the French navy had been so effectually crippled and reduced by the decisive victory of the 12th of April,

[29] Naval Chronicle, vol. xxv, p. 404.
[30] Ibid. Yet here also the gossip of the day, as reflected in the Naval Atalantis, imputed the chief credit to Young, the captain of the flag-ship. Sir Gilbert Blane stated, many years later, "When it was close upon sunset, it became a question whether the chase should be continued. After some discussion between the admiral and captain, at which I was present, the admiral being confined with the gout, it was decided to persist in the same course with the signal to engage to leeward." United Service Journal, 1830, Part II, p. 479.
[31] Rodney was a strong Tory. Almost all the other distinguished admirals of the day, notably Keppel, Howe, and Barrington, were Whigs,—a fact unfortunate for the naval power of England.

as to be no longer in a condition to contest with Great Britain the empire of the seas." This is nonsense, excusable in 1782, but not to the calm thought of after days. The favorable terms obtained were due to the financial embarrassment of France, not to her naval humiliation; and if there was exaggeration in the contention of the advocates of peace that England could not save Jamaica, it is probable that she could not have recovered by arms the other islands restored to her by the treaty.

The memory of De Grasse will always be associated with great services done to America. His name, rather than that of Rochambeau, represents the material succor which France gave to the struggling life of the young Republic, as Lafayette's recalls the moral sympathy so opportunely extended. The incidents of his life, subsequent to the great disaster which closed his active career, cannot be without interest to American readers.

After the surrender of the "Ville de Paris," De Grasse accompanied the English fleet and its prizes to Jamaica, whither Rodney repaired to refit his ships, thus appearing as a captive upon the scene of his intended conquest. On the 19th of May he left the island, still a prisoner, for England. Both by naval officers and by the English people he was treated with that flattering and benevolent attention which comes easily from the victor to the vanquished, and of which his personal valor at least was not unworthy. It is said that he did not refuse to show himself on several occasions upon the balcony of his rooms in London, to the populace shouting for the valiant Frenchman. This undignified failure to appreciate his true position naturally excited the indignation of his countrymen; the more so as he had been unsparing and excessive in denouncing the conduct of his subordinates on the unlucky 12th of April.

"He bears his misfortune," wrote Sir Gilbert Blane, "with equanimity; conscious, as he says, that he has done his duty. . . . He attributes his misfortune, not to the inferiority of his force, but to the base desertion of his officers in the other ships, to whom he made the signal to rally, and even hailed them to abide by him, but was abandoned." [32]

This was the key-note to all his utterances. Writing from the English flag-ship, the day after the battle, he "threw upon the greater part of his captains the misfortunes of the day. Some had disobeyed

[32] Rodney's Life, vol. ii, p. 242.

449

his signals; others, and notably the captains of the 'Languedoc' and 'Couronne,' that is to say his next ahead and astern, had abandoned him." [33] He did not, however, confine himself to official reports, but while a prisoner in London published several pamphlets to the same effect, which he sent broadcast over Europe. The government, naturally thinking that an officer could not thus sully the honor of his corps without good reason, resolved to search out and relentlessly punish all the guilty. The captains of the "Languedoc" and "Couronne" were imprisoned as soon as they reached France, and all papers, logs, etc., bearing upon the case were gathered together. Under all the circumstances it is not to be wondered at that on his return to France, De Grasse, to use his own words, "found no one to hold out a hand to him." [34] It was not till the beginning of 1784 that all the accused and witnesses were ready to appear before the court-martial; but the result of the trial was to clear entirely and in the most ample manner almost everyone whom he had attacked, while the faults found were considered of a character entitled to indulgence, and were awarded but slight punishment. "Nevertheless," cautiously observes a French writer, "one cannot but say, with the Court, that the capture of an admiral commanding thirty ships-of-the-line is an historical incident which causes the regret of the whole nation." [35] As to the conduct of the battle by the admiral, the Court found that the danger of the "Zélé" on the morning of the 12th was not such to justify bearing down for so long a time as was done; that the crippled ship had a breeze which was not then shared by the English, five miles away to the southward, and which carried her into Basse Terre at ten A.M.; that the engagement should not have been begun before all the ships had come into line; and finally, that the fleet should have been formed on the same tack as the English, because, by continuing to stand south, it entered the zone of calms and light airs at the north end of Dominica.[36]

De Grasse was much dissatisfied with the finding of the Court, and was indiscreet enough to write to the minister of marine, protesting against it and demanding a new trial. The minister, acknowl-

[33] Chevalier, p. 311.
[34] Kerguelen: Guerre Maritime de 1778. Letter of De Grasse to Kerguelen, p. 263.
[35] Troude: Batailles Navales. It is interesting to note in this connection that one of the ships near the French admiral, when he surrendered, was the "Pluton," which, though the extreme rear ship, had nevertheless thus reached a position worthy of the high reputation of her captain, d'Albert de Rions.
[36] Troude, vol. ii, p. 147.

edging his protest, replied in the name of the king. After commenting upon the pamphlets that had been so widely issued, and the entire contradiction of their statements by the testimony before the Court, he concluded with these weighty words:—

"The loss of the battle cannot be attributed to the fault of private officers.[37] It results, from the findings, that you have allowed yourself to injure, by ill-founded accusations, the reputation of several officers, in order to clear yourself in public opinion of an unhappy result, the excuse for which you might perhaps have found in the inferiority of your force, in the uncertain fortune of war, and in circumstances over which you had no control. His Majesty is willing to believe that you did what you could to prevent the misfortunes of the day; but he cannot be equally indulgent to your unjust imputations upon those officers of his navy who have been cleared of the charges against them. His Majesty, dissatisfied with your conduct in this respect, forbids you to present yourself before him. I transmit his orders with regret, and add my own advice to retire, under the circumstances, to your province."

De Grasse died in January, 1788. His fortunate opponent, rewarded with peerage and pension, lived until 1792. Hood was also created a peer, and commanded with distinction in the early part of the wars of the French Revolution, winning the enthusiastic admiration of Nelson, who served under him; but a sharp difference with the admiralty caused him to be retired before achieving any brilliant addition to his reputation. He died in 1816, at the great age of ninety-two.

[37] That is, commanders of single ships.

14

Critical Discussion of the Maritime War of 1778

The war of 1778, between Great Britain and the House of Bourbon, which is so inextricably associated with the American Revolution, stands by itself in one respect. It was purely a maritime war. Not only did the allied kingdoms carefully refrain from continental entanglements, which England in accordance with her former policy strove to excite, but there was between the two contestants an approach to equality on the sea which had not been realized since the days of Tourville. The points in dispute, the objects for which the war was undertaken or at which it aimed, were for the most part remote from Europe; and none of them was on the continent with the single exception of Gibraltar, the strife over which, being at the extreme point of a rugged and difficult salient, and separated from neutral nations by the whole of France and Spain, never threatened to drag in other parties than those immediately interested.

No such conditions existed in any war between the accession of Louis XIV. and the downfall of Napoleon. There was a period during the reign of the former in which the French navy was superior in number and equipment to the English and Dutch; but the policy and ambition of the sovereign was always directed to continental extension, and his naval power, resting on inadequate foundations, was ephemeral. During the first three-quarters of the eighteenth century there was practically no check to the sea power of England; great as were its effects upon the issues of the day, the absence of a capable rival made its operations barren of military lessons. In the later wars of the French Republic and Empire, the apparent equality in numbers of ships and weight of batteries was illusive, owing to the demoralization of the French officers and seamen by causes upon which it is not necessary here to enlarge. After some years of courageous but impotent effort, the tremendous disaster of Trafalgar proclaimed to the world the professional inefficiency of the French and Spanish navies, already detected by the keen eyes of Nelson and his brother officers, and upon which rested the contemptuous confidence that characterized his attitude, and to some extent his tactics, toward them. Thenceforward the emperor "turned his eyes from the only field of battle where fortune had been unfaithful to him, and deciding to pursue England elsewhere than upon the seas, undertook to restore his navy, but without reserving to it any share in a strife become more than ever furious. . . . Up to the last day of the Empire he refused to offer to this restored navy, full of ardor and confidence, the opportunity to measure itself with the enemy." [1] Great Britain resumed her old position as unquestioned mistress of the seas.

The student of naval war will therefore expect to find a particular interest in the plans and methods of the parties to this great contest, and especially where they concern the general conduct of the whole war, or of certain large and clearly defined portions of it; in the strategic purpose which gave, or should have given, continuity to their actions from first to last, and in the strategic movements which affected for good or ill the fortunes of the more limited periods, which may be called naval campaigns. For while it cannot be conceded that the particular battles are, even at this day, wholly devoid of tactical instruction, which it has been one of the aims of the preceding pages to elicit, it is undoubtedly true that, like all the tactical systems of history, they have had their day, and their present usefulness to the student is rather in the mental training, in the forming of correct tactical habits of thought, than in supplying models for close imitation. On the other hand, the movements which precede and prepare for great battles, or which, by their skilful and energetic combinations, attain great ends without the actual contact of arms, depend upon factors more permanent than the weapons of the age, and therefore furnish principles of more enduring value.

[1] Jurien de la Gravière: Guerres Maritimes, vol. ii, p. 255.

In a war undertaken for any object, even if that object be the possession of a particular territory or position, an attack directly upon the place coveted may not be, from the military point of view, the best means of obtaining it. The end upon which the military operations are directed may therefore be other than the object which the belligerent government wishes to obtain, and it has received a name of its own,—the objective. In the critical consideration of any war it is necessary, first, to put clearly before the student's eye the objects desired by each belligerent; then, to consider whether the objective chosen is the most likely, in case of success, to compass those objects; and finally, to study the merits or faults of the various movements by which the objective is approached. The minuteness with which such an examination is conducted will depend upon the extent of the work which the inquirer proposes to himself; but it will generally conduce to clearness if an outline, giving only the main features unencumbered by detail, should precede a more exhaustive discussion. When such principal lines are thoroughly grasped, details are easily referred to them, and fall into place. The effort here will be confined to presenting such an outline, as being alone fitted to the scope of this work.

The principal parties to the War of 1778 were, on the one hand, Great Britain; on the other, the House of Bourbon, controlling the two great kingdoms of France and Spain. The American colonies, being already engaged in an unequal struggle with the mother-country, gladly welcomed an event so important to them; while in 1780 Holland was deliberately forced by England into a war from which she had nothing to gain and all to lose. The object of the Americans was perfectly simple,—to rid their country out of the hands of the English. Their poverty and their lack of military sea power, with the exception of a few cruisers that preyed upon the enemy's commerce, necessarily confined their efforts to land warfare, which constituted indeed a powerful diversion in favor of the allies and an exhausting drain upon the resources of Great Britain, but which it was in the power of the latter to stop at once by abandoning the contest. Holland, on the other hand, being safe from invasion by land, showed little desire for anything more than to escape with as little external loss as possible, through the assistance of the allied navies. The object of these two minor parties may therefore be said to have been the cessation of the war; whereas the principals hoped from its continuance certain changed conditions, which constituted their objects.

With Great Britain also the object of the war was very simple. Having been led into a lamentable altercation with her most promising colonies, the quarrel had gone on step by step till she was threatened with their loss. To maintain forcible control when willing adhesion had departed, she had taken up arms against them, and her object in so doing was to prevent a break in those foreign possessions with which, in the eyes of that generation, her greatness was indissolubly connected. The appearance of France and Spain as active supporters of the colonists' cause made no change in England's objects, whatever change of objective her military plans may, or should, have undergone. The danger of losing the continental colonies was vastly increased by these accessions to the ranks of her enemies, which brought with them also a threat of loss, soon to be realized in part, of other valuable foreign possessions. England, in short, as regards the objects of the war, was strictly on the defensive; she feared losing much, and at best only hoped to keep what she had. By forcing Holland into war, however, she obtained a military advantage; for, without increasing the strength of her opponents, several important but ill-defended military and commercial positions were thereby laid open to her arms.

The views and objects of France and Spain were more complex. The moral incentives of hereditary enmity and desire of revenge for the recent past doubtless weighed strongly, as in France did also the sympathy of the *salons* and philosophers with the colonists' struggle for freedom; but powerfully as sentimental considerations affect the action of nations, only the tangible means by which it is expected to gratify them admit of statement and measurement. France might wish to regain her North American possessions; but the then living generation of colonists had too keen personal recollection of the old contests to acquiesce in any such wishes as to Canada. The strong inherited distrust of the French, which characterized the Americans of the revolutionary era, has been too much overlooked in the glow of gratitude which followed the effectual sympathy and assistance then given; but it was understood at the time, and France felt, that to renew those pretensions might promote, between people of the same race only recently alienated, a reconciliation by just concessions, which a strong and high-minded party of Englishmen had never ceased to advocate. She therefore did not avow, perhaps did not entertain, this object. On the contrary, she formally renounced all claim to any part of the continent which was then, or had recently been, under the power of the British crown, but stipulated for freedom of action in conquering and retaining any of the West India Islands, while all the other colonies of Great Britain were, of course, open to her attack. The principal objects at which France aimed were therefore the English West Indies and that control of India which had passed into English hands, and also to secure in due time the independence of the United States, after they had wrought a sufficient diversion in her favor. With the policy of exclusive trade which characterized that generation, the loss of these important possessions was expected to lessen that commercial greatness upon which the prosperity of England depended,—to weaken her and to strengthen France. In fact, the strife which should be greater may be said to have been the animating motive of France; all objects were summed up in the one supreme end to which they contributed,—maritime and political superiority over England.

Preponderance over England, in combination with France, was also the aim of the equally humbled but less vigorous kingdom of Spain; but there was a definiteness in the injuries suffered and the objects specially sought by her which is less easily found in the broader views of her ally. Although no Spaniard then living could remember the Spanish flag flying over Minorca, Gibraltar, or Jamaica, the lapse of time had not reconciled the proud and tenacious nation to their loss; nor was there on the part of the Americans the same traditional objection to the renewal of Spanish sovereignty over the two Floridas that was felt with reference to Canada.

Such, then, were the objects sought by the two nations, whose interposition changed the whole character of the American Revolutionary War. It is needless to say that they did not all appear among the causes, or pretexts, avowed for engaging in hostility; but sagacious English opinion of the day rightly noted, as embodying in a few words the real ground of action of the united Bourbon Courts, the following phrase in the French manifesto: "To avenge their respective injuries, and to put an end to that tyrannical empire which England has usurped, and claims to maintain upon the ocean." In short, as regards the *objects* of the war the allies were on the offensive, as England was thrown upon the defensive.

The tyrannical empire which England was thus accused, and not unjustly, of exercising over the seas, rested upon her great sea power, actual or latent; upon her commerce and armed shipping, her commercial establishments, colonies, and naval stations in all parts of the world. Up to this time her scattered colonies had been bound to her by ties of affectionate sentiment, and by the still stronger motive of self-interest through the close commercial connection with the mother-country and the protection afforded by the constant presence of her superior navy. Now a break was made in the girdle of strong ports upon which her naval power was based, by the revolt of the continental colonies; while the numerous trade interests between them and the West Indies, which were injured by the consequent hostilities, tended to divide the sympathies of the islands also. The struggle was not only for political possession and commercial use. It involved a military question of the first importance,—whether a chain of naval stations covering one of the shores of the Atlantic, linking Canada and Halifax with the West Indies, and backed by a thriving seafaring population, should remain in the hands of a nation which had so far used its unprecedented sea power with consistent, resolute aggressiveness, and with almost unbroken success.

While Great Britain was thus embarrassed by the difficulty of maintaining her hold upon her naval bases, which were the defensive element of her naval strength, her offensive naval power, her fleet, was threatened by the growth of the armed shipping of France and Spain, which now confronted her upon the field which she had claimed as her own, with an organized military force of equal or superior material strength. The moment was therefore favorable for attacking the great Power whose wealth, reaped from the sea, had been a decisive factor in the European wars of the past century. The next question was the selection of the points of attack—of the principal *objectives* upon which the main effort of the assailants should be steadily directed, and of the secondary objectives by which the defence should be distracted and its strength dissipated.

One of the wisest French statesmen of that day, Turgot, held that it was to the interest of France that the colonies should not achieve their independence. If subdued by exhaustion, their strength was lost to England; if reduced by a military tenure of controlling points, but not exhausted, the necessity of constant repression would be a continual weakness to the mother-country. Though this opinion did not prevail in the councils of the French government, which wished the ultimate independence of America, it contained elements of truth which effectually moulded the policy of the war. If benefit to the United States, by effecting their deliverance, were the principal object, the continent became the natural scene, and its decisive military points the chief objectives, of operations; but as the first object of France was not to benefit America, but to injure England, sound military judgment dictated that the continental strife, so far from being helped to a conclusion, should be kept in vigorous life. It was a diversion ready made to the hand of France and exhausting to Great Britain, requiring only so much support as would sustain a resistance to which the insurgents were bound by the most desperate alternatives. The territory of the thirteen colonies therefore should not be the principal objective of France; much less that of Spain.

The commercial value of the English West Indies made them tempting objects to the French, who adapted themselves with peculiar readiness to the social conditions of that region, in which their colonial possessions were already extensive. Besides the two finest of the Lesser Antilles, Guadeloupe and Martinique, which she still retains, France then held Sta. Lucia and the western half of Hayti. She might well hope by successful war to add most of the English Antilles, and thus to round off a truly imperial tropical dependency; while, though debarred from Jamaica by the susceptibilities of Spain, it might be possible to win back that magnificent island for an allied and weaker nation. But however desirable as possessions, and therefore as objects, the smaller Antilles might be, their military tenure depended too entirely upon control of the sea for them to be in themselves proper objectives. The French government, therefore, forbade its naval commanders to occupy such as they might seize. They were to make the garrisons prisoners, destroy the defences, and so retire. In the excellent military port of Fort Royal, Martinique, in Cap Français, and in the strong allied harbor of Havana, a fleet of adequate size found good, secure, and well-distributed bases; while the early and serious loss of Sta. Lucia must be attributed to the mismanagement of the French fleet and the professional ability of the English admiral. On shore, in the West Indies, the rival powers therefore found themselves about equally provided with the necessary points of support; mere occupation of others could not add to their military strength, thenceforth dependent upon the numbers and quality of the fleets. To extend occupation further with safety, the first need was to obtain maritime supremacy, not only locally, but over the general field of war. Otherwise occupation was precarious, unless enforced by a body of troops so large as to entail expense beyond the worth of the object. The key of the situation in the West Indies being thus in the fleets, these became the true objectives of the military effort; and all the more so because the real *military* usefulness of the West Indian ports in this war was as an intermediate base, between Europe and the American continent, to which the fleets retired when the armies went into winter quarters. No sound strategic operation on shore was undertaken in the West Indies except the seizure of Sta. Lucia by the English, and the abortive plan against Jamaica in 1782; nor was any serious attempt against a military port, as Barbadoes or Fort Royal, possible, until naval preponderance was assured either by battle or by happy concentration of force. The key of the situation, it must be repeated, was in the fleet.

The influence of naval power, of an armed fleet, upon the war on the American continent has also been indicated in the opinions of Washington and Sir Henry Clinton; while the situation in the East Indies, regarded as a field by itself, has been so largely discussed under the head of Suffren's campaign, that it needs here only to repeat that everything there depended upon control of the sea by a superior naval force. The capture of Trincomalee, essential as it was to the French squadron which had no other base, was, like that of Sta. Lucia, a surprise, and could only have been effected by the defeat, or, as happened, by the absence of the enemy's fleet. In North America and India sound military policy pointed out, as the true objective, the enemy's fleet, upon which also depended the communications with the mother-countries. There remains Europe, which it is scarcely profitable to examine at length as a separate field of action, because its relations to the universal war are so much more important. It may simply be pointed out that the only two points in Europe whose political transfer was an object of the war were Gibraltar and Minorca; the former of which was throughout, by the urgency of Spain, made a principal objective of the allies. The tenure of both these depended, obviously, upon control of the sea.

In a sea war, as in all others, two things are from the first essential,—a suitable base upon the frontier, in this case the seaboard, from which the operations start, and an organized military force, in this case a fleet, of size and quality adequate to the proposed operations. If the war, as in the present instance, extends to distant parts of the globe, there will be needed in each of those distant regions secure ports for the shipping, to serve as secondary, or contingent, bases of the local war. Between these secondary and the principal, or home, bases there must be reasonably secure communication, which will depend upon military control of the intervening sea. This control must be exercised by the navy, which will enforce it either by clearing the sea in all directions of hostile cruisers, thus allowing the ships of its own nation to pass with reasonable security, or by accompanying in force (convoying) each train of supply-ships necessary for the support of the distant operations. The former method aims at a widely diffused effort of the national power, the other at a concentration of it upon that part of the sea where the convoy is at a given moment. Whichever be adopted, the communications will doubtless be strengthened by the military holding of good harbors, properly spaced yet not too numerous, along the routes,—as, for instance, the Cape of Good Hope and the Mauritius. Stations of this kind have always been necessary, but are doubly so now, as fuel needs renewing more frequently than did the provisions and supplies in former days. These combinations of strong points at home and abroad, and the condition of the communications between them, may be called the strategic features of the general military situation, by which, and by the relative strength of the opposing fleets, the nature of the operations must be determined. In each of the three divisions of the field, Europe, America, and India, under which for sake of clearness the narrative has been given, the control of the sea has been insisted upon as the determining factor, and the hostile fleet therefore indicated as the true objective. Let the foregoing considerations now be applied to the whole field of war, and see how far the same conclusion holds good of it, and if so, what should have been the nature of the operations on either side.

In Europe the home base of Great Britain was on the English Channel, with the two principal arsenals of Plymouth and Portsmouth. The base of the allied powers was on the Atlantic, the principal military ports being Brest, Ferrol, and Cadiz. Behind these, within the Mediterranean, were the dock-yards of Toulon and Cartagena, over against which stood the English station Port Mahon, in Minorca. The latter, however, may be left wholly out of account, being confined to a defensive part during the war, as the British fleet was not able to spare any squadron to the Mediterranean. Gibraltar, on the contrary, by its position, effectually watched over detachments or reinforcements from within the Straits, provided it were utilized as the station of a body of ships adequate to the duty. This was not done; the British European fleet being kept tied to the Channel, that is, to home defence, and making infrequent visits to the Rock to convoy supplies essential to the endurance of the garrison. There was, however, a difference in the parts played by Port Mahon and Gibraltar. The former, being at the time wholly unimportant, received no attention from the allies until late in the war, when it fell after a six months' siege; whereas the latter, being considered of the first importance, absorbed from the beginning a very large part of the allied attack, and so made a valuable diversion in favor of Great Britain. To this view of the principal features of the natural strategic situation in Europe may properly be added the remark, that such aid as Holland might be inclined to send to the allied fleets had a very insecure line of communication, being forced to pass along the English base on the Channel. Such aid in fact was never given.

In North America the local bases of the war at its outbreak were New York, Narragansett Bay, and Boston. The two former were then held by the English, and were the most important stations on the continent, from their position, susceptibility of defence, and resources. Boston had passed into the hands of the Americans, and was therefore at the service of the allies. From the direction actually given to the war, by diverting the active English operations to the Southern States in 1779, Boston was thrown outside the principal theatre of operations, and became from its position militarily unimportant; but had the plan been adopted of isolating New England by holding the line of the Hudson and Lake Champlain, and concentrating military effort to the eastward, it will be seen that these three ports would all have been of decisive importance to the issue.

South of New York, the Delaware and Chesapeake Bays undoubtedly offered tempting fields for maritime enterprise; but the width of the entrances, the want of suitable and easily defended points for naval stations near the sea, the wide dispersal of the land forces entailed by an attempt to hold so many points, and the sickliness of the locality during a great part of the year, should have excepted them from a principal part in the plan of the first campaigns. It is not necessary to include them among the local bases of the war. To the extreme south the English were drawn by the *ignis fatuus* of expected support among the people. They failed to consider that even if a majority there preferred quiet to freedom, that very quality would prevent them from rising against the revolutionary government by which, on the English theory, they were oppressed; yet upon such a rising the whole success of this distant and in its end most unfortunate enterprise was staked. The local base of this war apart was Charleston, which passed into the hands of the British in May, 1780, eighteen months after the first expedition had landed in Georgia.

The principal local bases of the war in the West Indies are already known through the previous narrative. They were for the English, Barbadoes, Sta. Lucia, and to a less degree Antigua. A thousand miles to leeward was the large island of Jamaica, with a dock-yard of great natural capabilities at Kingston. The allies held, in the first order of importance, Fort Royal in Martinique, and Havana; in the second order, Guadeloupe and Cap Français. A controlling feature of the strategic situation in that day, and one which will not be wholly without weight in our own, was the trade-wind, with its accompanying current. A passage to windward against these obstacles was a long and serious undertaking even for single ships, much more for larger bodies. It followed that fleets would go to the western islands only reluctantly, or when assured that the enemy had taken the same direction, as when Rodney went to Jamaica after the Battle of the Saints, knowing the French fleet to have gone to Cap Français. This condition of the wind made the windward, or eastern, islands points on the natural lines of communication between Europe and America, as well as local bases of the naval war, and tied the fleets to them. Hence also it followed that between the two scenes of operations, between the continent and the Lesser Antilles, was interposed a wide central region into which the larger operations of war could not safely be carried except by a belligerent possessed of great naval superiority, or unless a decisive advantage had been gained upon one flank. In 1762, when England held all the Windward Islands, with undisputed superiority at sea, she safely attacked and subdued Havana; but in the years 1779-1782 the French sea power in America and the French tenure of the Windward Islands practically balanced her own, leaving the Spaniards at Havana free to prosecute their designs against Pensacola and the Bahamas, in the central region mentioned.[3]

Posts like Martinique and Sta. Lucia had therefore for the present war great strategic advantage over Jamaica, Havana, or others to leeward. They commanded the latter in virtue of their position, by which the passage westward could be made so much more quickly than the return; while the decisive points of the continental struggle were practically little farther from the one than from the other. This advantage was shared equally by most of those known as the Lesser Antilles; but the small island of Barbadoes, being well to windward of all, possessed peculiar advantages, not only for offensive action, but because it was defended by the difficulty with which a large fleet could approach it, even from so near a port as Fort Royal. It will be remembered that the expedition which finally sat down before St. Kitt's had been intended for Barbadoes, but could not reach it through the violence of the trade-wind. Thus Barbadoes, under the conditions of the time, was peculiarly fitted to be the local base and depot of the English war, as well as a wayside port of refuge on the line of communications to Jamaica, Florida, and even to North America; while Sta. Lucia, a hundred miles to leeward, was held in force as an advanced post for the fleet, watching closely the enemy at Fort Royal.

In India the political conditions of the peninsula necessarily indicated the eastern, or Coromandel, coast as the scene of operations. Trincomalee, in the adjacent island of Ceylon, though unhealthy,

---

[3] It may be said here in passing, that the key to the English possessions in what was then called West Florida was at Pensacola and Mobile, which depended upon Jamaica for support; the conditions of the country, of navigation, and of the general continental war forbidding assistance from the Atlantic. The English force, military and naval, at Jamaica was only adequate to the defence of the island and of trade, and could not afford sufficient relief to Florida. The capture of the latter and of the Bahamas was effected with little difficulty by overwhelming Spanish forces, as many as fifteen ships-of-the-line and seven thousand troops having been employed against Pensacola. These events will receive no other mention. Their only bearing upon the general war was the diversion of this imposing force from joint operations with the French, Spain here, as at Gibraltar, pursuing her own aims instead of concentrating upon the common enemy,—a policy as shortsighted as it was selfish.

offered an excellent and defensible harbor, and thus acquired first-rate strategic importance, all the other anchorages on the coast being mere open roadsteads. From this circumstance the trade-winds, or monsoons, in this region also had strategic bearing. From the autumnal to the spring equinox the wind blows regularly from the northeast, at times with much violence, throwing a heavy surf upon the beach and making landing difficult; but during the summer months the prevailing wind is southwest, giving comparatively smooth seas and good weather. The "change of the monsoon," in September and October, is often marked by violent hurricanes. Active operations, or even remaining on the coast, were therefore unadvisable from this time until the close of the northeast monsoon. The question of a port to which to retire during this season was pressing. Trincomalee was the only one, and its unique strategic value was heightened by being to windward, during the fine season, of the principal scene of war. The English harbor of Bombay on the west coast was too distant to be considered a local base, and rather falls, like the French islands, Mauritius and Bourbon, under the head of stations on the line of communications with the mother-country.

Such were the principal points of support, or bases, of the belligerent nations, at home and abroad. Of those abroad it must be said, speaking generally, that they were deficient in resources,—an important element of strategic value. Naval and military stores and equipments and, to a great extent, provisions for sea use, had to be sent them from the mother-countries. Boston, surrounded by a thriving, friendly population, was perhaps an exception to this statement, as was also Havana, at that time an important naval arsenal, where much ship-building was done; but these were distant from the principal theatres of war. Upon New York and Narragansett Bay the Americans pressed too closely for the resources of the neighboring country to be largely available, while the distant ports of the East and West Indies depended wholly upon home. Hence the strategic question of communications assumed additional importance. To intercept a large convoy of supply-ships was an operation only secondary to the destruction of a body of ships-of-war; while to protect such by main strength, or by evading the enemy's search, taxed the skill of the governments and naval commanders in distributing the ships-of-war and squadrons at their disposal, among the many objects which demanded attention. The address of Kempenfeldt and the bad management of Guichen in the North Atlantic, seconded by a heavy gale of wind, seriously embarrassed De Grasse in the West Indies. Similar injury, by cutting off small convoys in the Atlantic, was done to Suffren in the Indian seas; while the latter at once made good part of these losses, and worried his opponents by the success of his cruisers preying on the English supply-ships.

Thus the navies, by which alone these vital streams could be secured or endangered, bore the same relation to the maintenance of the general war that has already been observed of the separate parts. They were the links that bound the whole together, and were therefore indicated as the proper objective of both belligerents.

The distance from Europe to America was not such as to make intermediate ports of supply absolutely necessary; while if difficulty did arise from an unforeseen cause, it was always possible, barring meeting an enemy, either to return to Europe or to make a friendly port in the West Indies. The case was different with the long voyage to India by the Cape of Good Hope. Bickerton, leaving England with a convoy in February, was thought to have done well in reaching Bombay the following September; while the ardent Suffren, sailing in March, took an equal time to reach Mauritius, whence the passage to Madras consumed two months more. A voyage of such duration could rarely be made without a stop for water, for fresh provisions, often for such refitting as called for the quiet of a harbor, even when the stores on board furnished the necessary material. A perfect line of communications required, as has been said, several such harbors, properly spaced, adequately defended, and with abundant supplies, such as England in the present day holds on some of her main commercial routes, acquisitions of her past wars. In the war of 1778 none of the belligerents had such ports on this route, until, by the accession of Holland, the Cape of Good Hope was put at the disposal of the French and suitably strengthened by Suffren. With this and the Mauritius on the way, and Trincomalee at the far end of the road, the communications of the allies with France were reasonably guarded. England, though then holding St. Helena, depended, for the refreshment and refitting of her India-bound squadrons and convoys in the Atlantic, upon the benevolent neutrality of Portugal, extended in the islands of Madeira and Cape Verde and in the Brazilian ports. This neutrality was indeed a frail reliance for defence, as was shown by the encounter between Johnstone and Suffren at the Cape Verde; but there being several possible stopping-places, and the enemy unable to know which, if any, would be used, this ignorance itself conferred no small security, if the naval commander did not trust it to the neglect of proper disposition of his own force, as did Johnstone at Porto Praya. Indeed, with the delay and uncertainty which then characterized the transmission of intelligence from one point to another, doubt where to find the enemy was a greater bar to offensive enterprises than the often slight defences of a colonial port.

This combination of useful harbors and the conditions of the communications between them constitute, as has been said, the main strategic outlines of the situation. The navy, as the organized force linking the whole together, has been indicated as the principal objective of military effort. The method employed to reach the objective, the conduct of the war, is still to be considered.[4]

Before doing this, a condition peculiar to the sea, and affecting the following discussion, must be briefly mentioned; that is, the difficulty of obtaining information. Armies pass through countries more or less inhabited by a stationary population, and they leave behind them traces of their march. Fleets move through a desert over which wanderers flit, but where they do not remain; and as the waters close behind them, an occasional waif from the decks may indicate their passage, but tells nothing of their course. The sail spoken by the pursuer may know nothing of the pursued, which yet passed the point of parley but a few days or hours before. Of late, careful study of the winds and currents of the ocean has laid down certain advantageous routes, which will be habitually followed by a careful seaman, and afford some presumption as to his movements; but in 1778 the data for such precision were not collected, and even had they been, the quickest route must often have been abandoned for one of the many possible ones, in order to elude pursuit or lying-in-wait. In such a game of hide-and-seek the advantage is with the sought, and the great importance of watching the outlets of an enemy's country, of stopping the chase before it has got away into the silent desert, is at once evident. If for any reason such a watch there is impossible, the next best thing is, not at-

[4] In other words, having considered the objects for which the belligerents were at war and the proper objectives upon which their military efforts should have been directed to compass the objects, the discussion now considers how the military forces should have been handled; by what means and at what point the objective, being mobile, should have been assailed.

tempting to watch routes which may not be taken, to get first to the enemy's destination and await him there; but this implies a knowledge of his intentions which may not always be obtainable. The action of Suffren, when pitted against Johnstone, was throughout strategically sound, both in his attack at Porto Praya and in the haste with which he made for their common destination; while the two failures of Rodney to intercept the convoys to Martinique in 1780 and 1782, though informed that they were coming, show the difficulty which attended lying-in-wait even when the point of arrival was known.

Of any maritime expedition two points only are fixed,—the point of departure and that of arrival. The latter may be unknown to the enemy; but up to the time of sailing, the presence of a certain force in a port, and the indications of a purpose soon to move, may be assumed as known. It may be of moment to either belligerent to intercept such a movement; but it is more especially and universally necessary to the defence, because, of the many points at which he is open to attack, it may be impossible for him to know which is threatened; whereas the offence proceeds with full knowledge direct to his aim, if he can deceive his opponent. The importance of blocking such an expedition becomes yet more evident should it at any time be divided between two or more ports,—a condition which may easily arise when the facilities of a single dock-yard are insufficient to fit out so many ships in the time allowed, or when, as in the present war, allied powers furnish separate contingents. To prevent the junction of these contingents is a matter of prime necessity, and nowhere can this be done so certainly as off the ports whence one or both is to sail. The defence, from its very name, is presumably the less strong, and is therefore the more bound to take advantage of such a source of weakness as the division of the enemy's force. Rodney in 1782 at Sta. Lucia, watching the French contingent at Martinique to prevent its union with the Spaniards at Cap Français, is an instance of correct strategic position; and had the islands been so placed as to put him between the French and their destination, instead of in their rear, nothing better could have been devised. As it was, he did the best thing possible under the circumstances.

The defence, being the weaker, cannot attempt to block *all* the ports where divisions of the enemy lie, without defeating his aim by being in inferior force before each. This would be to neglect the fundamental principles of war. If he correctly decide not to do this, but to collect a superior force before one or two points, it becomes necessary to decide which shall be thus guarded and which neglected, —a question involving the whole policy of the war after a full understanding of the main conditions, military, moral, and economic, in every quarter.

The defensive was necessarily accepted by England in 1778. It had been a maxim with the best English naval authorities of the preceding era, with Hawke and his contemporaries, that the British navy should be kept equal in numbers to the combined fleets of the Bourbon kingdoms,—a condition which, with the better quality of the *personnel* and the larger maritime population upon which it could draw, would have given a real superiority of force. This precaution, however, had not been observed during recent years. It is of no consequence to this discussion whether the failure was due to the inefficiency of the ministry, as was charged by their opponents, or to the misplaced economy often practised by representative governments in time of peace. The fact remains that, notwithstanding the notorious probability of France and Spain joining in the war, the English navy was inferior in number to that of the allies. In what have been called the strategic features of the situation, the home bases and the secondary bases abroad, the advantage upon the whole lay with her. Her positions, if not stronger in themselves, were at least better situated, geographically, for strategic effect; but in the second essential for war, the organized military force, or fleet, adequate to offensive operations, she had been allowed to become inferior. It only remained, therefore, to use this inferior force with such science and vigor as would frustrate the designs of the enemy, by getting first to sea, taking positions skilfully, anticipating their combinations by greater quickness of movement, harassing their communications with their objectives, and meeting the principal divisions of the enemy with superior forces.

It is sufficiently clear that the maintenance of this war, everywhere except on the American continent, depended upon the mother-countries in Europe and upon open communication with them. The ultimate crushing of the Americans, too, not by direct military effort but by exhaustion, was probable, if England were left unmolested to strangle their commerce and industries with her overwhelming naval strength. This strength she could put forth against them, if relieved from the pressure of the allied navies; and relief would be obtained if she could gain over them a decided preponderance, not merely material but moral, such as she had twenty years later. In that case the allied courts, whose financial weakness was well known, must retire from a contest in which their main purpose of reducing England to an inferior position was already defeated. Such preponderance, however, could only be had by fighting; by showing that, despite inferiority in numbers, the skill of her seamen and the resources of her wealth enabled her government, by a wise use of these powers, to be actually superior at the decisive points of the war. It could never be had by distributing the ships-of-the-line all over the world, exposing them to be beaten in detail while endeavoring to protect all the exposed points of the scattered empire.

The key of the situation was in Europe, and in Europe in the hostile dock-yards. If England were unable, as she proved to be, to raise up a continental war against France, then her one hope was to find and strike down the enemy's navy. Nowhere was it so certainly to be found as in its home ports; nowhere so easily met as immediately after leaving them. This dictated her policy in the Napoleonic wars, when the moral superiority of her navy was so established that she dared to oppose inferior forces to the combined dangers of the sea and of the more numerous and well-equipped ships lying quietly at anchor inside. By facing this double risk she obtained the double advantage of keeping the enemy under her eyes, and of sapping his efficiency by the easy life of port, while her own officers and seamen were hardened by the rigorous cruising into a perfect readiness for every call upon their energies. "We have no reason," proclaimed Admiral Villeneuve in 1805, echoing the words of the emperor, "to fear the sight of an English squadron. Their seventy-fours have not five hundred men on board; they are worn out by a two years' cruise." [5] A month later he wrote: "The Toulon squadron appeared very fine in the harbor, the crews well clothed and drilling well; but as soon as a storm came, all was changed. They were not drilled in storms." [6] "The emperor," said Nelson, "now finds, if emperors hear truth, that his fleet suffers more in a night than ours in one year. . . . These gentlemen are not used

[5] Orders of Admiral Villeneuve to the captains of his fleet, Dec. 20, 1804
[6] Letter of Villeneuve, January, 1805.

to the hurricanes, which we have braved for twenty-one months without losing mast or yard." [7] It must be admitted, however, that the strain was tremendous both on men and ships, and that many English officers found in the wear and tear an argument against keeping their fleets at sea off the enemy's coast. "Every one of the blasts we endure," wrote Collingwood, "lessens the security of the country. The last cruise disabled five large ships and two more lately; several of them must be docked." "I have hardly known what a night of rest is these two months," wrote he again, "this incessant cruising seems to me beyond the powers of human nature. Calder is worn to a shadow, quite broken down, and I am told Graves is not much better." [8] The high professional opinion of Lord Howe was also adverse to the practice.

Besides the exhaustion of men and ships, it must also be admitted that no blockade could be relied on certainly to check the exit of an enemy's fleet. Villeneuve escaped from Toulon, Missiessy from Rochefort. "I am here watching the French squadron in Rochefort," wrote Collingwood, "but feel that it is not practicable to prevent their sailing; and yet, if they should get by me, I should be exceedingly mortified. . . . The only thing that can prevent their sailing is the apprehension that they may get among us, as they cannot know exactly where we are."

Nevertheless, the strain then was endured. The English fleets girdled the shores of France and Spain; losses were made good; ships were repaired; as one officer fell, or was worn out at his post, another took his place. The strict guard over Brest broke up the emperor's combinations; the watchfulness of Nelson, despite an unusual concurrence of difficulties, followed the Toulon fleet, from the moment of its starting, across the Atlantic and back to the shores of Europe. It was long before they came to blows, before strategy stepped aside and tactics completed the work at Trafalgar; but step by step and point by point the rugged but disciplined seamen, the rusty and battered but well-handled ships, blocked each move of their unpractised opponents. Disposed in force before each arsenal of the enemy, and linked together by chains of smaller vessels, they might fail now and again to check a raid, but they effectually stopped all grand combinations of the enemy's squadrons.

[7] Letters and Despatches of Lord Nelson.
[8] Life and Letters of Lord Collingwood.

The ships of 1805 were essentially the same as those of 1780. There had doubtless been progress and improvement; but the changes were in degree, not in kind. Not only so, but the fleets of twenty years earlier, under Hawke and his fellows, had dared the winters of the Bay of Biscay. "There is not in Hawke's correspondence," says his biographer, "the slightest indication that he himself doubted for a moment that it was not only possible, but his duty, to keep the sea, even through the storms of winter, and that he should soon be able to 'make downright work of it.' " [9] If it be urged that the condition of the French navy was better, the character and training of its officers higher, than in the days of Hawke and Nelson, the fact must be admitted; nevertheless, the admiralty could not long have been ignorant that the number of such officers was still so deficient as seriously to affect the quality of the deck service, and the lack of seamen so great as to necessitate filling up the complements with soldiers. As for the *personnel* of the Spanish navy, there is no reason to believe it better than fifteen years later, when Nelson, speaking of Spain giving certain ships to France, said, "I take it for granted not manned [by Spaniards], as that would be the readiest way to lose them again."

In truth, however, it is too evident to need much arguing, that the surest way for the weaker party to neutralize the enemy's ships was to watch them in their harbors and fight them if they started. The only serious objection to doing this, in Europe, was the violence of the weather off the coasts of France and Spain, especially during the long nights of winter. This brought with it not only risk of immediate disaster, which strong, well-managed ships would rarely undergo, but a continual strain which no skill could prevent, and which therefore called for a large reserve of ships to relieve those sent in for repairs, or to refresh the crews.

The problem would be greatly simplified if the blockading fleet could find a convenient anchorage on the flank of the route the enemy must take, as Nelson in 1804 and 1805 used Maddalena Bay in Sardinia when watching the Toulon fleet,—a step to which he was further forced by the exceptionally bad condition of many of his ships. So Sir James Saumarez in 1800 even used Douarnenez Bay, on the French coast, only five miles from Brest, to anchor the in-shore squadron of the blockading force in heavy weather. The

[9] Burrows: Life of Lord Hawke.

positions at Plymouth and Torbay cannot be considered perfectly satisfactory from this point of view; not being, like Maddalena Bay, on the flank of the enemy's route, but like Sta. Lucia, rather to its rear. Nevertheless, Hawke proved that diligence and well-managed ships could overcome this disadvantage, as Rodney also afterward showed on his less tempestuous station.

In the use of the ships at its disposal, taking the war of 1778 as a whole, the English ministry kept their foreign detachments in America, and in the West and East Indies, equal to those of the enemy. At particular times, indeed, this was not so; but speaking generally of the assignment of ships, the statement is correct. In Europe, on the contrary, and in necessary consequence of the policy mentioned, the British fleet was habitually much inferior to those in the French and Spanish ports. It therefore could be used offensively only by great care, and through good fortune in meeting the enemy in detail; and even so an expensive victory, unless very decisive, entailed considerable risk from the consequent temporary disability of the ships engaged. It followed that the English home (or Channel) fleet, upon which depended also the communications with Gibraltar and the Mediterranean, was used very economically both as to battle and weather, and was confined to the defence of the home coast, or to operations against the enemy's communications.

India was so far distant that no exception can be taken to the policy there. Ships sent there went to stay, and could be neither reinforced nor recalled with a view to sudden emergencies. The field stood by itself. But Europe, North America, and the West Indies should have been looked upon as one large theatre of war, throughout which events were mutually dependent, and whose different parts stood in close relations of greater or less importance, to which due attention should have been paid.

Assuming that the navies, as the guardians of the communications, were the controlling factors in the war, and that the source, both of the navies and of those streams of supplies which are called communications, was in the mother-countries, and there centralized in the chief arsenals, two things follow: First, the main effort of the Power standing on the defensive, of Great Britain, should have been concentrated before those arsenals; and secondly, to maintain such concentration, the lines of communication abroad should not have been needlessly extended, so as to increase beyond the strictest necessity the detachments to guard them. Closely connected with the last consideration is the duty of strengthening, by fortification and otherwise, the vital points to which the communications led, so that these points should not depend in any way upon the fleet for protection, but only for supplies and reinforcements, and those at reasonable intervals. Gibraltar, for instance, quite fulfilled these conditions, being practically impregnable, and storing supplies that lasted very long.

If this reasoning be correct, the English dispositions on the American continent were very faulty. Holding Canada, with Halifax, New York, and Narragansett Bay, and with the line of the Hudson within their grip, it was in their power to isolate a large, perhaps decisive, part of the insurgent territory. New York and Narragansett Bay could have been made unassailable by a French fleet of that day, thus assuring the safety of the garrisons against attacks from the sea and minimizing the task of the navy; while the latter would find in them a secure refuge, in case an enemy's force eluded the watch of the English fleet before a European arsenal and appeared on the coast. Instead of this, these two ports were left weak, and would have fallen before a Nelson or a Farragut, while the army in New York was twice divided, first to the Chesapeake and afterward to Georgia, neither part of the separated forces being strong enough for the work before it. The control of the sea was thus used in both cases to put the enemy between the divided portions of the English army, when the latter, undivided, had not been able to force its way over the ground thus interposed. As the communication between the two parts of the army depended wholly upon the sea, the duty of the navy was increased with the increased length of the lines of communication. The necessity of protecting the seaports and the lengthened lines of communication thus combined to augment the naval detachments in America, and to weaken proportionately the naval force at the decisive points in Europe. Thus also a direct consequence of the southern expedition was the hasty abandonment of Narragansett Bay, when D'Estaing appeared on the coast in 1779, because Clinton had not force enough to defend both it and New York.[10]

[10] Of this Rodney said: "The evacuating Rhode Island was the most fatal measure that could possibly be adopted. It gave up the best and noblest harbor in America, from whence squadrons, in forty-eight hours, could blockade the three capital cities of America, namely, Boston, New York, and Philadelphia." The whole letter, private to the First Lord of the Admiralty, is worth reading. (Life of Rodney, vol. ii, p. 429.)

In the West Indies the problem before the English government was not to subdue revolted territory, but to preserve the use of a number of small, fruitful islands; to keep possession of them itself, and to maintain their trade as free as possible from the depredations of the enemy. It need not be repeated that this demanded predominance at sea over both the enemy's fleets and single cruisers,—"commerce-destroyers," as the latter are now styled. As no vigilance can confine all these to their ports, the West Indian waters must be patrolled by British frigates and lighter vessels; but it would surely be better, if possible, to keep the French fleet away altogether than to hold it in check by a British fleet on the spot, of only equal force at any time, and liable to fall, as it often did, below equality. England, being confined to the defensive, was always liable to loss when thus inferior. She actually did lose one by one, by sudden attack, most of her islands, and at different times had her fleet shut up under the batteries of a port; whereas the enemy, when he found himself inferior, was able to wait for reinforcements, knowing that he had nothing to fear while so waiting.[11]

Nor was this embarrassment confined to the West Indies. The nearness of the islands to the American continent made it always possible for the offence to combine his fleets in the two quarters before the defence could be sure of his purpose; and although such combinations were controlled in some measure by well-understood conditions of weather and the seasons, the events of 1780 and 1781 show the perplexity felt from this cause by the ablest English admiral, whose dispositions, though faulty, but reflected the uncertainties of his mind. When to this embarrassment, which is common to the defensive in all cases, is added the care of the great British trade upon which the prosperity of the empire mainly depended, it must be conceded that the task of the British admiral in the West Indies was neither light nor simple.

In Europe, the safety of England herself and of Gibraltar was gravely imperilled by the absence of these large detachments in the Western Hemisphere, to which may also be attributed the loss of Minorca. When sixty-six allied ships-of-the-line confronted the thirty-five which alone England could collect, and drove them into their harbors, there was realized that mastery of the Channel which

<hr />

[11] The loss of Sta. Lucia does not militate against this statement, being due to happy audacity and skill on the part of the English admiral, and the professional incapacity of the commander of the greatly superior French fleet.

Napoleon claimed would make him beyond all doubt master of England. For thirty days, the thirty ships which formed the French contingent had cruised in the Bay of Biscay, awaiting the arrival of the tardy Spaniards; but they were not disturbed by the English fleet. Gibraltar was more than once brought within sight of starvation, through the failure of communications with England; and its deliverance was due, not to the power of the English navy suitably disposed by its government, but to the skill of British officers and the inefficiency of the Spaniards. In the great final relief, Lord Howe's fleet numbered only thirty-four to the allied forty-nine.

Which, then, in the difficulties under which England labored, was the better course,—to allow the enemy free exit from his ports and endeavor to meet him by maintaining a sufficient naval force on each of the exposed stations, or to attempt to watch his arsenals at home, under all the difficulties of the situation, not with the vain hope of preventing every raid, or intercepting every convoy, but with the expectation of frustrating the greater combinations, and of following close at the heels of any large fleet that escaped? Such a watch must not be confounded with a blockade, a term frequently, but not quite accurately, applied to it. "I beg to inform your Lordship," wrote Nelson, "that the port of Toulon has never been blockaded by me; quite the reverse. Every opportunity has been offered the enemy to put to sea, for it is there we hope to realize the hopes and expectations of our country." "Nothing," he says again, "ever kept the French fleet in Toulon or Brest when they had a mind to come out"; and although the statement is somewhat exaggerated, it is true that the attempt to shut them up in port would have been hopeless. What Nelson expected by keeping near their ports, with enough lookout ships properly distributed, was to know when they sailed and what direction they took, intending, to use his own expression, to "follow them to the antipodes." "I am led to believe," he writes at another time, "that the Ferrol squadron of French ships will push for the Mediterranean. If it join that in Toulon, it will much outnumber us; but I shall never lose sight of them, and Pellew (commanding the English squadron off Ferrol) will soon be after them." So it happened often enough, during that prolonged war, that divisions of French ships escaped, through stress of weather, temporary absence of a blockading fleet, or misjudgment on the part of its commander; but the alarm was quickly given, some of the many frigates caught sight of them, followed to detect their probable destination, passed the word from point to point and from fleet to fleet, and soon a division of equal force was after them, "to the antipodes" if need were. As, according to the traditional use of the French navy by French governments, their expeditions went not to fight the hostile fleet, but with "ulterior objects," the angry buzz and hot pursuit that immediately followed was far from conducive to an undisturbed and methodical execution of the programme laid down, even by a single division; while to great combinations, dependent upon uniting the divisions from different ports, they were absolutely fatal. The adventurous cruise of Bruix, leaving Brest with twenty-five ships-of-the-line in 1799, the rapidity with which the news spread, the stirring action and individual mistakes of the English, the frustration of the French projects[12] and the closeness of the pursuit,[13] the escape of Missiessy from Rochefort in 1805, of the divisions of Willaumez and Leissegues from Brest in 1806,—all these may be named, along with the great Trafalgar campaign, as affording interesting studies of a naval strategy following the lines here suggested; while the campaign of 1798, despite its brilliant ending at the Nile, may be cited as a case where failure nearly ensued, owing to the English having no force before Toulon when the expedition sailed, and to Nelson being insufficiently provided with frigates. The nine weeks' cruise of Ganteaume in the Mediterranean, in 1808, also illustrates the difficulty of controlling a fleet which has been permitted to get out, unwatched by a strong force, even in such narrow waters.

No parallel instances can be cited from the war of 1778, although the old monarchy did not cover the movements of its fleets with the secrecy enforced by the stern military despotism of the Empire. In both epochs England stood on the defensive; but in the earlier war she gave up the first line of the defence, off the hostile ports, and tried to protect all parts of her scattered empire by dividing the fleet among them. It has been attempted to show the weakness of the one policy, while admitting the difficulties and dangers of the other. The latter aims at shortening and deciding

[12] The plan of campaign traced by the Directory for Bruix became impossible of execution; the delay in the junction of the French and Spanish squadrons having permitted England to concentrate sixty ships in the Mediterranean.—Troude, vol. iii, p. 158.

[13] The combined squadrons of France and Spain, under Bruix, reached Brest on their return only twenty-four hours before Lord Keith, who had followed them from the Mediterranean. (James: Naval History of Great Britain.)

the war by either shutting up or forcing battle upon the hostile navy, recognizing that this is the key of the situation, when the sea at once unites and separates the different parts of the theatre of war. It requires a navy equal in number and superior in efficiency, to which it assigns a limited field of action, narrowed to the conditions which admit of mutual support among the squadrons occupying it. Thus distributed, it relies upon skill and watchfulness to intercept or overtake any division of the enemy which gets to sea. It defends remote possessions and trade by offensive action against the fleet, in which it sees their real enemy and its own principal objective. Being near the home ports, the relief and renewal of ships needing repairs are accomplished with the least loss of time, while the demands upon the scantier resources of the bases abroad are lessened. The other policy, to be effective, calls for superior numbers, because the different divisions are too far apart for mutual support. Each must therefore be equal to any probable combination against it, which implies superiority everywhere to the force of the enemy actually opposed, as the latter may be unexpectedly reinforced. How impossible and dangerous such a defensive strategy is, when not superior in force, is shown by the frequent inferiority of the English abroad, as well as in Europe, despite the effort to be everywhere equal. Howe at New York in 1778, Byron at Grenada in 1779, Graves off the Chesapeake in 1781, Hood at Martinique in 1781 and at St. Kitt's in 1782, all were inferior, at the same time that the allied fleet in Europe overwhelmingly outnumbered the English. In consequence, unseaworthy ships were retained, to the danger of their crews and their own increasing injury, rather than diminish the force by sending them home; for the deficiencies of the colonial dock-yards did not allow extensive repairs without crossing the Atlantic. As regards to comparative expense of the two strategies, the question is not only which would cost the more in the same time, but which would most tend to shorten the war by the effectiveness of its action.

The military policy of the allies is open to severer condemnation than that of England, by so much as the party assuming the offensive has by that very fact an advantage over the defensive. When the initial difficulty of combining their forces was overcome,—and it has been seen that at no time did Great Britain seriously embarrass their junction,—the allies had the choice open to them where, when, and how to strike with their superior numbers. How did they avail themselves of this recognized enormous advantage? By nibbling at the outskirts of the British Empire, and knocking their heads against the Rock of Gibraltar. The most serious military effort made by France, in sending to the United States a squadron and division of troops intended to be double the number of those which actually reached their destination, resulted, in little over a year, in opening the eyes of England to the hopelessness of the contest with the colonies, and thus put an end to a diversion of her strength which had been most beneficial to her opponents. In the West Indies one petty island after another was reduced, generally in the absence of the English fleet, with an ease which showed how completely the whole question would have been solved by a decisive victory over that fleet; but the French, though favored with many opportunities, never sought to slip the knot by the simple method of attacking the force upon which all depended. Spain went her own way in the Floridas, and with an overwhelming force obtained successes of no military value. In Europe the plan adopted by the English government left its naval force hopelessly inferior in numbers year after year; yet the operations planned by the allies seem in no case seriously to have contemplated the destruction of that force. In the crucial instance, when Derby's squadron of thirty sail-of-the-line was hemmed in the open roadstead of Torbay by the allied forty-nine, the conclusion of the council of war not to fight only epitomized the character of the action of the combined navies. To further embarrass their exertions in Europe, Spain, during long periods, obstinately persisted in tying down her fleet to the neighborhood of Gibraltar; but there was at no time practical recognition of the fact that a severe blow to the English navy in the Straits, or in the English Channel, or on the open sea, was the surest road to reduce the fortress, brought more than once within measurable distance of starvation.

In the conduct of their offensive war the allied courts suffered from the divergent counsels and jealousies which have hampered the movements of most naval coalitions. The conduct of Spain appears to have been selfish almost to disloyalty, that of France more faithful, and therefore also militarily sounder; for hearty co-operation and concerted action against a common objective, wisely chosen, would have better forwarded the objects of both. It must be admitted, too, that the indications point to inefficient administration and preparation on the part of the allies, of Spain especially; and that the quality of the *personnel* [14] was inferior to that of England. Questions of preparation and administration, however, though of deep military interest and importance, are very different from the strategic plan or method adopted by the allied courts in selecting and attacking their objectives, and so compassing the objects of the war; and their examination would not only extend this discussion unreasonably, but would also obscure the strategic question by heaping up unnecessary details foreign to its subject.

As regards the strategic question, it may be said pithily that the phrase "ulterior objects" embodies the cardinal fault of the naval policy. Ulterior objects brought to nought the hopes of the allies, because, by fastening their eyes upon them, they thoughtlessly passed the road which led to them. Desire eagerly directed upon the ends in view—or rather upon the partial, though great, advantages which they constituted their ends—blinded them to the means by which alone they could be surely attained; hence, as the result of the war, everywhere failure to attain them. To quote again the summary before given, their object was "to avenge their respective injuries, and to put an end to that tyrannical empire which England claims to maintain upon the ocean." The revenge they had obtained was barren of benefit to themselves. They had, so that generation thought, injured England by liberating America; but they had not righted their wrongs in Gibraltar and Jamaica, the English fleet had not received any such treatment as would lessen its haughty self-reliance, the armed neutrality of the northern powers had been allowed to pass fruitlessly away, and the English empire over the seas soon became as tyrannical and more absolute than before.

Barring questions of preparation and administration, of the fight-

[14] The high professional attainments of many of the French officers is not overlooked in this statement. The quality of the *personnel* was diluted by an inferior element, owing to the insufficient number of good men. "The *personnel* of our crews had been seriously affected by the events of the campaign of 1779. At the beginning of 1780 it was necessary either to disarm some ships, or to increase the proportion of soldiers entering into the composition of the crews. The minister adopted the latter alternative. New regiments, drawn from the land army, were put at the disposal of the navy. The corps of officers, far from numerous at the beginning of hostilities, had become completely inadequate. Rear-Admiral de Guichen met the greatest difficulty in forming the complements, both officers and crews, for his squadron. He took the sea, February 3, with ships 'badly manned,' as he wrote to the minister." (Chevalier: Hist. de la Marine Française, p. 184.) "During the last war [of 1778] we had met the greatest difficulty in supplying officers to our ships. If it had been easy to name admirals, commodores, and captains, it had been impossible to fill the vacancies caused by death, sickness, or promotion among officers of the rank of lieutenant and ensign." (Chevalier: Marine Française sous la République, p. 20.)

ing quality of the allied fleets as compared with the English, and looking only to the indisputable fact of largely superior numbers, it must be noted as the supreme factor in the military conduct of the war, that, while the allied powers were on the offensive and England on the defensive, the attitude of the allied fleets in presence of the English navy was habitually defensive. Neither in the greater strategic combinations, nor upon the battlefield, does there appear any serious purpose of using superior numbers to crush fractions of the enemy's fleet, to make the disparity of numbers yet greater, to put an end to the empire of the seas by the destruction of the organized force which sustained it. With the single brilliant exception of Suffren, the allied navies avoided or accepted action; they never imposed it. Yet so long as the English navy was permitted thus with impunity to range the seas, not only was there no security that it would not frustrate the ulterior objects of the campaign, as it did again and again, but there was always the possibility that by some happy chance it would, by winning an important victory, restore the balance of strength. That it did not do so is to be imputed as a fault to the English ministry; but if England was wrong in permitting her European fleet to fall so far below that of the allies, the latter were yet more to blame for their failure to profit by the mistake. The stronger party, assuming the offensive, cannot plead the perplexities which account for, though they do not justify, the undue dispersal of forces by the defence anxious about many points.

The national bias of the French, which found expression in the line of action here again and for the last time criticised, appears to have been shared by both the government and the naval officers of the day. It is the key to the course of the French navy, and, in the opinion of the author, to its failure to achieve more substantial results to France from this war. It is instructive, as showing how strong a hold tradition has over the minds of men, that a body of highly accomplished and gallant seamen should have accepted, apparently without a murmur, so inferior a rôle for their noble profession. It carries also a warning, if these criticisms are correct, that current opinions and plausible impressions should always be thoroughly tested; for if erroneous they work sure failure, and perhaps disaster.

There was such an impression largely held by French officers of that day, and yet more widely spread in the United States now, of the efficacy of commerce-destroying as a main reliance in war, especially when directed against a commercial country like Great Britain. "The surest means in my opinion," wrote a distinguished officer, Lamotte-Picquet, "to conquer the English is to attack them in their commerce." The harassment and distress caused to a country by serious interference with its commerce will be conceded by all. It is doubtless a most important secondary operation of naval war, and is not likely to be abandoned till war itself shall cease; but regarded as a primary and fundamental measure, sufficient in itself to crush an enemy, it is probably a delusion, and a most dangerous delusion, when presented in the fascinating garb of cheapness to the representatives of a people. Especially is it misleading when the nation against whom it is to be directed possesses, as Great Britain did and does, the two requisites of a strong sea power,—a widespread healthy commerce and a powerful navy. Where the revenues and industries of a country can be concentrated into a few treasure-ships, like the flota of Spanish galleons, the sinew of war may perhaps be cut by a stroke; but when its wealth is scattered in thousands of going and coming ships, when the roots of the system spread wide and far, and strike deep, it can stand many a cruel shock and lose many a goodly bough without the life being touched. Only by military command of the sea by prolonged control of the strategic centres of commerce, can such an attack be fatal;[15] and such control can be wrung from a powerful navy only by fighting and overcoming it. For two hundred years England has been the great commercial nation of the world. More than any other her wealth has been intrusted to the sea in war as in peace; yet of all nations she has

[15] The vital centre of English commerce is in the waters surrounding the British Islands; and as the United Kingdom now depends largely upon external sources of food-supply, it follows that France is the nation most favorably situated to harass it by commerce-destroying, on account of her nearness and her possession of ports both on the Atlantic and the North Sea. From these issued the privateers which in the past preyed upon English shipping. The position is stronger now than formerly, Cherbourg presenting a good Channel port which France lacked in the old wars. On the other hand, steam and railroads have made the ports on the northern coasts of the United Kingdom more available, and British shipping need not, as formerly, focus about the Channel.

Much importance has been attached to the captures made during the late summer manœuvres (1888) by cruisers in and near the English Channel. The United States must remember that such cruisers were near their home ports. Their line of coal-supply may have been two hundred miles; it would be a very different thing to maintain them in activity three thousand miles from home. The furnishing of coal, or of such facilities as cleaning the bottom or necessary repairs, in such a case, would be so unfriendly to Great Britain, that it may well be doubted if any neighboring neutral nation would allow them.

Commerce-destroying by independent cruisers depends upon wide dissemination of force. Commerce-destroying through control of a strategic centre by a great fleet depends upon concentration of force. Regarded as a primary, not as a secondary, operation, the former is condemned, the latter justified, by the experience of centuries.

ever been most reluctant to concede the immunities of commerce and the rights of neutrals. Regarded not as a matter of right, but of policy, history has justified the refusal; and if she maintain her navy in full strength, the future will doubtless repeat the lesson of the past.

The preliminaries of the peace between Great Britain and the allied courts, which brought to an end this great war, were signed at Versailles, January 20, 1783, an arrangement having been concluded between Great Britain and the American Commissioners two months before, by which the independence of the United States was conceded. This was the great outcome of the war. As between the European belligerents, Great Britain received back from France all the West India Islands she had lost, except Tobago, and gave up Sta. Lucia. The French stations in India were restored; and Trincomalee being in the possession of the enemy, England could not dispute its return to Holland, but she refused to cede Negapatam. To Spain, England surrendered the two Floridas and Minorca, the latter a serious loss had the naval power of Spain been sufficient to maintain possesssion of it; as it was it again fell into the hands of Great Britain in the next war. Some unimportant redistribution of trading-posts on the west coast of Africa was also made.

Trivial in themselves, there is but one comment that need be made upon these arrangements. In any coming war their permanency would depend wholly upon the balance of sea power, upon that empire of the seas concerning which nothing conclusive had been established by the war.

The definitive treaties of peace were signed at Versailles, September 3, 1783.

Index

485

1756-1763, 262, 281, 284; effect of commercial interests on the results at Yorktown, 348; great centre of English, 481 (note); policy of Great Britain as to neutral, 482.

Commerce-Destroying (Cruising Warfare), a strategic question, 7; dependence on geographical position, 27; diffusion of effort, 27; disadvantageous position of United States, 28, 481 (note); Spanish treasureships, 36, 45, 184, 231, 276, 279; English and Dutch commerce defy, 45, 116-117, 118, 183, 203, 262, 280, 281, 282, 481; Charles II. resorts to it as a substitute for great fleets, 115; disastrous results, 116; discussion of, as a principal mode of warfare, 116-119; dependent upon a near base or upon powerful fleets, 116, 174, 203, 277; illustrations, 1652-1783, 117-119; injurious reaction on the nation relying upon it, 119; illustrations, 119-121; mistaken conclusions drawn from American privateering in 1812, and from the Confederate cruisers, 120, 121; effect of great navies, 121; illustrations, after battle of Solebay, 131; after battle of Texel, 136; decline of Dutch navy, 142, and consequent increase of commerce-destroying by French privateers, 149; in the war of 1689-1697, discussion, 172-175; in the war of 1702-1713, 202-204; in war of 1739-1748, 247; in Seven Years' War, 260, 262, 274, 277, 279, 280-281 (discussion), 290 (note); in American Revolution, 303, 339, 348, 355, 358, 362 (and note), 363, 395, 396, 403, 411, 474, 481 (and note); French privateering, 117, 119, 149, 173, 174, 203, 247, 277, 280-281; peculiar character of French privateering, 1689-1713, 173-175, 203, 204.

Conflans, French Admiral, commands fleet intended for invasion of England, 264; sails from Brest, 265; encounters Hawke and is defeated by him, 266-268.

Cornwallis, British General, wins battle of Camden, 339; overruns Southern States, 340; marches into Virginia, 341; takes position at Yorktown, 344; surrounded by enemies, 345; capitulates, 346.

Cornwallis, Captain British navy, gallant conduct in Hood's action at St. Christopher, 422.

Corsica, island of, naturally Italian, 28; a dependency of Genoa, 179; Genoa cedes fortified harbors to France, 257; whole island ceded to France, 295; strategic value, 295.

Cromwell, Oliver, naval policy of, 52; issues Navigation Act, 52; condition of navy under, 52, 53, 88, 112; takes Jamaica, 52; takes Dunkirk, 91.

D'Aché, French Commodore, reaches India, 271; first and second battles with Pocock, 272; ill-will to the French governor, Lally, 271, 273; goes to the Isle of France, 273; return to the peninsula, and third battle with Pocock, 274; abandons the peninsula, 274.

De Barras, French Commodore, commands French squadron at Newport, and takes part in operations against Cornwallis, 346-348.

De la Clue, French Commodore, sails from Toulon to join Brest fleet, 263; encounters and beaten by Boscawen, 264.

D'Estaing, French Admiral, transferred from the army to the navy, 328; long passage from Toulon to the Delaware, 317; fails to attack the British fleet in New York, 319; runs British batteries at Newport, 319; sails in pursuit of Howe's fleet, and receives injuries in a gale, 320; goes to Boston, 320; foiled by Howe on all points, 321; goes to West Indies, 322; failure at Sta. Lucia, 323; capture of St. Vincent and Grenada, 324; action with Byron's fleet, 324-328; professional character, 328-331; ineffectual assault on Savannah, 332; return to France, 332.

D'Estrées, French Admiral, commands French contingent to the allied fleet at Solebay, 130; at Schoneveldt, 134; at the Texel, 134; equivocal action at the battle of the Texel, 135, 138; notice of, 152.

De Grasse, French Admiral, sails from Brest for West Indies, 339; partial action with Hood off Martinique, 339, 340; takes Tobago, and goes thence to San Domingo, 340; determines to go to Chesapeake Bay, 345; thoroughness of his action, 345, 348; anchors in Lynnhaven Bay, 345; skilful management when opposed by Graves, 346; share in results at York-

France, 219; allows the navy to decay, 215, 220, 222, 223; death, 223.

France. See under Colonies, Commerce, Commerce-Destroying, Geographical Position, Government, Inhabitants, character and number of Naval Policy, Naval Tactics, Sea Power, Strategy.

Frederick, King of Prussia, seizes Silesia, 231; Silesia ceded to, 245; opens Seven Years' War, 258; desperate struggle of, 260, 269; losses in the war, 286; results of the war to, 286; partition of Poland, 296.

Gardiner's Bay, Long Island, useful as a base of operations to an enemy of the United States, 189; station of English fleet, 342.

Geographical Position, its effect upon the sea power of countries, 25-30.

Gibraltar, strategic question, 10; taken by Rooke, 187; strategic value, 188; value to England, 26, 28, 195, 262, 290, 367; offers to restore to Spain, 208, 262; attacks on, 188, 216, 364; siege of, 358-365.

Government, character and policy of, effect upon the sea power of countries, 50-76; English, 51-58; Dutch, 58-60; French, 60-70; United States, 72-76.

Graves, British Admiral, commanding in New York, sails to relieve Cornwallis, 345; out-manœuvred by De Grasse, 346; criticisms on, 346, 347.

Graves, British Captain, afterward admiral, urges Rodney to attack French squadron anchored in Newport, 351; second to Nelson at Copenhagen, 351 (note); blockading on French coast, 470.

Great Britain. See England.

Hannibal. See Second Punic War, 11-18.

Havana, strategic value of, 278, 462, 464; taken by the English, 278; restored at Peace of Paris, 283, 285.

Hawke, Sir Edward, afterward Lord, British Admiral, distinguishes himself at the battle of Toulon, 236; captures a French squadron, 240-241; seizes French shipping in the Atlantic, 251; relieves Byng in the Mediterranean, 256; blockade of Brest, 264, 471; brilliant action in Quiberon Bay, 265-268; maxim as

to strength of English fleet, 468.

Henry IV., of France, policy, of 51, 60, 80.

Herbert, British Admiral, commands allied English and Dutch fleets at battle of Beachy Head, 162.

Holland. See under Colonies, Commerce, Commerce-Destroying, Geographical Position, Government, Inhabitants, character and number of, Naval Policy, Naval Tactics (Ruyter's), Sea Power, Strategy.

Hood, Sir Samuel, afterward Lord, British Admiral, trait of subordination in, 314 (note); action with De Grasse off Martinique, 339; sent by Rodney to America with fourteen ships, 345, 346; second in command in action off Chesapeake, 348; temporary chief command in West Indies, 418; brilliant action at St. Christopher's Island, 420-426; junction with Rodney, 428; partial action of April 9, 1782, 430-432; at battle of the Saints, 436-442; De Grasse's flag-ship strikes to his, 438; opinion as to Rodney's failure to pursue his advantage, 445; captures four French ships, 446; later career and death, 451.

Hoste, Paul, work on naval tactics, 67, 130, 162, 164.

Howe, Lord, British Admiral, naval policy of, 7; at Philadelphia, 318; at New York, 318; at Newport, 319; energy and skill of, 320, 321; commands Channel fleet, 363; relieves Gibraltar, 365; a whig in politics, 448; opinion as to blockades, 470.

Howe, Sir William, British General, commander-in-chief in America, 302; expedition to the Chesapeake, 302, 417, 473; indolence of, 321.

Hughes, Sir Edward, British Admiral, arrives in India, 307; takes Negapatam and Trincomalee, 307; first meeting with Suffren, 379; task in India, 380; first battle with Suffren's squadron, 381-385; second battle with Suffren, 388-393; contemporary criticisms on, 393; third battle with Suffren, 398-400; tactics of, 382, 400, 404, 407, 413; slowness of, loses Trincomalee, 401-402; fourth battle with Suffren, 404-407; praise bestowed by, upon his captains, 407; goes to Bombay from Coromandel coast, 409; returns to Madras, 412; supports Eng-

Cape of Good Hope, 373; action, with British squadron at the Cape Verde Islands. 373, 374; military discussion of his conduct, 376-378; arrival in India, 379; lack of seaports on which to base operations, 307, 380; first battle with squadron of Sir Edward Hughes, 381-384; tactics in the action, 384-386; estimate of the strategic situation in India, 376, 385, 395, 396, 414, 416; second battle with Hughes, 388-391; tactics in it, 391-393; strategic action, 394, 396, 398, 401-404, 409-411, 413-414, 415, 467; military character, 396, 398, 401, 407, 415, 416; third battle with Hughes, 398-400; takes Trincomalee, 402; activity of, 401, 402, 408, 413, 416; fourth battle with Hughes, 403-407; wreck of two of squadron, 408; goes to Sumatra, 411; returns to Trincomalee, 412; relieves Cuddalore besieged by the English, 413; fifth battle with Hughes, 413; conclusion of peace, 414; return to France, 415; rewards, 415; later career and death, 416.

Tourville, French Admiral, commands at the battle of Beachy Head, 161; sluggish pursuit of the enemy, 164; military character, 165; celebrated cruise in 1691, 167; commands at battle of La Hougue, 169; tactics and brilliant defence at La Hougue, 169; destruction of French ships, 170; supports the army in Catalonia, 172; destroys or disperses a great English convoy, 173; death, 187.

Trafalgar, Battle of, final act of a strategic combination, 10, 20 (note); tactics at, 10, 312; effects of, 41; Nelson's position at, 311, 315; Collingwood's action after Nelson's death, 316.

Trincomalee, in Ceylon, Dutch influence in, 84; passes into the hands of the English, 307, 380; effect upon the contest in India, 307, 379 (note), 380, 381 (note), 385, 388, 393, 402, 404, 409, 412; strategic value of, 380, 388, 395, 402, 409, 463, 464, 465; taken by Suffren, 402; restored to Holland at peace of 1783, 482.

Two Sicilies, the, acquired by Austria, 211; foundation of Bourbon Kingdom of, 219; forced by British fleet to withdraw troops from Spanish army, 232, 269.

United Provinces. See Holland.

Vernon, British Admiral, takes Porto Bello, is repulsed from Cartagena and Santiago de Cuba, 230.
Villeneuve, French Admiral, Trafalgar, campaign, 20, 21 (note), 469; at the battle of the Nile, 69; suicide, 358.

Walpole, Sir Robert, prime minister of England, 211, 213; peace policy of, 213, 215; naval demonstrations, 215; struggle with the war party in England, 218, 220, 221; neutrality causes Austria to lose the two Sicilies, 219; forced into war with Spain, 221; accord with Fleuri, 213, 215; confidence betrayed by Fleuri, 219; driven from office, 223, 231; death, 223.
War, Second Punic, influence of sea power upon, 11-18.
Wars, American Revolution, 301-352; Anglo-Dutch, second, 93-116; Anglo-Dutch, third, England in alliance with France, 126-141; Austrian Succession, 231-245; France against Holland, Germany, and Spain, 1674-1678, 140-150; Great Britain against Spain, 221-245; League of Augsburg, 157-175; Maritime War of 1778, 308-482; Polish Succession, 218; Russia and Sweden, 204; Seven Years', 256-283; Spanish Succession, 1702-1713, 183-194.
Washington, George, at Pittsburg and in Braddock's expedition, 251; opinion as to the line of the Hudson, 301 (note); comments on D'Estaing's cruise, 322 (note); despatches to De Grasse, 340; meeting with Rochambeau, 344; result of their deliberations, 344; marches from New York to Virginia, 345; opinions as to the influence of sea power on the American Revolution, 352-355.
William III., naval policy of, 59, 171; becomes ruler of Holland, 133; general policy, 59, 149, 150, 155, 157, 158, 171, 180-182, 184; expedition to England, 158; becomes King of England, 53, 158; difficulties of his position, 159; goes to Ireland, 161; dies, 182.